The GIANT Encyclopedia of Science Activities

The GIANT Encyclopedia of Science Activities for Children

More than 600 Science Activities

Edited by Kathy Charner

Illustrated by Rebecca Grace Jones

Viva Books Private Limited

New Delhi • Mumbai • Chennai • Kolkata • Bangalore

First Indian Edition 2004

Reprinted 2006

VIVA BOOKS PRIVATE LIMITED

- 4262/3 Ansari Road, Daryaganj, New Delhi 110 002
  E-mail: viva@vivagroupindia.net
- 215-216 New Apollo Estate, 2nd Floor, Mogra Lane, Andheri (E), Mumbai 400 069
  E-mail: vivamumbai@vivagroupindia.net
- Jamal Fazal Chambers, 26 Greams Road, Chennai 600 0067
  E-mail: vivachennai@vivagroupindia.net
- B-103, Jindal Towers, 21/1A/3, Darga Road, Kolkata-700 017
  E-mail: vivakolkata@vivagroupindia.net
- 7 GF, Sovereign Park Apts., 56-58 K. R. Road, Basavanagudi, Bangalore 560 004
  Email: vivabangalore@vivagroupindia.net

Published by arrangement with

Gryphon House, Inc.
10726 Tucker Street
Beltsville MD 20705

Cover Illustration: Beverly Hightshoe
Text Illustrations: Rebecca Grace Jones

ISBN 81-7649-861-0

Published by Vinod Vasishtha for Viva Books Private Limited, 4262/3 Ansari Road, New Delhi 110 002 and printed and bound at Saurabh Printers Pvt. Ltd., NOIDA.

Dedication

To all the teachers of young children, especially those who contributed to this book

To the creativity of Rosanna Demps and Mike Freeman

To the joint efforts of the editorial team

Table of Contents

Table of Contents

Table of Contents

Table of Contents

Table of Contents

Table of Contents

Table of Contents

Introduction

Children as Scientists

Children are born curious. This curiosity is the key to learning anything, including science. Children want to know how things happen, why they happen as they do, what will happen if—and lots more. Teachers of young children need only to activate their curiosity, providing the opportunities and materials necessary to find out the answers to their questions in the world of science. This book is filled with opportunities for children to learn the how, the why, the what happens now, and many other unique and interesting parts of science. In addition, since the activities in this book have already been used successfully by teachers, the reader can be confident that the activities will "work."

The Building Blocks of Science

In addition to curiosity, the science skills developed and encouraged by the activities in this book include communication, observation, estimation, measurement, cause and effect, investigation and evaluation. A critical part of science learning is communicating the results of the experiment. Drawing a picture, writing or dictating the results of the activity and charting the results are just three examples of how children learn to communicate what they have experienced in activities. From a simple game of "I Spy" to careful observation with a magnifying glass, the ability to look and see things, then look again to see what might have been missed, is an important part of this book. Whether you call it guessing or estimating, it's all the same. Learn the fun of guessing what might happen and then finding out what does happen. Measuring the results of activities is another important part of science, and children love to measure things, from each other to whales. Give them rulers, balance scales, paper inchworms, cups, measuring tapes and other devices so they can measure to their hearts' content. We call it cause and effect; children might say _______ always happens when I do ___________. Encourage the children to try something over and over so they will learn for themselves that when a process is repeated, the same results often occur. Understanding cause and effect is an essential scientific skill. Children's natural curiosity drives them to find out why something happens the way it does, to investigate a situation, to examine the results of an activity, to answer the questions they have. The activities in this book help children investigate those questions and find out the answers. Evaluating an activity or the results of an activity is another critical building block of science knowledge. This book is filled with opportunities for children to evaluate activities and the science knowledge they learned from the activities. These skills also develop creative thinking, an essential skill for science (and everything else!).

Set Up for Success in Science

The following ideas will help children be successful in their scientific explorations:

- Approach science activities with enthusiasm.
- Set up child-directed activities so the children can experiment on their own, at their own pace.
- Encourage children to repeat an activity over and over, until the learning makes sense, the fun wears off, the repetition becomes boring, etc.
- Make take-home versions of the activities so the children can try them at home, or show them to their families.
- Introduce the children to a developmentally appropriate version of the scientific method:
  ASK—What will happen if . . .
  GUESS—I think this will happen . . .
  TRY—Test to see if your guess is what really happens.
  ANSWER—This is what happened.
  (See *Let's See What Happens* on page 416 for additional information.)
- Use picture directions (also known as rebus directions) as often as possible. That way children will be able to do the activity on their own.
- Rotate durable science "tools," such as magnifying glasses, balance scales, magnets and magnetic wands, animals, plants and measuring tapes (or nonstandard measuring devices like a hand print covered in clear contact paper or an unsharpened pencil) in and out of the science center.
- Include materials not usually associated with science—like paper, markers and crayons (for drawing, writing or dictating and charting results), bells (for finding out which ones have a high sound and which ones a low sound), tape (for checking its ability to hold different materials) and magazines (for challenging the children to find pictures that relate to a science activity). The list can go on and on. Put any material into the science center and encourage children to use their natural curiosity and science skills to learn about it, then communicate this learning through drawings, charts, stories and more. (See *Science Centers in the Early Childhood Classroom* on page 405 for more suggestions.)

Using Children's Interest as a Starting Point

One day the children notice that the leaves on the trees are changing from green to brilliant oranges and reds, or that the plants in the classroom are drooping, or that some books are starting to wear out and others are not. Children are naturally curious about these kinds of everyday occurrences. Use their curiosity to investigate these events, turning them into "teachable moments." Begin by looking at the table of contents and the index to find activities that can help you and the children discover why things happen the way they do, what to expect the next time the same thing happens, and how to communicate what you know and find out what you don't.

Introduction

How to Use This Book

Age
The age listed is a suggestion. Each teacher is the best judge of the appropriateness of an activity, based on his or her prior knowledge of the children and the children's responses to the activity.

Science skills
The science skills and learning objective of the activity are found under this heading.

Materials
This section contains a list of everything you will need to complete each activity. Most materials are already in a typical classroom. Other materials might need to be purchased from stores or donated by parents.

What to do
The directions for the activities are presented in a step-by-step format. When necessary, patterns and illustrations accompany the activity.

More to do
Ideas for extending the science activity into another science activity or into other areas of the curriculum are included in this section. Many activities include suggestions for integrating the science activity into areas such as math, dramatic play, art, blocks, a field trip, cooking, snack and language.

Related books (and songs)
A list of children's books (and sometimes songs) that relate to the science activity are included in this section.

Original songs (and poems)
Songs and poems written by the teachers who submitted the activities appear here. The songs use familiar melodies; just the words are new.

Index
There is a comprehensive index at the end of this book.

Just listen as the children express their curiosity, then use this book as a tool to begin to satisfy their thirst for knowledge.

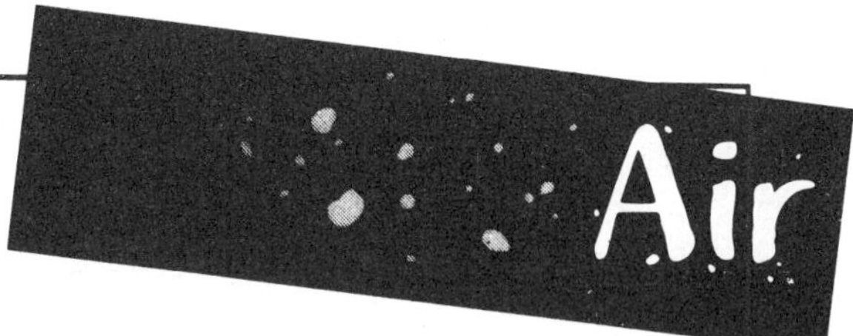

3+

Across the Water

Science skills

Children use observation to identify differences and recognize similarities, and they see how cause and effect works.

Materials

Jelly roll pans, or any flat metal or plastic lid with sides
Water
Styrofoam packing pieces
Food coloring

What to do

1. Place each pan on a table.
2. Pour in a small amount of water to cover the bottom of the pans.
3. The children can make ripples on the water by blowing gently. Give a name to this wind (gentle breeze, light wind).
4. Two children can stand across the table from each other and blow pieces of Styrofoam back and forth. Investigate to find out what other objects can be moved by the wind on the water.
5. Observe the change in the water as you add drops of food coloring. Swirl the water around and watch as it gradually turns a different color.
6. Compare gentle wind to strong wind by letting two children stand on the same side of the table and blow. Give names to the strong wind (blustery, windy, gale, storm, etc.). After your storms, there will be cleaning up to do!

Linda Ann Hodge, Minnetonka, MN

3+

Bubble Wand Magic

Science skills

Children use all their senses to observe details and to recognize and identify similarities and differences.

Materials

Pipe cleaners, one per child
Several wide mouth containers of soapy bubble liquid

Air

1.

2.

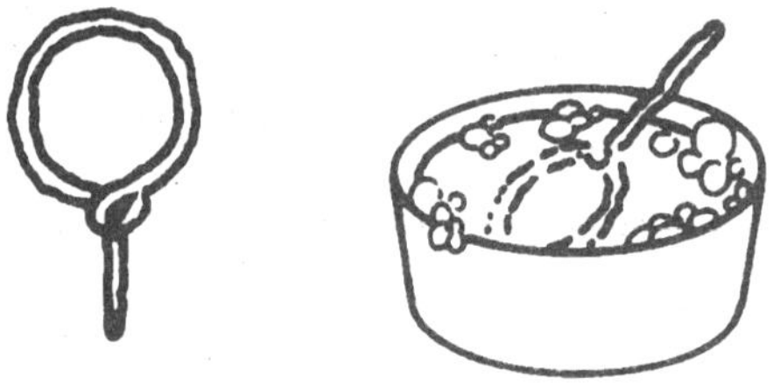

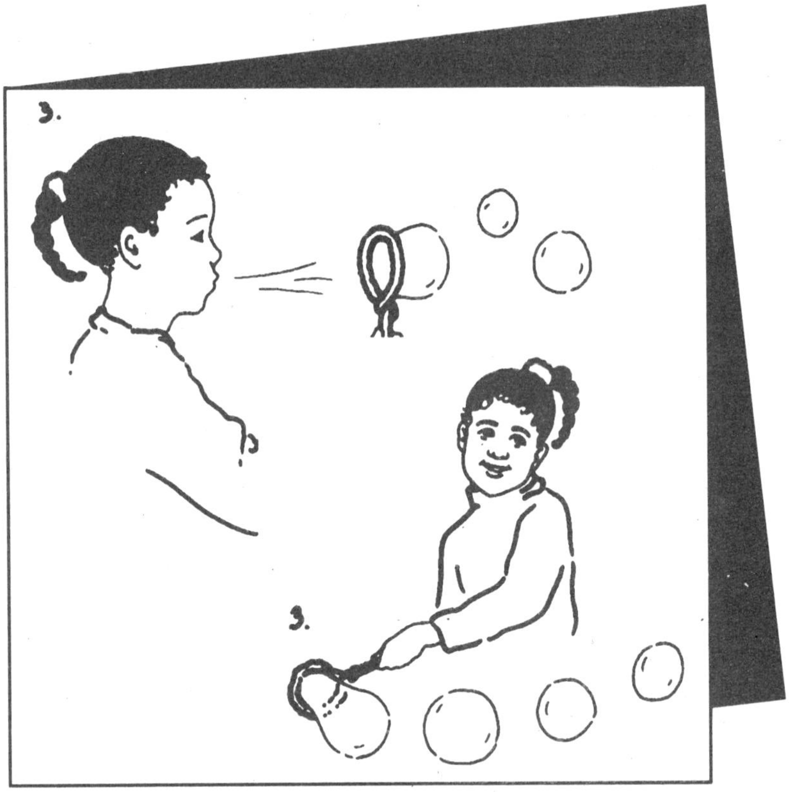

What to do

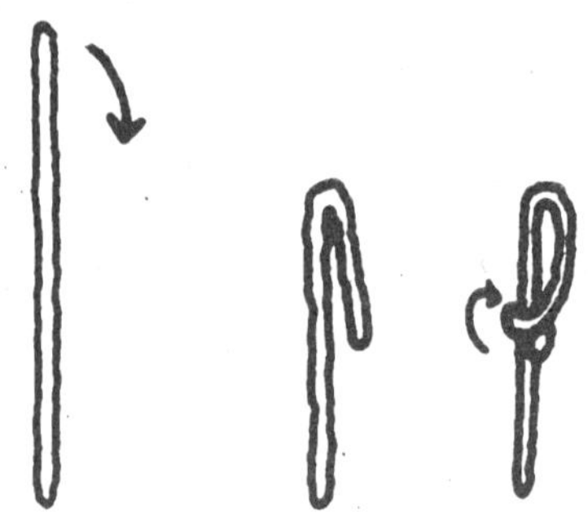

1. Give each child a pipe cleaner. Show them how to bend and twist the pipe cleaner to form a loop at the end.
2. The children make bubbles by blowing on the wand circle and by sweeping the wand through the air. Which method makes bigger bubbles? Which method makes more bubbles?
3. Practice making bubbles indoors, if you wish. Compare this to the movement of the bubbles outdoors on a slightly breezy day.
4. Can the children catch and hold the bubbles on the saturated bubble wands? Can they do the same thing using their dry hands? Why?
5. For a simpler version, an adult makes bubbles and challenges the children to touch them, catch them and jump on them.

Original poem

Bubbles floating in the air,
Bubbles floating everywhere.
And the only time they stop,
Is when the bubbles pop! pop! pop!

Related book

Piggyback Songs: New Songs to the Tune of Childhood Favorites by Jean Warren

Christina Chilcote, New Freedom, PA

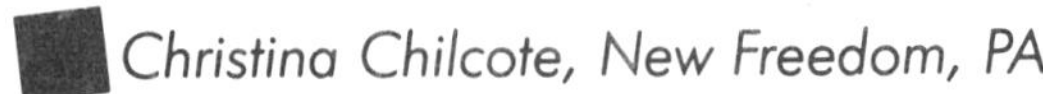

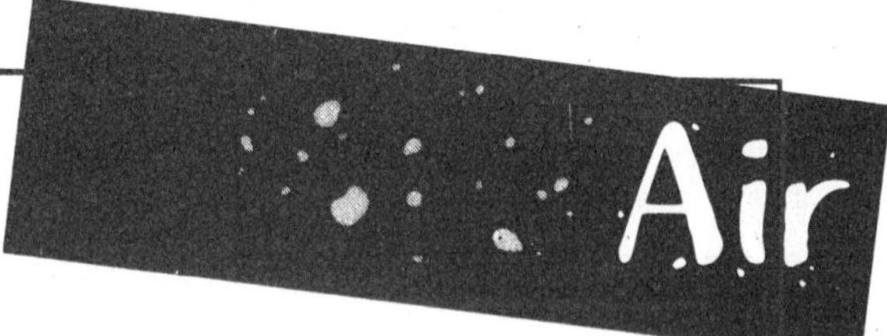

3+ Bumper Pool

Science skills

Children practice observation skills and have an opportunity to see cause and effect.

Materials

Small Styrofoam balls, 1″ to 1½″ (2.5 cm to 3.75 cm)
Large package of straight plastic straws

What to do

1. Be sure the water table is clean and dry.
2. Place Styrofoam balls in the water table.
3. Give each child a straw.
4. Encourage the children to blow the balls around the table and bump other balls by blowing into the straws.

More to do

More science: For a small group you can place large cookie sheets at the table. Give the children a couple of balls each, and have the children race the balls from one end of the cookie sheet to the other by blowing. Show the children how they can move more than one ball by moving their heads back and forth as they blow.

Rinnie Wells, Norman, OK

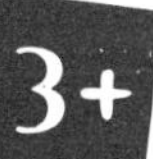

3+ Feather Race

Science skills

Children see the effects of air pressure.

Materials

Feathers, one for each child
Straws, one for each child

What to do

1. Talk with the children about air.
2. Let the children put their hands to their mouths and blow to feel the air on their hands.

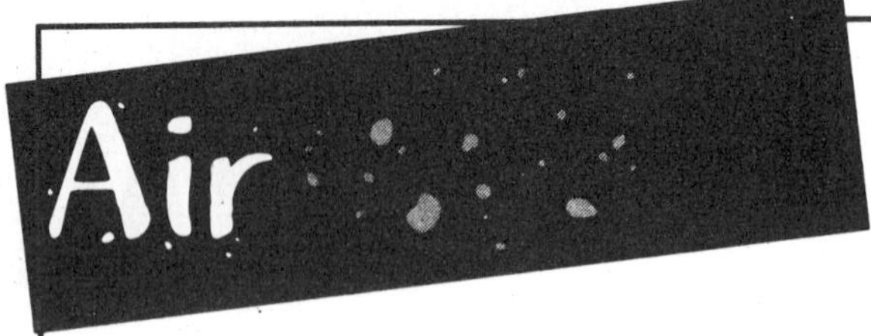

3. Explain that they are going to use air to play a game.
4. Give each child a straw with a feather placed in one end.
5. At the count of three, the children blow into their straws and see whose feather flies the farthest.

More to do

Art: Let the children paint with feathers and tempera paint.

Math: To work math into the feather experiment, measure the distance each feather went and make a graph with your results.

Cindy Winther, Oxford, MI

Blowing Bubbles

Science skills

Children observe that air occupies space, and they practice fine motor skills.

Materials

Plastic straws
Small plastic cups or margarine containers
Dishwashing detergent or baby shampoo
Water

What to do

1. Cut the straws in 4" (10 cm) lengths.
2. Fringe one end of each straw piece by snipping it several times about ¼" (6 mm).
3. Mix one teaspoon (5 ml) of detergent or baby shampoo with one cup (250 ml) of water; pour ½" (13 mm) of the mixture into the containers.
4. Demonstrate blowing by holding a piece of paper and watching it move as you blow.
5. Have children do the same.
6. Dip the fringed end of the straw into the solution and blow gently to form a bubble. Tell the children that the air is now trapped inside the soap film.
7. Give each child a straw and a container of soapy solution.
8. Instruct them to dip the cut end into the solution, then blow gently.

Mary Jo Shannon, Roanoke, VA

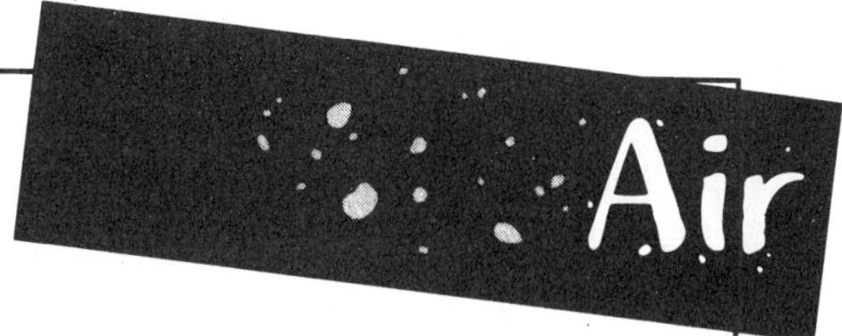

3+ Water in your Breath

Science skills

Children learn about water vapor with this simple activity.

Materials

Small mirror

What to do

1. Let each child take a turn holding a small mirror close to his lips.
2. Have each child open his mouth as wide as he can and blow out.
3. A foggy spot will form on the mirror.
4. Touch the spot.
5. The spot is liquid water.
6. Explain to the children that water vapor is in your body and when you blow out, the water vapor in your breath hits the cold mirror. The water condenses and changes into liquid water and forms the spot on the mirror.

Cindy Winther, Oxford, MI

3+ Magical Air

Science skills

Children observe a surprising and fun experiment, learn about cause and effect and draw conclusions.

Materials

Balloons
Water table or clear plastic bin
Paper towels
Paper airplanes
Transparent glass or plastic cup

What to do

1. Show a blown-up balloon. Ask, "What is in the balloon? How did it get there?"
2. Fly a paper airplane. Ask, "What makes the airplane stay up?"
3. Ask children to stand up and spread out so no one is touching anyone else. Say, "Let's see what happens if you move your arms like this. (Make small circles with arms). "What do you feel?"

Air

4. Ask children to give other examples of air (blowing bubbles in water, flying kites, trees blowing in the wind, etc.).
5. Sit down with the children. Say, "Yes, air is here even if we can't see it. It takes up space. Let's do an experiment. What do you think will happen if I crumple up this paper towel, put it in this glass and turn the glass upside down in water?" Almost all children will say that the towel will get wet.
6. Say, "OK, let's see." Place the crumpled paper towel inside the glass. Turn it upside down and push it straight down in the water. Check the towel. It doesn't get wet.
7. Discuss the children's thoughts about the reason for this. Yes, air really is there even though we can't see it. It does take up space.
8. Let the children repeat the experiment for themselves. Have materials on hand so children can experiment in small groups.
9. Tell parents what you did since children get so excited about this "magic" they may want to try it again at home.

Sharon F. Milner, Carrollton, GA

Bubble Works

Science skills

With these great bubble ideas, children practice observation, language and measuring skills.

Materials

Homemade bubble solution:
2 cups (500 ml) water
¼ cup (60 ml) glycerine
2 tablespoons (30 ml) liquid dish soap

Straws, one per child
Light colored paper
Ruler
Prism
Low-sided tub

What to do

1. Blow bubbles and catch them on a sheet of paper. They will pop upon contact with the paper but they will leave imprints.
2. Measure the bubbles' sizes using rulers or your own instruments of measure.
3. Use a prism to make the rainbow colors that you see inside a bubble
4. Let children try a variety of items to make bubbles with, including paper/plastic tubes, slotted spoons, colanders, etc.
5. Make a bubble pipe. (You will need a polystyrene cup, a straw and a pencil.) Punch a hole in the base of the cup and insert the straw. Put some bubble solution into the cup. The children can blow bubbles from their own bubble pipes.
6. Make My Bubble Books. Draw or paint bubbles of different colors and sizes.
7. Where is the bubble? The teacher blows a bubble and the children describe where it goes and where it lands. Children take turns blowing bubbles and telling where their bubbles go
8. Put soapy water in tubs or a sensory table with egg beaters.

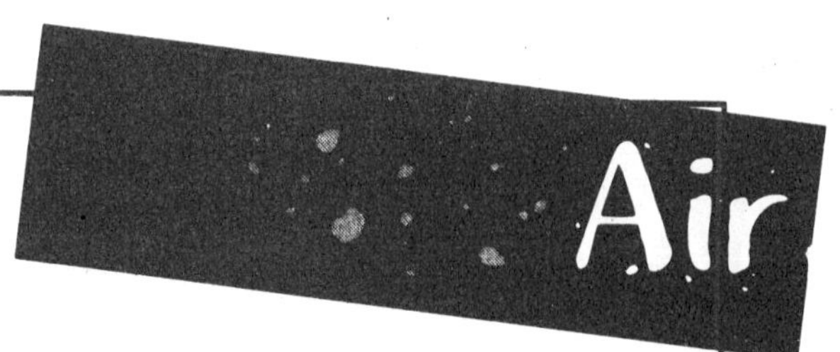

Original song

Bubbles (sing to the tune of "Twinkle, Twinkle, Little Star")

Bubbles, bubbles up so high,
Floating, floating in the sky.
Filled with colors, filled with air,
Popping here, popping there.
Bubbles, bubbles up so high,
Floating, floating in the sky.

Sandra Nagel, White Lake, MI

3+

Liquid Starch Bubbles

Science skills

The children mix an interesting bubble solution.

Materials

Smocks
Liquid starch
Glitter
Individual trays
Dish soap (Ivory works best)
Bubble wands

What to do

1. Arrange the trays on the table.
2. Pour some liquid starch onto each tray along with a squirt of dish soap.
3. Sprinkle in the glitter.
4. Give each child a tray and a bubble wand. They may scoop some of the mixture into their wands.
5. At first, the ingredients will be soupy and may splatter, but the mixture will thicken

More to do

Cooking: Make pudding for a snack. The children will see the powder stage, add milk and see the liquid stage, then chill it to see the solid stage.
More science: A cornstarch goop table can be open at the same time, consisting of cornstarch and water. The children can distinguish between liquids and solids.
Movement: Use a parachute to pretend the class is one giant bubble. The group stands around the parachute and shakes rapidly. On the count of three, raise the parachute in the air, then watch the bubble quickly disappear.

Original poem

I Am a Bubble, Big and Round

I am a bubble, big and round.
I float in the air not on the ground.
The children love to hop and see
If they can pop me!

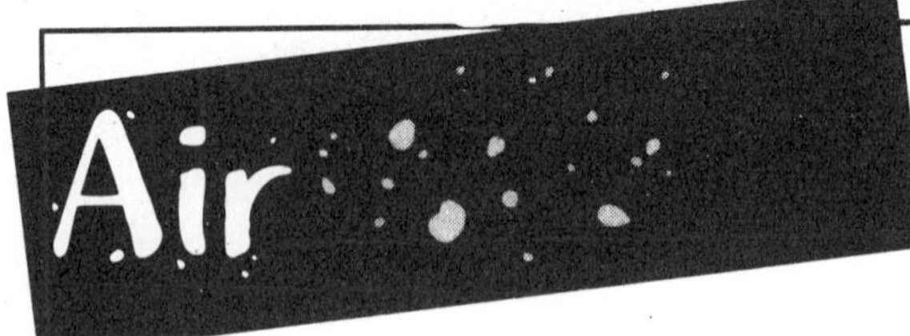

Related book
Children's Museum of Activity Book: Bubbles
by Benny Zubrowski

Kelly Cassidy, Voluntown, CT

Twirlybirds

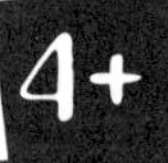

Science skills
Children practice following directions and using fine motor skills.

Materials
Strips of construction paper, ¾" x 7" (19 mm x 17.5 cm)
Paper clips

What to do
1. Give each child a strip of construction paper and show them how to fold their twirlybirds, following the steps below. (Twirlybirds can be premarked with fold lines, prefolded or even premade for very young children.)
2. Each paper is folded in half. The strip is now ¾" by 3½" (19 mm x 8.75 cm).
3. About 1" of one end is folded down at a 45 degree angle.
4. About 1" of the unfolded end is folded in the opposite direction at a 45 degree angle.

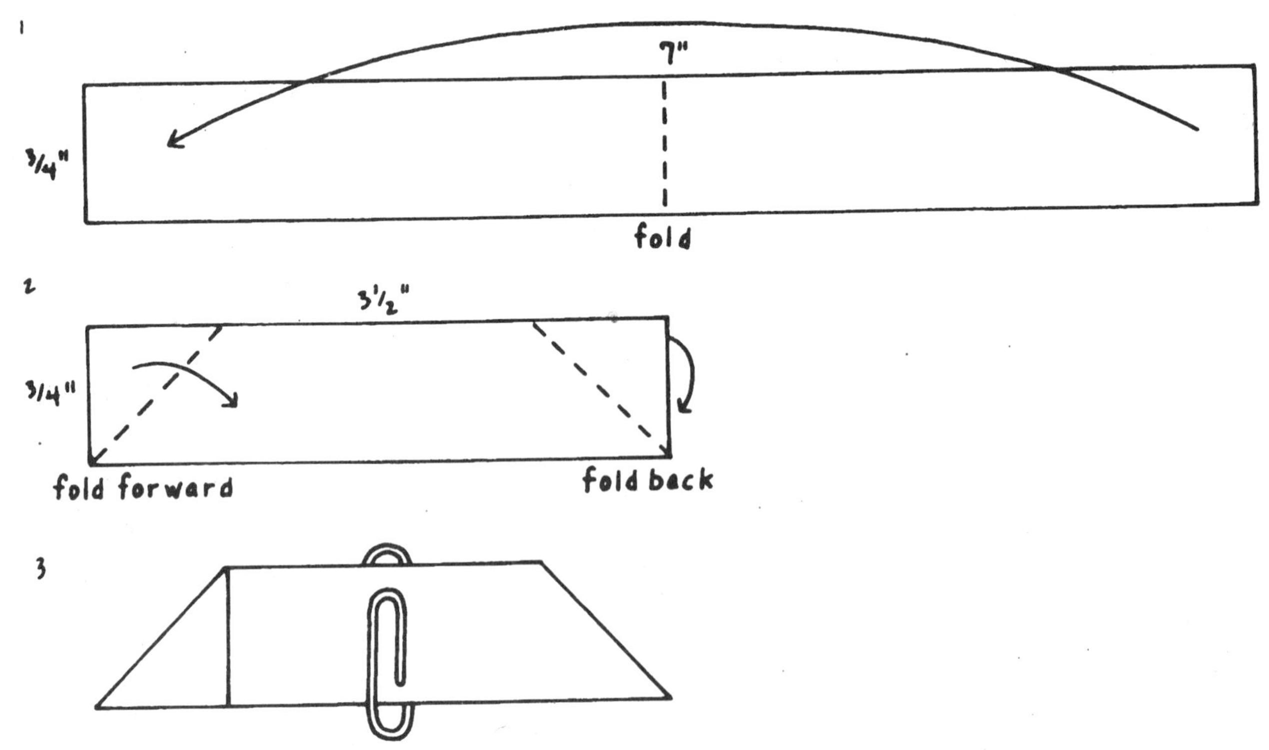

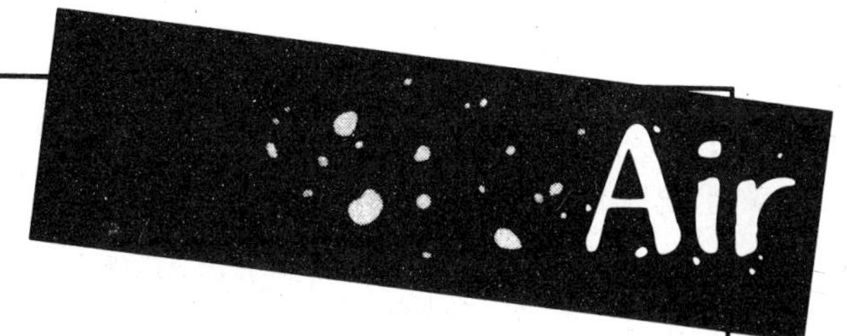

5. Attach the paper clip to the middle fold and open the two end "wings" slightly.
6. Invite the children to toss their twirlybirds in the air and see them swirl to the ground.

More to do

More science: If double maple seeds have been collected in advance, their whirling descent can be compared to the children's twirlybirds.

Original poem

Five little helicopters starting to soar,
One took a trip and then there were four.
Four little helicopters zooming past a tree,
One zoomed away and then there were three.
Three little helicopters twirling in the blue,
One landed on the ground and then there were two.
Two little helicopters flying just for fun,
One flew away and then there was one.
One little helicopter moving toward the sun,
It flew so far that then there were none!

Related books

Budgie the Little Helicopter by Sarah Ferguson, Duchess of York
Harry's Helicopter by Joan Anderson

Christina Chilcote, New Freedom, PA

4+

Air Pressure Push

Science skills
The children learn to recognize cause and effect.

Materials

Large plastic drinking straws
Cotton balls or ping pong balls
Lid of a large cardboard gift box, approximately 11" x 17" (28 cm x 42 cm)

What to do

1. Place the upside down gift box lid on a table.
2. Place a few cotton balls or ping pong balls in the gift box lid.
3. Give straws to the children.
4. Have the children take turns standing at one narrow end of the lid, pointing their straws at the ball and blowing into the straw.

5. Ask the children what they observed. Did the balls move? Why?
6. Divide the children into two groups. Have one group stand at each narrow end of the lid. Ask them to point their straws at the balls and blow.
7. Ask the children what they observed. Did the balls move? Why?
8. If four children are participating, place one at each side of the lid. Have them point their straws at the balls and blow.
9. Ask the children what they observed this time. Did the balls move? Why?

More to do

Games: Play air pressure soccer by turning the upside down box lid into a soccer field. Draw lines across the lid widthwise in three places, 2" (5 cm) from each narrow end and exactly in the middle of the lid. Give straws to two to four children. Divide the children into two teams. Place one team at each narrow end of the lid. Place a cotton ball in the center of the lid. When the teacher says "Go!" each team tries to blow the ball into the opposite end zone. The game is over when three goals have been scored. Group the other children into teams and let them have a turn.

Related book

Wind Garden by Angela McAllister

Christina Chilcote, New Freedom, PA

Blow Wind, Blow!

4+

Science skills

The children observe cause and effect, and they try to make predictions.

Materials

Hand-held hair dryer with at least two settings

Classroom objects (include some objects that can be blown easily by the air from the hair dryer and some that cannot), such as:

- Tissue
- Crayon
- Wooden block

What to do

1. Begin the activity with a discussion about wind as air that's moving very fast. Explain how a little wind is called a breeze and a lot of wind is sometimes called a gust.
2. Show children the hair dryer and ask if they know what it is and what it is used for. Turn on the hair dryer and demonstrate how it blows things with air. (Watch for those children who may be frightened by the sound.)

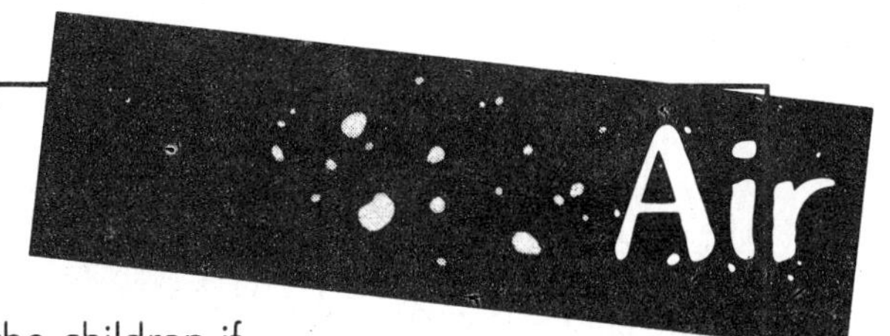

3. Demonstrate the low and then the high settings of the hair dryer. Compare each to a breeze and a gust, respectively.
4. Bring out the lightest of the classroom objects and ask the children if they think a "breeze" or a "gust" will blow it. Using the lowest setting, blow the object across the floor. Bring out another object and repeat the predicting and experimenting. Continue with the remaining items, making sure at least one of the objects is too heavy to move even with the highest setting.
5. Direct the children to choose other items from the classroom to bring to the circle. Ask them to predict whether their choice can be blown by a breeze or a gust. Test their predictions from all angles, since some items can or cannot be moved based on their position.
6. As a transition, tell the children that when the wind blows them, they can leave the circle and go to the next activity. Using the lowest setting on the dryer, gently aim the air flow at each child.

More to do

Art: Use the hair dryer at the art table (with adult guidance) to blow washable watercolors across paper. First put the paper into the bottom of a box to keep splatters contained.
Math: To play a number game, spread out a grouping of objects. Using the hair dryer, blow away a few of the objects. Count how many are left.

Related books

The Wind Blew by Pat Hutchins
Who Took the Farmer's Hat? by Joan L. Nodset

Vickie L. Schneider, Oshkosh, WI

Bubble Shapes

Science skills
Children categorize bubble wands based on their effectiveness as bubble blowers.

Materials

Wire coat hangers
Duct tape
Dishpan or large plastic dish
Wire clippers
Plastic straws
String

Homemade Bubble Solution:
2 cups (500 ml) dishwashing detergent
1 ½ quarts (1.5 liters) water
¾ cup (175 ml) white corn syrup
Mix all ingredients well. Cover and let settle overnight at room temperature.

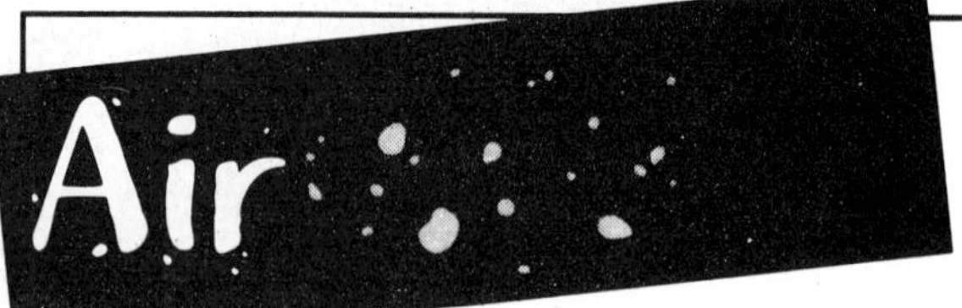

What to do

1. The day before doing this activity, make up the bubble solution.
2. The next day, clip open the coat hangers and cut off the hooks. Twist the two ends together to make a handle, reinforcing with duct tape. Bend the bubble wands into unique shapes.
3. Attach string through plastic straws for a wiggly wand.
4. Bend and connect the straws into three-dimensional shapes for making unusual bubbles.
5. Pour solution in large pan. Set the pan outside and let the children experiment with the wands and with other common household items, such as rubber lid tops, wire whisk, plastic cookie cutters, plastic colander, plastic soft drink rings, sifters, funnels.
6. Children may categorize wands and bubble makers into groups of good wands/bad wands or best bubble makers.

More to do

More science: Cut a long sheet of paper from a roll and lay it on the ground. Let the children blow bubbles onto the paper to observe splat patterns of different-sized bubbles. ▪ Separate the bubble solution into smaller bowls. Add 1 teaspoon of liquid tempera paint to each bowl, using a variety of colors. Mix. Blow colored bubbles onto white or light-colored paper and observe splat patterns.

Related book

Bubble Trouble by Mary Packard

Susan R. Forbes, Holly Hill, FL

Invisible But Real

4+

Science skills

Children predict and observe the effect of air pressure on various objects.

Materials

Styrofoam packaging pieces
Book
Pail of water
Hand fan
Balloon

What to do

1. Scatter Styrofoam pieces on the floor in a circle slightly larger than the book.
2. Gently drop the book into the center of the circle. Pieces will scatter. What made them move? Air was pushed out of the way by the falling book.
3. Scatter the pieces in front of an open door. Guess what will happen when the door closes. Test the theory by pushing the door hard.
4. Use a hand fan to make the pieces move.
5. Blow up a balloon. It is filled with air.

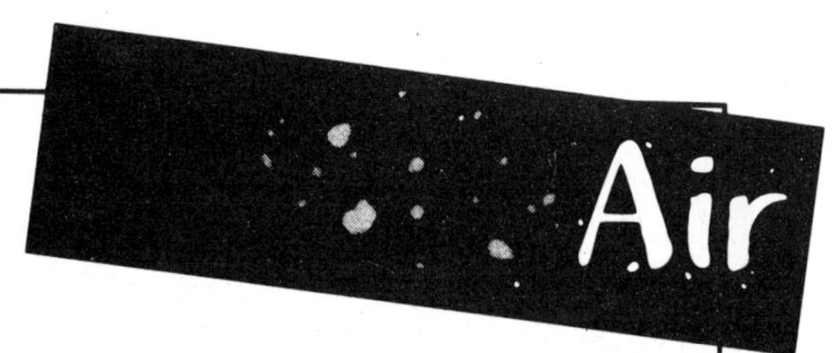

6. Push the balloon down in a pail of water. Water is pushed out of the way and rises.
7. Put a light-weight book on top of a flat balloon and then blow up the balloon. The book is lifted by the air!

More to do

Art: Paint a picture by blowing the paint around with a straw.
More science: Make a windsock with a 9" x 12" (22.5 cm x 30 cm) construction paper cylinder decorated at one end with tissue paper streamers. ▪ Make kites from paper grocery bags and test them on a windy day.
Sand and water table: Use a bulb baster to transfer colored water from one bowl to another. Air inside keeps water out. You have to squeeze out the air to make room for water.

Related books

The Magic Kite by Kira Daniel
The Windy Day by Janet Craig

Sandra Gratias, Perkasie, PA

4+

The Air Table

Science skills

Children observe the effects of various wind makers on different objects and use classification skills to organize those objects.

Materials

Wind Makers:
Foot air pump (easier for young children)
Hand fan
Air noise makers
Straw painting
Hand air pump
Balloons
Paper bags

Movers:
Feathers
Metal
Short pieces of ribbon
Blocks
Paint
Any other items in the room

What to do

1. Have all the materials available, and wait for a windy day.
2. Talk about the wind and about air. Air is all around us; we breathe and can fill a bag or a balloon with it. Air moves some things.
3. Introduce the wind makers to the children (balloons require close adult supervision). Let them experiment with the wind makers. For younger children, a foot pump is much easier to use than a hand pump.
4. Place the classroom objects on a table. Give the children time to experiment with each and

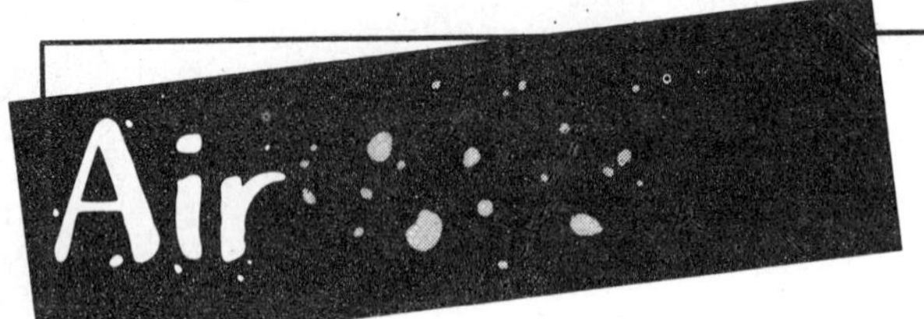

to see which items can be moved by the air created by the various wind makers and which cannot. Encourage children to categorize items.

More to do

Art: Make wind chimes and hang them outdoors near a classroom window. ▪Make wind paintings by moving liquid on a level paper with air from a wind maker. ▪Make decorative hand fans with poster board and tongue depressors.

Tom Gordon, Slippery Rock, PA

The Tortoise and the Hare

4+

Science skills

In the race between the two fabled animals, children observe the effect of wind and make predictions about who will win and why.

Materials

Two 10" (25 cm) circles of poster board, one with the picture of a rabbit on it, one with the picture of a turtle on it
Several sheets of newspaper
Chalk or masking tape
The Tortoise and the Hare fable
Indoors—a 15′ x 6′ (5 m x 2 m) non-carpeted, open area
Outdoors—a 15′ by 6′ (5 m x 2 m) smooth surface (concrete, asphalt, etc.)

What to do

1. Mark the starting line with chalk or masking tape. Ten feet (3 m) away mark the finish line in the same manner.
2. Tell or read the fable *The Tortoise and the Hare*.
3. Lay the poster board circles on the starting line about 3′ (1 m) apart.
4. Two children are each given a double sheet of newspaper. They use the newspaper to fan the air behind their animal and make their animal move. The first animal across the finish line wins the race.
5. Have the children experiment with the shape of the newspaper. Which shape is the most efficient mover of air—a flat sheet, a sheet folded in half or a sheet pleated into a fan?

Christina Chilcote, New Freedom, PA

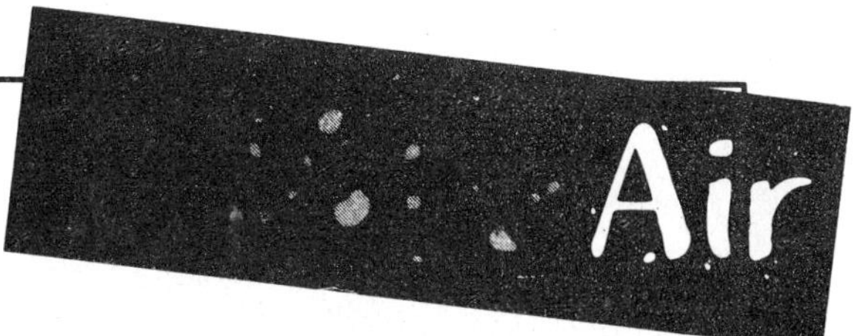

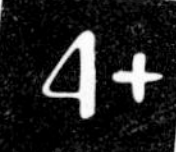

There She Blows!

Science skills

Children observe objects of different weights and sizes being moved by wind power.

Materials

Small electric fan or blow dryer
Masking tape
Assortment of lightweight items, such as:

- Cottonballs
- Wads of paper
- Packing nuts
- Leaves
- Ping pong balls
- Styrofoam cups
- Feathers
- Paper cups

Long smooth table or other flat surface
Marker
Assortment of heavy items

What to do

Note: Constant adult supervision is required for this activity.

1. Place fan or blow dryer at one end of table.
2. Place masking tape across the other end of table for the "Finish Line."
3. Ask the children to place objects in a row in front of vortex of fan while the fan is turned off.
4. Have the children guess which object will cross the finish line first.
5. Turn the fan on and observe.
6. Discuss wind force versus the weight and density of the objects.

More to do

Fine motor skills: Encourage children to create their own fans out of half sheets of construction paper folded back and forth.

Games: Create mazes and obstacles for objects to be blown through, over, under, around, etc. to encourage concepts of spatial relationships and construction.

Dani Rosensteel, Payson, AZ

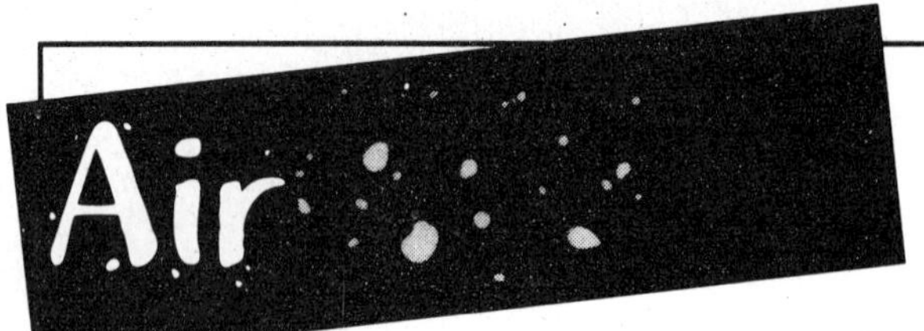

Wind Whirlers

4+

Science skills
Children make a wind toy and observe as the wind plays with it, and they practice fine motor skills.

Materials

Discarded miniblinds (lead-free, vinyl or aluminum), from a local thrift store
Hole punch
Large beads
Markers
String
Yarn

What to do

1. Before you make the wind whirlers, disassemble the blinds and sterilize them in bleach water. Allow to dry. Then, cut the slats into 6" (15 cm) pieces, rounding off the edges. Now punch a hole in the center of each slat.
2. Place the beads and slats on a table for children to string.
3. An adult ties one bead to the end of the yarn, and then instructs children to alternate slats and beads. Children can take turns stringing one classroom whirler, or each child may work on his own.
4. Allow the children to string as long as they like.
5. Top off the string with a loop for hanging, and mark each child's name on a slat.
6. Hang the whirler outside and watch the wind play!

Dani Rosentsteel, Payson, AZ

Jet Balloon Races

Science skills
Children have fun observing balloon races and predicting how far each balloon will go.

Materials

Balloons, all the same size
2 pieces of smooth string, each at least 10' (3 m) long
Masking tape
2 wooden chairs
1" (2.5 cm) piece of large plastic drinking straw, 1 per balloon

What to do

1. Tie one end of each string to the back of each chair.
2. Explain that as the air rushes out of a blown up balloon, it will push the balloon in the opposite direction.
3. Blow up two balloons to approximately the same size. Pinch the ends closed but do not tie off. Tape a piece of plastic drinking straw to the side of each balloon.
4. Thread the untied end of the string through the straw so that the balloon is close to the chair. Make sure that the untied end of the balloon is facing away from the chairs.
5. Hold the strings taut. At "ready, set, go," release the balloons. Which balloon goes farthest?
6. If one string is held horizontally, while the other string is held at an ascending angle, which wins? If one string is held horizontally, while the other string is held at a descending angle, which wins? If the strings are held at the same level and the second balloon is blown up to twice the size of the first balloon, which wins? After each experiment, ask the children why they think the results they observed happened.

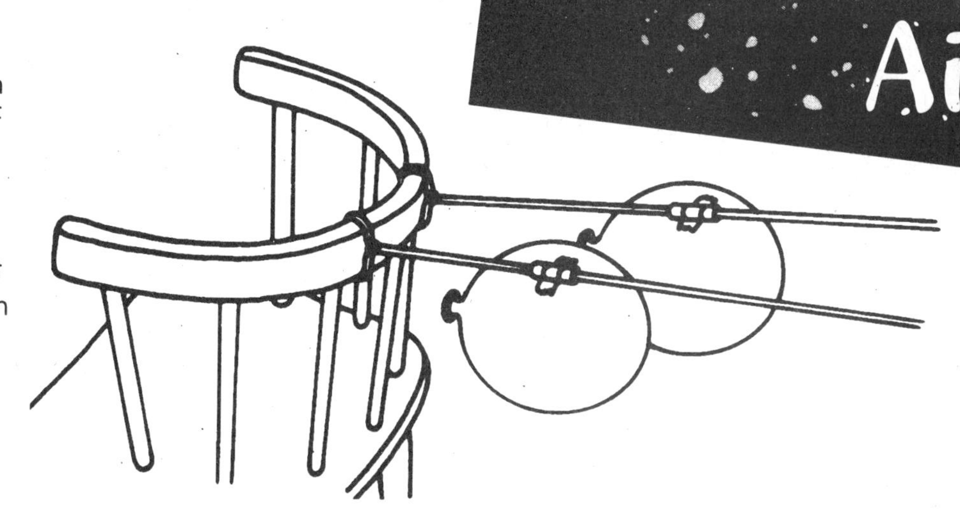

Related book

Curious George Gets a Medal by H. A. Rey

Christina Chilcote, New Freedom, PA

Parachutes

Science skills

Children make their own parachutes and fly them to observe and predict air flow.

Materials

Unbleached muslin fabric, cut into 8" (20 cm) circles
Fabric markers or crayons
Yarn or thin string, cut into 18" (45 cm) pieces, 4 pieces for each parachute
Large-eyed needles
Empty thread spools (may be purchased from craft supply catalogs or stores)

What to do

1. The children use the markers or crayons to decorate their circles of muslin.
2. Thread a piece of string or yarn through a needle. You will need to tie a piece of the string

Air

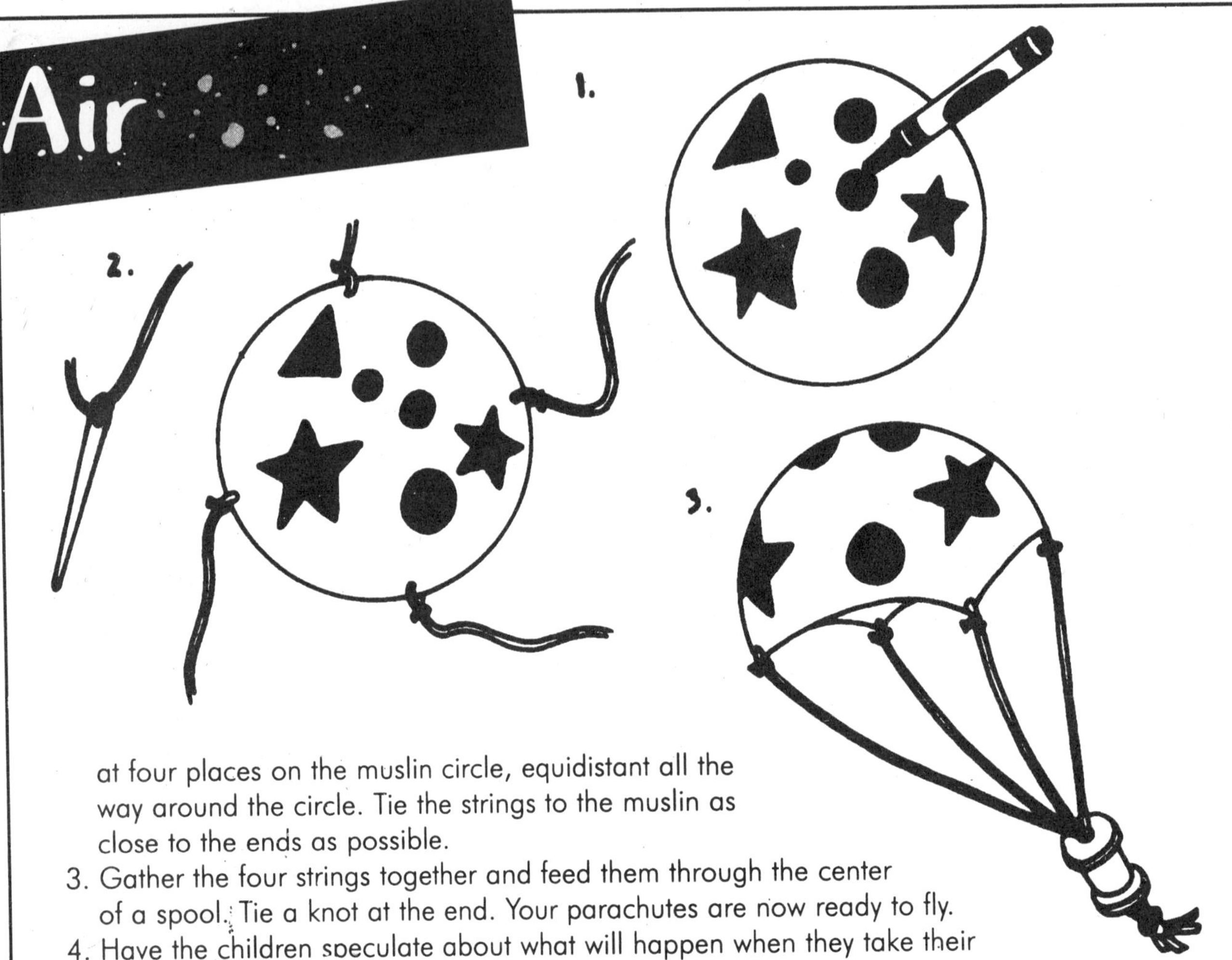

at four places on the muslin circle, equidistant all the way around the circle. Tie the strings to the muslin as close to the ends as possible.

3. Gather the four strings together and feed them through the center of a spool. Tie a knot at the end. Your parachutes are now ready to fly.
4. Have the children speculate about what will happen when they take their parachutes outside and toss them into the air.
5. Go outside and launch them by throwing them into the air. It helps if it is a breezy day. Explain to them that the material is catching the air, holding the parachutes up, then allowing them to drift gently down. (Make sure the children give each other some space so that no one gets hit by a parachute.)
6. You could have races to see which parachute goes the farthest or floats the longest.

More to do

Language: Have the children dictate a sentence about their parachute-flying experience. Sentences can be written on a chart story tablet and read by the whole class, or each child's sentence could be put on a separate piece of paper that she could then illustrate. Bind these pages together and give the collection a title, such as Our High Flying Adventure. Keep the book available in your classroom library.

Related books

Airplanes and Flying Machines illustrated by Donald Grant
Hot-Air Henry by Mary Calhoun

Deborah A. Chaplin, Hot Springs, VA

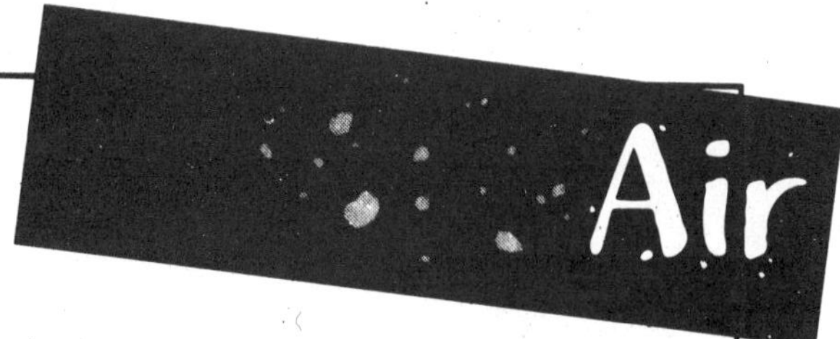

Bubble Paint

Science skills

Children learn observation, using all the senses to find air and wind.

Materials

Chalkboard
Pinwheel
Liquid soap
Enamel pan, 9" x 12" (22.5 cm x 30 cm)
Water
The Wind Blew by Pat Hutchins
Balloon
Tissues
Liquid tempera paint in blue, purple or red
Straws
White or manila paper

What to do

1. Read *The Wind Blew.*
2. Ask the children if they can see the wind.
3. Ask how we know about wind if we can't see it. Do the following quick activities to show the children the effects of wind.
4. Wet a small chalkboard and let children blow on it and observe the drying.
5. Blow up a balloon and release it.
6. Blow on a pinwheel.
7. Give each child a tissue to place over her face. Show how to blow and then catch it.
8. Blow bubbles and let the children catch them.
9. Now that they have practiced blowing air, fill the pan with water about an inch (2.5 cm) from the top.
10. Add the liquid soap, about 1 cup (250 ml).
11. Stir in the paint, about 1 cup (250 ml).
12. Give each child a straw and let them blow together into the water.
13. Bubbles will rise above the top of the pan. Gently cover bubbles with the paper.
14. Remove to a place to dry.

More to do

Art: Bubble prints make a great background for under sea pictures: sponge print fish, add leaves, glue sand and shells on the bottom.
More science: Make homemade kites and fly them outdoors.
Movement: Using scarves, the children dance to music.

Related book

Gilberto and the Wind by Marie Hall Ets

 *Teresa J. Nos, Baltimore, MD*

Alphabet

Floating Names

4+

Science skills

Children practice name and letter recognition while learning about the floatation and absorption properties of sponges.

Materials

Alphabet sponges, purchased at a craft store

Water table

What to do

Place a supply of alphabet sponges at the water table. Let the children experiment with the sponges, squeezing them, submerging them, etc. Encourage each child to spell her name with the sponges.

More to do

Sand and water table: Supply other objects at the water table for the children to experiment with. See if the objects float or sink.

Related book

Underwater Alphabet by Jerry Pallotta

Joyce Montag, Slippery Rock, PA

Magic Painting

Science skills

Children observe their names magically disappear after they have written them with water.

Materials

Clear plastic cup for each child
Pitcher of water
Large cement area
Tempera paintbrush for each child
Towels
Sunny day

What to do

1. Tell the children you are going to show them how to "magic paint."
2. Take the children out to a cement area in the sun.
3. Using water and a tempera paintbrush, paint your name on the cement.
4. Wait for a few minutes and watch as the letters disappear like magic.

5. Give each child a cup half filled with water and a tempera brush and let them "magic paint" their name and other letters of the alphabet on the cement.
6. Ask the children if they know what happened to the water; why did it disappear?
   Hint: Keep a pitcher full of water close by for refills; towels are handy for water spilled on clothes.

More to do

More science: Discuss the water cycle with the children and talk about evaporation. Do the following experiment. Write each child's name on her cup. Draw a line about three-quarters of the way up on each child's plastic cup with a permanent marker. Fill each cup to the line. Put some of the cups in a sunny spot in the classroom and some in a closet. Each day, check and see how much water has evaporated from each cup. Compare how much water evaporates in the sun and in the closet. The children can dictate stories about what happened to the water in their cups.

Barbara Saul, Eureka, CA

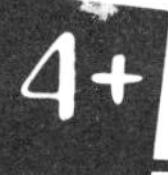
4+

The Vanishing Z

Science skills
Evaporation makes the Z vanish as the children watch.

Materials

One sheet of dark colored construction paper
Cotton swab

What to do

1. Wet the cotton swab.
2. Using the wet end of the swab, write a large letter Z in the center of the construction paper. Write it lightly so it will evaporate quickly, but make sure it is visible to the children.
3. Then slowly sing the ABC song like this:
   A B C D E F G H I J K L M N O P Q R S T U V W X Y...Where's Z?
4. Hold up the paper and show the children that the Z has vanished. Continue singing: "Z is no longer there, it evaporated in the air."
5. Explain to the children about evaporation.

More to do

More science: Give the children construction paper, cotton swabs and water. Let them draw their own vanishing pictures.

Dotti Enderle, Houston, TX

Animals

A-Hunting We Will Go

3+

Science skills

Learning about animal habitats is fun with this game.

Materials

Imaginations

What to do

1. Take the children on an imaginary animal hunt. All should sit in chairs with hands on their knees.
2. As the hunt begins, show them how to slap their knees alternately to simulate a person walking.
3. The children repeat each line after you say it and imitate your hand movements.
4. Chant this animal hunt poem as you slap your knees.

We're going on an animal hunt.
We're going to get some big ones.
I'm not afraid!
Oh, no!
What's that up ahead?
*It's a river.**
Can't go around it. (try other prepositions, too, for example, over or through)
Can't go under it.
We'll have to swim it.

* Suggestions for animal habitats:

Bird	Tree	Monkey	Tree
Lion	Grass	Tiger	Grass
Bear	Cave	Goat	Mountain
Bobcat	Mountain	Snake	River
Fish	River	Octopus	Ocean
Whale	Ocean		

5. Pause after the first verse and ask what kind of animals live in the river. Allow for some discussion and then suggest that the children attempt to catch some of those types of animals as you swim across the river.
6. Make swimming motions and pretend you are picking up various fish and water creatures and putting them in a sack. Wipe your forehead with your hand, shake your arms and begin slapping your knees again as you say the next verse of the poem.
7. Continue as you explore a variety of animal habitats, until you feel you have gathered enough animals or the children's interest begins to wane. Stop your safari in a nice field for

lunch and, over your pretend meal, discuss the animals you have collected during your adventure. Here are some questions you could ask to stimulate conversations. Where did we get the snakes? What lived in the tall grass? What did you find under the rocks in the river?

8. Discuss what you should now do with your collection of animals. Should you put them in a zoo or release them back into the wild? Maybe you can take them home with you in your backpack, or just let them loose to roam around the room.

More to do

Art: Cut out magazine pictures of a variety of animals and use them to make a collage to represent what you found on your animal hunt. ▪ The children can make their own binoculars for use on your jungle safari. Have them decorate two toilet paper rolls in any manner they wish. Avoid using glitter or glued-on materials since these will be used near the eyes and such materials often fall off. Tape or staple the two tubes together to form a pair of binoculars. Punch two holes in the ends and tie on some string or yarn so that the binoculars can be worn around the children's necks.

Language: Make a simplified lift-the-flap book about your jungle adventures. Cut out magazine pictures of jungle animals and glue them to an 8" x 10" (20 cm x 25 cm) piece of paper. Have the children draw a representation of that animal's habitat, such as grass for a snake or a tree for a bird. Cut the picture of the habitat out and create a flap to fit over and hide the animal picture. Affix the cutout to the 8" x 10" paper using glue or a metal brad. Now you can lift the flap to find out which jungle animals live in which habitat. Create a cover and bind the pages together into a book.

Related books and recording

A Creepy Crawly Song Book by Hiawyn Oram
Crocodile Beat by Gail Jorgensen
Hippo Lemonade by Mike Thaler
Into the Jungle by Judy Hindley
Jane Yolen's Old MacDonald Songbook by Jane Yolen
Jungle Walk by Nancy Tafuri
Nanta Lion's Search and Find Adventure by Susan McDonald
Stop That Noise by Paul Geraghty
The Tiger Who Lost His Stripes by Anthony Paul
Who is the Beast? by Keith Baker
"The Animal's Lullaby" by Tom Paxton

Mr. & Mrs. Mouse

Science skills

A mouse family teaches children to observe and ask questions about hibernation and nature.

Materials

Old aquarium, ¼ full of bedding and cedar chips (clean every four weeks)
Some type of wire mesh lid
Water bottle
Mouse food purchased at pet store
Cardboard tubes (toilet paper, paper towel)
Male and female mouse, pet store purchased

What to do

1. Prepare cage and add mice. Remember, tolerance is the name of the game for adults when mice are in the classroom, because with patience, a wonderful experience takes place.
2. This project is perfect for the winter season! Children often question what happens to animals in the cold and snow. These mice will provide your classroom with a first-hand visual experience of the answer. The more tubes you put in the cage, the more tunnels the mice create and the more tearing they do. Their homes become very elaborate.
3. You seldom see them work, just like the burrowing animals outside in the winter. But the children witness the creative structures that are built and how animals outside protect themselves from the elements.

More to do

More science: If you are lucky enough for Mr. and Mrs. Mouse to become parents, your children will witness a very supportive, caring and loving animal mother. Mr. Mouse should be removed from the cage at this time. Mrs. Mouse needs a clean cage and lots of cardboard to keep her babies hidden and secluded in the tunnels and bedding. She cares for them constantly. As the babies get older the mother starts revealing them slowly to the outside world. What an exciting learning time for the children! Consult your pet store about taking the mice and babies back. It is a completion to your unit that the children will accept.

Related book

The *Frederick* books by Leo Lionni

Diane L. Shatto, Kansas City, MO

Animal Sound Matching

3+

Science skills

The children use auditory and visual cues to identify animals.

Materials

Tape recorder
Cassette tape
Pictures of animals

What to do

1. Make or purchase a tape with animal sounds.
2. Play the tape for the children.
3. Let them identify animals making the sounds.
4. Then let the children make the animal sounds for the tape as the teacher holds up a picture of each animal.
5. Encourage the children to make up a story about animals, adding in animal sounds when needed. Put it on tape.

Related books and recordings

Early Morning in the Barn by Nancy Tafuri
Let's Go Home, Little Bear by Martin Waddell and Barbara Firth
"I Bought Me a Rooster"
"Old MacDonald Had a Farm"

Sherri Scott, Hermitage, TN

3+

Hibernating Bears

Science skills
Children learn about hibernation and nature and use fine motor skills.

Materials

Video about bears and hibernation
Empty boxes
Leaves
Toy teddy bears
Fake moss
Glue

What to do

1. During circle time discuss animals such as bears that become lethargic and hibernate during the cold winter months.
2. If possible, show the children a video on hibernating animals.
3. Have each child bring her favorite teddy bear from home, and supply each child with an empty box.
4. Tell the children they will be making homes for their bears to rest in for the winter.
5. Each child uses glue, fake moss and leaves to decorate their empty box and turn it into a cave.
6. Sing the Hibernating Bear song (below).

Original poem

Hibernating Bear (sing to the tune of Three Blind Mice)
Hibernating bear, hibernating bear.
Winter's drawing near, winter's drawing near.
Fill up your belly with something warm,
Then curl up and sleep all safe from the storm.
Hibernating bear, hibernating bear.

Related book
We're Going on a Bear Hunt by Michael Rosen

Lisa M. Lang, Parkersburg, WV

Peek-a-Boo Owl Puppets

Science skills
Using an owl puppet they made themselves, children learn about the owl's habitat.

Materials
Empty toilet tissue tubes, one for each child
Glue
White dot stickers, about ¾" (19 mm) in diameter
Green tissue paper squares
Scissors

What to do
1. Draw an oval shape on one side of the toilet tissue tube, about 1 inch (2.5 cm) in diameter. Draw it near the center of the tube.
2. Poke a hole with scissors into the oval for a starting point. Let the children finish cutting out the oval. (Pre-cut these for younger children.)
3. Roll the tissue paper squares into balls and glue them onto the top half of the tube.
4. On the white circle sticker dots, draw an owl.
5. Place the owl sticker on your pointer fingernail, then stick your finger up into the tube and out of the oval hole. Your owl is now perching in his tree home.
6. Use these puppets while you sing the following song:

   Little Owl (sing to the tune of "Frère Jacques")
   Little owl, little owl,
   In the tree, in the tree.
   Whoo-oo are you looking for?
   Whoo-oo are you looking for?
   Is it me? Is it me?

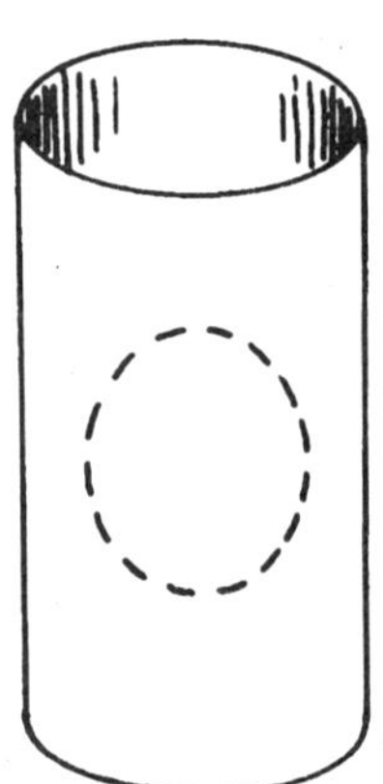
Draw and cut oval hole out of toilet tissue tube.

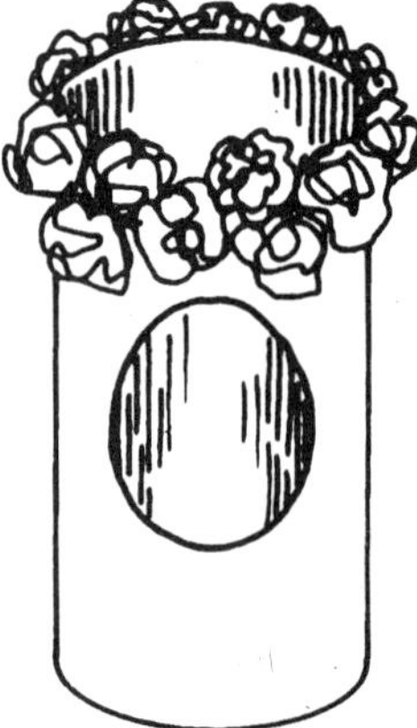
Decorate top of tube with tissue paper balls.

Place owl sticker on fingernail.

Related books
Owl at Home by Arnold Lobel
Owl Babies by Martin Waddell
Owl Moon by Jane Yolen

Valerie Chellew, Marshfield, WI

3+

Animal Pieces

Science skills
Children practice observation and classification skills as they match parts to wholes.

Materials
Line drawings of parts of animals: beaks, claws, tail, neck, legs, mouths, eyes
Pictures of whole animals
Glue
Cardboard pieces, 4" x 6" (10 cm x 15 cm)

What to do

1. Make two sets of cards. The first set is made by gluing drawings of parts of animals onto the cardboard. The second set is made by gluing pictures of whole animals onto cardboard.
2. The children sit on the carpet, and you pass out the animal piece cards, one per child.
3. Place whole animal cards on a chalkboard rail or wall chart pockets.
4. Children take turns matching the animal parts with the whole animal pictures.

Susan R. Forbes, Holly Hill, FL

3+

Putting Life in Order

Science skills
Children observe the life cycle of frogs first-hand and practice classification and ordering skills.

Materials
Fish net, from local pet store
Plastic peanut butter jar, thoroughly cleaned and rinsed
3 or 4 milk jugs, gallon size (4 L), or similar containers
One five-gallon (20-liter) fish tank (or larger)
Several tadpoles acquired from a local pond or stream
Poster board
Markers

What to do

1. If you can, go on a field trip to find some tadpoles (for instructions, see More to do, below). If not, then visit a local pond or stream yourself and collect some tadpoles.
2. Upon returning to your classroom, place your newly acquired tadpoles in your fish tank. Heating it is not necessary, as the tadpoles are at home in cold water. Add a few leaves, twigs or rocks taken from the same pond as the tadpoles. (Using plants or rocks acquired elsewhere may introduce an unfamiliar and therefore deadly form of bacteria into the tadpoles' environment.)
3. Make a simple graph on your poster board. There should be four columns, one for each stage of a tadpole's life. The headings should read: 1. Eggs, 2. Tadpole Stage One, 3. Tadpole Stage Two, 4. Frog.
4. As your tadpoles grow and develop, keep track of their progress by having the children draw pictures of their changing development. Attach the pictures to the poster board graph under the appropriate heading. If you were not able to collect any frog eggs, you will need to supply a picture of the eggs. If possible, take photos of the tadpoles as they grow and post them on the graph also. You can feed your tadpoles a combination of live weeds, grasses (from the same pond where you found the tadpoles) or you can get pre-mixed tadpole food at your local pet store.
5. Emphasize that the development of the tadpoles always happens in the same order. Even though the tadpoles may differ in size and appearance, they go through the developmental stages in the same order. Review the growth graph daily.
6. After the children seem to fully understand the various stages of a tadpole's growth, make a small set of pictures for each child. The cards should depict the same stages of development as the graph.
7. Ask each child to place the pictures in the correct order. They can then compare their cards to the graph to check their work.
8. After your tadpoles have matured into frogs, discuss what you should do with them. Should you keep them as classroom pets or return them to their own environment? Have the children vote on what you should do. If you decide to return the tadpoles to the wild, plan another trip to their original pond or stream and have a "Letting Go" celebration.

More to do

Games: Have Frog Jumping races. The children will enjoy hopping from start to finish. Remind them to move like the frogs. ▪ Play a good old fashioned game of Leap Frog. Many of the children in your classroom will have no prior knowledge of this fun and physically demanding game. Remind the children to be careful while hopping over each other's heads.

Language: Make a book about the stages of your tadpoles' development. Ask the children to draw pictures and write or dictate short descriptive sentences about each stage of development. Bind the pages together into a book. Invite the children to brainstorm a title for the story. In our classroom we finally settled on "The Story of Wiggly and How He Grew." We limited ourselves to writing about one specific tadpole.

More science: If permitted, take the children on a field trip to catch the tadpoles. Check the pond or stream before taking the children to make sure tadpoles are actually there. Then provide some children with a small net (like the ones you find at a pet store). Carefully supervise as the children attempt to scoop up the tadpoles. Don't keep too many. Five or eight tadpoles should sufficiently support this activity. If you overload your tank, you will have problems keeping the tank sufficiently clean. Also, collect a few frog eggs if you can. Although these will probably not hatch, they are useful for helping children successfully order the life of a frog. Put the tadpoles in a clean and thoroughly rinsed peanut butter jar. At the same time, collect three or four gallons of water from the same area as the tadpoles. Be sure to scoop up some dirt, leaves and mud from the bottom. Your tadpoles will find food there.

Related books

An Extraordinary Egg by Leo Lionni
Felix and the 400 Frogs by Jon Buller and S. Schade
Frog on His Own by Mercer Mayer
Frogs and Toads and Tadpoles, Too by Alan Fowler
From Tadpole to Frog by Wendy Pfeffer
Jump, Frog, Jump! by Robert Kalan
Tadpole and Frog by Christine Back and Barrie Watts

Virginia Jean Herrod, Columbia, SC

3+

Snowshoe Hare's Surprise

Science skills

Children observe the surprising color change of a snowshoe hare in winter and spring.

Materials

Tan construction paper or large brown grocery bags
Pattern of sitting snowshoe hare
Pencil
Scissors
12 mm wiggle eyes
White drawing or construction paper
Pink, brown and black markers
Scotch tape or small amount of white glue
White crayon

What to do

1. Find the area on a globe where the snowshoe hare lives. It can be found in Alaska, Canada and the Northern United States and also southward to the Great Lakes, the Rockies and the Appalachians.
2. Compare the summer food and winter food of the snowshoe hare.
3. Use the word "camouflage" in reference to the snowshoe hare. How are other animals camouflaged with their environment?
4. Engage the children's creativity and bring the snowshoe hare to life by making puppets.
5. Trace hare pattern on brown paper. Trace the same pattern on white paper. Cut out the brown and white hares. Cut a brown tab 2" (5 cm) long by 1" (2.5 cm) wide.
6. Color tips of ears black on both hares.
7. Trace legs and ear line between ears. Use brown marker on brown hare, black on white hare.
8. Color nose, mouth and one ear pink on both brown and white hare.
9. Draw eye with brown marker, color inside with pink marker then glue on wiggle eye in center on both brown hare and white hare.

Animals

10. Color with white crayon on brown hare only. Color around pink on ear, edge of other ear, around marker line of eye and paws.
11. Color brown fur lines on brown hare; pencil fur lines on white hare.
12. Add pencil whiskers on both brown and white hares.
13. Glue tab at face area, under brown hare, on top of white hare on reverse side. Fold and cut notch if desired.
14. Fold bottom flaps under so they overlap, the brown hare faces forward.
15. Then when brown hare grows longer white fur and changes to all white for winter, flip white hare forward. Now bottom flap will face outward on both hares. White flap will depict snow and the ground and hare will still stand up. When it is spring again, flip brown hare forward. The change of color of snowshoe hare is the surprise.

More to do

Art: Let children form a flat or three-dimensional snowshoe hare out of clay (modeling clay) or gray clay that can be glazed and fired, or out of playdough.

Dramatic play: Dramatize the zigzag hopping, the freezing like a statue and other traits of the snowshoe hare. Other children could be a fox, lynx, mountain goat, owl, golden eagle, plover and other arctic animals or birds. The snowshoe hare should have different reactions to each depending on whether the animal or bird is friendly or a predator.

More science: Using pictures from books or magazines, compare the shape and size and color of cottontail rabbits, jack rabbits, lop-eared rabbits, European rabbits, Arctic hares, jumping hares, pygmy rabbits, Vienna blue rabbits and snowshoe hares. What kind of rabbit do you have in your area? ▪ Discuss animals that hibernate. Which animals sleep part of the winter? The snowshoe hare does not hibernate at all. ▪ Compare the feet of animals and their tracks left in the snow. You can play a matching game to match tracks with pictures of animals, perhaps using a flannel board. The large wide feet of the snowshoe hare give it its name.

Original song/poem

The Snowshoe Hare

(sing to the tune of "The Farmer in the Dell")

The snowshoe hare is brown.
That is his summer coat.
He nibbles on some grass and leaves,
And then he eats some fruit.

His white fur starts to grow
Thicker and longer in the fall,
Until you cannot see the brown
Anywhere at all.

The tips of his ears are black,
And the snow falls all around.
He looks like a white statue
That doesn't make a sound.

His favorite time is night
When danger is not near.
Then he can eat and jump and dance
Without any fear.

Little Bunny

I see a little bunny
In the garden near.
And I walk very quietly
So that he won't hear.

But when I'm almost to him
He looks and hops away.
I wish he would be my pet.
Maybe he'll be back some day.

Related book

Summer Coat, Winter Coat: The Story of the Snowshoe Hare by Doe Boyle

 *Mary Brehm, Aurora, OH*

The Little Red Barn

3+

Science skills

The children learn about the farm life of animals through a field trip and their own dramatic play.

Materials

Poster board
Small plastic farm animals and other toy farm pieces
Farm-style dress-up clothes

What to do

1. Take a trip to a farm. Talk with a farmer and/or schedule a farm animal visit.
2. Make a "What Happens in a Barn?" poster. Ask the children the question after taking a field trip to a farm. Record their answers.
3. Add small farm animals, toy barns, tractors, trucks, etc. to the block area and add farming clothing to the dramatic play area so that the children can imaginatively play out the barn information they have learned.

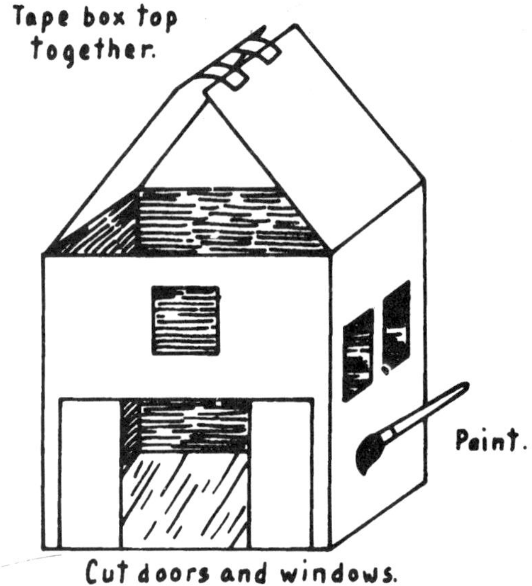

More to do

Dramatic play: The teacher holds the box top flaps up and tapes them together to resemble a barn roof. Keep a slight gap at the peak of the roof to let lighting in. Cut front and back doors if desired. The doors can be cut to open and shut or can be completely cut out so that only doorways remain. Windows can be cut the same way. Place the box on drop cloths and let the children paint the box. Teachers can add defining touches if desired but this should be as child-directed as possible. Allow the box to dry for several hours. After the box is dry, add a bale of hay or straw to box bottom to create the flooring inside of a barn. Add planters as animal troughs for stuffed animals.

Related books and song
E-I-E-I-O by Gus Clarke
Inside a Barn in the Country by Alyssa Satin Cappucilli
No Moon, No Milk by Chris Babcock
Pet the Baby Animals by Lucinda McQueen
"Old MacDonald"

 *Tina R. Woehler, Flower Mound, TX*

3+ Sorting Farm, Zoo and Woods Animals

Science skills
In learning about animal habitats, children practice sorting and classification skills.

Materials
Small plastic animal figures
Small cardboard boxes with pictures pasted in the bottom and word labels attached: Barn, farm, cage, zoo, trees, woods

What to do
After lessons in which you introduce animals that live on a farm, in the zoo or in the woods, arrange this individual activity to reinforce the concepts. Put the various animals in a basket and let the children sort them according to where they live.
Alternative: Use laminated pictures of animals and compartments of a muffin tin as habitats.

 *Mary Jo Shannon, Roanoke, VA*

3+ Warm Whales

Science skills
In a fun experiment, children use all their senses to observe and predict the outcome.

Materials
Favorite book about whales
Cold water
Solid cooking shortening
Boot or mitten with removable insulated liner
2 medium-size bowls
Paper towels

What to do
1. At circle time, read your favorite book about whales.

2. Discuss how some whales live in very cold water. How do they stay warm? How do people stay warm?
3. Explain that people can wear extra layers of clothing. Show the boot or mitten and remove the liner. Discuss how this extra layer keeps people warm.
4. Since whales don't wear clothes, how do they stay warm in the very cold water?
5. Here's a fun way to demonstrate how they do it: Fill 2 bowls three-quarters full with cold water. Ask a child to place one hand in each of the bowls. How does it feel? Both hands are cold. Now the teacher completely covers one of the child's hands with shortening. Place this hand in one of the bowls and place the other hand in the other bowl. Which hand feels cold? The hand covered with shortening is protected from the cold. Whales are also protected from the cold with a layer of fat called "blubber." Using paper towels, clean off the child's shortening-covered hand.

More to do

Home living: Have many types of clothing available in this center so the children can practice dressing in layers: T-shirts, sweaters, sweatshirts, boots, socks, mittens, etc.

More science: Fill a clear plastic soda container, 12 to 20 oz. (375 ml to 625 ml), label removed, half full of water. Add a few drops of blue food coloring. Add baby oil to fill the container to about one inch (2.5 cm) from the top. Screw on the cover tightly and shake to mix. Holding the bottle on its side, rock it gently to make "waves" appear.

Original poem

Blubber

Here's a tale of a whale,
Who was never cold!
Not a bit, not even a little chilly,
So I'm told!

To stay warm, people wear clothes,
And can even try rubber!
But whales wear a wonderful thing
Called blubber!

Related books

Animals Should Definitely Not Wear Clothing by Judi Barrett
Going on a Whale Watch by Bruce McMillan
Whales by Gail Gibbons

Kathy A. Lone, Sioux Falls, SD

3+

Hidden Animals

Science skills
Children observe first-hand how animals protect themselves from predators in nature.

Materials
Sand
Bucket
Red and beige construction paper

What to do
1. Ahead of time, fill a bucket or bin with sand. Cut about 30 half-inch (13 mm) squares from the construction paper, 15 of each color.
2. Talk with the children about how in nature, plants and animals blend in with their environment. This is their protection from predators.
3. Show the children the red and beige squares. Count them so the children see that there is an equal number of each. Then mix the squares up in the sand.
4. Set a timer for one minute. Children sift through the sand and try to find the red and beige squares.
5. When the timer goes off, count to see how many of each color were found.
6. Relate the results back to the concept of plants and animals blending in with their environment. To reinforce this point, play the game again, this time telling the children to pretend that they are hungry lions, and that the squares are little mice that lions love to eat. Note that the "beige mice" are the ones who more often escape the hungry lions!
7. As an option, substitute white packing material for sand and use red and white paper.

More to do
Art: Draw animals on colored construction paper using the same color marker and then a different color marker. Note that the differently colored animals are easier to see.
More science: Hide plastic animals in the classroom by setting them against backgrounds that match or blend in with their colors. They're camouflaged!

Related book
The Mixed-Up Chameleon by Eric Carle

Suzanne Pearson, Winchester, VA

Animals

Learning About the Farm

3+

Science skills
With fine motor skills and encouragement to ask questions about nature, children create farm scenes.

Materials

Construction paper, wide variety of colors
Glue or paste
Farm animal stickers
Red and black felt
Yellow crayons
Cotton balls
Brown fingerpaint or tempera paint
Short and long pieces of straw
Black markers or crayons

What to do

1. Talk with the children about what living on a farm might be like and how it would differ from living in a city. You can also talk about driving farm equipment instead of cars.

2. Talk about where the food we buy at the store comes from and how it is grown. You can discuss the different types of weather farmers need to have their crops grow and when they might be harvested.
3. On day one of your farm discussion, cut large pig shapes from pink construction paper and let each child paint brown mud on their pig. Give each child a sheet of manila construction paper with a cow drawn on it. Let the children cut or tear black and white squares or spots from construction paper and paste them onto the cows.
4. On day two, give each child a piece of manila construction paper with a scarecrow drawn on it, or let them draw their own scarecrows. Give them precut clothes (hat, shirt, pants) cut from various colors of construction paper to paste on the scarecrow, or let them cut or tear their own version of clothes to paste on. Glue pieces of straw to the ends of arms and legs. As an option, tear small pieces of paper to paste on clothes as patches.
5. On day three, draw lambs on white construction paper, and give one to each child. Cover the lamb with glue and give each child cotton balls to pull apart and paste on the lamb. Use a black marker or crayon to add the face.
6. On day four, help the children cut large barns from red construction paper. Each child can paste her barn onto a piece of manila paper and then add stickers of different farm animals. The animals can be in or out of the barn. Perhaps she'll want to glue some or all of the previous day's projects onto the scene.
7. On day five, encourage the children to draw large nests on manila paper. Give them white or brown oval shapes for eggs to paste in the nest, or let the children cut out or tear out their own eggs. Count out how many eggs are in each nest and write the number under the nest.
8. On day six, cut one large and one small red rectangle and one large and one small black circle for each child from construction paper. Paste the pieces together on a sheet of manila paper to make a tractor. Let the children also take turns putting together similar shapes from felt to make tractors. Small groups of two to three children can work together.
9. On day seven, cut out vegetables from construction paper, such as green beans, green pea pods, red tomatoes, yellow ears of corn. Give each child one of each vegetable to make a "sunshine garden." Let each child paint the bottom area of a piece of manila paper brown for soil. Paste the vegetables over the soil after the paint dries. Encourage the children to decorate their pictures further, perhaps adding a big bright sunshine or some clouds, grass or flowers.
10. On day eight, cut out more vegetables from construction paper, like orange carrots, brown potatoes, brown onions, red radishes. Give each child one of each vegetable to make an underground garden. Cover a piece of manila paper with brown paint. When it dries, the children can paste their vegetables on it. Alternatively, children could paste these underground vegetables onto their pictures from the day before.

More to do

Math: Count the eggs each child put in his nest. Compare each nest to see which has more or fewer eggs.

More science: Plant bean seeds and watch them grow in your classroom.

Movement: For a gross motor activity, pretend to be farm cats. Stretch, slink, paw the ground, crawl, arch your backs up and down, and go to sleep. ▪ Pretend to be scarecrows bending and swaying in the wind. Talk about why farmers use scarecrows.

Animals

Related books and rhymes

Big Bird's Farm by CTW (Sesame Street Staff)
Big Red Barn by Margaret Wise Brown
Eating the Alphabet: Fruits and Vegetables from A to Z by Lois Ehlert
Going to Sleep on the Farm by Wendy Cheyette Lewison
I'm Going to Be a Farmer by Edith Kunhardt
Jack's Garden by Henry Cole
Mary Had a Little Lamb by Sara Josepha Hale
Mouse and Mole and the Year-Round Garden by Doug Cushman
Old MacDonald Had a Farm illustrated by Pam Adams
One Cow Moo Moo by David Bennett
Rockabye Farm by Diane Johnston Hamm
Spot Goes to the Farm by Eric Hill
The Supermarket by Gail Gibbons
Nursery Rhymes:
"Baa Baa Black Sheep"
"Farmer in the Dell"
"Little Boy Blue"
"Mary Had a Little Lamb"
"Old MacDonald Had a Farm"

Diane K. Weiss, Fairfax, VA

A Bully in the Tank

Science skills

Children make observations and predictions; working together builds their sense of community.

Materials

Beta fish
4 to 6 feeder goldfish
2 ½ gallon (10 L) fish tank that can be divided with glass dividers

What to do

1. Talk to the children about what it means to be a bully. Ask the children what usually happens to bullies.
2. Show them the two different types of fish. Explain that Beta fish are known to be aggressive just like bullies, and explain that the smaller goldfish are kind to each other.
3. Set up the tank on a table in front of the group, with the tank dividers handy.
4. Discuss with the children whether they think the teacher should put all of the fish together.
5. If children reply "yes," then remind them that the Beta fish can be mean.
6. If children insist on putting all the fish together, go ahead and put them all together.
7. Encourage the children to count the fish and draw a picture of each fish on a large piece of paper. Hang up the paper so that as the days go by the children can map the progress of the goldfish. Each day, or as things start to happen again, bring the tank over and ask the children

what should be done about the Beta fish being a bully.

8. When children come up with ideas to separate or punish the Beta fish, show them the tank divider. Then explain that it would keep the fish separate but they would still be able to see each other so the mean fish would not get lonely.
9. Separate the fish with the divider. The children may then be interested in talking about how people who are bullies should be treated, as well as what they can do in school or at home when someone is a bully.

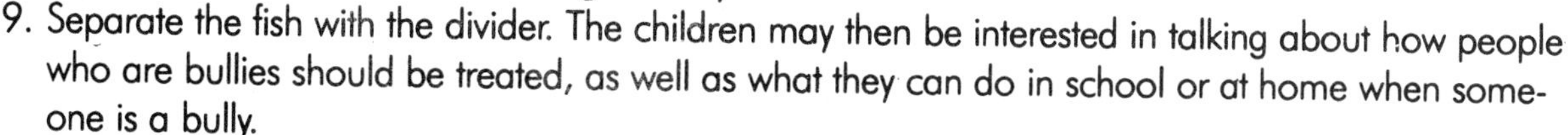

10. The teacher can then use the saying: "get along" (with hands held together) or "get along" (with hand doing a brushing motion to show that the person should leave) to remind the children of their experience with the fish.

 *Melissa Browning, Milwaukee, WI*

3+

An Animal in Your Hand

Science skills
The children are encouraged to make observations about animals and to use fine motor skills.

Materials

Paper lunch bags
Wiggle eyes
Construction paper
Markers
Scotch tape
Pipe cleaners
Tissue paper
Scissors
Glue

What to do

1. Read a book about a particular animal or discuss the animal of the week.
2. Each child may decide on an animal puppet to make (he may decide to make the animal from the story you read or something else).
3. Ask each child to name materials they might need to make the puppet (keeping in mind the different body parts).
4. Assist the children in making their puppets: have ready pictures of the particular animal, and answer questions about the shape, size and location of the animal's body parts.

More to do

Dramatic play: Use the puppets to make a puppet show. ▪ Use the puppets for problem solving, to explore emotions and to boost imagination.
Field trip: Go on a nature walk and try to observe real animals.
Special days: On a certain day, children can bring in their pets and talk about how they are different (appearance, food they eat, where they sleep, what they do) and what is the same about all the pets.

 *Billie Miteva, Pomona, NJ*

Animals

Born or Hatched? 3+

Science skills

Children develop observation skills and learn to classify animals.

Materials

Index cards, 3" x 5" (7.5 cm x 12.5 cm)
Pictures of birds, snakes, lizards, dinosaurs, puppies, kittens, mice, horses, etc.
Two bags, one labeled with a picture of an egg that says "Hatched" and one with a picture of a baby that says "Born"

What to do

1. Draw or find pictures of animals to be classified.
2. Glue the pictures to the index cards.
3. Cover the cards with clear contact or laminate.
4. Use clear contact to attach the picture of an egg to one bag and the picture of the baby to the other bag. Print the words "Born" and "Hatched" on the appropriate bag.
5. The children take the top card and classify. This activity and discussion about each card should be done as a group. Then the children can repeat it on their own as a reinforcement activity.

Phyllis Esch, Export, PA

Earthlings A to Z 3+

Science skills

Children learn about the animals in alphabetical order.

Materials

Globe
Library books on animals

What to do

1. Set aside one day of the week to be "Meet an Earthling" day, then introduce a different animal each week.
2. Use the following list of "earthlings," or make your own:

A-ant	I-iguana	Q-quail
B-bear	J-jaguar	R-rooster

C-cat	K-kangaroo	T-tiger
D-donkey	L-lion	U-unicorn
E-elephant	M-mouse	V-vulture
F-fish	N-newt	W-whale
G-gorilla	O-octopus	X-is in ox
H-horse	P-polar bear	Y-yak
	S-seal	Z-zebra

3. Explain to the children that everyone who lives on the earth is an earthling. We all share the earth and need to learn about it and care for one another. Read a story about an earthling.
4. On the globe, locate where the different earthlings live.

More to do

Alphabet: This activity lends itself to a study or refresher on the letters of the alphabet.

Art: Draw, paint or look in books and magazines for pictures of the earthlings. Hang them up in the room.

Field trip: Take a trip to the zoo. Learn about people who care for animals such as veterinarians, zookeepers, farmers, etc. Invite one of them to come and speak with the children.

Related books

Biggest, Strongest, Fastest by Steve Jenkins
Dear Children of the Earth by Schim Schimmel
I Love You, Mouse by John Graham
Polar Bear, Polar Bear, What Do You Hear? by Bill Martin, Jr.
Quick as a Cricket by Audrey Wood

Susan Rinas, Parma, OH

3+

Whose Baby?

Science skills
The children learn classification and visual skills in this matching game.

Materials

Magazine pictures of both young and mature animals
Oaktag cards, 6″ x 8″ (15 cm x 20 cm)
Scissors
Glue
Are You My Mother? by P. D. Eastman

What to do

1. Cut out the pictures of young and mature animals. Glue them on to oaktag cards.
2. The children sit in a circle on the floor; give each child a card.
3. The teacher holds a card first and asks either "Who has my baby?" or "Who has my

mother/father?". The child with the correct card brings it up to the teacher to make a match.

4. The game proceeds round-robin fashion with each initiating child asking either "Who has my baby?" or "Who has my mother/father?".
5. Read *Are You My Mother?*.

More to do

More science: Set out the cards on a table. Children may work at matching the cards during center time.

Related book

Animals Born Alive and Well by Ruth Heller

Susan R. Forbes, Holly Hill, FL

Pet Prints

3+

Science skills

In this delightful game, children hone their observation skills, and compare and contrast similar items.

Materials

Ink pads or paint and a pan
Paper
Photos of animals or similar pictures from magazines
Contact paper

What to do

1. Send the children home with an ink pad or paint and a pan and four pieces of paper. Attach a note asking parents to assist their child in making four paw prints of their pet or a friend or neighbor's pet. Also request that they send in a photo of their pet.
2. Collect the the paw prints and cover with contact paper for durability. Match the photos to the prints and mark the backs of the photos with stickers or colored shapes similar to those on the paw prints. This will enable the children to check their answers at a self-directed center.
3. At a center or during circle time bring out several of the paw prints and spread them out for all to see. Discuss their differences and similarities, sizes and shapes, etc. Begin to guess what kinds of animals would leave such footprints.
4. One by one, show the children's photos that the children brought in and begin to match the prints to the photos.
5. Put the pet prints and the matching photos on a table or leave them on the carpet during free play so the children can use them as a self-directed activity.
6. Children can also make prints of their own bare feet with paint. When the footprints are dry and covered with contact paper, the children try to find the prints that match their own feet.

Related book
The Snowy Day by Ezra Jack Keats

Ann Gudowski, Johnstown, PA

3+

5 Cave Critters

Science skills
Through a flannel board story, children become interested in the environment and nature.

Materials

Five Cave Critters flannel board story
Flannel board pieces (created in advance): crawfish, blind cave fish, a bat, red spotted salamander, a cave cricket, a large cave shape that all of the creatures will fit into
Large flannel board

What to do

1. Prepare all of your flannel board pieces, perhaps even laminate them.
2. It is really fun to start your circle time with this flannel board story:

Five Cave Critters

When walking through an old, damp cave,
I knew that I must be extremely brave.
For I was told that I would see,
Five different cave creatures right before me.

Water was trickling at my feet.
A crawfish snapped, it was really neat.
Next, I would see, down by the pool,
A blind cave fish, an orange jewel.

I heard a squeak and up I looked,
A baby bat in the rock was hooked.
Down on the floor, running through my light,
Was a red spotted salamander, twinkling bright.

As I walked deeper into the cave,
A cave cricket hopped, but I was sooo brave.
Five unique creatures, I was lucky to see,
Maybe there are more, "Want to come with me?"

3. Copy the above story onto index cards so that it is easy to handle and not as obvious as a large sheet of paper during circle time.
4. Next, line up all the flannel board objects in the order in which you plan to use them. This helps to keep everything running smoothly.

5. Quickly prepare the children for a great surprise. Don't share anything about what they will be learning until after the story.
6. Start the story immediately. Be very enthusiastic!
7. After the story is completed ask the children open-ended questions to encourage their
participation. This is an excellent way for children to share their thoughts and interests.
8. Encourage the children to handle and look at all the flannel board pieces. This gives them further opportunity to ask questions.

More to do

Art: Offer the children a variety of activities. Two favorites are bat ears and toilet paper tube bats. Make the bat ears by first drawing two bat's ears (which look like fat tear drops), making a head band to fit the child and then attaching the ears with the points facing out to the sides. The children can make the toilet paper tube bats by painting their toilet paper tubes a dark color (black, gray or brown). Allow them to dry, and then the children can cut out wings from tissue paper in a dark color. You can explain that the paper is fragile just like the bat wings. Then cut out a face, draw its features and attach both the wings and the face with white glue. Finally, hang the bats from the ceiling in your classroom.

Dramatic play: Turn the dramatic play center into a giant cave. Use a dark colored blanket to cover the shelves in which you create "the cave." Keep a crate of important items you must never forget when cave exploring: flashlights, hard harts, binoculars, magnifying glasses, notepads and pencils for noting or drawing about all the lovely things you will see. Create a cave atmosphere with plastic creatures and flannel ponds, etc. Add small fossils and magnifying glasses, informative books (with lots of great pictures) from the local library, flash cards, pamphlets on local caves and other hands-on materials.

Related books

Beast Feast by Douglas Florian
Stellaluna by Janell Cannon
Under the Ground by Gallimond Jeunesse

Debora L. Stuck, Nixa, MO

Animal Matching Game

Science skills

Children develop memory by playing matching card games.

Materials

2" x 3" (5 cm x 7.5 cm) cards (cut them from old manila file folders or from scrap cardstock available from copy shops)

Stickers of animals, insects or birds, two of each (sets of stamps are free from the National Wildlife Association if you subscribe to Ranger Rick or Your Big Backyard)

What to do

1. Center one sticker on each card.
2. Separate the cards into two decks, so one of each picture is in each deck. Then mix or shuffle each deck separately.
3. Lay out cards from one of the decks in a row.
4. Draw cards from the other deck, matching them to the ones that are laid out.

More to do

Games: Play Concentration. Shuffle all the cards together and lay them face down in rows. At each turn, players turn over cards, hoping to find a match. Players remove matched cards. If the turned cards don't match, they are turned face down in the same place. The idea is for players to remember the position of the cards.

Mary Jo Shannon, Roanoke, VA

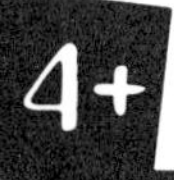

4+

What Do I Eat?

Science skills

Children sort and classify as they learn what foods different animals eat.

Materials

Pictures of a variety of animals
Plastic or real animal foods such as an acorn, carrot, hay, dog bone, birdseed, log chewed by a beaver, beehive, small snail shell, rubber worm
Table

What to do

1. Lay the pictures of the animals on the table and place the food items on the table also.
2. Children work at matching the food and the pictures.

More to do

Games: Make a file folder game using the same principle, only this time using pictures of animals and the places that they usually sleep or live. ▪ On a large piece of cardboard, trace or draw the continents, color them in different colors and write the names of each on them. Then provide small pictures of animals for the children and talk about where the animals originally come from. Write the name of the continent on the back of each so the children can check their work. This activity is a wonderful way to introduce the children to the geography of the world, especially if you are planning a trip to the zoo, where continent maps are usually posted for each animal.

Melissa Browning, Milwaukee, WI

Animal Tracks

4+

Science skills

Children develop a total picture of an animal using observation, classification, imagination and predicting skills.

Materials

Masking tape
Pictures of animals, drawings or cut from magazines
Pictures of animal tracks to copy

What to do

1. Using masking tape, form animal tracks on your classroom or gym floor. You can form the tracks with tape or copy tracks you've drawn on paper and then tape to the floor. Begin tracks on one side of the room and work them toward the opposite wall. Let them zigzag and cross each other.
2. Tracks should end at the opposite wall, where the children will find a picture of the animal hung at their eye level. Remember that a human is an animal also.
3. Instruct children to follow a set of tracks to an animal picture. After the children name the animal, ask them if they can show you how they think this animal would move? What would it eat? Where would it live? Can they make a sound like this animal picture?
4. At circle time, share information on each animal with the children. Record children's remarks and discoveries on a piece of paper to be posted next to each animal picture.

More to do

More science: You can ask each child to adopt an animal until next class. Assign each child an animal and ask him to find out one fact about his animal. During the next class, he can share his knowledge with everyone. Have an encyclopedia on hand in case someone forgets. The new facts can be added to your lists posted next to each animal.

Related recording

"Animal Action" on *Kids in Motion* by Greg and Steve

Connie Heagerty, Trumbull, CT

4+

Bats

Science skills
Children's curiosity about the environment and nature is encouraged, especially about bats.

Materials

Flashlight
Tree, silk or real
Black paint
Bat stencils for tracing, different sizes
Black construction paper
Discarded refrigerator box
String
Large paintbrushes
Paper hole punch
Stellaluna by Janell Cannon

What to do

1. Read *Stellaluna* to the children. Talk about the habitats of bats, what bats eat and why bats hang upside down.
2. Children trace around bat stencils onto black construction paper, then cut out and punch a hole in the bottom of a bat. Attach string so the bats can hang upside down from your indoor or outdoor trees.
3. Make a cave. You and the children can set up the dramatic play area as a camping center with the cave as one of the props. Let the children paint the outside of a refrigerator box with black paint. Hang some of the stencil bats inside the cave. Children can look into the box with a flashlight, or carefully crawl into the box to look at the bats.

More to do

More science: Compare bat habitats to those of other animals. Find pictures of animal habitats and make a mural. ▪ Collect a live insect collection. ▪Make a chart graphing other animals that fly, hang upside down, hibernate and live in caves and trees.
Snack: Children can make and eat a bat fruit salad.

Related book and magazines

Bat Jamboree by Kathi Appelt
Ranger Rick and *Your Big Backyard*, National Wildlife Association

Cheryl Collins, Hughson, CA

Animals

Cuddly Koala Puppet

4+

Science skills

With the fun of making a puppet, children learn observation, sequencing, fine motor and visual skills.

Materials

Old white shag rug or white fake fur
Brown lunch bags
Scissors
Medium-point black marker
Pink marker
Brown and black construction paper
Pink, white and black crayons
White glue
15 mm wiggle eyes

What to do

1. Discuss facts about the koala. Compare the koala's hands and feet with human hands and feet.
2. Cut white fur for ears and under chin area ahead of time.
3. Make patterns for the head (with ears), arm, body and leg. Trace two arms and two legs.
4. Make body pattern slightly larger than the front of a lunch bag.
5. Cut the body parts out of brown construction paper. Glue them onto the front of the upside-down bag.
6. Cut the nose out of black construction paper.

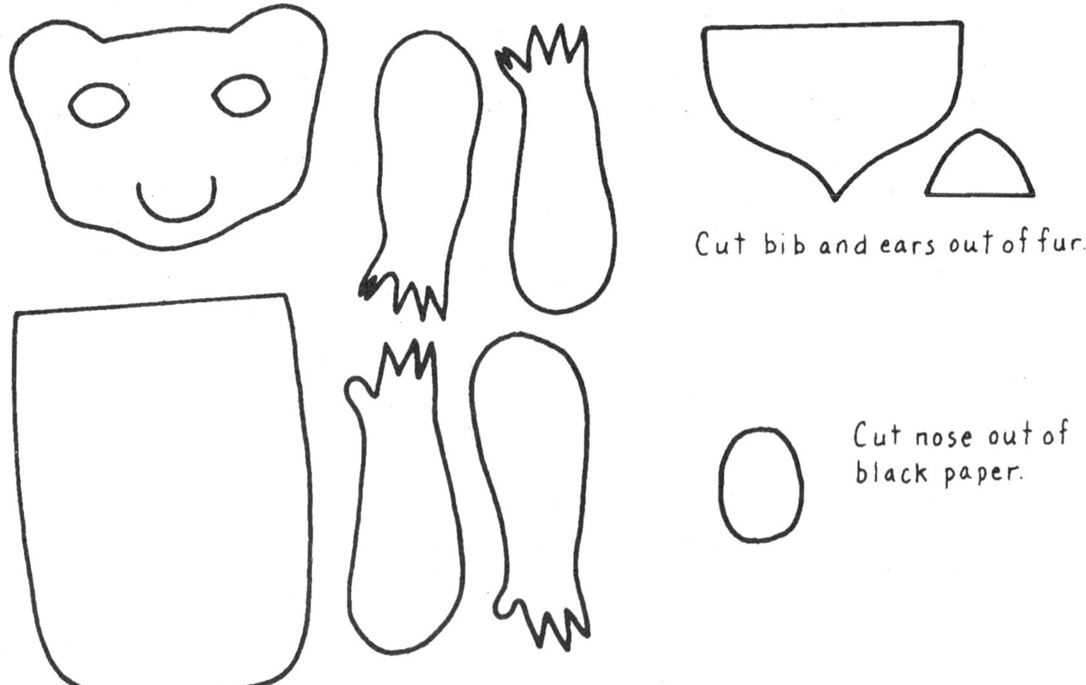

7. Use black marker to color claws on arms and legs.
8. Draw a mouth on the head with black crayon, then white crayon.
9. Use pink to color the tongue and white on the sides for cheeks.
10. Glue on wiggle eyes. Draw around wiggle eyes with black crayon, or the children can draw eyes first, then glue wiggle eye to each center.
11. Dab pink on fur tips of ears with pink marker.
12. Glue the nose to the head, and a fur piece onto each ear. Then glue the head to the top of the upturned bag and a fur piece under the "chin."
13. Glue arms between bag folded areas, sloped upward.
14. Glue legs with toes pointing in toward the other leg.
15. Put a blacker marker line to show where the two toes are grown together as one, but with two claws.

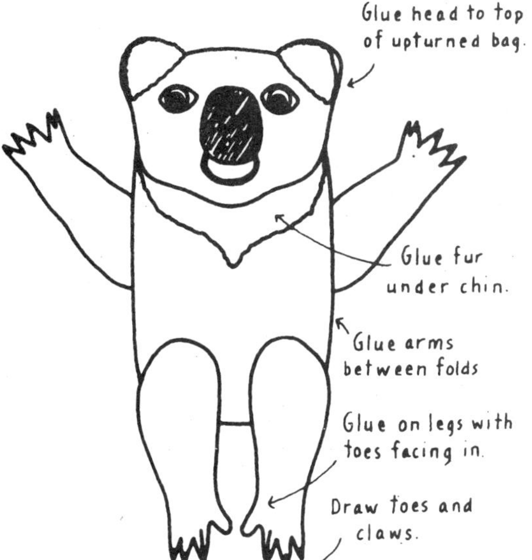

More to do

Dramatic play: Dramatize being a baby koala, growing and climbing, sleeping and eating.

More science: Find Australia on a map or globe. Let the children fly a small airplane from where they live to Australia. Show pictures of other unusual animals that live in Australia. ▪Name other animals that have pouches. ▪Discuss the reason koalas are not found in most zoos (only in the San Diego and Los Angeles zoos outside of Australia because eucalyptus trees will grow there).

Original song

Oh, Have You Seen a Koala?
(sing to the tune of "Oh Have You Seen the Muffin Man")

Oh, have you seen a koala, a koala, a koala?
Oh, have you seen a koala? She lives very far away.

Oh, yes, I've seen a koala, a koala, a koala.
Oh, yes, I've seen a koala. She lives in Australia.

Oh, have you seen her baby, her baby, her baby?
Oh, have you seen her baby? She carries him in her pouch.

Oh, maybe I'll see her baby, her baby, her baby
Oh, maybe I'll see her baby when he crawls out of her pouch.

Animals

The Furry Koala and Her Baby

The mama koala climbs up toward the sky.
In a eucalyptus tree where she's high and dry.

She smells each leaf before she will eat it.
Her strong muscles and claws help her to reach it.

She has a pouch where her new baby will grow.
The baby is always with the mommy, you know.

When the baby is too big for mommy's warm pouch
He'll hold on mommy's fur like the back of a couch.

Once in a while mom climbs down from the tree
Then on the ground, she walks very awkwardly.

Back in the tree they both sleep all the day
Then awake at night, they climb and swing and play.

The leaves give mommy water so she doesn't need to drink.
The koala has brownish-gray fur, and looks cuddly, I think.

Mary Brehm, Aurora, OH

Hamsters Play While We Sleep

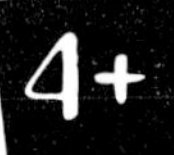

Science skills
By observing a real hamster in the classroom, children learn about the habits of nocturnal animals.

Materials

Hamster in cage
White construction paper
Yellow crayons
Paintbrushes
Chart paper
Black marker
Black paint diluted with water

What to do

1. Bring in a hamster in a cage and have the children observe its behavior for several days.

2. As the observations flow, record each one on a large sheet of paper entitled, "What we observe about our hamster." Encourage the children to discuss the hamster's sleeping patterns. Introduce the word nocturnal (active at night).
3. For each child write: "Hamsters are nocturnal" on a white piece of construction paper and help him to read the sentence. Explain what it means.
4. Reinforce the concept. Have each child color a yellow hamster in the center of the page underneath the words. Encourage the children to press down hard with their crayon and color their hamster completely.
5. Crease the paper and fold the sentence back. Then have the children paint over the hamster picture and the entire page with the diluted black paint.
6. The hamster will shine through the black night. Hamsters are nocturnal!
7. Brainstorm a list of other animals that are nocturnal, for example, raccoons or bats.

More to do

More science: Darken the room and challenge the children to attempt to locate an object in the dark. What are the challenges of working in the dark? Talk about ways nocturnal animals adapt. For instance, hamsters have an excellent sense of smell. Bats have sensitive ears and echo-location.

Snack: Serve dry cereal mixed with nuts and seeds for a delicious hamster snack.

Ann Flagg, Clarion, PA

4+

Horse Sense

Science skills

This activity fosters children's observation and classification skills.

Materials

Plastic model of a horse
Velcro strips, cut into ¼" (6 mm) square pieces
Piece of poster board approximately as wide and long as the horse model
Smaller pieces of poster board for one-word labels
Small container for the labels

What to do

1. Before introducing this activity to the children, select the vocabulary you wish to introduce, such as mane, tail, back, neck, foreleg, hoof, etc.
2. Make a small printed label with each vocabulary word and laminate it for long wear. Attach Velcro pieces to the back of the label cards and to the corresponding point on the model horse's body.
3. Make a chart with an outline drawing of a horse and the vocabulary words written on or near the correct body part, mounted on poster board and laminated for long wear.

4. Introduce the model horse and explain that here is a name for each part of a horse's body. Remove the labels from their container and point out that each label word matches a word on the chart. Note that it is not necessary for the child to be able to read the words, only to match them.
5. Using the Velcro patches, attach each label to the point on the horse's body corresponding to the point where the word occurs on the chart, reading each word aloud as you go.
6. Check your work by looking at the chart to see that the words on the horse's body are in the same positions on the chart.
7. Return the labels to their container and invite the children to choose this activity during free choice time.

More to do

More science: After a child has practiced with the chart, ask her if she would like to try to label the model correctly by reading the label words and attaching them without help from the chart. Let the child then use the chart the check her work. ▪ Use models of different animals and introduce different vocabulary. There are excellent models of other farm animals, dinosaurs and human bodies commercially available. ▪Make copies of your outline drawing with blank lines where the labels should go and let older children write the name of each body part in the correct space after matching the labels to the model.

 *Susan Jones Jensen, Norman, OK*

Rocky Raccoon Puppet

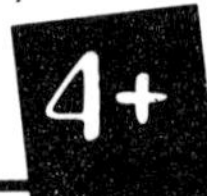

Science skills

With the fun of making a raccoon puppet, the children learn observation, sequencing, fine motor and visual skills.

Materials

Ranger Rick magazines
Black, brown, pink and white crayons or tempera paints
Scissors
White glue
Large brown bags
Brown lunch bags
Pencil
20 mm wiggle eyes

What to do

1. Let children look at several issues of *Ranger Rick* magazine.
2. Discuss traits of the raccoon. The name raccoon means "the washer." Raccoons like to wash their food before eating it. They eat tadpoles, minnows, corn, fruit, nuts, vegetables and garbage. They have 40 teeth, nimble fingers and are very curious animals. Baby raccoons can climb before they can even see. Raccoons have "masks" and stripes on their tails.
3. Trace the patterns for the head, tail, leg and jaw of a raccoon on the large brown bags and cut out.

4. Using a brown lunch bag for the body, draw and color the pink tongue on the jaw; color black around the edge. Add white teeth.
5. Crayon black and brown features on the head: mask, nose, top of legs, paws.
6. Add white on the face; then glue on eyes. Make pencil whiskers. Color black stripes both sides.
7. Glue head on top bag flap (the bag is upside down).
8. Glue jaw under bag flap.
9. Glue on arms, legs and tail.
10. Add black fur marks.

More to do

Dramatic play: Have raccoon puppet show using the puppets the children made. ▪Children can dramatize being raccoons. Pretend to wash food, climb trees, take a lid off of a garbage can, find a shiny object, etc.

More science: Baby raccoons are called kits. Other animal baby names are owlet, cub, pup, cygnet, duckling. What animal babies have these names? ▪Raccoons are nocturnal: they hunt for food at night. Discuss other nocturnal animals.

Original song and poem

Little Raccoon (sing to the tune of "Frère Jacques")

Little raccoon, little raccoon,
By the light of the moon,
By the light of the moon.
Your eyes look like a fluorescent green,
You are the cutest thing I've seen,
Little raccoon, little raccoon.

Little raccoon, little raccoon,
Awake at night,
Awake at night.
Your tail is striped and you look mean,
Like a robber on Halloween,
Little raccoon, little raccoon.

Animals

Brown Raccoon at Night

Brown raccoon hunts in the light of the moon
For his food—he'll find some soon.
He will eat just about anything—fruit, nuts,
Veggies or even a bird wing.
You can spot him with his mask and striped tail.
He may even hunt in your garbage pail.

Take the food to the stream near by,
Slosh it in water so your throat won't be so dry.
Run, little raccoon, so wild and so free,
Then with your nimble paws climb a tree.
Take a nap in the early morning light,
Getting ready to prowl again the next night.

Mary Brehm, Aurora, OH

4+

Sea Animal Sensations

Science skills
Children practice predicting and inferring to guess an animal correctly in a game.

Materials
None

What to do

1. While children are sitting in a circle, sing the following song to the tune "I'm a Little Teapot":
   I'm a little sea animal thin and smooth.
   I have two fins, they help me move.
   When I want to have fun I wiggle my tail,
   Swim in the water and go for a sail.
2. Ask the children to think of a sea animal they would like to be if they lived in the sea.
3. Choose one child to go into the circle and act out her sea animal.
4. Let the children guess what sea animal they think that child is.
5. Once someone guesses the type of sea animal the child was, that person goes into the center and acts out her sea animal.

More to do

Music: Make up various songs that go with the sea animals that were acted out, for example:
I'm a little sea animal _________ *and* ________.
I have two __________, *and they help me* ________.
When I want to have fun I wiggle my ________.
I swim in the water and go for a ________.

Related book
The Ocean Alphabet Book by Jerry Palotta

Stephanie Person, Kingsburg, CA

Animals

What Animal Is It?

4+

Science skills

Children reconstruct a mystery animal from its bones and learn observation and ordering skills.

Materials

Whole chicken, cooked

Stickers or pictures of 4 or 5 different animals, including a chicken

What to do

1. After baking or boiling the whole chicken, remove the meat from the bones.
2. Wash and dry the bones well (microwaving helps the bones dry quickly).
3. Display the bones on a science table.
4. Discuss how scientists had trouble reassembling bones into the proper animal when they first discovered dinosaur bones.
5. Show the pictures of animals; one must be a chicken.
6. Children try to reassemble the bones and guess which animal the bones came from.
7. Record their guesses. Tell them there is a hint in the bones. (Birds are the only animal to have a wishbone. Children are usually familiar with that from Thanksgiving.)
8. Reveal the correct answer.
9. Correct guesses get dinosaur stickers.

More to do

Games: Hide real or paper bones in the classroom and go on a bone hunt.

Teresa J. Nos, Baltimore, MD

What Do Squirrels Eat?

Science skills

Through observation and experimentation children learn what squirrels eat.

Materials

Book about squirrels

Crackers

Nets

Bread crumbs

What to do

1. Read the class a book about squirrels.
2. Discuss what squirrels might like to eat.
3. Try feeding different types of nuts and crackers or bread crumbs to squirrels. Observe which type of foods squirrels eat.
4. Discuss with the children which foods squirrels ate. Write an experience story with children.

More to do

Art: Children draw pictures of squirrels eating or make collages using cut-out squirrels and real nuts.

Deborah Hannes Litfin, Forest Hills, NY

Gator Gait

Science skills

In making an alligator headband and acting out alligator movements, the children's curiosity about the natural world is encouraged.

Materials

Cardboard egg cartons (one carton will supply three children)
Oaktag
Green paint
Wiggle eyes
Scissors
Green paper
Glue
Chart paper with "Gator Gait" (next page) written on it

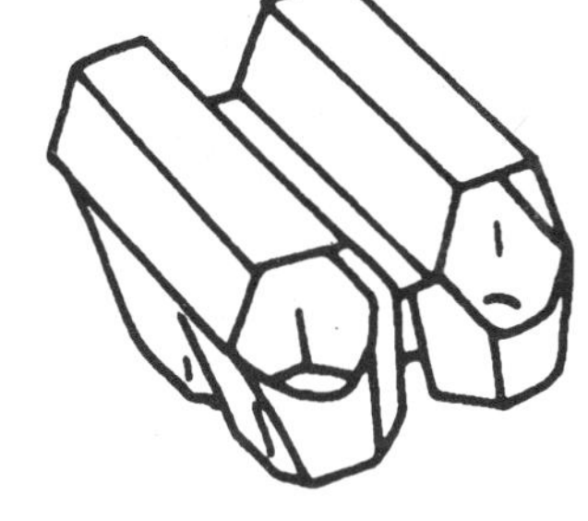

What to do

1. Cut the cardboard egg cartons, with top still attached, into three equal sections. Give each child one section.

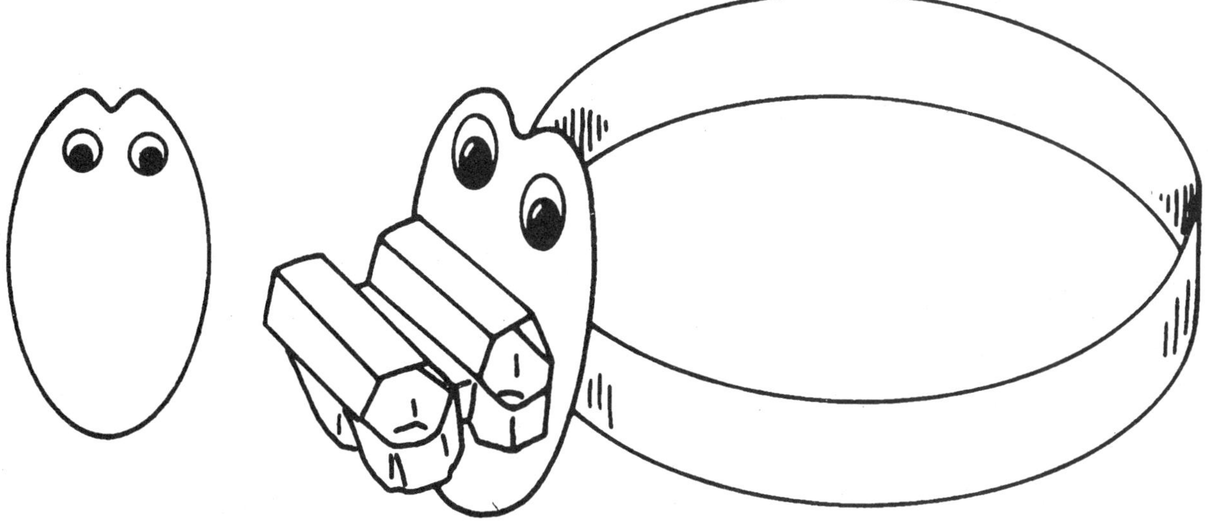

This is the alligator's mouth.

2. On the oaktag trace one oval for each child. This will be the alligator's head. The size of the oval should be 6" x 3½" (16.5 cm x 9 cm) with an indention in the top of the oval, forming the bulging alligator eyes. The children can cut out the mouths.
3. Have the children paint both the mouth and head green (paint on the side of the oval that now bulges upward).
4. While the alligators are drying, the children make headbands using the green paper. Show them how to fold the paper in half lengthwise, then in half twice more, and cut on the creased lines. Pair off children to help each other measure their heads for headbands using the green strips they just cut out. They glue the strips together to form their headbands.
5. Once the alligators are dry, the children will glue the mouth onto the center of the head, then glue two plastic eyes in the center of the bulges at the top of the head, and then glue their headband to the back of the head.
6. While the glue is drying read "Gator Gait" to the children. Go through the motions while reading together with the class. Now sing "Gator Gait" and do the actions. Ask children to tell you what they learned about the alligator from the song. For example, they should be able to tell you where it lives, how it moves, etc.
7. After the alligator discussion, the children put on their gator headbands. Now sing and act out "Gator Gait" once more together.

Original song

"Gator Gait" (sing to the tune of "Three Blind Mice")

Say, "Let's do the gator gait!"

See the little gators, see the little gators
Doing the gator gait, doing the gator gait
They slither and slide (hands together, arms out in front weaving back and forth)
They sneak and spy (cup hand over forehead, crouching shoulders and head)
With a snap (alligator's mouth, opening and closing hands, together then apart, then close with a clap) and a swap (alligator's tail thrashing back and forth in water—wiggle bottom back and forth)
And a splish and a splash (imitate tromping through water on all fours)
Scurrying through the tall swampy grass (imitate hurrying through tall grass, pushing it aside with your arms like doing the dog paddle)
See the little gators, see the little gators
(Shout) Doing the gator gait!

Related book

There's an Alligator Under My Bed by Mercer Mayer

Kathy Brand, Greenwood Lake, NY

Fish and Frogs

Science skills

Children learn about pond life, and their social development is enhanced with a small research project.

Materials

Fish Is Fish by Leo Lionni
Chart paper or chalkboard
Pocket chart
Fish and frog references—pictures and informational books

What to do

1. If possible, read a poem or book about frogs.
2. Invite children to tell what they know about frogs, ponds and fish. Record this on a chart or chalkboard. This could be one day's lesson, or you might continue if interest is high.
3. Read Leo Lionni's *Fish Is Fish*. Discuss aspects of the story such as how we all change as we grow, certain animals have to live in certain places to survive, we can still be friends with others even if they are different than we are, etc.
4. Ask the children to list how fish and frogs are different and how they are the same. This can be recorded on a chart or board.
5. Have animal reference books and picture encyclopedias available in the classroom. Divide the class into small groups. Each group can research one of the following areas: fish life cycle, natural fish food, natural fish enemies and how frogs are helpful, etc. Each group member might have a job such as researcher, recorder and reporter. Children should be allowed about two days to research and record their findings.
6. When the research is completed each group will have a turn sharing the facts they learn with the class. Visuals such as books and pictures are encouraged. As each group reports orally, record research findings on a big poster.

More to do

Art: Children can draw pictures of pond life, a fish hatchery or any other fish or frog story they care to depict with crayons. ▪ The children could also do a watercolor wash of blue, green, brown or other colors.

Games: In groups children could make up riddles about different types of fish and amphibians and have the others try to guess what animal it is.

More science: Read *The Little Turtle* by Vachel Lindsay to demonstrate one of the minnow's natural enemies. ▪ Set up a goldfish bowl or tank in the classroom. Discuss the care and feeding of the goldfish.

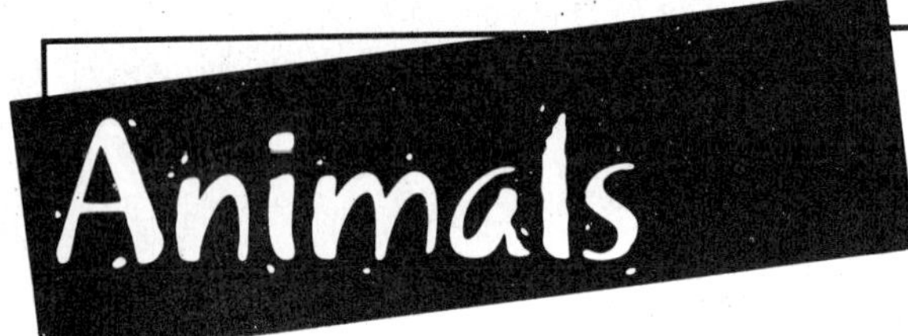

Related books
Fish Is Fish by Leo Lionni
The Little Turtle by Vachel Lindsay

 *Jeannie Gunderson, Caspar, WY*

Frog Information in a Can

5+

Science skills
Learning frog facts encourage children's interest in nature.

Materials

Pringles can, empty
Large wiggle eyes
Scissors
Construction paper
Glue
Index cards, cut into 1" x 5" (2.5 cm x 7.5 cm) strips

What to do

1. Make a frog by covering the Pringles can with green paper. Glue on the wiggle eyes, a frog mouth and frog legs. Cut a slit in the mouth (the lid) wide enough for the strips to slide in or out.
2. As you learn about frogs, have children dictate information about frogs. Begin each sentence with the word "Frogs." For example: "Frogs hop." "Frogs eat bugs." "Frogs like to live near a pond." "Frogs have long tongues."
3. Place the strips in the frog can. Pull them out one at a time and read them with the children.
4. As a variation, write some strips that are not true, such as "Frogs eat berries." "Frogs have six legs." Mix these with the true statements. Tell children the frog can only eat the true statements. Read the statements and have children decide if the statement can be fed to the frog.
5. Place the frog can in the science area so children can use it independently.

More to do

Math: Children practice estimation and counting skills when you put frog counters or gummy frog candies in a small jar. Put in a different number each day. Count the frogs each day after all have guessed, and let the children jump like frogs as many times as the number of frogs. Having a big difference in the number from day to day allows the children to experience the idea that larger numbers fill more of the jar. ▪Help each child cut out a lily pad shape, about 9" x 12" (22.5 cm x 30 cm), from green construction paper. Have each child put 12 frog stickers on his lily pad. Roll a pair of dice. A child counts the dots and tells how many there are. Children use frog counters or buttons to cover that number of frog stickers on their lily pads. As a variation, cover all the frog stickers with buttons or frog counters and remove the number that is called out. How many are left?

Snack: The children can make Frogs on a Log by cutting two-inch pieces of celery and filling the celery's cavity with peanut butter or cheese spread. Then place a gummy frog on each log, using the peanut butter to hold the frog in place.

Original song

Sing to the tune of "Twinkle Twinkle Little Star."

Little green frog likes to hop,
Hop and hop and hop and hop.
Hopping here, hopping there
Hopping, hopping everywhere.
Little green frog likes to hop,
Hop and hop and hop and stop.

Related books and recording

Frog and Toad are Friends by Arnold Lobel
Frog: See How They Grow Book by Tim Taylor
Jump, Frog, Jump! by Robert Kalan
The Mysterious Tadpole by Steven Kellogg
Tuesday by David Wiesner
"Five Green and Speckled Frogs" (available on many children's music albums and in song books in your library)

 *Barbara F. Backer, Charleston, SC*

5+

Life Cycles

Science skills
Children work on their sequencing skills.

Materials

Life cycle pictures from old science books
Glue
Flannel board
Construction paper, various colors
Felt

What to do

1. Cut out pictures showing the life cycle of a frog, butterfly, chicken, robin, etc.
2. Mount the stages of each on a piece of construction paper, using a different color for each animal.
3. Laminate the pictures, then back them with felt.
4. Let the children pick an animal or insect and arrange the pictures of its life cycle in proper sequence on the flannel board.

More to do

Games: Have a child dramatize a stage in the life cycle of one of the animals. The other children can guess which stage and which animal it is.

Related book and recordings

Chickens Aren't the Only Ones by Ruth Heller

Animals

"Baby Bird," *Wee Sing Children's Songs and Fingerplays*
"Egg to Chick," "Butterfly Song" and "Pollywogs," *Animals*, Sing and Learn

Jackie Wright, Enid, OK

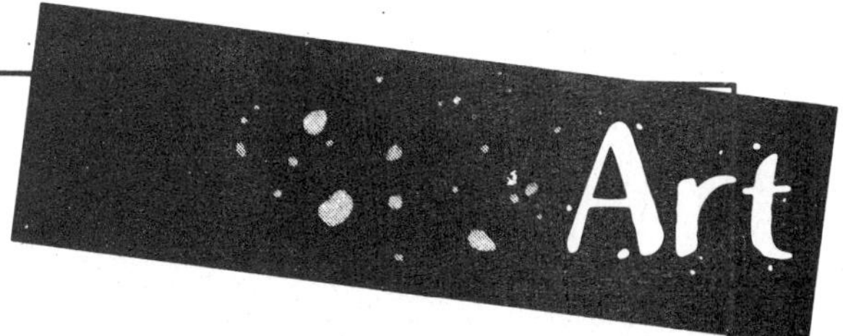

3+

Blossom Study Tablecloth

Science skills

Children use fine and gross motor skills to create art from nature.

Materials

Flat, hard work surface such as a concrete floor
Plain white tablecloth or white sheet
Hammer
Permanent marker, optional
Paper grocery bags
Collection of fresh flowers, blossoms and leaves
Table knife

What to do

1. Spread the grocery bags out on a concrete floor or other hard work surface. The work surface should be able to take extremely hard pounding with a hammer.
2. Spread half of the tablecloth out over the grocery bags. Let the other half spread out on the floor for the moment.
3. Arrange the collection of flower blossoms and leaves over the grocery bag half of the tablecloth. Ignore the other half for now. Encourage the children to group and arrange blossoms and leaves by color, type, size or other scientific observation. Some scientists like to arrange the blossoms in order from small to large or by groups of color. Others like to make a pattern or combination of both. Any grouping ideas are okay.
4. Now fold the other half of the tablecloth carefully and gently over the arranged and grouped flower blossoms and leaves. Two people may be needed so that the blossoms don't blow away.
5. Next, feel where covered blossoms are with your fingers. When you find them, pound on them with a hammer until the juices and colors soak through the fabric. Be careful not to pound so long and hard that you make a hole.
6. Move on to other blossoms and leaves, continuing to hammer until all the blossoms have been pounded and their colors have soaked into the tablecloth.
7. Open the tablecloth. Scrape the plant bits and pieces away with a table knife and brush extra bits away with the palm of the hand.
8. Cover a table with the cloth, showing the naturally colored fabric.
9. To compliment the tablecloth, place a vase of flowers in the center of the table, the same kinds of flowers used in the project. To launder the tablecloth, wash it in cold water only. Even so, colors will fade significantly. Do not use bleach. Dry on low.

More to do

Language: Write the names of the flowers and leaves directly on the tablecloth with a permanent marker. Make lines around the plant impressions with the permanent marker to help highlight groupings or plant varieties.

More art: Create napkins or a table runner using the same directions.

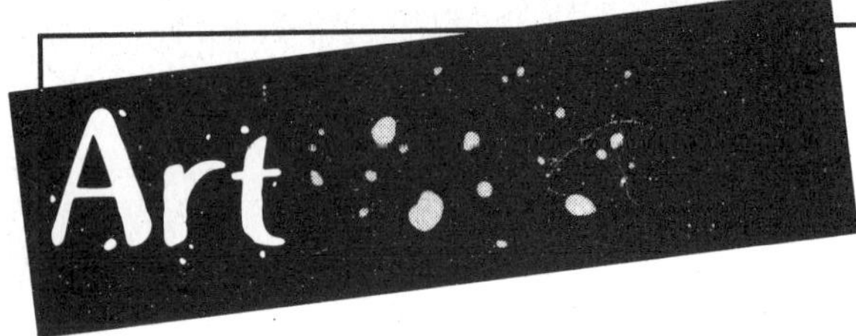

Original poem

Billowy Pillowies

Cherry blossoms, pink and billowy
Apple blossoms, white and pillowy.
Every tree all soft and fluttery
Filled with flowers sweet and puffery.
Then the wind becomes all blowy,
Blossoms fly like winter snowy.
Now my hair's all billowy pillowy,
And my clothes are fluffery puffery.
See the ground, just like snow,
That's how billowy pillowies go.

 *MaryAnn F. Kohl, Bellingham, WA*

Tie-Dye Weaving

Science skills

This artistic activity teaches observation and fine motor skills.

Materials

12" (30 cm) strips of cotton muslin, 1" (2.5 cm) wide, prewashed
Bowls or buckets for dye
Food coloring, as many colors as you desire
Water
Rubber or latex gloves
Outdoor wire fence or chicken wire loom

What to do

1. Tie each strip with two knots that are tight enough to resist the dye, but loose enough to untie later.
2. Mix food color and water in bowls or buckets.
3. Allow children to dip the muslin strips into the first color.
4. Squeeze the excess dye out of the muslin into the bowl or bucket.
5. Repeat in at least one more color (you may want to use primary colors only).
6. Hang to dry.
7. Untie the knots when the strips are dry.
8. Weave the strips into a fence or loom.

Cathy Costantino, Carol Patnaude, Lynn R. Camara, Warwick, RI, and Darlene Maloney, East Greenwich, RI

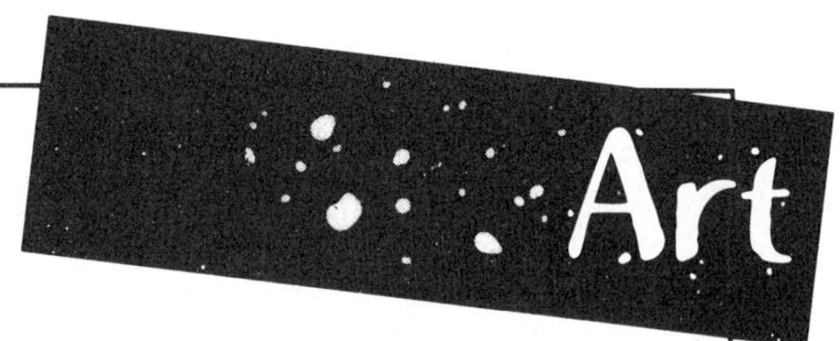

3+

Sun Prints

Science skills

Children make predictions, observe cause and effect and check their predictions.

Materials

Dark-colored construction paper
Collection of classroom objects, such as scissors, crayons, blocks
Sunlight

What to do

1. As the children are seated for circle time, discuss the collection of objects in relation to their shapes.
2. Ask each child to select a few items and place them on a dark-colored piece of construction paper.
3. Encourage the children to predict what will happen to the construction paper when it is placed in the direct sunlight.
4. Put these papers with the objects on them in direct sunlight. This can be done indoors by a window in the direct sun, or outdoors.
5. After a few minutes, the children can remove the objects to discover what happened to the paper.
6. Discuss why the shapes of the objects remain on the paper even though the objects have been removed (the sunlight faded the paper). Compare the results to the children's predictions.

More to do

More art: Without the children, prepare different prints and have the children guess what objects were used to make those prints.

More science: Do this activity during different seasons of the year and discover why it takes longer for the print to appear in winter than in summer.

Related book

What Makes a Shadow? by Clyde Robert Bulla

Sandra Fisher, Kutztown, PA

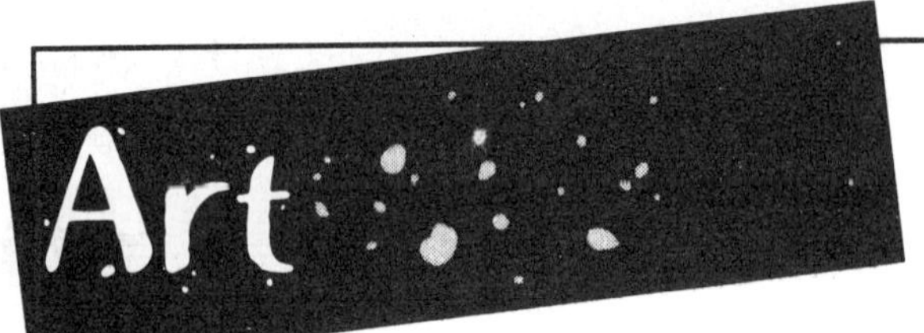

Magic Pictures

3+

Science skills

The children observe evaporation as they create designs and pictures.

Materials

Water
Salt
Cotton swabs
Plastic cups
Dark paper

What to do

1. Let each child make his own solution for painting by mixing 1 cup (250 ml) of water with 2 tablespoons (30 ml) salt. Talk about the changes as the children mix.
2. Ask where the salt went, then explain that it dissolved.
3. Let the children paint a design on dark paper using cotton swabs.
4. Set it in a sunny spot to dry. Check the paintings from time to time. Ask what is happening. Talk about evaporation. The children will find it fascinating when the salt designs magically appear.

Related book

Rain, Drop, Splash by Alvin Tressett

Cindy Winther, Oxford, MI

Sand Sketching

Science skills

As they make delicate designs, children practice observation and fine motor skills.

Materials

Clean or silicone sand, about 4 cups (1 liter)
Cookie sheet or lasagna pan, 8" x 11" (20 cm x 27.5 cm)
3 sturdy sticks, 12" (30 cm) long, or a ⅜" (10 mm) dowel
String or yarn, about 18" (45 cm) long
Pointed stone or mason plumbob tool

What to do

1. Pour the sand into the sheet or pan.
2. Place the three sticks into the sand, positioning their bottom ends in tripod position.
3. Bring the top ends of the sticks together and wrap several times with string.
4. Drop the remaining string down the center of tripod.
5. Tie the pointed rock or plumbob point down to the string so its tip touches the sand gently.
6. Adjust the sticks to allow free movement of the pendulum, so the point sketches the sand and continues to move.
7. Encourage the children to gently push the end of the pendulum to set it into motion and make a design.
8. Erase the sketch by smoothing the sand, and begin again.

Dani Rosensteel, Payson, AZ

3+

Shell Prints

Science skills

Children use creativity and visual skills to make a picture.

Materials

Medium or large size shells
Pie tins or paint pans
Paintbrushes
Smocks
Paints, any color
Paper

What to do

1. Let each child choose a shell and paint it with a brush or roll it in a shallow pan of paint.
2. He puts the shell in the middle of a piece of paper.
3. Let the child begin to roll the shell around the paper or crumple the paper around the shell.
4. Remove the shell from the paper and allow the print to dry.

More to do

More art: Children can choose other objects from the room or home to cover with paint and make prints.

Ann Gudowski, Johnstown, PA

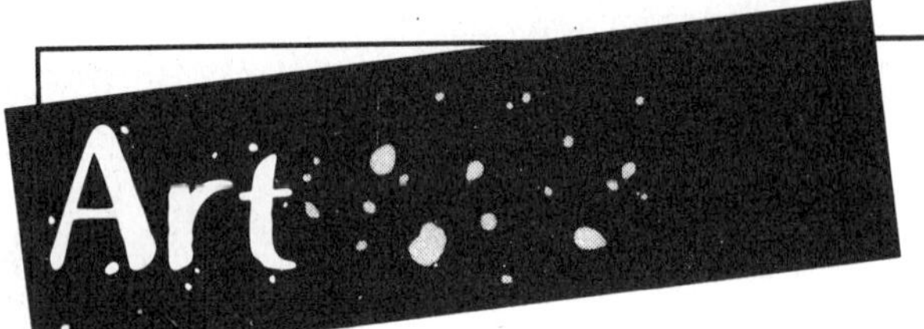

Nature Rubbings

3+

Science skills

This art project will stimulate children's interest in and curiosity about the environment and nature, as well as help them develop fine motor skills.

Materials

Paper
Crayons or colored chalk

What to do

1. Explain to the children that they will be going on an outside art walk.
2. Demonstrate how to make rubbings, by placing paper over an object, such as a leaf, and gently rubbing back and forth with crayon or chalk to make an image.
3. As your class interacts with the environment, make rubbings of tree bark, the sidewalk, a fallen leaf, twigs, the grass, tires, etc.

More to do

More art: Make a classroom book or bulletin board display of your art walk rubbings.
More science: Collect various nature artifacts such as fallen tree bark, dead leaves and dried bugs and observe with magnifying glasses.

 *Patricia Moeser, McFarland, WI*

Chalk Scraping Prints

Science skills

Children learn that chalk dust floats.

Materials

Newspapers
Different colored chalk (sidewalk chalk is best)
Children's scissors
Shallow pan of water
Manila or ditto paper cut into shapes, if desired

What to do

1. Prepare the area by spreading out newspapers and filling the shallow pan with water.
2. Show children how to hold chalk over the water and use the scissors to scrape the different

colored chalk so the dust floats on top.

3. Keep scraping chalk until you have many colors floating on top of the water. Three or four children may scrape at one time.

4. Take the manila or ditto paper and lay it gently on top of the water. Do not push it under!
5. Pick it up carefully and you have a print. Allow to dry. Four or five prints may be made before it is necessary to change the water (all the chalk dust goes to the bottom as you put the paper on).

More to do

More art: This project can be adapted to any season or holiday by cutting the paper into appropriate shapes. For example, at Easter, the paper could be cut into egg or bunny shapes and for spring or summer projects into flowers.

 *Leslie B. Brunner, Hot Springs, VA*

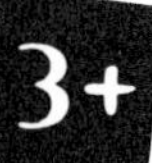

Invisible Design

Science skills

Children compare and contrast different painting techniques.

Materials

Cooking oil in a cup
Brushes
Window or light source
Butcher paper
Water in a cup

What to do

1. Paint with cooking oil on butcher paper.
2. Hold the design up to the light to make the art visible.
3. With a paintbrush full of water, paint over the oil design. Paint on the untouched paper too.
4. Look at the way oil and water act together.

More to do

More art: Using a damp sponge, try to wipe the oil design away. ▪ Paint with watercolors on the oil and water designs. ▪Draw with permanent felt pens on the oil and water designs.

 *Nancy Gardner, Weymouth, MA*

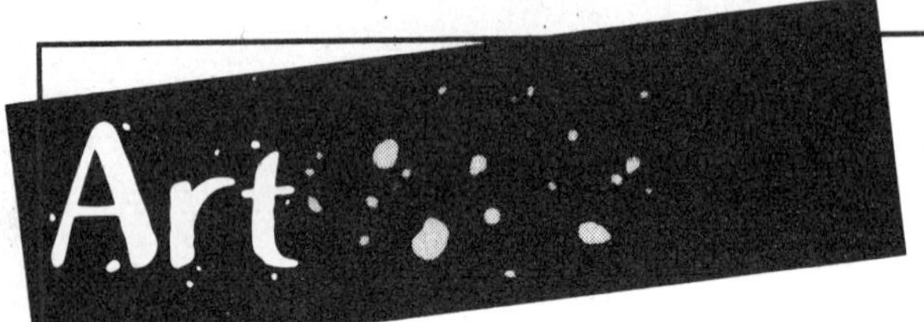

Invisible Paint

4+

Science skills

Children practice writing their names and using observation skills.

Materials

Candles, the clear emergency kind (break in half to extend use)
Plain art paper and pencils
Watercolors

What to do

1. Help the children practice writing their names on the paper.
2. Give each child a candle to draw with. Let them know that even though they cannot see their writing now, they will be able to see it later. (The more wax they use the better). Encourage them to try writing their own names with the candle.
3. Allow the child to paint watercolors over the entire page to reveal the secret designs and shapes.
4. Hang to dry.

More to do

More art: Try same activity on fabric!

Dani Rosensteel, Dayson, AZ

Berry Purple Paint

Science skills

Children have fun with natural dyes and observe cause and effect relationships.

Materials

Brown onion skins
Stove
Juice from 1 package of canned blueberries
Stapler
Three 2" x 3" (5 cm x 7.5 cm) strips of white cotton or flannel per child
One cardboard strip per child, 1½" x 8" (3.5 cm x 20 cm)
Pan of water
Juice from a can of beets
Newsprint

What to do

1. Boil onion skins in water to cover to create a brown liquid. Remove skins.
2. Place bowls of beet, berry and onion juice on the table. Look at the foods they came from. Name the colors. Let each child dip a strip of cloth into the beet juice, remove it and squeeze it out. Note the color.
3. Each child may do the same with two more pieces of cloth, one for the blueberry and one for the onion skin juice. Spread the strips out on newsprint to dry.
4. Staple the fabrics onto a strip of cardboard to take home.
5. Talk about how Native Americans and early settlers made their own dyes and inks.

More to do

More science: Dye some craft sticks, tongue depressors or flat wooden craft shapes with the natural dyes and use them for making pictures and constructions.

Related books

Charlie Needs a Cloak by Tomie dePaola
The Legend of the Indian Paintbrush by Tomie dePaola

Sandra Gratias, Perkasie, PA

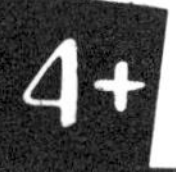

4+

Easy and Inexpensive Block Printing

Science skills

Children practice fine motor skills while creating a gift.

Materials

Paper cutter
White paper, 9″ x 12″ (22.5 cm x 30 cm)
One #2 pencil with a medium point for teacher
Newspaper
Rolling pin
One tube of pink or red water-soluble ink for block printing
White Styrofoam meat trays, one per child
Pencils for the children
Red crayons
One 4″ long brayer (roller)
Flat metal or baked enamel tray or cookie sheet

What to do

1. Use the paper cutter to cut off the sides and any excess from the trays so that they are uniform in size.
2. Fold the 9″ x 12″ paper in half to be 6″ (15 cm) wide. Open and write with a red crayon "I love you," and sign your own name in pencil.
3. Cut more paper the same size as the trays and let the children practice their designs for a card cover with pencils.
4. With pencil, the children draw the same design on the Styrofoam. Do not use letters, as they will be reversed.

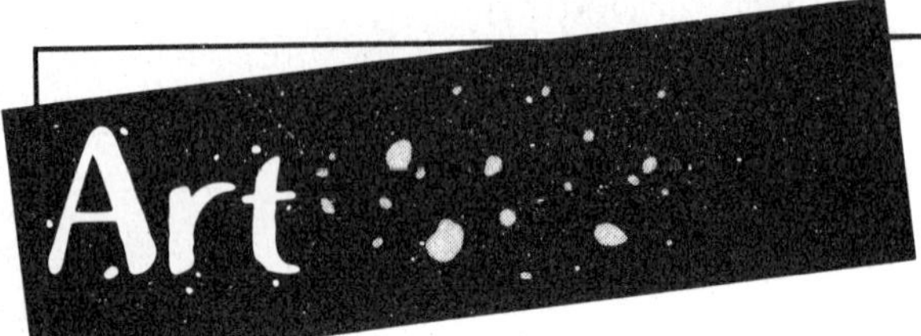

5. The indentations left by the pencil will be white when printed. If the grooves are not deep enough, an adult should retrace the design on the Styrofoam with a sharper #2 pencil.
6. Cover the work area with newspaper.
7. Squeeze a little ink onto the metal tray, then roll the brayer in it until it is coated.
8. Roll the brayer onto Styrofoam design until uniformly coated.
9. With ink side down, center the tray on the cover of the card and roll on top of it with a rolling pin, using some pressure. Lift off and let the print dry.

More to do

Games: Put three to five dry block print trays on the floor. Let the children try to throw a beanbag onto or touching one or more trays. Give the child three or four beanbags with which to try. Keep score beside each name on chart or chalkboard. This will encourage letter and numeral recognition. ▪ Line up the dry block prints on an easel at circle time. Children close their eyes and the teacher removes one design. The children try to figure out which design is missing. As a greater challenge, rearrange the remaining designs. This helps to develop memory. ▪ Use the prints as a matching game. Give a child a dry block print design. Ask him to find the card that matches the design he was given.

Math: Count all the circles (or squares or Valentine shapes) on the group of several designs. ▪ Use block printing as a review of the various shapes that the children have learned (square, triangle, diamond, etc.). Each child could block print a different shape and then name it.

More art: Use the same technique but vary the design and color of block printing ink to make cards for Mother's Day, Father's Day, Easter, Christmas, Hanukkah or any other occasion. ▪ Block print a border or mural for a bulletin board. Either reuse one design over and over or use many children's designs. ▪ Block print designs on a large sheet of paper and use as wrapping paper for a special parent gift. ▪ Use cards made by block printing as invitations to a school activity or open house. ▪ Design a picture to block print, not necessarily a card. For example, make a snowman and snowflake scene, perhaps using a larger piece of Styrofoam.

Original poems

A Valentine for Mommy and Daddy

I love you, Mommy.
I love Daddy, too,
And I want to make
A Valentine for you.

I'll get some paper and
Draw a heart.
I want it to be pretty.
How do I start?

Maybe some stickers,
Some yarn or lace,
Perhaps draw an animal
Or a funny face.

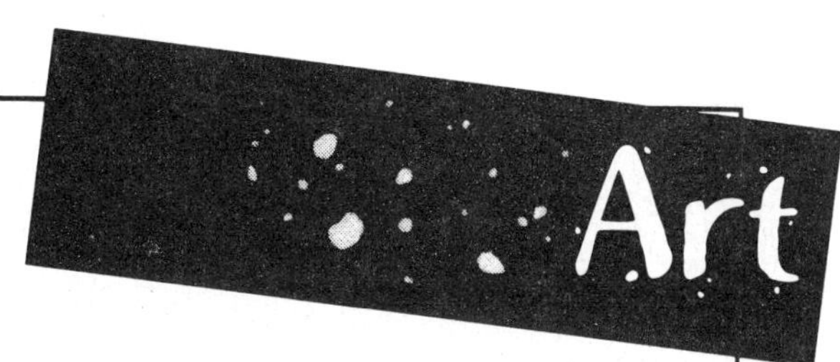

I'll color with crayons,
Paint or glitter and glue.
Then make some x's and o's to say,
"I love you."

Making Valentines

I like to cut out Valentines
And decorate them with lace.
Some are very beautiful,
Others have a funny face.

I make them for my friends
And for my grandparents, too.
I'm working on a red shiny one
Just especially for you.

Each Valentine is different.
I use paper of every kind.
When you open up the envelope
You never know what you'll find.
Oh, it's fun to get some cards
On happy Saint Valentine's Day
But the most fun of all
Is giving them away.

A Letter to Santa

It's so hard to wait for Christmas
It takes so long to get here
I think that Merry Christmas
Is the best holiday of the year.

I just think and think about
The toys I like the very best
And Mommy writes a list for me
Like a ball, bike or treasure chest.

Then my daddy looks at my letter.
He reads it over twice,
And tells me it's a long list
So I'd better be real nice.

I get a big fat envelope
My letter can't be too wide.
And I fold it up just so
Then it can hide inside.

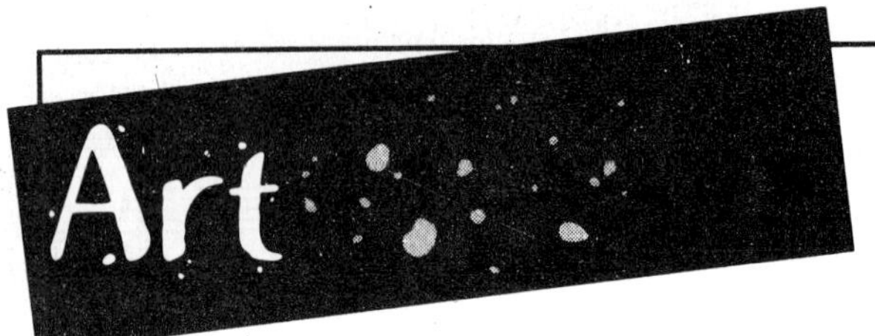

My mother lets me lick the stamp,
And she puts the address on.
Then I take it to our mailbox
I wonder if the postman's gone?

I won't know 'til Christmas
If Santa got my letter all right,
But I'll hang up my stocking and hope.
Gee, I just can't sleep tonight.

Mary Brehm, Aurora, OH

Native American Sand Art

Science skills
Children use small motor skills in this activity.

Materials

Sandpaper
Oven or toaster oven
Cookie sheet
Crayons
Hot pad

What to do

1. Discuss Native American symbols. Draw some on the chalkboard. Explain that Native Americans would often draw a picture to symbolize a word or an event.
2. Give each child a piece of sandpaper, cut to whatever size will fit your toaster oven. Have the children draw pictures and symbols on the sandpaper using crayons. Press hard.
3. Place the drawings on a cookie sheet with heavy items on the edges of the pictures so they will not curl from the heat. Heat each sheet in the oven at 350° F (180° C) for 20 minutes.
4. Observe with the children the changes in their pictures.
5. Make a construction paper frame for these shiny works of art!

More to do

More art: For a variation of the above project, after you remove the pictures from the oven and cookie sheet, immediately place a white piece of paper over the top and rub with your hand. The melted crayon will rub off onto the paper, making a print.

Sand and water table: Place damp sand in your table and encourage the children to use their fingers or a stick to draw pictures and symbols in it.

Valerie Chellew, Marshfield, WI

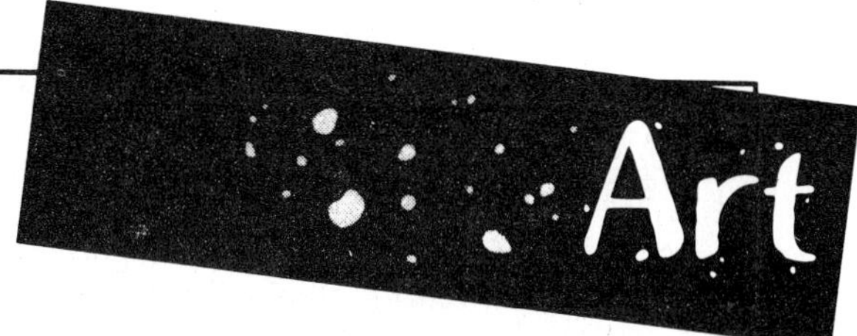

4+

Solar Crayons

Science skills
Children observe solar energy and learn cause and effect.

Materials

Broken crayons
Wooden hammers or wooden blocks
Warm, sunny day
Resealable plastic bags, quart or liter size
Aluminum muffin tins

What to do

1. Children place a handful of broken crayon pieces of a single color into a resealable plastic bag and seal it up.
2. Pound the bag with a hammer or block until the crayons are well crumbled.
3. Empty the bags into individual muffin tins. Use a separate tin for each color.
4. Place the tins in a sunny area and check them periodically for signs of melting.
5. When the crayon bits have melted into one mass, let them cool overnight. Give each child his recycled solar crayon.

More to do

More art: Draw designs with the cooled crayons.
More science: Make a solar hotdog grill as follows: Cut a cardboard oatmeal box in half lengthwise and line it with foil. Skewer a pre-cooked hotdog with a long wooden skewer and put it in the box. Place in a sunny spot. Rotate the skewer occasionally. The hotdog is done when it sweats.

 *Teresa J. Nos, Baltimore, MD*

4+

Spin Art

Science skills
Children use all their senses to observe centrifugal force.

Materials

Old record player/turn table
Lots of paint colors
Syringes without the needles, optional
Paint aprons
Sheet of plastic, large enough to cover the record player
Lots of cheap paper plates
Squeeze bottles
Basters

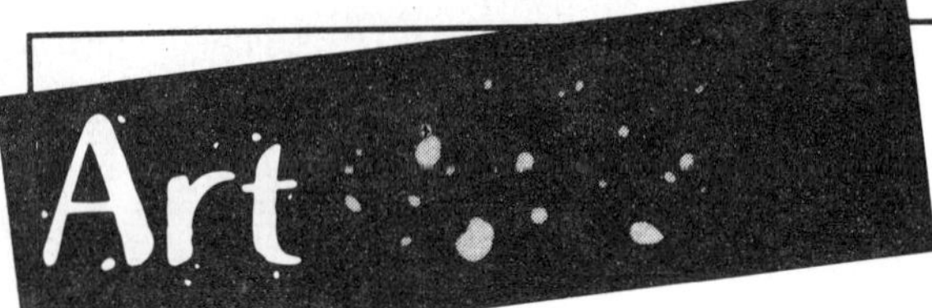

What to do

1. Find an area out of the way in the classroom so that you can do this activity for a while.
2. Place the sheet of plastic over the record player with the spindle (through which the record would normally be placed) poking through. This is a safety precaution, to ensure that no liquid makes contact with the record player itself.
3. Write the children's names on the paper plates. Put a paper plate on the spindle of the record player by pressing the spindle through the center of the plate.
4. With constant adult supervision turn the record player on. The plate spins.
5. Let the children squeeze small amounts of paint onto the plate with squeeze bottles, syringes or basters, and watch the colors move and spin.
6. Turn the record player off after every plate. Hang the plates to dry.
7. Remember to unplug the record player.
8. Discuss the circular motion and how liquid responds to the circular motion.

Dani Rosensteel, Payson, AZ

Textures

Science skills

Children make observations about their environment as they create a rubbed picture.

Materials

Newsprint
Textures (tree bark, asphalt, leaves, etc.)
Dark crayon or charcoal

What to do

1. Give each child or pair of children a piece of newsprint paper and a dark crayon or charcoal.
2. With a few minor instructions, send the children around the room or playground looking for textures to rub.
3. As the children lose interest, bring them back together for show and tell and a discussion of the different textures around us.
4. Discuss which textures make good rubbings and which ones do not.

More to do

More art: Give each child a pre-drawn picture with large areas (for example, building with a roof, tree, grass, dirt, car, animals, etc.). Instruct each child to use a variety of colors and fill in each area with a texture rubbing, trying to reproduce the look of boards, ground, etc. Display the finished products.

Wanda K. Pelton, Lafayette, IN

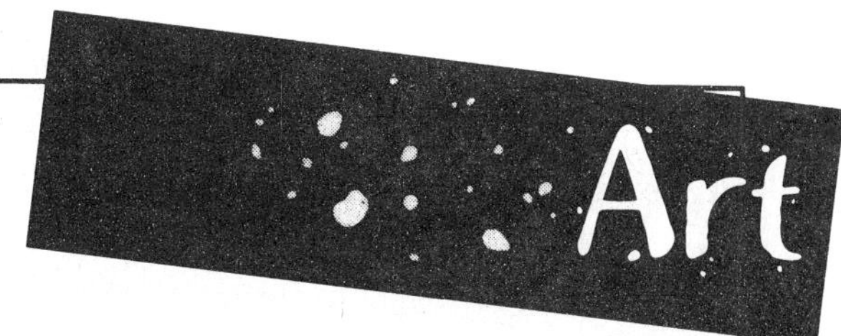

4+

Watching Absorption

Science skills
Children practice observation and use fine motor skills.

Materials

White paper towels, napkins or tissue paper
Eyedroppers
Muffin tin of water with food color added, different color in each tin

What to do

1. Cover your workspace very well because food color is permanent.
2. Children will fold the white paper towel or other paper and drop on the colors with the eyedroppers.
3. Colors will be observed to move, especially on the paper towel. Some colors will combine to make a new color.
4. Write names with a ballpoint pen, because markers will bleed on the paper.
5. Open very carefully! When dry, these pretty papers can be used for wrapping packages!

Hint: When using tissue paper, help the child fold it as small as possible and do not attempt to completely unfold the tissue until it is dry.

More to do

More science: Encourage the children to watch the color move up the eyedropper. This will use eye muscles to track the water movement. Children will learn to coordinate their fingers with the filling and emptying of the dropper with air and colored water (fine motor functions), and to concentrate while placing the colors where they desire (eye/hand coordination).

 *Linda Ann Hodge, Minnetonka, MN*

5+

Oil Design

Science skills
Children make observations and draw conclusions.

Materials

Pan, 11" x 14" (27.5 cm x 35 cm)
Food coloring
Cooking oil in small pan
White construction paper
Water
Cotton swabs
Wax paper
Clothespins

What to do

1. Prior to the lesson, fill the 11" x 14" pan half full with colored water.
2. Give each child a piece of wax paper to use as a work surface and a cotton swab. Ask them to dip their cotton swabs into the pan with cooking oil.
3. Take this oil-soaked cotton swab and draw on the white paper, creating a design. Make sure there is always enough oil on the cotton swab.
4. When the design is complete, attach a clothespin to one end of the paper.
5. The child picks up the paper with the clothespin, puts the paper in the pan of colored water and pulls it through the pan so the entire paper is submerged.
6. Remove the paper and allow it to dry.
7. Discuss why the colored water did not adhere to the oil designs—because oil and water do not mix.

More to do

More art: Children can write secret codes or messages or make secret designs for their friends. The recipient can read the message by placing the paper in colored water.

Sandra Fisher, Kutztown, PA

Peas & Toothpicks Sculpture

Science skills

Children develop fine motor skills as they build a sculpture.

Materials

Whole dried peas
Round toothpicks
Paper plates

What to do

1. Soak the peas overnight in enough water to cover. They should be firm, but soft enough for a toothpick to be pushed in easily. Keep the peas covered so they won't dry out.
2. At the art table, lay out the peas and toothpicks. Each child gets a paper plate on which to build his sculpture.
3. Demonstrate how to push the toothpicks into the peas gently. The children may tend to connect one after another into a long line. You may need to guide them to build a more three-dimensional building. It would be helpful to have examples previously made for them to look at.
4. Allow the sculptures to dry. As the peas dry they will create a firm bond to the toothpicks.

Valerie Chellew, Marshfield, WI

3+

Bathing Babies

Science skills

With the fun of play in warm, soapy water, children learn about water safety and practice fine motor skills.

Materials

Several baby dolls
Water table or baby tubs
Wash cloths
Bathtub safety seats
Towels
Warm water
Baby soap and/or shampoo bottles (trial size)
Rinsing cups
Water thermometers

What to do

1. Fill water table or tub with warm soapy water.
2. Add toys, wash cloths, sponges, cups and thermometers to water along with dolls.
3. Talk about how to hold the baby while bathing or show the bathtub safety seat and discuss how they help keep babies safe and other water safety tips.
4. Allow the child to use soap/shampoo to give the baby a bath, rinse, sing, play in water, etc.
5. Towel dry the babies and you're done. Babies are all clean!

More to do

Home living: To enhance fine motor skills, allow the children to try to diaper and dress the dry baby dolls after bathing them. ▪ Expand self-help skills by allowing the children to dress themselves this week as the opportunity arises. Use circle time to practice putting on socks, shoes, coats, sweaters, hats, mittens, etc.

 *Tina R. Woehler, Flower Mound, TX*

3+

Lotion Play

Science skills

In this wonderfully messy activity children use their senses and develop fine motor skills.

Materials

Trays or clean tabletop
Baby lotion (hypo-allergenic)
Old combs, toothbrushes, frosting spreaders, paintbrushes, etc.

What to do

1. Put the lotion onto the surface, about two table spoons (30 ml) per child.
2. Add any object that you might manipulate the lotion with.
3. Allow the children to use their hands to spread, draw and rub lotion on the tray surface or on their bodies.
4. Observe and talk about the texture, smell, sight, etc., while exploring takes place.
5. Add more lotion as it dries or gets absorbed into the children's skin.
6. Wash excess lotion off with soap and water after play is complete.
7. Clean the tabletop with dry paper towels and damp sponges. Trays may be washed in warm soapy water.

Tina R. Woehler, Flower Mound, TX

Baby Food Experiment

Science skills

As they eat, children use communication skills and record data.

Materials

Canned carrots, green beans, peaches and pears
Can opener
Food processor
Baby spoons, one per child
Empty, clean baby food jars with labels, the same kinds as the above listed foods
Fresh bananas
Large spoon
Plates

What to do

1. Place the contents of the can in the food processor, one type of food at a time. Blend until smooth.
2. Place food in the empty jar with the appropriate label.
3. Talk about how the canned items were pre-cooked and preserved and are ready for processing to make baby foods.
4. Introduce the fact that a baby usually has no teeth when she begins to eat solid foods; that's why her foods must be smooth.
5. Place each food in the processor and blend until you have made enough food for all the children.
6. Serve each food to the children and allow them to eat it with the baby spoons.
7. Discuss the textures, tastes, smells, etc., as they eat the food.
8. A tasting chart can be made for each food tasted per child. Record likes and dislikes.

More to do

Home living: Add baby spoons, bibs, highchairs, plates, etc. to the center for pretend baby feeding.

More science: Invite a parent with a real infant to visit the classroom and allow the children to watch as the infant is fed. Talk about portion sizes and spoonfuls used. Note how long it took the baby to eat the food, too. ▪ If children are interested in the texture of baby food, allow them to play with it in mess trays using baby spoons, scoops, etc.
Snack: Make warm milk and other foods that infants drink (use whole milk for best results).

Related book
Here Come the Babies by Catherine Anholt

Tina R. Woehler, Flower Mound, TX

Seashell Art

3+

Science skills

The children classify objects, learn numbers and discuss nature.

Materials

Seashells of all shapes and sizes and/or small pieces of driftwood from the beach or craft store
Cardboard cut into pieces of various sizes
Poster paint or watercolors
White glue
Fishing wire
Optional: a power drill, small wiggle eyes

What to do

1. Divide the children into small groups.
2. Give each group of children some seashells. If you do this project as a follow-up to a trip to the beach, let the children use the shells they collected themselves.
3. Have the groups sort and classify the seashells and tell what their classifications are (colors, shapes, etc.).
4. Ask the children to count the shells in each category and write the number down. Let them take turns reporting their findings to the class.
5. Discuss what animals lived in the shells.
6. Let the children do one or more of the following activities with their shells: paint their shells with poster paint or watercolors; glue shells onto the cardboard to make a sculpture; make shell creatures by gluing shells together and gluing eyes on the shells; have an adult drill holes in the shells and driftwood and then use the fishing wire to tie the shells to the driftwood to make shell mobiles; use the drilled shells to make jewelry.
7. Discuss how Native Americans used shells for money and jewelry. Show the children pictures and read them related books.

More to do

Field trip: Take the children to a museum to see Native American art.
Language: Encourage the children to dictate a story about who they think lived in the shells and how they think the shells ended up on the beach.

Barbara Saul, Eureka, CA

Winter Beach Party

Science skills

This activity allows children to practice fine motor skills and fosters social development.

Materials

Lawn chair
Seashells
Sand bucket and shovel
The Rainbow Fish by Marcus Pfister
Hula hoop
Dowel
String for fishing pole
Sunglasses
Other books about beaches, oceans and fish
Beach towels
Paper
Paper fish, with paper clip attached to each
Magnet
Crayons or markers

What to do

1. Greet children wearing sunglasses and sitting in a lawn chair.
2. Display books about fish, sea and beaches on a table decorated with the bucket, shovel and seashells.
3. Children can sit on beach towels on the floor.
4. Read *The Rainbow Fish* with the children.
5. Create an ocean using a hula hoop on the floor. Put the paper fish, each containing a paper clip in the "ocean." Each child now has the opportunity to go fishing. The pole is a wooden dowel with string and a magnet used to catch the fish. Children can color fish now or at home.
6. Sing "Row, Row, Row Your Boat." Pair the children and ask each pair to join hands and sit face-to-face on the floor. Sing the song as the children rock back and forth, rowing their boats.
7. Complete the beach party by giving each child a seashell and the fish caught earlier.

Original poem

The Whale
(adapted from Juba This, Juba That by Virginia Tashjian)

If you ever, ever, ever (clap each word which repeats)
Meet a whale, whale, whale,
You must never, never, never
Touch its tail, tail, tail.
If you ever, ever, ever
Touch its tail, tail, tail,
You will never, never, never
Meet another whale, whale, whale.

Joan Bowman, Bensalem, PA

A Day at the Beach

4+

Science skills

With sand and water play, children use their fine and gross motor skills and have an opportunity for social development.

Materials

Sand (take children to the beach or use a large sand box)
Old spoons or plastic sand shovels
Sand pails or plastic bowls
Water

What to do

1. Divide the children into small groups.
2. Tell the children that they are going to have a contest to see who can build the biggest sand castle in a set amount of time (try 10 minutes).
3. At the end of the activity have the children admire each other's work and give a small award to all.
4. Now tell the children that they are going to have a contest to see who can dig the deepest hole in a set amount of time.
5. At the end of the activity, encourage the children to admire each other's holes. If this activity is done at the beach, see if any of the children hit water when they dug their holes and discuss why they found water.

More to do

Language: When the children return to class, have them draw pictures of their sand castles and dictate experience stories about them. Make a class book with the stories.
More science: Make a whole community out of sand. Have the children brainstorm what buildings belong in a community and have each group build some of the buildings and roadways in the community.

Related book

Big Al by Andrew Clements

Barbara Saul, Eureka, CA

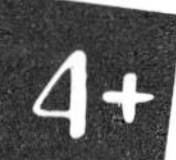

Sand Candles

Science skills

This activity develops the children's fine motor skills.

Materials

Candle wax or paraffin (clear wax can be colored by adding a crayon to it while it is hot)
An old pot or large can
Heat source (campfire, hot plate or stove)
String cut into 7" (17.5 cm) lengths
Small sticks, from 4" to 7" (10 cm to 17.5 cm) long, or try dowels or old pencils
Sand, at the beach or in a sandbox or dishpan

What to do

1. Put candle wax or paraffin in the pot or can and heat until the wax turns to liquid.
2. Tie a string onto the center of each stick, dowel or pencil.
3. Ask each child to dig a small hole in the sand, 3 to 6 inches (7.5 cm to 15 cm) deep.
4. An adult will pour the hot wax into the sand hole.
5. Help each child take the pencil and string and put the string into the hot wax, holding it on the top with the pencil. Rest the pencil on the opening to support the string until the wax cools. This will be the candlewick.

Melt wax in pot.

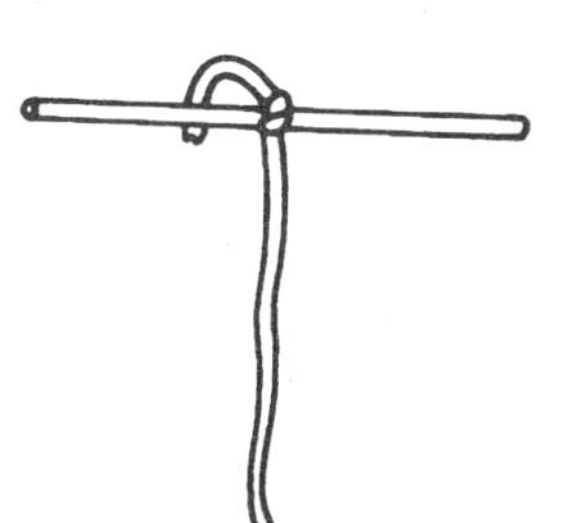

Tie string to stick.

Dig hole in sand.

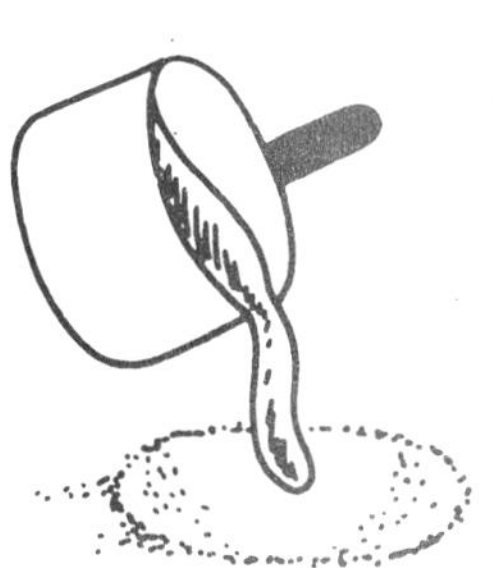

Pour wax into the sand.

Put string in wax and rest stick on opening.

Dig out candle

Trim wick.

Dip candle into hot wax.

6. After the wax sets and cools, let each child dig his or her candle out of the sand.
7. Cut the strings to the proper length for a candlewick.
8. After the children take their candles out of the sand, an adult can dip each one once in hot wax (using the wick as a handle). This assures that the sand will not fall off of the candle.

More to do

Art: Let each child make a wax hand print. Instead of digging a hole, each child can make her hand impression in the sand, fill it with wax and dig it out. You can also make footprints like this. These impressions make great gifts.

Barbara Saul, Eureka, CA

Sea Collage

Science skills

This is an artistic activity to develop children's fine motor skills.

Materials

Heavy white cardboard about 6" x 9" (15 cm x 22.5 cm), or matboard or foam board scraps or cut-up gift boxes
White glue
Bits of driftwood
Sand
Sponges
Blue and green dry tempera paint
Small shells
Pebbles from the beach

What to do

1. This activity is good to use in the fall as children talk about their beach trips and bring their collections to school. The collages may inspire group conversation about the sea. Science discussion should include the textures involved, noting how the churning waters and sand smoothes the stones, driftwood and shells.
2. Use a damp sponge dipped in the dry paint to color the cardboard slightly. Wipe the sponge gently across the surface to suggest waves.
3. Dribble white glue on the cardboard.
4. Arrange the shells, pebbles and driftwood on the glue.
5. Sprinkle the entire collage with sand.
6. Allow it to dry, then hold it upright and tap to remove excess sand.

More to do

More science: If you can arrange to use a rock tumbler, the children could see the churning of the sea and sand in action.

Mary Jo Shannon, Roanoke, VA

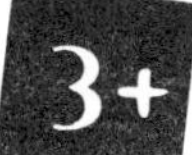

Going on a Bear Hunt

Science skills

Children practice counting and working together to bring the bear to its cave.

Materials

Brown paper ovals, each with a bear paw print on it, about 10″ (25 cm)
Six slips of paper numbered 1 through 6 in a small box or paper bag
Tape
We're Going on a Bear Hunt by Michael Rosen
Optional: picture of a house, a brown bear, a stream, mountains, a forest and a meadow

What to do

1. Discuss a brown bear's habitat with the class and read *We're Going on a Bear Hunt.*
2. Tape the bear paw prints to the floor in a track, starting at "home" (a picture of a house could be taped next to the first paw print) and ending at the bear's cave (a picture of a brown bear could be taped next to the last paw print). Along the way, pictures of a stream, mountains, etc. can be taped next to various paw prints.
3. One child becomes the bear, while other children take turns drawing numbers from the box or bag. The "bear" can advance only as many paw prints as the number drawn. The whole class helps count the steps. By the time the last number is pulled, the "bear" should reach his home.

More to do

More science: This activity can lead to a discussion of identifying various animal tracks. Good books for this discussion include *Whose Footprints?* by Molly Coxe and *Crinkleroot's Book of Animal Tracks and Wildlife Signs* by Jim Arnosky.

Related books

Bear by John Schoenherr
Sleepy Bear by Lydia Dabcovich

Christina Chilcote, New Freedom, PA

Bear's Snack Time

Science skills

As children eat a bear's snack, they are encouraged to ask questions about nature.

Materials

One small paper plate and paper cup per child
Blueberries
Apple slices
Walnuts
Goldfish crackers
Bottles of spring water
Blueberries for Sal by Robert McCloskey
Carrot sticks
Squeeze bottle of honey
Napkins or paper towels

What to do

1. This activity could culminate in a discussion on a bear's diet: fruit, nuts, berries, roots, fish and meat.
2. Read *Blueberries for Sal* to the children.
3. Serve each child a "bear snack"—fruit (blueberries, apple slices), nuts (walnuts), roots (carrot sticks), and fish (goldfish crackers). Add a dab of honey on each plate. Give cups of cool spring water. Be prepared to hear growling!
   Note: in some rare instances, children can have an allergic reaction to honey or nuts. Check with parents before you serve honey or nuts.

More to do

More science: Compare the food in the bear's snacktime to the food other animals eat.
Snack: Have a rabbit snacktime (carrots, lettuce, strawberries, etc.). Have a bird snacktime (sunflower seeds, blueberries or raspberries, gummi worms, etc)

Original song

Sing to the tune of *"Frère Jacques."*

Berries and fruit
Meat and root
Help bears grow,
Grow, grow, grow.
Eat a little fish,
Some honey if you wish,
And grow, bears, grow.
Grow, bears, grow.

Related books and recording

The Bear That Heard Crying by Natalie Kinsey-Warnock and Helen Kinsey
Every Autumn Comes the Bear by Jim Arnosky
"The Teddybears Picnic"

Christina Chilcote, New Freedom, PA

What Do Bears Eat?

Science skills
Children develop their use of language in this activity.

Materials
A variety of berries
Assortment of nuts
Honey

What to do
1. Talk about what bears eat and where bears find their food.
2. Have a bear food tasting party.

More to do
Math: Make a graph of the children's food preferences.

Related book
Jamberry by Bruce Degen

Holly Dzierzanowski, Austin, TX

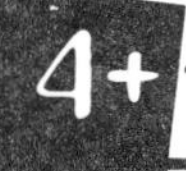

Bears

Science skills
Children practice communication skills as they discuss and learn about bears.

Materials
Pictures or a book showing different kinds of bears
Paper bags and brown construction paper
"Grandpa Bear's Lullaby" by Jane Yolen from *Dragon Night and Other Lullabies*
Glue
Scissors

What to do
1. Display the pictures of the different kinds of bears so that all children can view them. Ask the following questions: What are these? (Bears) Does anyone know the names of these bears? (Polar bear, Black bear, Grizzly bear, Brown bear, etc.) How are the bears different and the same?

2. Tell the children that bears can walk on two legs and also on all four. Children can imitate a bear walking each way.
3. Discuss the term "hibernation."
4. Read the poem "Grandpa Bear's Lullaby" to help explain hibernation.
5. Sing "Going on a Bear Hunt" or "The Bear Went Over the Mountain." When singing the latter, walk like a bear.
6. Open a paper lunch bag and fold it in half. Have children rip pieces of brown construction paper and glue it on three sides of the bag so it looks like a cave. Have the children cut out a picture of a sleeping bear and glue it inside the paper bag. The children have their own hibernating bear.

More to do

Dramatic play: Have the children bring in their favorite teddy bear, along with a beach towel, pair of sunglasses and a hat. Read *Teddy Bear's Picnic* and then have a teddy bear picnic for snack or lunch.

Related book and song

Teddy Bear's Picnic by Jimmy Kennedy
"The Bear Went Over the Mountain"

Susan L. Mahoney, Patuxent River, MD

3+

For the Birds

Science skills
The children practice fine and gross motor skills as they observe and classify.

Materials

String cut in various lengths
Dried grasses (available at craft or florist shops)
Cardboard
Yarn cut in pieces
Raffia cut in pieces

What to do

1. Beforehand, hide the materials listed above in various places either inside or outside on the playground. Go on a bird nest hunt with the children so there will be a real one in the classroom that they can examine.
2. Talk about nests as homes for birds.
3. Explain to the children how the bird builds its nest—one stick, piece of paper, scrap of yarn at a time—and that birds have to hunt to find the materials they need.
4. Back in the classroom, tell the children it is their turn to build a nest and that everything they need is hiding somewhere in the classroom (or yard).
5. Allow the children to create birdnests with the materials they find.
6. Challenge older children to construct a nest like the birds do, one piece of material at a time, so that they have to fly back and forth repeatedly, gathering materials.

More to do

Games: Use pictures of birds for matching games.
More science: Play a tape of real bird songs for the children. ▪ Visit a local aviary or a well-stocked bird-oriented pet store. ▪ Use binoculars to watch birds as they fly and work on their nests. ▪ Talk about other animals and where they live. Also talk about birds that do not live in nests. ▪ Collect a variety of pictures of birds and other animals. Have the children sort the pictures into two categories: birds and not birds.
Music and movement: Do creative movement exercises in which the children fly to music.

Original poem

A twig, some grass, a piece of string,
A bird's nest built up in a tree.
Wait awhile, the eggs will hatch.
And there will be babies to see!

Birds fly high, up in the sky.
Graceful wings in flight.

They search for food and things to eat,
And return to their nest at night.

 *Linda Ford, Sacramento, CA*

Helping Birds Build Their Homes

Science skills
Children use numbers, observation and fine motor skills.

Materials
Scraps of yarn about 2" to 4" (5 cm to 10 cm) long
Lint from clothes dryer

What to do
1. In early spring, read about birds building nests, then plan this activity to assist them.
2. Let the children count ten pieces of yarn, then tie a longer piece of yarn around the bundle in the middle.
3. Tie a piece of yarn around a ball of lint.
4. Tie all these materials to bushes on the playground and watch them disappear as birds look for materials to build nests.

More to do
More science: Examine the yarn and the lint with a magnifying glass. Introduce the term "fiber." Discuss how washing and drying clothes removes some of the fibers from the material. Relate this to clothing wearing out. What else removes fibers? (friction) Which parts of clothing wear out first? (knees, elbows) Why?

 *Mary Jo Shannon, Roanoke, VA*

Weaving a Nesting Branch for the Birds

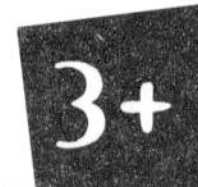

Science skills
Children are fascinated to see that their creations are helping the birds to build homes.

Materials
Forked branches
String or twine
Odds and ends such as cotton, sheep's wool, yarn scraps, animal fur, string, thread, ribbon

What to do

1. Collect forked branches, one per child, of a size easily handled by the children. Show the children how to wrap string or twine around and around the fork of their branch, fairly tightly.
2. Then the children weave the odds and ends in and out loosely.
3. Hang the branch outside where birds can safely find the bits to use in building their nests and where children can watch the birds.

More to do

Games: Play the circle game "Bluebird."
More science: Children make individual nesting balls to take home by stuffing old onion bags. ▪ Look at a collection of nests to see how differently they are made and to see bits of litter that the birds have used in addition to natural materials. ▪ Take a walk during the winter to see abandoned nests in the trees. ▪ Feed the birds year round. Make bird feeders from milk cartons or by covering white pine cones with peanut butter and rolling in seeds.

Related books and songs

Have You Seen Birds? by Joanne Oppenheim
Mr. and Mrs. Bird and Their Family by Daniel Boillat
Mr. and Mrs. Bird Build a Nest by Daniel Boillat
A Year of Birds by Ashley Wolff
"All the Birds Sing" from *Sing Through the Seasons*
"Spring Is Coming" from *Pentatonic Songs* by Elizabeth Lebret

Linda Atamian, Charlestown, RI

3+

Bird Nests

Science skills
The children use fine motor activity to build a real bird's nest, and they are encouraged to wonder about nature.

Materials

Cup (250 ml) of soil, or more
Spoon
Assortment of grasses
Water
Straw
Paper

What to do
1. Mix the soil and water with a spoon until it holds together.
2. Make a nest shape from grasses and straw.
3. Put mud under and in nest until the nest holds together.
4. Place the nest on paper to dry.

More to do

More science: Take a nest nature walk and look in trees to see how many and what kinds of nests are there. Read and look at books to see various nests and birds that build them. ▪ Invite a carpenter to the classroom to build a simple birdhouse to put out for the birds.

 *Marilyn Harding, Grimes, IA*

Bird Watching Binoculars

Science skills

Children develop observation skills using binoculars that they make.

Materials

Cardboard tubes, cut into 6" (15 cm) lengths
Yarn or string, cut into 2' (60 cm) lengths
Black paint
A children's book about birds
White glue
Hole punch
Brushes
A bird identification guide for the teacher

What to do

1. Tell the children that they are going to make binoculars to watch birds with.
2. Ask each child to paint two tubes black.
3. Help each child glue the two tubes together side-by-side.
4. Read the children the book about birds while the glue dries.
5. Use the hole punch to make holes in the outside edges of the cardboard tubes.
6. Tie one end of the yarn to one hole and the other end to the opposite hole, to make straps to put over the children's heads to hold their binoculars around their necks.
7. Take the children on a bird watching walk. Write down which birds and how many of each kind they see.
8. Set up a bird watching area out of one of the classroom windows. Put out birdseed and put the binoculars by the window for the children to observe the birds.

More to do

Field trip: Schedule a field trip to a local wildlife area or zoo to watch the birds.

Language: When the class returns to the room, write a class story about the birds the children saw, and make a graph.

Math: Count how many of each kind of bird the children saw.

Barbara Saul, Eureka, CA

4+

Birds of a Feather

Science skills
Children use all their senses to observe bird feathers and are encouraged to ask questions about them.

Materials

Variety of feathers from one type of bird, such as body, wing, tail and down feathers (these can be obtained easily from pet shops or bird owners, but be sure to get clean feathers)
Magnifying glasses
Balance or scale and gram weights (for older children)
Note: Down feathers are very fragile and "ball up" if handled roughly. The easiest way to transport them from the bird to the class is to lay them gently on a piece of felt, then peel them off as they are needed for the activities.

What to do

1. Look at the feathers without magnification. Observe and discuss similarities and differences in size, shape, color and texture. Following are some observations, in addition to color, that children may make. Wing feathers are slightly curved. The quill on a tail or wing feather is long and thick to anchor it securely to the bird's body. These feathers are used to steer the bird in flight and have to endure a great deal of pressure from the air. The quills on body feathers are small. These feathers protect the bird from weather and sun. They don't push against the air to help the bird fly, so they do not have to be attached as securely as wing and tail feathers. Down feathers are fluffy and sticky with very little quill. These are usually hidden under the other feathers and help keep the bird warm.
2. Allow children to touch the feathers. Which are softest?
3. Drop different feathers from equal heights and observe how they fall. Some spin, some float. All feathers do not fall at the same speed.
4. Use magnifying glasses to observe the feathers. Children can describe or draw what they see.
5. Older children may want to determine how many feathers it takes to weigh a gram. Estimate the number of feathers it will take. Use a balance and a one gram weight to check predictions. Do feathers weigh very much?

More to do

Art: Use feathers as paintbrushes to paint pictures about birds or nature. ▪ Explain that feathers from large birds were used as pens long ago. Use large feathers and paint or ink to practice writing and drawing. ▪ Use decorative feathers purchased from a craft store to glue onto an outline drawing of a bird.
More science: Compare and contrast feathers from different breeds of birds for size, color, texture, etc. ▪ Look at pictures of birds (or look at a real bird) and discuss which feathers are clearly visible when a bird is at rest. Feathers tend to blend together on a bird and downy feathers are rarely visi-

ble. ▪ Observe a pet bird, a bird outside the classroom or a bird at the zoo preening or grooming itself. Birds take good care of their feathers so they stay healthy and are always ready to fly.

Related book
How to Hide a Parakeet and Other Birds by Ruth Heller

Kim Arnold, Big Flats, NY

Christmas Tree for the Birds

Science skills
Children use their fine motor skills to make a gift for the birds, then observe as the birds eat the gift.

Materials
Yarn, cord and blunt needle
Dry cereal
Pine cones
Solid shortening, such as Crisco
Fruit and berries
Bird identification books
Tape
Pipe cleaners
Peanut butter
Birdseed
Popcorn

What to do

1. Cut lengths of yarn and wrap the ends with tape. Let the children string dry cereal and then tie the ends of the yarn together.
2. Twist pipe cleaners around pinecones to make a handle. Mix together half peanut butter and half shortening. (Birds need fat to stay warm. Peanut butter needs to be mixed with solid shortening so their beaks don't stick.) Spread this mix on the pine cones. Roll them in birdseed.
3. Using a blunt needle and cord, thread fruit, popcorn and berries.
4. Decorate an outdoor tree or bush that you can observe from inside with these bird treats.
5. Watch and identify the variety of bird (or squirrel) visitors.

More to do
Art: Paint with feathers.
More science: Set up the science table with birdfeeders, bird books and feathers. ▪ Dissect a bird nest. List what's found inside.

Related books
Are You My Mother? by P. D. Eastman
Have You Seen Birds? by Jeanne Oppenheim

Teresa J. Nos, Baltimore, MD

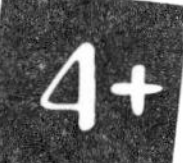

Downy Duckling Puppet

Science skills

Making a puppet encourages children to use fine motor skills and ask questions about birds.

Materials

Brown lunch bags
Tan, gold and brown construction paper
White glue
Pencil
Brown and black markers
Scissors
12 mm wiggle eyes
Duckling pictures

What to do

1. Compare pictures of yellow pond ducklings and brown mallard ducklings.
2. Enlarge the patterns.
3. Trace the patterns on appropriate colors of construction paper and cut out.
4. Using the lunch bags upside down, glue the bottom beak under bag flap.
5. Glue the round head on the topside of the bag flap.
6. Trim off the corners of the bag so only the circular head shows.
7. Glue the top beak (gold) on the head circle. It should be slightly smaller than the bottom beak.
8. Round the bottom of bag.
9. Glue on the brown back.
10. Glue the brown wings in between side folds.

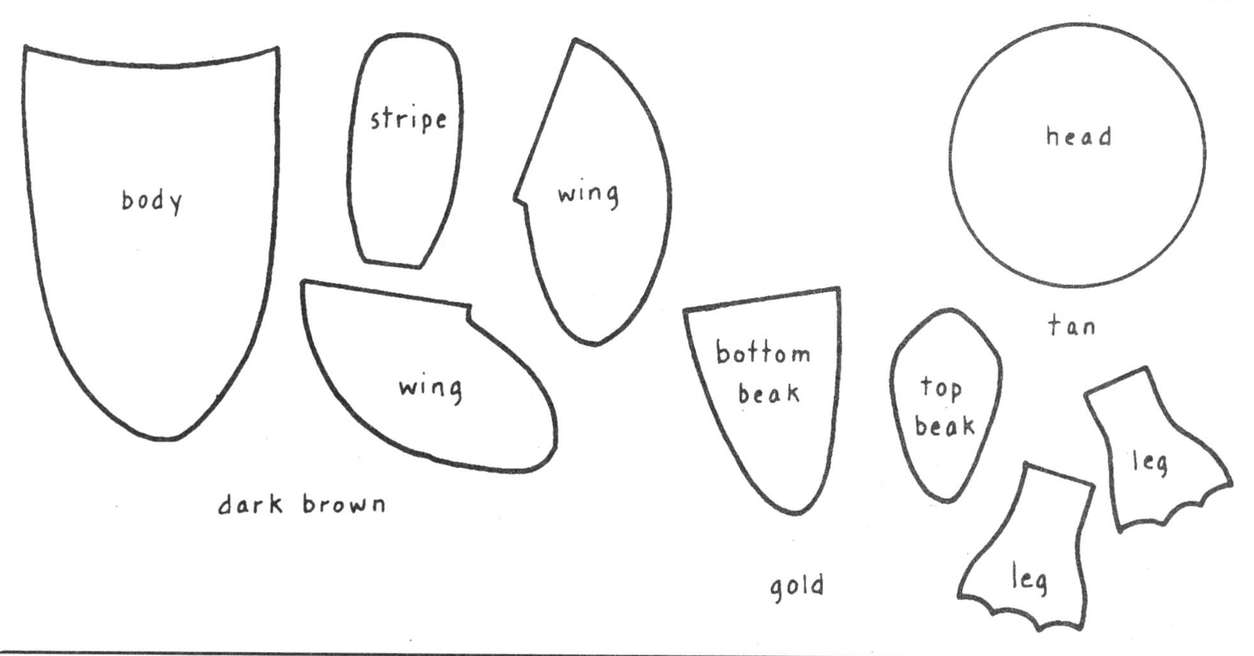

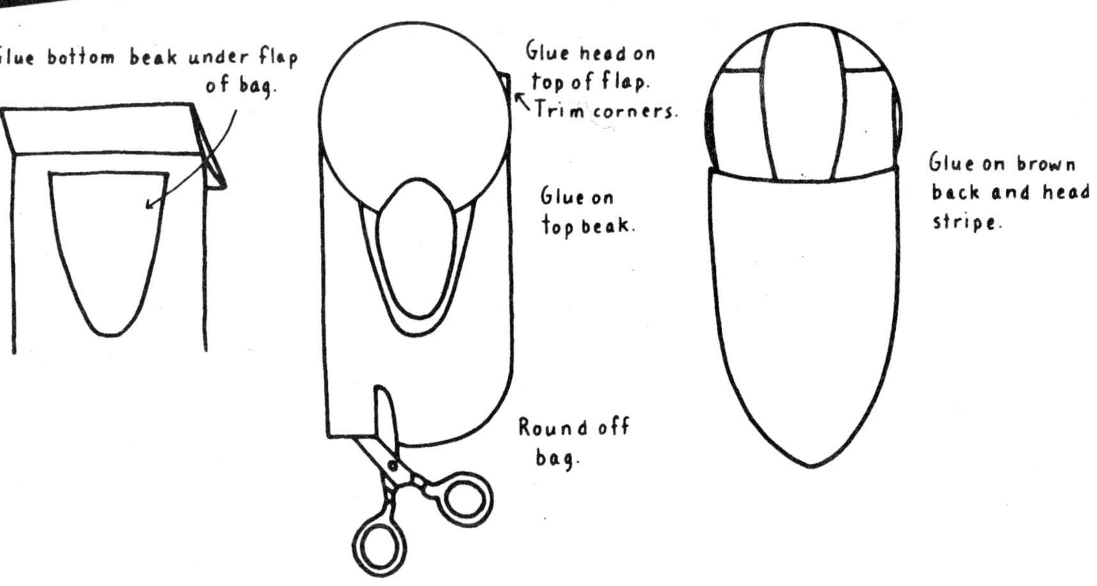

11. Glue the legs underneath body front.
12. Color with brown marker on the head and body. Allow some lighter background paper to show, resembling downy feathers.
13. Glue on the 12 mm wiggle eyes.
14. Make two nostril ovals on the top beak with a pointed black marker.

More to do

Games: Children squat and try to walk like ducklings and flap their arms like wings. ▪ Each child dramatizes being a different animal. Others guess what they are. ▪ Children can use duckling puppets as they sing songs or chant poems about ducklings.

More science: Show a real duck egg and compare it with a chicken egg, a bird egg, a goose egg and, if possible, an ostrich egg. ▪ Bring in pictures showing the shape and coloring of other ducks such as the Hooded Mergonser Duck, the Pintail Duck, the Ringed Teal Duck, the Shoveller Duck, the Spot-billed Duck and the Ruddy Duck. Show carved wooden models or plush toys. ▪ Discuss why the female duck's plumage is not as pretty and bright as the male's.

Original poems

Fuzzy Ducky

Little fuzzy ducky yellow,
You're a funny little fellow.
You say quack quack when you talk
And you wiggle waddle when you walk.

You swim around the pond with ease.
Your feet are webbed and you have no knees.
Then quick as a wink, bobbing down you go,
Looking for some worms below.

I'll come and watch you every day
'Cause that's more fun than other play,
And bring some crumbs and throw them, too.
Gee, I wish that I were you.

Animal Fair

I like to pretend
I'm in an animal fair.
I can be most anything
Like a lion, giraffe or bear.

I walk with stiff legs
And hold my head up high
And I think I am a giraffe
Eating leaves off trees in the sky.

I make my arms into a trunk
And hunch my back up round.
An elephant's trunk sways to and fro
Just inches from the ground.

I put my feet together
And hop just like a bunny,
Then hold my hands up high for ears.
I wonder if I look funny?

I try to be a little duck
But that's the hardest of all.
I sit down on my heels and walk,
And every time I fall.

I look for all the animals
In books and on TV—
There are so many creatures
I can pretend to be.

Related books

Make Way for Ducklings by Robert McCloskey

Mary Brehm, Aurora, OH

Birds

Make a Bird Book

4+

Science skills

Children practice observation and fine motor skills.

Materials

Construction paper, white and other colors
Crayons, markers, pencils
Stapler
Date stamp

What to do

1. Encourage the children to design pages for a bird book. They may want to draw outlines of birds on some of the pages, to be colored in according to the colors of birds they see. In this book, they will be able to record the birds they observe, depending on their ages, by drawing pictures or writing words to describe the birds.
2. Let the children put the pages in the order they want.
3. An adult staples the pages together to make a book.
4. Help the children write their names on the front of their books.
5. Set up a bird-watching area in the classroom.
6. Tell the children that they are going to take turns watching birds. This activity can be one of your learning centers.
7. When the children see birds, ask them to finish a page of their bird book by adding bird beaks, tails and feet and colors to their bird outlines, or by writing words (for example: gray, small, long tail feathers) or making any other type of bird-descriptive picture they wish.
9. Stamp the date on the page (or let the children do it).
10. Let an adult write the place the bird was seen (playground, garden, etc.).

More to do

Math: Make a bird counting chart, and show the children how to make lines for every bird they see. Each day or week, ask the children to count how many birds they see.

More science: Have the children make bird books to take home and complete with their families. ▪ Explain to the children about bird and animal migration and watch for migrating birds flying overhead. Talk about when the birds most often appeared and see if the children can figure out why certain birds are seen at certain times and not at other times.

Barbara Saul, Eureka, CA

4+

Dazzling Quetzal Bird

Science skills

Children use fine motor skills to create a picture of a dazzling creature.

Materials

3″ x 5″ (7.5 cm x 15 cm) index cards
Pencil
White glue
Short white feathers
Markers: yellow, light green, orange, red, brown, dark green
Pattern of quetzal bird
White drawing paper
Green glitter
Long green feathers
7 mm wiggle eyes

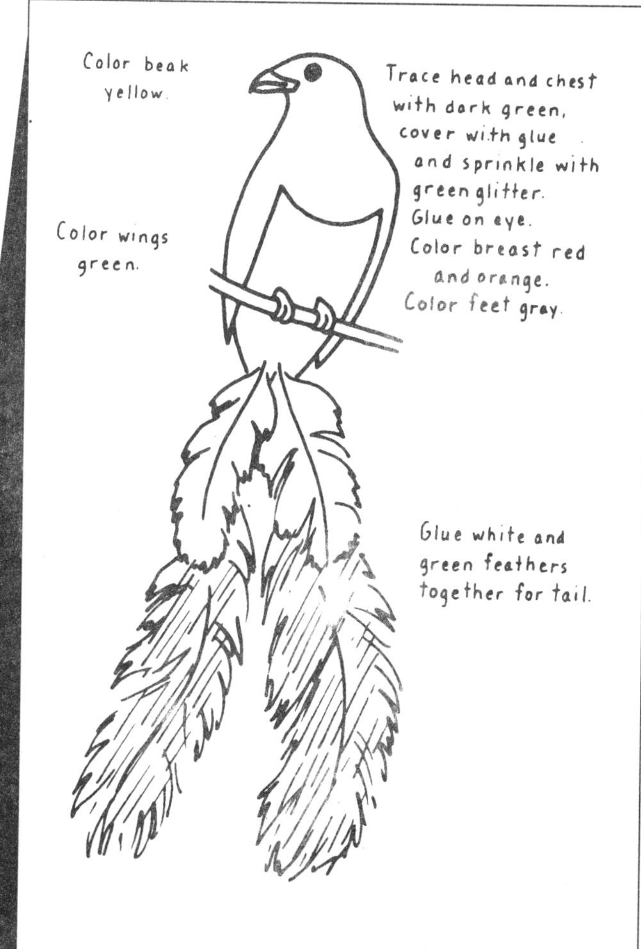

What to do

1. Put one line of information on each of several index card. A child picks a card and the teacher reads the information, for example: quetzal birds live in the Central American and Mexican rain forests; quetzal birds are very colorful; male quetzals are the brightest color; fathers take their turn sitting on eggs; quetzals nest in holes in trees; the green quetzal tail feather is two feet long; the quetzal is pictured on the stamps and coins of Guatemala; the male quetzal jumps off the branch backwards to fly; only Aztec Indian noblemen were allowed to decorate their clothes with green quetzal feathers; quetzals catch falling fruit or insects to eat.
2. Before you start this project, find a good picture of a quetzal bird to use as a pattern. Then trace the pattern onto sheets of white paper, one for each child, and help them make their own quetzal puppets.
3. Color the feet with pencil.
4. Color yellow on the head crown and beak.
5. Color the breast red first, then orange on top of the red.
6. Color the side feather wing area with a light green marker.

7. Trace the head and v-shaped neck with dark green, then cover the center of the head with white glue and sprinkle on green glitter.
8. Glue on the eyes.
9. Glue the white and green feathers together for the tail feathers.
10. Glue the top half of the white feather to form the quetzal tail at the base of the drawing.

More to do

Math: Children sort feathers by size and count them.

More science: Find Guatemala on the globe; find Mexico. ▪ Visit a bird aviary. ▪ Show the children pictures of various birds. Discuss the variety of colors and shapes.

Original song and poem

Did You Ever See a Quetzal Bird?

(sing to the tune of "Did you Ever See a Lassie")

Verse 1: Did you ever see a quetzal bird from Central America? He looks this way . . .

Verse 2: Did you ever see his two green feathers
hanging down from his tail? He sits this way . . .

The Male Quetzal Bird

The quetzal bird is very bright green.
He is the most unusual bird you've ever seen.
His two green feathers hang low below the limb
On which he is sitting, viewing the trees around him.
When he goes in a hole that is his nest in a tree.
The tip of his tail feathers you can still plainly see.
When he wants to soar high in the blue, blue sky
He has to fall backward before he can fly.
An orange-red breast and yellow feather crown has he.
The male quetzal bird is the crown jewel of bird royalty.

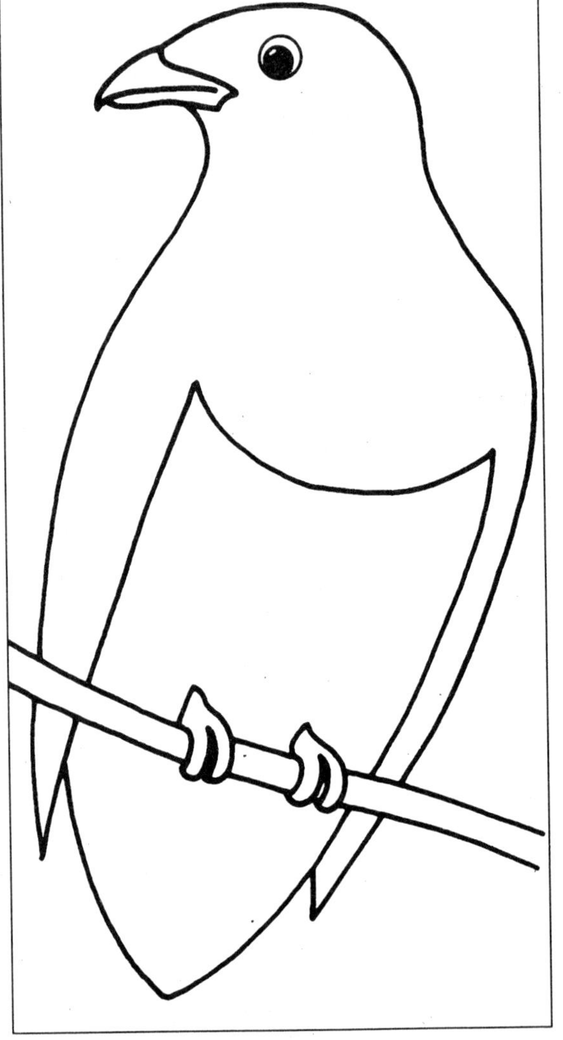

Related books

A Is for Animals by David Pelham

Incredible Animals A to Z, National Wildlife Federation

Mary Brehm, Aurora, OH

3+ In a Heartbeat

Science skills
Children experience the beating of their own hearts.

Materials

Upbeat music
Stethoscope
Slow, soothing music
Alcohol wipes

What to do

1. At circle time, ask the children if they can show you where their hearts are. Ask the children to place their hands over their hearts and feel the beat.
2. Tell the children that the heart is a muscle that pumps blood throughout the body.
3. Put on some upbeat music and have the children stand and jog or dance in place for two minutes. Ask them to stop and feel their heartbeats this time.
4. Have children lie down and close their eyes for two minutes while you play some slow, soothing music. Ask them to check their heartbeats again.
5. If you have a stethoscope, let the children take turns listening to their heartbeats (use the alcohol wipes on the ear pieces and then wipe them dry between uses). You can ask children to imitate their heartbeats by clapping, jumping, etc.

Related book

Magic School Bus, Inside the Human Body by Joanna Cole

Connie Heagerty, Trumbull, CT

3+ Eyeglasses

Science skills
With observation and fine motor skills, children are encouraged to ask questions about eyes and vision.

Materials

Magazine pages with pictures
Eyeglasses
Microscope
"Spy" glasses
Small toy or real bug
Magnifying glasses
Binoculars

What to do

1. Say "You asked why I (teacher) and some children wear glasses. They help us to see better. We will look and see."
2. Pass around magazine pages with figures on them. Look at them normally.
3. Ask the children to look at them with eyeglasses, then with the magnifying glasses. "What's different? That's right—they're bigger."
4. Observe a small toy or real bug through the microscope.
5. Look at objects all around through spy glasses and binoculars.

Original song

Sing to the tune of "Frère Jacques."

I wear glasses, I wear glasses
To help me see, to help me see.
Everything looks bigger, everything looks better
Like it should be, like it should be.

Related book

Arthur by Amanda Graham

Marilyn Harding, Grimes, IA

Bendable Bones

Science skills

Children observe as something hard and brittle becomes bendable.

Materials

Chicken bones
Vinegar
Water
Containers

What to do

1. Place the chicken bones into two different containers, one with vinegar and one with water.
2. Test the bones each day for about a week. See if they can bend easily.
3. The bones in the vinegar become bendable as the calcium dissolves.

Related book

The Skeleton Inside You by Philip Balestrino

Andrea Clapper, Cobleskill, NY

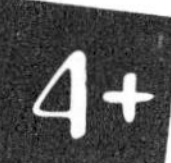

Insides Out

Science skills
Children use fine motor skills and observation.

Materials

Large light-colored sweatshirt
Various colored calico
Scissors
Iron-on bonding material, such as "Wonder Under"
Pattern for organs
Iron
Fabric puffy paint

What to do

1. Wash and dry the sweatshirt.
2. Make paper patterns for organs and cut them out of calico (red for heart, blue for lungs, purple for liver, green for stomach, brown for intestines, yellow for kidneys).
3. Iron these onto the sweatshirt using the bonding material.
4. Outline the organs with the puffy paints and label them
5. Let the sweatshirt dry thoroughly.
6. Wear it in class to show what you'd look like inside out!

More to do

Dramatic play: Fill a box with medical props and bandaids so children can play hospital.
More science: Copy patterns and directions for parents to duplicate this activity on a child's T-shirt. ▪ Display models of the invisible man and woman on science table.

 *Teresa J. Nos, Baltimore, MD*

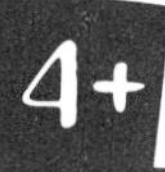

All Thumbs?

Science skills
Encourages children's interest in nature and allows them to practice fine motor skills.

Materials

Snug pair of infant socks
A variety of 10 to12 small objects in a range of shapes and textures (e.g., a shell, a button, a paper clip)

What to do

1. Place the objects on a table and encourage the children to handle each item. Ask them to observe how their fingers and thumbs help them with this task.
2. Ask, "What do you think it would be like to pick things up without using your fingers or thumbs?" Allow time for responses.
3. Place a snug but not tight or binding infant sock over each hand of a child volunteer. Ask the child to pick up a few of the objects, one at a time. Promote comparisons with questions such as, "Which are easier to pick up, the smooth things or the bumpy ones?" Repeat this step with the remaining children.
4. After each child has had a turn, continue the activity by displaying pictures of animals that function without the use of fingers or thumbs. Discuss the ways in which these animals compensate.

More to do

Art: Invite your budding artists to illustrate lots of varied and unusual ways they might pick up small items if they did not have the use of their fingers and thumbs.

Related book

Hand, Hand, Fingers, Thumb by A. Perkins

 *Marji E. Gold-Vukson, West Lafayette, IN*

Pasting Puzzles

Science skills

Children use their predicting and inferring skills and practice fine motor activity.

Materials

Magazine pictures of people of various ages, both genders and differing body types
Envelope for each picture
Glue sticks
Construction paper

What to do

1. Cut the pictures into two, three or four pieces (use straight cuts).
2. Use the envelopes to keep the puzzle pieces together.
3. Give each child an envelope and a piece of construction paper large enough to hold the complete picture. Give younger children the puzzles with fewer pieces.
4. Let the children assemble the puzzles on the paper.
5. When the puzzles are complete, they may glue the pieces in place.

More to do

Language: Name body parts, gender of the person pictured and possible role (mommy, daddy, big brother, sister, baby, grandmother, etc.). This activity provides an opportunity for children to

develop perceptual awareness of body parts, fine motor control and hand-eye coordination.

 *Mary Jo Shannon, Roanoke, VA*

4+ Skin Match

Science skills
Children use classification and inferring skills and fine motor skills.

Materials

2" (5 cm) square pieces of animal "skin" samples: wallpaper, cloth samples like fake fur, reptile print, fish scales, lobster shell, chamois, leather, feathers, pieces of tree bark
Glue
Cardboard pieces, 4" x 6" (10 cm x 15 cm)
Pictures of animals
Pictures of fruits and vegetables

What to do

1. Glue the skin samples onto the cardboard, one per piece.
2. Cut out pictures of whole animals, and glue them on cards, again, one per piece.
3. Ask the children to match the skin samples with the cards of the whole figures.

More to do

More science: Encourage the children to categorize skin sample cards by common characteristics: soft, smooth, rough, etc. ▪ Have a magnifying glass available to observe sample cards and children's own skin.

Related book

Animals Should Definitely Not Wear Clothing by Judi Barrett

 *Susan R. Forbes, Holly Hill, FL*

4+ Tickle My Arm

Science skills
With lots of giggles children will work on social development.

Materials

A partner

What to do

1. At group time, buddy up for this silly, fun experiment in body awareness.

2. Taking turns, have one child close her eyes and lay her arm on the second child's lap.
3. Encourage the second child gently and slowly to tickle the inside of the first child's arm.
4. The first child tries to guess when the tickle reaches the area of the arm inside the elbow and says "stop."
5. The second child stays at the spot while the first child opens her eyes and sees how close her guess was.
6. Switch partners (no peeking!).

Dani Rosensteel, Payson, AZ

X-Ray Puzzle

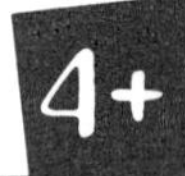

Science skills
Children use observation and inferring skills.

Materials

A book with large pictures of the human skeleton
Window
Manila envelopes
Old X-rays
Scissors
Tape or gum adhesive

What to do

1. Read the book about skeletons to the children. Let them look closely at the pictures.
2. Collect discarded X-rays from a hospital or doctor's office.
3. Cut X-rays with scissors into various shapes.
4. The children assemble the X-rays at a window using tape or gum adhesive.
5. Remove the adhesive before returning the pieces to the envelopes.

Related book

A Book About Your Skeleton by Ruth Belov Gross

Susan R. Forbes, Holly Hill, FL

Bag Bodies

Science skills
Children learn fine motor skills and are encouraged to ask questions about nature.

Materials

Look Inside Your Body by Denice Patrick

For each child you will need:

Large brown grocery sack
String
Tagboard circle
Red balloon
Brown yarn
Hanger
Dried hollow noodles or straw sections
Gray yarn
Two oval sponges
Masking tape

What to do

1. Read the book about the body.
2. Cut up the middle of a grocery bag and in a circle around the bottom.
3. Write (child's name) Body on the outside of the bag.
4. Bend and attach a hanger to the inside of the bag.
5. String noodles or straw sections, and hang them from the hanger to form a spine.
6. Decorate the tagboard circle to look like a child's head. Glue a gray yarn brain to the top of the head.
7. Blow up the red balloon to heart size, tie it off and attach it to the inside of the bag with masking tape.
8. Hot glue two oval sponges to the inside of the bag to form lungs. Sponges must be completely dry.
9. Glue brown yarn intestines near the bottom inside of the bag.

More to do

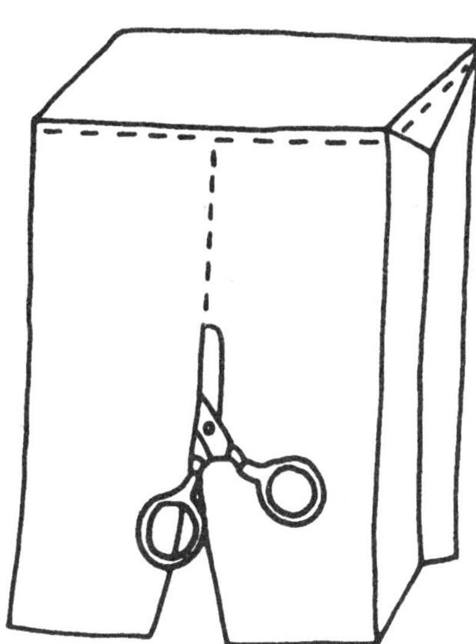

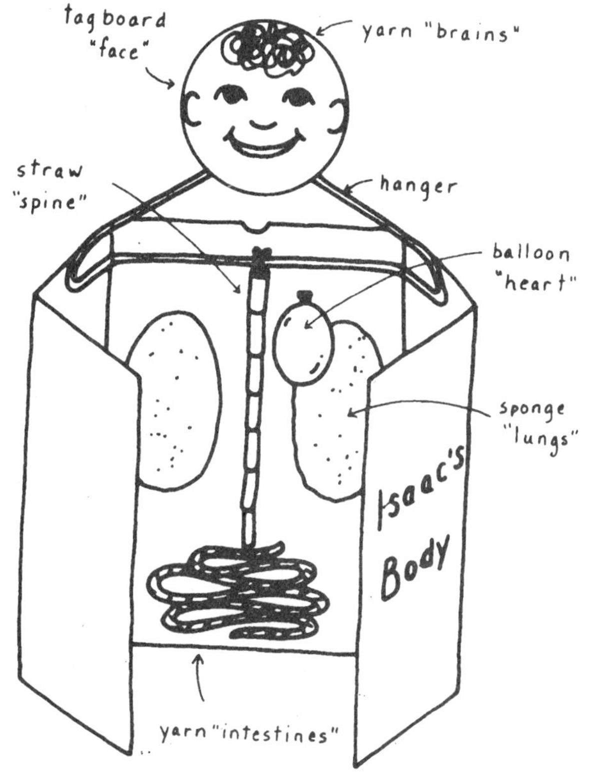

Bookmaking: Create "All About Me" books with name, family picture, self-portrait, home, address, etc.
Circle time: Learn fingerplays about the body.
Games: Exercise the body when you discuss the heart.
Math: Graph children by characteristics such as eye color, hair color, etc.
Music: Sing songs about the body.

Kimberle S. Byrd, Kalamazoo, MI

Bumps and Bruises

Science skills
Children learn from their own bodies through observation.

Materials

Five pieces of white paper
Crayons or markers
Book or poster that shows the veins and arteries of the human body

What to do

1. Beforehand, draw a circle on each of the five pieces of paper, and color and number them.
2. Show the children the book or poster picture of the veins and arteries of the body. Explain that the job of the veins and arteries is to carry the blood throughout the body. Have the children look at the inside of one of their wrists. Sometimes we can see some of the veins!
3. Explain that right under and very close to the skin are something called blood vessels. They are like veins, but much smaller.
4. Ask the children to stretch out their legs and look for any "colored marks or circles." (This is easiest if it is "shorts" season, but pant legs can be rolled up.)
5. Ask if anyone knows the name of these "colored circles" (bruises).
6. Explain that bruises occur when the blood vessels break under the skin. When a blood vessel breaks, it bleeds and the blood goes into the skin. This is how the bruise gets its color.
7. Ask the children if they can think of ways the blood vessels could get broken under our skin (falls, bump into things, etc.).

More to do

Art: Ask the children to trace their hands on black construction paper and use scissors to cut out the handprints. Provide white straws that have been cut into 1" (2.5 cm) pieces (older children can cut their own straws). The children can then create "veins" by gluing the straws on to the handprint.
Cooking: Bring in "bruised" fruit such as apples, bananas and pears. Use child-safe knives and ask the children to remove the bruised skin area of the fruit. Examine and discuss how they think fruit could get bruised. Help the children peel and cut the fruit to make a fruit salad. Serve for a snack.

Original song

Bumps and Bruises

(sing to the tune of "London Bridge")

Bumps and bruises by falling down,
Hitting the ground,
Running around.
Bumps and bruises by falling down,
That's how they happen!

Related book

How It Works: The Human Body by Kate Barnes

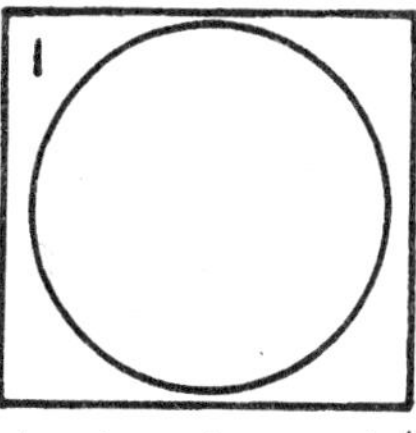

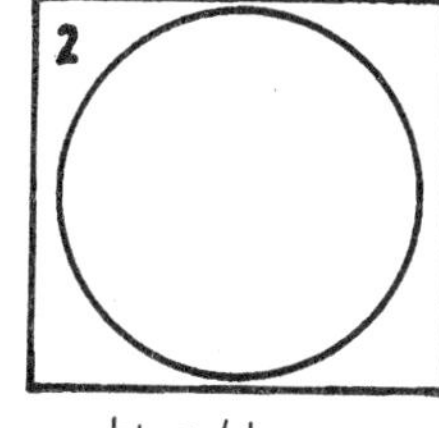

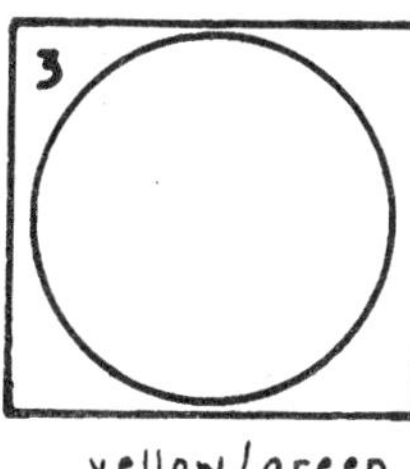

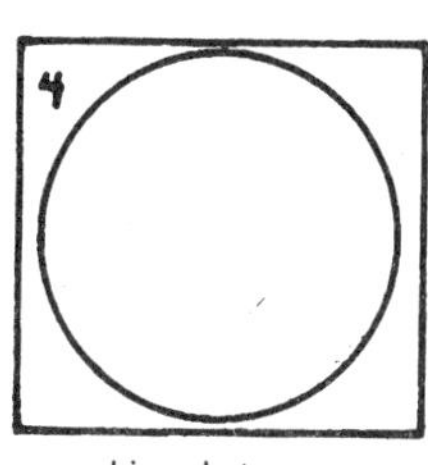

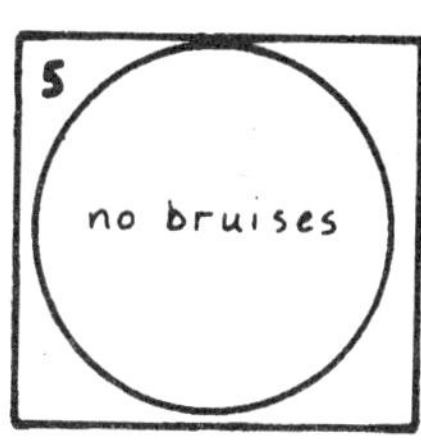

Kathy A. Lone, Sioux Falls, SD

5+

Fingerprint Fun

Science skills

Children use observation and classification skills.

Materials

Ink pad
Magnifying glasses
Paper, two small pieces per child

What to do

1. Ask each child to press a pointer finger on the ink pad and then press the fingerprint on one small piece of paper. Repeat with the other pointer finger.
2. Encourage the children to explore their fingerprints with the magnifying glasses.
3. Explore other children's fingerprints.
4. Mix up the pieces of paper and try to find the matching fingerprints.

More to do

Language: Make a class book for each child containing the sentence, "The unique thing about me is ________.".

Math: Measure hands with links, cubes, etc.
More science: Discuss the fact that each person's fingerprints are different and that this tells us apart. Discuss how we all look different and are unique.

Related books
Bein' With You This Way by W. Nikola-Lisa
Here Are My Hands by Bill Martin, Jr. and John Archambault

Amy B. Lieberman, Oxford, MA

Family Likenesses

Science skills
Children classify, graph and think about similarities and differences.

Materials
Paper
Pencils

What to do
1. Show the children how to make a chart of their family members. Help the children list their parents, siblings and put their own name down one side of the paper.
2. Across the top, put categories: hair, eyes, skin color and height.
3. Break the categories down even more, for example, under hair, put blonde, brunette and black. Under eyes, put green, blue, brown and hazel. For skin, put light medium and dark and under height, put short, medium and tall.
4. Draw lines vertically and horizontally to make boxes for the categories.
5. Make an X in the box across each of the choices that fit your parents, your siblings and yourself.
6. Do you have physical likenesses of both your parents?
7. Add other family members, such as grandparents, aunt and uncles to the chart.
8. After everyone is through, take some time to let each child show her chart. Help her identify similarities and differences among people listed. We are each unique but we also share some common family traits, don't we?

Related books
Are You My Mommy? by Carla Dijs
Are You My Mother? by P. D. Eastman
Black, White, Just Right! by Marguerite W. Davol

Monica Hay-Cook, Tucson, AZ

3+ Kitten Song

Science skills
Children learn about kittens with two songs and are encouraged to ask questions about nature.

Materials
A copy of the song below, illustrated with kittens

What to do
After learning about pets, introduce the nursery rhyme, "The Three Little Kittens." Discuss what is real and what is make believe. Do kittens really wear mittens? Do kittens really have four paws? Then sing this song to the tune of "I'm a Little Teapot."

I'm a little kitten, I have four paws.
I don't have fingers but I do have claws.
My body is covered with soft, soft fur.
I like to meow and I like to purr.

 *Angela M. Williamson, Seven Devils, NC*

3+ Three Little Kittens

Science skills
Children use fine motor skills.

Materials
White construction paper, 12" x 7" (30 cm x 17.5 cm)
Scissors
Paintbrush
Crayons
Watercolor paint

What to do
1. Discuss various kinds and colors of real cats such as Calico, Tiger, Persian, Siamese.
2. Following are some traits of all cats: they like to play; they are curious; they make good pets; they like to stay clean; they like to sleep in the daytime; they like to roam and hunt for food at night. Cats are members of the same family as lions, tigers, panthers, cougars, jaguars and pumas. Mother cats pick up kittens by the backs of their necks and carry them in their mouths. This does not hurt the kittens because the skin is loose. (Have children feel their

Cats

elbow skin when their arms are extended and help them to realize that this does not hurt.) Cats have feelings: a purring cat is happy; if the fur on a cat's back stands up and it spits or claws, it is angry; a hungry cat's "meow" sounds different from the "meow" of fear. The claws of most cats can be hidden in their paws—the Siamese cat cannot do this. If a cat falls from a high place, it can twist or flip in mid-air and will always land on its cushioned paws.

3. Now help the children make their own paper cats by folding the white paper into thirds.
4. Make a cat pattern and trace it into the folded construction paper (you could do the tracing or the children could do it).
5. Cut the pattern out triple thick. Be sure the pattern touches both folds.
6. Unfold the paper and add crayon features.
7. Paint the cats with watercolor as desired, let dry.
8. Fold tails back and stand up.

More to do

Dramatic play: Dramatize "Three Little Kittens" or modify the above paper cat project by adding three pairs of mittens to the cutouts.

Field trip: Visit a pet shop and discuss the care of cats and kittens.

Movement: Pretend to be cats. Crawl, climb, pounce!

Snack: Make cat-shaped sugar cookies. Frost and decorate.

Special days: Have cat day—bring a cat object, a cat toy or plush cats for show and tell. Perhaps someone's parent could bring in their pet cat as a surprise.

Original poems

Five Little Kittens Fingerplay

Five little kittens were playing one day.
The first little kitten jumped in the hay.
The second little kitten climbed up a tree.
The third little kitten chased a bumble bee.
The fourth little kitten went pounce, pounce, pounce.
The fifth little kitten caught a little gray mouse.
Then all the little kittens came calling mew,
mew, mew.
I think little kittens are cute, don't you?

Calico Cat

Soft calico cat, pretty calico cat,
Your splotches hide where you are at.
Please little cat won't you come into view?
Though I can't see you, I hear mew, mew, mew.

I like your colors, brown, black and gold
You bring good luck, so I am told.
Here's some milk for my favorite pet
Now I can see you, when the food you get.

Lick your paws when you are through
And clean your mouth and whiskers, too.
Then climb up and sleep in my lap.
I'll pet you while you take a nap.

Related books

Kittens Are Like That by Jan Pfloog
The Little Kitten by Judy Dunn

Mary Brehm, Aurora, OH

Cat Moves

Science skills
With imagination and imitation, children practice observation and large motor skills.

Materials
Copy of the poem on a large piece of tagboard
Sentence strips, cut into phrases of the poem, for example, "Sleepy Cats" on one and "Creepy Cats" on another
Large open area, inside or outside

What to do
1. Read the following poem aloud to the children.
   Cats
   Sleepy cats
   Creepy cats
   Purry cats
   Furry cats
   Mousy cats
   Housey cats
   Ruggy cats
   Huggy cats
2. Reread the poem and have the children act out each line, for example at "Sleepy cats," children curl up like a cat and pretend to sleep.
3. Ask the children to think of more movements that cats make. Allow them to demonstrate their movements, and let their classmates make those moves.
4. Afterwards, reread the poem and talk to the children about rhyming words.
5. Pass out a sentence strip to each of eight children. Have each child try to find the child who has the rhyming word that goes with theirs (ex: ruggy - huggy). Repeat until each child has had a turn.

More to do
Art: Let each child pick one line of the poem to illustrate. Adults can write the line for younger children while older children can copy the words themselves.
Special day: Invite parents to bring pet cats for visits to the classroom.

Related book
Hannah and Jack by Mary Nethery

 *Barbara Saul, Eureka, CA*

3+

Squish Bags of Color

Science skills

Children observe colors being mixed and use their fine motor skills in this tactile experience.

Materials

Resealable plastic bags, 12
Clear hair gel
Scissors
White construction paper, one piece per child
Construction paper circles of red, yellow, blue, green, purple and orange
Red, blue and yellow paint
Duct tape
Glue
Marker

What to do

1. Put 1 part red and 2 parts yellow paint into a resealable plastic bag with a ¼ cup (60 ml) of the hair gel.
2. Seal the bag and secure the top with duct tape.
3. Ask a child to squish the bag to mix the colors. What happens?
4. Repeat steps 1 to 3, using 2 parts yellow and 1 part blue in a bag with media mix, and then with equal parts of red and blue in a bag until all the bags are used.
5. Help the children chart the results with construction paper circles and glue on a piece of white paper, using + and = signs, for example, red + yellow = orange.

More to do

Art: Snip the corner of the resealable plastic bags and encourage the children to squeeze out the paint, making designs on finger paint paper or other shiny paper. This way the contents of the bags will not be wasted.

Original song

Colors (sing to the tune of "If You're Happy and You Know It")

Yellow and blue make green (the next part is said instead of clapping), *don't you see*
Yellow and red make orange, don't you see
Red and blue make purple,
Don't you see, don't you see?
All the colors you can make with these three!

Related books

A Color of His Own by Leo Lionni
Mouse Paint by Ellen Stoll Walsh
White Rabbit's Book of Color by Alan Baker

Glenda Manchanda, Bemidji, MN

Rose-Colored Glasses

3+

Science skills

The world looks different as children observe it through tinted glasses.

Materials

Glasses pattern
Scissors
Tape
Rolls of colored cellophane (available at art supply stores)
Pencils
Tagboard or card stock
Sequins, glitter, glue and markers, optional

What to do

1. Trace the glasses pattern onto pieces of tagboard.
2. Cut the pattern out, including the "lens" areas. Steps 1 and 2 should be done by an adult for very young children.
3. Cut out two pieces of colored cellophane to fit over the lenses of each pair of glasses.
4. Tape the cellophane to the inside of each lens.
5. Let the children decorate the outside of their spectacles with glitter, sequins or markers.
6. Encourage them to explore their environment using their colored spectacles.
7. Ask them to trade their glasses for some of another color and see what everything looks like.

More to do

More science: Instead of glasses, make hand-held magnifying glasses. Put the colored glasses at a center and let the children explore looking through them. Show the children how to overlay two colors together to make a new color.

Barbara Saul, Eureka, CA

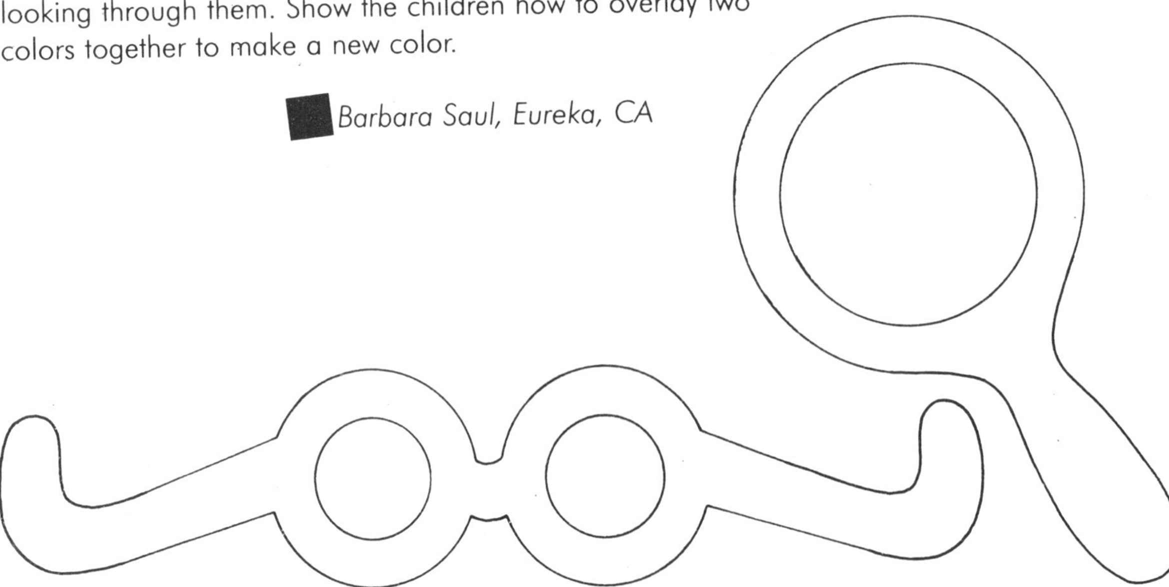

3+

Mixing Colors With Finger Paints

Science skills

Children enjoy finger painting as they practice observation and fine motor skills.

Materials

Painting shirts
Easel paper
Finger paints in primary colors: red, blue and yellow
Colored construction paper
Dish tub of warm clear water
Color wheel, optional
Tables covered with butcher paper or newspaper
Finger painting paper
Sponge and bowl of water
Dish tub of warm soapy water
Cloth or paper towels

What to do

1. Tell the children that there are three primary colors: red, blue and yellow. Explain the word "primary" means first and these colors are the first colors because when they are mixed together, they make other colors called secondary (second) colors. Tell them that today they are going to mix two of the primary colors to find out what secondary colors they make.
2. Divide the children into small groups.
3. Taking one group at a time, ask the children to put on painting shirts and roll up their sleeves.
4. On a covered table, place a sheet of easel paper and on top of that, a smaller sheet of finger painting paper.
5. Write the child's name on the back of the finger painting paper.
6. Wet each paper with a wet sponge and let the child pick two colors. Put 1 tablespoon (15 ml) of each color on his paper. If you are using tempera, also add 1 tablespoon (15 ml) of liquid starch.
7. Let the children use their hands to mix the paint and create a new color.
8. When the children are finished, lift the painting by the easel paper to dry elsewhere.
9. At another table, have an adult help each child make hand prints on the colored construction paper before the paint on their hands dries.
10. Ask each child as he finishes to wash his hands in the warm soapy water, then rinse in the clear water and wipe on a towel.

Mixing Colors With Frosting

3+

Science skills
Children observe color mixing by making their own tasty treats.

Materials

Graham crackers
Food coloring
White frosting
Toothpicks

What to do

1. Talk to the children about mixing colors. Ask them if they know which colors combine to make green, purple and orange. If they don't know, tell them that they are going to find out by experimenting with color mixing.
2. Demonstrate how to color the white frosting by adding food coloring to it. Mix batches of red, blue and yellow frosting.
3. Give each child a graham cracker and a toothpick.
4. Let each child choose two of the frosting colors to put on his graham cracker (use about 1 teaspoon or 5 ml of each color per graham cracker).
5. Let the children mix their colors with their toothpicks to see what secondary colors appear.
6. After the children tell you what color they made, let them eat their treat.
7. Steps 1-6 may be repeated with different color combinations.
8. For a follow-up, write a whole-class chart or story about which colors mixed together to make new colors.

More to do

Art: Ask the children which colors look warm, which colors seem cool? Encourage the children to color with just warm colors or just cool colors. Display the pictures and ask the children to dictate stories about them.
Math: Make a graph of the children's favorite colors.

Related books

Little Blue and Little Yellow by Leo Lionni
Lunch by Denise Fleming
Rainbow of My Own by Don Freeman
Who Said Red? by Mary Serfozo

Barbara Saul, Eureka, CA

My Own Colors

Science skills
Children use their senses and observe colors.

Materials

Samples of Formica or other counter materials or linoleum (often available free of charge at large hardware stores)
Metal rings

What to do

1. Slip several samples on the metal ring and clip it closed.
2. For the youngest children, make sure the samples have rounded, not sharp, edges. These are the perfect size for small hands to carry. They are indestructible and wash up easily and make a satisfying noise when shaken.
3. Use the sample booklets to play an "I Spy the Color" game. Children take turns choosing one of the samples as the color everyone will look for.

Related books and recording

A Color of His Own by Leo Lionni
Color Dance by Ann Jonas
Mouse Paint by Ellen Stoll Walsh
"The World Is a Rainbow," by Greg and Steve

Tracie O'Hara, Charlotte, NC

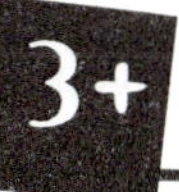

Playdough Color Mixing

Science skills
Children make observations and practice predicting, comparing and using fine motor skills.

Materials

Favorite playdough recipe and the ingredients
Red paste food coloring (available at cake decorating or craft stores; it will produce the correct color to make orange and purple)
Yellow and blue food coloring
Plastic gloves
Simple color chart

What to do

1. Mix the playdough according to directions, omitting the food coloring, and divide it into three equal portions. Note: Older children may enjoy making the play dough and adding the color with the teacher. You may use an entire batch of playdough for each color depending on the number of children in your class.
2. Put the plastic gloves on (to prevent coloring hands), and add red paste coloring to one portion of the playdough by kneading the color into the dough.
3. Add blue and yellow food coloring to each of the other playdough portions in the same manner. You will have three portions of playdough: one yellow, one red and one blue.
4. Gather the children at a table and give each child one small piece each of yellow and blue playdough.
5. Encourage the children to mix the colors. As they are working, ask questions to stimulate their thinking and to focus their observation. What is happening as you mix? What is the result?
6. Continue with steps 4 and 5 until the children have also mixed yellow and red, and blue and red.
7. Use a simple color chart to check the results.

More to do

Art: At the easel, have yellow, blue and red paints available for the children to mix. Are the results the same as the playdough experiment?

More science: Help the children make a color chart of their own using construction paper, markers or colored glue.

Related books

A Color of His Own by Leo Lionni
Mouse Paint by Ellen Stoll Walsh
White Rabbit's Color Book by Alan Baker

Glenda Manchanda, Bemidji, MN

Color Magic

Science skills

Children observe cause and effect as they watch colors combine.

Materials

Colored transparent book report covers
Overhead projector

What to do

1. Cut the transparent book report covers to fit on the overhead projector.
2. Place a blue cover on the projector. This will reflect the color on the wall.
3. Place a yellow cover on the top of the blue one while singing the following song to the tune of Frère Jacques:

Blue and yellow, blue and yellow,
That makes green, that makes green.
Colors come together, colors come together,
As you see, as you see.

4. Repeat the song using other color combinations.

More to do

More science: Cut the transparencies into various shapes (circles, squares, triangles). Reinforce identifying shapes as well as colors.

Dotti Enderle, Houston, TX

Color Collage

Science skills
Children must be sharp-eyed observers, and they practice fine motor skills.

Materials

Magazines
Glue or gluesticks
Hailstones and Halibut Bones by Mary O'Neill
Scissors (if skill level permits)
Cardboard figures of various objects

What to do

1. You can use this activity to introduce colors. The teacher makes large figures beforehand, one figure for each color. Examples:
   apple—red
   pumpkin—orange
   tree—green
   top hat—black
   sheep—white
   sun—yellow
   grapes—purple
   car—blue
   ballet slipper—pink
   bear—brown
2. Introduce a color by reading the poem about the color from Hailstones and Halibut Bones.
3. Encourage children to find items in the color discussed, for example, clothes, toys other objects in the classroom.
4. Give the children magazines and tell them to locate items in the magazine of the color discussed. If the children are able to cut, have them cut out the objects. If not, they can tear items or the teacher can cut them. Teacher may have to trim pictures to show a certain color.
5. Ask the children to glue the cut pieces onto your teacher-made shape until the entire shape is filled with the color. Repeat with the rest of the shapes.
6. Laminate and display the shapes in your classroom. You can make these figures each year to introduce colors, instead of purchasing the commercial color figure sets.

More to do

Language: Ask the children to dictate a sentence about the items they found and have the sentences follow a pattern. For example, Tommy found a red block. Eric found a red shirt. Write the

sentences on chart story paper and distribute one to each child. Encourage the children to find their word on the chart story. Try to concentrate on the color words and children's names. ▪ As a cumulative activity after all the colors have been introduced, make a book for the classroom library entitled *Our Favorite Colors*. The children can dictate a sentence using a pattern. For example, Mary said, "My favorite color is blue. The sky is blue, my shirt is blue and my lunch box is blue." The pattern should have the name of the child, name of the favorite color and a list of three things that are that color. The children can illustrate their sentences. Bind pages together and put into a book for your classroom library.

Math: Give the children items that are of varying colors, for example, buttons. Have them sort the items by color. The children can use unifix cubes and make a color pattern.

 *Deborah Chaplin, Hot Springs, VA*

Color Detectives

Science skills

Children use observation and large motor skills.

Materials

Cardboard magnifying glasses (enough for each child in the class)

What to do

1. Plan a color day each month. On that day the children may either wear or bring something in that is the color of the month.
2. The art activity as well as snack is centered around the color of the month on that day. For example, if the color is yellow, you might have bananas and lemonade for snack.
3. At circle time, each child has a chance to show what they brought or wore with the special color.
4. Then explain that you need some color detectives to help find all the red (or yellow, etc.) in the classroom. More than likely, every child's hand will go up! Give each child a magnifying glass to help search for the color.

Related book

Colors & Things by Tana Hoban

Cindy Winther, Oxford, MI

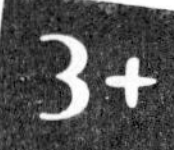

Colors, Colors Everywhere

Science skills
All their senses are put to work as children make observations and use fine motor skills.

Materials
Index cards with a different color on each side

What to do
1. Give each child a colored card. One side has a common color, such as blue, brown or green. The other side has a less common color, such as red, orange or purple.
2. Head out for a nature walk and challenge each child to find natural items that match the colors on their card. (Encourage children not to pick every plant that matches.) Hint: children respond well to new words for Go and Stop or Come Back. For example, "peanut butter" might mean Go and "banana split" could mean Come Back or Stop. This encourages good listening skills.
3. Children can return for a new color card after matching items to their first card.
4. Periodically call a "time out to share" for the group. The teacher names a color and the children take turns sharing what they found to match (for example: Blue—sky, flower, rock, water).

More to do
Language: Read color poems from *Hailstones and Halibut Bones* by Mary O'Neill, and discuss the feelings created or inspired by different colors.
More science: Create a chart showing natural items and colors.

	Leaf	Flower	Rock	Bark
Red	X	X	X	
Blue			X	X
Green	X	X		

Karen Johnson, Grand Rapids, MI

Watercolors

3+

Science skills

Children practice observation and prediction and inference skills.

Materials

Two resealable plastic bags
Ice water
Hot water
Red food color

What to do

1. Pour 1 cup (250 ml) of ice water into a resealable plastic bag.
2. Drop in 3 drops of red dye, zip it shut and try not to jiggle the bag.
3. Watch what happens to the red dye. Check the time to see how long it takes the dye to turn all the water red.
4. The children are observing the process called "diffusion" which will cause the two different kinds of molecules to mix. The red dye molecules will spread from where there are more of one kind to where there are fewer of the same kind.
5. Next, pour 1 cup (250 ml) of hot tap water into another bag. Add 3 drops of red dye and seal. Observe how long it takes the dye to turn the water red. Are there differences depending on water temperature?

Cindy Winther, Oxford, MI

Where Are the Colors?

Science skills

Children use all their senses to observe the relationship between color and light.

Materials

Scarf, fabric or washcloth
Drawstring bag
Flashlight

What to do

1. Put the fabric into the bag and draw it closed.
2. Let the children guess the color of the cloth. Allow them to feel it, smell it, listen to it, but not see it.

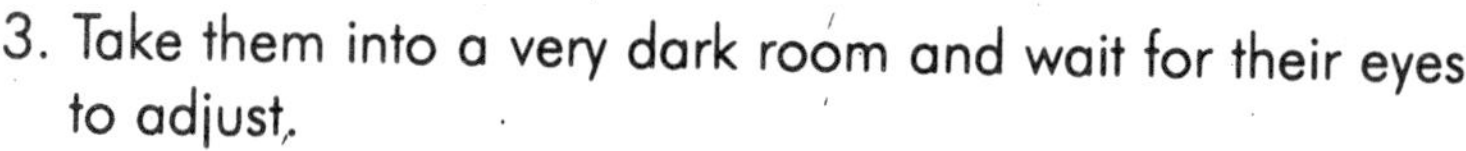

3. Take them into a very dark room and wait for their eyes to adjust.
4. Pull out the cloth. Can they see the color?
5. Admit a small amount of light. Does that help?
6. Shine the flashlight on the cloth. You must have light to see color.

More to do

More science: Explore shadows. How are they made? Why are they black? In the absence of light, there is no color. ▪ Experiment with mixing colors and adding white and black. ▪ Try doing puzzles, stringing beads and drawing while blindfolded. This kind of activity also builds an awareness of handicaps. Try using a cane to get around the room while blindfolded.

Related books

Brown Bear, Brown Bear, What Do You See? by Bill Martin, Jr.
The Colors by Monique Felix
White Rabbit's Color Book by Alan Baker

Sandra Gratias, Perkasie, PA

3+

Yellow + Blue = Green

Science skills
Children use fine motor skills and observe how colors mix.

Materials

Resealable plastic sandwich bags, one per child
Yellow finger paint
Duct tape
Spoon
Blue finger paint

What to do

1. For each child, put one tablespoon (15 ml) of yellow finger paint into one side of a sandwich bag, and one tablespoon of blue finger paint into the other side of the bag.
2. Seal and tape the top of the bag.
3. Encourage the children to gently squish both sides of the bag to combine the two colors. What color do they create?

More to do

Art: Finger paint with yellow and blue finger paint, mixing to make green.
Cooking: Make instant pudding and add yellow and blue food coloring to make green pudding, or add food coloring to cream cheese.
More science: Use yellow and blue food coloring and water in an ice cube tray to make green.

Related books and recordings

Colors Everywhere by Tana Hoban

Green Bear by Alan Rogers
Little Blue and Little Yellow by Leo Lionni
Mouse Paint by Ellen Stoll Walsh
Red Day, Green Day by Edith Kunhardt
"Colors" by Hap Palmer
"Parade of Color" by Hap Palmer

 *Kaethe Lewandowski, Centreville, VA*

Find Your Color Game

Science skills
In this matching game, children use observation, fine motor and classification skills.

Materials

Brown Bear, Brown Bear, What Do You See? by Bill Martin
Wooden board
Basket
Color chips or paint samples from a paint store
Cup hooks
Hole punch

What to do

1. Read *Brown Bear, Brown Bear, What Do You See?* to the children.
2. Give each child a color chip, then ask each child to find something in the room that is the same color as his chip. Children take turns naming their color and finding an object in the room that is the same color.
3. Take a wooden board and screw the cup hooks into the board.
4. Have available a set of color chips that duplicates the children's. Punch a hole in each chip and laminate it. (Formica color chips also work well.) Put the duplicate set of chips into a basket.
5. Ask the children to search through the basket for a matching color chip and then hang their pair on a hook.

Flash of Color

Science skills
Children practice observation skills with a beautiful light display.

Materials

Scissors
Flashlights
Colored plastic wrap or colored cellophane
Rubber bands

What to do

1. Cut squares of plastic wrap or cellophane large enough to fit over the heads of the flashlights and secure with rubber bands.
2. The children turn on the flashlights and shine the colored light beams around the room.
3. Other activities children can try include matching a blue beam to a blue object; trying to mix colors by shining two different colored beams on one spot; shining the light beam on a mirror and trying to make the reflection hit a predetermined target in the room; and experimenting with the overhead lights on and off. Is one condition better than another?

More to do

Art: The children can mix tempera colors, finger paint colors or food coloring to further experiment with color mixing.

More science: The children can make a pair of binoculars from empty toilet paper tubes and colored cellophane. They will see the world through different colors. ▪ Help children use the overhead projector to discover concepts of light and reflection. By moving the lens cover around, children will discover more about reflecting light. ▪ What other things will make a reflecting light? (Shiny spoon, a stainless steel tea kettle, even one child's book bag, as we discovered.)

Related books and recording

Light by Donald Crews
Round Trip by Ann Jonas
"This Little Light of Mine" by Raffi and various other recording artists

Diane Billings, Marietta, GA

Magic Color Flow

Science skills
Children observe colors and how they diffuse.

Materials

Paper towels
Clear plastic cups
Resealable plastic sandwich bags
Watercolor markers
Water
Tape

What to do

1. Give each child one paper towel and their choice of a colored marker.
2. Encourage the children to draw on the paper towel with the marker.
3. When each child is finished with his picture, ask him to put the paper towel into a clear plastic cup half-filled with water.
4. Discuss the results with the children. (The color from the marker will diffuse into the water creating a jewel-like color in the water.)

5. Encourage each child to squeeze out his paper towel and unfold it. The lines of the drawing will have blurred and softened; the color will have spread throughout the towel (diffusion again).
6. You can then pour the water into a resealable plastic sandwich bag and tape it to the window as a sun catcher. If your theme is rainbows, each child could make one color of the rainbow, then display the sun catchers together as a rainbow in your window. (This is an excellent activity to do at an outdoor table on a nice day.)
7. Talk about the concept of diffusion which describes the way the color spreads through the water and the paper towels.

More to do

More science: The children can use two or more paint colors to experiment with color mixing.

Kim Merritt, Tallahassee, FL

Color Walk

Science skills

Children make observations, ask questions about nature and practice fine and large motor skills.

Materials

Crayons, one per child
Cardboard
Marker
A place to walk in nature
Tape
Paper, optional

What to do

1. Give each child a crayon and tell him that on the walk he should look for and gather items the same color as his crayon.
2. Using a large piece of cardboard and tape, make a display of the crayons and the items that the children found to match. Alternatively, children could use their crayons to do rubbings of the items they find, rather than disturb nature by collecting the items.

More to do

Art: Encourage children to use crayons and paper on a nature walk to get a variety of textured rubbing samples.

Melissa Browning, Milwaukee, WI

Colorful Nature Walk

Science skills
Children use all their senses for observation and also work on fine motor and classification skills.

Materials
A paper bag for each child
Markers, optional

What to do
1. Give a bag to each of the children. They may wish to decorate their bags.
2. Explain to the children that you are going to go on a nature walk, but this is not just an ordinary nature walk. It is a color nature walk! Tell the children that they will look for colorful natural items, such as a red leaf, a green piece of grass, etc.
3. Younger children can collect all of the colors. Older children can be grouped into "color teams," each assigned a specific color to look for. For example, the yellow team collects only yellow items.
4. Let the children explore the natural environment and have fun collecting.
5. Once back in the classroom, each child or group discusses what they found.
6. This is a great activity to do in the fall and spring to explore the seasons as well as reinforce color recognition!

More to do
Art: Make u collage with the items that were collected.
Language: Ask the children to record, in small books, what they collected. Younger children can draw pictures and dictate words. Older children can use inventive spelling to write the words.
Math: Make a graph of how many items the children found for each color.

Related books
Planting a Rainbow by Lois Ehlert
Red Leaf, Yellow Leaf by Lois Ehlert

Amy B. Lieberman, Oxford, MA

Mixing Colors Magic

3+

Science skills

In this activity, children use observation and prediction.

Materials

Red, yellow and blue paint
Paper for each child

What to do

1. Discuss the "magic" of mixing colors. Using paint, demonstrate to the children what happens when you mix two primary colors.
2. Give each child a small amount of paint in a primary color on one side of the paper and a small amount of another color on the other side.
3. Ask each child to fold his paper closed and press down from top to bottom.
4. Open the paper and see the colorful blots in a new color that the children have created.
5. Ask the children what picture they see in their painting and label the picture for them.
6. Cut the paintings into butterfly shapes and hang them around your room.

Related books and recording

Babar's Book of Color by Laurent De Brunhoff
Little Blue and Little Yellow by Leo Lionni
"Colors Song" by Hap Palmer

Suzanne Maxymuk, Cherry Hill, NJ

Rainbow Iceberg

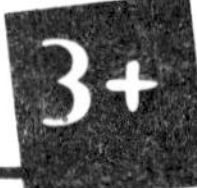

Science skills

An exciting experiment that allows children to observe color mixing.

Materials

Rock salt
Small bucket
Freezer
Paint aprons
Measuring cup
Water
Large bowl
Food coloring

What to do

1. Pour ½ cup (125 ml) salt into the bottom of the bucket. Fill the bucket with water and place in the freezer overnight.
2. The following day, take the bucket out of the freezer and turn it upside down in the large bowl. Ask the children to put on aprons.
3. The adult squeezes drops of food color onto the block of ice.
4. Encourage the children to touch, pet, feel and observe the ice as it melts and the colors blend. Discuss the melting ice and blending colors and ask for the children's predictions about what will happen to the ice and why. Remember that food coloring may stain skin and clothing.

Dani Rosensteel, Payson, AZ

Color Exploration

Science skills

Children observe and use prediction and inference skills in this experiment.

Materials

Small clear plastic cups
Protected area (floor, tub, tabletop, etc.)
Red, yellow and blue dye

What to do

1. Fill three cups with clear water.
2. Dye each with a different primary color.
3. Let the children experiment by pouring some of the colored water into the clear cups.
4. Encourage them to mix the colors and try to discover which two colors make orange, purple and green. Did they create anything else?

More to do

Art: Once the children discover the color combinations for the secondary colors, move this concept into other areas. Make pictures by drawing with one color crayon or markers over another color. • Try blot/squash painting with two primary colors.
Food: Try mixing frostings of different primary colors to frost cookies with secondary colors.

Related books

A Color Sampler by Kathleen Westray
Color by Ruth Heller
Purple, Green, and Yellow by Robert Munsch

Wanda K. Pelton, Lafayette, IN

Color Dots

4+

Science skills

Children use fine motor skills and make observations about color.

Materials

4 small bottles of food coloring
8 index cards
8 clear plastic punch cups
Red, yellow, blue and green 1" (2.5 cm) dots, purchased from stationery store

What to do

1. Set this activity up as a center. Fill each punch cup half-full with water. Assemble the cups in a row.
2. Create color cards by sticking color dots onto the blank cards, one color per card. Place one color card on the table in front of each cup.
3. Instruct the children to drop the same number of food coloring drops on the corresponding color cards into each cup and observe the resulting color.

More to do

Art: Children can experiment mixing colors using tempera paint.

Related book

Mouse Paint by Ellen Walsh

Joyce Montag, Slippery Rock, PA

Color Mixing

Science skills

Fine motor skills come in handy as children observe colors they mix.

Materials

Newspaper
Food coloring or watercolor paints in red, blue and yellow
Ice cube trays
Eyedroppers

What to do

1. Place newspaper on tables.
2. Fill half of the ice cube sections with water colored with food coloring or liquid watercolor paints.

3. With the eyedroppers, the children can mix colors in the empty sections.
4. Add an assortment of clear containers for additional mixing.

More to do

Art: You might try other color mixing activities with the children: finger painting, easel painting, plastic color panels.

Audrey F. Kanoff, Allentown, PA

Color, Shape and Texture

Science skills

Children use their observation skills to group and classify different items.

Materials

Two pieces of construction paper of contrasting colors, for example, orange and green
Cardboard shapes (prepared by an adult), 2" (5 cm) circles and 4" (10 cm) squares
Pencils
One piece of sandpaper
Children's scissors

What to do

1. Children trace the circles, two on orange and one on green construction paper, and one on brown sandpaper.
2. The children trace the squares, two on orange and one on green construction paper, and one on brown sandpaper.
3. Ask the children to cut out the circles and squares. (An adult should probably cut out the sandpaper circles and squares.)
4. The children mix up the squares and circles and put them in a pile.
5. Ask whether these things make a group. Children may think of a group of colored objects or a group of shapes. How could they be put into smaller groups that are more alike? (For instance, they might use color as a basis for grouping.) Are there any other ways of grouping the objects? (They could be put in smaller groups by shape.) Are there any other ways of grouping the objects? By texture?

More to do

More science: Discuss the similarities and differences of the shapes. ▪ Ask the children to sort the shapes by sight and then by touch only.

Related books

Color by Ruth Heller
Sorting by Henry Pluckrose
Sorting and Sets by Sally Hewitt
Texture by Karen Bryant-Mole

Elizabeth Thomas, Hobart, IN

Color Frames

4+

Science skills
Children use observation and fine motor skills.

Materials

Blue, red and yellow cellophane
Scissors
Hole punch
Construction paper in blue, red and yellow
Glue
Yarn or string

What to do

1. Before class, cut one red, blue and yellow 4" (10 cm) construction paper square per child. Fold each in half and cut out the center, leaving a 1" (2.5 cm) frame. Next cut out one 3½" (8.5 cm) square of red, blue and yellow cellophane per child.
2. Give each child one set of colored cellophane and one set of construction paper squares. Ask the children to match the cellophane color to its corresponding construction paper frame.
3. Glue the cellophane to its frame. Instruct children to put glue only on the construction paper.
4. Punch a hole in the center of the top of each frame. String all three frames loosely together.
5. Let children experiment by holding the colors up to their eyes and looking at objects in the room. Encourage them to combine colors and look through two or three at a time.
6. Give children a flashlight and let them shine it through the cellophane colors. Use a white surface such as a wall, floor or piece of construction paper to reflect colors onto. Encourage children to combine colors. Ask them what colors they see if they shine light through both the yellow and blue frames.
7. At circle time talk about how red, yellow and blue are primary colors from which all other colors can be made. Ask children to describe the different colors they made by combining the primary colors.

Related book

Is It Red? Is it Yellow? Is It Blue? by Tana Hoban

Connie Heagerty, Trumbull, CT

Color Magnifying Glasses

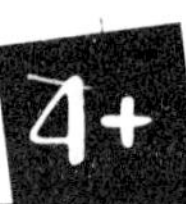

Science skills
Children use fine motor skills, then explore colors around the classroom.

Materials

Is It Red? Is It Yellow? Is It Blue? by Tana Hoban
Magnifying glass pattern
Tagboard or heavy weight paper
Glue sticks
Yellow, blue and red cellophane

What to do

1. Read *Is It Red? Is It Yellow? Is It Blue?* Discuss the signs and the different colors.
2. Ahead of time, prepare six magnifying glass patterns for each child. Help the children create their own red, blue and yellow magnifying glasses at their desks.
3. For each magnifying glass, use two magnifying glass patterns. Place one magnifying glass down and glue along the round part of the magnifying glass and handle.
4. Place a piece of cellophane down on the magnifying glass. Then glue around the second magnifying glass, and place on top of the first magnifying glass and cellophane.
5. The children cut the excess cellophane from around the magnifying glass.
6. Repeat this process, making magnifying glasses with each of the other two colors.
7. Using these magnifying glasses, the children view the things in the classroom as blue, red and yellow.
8. Point out to the children that they can create other colors by placing the magnifying glasses on top of one another.

More to do

Math: Create a class graph titled "Our Favorite Colors."

 *Susan Mahoney, Patuxent River, MD*

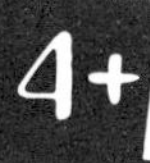

Mix It Up

Science skills
Children make predictions and observe color mixing changes.

Materials

2 half-gallon (2 L) containers of colored water, one blue and one red
1 package small, clear plastic dosage-type cups (available at medical supply shops or party supply stores)
4 small serving trays
4 medicine or eyedroppers
8 small (8 oz. or 250 ml) clear plastic drinking cups
Sponge

What to do

1. In advance, mix up two batches of colored water (3-5 drops of food coloring per half gallon are sufficient).
2. Set out the four trays. Each tray should contain 2 8-oz. cups, 4 to 5 smaller cups and 1 medicine or eyedropper.
3. Fill the 8 oz. cups halfway with one of the two water solutions.
4. Allow the children to mix the waters to form a new color.
5. Dispose of the water after each child finishes so that the next child has fresh water.

More to do
Art: Mix colors by melting crayons.

Related books
Color Dance by Ann Jonas
The Color Kittens by Golden Books Staff
Little Blue and Little Yellow by Leo Lionni
Mouse Paint by Ellen Stoll Walsh

Linda Ford, Sacramento, CA

Mix It Up Again

Science skills
By conducting their own experiments, children create, observe and make predictions about the colored light flowing into their classroom.

Materials
Transparent colored florist or craft wrap (red, yellow, blue)
Tape
A sunny window
3 to 6 pieces of shirt cardboard

What to do
1. Tape a 1′ (30 cm) square section of colored transparent wrap to a sunny window.
2. Use the shirt cardboard to make color paddles by first folding the cardboard in half, then cutting out a "window." Then unfold. Tape transparent wrap over this cutout hole. Refold and tape the cardboard shut. Make at least one color paddle for each color.

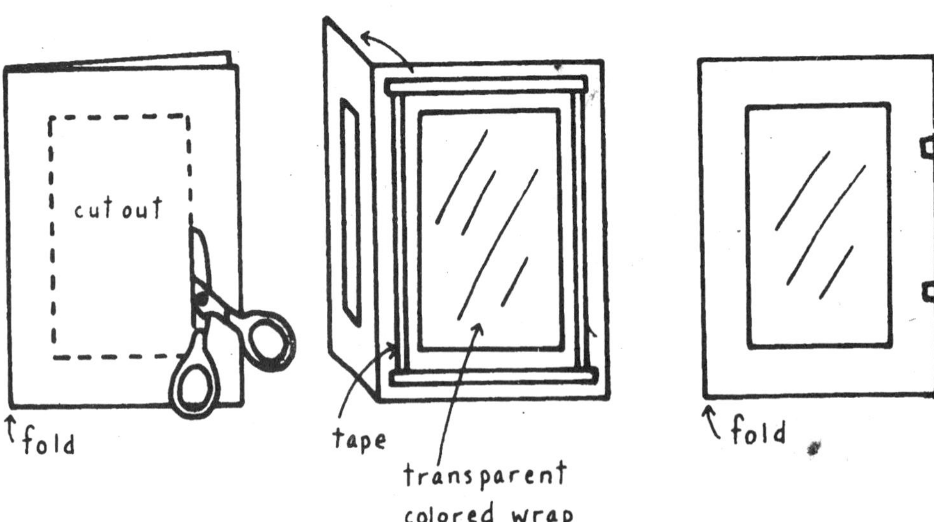

3. When the sun hits your window it should cast a patch of colored sunlight through the transparent wrap into the classroom.
4. Encourage the children to hold the color paddles up to the window to mix and change the colors.

Original poem

A little red and then some blue,
What do you think they're going to do?
Mix some yellow and some blue,
Color mixing is fun to do!

Related books

Color Dance by Ann Jonas
The Color Kittens by Golden Books Staff
Do You Know Colors? by Katherine Howard
Little Blue and Little Yellow by Leo Lionni
Mouse Paint by Ellen Stoll Walsh

Linda Ford, Sacramento, CA

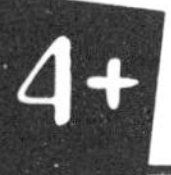

Somewhere Over Newton's Rainbow

Science skills
Children observe what a great scientist first discovered long ago.

Materials

Picture of Sir Isaac Newton, optional
Men's old white dress shirts or lab coats for dress-up
One plastic prism

What to do

1. If possible, show a picture of Sir Isaac Newton and explain that he was a great scientist. Talk about what a scientist is (an expert in science, someone who observes, studies and does experiments to find out more about things in the world). If possible, have the children dress up in lab coats like real scientists. Tell the children you are going to do the following experiment, first done by Newton.
2. Locate a window in your school or classroom where direct sunlight is pouring in. Cover the window or pull down a shade so only a small beam of light comes through. Hold the prism point down in the beam so that the children can see a rainbow. Explain that when white light from the sun passes through the prism and is broken up into different colors, a rainbow appears. Allow each child time to explore using the prism.

More to do

Games: Sing "The Rainbow in the Dell" to the tune of "The Farmer in the Dell." Make red,

orange, yellow, green, blue and violet construction paper circles and a drawing of a rainbow. Attach yarn to the rainbow and the circles individually to make them into necklaces. Select a child to wear the rainbow. Distribute the other color necklaces. Ask the child wearing the rainbow to select the first color. For example, "The rainbow takes the red, the rainbow takes the red. Hi-ho the derry-o, the rainbow takes the red." Continue until all the colors have been selected, then let each color go away until "the rainbow stands alone." Repeat the game until each child has had a turn.

Math: Make a bar graph illustrating each child's favorite color of the rainbow. The children can use Unifix or wooden cubes to duplicate the graph.

Related books

Harold and the Purple Crayon by Crockett Johnson
Mary Wore Her Red Dress, and Henry Wore His Green Sneakers by Merle Peek
Planting a Rainbow by Lois Ehlert
Who Said Red? by Mary Serfozo

Ann M. Ferruggia, Voorhees, NJ

Secondary Color Wheel

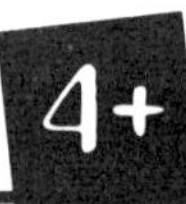

Science skills
Children observe how new colors appear.

Materials

Large circle cut from poster board, divided into 6 wedges
3 glass jars (baby food jars work well)
Red, yellow and blue acrylic paint
Small circles cut from manila paper, divided into 6 wedges, one per child
Crayons or markers

What to do

1. Tack the large color wheel to the bulletin board.
2. The teacher, using primary colors, paints three of the segments red, blue and yellow.
3. Using the glass jars, the teacher demonstrates mixing the primary colors to create three new colors: green, orange and purple.
4. After a class discussion, the "new" colors may be added to the appropriate places on the color wheel.
5. Give the children small color wheels which they may try coloring with crayons or markers to match those on the large color wheel.

Elaine Commins, Atlanta, GA

The Amazing Color-Blending Bottles

Science skills
Children observe the mixing of secondary colors.

Materials

3 clear glass one-gallon (1 L) apple juice bottles
Red, yellow and blue food coloring in droppers or squeeze bottles
Water
Long, slender stir stick

What to do

1. Before class, soak the labels off and thoroughly wash the glass bottles. Fill each almost to the top with water.
2. Discuss with the children the blending and mixing of primary colors to create secondary colors. Then ask all the children to gather around the bottles of water.
3. Slowly put 6 drops of yellow food color into the water and watch as it streaks. Use the long stick to swirl it a bit and see how the color becomes unified. Wait for the water to become still.
4. Slowly add 3 drops of red food coloring and watch as streaks of orange appear. Eventually, swirl the water again to see the unified orange color appear.
5. Continue this method with the other two bottles to make green and purple. For the second bottle, use 6 drops of yellow with 2 or 3 drops of blue to make green. For the third bottle, use 3 or 4 drops of red and 2 or 3 of blue to make purple.

More to do

More science: Ask for suggestions of other colors to add after the secondary colors are made (brown and black are easy to achieve). ▪ For a learning center, have available baby food jars; pitchers of water; a bucket for dumping used water; bottles of red, yellow, blue and white liquid tempera paint; and small stir sticks. Children experiment with mixing colors in jars half filled with water to create secondary colors as well as shades of colors using the white. ▪ Shine a flashlight through the bottles during the different steps of the process.
Music: Play soft, relaxing music in the background. Children may lie on the floor in a semicircle facing the bottles. Ask the children what they observe about quiet time with the addition of a color to focus on.

Related books and recording

Color by Ruth Heller
Do You Know Colors? by Katherine Howard
"Colors" by Hap Palmer

Linda J. Becker, Rochester, MN

Tissue Color Mix

5+

Science skills
Children observe changes in mixed colors and use fine motor skills to create a picture.

Materials
Colored art tissue paper
Liquid starch
White paper
Scissors
Paintbrush
Water for rinsing

What to do

1. Cut art tissue into a variety of shapes.
2. Dip a paintbrush into liquid starch and use it like glue to paint and stick tissue shapes to white paper.
3. Overlap shapes to create new colors. Rinse the brush in clear water between painting over the tissue paper colors. This will keep the colors bright.

More to do
Art: Use starch to brush tissue pieces onto clear plastic wrap. Then dry and tape the picture to a sunny window. ▪ Use liquid starch to glue tissue pieces to wax paper. ▪ To color Easter eggs, brush over the tissue shapes on the eggs with liquid starch. Allow to dry; remove the tissue paper and see the colored egg!
More science: Layer the following colored tissues to make new colors: magenta over yellow to create red; bright blue over yellow to create green; magenta over bright blue to create purple; combinations of all three to create black.

Nancy Gardner, Weymouth, MA

Vegetable Dyes

Science skills
Children observe absorption using colored liquids.

Materials
1 carrot
1 red cabbage
3 sandwich-size resealable plastic bags
Strips of various fabrics: cotton, wool felt, synthetics
1 beet
Grater
3 clear cups
Warm water

What to do

1. Grate about ⅛ cup each of the carrot, beet and cabbage. Keep them separate.
2. Put each into a resealable plastic bag and add ¼ cup (40 ml) of warm water.
3. Press and squish for 2 to 3 minutes, until the water is colored.
4. Empty each colored liquid into separate clear cups.
5. Use cotton strips, wool felt strips and synthetic strips of material. Dip each type of cloth into all 3 dyes. Measure which type of cloth absorbed the most and the least.

More to do

Art: You can use these vegetable liquids as watercolor paints and discuss with the children which vegetable made dark colored paint, light colored paint, etc.

Snack: The children can also use the liquid to color hardboiled eggs by adding ¼ cup (60 ml) vinegar to each colored liquid. Enjoy the colored eggs for snack.

Laura Claire-Gremett, San Jose, CA

Shaker Pudding

3+

Science skills

In this fun and delicious project, children practice observation and small and large motor skills.

Materials

Baby food jars, one for each child
Milk
Pudding mix
Spoons, popsicle sticks or tongue depressors

What to do

1. Each child needs a small, screw-top jar.
2. Put about 3 tablespoons (45 ml) of dry pudding in each jar and add the same amount of milk.
3. Screw on the lid to the jar.
4. Let the children shake, shake, shake! Play your favorite dancing music. This can be a great movement activity for a rainy day! Play Greg and Steve's song, "Popcorn," substituting pudding for the title, and shake it up!
5. Take off the lid and—ta dah! Pudding! Depending on the size of the mouth of the jar, a popsicle stick or a tongue depressor may be a good alternative to a spoon.

More to do

More cooking: Use vanilla pudding and a few drops of food color to tie this activity in to a color or holiday theme. Put the pudding in a paper cup, add a popsicle stick and put it in the freezer, and you have a frozen treat.

Tracie O'Hara, Charlotte, NC

Let's Make Bread!

3+

Science skills

In this very tactile project, children use all their senses to make observations, and they use fine motor skills.

Materials

Large clean plastic bucket
3 packets yeast
Measuring cups and spoons
5 lbs. (2.5 kg) whole wheat flour
Warm water
1 cup (250 ml) honey
Salt
Large mixing spoons

Marker
Newsprint paper (not newspaper!)
Butter at room temperature
Oven
Metal coffee tins: three 3-lb. (1½ kg) tins, four 2-lb. tins (1 kg) and six 1½-lb. tins (750 gm), or a mixture
2-3 cups (500-750 ml) of wheat germ, sunflower seeds or nuts
Recipe written on large paper with pictures so the children can "read" it as they make the bread (also called a rebus)

What to do

1. Ask the children to measure into a large plastic bucket: 2 quarts (2 L) warm water, 3 packets yeast, 1 cup honey, then mix. Explain that this is the "magical mixture" that will make their bread grow. Let them smell the mixture.
2. Measure and mix in 3 tablespoons (45 ml) of salt and the sunflower seeds, nuts, wheat germ or whatever you decide to add to your bread.
3. Add enough whole wheat flour to make this a stiff dough. The children will be able to do all but the mixing at the end when the dough becomes too stiff. Mark the level of the dough on the outside of the bucket with a marker, cover it with a lid or some newsprint and put the bucket in a sink of hot water. The dough will rise in 30 minutes to one hour.
4. Check to see how the magic yeast has made the dough grow.
5. Ask the children to wash, then flour, their hands. Put the dough out on floured newsprint in handfuls for the children to knead. Keep their hands floured and demonstrate for them how to knead.
6. Butter the coffee tins and divide the dough among them.
7. Cover the tins and put them in hot water in the sink for 15 to 20 minutes. The dough should rise to the top but not over the edges.
8. Bake at 375°F (190°C) for about one hour.
9. Enjoy the warm bread for an afternoon snack.

More to do

More cooking: If available, arrange some dried wheat stalks from a field in a decorative container in the classroom. ▪ Get grains of wheat from a health food store and grind some in a blender to show where the flour comes from.

Original song

Sing this song to the tune of "This Is the Way We Wash Our Clothes."

This is the way we mix our bread, mix our bread, mix our bread (stir with spoon). This is the way we mix our bread so early (Monday) morning.
This is the way our bread rises up (squat down and grow the way the bread does)...
This is the way we knead our bread (make exaggerated kneading motions)...
This is the way our bread rises up...
Our bread goes in the oven to bake.
This is the way we eat our bread....

Shirley Story, Lenoir, NC

Cooking Yummy Chocolate Tofu Pudding

3+

Science skills

Cooking and tasting are fun ways to learn about a new food.

Materials

Dry soybeans
½ cup (125 ml) honey
4 tablespoons (60 ml) unsweetened cocoa powder
One 19-ounce (580 ml) package of firm silken tofu, chilled and cubed
Blender
1 teaspoon (5 ml) vanilla extract
Cups

What to do

1. Bring dry soybeans to show children. Save them to use for a craft project.
2. Show the children the tofu and explain that it is made from soybeans.
3. Chop the tofu and add to the blender.
4. Add remaining ingredients and blend.
5. Perhaps you could also mix up a batch of regular instant pudding, using milk, for taste comparisons. Explain to the children that some people do not eat any meat or animal products and that soybeans are an extremely healthful alternative source of protein.
6. Fill the cups with the tasty treat and chill, or eat right away.

 *Linda Atamian, Charlestown, RI*

Individual Egg Salads

Science skills

Children have fun using fine motor skills and observing as they make their own egg salad.

Materials

1 hardboiled egg per child
Mustard, mayonnaise, salt and pepper
Napkins
1 resealable plastic bag per child
Scissors
Crackers or bread

What to do

1. Give each child a hard-boiled egg and demonstrate how to peel it.
2. After the children have peeled their eggs, check for shells and give each child a plastic bag to put the egg into.

3. Let children hold the bag open as you put in a little mustard, mayonnaise, salt and pepper or other ingredients of your choice.
4. Zip the bags up and check for too much air or for leakage.
5. Encourage the children to squish the bag with their hands until it becomes egg salad.
6. Push everything down to one corner, cut the corner with scissors and squeeze the salad onto bread or crackers.

More to do

Language: Read and discuss *Chickens Aren't the Only Ones* by Ruth Heller.
Math: You and the children could discuss one-to-one correspondence as you hand out one egg per person and one plastic bag per person, etc.
More science: This activity may follow a discussion about animals that lay eggs and others that are born alive. It may also be used with a unit on farms and farm animals.

 *Leslie B. Brunner, Hot Springs, VA*

3+

Pizza Dough Play

Science skills
Children use all their senses to make observations and have an opportunity to practice fine motor skills as well as creativity.

Materials

Flour
Large bowls
Smooth, clean surface or mess trays
Plastic pizza cutters, cookie cutters, small rolling pins
½ cup (125 ml) measure
Water
Pizza pan
Colored playdough

What to do

1. Let each child measure ½ cup of flour and place it in a bowl.
2. Add enough water to make a dough with a consistency that is thick enough to be handled.
3. After washing their hands the children put flour on their hands and knead the dough on a surface or in a mess tray.
4. Discuss the textures of the dough as it is mixed. Remind children that this is a playdough pizza you are making; it is not to be eaten.
5. After it has been thoroughly combined, transfer the dough to the pizza pan, adding flour to the surface if the dough is too sticky.
6. Allow the children to manipulate the dough with their hands, rolling pins, pizza cutters, etc.
7. Re-apply flour to hands if dough continues to stick to hands; add flour to utensils if necessary.
8. Add colored playdough to dough to simulate pizza toppings. Discard all dough after play has ended.
9. On another day, make real pizzas for lunch by using a pizza crust mix purchased in many retail grocery stores. Just add desired toppings.

Cooking

More to do

Dramatic play: Turn that area into a pizza parlor with pizzeria props, pretend food, pizza pans, empty parmesan and grated pepper containers, etc. Make half of your pizzeria into a restaurant complete with a salad bar. Pre-paint shredded paper green to create lettuce. Add to a large bowl or water table and add pre-cut peppers, etc., for salad toppings. Add tongs for each salad item.

Field trip: Schedule a tour of a local pizzeria and talk to a pizza parlor or pizza delivery person. Ask for pizza props such as boxes, hats, sacks, insulated carriers, coupons, flyers, plates aprons, etc., to add to the dramatic play area.

Food: Order pizza for lunch. Choose the size and type and allow the children to collect the pizzas upon delivery.

Manipulatives: Make a pizza puzzle. Using a round piece of cardboard the size of a pizza pan, decorate the cardboard to look like a pizza. Cut it into slices. Allow the children to fit the pizza into the pizza pan to complete the puzzle. This can be done on a flannel board also.

Original song

On Top of a Pizza (sing to the tune of "On top of Old Smokey")

On top of a pizza,
All covered with cheese, (rub tummy)
I lost my pepperoni, (pretend to cry)
When somebody sneezed. (Achoo!)

It rolled off the table,
And onto the floor (point to the floor)
And then my pepperoni,
Rolled straight out the door! (Slam!)

Tina R. Woehler, Flower Mound, TX

Pizza Topping Taste Test

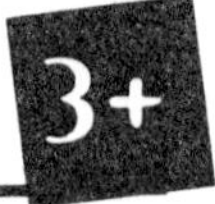

Science skills

In this taste test, children make observations and predictions and have an opportunity for language and vocabulary development.

Materials

Pepperoni slices
Cooked ground beef
Ham slices
Pineapple
Olives
Paper plates
Poster board
Grated pizza cheeses (cheddar, parmesan, provolone, mozzarella)
Canned mushrooms, drained
Green peppers, chopped
Anchovies
Napkins
Marker

What to do

1. Prepare pizza toppings beforehand or with the children.
2. Make a chart on poster board with every child's name on the left side. Make a space along the top of the poster board for each topping. Use a happy face for *liked* and a frown for *disliked* for each topping the children taste.
3. Distribute some of each of the toppings to each child.
4. Talk about the appearance, taste, smell and textures of the toppings as tasting occurs.
5. Record the responses on the poster board for each child and each topping. Which toppings were most popular? Least popular?

More to do

Snack: Prepare mini-pizzas for snack using ½ of an English muffin, pizza sauce, desired toppings and cheeses and bake in oven at 325°F (160°C) until cheese melts. ▪ Prepare fruit pizzas. Spread cookie dough from a tube onto an ungreased pizza pan, cook according to directions, then cool 15 minutes. Put whipped topping on the cookie on the pizza pan. Then add desired canned, chopped or freshly sliced fruits and slice. One roll of cookie dough is enough for 16 children.

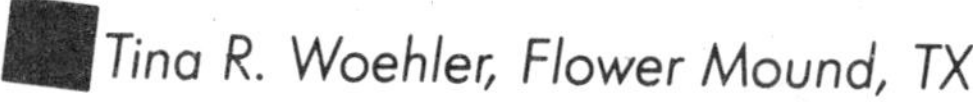

Tina R. Woehler, Flower Mound, TX

3+

Flavored Shaved Ice

Science skills

Another delicious experiment allows children to practice observation.

Materials

Ice shaver machine and accessories
Powdered drink mix, unprepared, presweetened
Cups
Water
Bowls
Spoons, one per child

What to do

1. Freeze the water in ice shaver containers according to the instructions on the box.
2. Turn the container upside down onto the palm of your hand and pour warm water over the container to loosen the ice from the container.
3. Place ice in the ice shaver machine.
4. Shave the ice into an empty container until there is enough ice for each child to have about ½ cup (125 ml).
5. Add a spoonful of drink mix to the shaved ice and mix.
6. Eat it up!

More to do

Sand and water table: Put shaved ice in trays or water table using scoops, spoons, shovel, trucks, etc.

Related book
The Ice Cream Store by Dennis Lee

Tina R. Woehler, Flower Mound, TX

What Can We Do With Playdough?

Science skills
Children make their own playdough, then embark on a variety of scientific experiences using observation, measuring and fine motor skills.

Materials
Playdough Recipe
½ cup (125 ml) salt
1 cup (250 ml) water
Food coloring
⅓ teaspoon (1-2 ml) flavoring: mint for green color, orange for orange color, almond for yellow color, cinnamon oil for red color, vanilla for no color at all, optional
1 cup (250 ml) flour
2 teaspoons (10 ml) cream of tartar
1 tablespoon (15 ml) oil
Double boiler pan
Wooden spoon
Butter knife
Wax paper
Closed plastic container with lid

What to do
This recipe is always soft and pliable. It makes a small amount of playdough for home use or triple the recipe for the classroom (that makes a 5″ or 12.5 cm ball). If you make this recipe with the children, take proper precautions when you cook the dough. If a child tastes the play-dough, it will taste salty but it will not harm him.

1. Let the children put the ingredients in the pan. For example, divide the 3 cups of flour for a triple recipe into ¼ cup (60 ml) amounts so each child can add one ingredient.
2. Mix the dry ingredients. Add oil, water and food coloring.
3. Put this mixture in the double boiler pan over hot water.
4. Cook and stir constantly for 3 minutes, until the mixture comes away from the sides of the pan.
5. Scrape the dough out of the pan with the butter knife.
6. After the playdough is cooked and partially cooled, let each child have a turn kneading it.
7. Put the ball of playdough on wax paper. Knead while warm, and then store it in an airtight container.

More to do
Art: Use playdough in craft projects to create a base to hold pipe cleaner flower stems. ▪ Make copies of the playdough recipe to send home and let each child take a small ball of playdough home as a gift. ▪ You can combine this recipe with other favorite classroom recipes as a gift for Mom and Dad. Each child can design her own recipe book cover.
Dramatic Play: Put playdough in the kitchen area to be used by four to six children during free play.

Fine motor: Give each child in the group a small amount of playdough and show them how to roll it into a long snake shape. Encourage children to make the shape of letters or numbers. ▪ Encourage the children to make three-dimensional fruit and vegetable shapes, such as a banana, apple, bunch of grapes, watermelon slice, carrots, potato, peas, string beans or an onion. Use the pretend food in the dramatic play center.
Math: Teach liquid measurement and dry measurement of ingredients. How many ¼ cups equals 1 cup? How many ⅓ cups equal 1 cup. ▪ Ask the children to make playdough balls of various sizes, then sort in them a row showing the gradual gradation of size, largest to smallest. Mix them up, then try doing smallest to largest. ▪ Put different size playdough balls on a balance scale. When does the scale balance? When does it tip to one side? Why? ▪ Take a walk and pick up leaves of various sizes and shapes. Back in the classroom, trace around the leaf and cut out a playdough cookie leaf.
More science: Give the children a box containing a comb, a screw, a large washer, a carved wooden or plastic building block, a large paper clip, puzzle piece, a piece each of plastic and canvas, a potato scrubber and any other safe object that has texture. You can also add several dull, sturdy plastic dinner knives for cutting the playdough and several plastic trays. Let the children experiment with the objects, using them to make shapes in the soft playdough. You can also add small wooden rolling pins and a spatula. ▪ Leave a small amount of playdough out for a day. What causes the crust to form? Leave it out for a week and discuss how it feels now. Could it be made into a new shape now? ▪ Compare the playdough recipe with another similar recipe such as cookie dough, bread dough or Christmas ornament dough. Which ingredients are the same and which are different?

Original poem

I Like to Play With Playdough

I like to play with playdough
And roll it in a ball.
Then poke it, push it, and pat it
And make anything at all.

Sometimes I make some cookies
And put them on a tray.
Other times I design a snowman
That does not melt away.

Now I'll make some numbers,
My favorite one is three.
Please come to the table
And make something with me.

Related book

From Kids With Love by Janis Hill and Laurie Patrick

Mary Brehm, Aurora, OH

A Baker's Balloon

3+

Science skills
Children are encouraged to make observations and use visual and fine motor skills.

Materials

Yeast
Sugar
Tall narrow bottle
Any other ingredients for a yeast bread or roll recipe
Magnifying glass
Warm water
Balloon
The Little Red Hen, any version

What to do

1. Read *The Little Red Hen.*
2. Tell the children that you are going to examine and experiment with the yeast a little bit before you bake. Look at the yeast under a magnifying glass. Smell and touch it.
3. Mix some yeast with sugar and warm water in the bottom of the bottle.
4. Secure the neck of the balloon over the bottleneck. Leave in a warm place.
5. Observe the bubbles in the bottle and watch the balloon begin to inflate.
6. Continue with your yeast bread-baking activity.

More to do

Art: Make masks of the characters from *The Little Red Hen*.
Storytelling: Act out the story. ▪ Invent a new story about what will happen the next time hen asks for help.

Original song

Sing and act out this song to the tune of "Here We Go Round the Mulberry Bush."

This is the way she plants the wheat, plants the wheat, plants the wheat.
This is the way she plants the wheat, the busy little red hen.

Add other verses, following the story line: cut the wheat, grind the wheat, carry the flour, mix the dough, knead the dough, bake the bread, eat the bread.

Related books

Bread, Bread, Bread by Ann Morris
Tony's Bread by Tomie DePaola

Sandra Gratias, Perkasie, PA

Pumpkin Bread

Science skills

Children use observation, measuring, communication and fine motor skills.

Materials

5 cups (1¼ kg) of sugar
1 cup (250 ml) applesauce
8 eggs
4 teaspoons (20 ml) baking soda
2 teaspoons (10 ml) cinnamon
½ teaspoon (2.5 ml) cloves
2 large bowls
Measuring cups and spoons
Wooden toothpick for testing doneness
1 cup (250 ml) margarine or butter, softened
1 cup (250 ml) vegetable oil
32 ounce can of pumpkin
2 teaspoons (10 ml) salt
1 teaspoon (5 ml) baking powder
7 cups (1¾ kg) of flour
Empty soup cans or small aluminum loaf pans
Large spoon
Oven

What to do

This recipe makes a loaf for each child to take home for Thanksgiving dinner.

1. With the children helping and taking turns, combine the sugar, softened margarine or butter, applesauce and oil. Mix until smooth.
2. Add the eggs one at a time, mixing well after each egg.
3. Blend in the pumpkin.
4. Combine all dry ingredients in a separate bowl, mix well and add the wet ingredients to the dry ingredients.
5. Pour the batter into greased soup cans or loaf pans.
6. Bake at 350°F (180°C) for about 1 hour and 10 minutes or until a wooden toothpick comes out clean.

More to do

Field trip: Go on a field trip to a pumpkin patch to pick your own pumpkins.

 *Lisa Shattuck, Johnson City, NY*

3+

Veggie Art

Science skills

As they create a delicious treat, children practice observation and classification skills.

Materials

One package of cream cheese at room temperature, or peanut butter

Paper saucers

Plastic knives, forks and spoons

Assortment of washed fresh vegetables that are colorful and interesting, for example, radishes, celery and carrot sticks, parsley, green beans, eggplant slices, sliced turnip, broccoli, spinach, cauliflower

What to do

1. Ask the children to spread the cream cheese or peanut butter generously over the saucer.
2. Arrange vegetables in interesting designs on the saucers.
3. Encourage the children to describe their designs with the class, naming vegetable colors, shapes, etc.
4. Eat the design for snack!

   Variation: Use fresh fruit rather than veggies, for example, cherries, grapes, pear halves, peach halves, orange rind rings, orange wedges, kiwi, etc.

More to do

More science: Use the veggie designs to begin a discussion on plants, or on our sense of taste, or on nutrition.

Easy Old-Fashioned Ice Cream

Science skills

During this delicious experiment, children observe, measure and practice sequencing and fine motor skills.

Materials

2½ cups (625 ml) brown sugar

3 bananas, mashed, optional

1 pint (500 ml) whipping cream

2 teaspoons (10 ml) vanilla

Ice cream maker (4 quart or 4 L size for this recipe), electric or hand crank (recommend hand crank for older children)

Crushed ice (available from fast food outlet or meat packing plant usually at no charge)

3 eggs

1 teaspoon (5 ml) salt

1 quart (1 L) milk

1 teaspoon (5 ml) almond flavoring

Pickling salt

Blender or hand beaters

Bowls, spatula, potato masher, measuring cups and spoons

What to do

1. As an introduction to this activity, you may wish to visit a dairy farm or plan a special trip to the grocery store. Or you could ask each child bring in an ingredient from home.
2. Mix the eggs and sugar. Involve the children in the measuring, stirring and cranking.

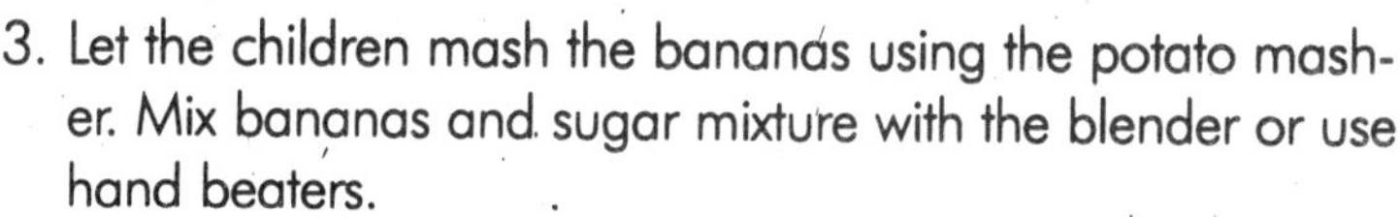

3. Let the children mash the bananas using the potato masher. Mix bananas and sugar mixture with the blender or use hand beaters.
4. Add cream, vanilla, salt and almond flavoring. Mix well.
5. Place the mixture in the ice cream canister and add enough milk to bring the liquid up to the fill line. Be careful not to fill above fill line.
6. Turn the dasher to make sure the mixture is well mixed. Note the consistency with the children. What does it look like?
7. Place the ice cream canister in the ice cream freezer. Add ice and salt, following the directions for your machine.
8. This ice cream takes about 45 minutes. Let your ice cream ripen in the ice cream freezer or in the deep freeze.
9. Serve ice cream at lunch time or as a snack. Discuss the changes that have happened with the children. Note that the ingredients have changed from liquid to solid, cool to cold, etc. Note: You can make strawberry ice cream by omitting bananas and adding 1 cup (250 ml) strawberry jam. Reduce sugar to 2 cups (500 ml). This ice cream is softer and creamier than store-bought ice cream.

More to do

Dramatic play: Set up an ice cream store and list everyone's favorite ice cream flavors on a big poster. Use paper cones and let children wear aprons. Make up a menu and ask the children how much things cost. Using play money enhances this activity.

Language: Make a list of all the interesting words to describe ice cream. You'll be surprised at what the children come up with.

Math: Graph everyone's favorite ice cream flavor on paper or on a chalkboard.

Sand and water table: Add any remaining ice to the water table. Do not use the ice to which salt has been added.

Related books

Two Cool Cows by Toby Speed
The Very Hungry Caterpillar by Eric Carle
When Winter Comes by Robert Maass

 *Mark Crouse, Port Williams, Nova Scotia, Canada*

Fun With Pudding

Science skills
Children measure and use fine motor skills.

Materials

Instant pudding mix, vanilla and chocolate
Cups
Napkins
Milk
Spoons
Wooden spoon

Electric mixer
Measuring cups
Bowls
Aprons

What to do

1. Gather all materials and set them up on a table. Review cooking rules, such as clean hands, aprons, taking turns, etc.
2. Discuss the steps in making pudding. To which food group does it belong?
3. Divide the class into groups and give each child a job. For example, two groups may prefer vanilla and two groups may want chocolate. Each child can have a job, such as pouring milk, measuring milk, opening the mix or placing ingredients in the bowl, and each child may use the electric mixer (supervised by the teacher). All of these activities should be guided by the teacher for best results.
5. Spoon the pudding into cups and serve with spoons and napkins.
6. Discuss what happened to the mix and the milk.

More to do

Language: Together make up a class story or poem about pudding, or about your pudding-making experiment.

Sand and water table: Using the measuring cup, practice measuring and pouring water or sand.

Related books

Pancakes for Breakfast by Tomie De Paola
Popcorn Book by Tomie De Paola

 *Karen Megay-Nespoli, Massapequa Park, NY*

Green Eggs?

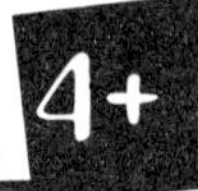

Science skills

Children observe, make predictions about changes and are encouraged to appreciate differences.

Materials

Green Eggs and Ham by Dr. Seuss
Butter
Green food coloring
Large clear glass bowl
Spatula or wooden spoon
Small paper plates or napkins and spoons or forks for each child
Chart tablet and marker
6 eggs
Electric frying pan
Fork or wire whisk
Paper towels
Platter

What to do

1. Read *Green Eggs and Ham.*

2. Ask the children to predict whether green eggs will taste any different from plain scrambled eggs. Write their predictions on chart paper.
3. Preheat the frying pan as you prepare the eggs for scrambling. Crack three of the eggs into the clear glass bowl and beat the eggs. Pour these eggs into the frying pan. Allow the children to watch the changes taking place as the eggs cook. When the eggs are done, place them on one side of the platter to cool.
4. Crack the remaining three eggs into the clear glass bowl. Add green food coloring and mix. Point out the changes in the eggs and the causes for these changes. Scramble the green eggs.
5. When you have cooked both the green and yellow eggs, allow the children to predict again whether or not there will be a difference in taste.
6. Give each child a small portion of each color egg and ask them to taste the eggs one at a time to determine if there is a difference in taste.
7. Check the class predictions.
8. Enjoy the rest of the eggs!

More to do

More science: Try other colors in scrambled eggs. ▪ Try coloring other foods, such as rice or mashed potatoes.

 *Lyndall Warren, Milledgeville, GA*

5+

The Way the Cookie Crumbles

Science skills
Children practice observation, measuring, predicting and fine motor skills.

Materials

Simple recipe for basic sugar cookies
Ingredients, enough for six bite-size cookies per child, and materials as outlined in the recipe
Aprons (optional)
Cookie cutters, one shape only
Three index cards, labeled, respectively, Sugar Cookies, No Sugar, No Leavening
Three plates
Large graph or chart paper with marker, set up to record information comparing the taste, color and smell of the cookies

What to do

1. In preparation for this baking experiment, ask the children to put on their aprons and carefully wash their hands.
2. Assist the children as they follow the recipe, baking three batches of cookies: one regular (control) batch, one batch that is identical to the first except that the sugar is omitted and one batch that is identical to the first except that the leavening (baking powder and/or soda)

is omitted. Keep the batches separated (by time or location) in the oven and on their cooling racks before moving them to the plates labeled with the index cards.

3. Give each child a "control" sugar cookie and ask the class to describe its taste, color, texture and smell. Record the responses in the appropriate areas of the chart. Repeat this step using the "no sugar" and "no leavening" cookies.
4. Ask the children to guess which of the three cookies would be the most popular with other children and to explain why.
5. Conduct a blind taste test, using volunteers from another class. Graph the results to determine whether your class's guess was correct. Discuss the outcome. Remember to point out that recipes are generally the result of experimentation!

More to do

Language: Encourage the children to brainstorm words to describe the taste, texture and smell of the cookies.

Related book

The Doorbell Rang by Pat Hutchins

Marji E. Gold-Vukson, West Lafayette, IN

Cooking Up Science in the Kitchen

5+

Science skills

In a delicious experiment, the children observe, discuss and use fine motor skills.

Materials

Instant pudding mix
Mixing bowl
Hand eggbeater
Milk
Measuring cup

What to do

1. Explain to your class how heat, cold and friction change the way food looks, tastes and feels. Ask the children to think of examples.
2. In two or more groups, the children stand around the table(s). Explain that they are going to help make pudding and that they will be observing many changes. Let them tell you what they do see before you get started (powdered mix, liquid milk).
3. Have the children guess what will happen when the two ingredients are mixed together, when the two ingredients are beaten together and when the finished mixture is chilled.
4. Follow the package directions on the pudding mix. Encourage the children to take turns mixing the pudding with the hand eggbeater.
5. Explain that the movement of the beater blades is causing the two ingredients to blend together, an example of friction.

6. Discuss the changes in the mixture and then chill the mixture. Observe, describe, eat and enjoy!

More to do

More science: Apples, pineapples and pears are easy to dry. Show your class prunes/plums, raisins/grapes, dried apricots and fresh ones. Discuss what has taken place with the dried fruit. Place the dry fruit in water over night. Observe and discuss what has taken place. ▪ Use heavy cream to make butter. Put the cream into clear plastic or glass containers with secure lids and ask the children to shake vigorously. Remove the lid to observe the various stages as the cream turns into butter.

 *Lois McEwan, Levittown, NY*

Cooking Up More Science in the Kitchen

Science skills

Children use all their senses to observe, and they make predictions and inferences.

Materials

One dozen eggs, or enough to feed your class
Whisk
Electric frying pan
Bowl
Butter
Chart paper and marker

What to do

1. Set up an electric frying pan in a safe area out of the children's reach but where they can observe. Supervise closely.
2. Ask the children to take turns cracking open the eggs and whisking them into the bowl. Observe and discuss appearance.
3. Coat the pan lightly with butter. Explain how the heat has turned the solid fat into a liquid.
4. Encourage the children to hypothesize what will happen to the eggs when they hit the hot pan. Write down their theories.
5. Cook the eggs. Observe the changes taking place. Compare the actual results with the children's hypotheses.

More to do

More science: Using extreme caution and supervising the activity closely, heat plain water in the electric frying pan. Place a thermometer in the water. At what temperature will it boil? What happens to the water if you let it boil for a long time? Discuss steam and evaporation. ▪ Use the boiling water to make instant gelatin, such as Jell-O. Let the children observe how the hot water dissolves the Jell-O. Chill the mixture overnight. Observe and discuss the changes that have taken place. ▪ Make ice cubes.

 *Lois McEwan, Levittown, NY*

Make a Recipe

5+

Science skills

Children learn about observation, prediction and cause and effect. They also develop fine motor skills.

Materials

Large mixing bowl
Paper
Readily available regular baking ingredients
Pens
Precut paper shapes of measuring cups and spoons, for the younger children

What to do

The idea here is first to have the children "create" recipes and then to make a "real" recipe. This will show the children how important precision and proportion of ingredients is in cooking, as well as the different effects of ingredients

1. At circle time, talk about recipes, ingredients and baking. Ask the children to think about something they would like to cook and about what types of ingredients the recipe requires.
2. Let them write or dictate their recipes on paper using words and pictures, such as ingredients, measuring cups and teaspoons. For young children, you can cut out magazine pictures of ingredients for them to choose from and paste on their paper.
3. With the children, pick one of the recipes to make together as a group.
4. Follow the steps the children have put in the recipe. Help them read the ingredients and directions and mix the ingredients in a bowl.
5. During the whole process, talk about the function of each ingredient, how it changes the mixture, what would happen if you added more or less flour, etc.
6. One part the children might find difficult is predicting the baking time. You could help them by setting a timer to their predicted time, pulling out the baked item and asking them if it seems done or what they think should be done next.
7. Another day, pick a recipe from a cookbook, read it with the children and follow the steps to bake the product.

More to do

Dramatic play: Provide play utensils for cooking and baking in this center.
Language: During circle time or other quiet indoor play time, work on a book of recipes for your school and place it in the book room.
Sand and water table: Water-table play can be used to experience and experiment with measuring cups and amounts (use words such as more, less, ingredient, liquid, solid, etc.) On a warm day, do this in a sandbox.

Billie Miteva, Pomona, NJ

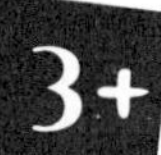

Day and Night Skies

Science skills
Here, children observe and use inference and fine motor skills.

Materials
Black paper, one piece for each child
Moon shapes
Cloud shapes
Glue
Sky-blue paper, one piece for each child
Sun shapes
Shiny star stickers

What to do

1. After discussing things the children can see when they look up in the sky during the day and night, give them each some pre-cut shapes and sky-blue paper.
2. Ask them to choose the shapes they see in the sky during the day and glue them on the blue paper.
3. Give the children the black paper and ask them to glue the moon shape and the star stickers all over.
4. After both papers dry, glue them back to back and hang them from the ceiling. The air will cause the papers to rotate from day to night. The nighttime stars will glitter and shine in the light.
5. As an alternative, provide the children with light-colored construction paper and encourage them to cut or tear out their own shapes for the day and nighttime sky pictures.

More to do
Art: Make a sky collage.
Math: The children can sort the shapes into categories relating to day and night.

 *Donna Austin, Lehighton, PA*

Fun With Flashlights

Science skills
Children experience cause and effect and practice observation, drawing conclusions and fine motor skills.

Materials
Blankets
Table
Flashlights of various kinds

Day & Night

What to do

1. Cover the table with blankets so they hang to the floor all around.
2. Place flashlights near the covered table and encourage the children to experiment with using the flashlights under the table.

More to do

Art: Make day and night pictures with chalk and black paper. Cut stars from aluminum foil or light colored paper to glue onto the night picture.
Cooking: Make pancakes for "breakfast."

Related book

Pancakes for Breakfast by Tomie dePaola

Marilyn Ewing, Richmond, TX

Twinkle, Twinkle, Little Star

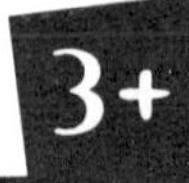

Science skills

This activity encourages children to talk about nature and their environment, and to use observation skills.

Materials

Styrofoam cup
Pin
Flashlight

What to do

1. Using a pin, poke holes in the bottom of a Styrofoam cup. If the children do this step, supervise closely.
2. Darken the classroom and shine the flashlight through the cup, creating a starry night on the ceiling.
3. Sing "Twinkle, Twinkle, Little Star."
4. Talk to the children about the night sky. Explain to them what stars really are, describe some of the constellations and talk about how long ago people used the stars to navigate on the seas.

More to do

More science: Help the children make their own planetariums with Styrofoam cups. Shine them on the ceiling and discuss the different designs.

Dotti Enderle, Houston TX

Day & Night

3+ Are You Sleeping?

Science skills

Children make a smooth transition to nap time by practicing auditory skills.

Materials

Small pillows
Blankets

What to do

1. Gather the children into a group.
2. Be sure each child has her small pillow and blanket.
3. The group sings the following song to the tune of "Frère Jacques":

   Are you sleeping, are you sleeping
   Little ______, Little ________,
   Morning bells are ringing, morning bells are ringing,
   Little ______, Little _______.

4. Fill in a child's name each time you sing the song. As each child hears her name, she lies down for nap time.

More to do

Dramatic play: Have a doll "getting ready for bed" activity. Each child takes a doll through her own bedtime routine. Have books available for nighttime stories, and end with a "Bedtime Snack" for the children.

Margaret Howard, McLean, VA

4+ Butterflies in a Net

Science skills

Children observe the earth's movement in this charming activity.

Materials

Butterfly shapes cut from dark paper
Tape
Butterfly net, or stretch a pair of nylons over a bent coat hanger frame and tape the end of the hanger

Day & Night

What to do

1. Tape butterflies in a bright sunny window. The sun should project the shapes on the floor.
2. Have the children "capture" (cover) the shadow butterflies with the net. Leave the net in place on top of the butterflies.
3. Check on the butterflies later. As the sun moves, the children will be amazed to see the butterflies escaping from the net. Ask the children to explain how this happened. Explain how the earth rotates and changes position.

More to do

Art: Trace black paper silhouettes of the children.
Dramatic play: Have a hand shadow or shadow puppet show.
Language: Have the children dictate or write their ideas about where the sun goes at night. Keep a journal.

Melanie Lemen, Clear Spring, MD

Day and Night

4+

Science skills

Children use their creativity and think about the differences between day and night.

Materials

What Makes Day and Night by Franklyn Branley
Paper plates, one whole and one half per child
Colored scraps of paper
Glue
Gold/silver stars, optional
Chart paper
1 gold fastener (brad)
Scissors
Markers

What to do

1. Read *What Makes Day and Night.*
2. Discuss night and day. Make a large chart on which to compare night and day. For example, talk about sights, sounds and jobs people can do in the day or night.
3. Give each child one whole and one half paper plate.
4. Secure the half plate to the whole plate with the brad fastener; the half must be movable.
5. On the bottom of the whole plate, draw day activities with people, sun, grass, etc. On the top draw night activities with the moon, stars. Encourage the children to use their imagination.

More to do

Language: Children fill two large circles (one night and one day) with pictures from magazines and newspapers, then discuss their choices of pictures.
Math: Count sun, moon and stars in books and on posters.

More science: Make a large chart of questions about night and day. Make another chart with the headings, What We Know and What We Would Like to Know.

Related books
The Day the Sun Danced by Edith T. Hurd
Night Becomes Day by Richard McGuire

Doris Jane Smith, Lincolndale, NY

Owling in the Light

Science skills
Children are encouraged to ask questions about nature.

Materials
Children as owls
Dark room
Flashlight
Rainy day

What to do
1. Sit with the children in a quiet, dark room.
2. Take a flashlight and slowly bring out the light of the moon in the middle of the circle on the ceiling.
3. Talk about the moon's light at night and how animals need it. Name some animals that would see the moon at night.

4. Discuss what happens to us if someone shines a flashlight in our eyes. How do we see? How do we feel?
5. Tell children they will be owls coming out at night. They will slowly and quietly fly around the room. Take the flashlight and shine it on an owl.
6. Discuss which light helps animals the most, light from nature or light from people?

More to do

More science: Name other animals the children could be. Then let them act out an animal at night in prey of another animal; freeze both with the light.

Related book

Owl Moon by Jane Yolen

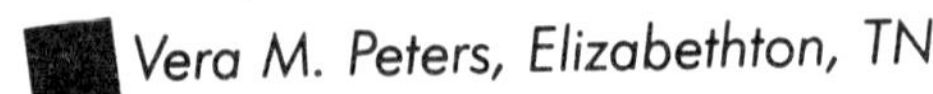

Vera M. Peters, Elizabethton, TN

3+

Chocosaurus

Science skills
Children make observations about dinosaurs as they create a tasty treat

Materials

Dazzle the Dinosaur by Marcus Pfister
Large bowl
Springform round pan
Candy kisses, wrapped
Cardboard or platter 16" x 16" (40 cm x 40 cm)
1 box brownie mix and ingredients
Wooden spoon
Aluminum foil
Buttercream frosting
Knife for cutting and frosting

What to do

1. Read the book *Dazzle the Dinosaur.* Tell the children you are going to make a special dinosaur like Dazzle that they can eat!
2. Pour the brownie mix into a bowl, and as the children pass the bowl and stir, sing to the tune of "Do You Know the Muffin Man":

   Oh do you know the dinosaur, the dinosaur, the dinosaur,
   Oh do you know the dinosaur whose name is Chocosaurus.

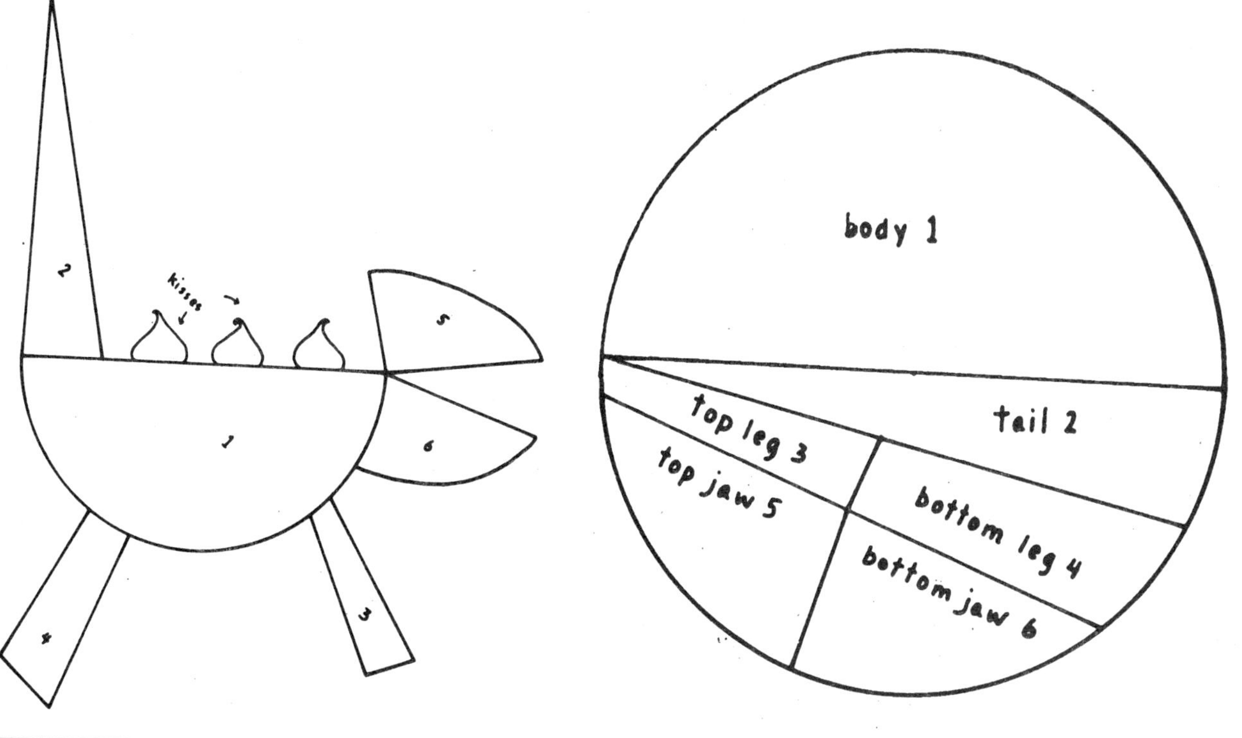

3. Pour brownie mix into a foil-lined springform pan and bake. Let cool. Show the children how you can cut a round cake and rearrange the pieces into a dinosaur.
4. Remove the cake from the pan and place it on the foil-covered cardboard. Let the children connect the cake pieces with frosting, then cover the entire Chocosaurus with the frosting.
5. Let each child come up and add a shiny chocolate kiss to the Chocosaurus' back, like the bony plates of a stegosaurus or Dazzle.
6. Eat and enjoy!

Holly Ciepluch, Whitefish Bay, WI

Tar Pit With Dinosaurs

3+

Science skills

In this fun and gooey project children are encouraged to ask questions about nature and to use fine motor skills.

Materials

Cornstarch, one boxful
Large bucket
Large plastic tray
Water
Black tempera paint
Set of plastic dinosaurs

What to do

1. In the bucket, mix one box of cornstarch with cold water until it is gooey.
2. Add black tempera to the water as you are stirring.
3. Place the "tar" into the large plastic tray.
4. Let the children help mix the "tar" together in the tray.
5. Put the dinosaurs into the "tar" and let the children creatively play with the mixture. You could add rocks, small plastic plants and a bowl for a water area.

Original songs

Pretend to be a dinosaur and sing to the tune of "I'm Being Swallowed by a Boa Constrictor":

I'm being swallowed up in the tar pit
I'm being swallowed up in the tar pit
I'm being swallowed up in the tar pit
And I don't like it very much!

Oh no, it's up to my foot,
Oh no, it's up to my knees, (waist, chest, chin...)
Oh no, it's up to my glob, glob, glob!

Vera M. Peters, Elizabethton, TN

3+

Pteranodon Mobile

Science skills
The children make observations and use fine motor skills.

Materials
Pteranodon pattern
Construction paper
Hole punch
Plastic clothes hangers
Cardboard
Scissors
Yarn

What to do

1. Copy a Pteranodon pattern onto cardboard and cut it out. This will serve as a stencil.
2. Let the children trace the stencil or draw a dinosaur freehand on construction paper. Each child will need three or more dinosaur shapes.
3. The children can watch you cut out the dinosaurs and punch a hole in each. The older children can cut them out themselves.
4. Cut a piece of yarn for each dinosaur, varying the lengths.
5. Show the children how to thread the yarn through the hole, and then you tie a knot in each to hold the yarn in place.
6. Tie the other end of the yarn to the clothes hangers. Hang and wait for a breeze to make the Pteranodons fly!

Related books
If the Dinosaurs Came Back by Bernard Most
Patrick's Dinosaurs by Carol Carrick
Time Train by Paul Fleischman
Time Flies by Eric Rohmann

 *Robin Works Davis, Keller, TX*

Dinosaurs

How Big Were They?

3+

Science skills

Children observe just how big dinosaurs were and practice large motor skills, too.

Materials

How Big Were the Dinosaurs? by Bernard Most
Tape measure, the longer the better
Open space
Sidewalk chalk or paper tape

What to do

1. Read *How Big Were the Dinosaurs?*
2. On the playground, school hallway or sidewalk, measure six foot (2 m) lengths, marking the measurement as you go.
3. Label the measurements in a manner similar to a time line, beginning with familiar objects and gradually getting longer, for example, car, school bus, elephant, whale, etc.
4. End with the measurements of selected dinosaurs.
5. This activity will help children visualize how big dinosaurs were.

More to do

Art: Sponge paint a wall-size dinosaur picture. ▪ Make fossil rocks from plaster of Paris.
Language: Depending on the age and ability of the children, research to find out if there are dinosaurs for each letter of the alphabet. Introduce them to the children.
Math: Create a bulletin board with hidden dinosaurs on it and count the dinosaurs.

Related books

Dinosaur Dance by Joe Noonan
Dinosaurs Came to Town by Dom Mansell

Wanda K. Pelton, Lafayette, IN

Make a Fossil

3+

Science skills

Children use their creativity, practice fine motor skills and are encouraged to ask questions about nature.

Dinosaurs

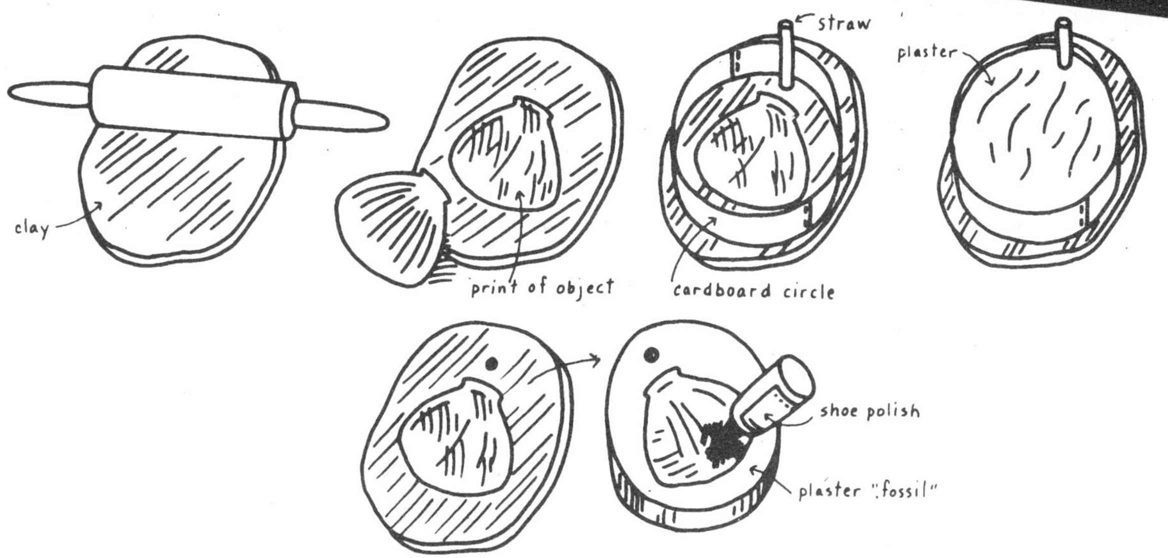

Materials

Modeling clay
Stapler
Plaster of Paris
Brown or black shoe polish
Objects to print, such as ferns, shells, large plastic dinosaurs or animals with clear footprints
Rolling pin
Cardboard strips 1½" (3.75 cm) thick
Pencil, stick or small pieces of plastic straws
Small rags

What to do

1. Roll out modeling clay to make one slab per child.
2. Allow the children to press one selected object into the slab, then remove the object, leaving a print.
3. Staple the cardboard strips together to make rings (like headbands). Place the rings firmly around the print and push them into the clay.
4. Prepare the plaster and pour it into the molds. Make a hanging hole with a pencil or stick before the plaster dries fully. If pieces of straws are available, press them into the modeling clay before you pour the plaster. They may be removed after the plaster dries.
5. After an hour, remove the mold from the clay and the cardboard.
6. Let the children stain their fossils with shoe polish.

Note: You could also use firm mud or firm ceramic clay.

Susan R. Forbes, Holly Hill, FL

Dig Up Dinosaurs

3+

Science skills

Children make observations, ask questions about nature and practice fine motor skills.

Materials

Bones (soup bones, soft poultry bones, large fish bones), bleached and dried
Sifters
Slotted spoons
Glue
Sand shovels
Bucket
Liquid laundry bleach
Sandbox
Cardboard
Paintbrushes
Safari hats, optional

What to do

1. Without the children, prepare the bones by boiling them in water with salt. Clean them and place them in a bucket of bleach for two hours, then remove them and place them in the sun to dry for a couple of days.
2. Bury the bones in the sandbox. Children use shovels, brushes, sifters and spoons to dig up the bones.
3. Each child glues his finds onto cardboard for display.

More to do

Math: Younger children may prefer to dig up small plastic dinosaurs and categorize them by color, size and shape. They may count sets as well. ▪ Extend this activity for older children to include math skills as follows: divide the sandbox into quadrants by attaching string in a criss-cross fashion (using thumb tacks) over the sandbox. Assign numbers to each quadrant. Prepare cardboard by writing the numeral for each square on the back of each piece. Assign one quadrant per child to dig up artifacts. Children may compare types and amounts of bones. They may reassemble the squares in order.

Related book

Giant Dinosaurs by Erna Rowe

Susan R. Forbes, Holly Hill, FL

Dinosaurs

3+

Dinosaur Habitats

Science skills

In the process of creating dinosaur habitats, children are encouraged to ask questions about nature and also to practice fine motor skills.

Materials

Foam meat trays, one for each child
Rocks
Toy dinosaurs
Sand
Plastic plants

What to do

1. Fill the meat trays with a layer of sand.
2. Pass out the materials to each child.
3. Let the children arrange the rocks, plants and dinosaurs to create dinosaur habitats.

Related books

Big Old Bones: A Dinosaur Tale by Carol Carrick
Bones, Bones, Dinosaur Bones by Byron Barton
Digging Up Dinosaurs by Aliki

 *Robin Works Davis, Keller, TX*

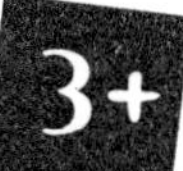

Digging Up Dinosaurs

Science skills

Children practice large motor and counting skills.

Materials

Sandbox with sand
Egg carton
12 small plastic dinosaurs

What to do

1. After talking about dinosaurs, hide twelve plastic dinosaurs in the sand.
2. Talk to the children about how archeologists dig for dinosaur bones.
3. The children take turns finding dinosaurs.
4. When all the dinosaurs have been found, there should be one dinosaur in each egg cup in the egg carton.

Dinosaurs

Related book
Dinosaurs by Claude Delafosse and James Prunier

 *Sandra Hutchins Lucas, Cox's Creek, KY*

Digging for Dinosaurs

3+

Science skills
Children have a chance to practice fine motor skills.

Materials
Plaster of Paris
Water
Cupcake pan lined with paper cups
Sand
Small plastic dinosaurs
Popsicle sticks

What to do

1. At least 24 hours before you plan to do this activity, make one mini dinosaur mountain for each child. Mix together 2 cups (500 ml) plaster of Paris and 5 cups (1.25 L) of sand. Add 2 cups (250 ml) of water and stir. Mixture should be fairly thick. Pour the mixture into a cupcake pan lined with paper cups. Put a plastic dinosaur in each cup while the plaster is still wet.
2. Explain to the children that they are going to become paleontologists (people who study life from long ago).
3. Give each child a mountain and a popsicle stick and explain that they are going to excavate the dinosaurs. Say that just like scientists, we must work slowly and carefully to scrape away the mountain.

More to do
Art: Let the children dip the plastic dinosaurs' feet into tempera paint and walk them across a long narrow strip of paper.

Related book
Digging Up Dinosaurs by Aliki

Cindy Winther, Oxford, MI

Dinosaur Eggs

3+

Science skills
Children observe changes.

Materials

One hard-boiled egg per child
A bowl for dipping
3 cups (750 ml) cold water
One envelope unsweetened drink mix in a bright color
Plastic wrap

What to do

1. Explain that dinosaurs hatched from eggs.
2. Let the children tap the eggs on a hard surface so that cracks form all over them.
3. Leave the shells on and set the eggs aside.
4. In the bowl, mix together the water and the drink mix. Add the cracked eggs.
5. Cover the bowl with plastic wrap and refrigerate for one day.
6. Take the eggs out of the water and peel. They look like dinosaur eggs!
7. Eat them!

Original poem

This chant is based on the book, *We're Going on a Bear Hunt* by Michael Rosen. Everyone sits in a circle. Establish a rhythm by clapping hands. Start the chant and have the children repeat each line after you.

Going on a Dino Egg Hunt

Chorus:
Going on a dino egg hunt! (repeat)
Going on a dino egg hunt (repeat)
Gonna find a big one! (repeat)

Oh look! (repeat)
What's that ahead? (repeat)
A swamp! (repeat)
Better go right through it. (repeat)
Squish, squish, squish, squish.

(Repeat chorus)

Oh, look! (repeat)
What's that ahead? (repeat)
A hot desert! (repeat)
Better go right through it! (repeat)
Pant, pant, pant, pant.

(Repeat chorus)

Oh, look! (repeat)
What's that ahead? (repeat)
An ocean! (repeat)
Better go right through it! (repeat)
Splash, splash, splash, splash.

(repeat chorus)

Oh look! (repeat)
What's that ahead? (repeat)
A grassland! (repeat)
Better go right through it! (repeat)
Swish, swish, swish, swish.

(repeat chorus)

But look! (repeat)
What's that ahead? (repeat)
A nest! (repeat)
But whose nest? (repeat)
An egg! (repeat)
But whose egg?
Tyrannosaurus Rex! Run!
Aaaaaaaaaaaagh!
Back through the grassland (repeat)
Back through the ocean (repeat)
Back through the hot desert (repeat)
Back through the swamp (repeat)
Back home again (repeat)
Whew!

Robin Works Davis, Keller, TX

Dinosaur Memory Game

Science skills
This activity enhances memory.

Materials
Pictures of dinosaurs
Card stock or construction paper
Clear contact paper or laminate

What to do
1. Draw or find pictures of dinosaurs.

2. Enlarge or reduce their size on a copier to fit the size of the cards or construction paper you are using. Make two copies of each picture.
3. Color the pictures and glue them on the cards or construction paper.
4. Cover them with clear contact paper or laminate.
5. Turn all cards picture-side down and play as a memory game. Turn over two cards and see if they match. If not, turn them over again and leave them where they were. If they do match, take the cards away. Continue searching for matches.

Phyllis Esch, Export, PA

4+

Fossils

Science skills
Children are encouraged to ask about nature and to practice fine motor skills.

Materials

Clay
Rolling pins
Mats
Harvest items (leaves, corn, acorns, twigs)

What to do

1. Provide children each with a handful of clay (playdough might work also) and ask them to roll it into a thin layer on their mats.
2. Let the children select two or three items with which to make fossil prints.
3. Assist the children in gently pressing the whole item down to make a print.
4. You might display the fossils in the science area, use them for further discussion or let the children take them home.

More to do

More science: Instead of harvest items, you can use toy dinosaurs' footprints. These you could also use to study the concept of same and different and to write stories about dinosaur adventures. ▪ This would be a good activity for a week when the topic is fossils or science or nature. Use the prints to study the parts of a particular plant or item, its texture, size, etc. You can talk about the making of real fossils.

Billie Miteva, Pomona, NJ

Gummy Dinosaurs

4+

Science skills

In this activity, children practice counting, sorting, fine motor skills and also social development.

Materials

Gummy dinosaur candies
Blackboard with chalk or chart paper and marker
Large clear plastic jar
Small counting cups, one for each child

What to do

Work in small groups. Ask the children to wash their hands before this activity.

1. Put the gummy dinosaurs into the clear plastic jar and ask the children to guess how many there are. Write their guesses or estimations on the blackboard or on chart paper.
2. Ask the children whether they think there are more dinosaurs of one color than there are of the other colors. Which color is it? Write the guesses.
3. Ask the children to think of ways you could find out how many there really are.
4. Pour the dinosaurs out of the jar and ask the children to sort them by color.
5. Make a graph to show which is the color of most of the dinosaurs. Talk about which type is longest, shortest, the same size as another type, etc.
6. Check these findings against the original hypotheses or guesses.
7. Ask the children if there are other ways to sort the dinosaurs.
8. Regroup the dinosaurs into one pile and ask the children to guess how many there are.
9. Working together as a group, count ten dinosaurs into each cup. Leave leftover dinosaurs on the table.
10. Show the children how to count the dinosaurs by tens.
11. Add the remaining dinosaurs to your total to find out how many dinosaurs there are.
12. Check your findings against the original hypotheses or guesses.
13. Have the children dictate a sentence each telling about your findings.
14. As an option, you could tell the children that they may have the gummy dinosaurs if they can figure out a fair way to distribute them.

More to do

More science: This method can be used at different times of the year with gummy worms, gummy bears, animal crackers, M&M's or jellybeans.

Snack: For snack, give the children dinosaur graham crackers.

Barbara Saul, Eureka, CA

4+

How Big Was a Dinosaur?

Science skills

In this activity children practice measuring, predicting and counting, as well as fine and large motor development, and they learn about space relationships and social development.

Materials

Large playground area
Yardstick, meter stick or tape measure
Ball of string, twine or yarn

What to do

1. Read the children a book that tells the length of different dinosaurs.
2. Ask the children to estimate which dinosaur was the biggest. Write down their hypotheses or make a graph showing a variety of dinosaurs and ask the children to mark the dinosaur that they think is the biggest.
3. Tell the children that today they are going to find out how big dinosaurs really were. Take the children out on the playground.
4. Ask one child to stand at the point from which the measuring will begin and hold one end of the string. Other children help measure while others unwind the string. With the yard or meter stick, measure where to cut off the string, depending on the type of dinosaur you are measuring.
5. When the string is laid out the entire length of the dinosaur, let the children stand or lie down alongside the string and count how many children it takes to make up the length of this dinosaur. Then let the children take turns standing at one end and walking heel to toe, counting how many of their foot lengths the dinosaur measures. Ask them if there are other ways to measure the length and let them try out their ideas.
6. Ask the children to brainstorm about objects they know of that are as long as this dinosaur ("it's as big as our car" etc.).
7. Write down the measurement.
8. Repeat steps 5 to 8 for different dinosaurs.
9. With the children, check your original hypothesis against the measurements. Discuss similarities and differences.
10. Write down a dictated statement from each child about what they learned about dinosaurs and/or about measurement with this experiment.

More to do

Art: Ask the children to draw or make clay models of two dinosaurs, showing the difference in sizes.

Dinosaurs

Related books

I Can Read About Prehistoric Animals by David Eastman

Story of Dinosaurs by David Eastman

 *Barbara Saul, Eureka, CA*

Skeletons

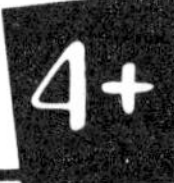

Science skills

Children are encouraged to ask questions about nature and practice fine motor skills.

Materials

Dinosaurs by Kathleen N. Daly

Large cardboard tubes (drapery material stores will give them for free)

Duct tape

What to do

1. Read the book *Dinosaurs* by Kathleen N. Daly.
2. Explain how dinosaurs are no longer alive, but museums have skeletons of dinosaurs. Ask if the children would like to create their own dinosaur skeleton.
3. Create a GIANT skeleton together, using long and short pieces of cardboard tubes duct-taped together.
4. Children can draw and cut out smaller bones to tape to the large skeleton frame.

 *Cindy Winther, Oxford, MI*

Dinosaur Dig

Science skills

Children observe and classify, use fine motor skills and work on social development.

Materials

Commercially made wooden dinosaur model, unassembled

Poster board

Contact paper or laminate

Packing material, such as Styrofoam chips

Container for model pieces and packing material

Large mat or plastic tablecloth

What to do

1. Before you introduce the activity to the children you will need to detach the dinosaur model pieces; trace the outline of each piece on the poster board, laying the pieces out randomly; laminate the poster board for long wear; bury the dinosaur "bones" in the packing material in the container.
2. Introduce the activity at a time when you are discussing dinosaurs. Explain that paleontologists dig for real dinosaur bones and that in the classroom the children will be able to dig for pretend bones.
3. Discuss the dinosaur being used. Present its name and information, such as the time and place it lived, what it ate and its approximate size.
4. Spread out the work mat and place the container with the "bones" and packing material, as well as the poster board on the mat.
5. Open the container, uncover several pieces and match them to their outlines, pointing out that they must match the outline exactly in both size and shape.
6. Replace the pieces you have taken out, being careful to bury them well in the packing material.
7. Replace any excess packing material in the container and fold the mat.
8. Place the activity where it is available to the children and invite them to choose it during free choice time. Be sure to emphasize that part of this activity is re-burying the "bones" so the work is ready for the next person.
9. After the activity has been available for some time and all who want to have had an opportunity to choose it, sit down with the entire group of children and, with their help in finding pieces, assemble the model in finished form. After you have displayed it in the classroom for a time, it may be taken apart, buried again and saved for next year.

More to do

Math: Number each piece of the model and place the same number on the corresponding outline to allow numeral matching as well as shape matching. Be sure to draw a line under potentially ambiguous numbers such as 6 and 16.

More science: Make the activity more challenging by mixing pieces from two different models in the same container and making two poster boards to which the pieces are to be matched. ▪ Choose dinosaurs that coexisted when they lived and discuss their possible relationship and the environment in which they lived.

Related books

David Dreaming of Dinosaurs by Keith Faulkner
The Dinosaur Alphabet Book by Jerry Pallotta
Tyrannosaurus Was a Beast by Jack Prelutsky

Susan Jones Jensen, Norman, OK

Those Dog-on Dinosaurs

5+

Science skills

Children make observations and use fine motor skills.

Materials

Books with pictures of dinosaur skeletons and human skeletons
Small dog bones or treats
Glue
Construction paper, large and small pieces
Markers or crayons
Outline of a dinosaur on paper
Scissors

What to do

1. Show the children pictures of dinosaur and human skeletons.
2. The children can use blank paper and refer to a completed example of this activity made by you or construction paper with an outline of a dinosaur on it. Those using the blank paper should lay the dog bones on the paper, forming their own outline of a dinosaur.
3. Glue these bones onto the paper.
4. With markers or crayons the children can add more detail to their pictures. Also, if they want to, the children can add additional pieces of colored construction paper for trees, grass, volcanoes, plants, clouds, etc., to enhance their pictures. They can either tear or cut the construction paper for these pieces.
5. Children use the paper with an outline on it in the same fashion as above, except they place the bones on the outline.

More to do

More science: Extend this activity by making fossils. Flatten out a small piece of modeling clay on wax paper. Choose an object such as a rock, a nut, a shell, a leaf, a pine cone, a stick or a small plastic dinosaur and press it into the modeling clay. Gently remove the object and an imprint should remain in the clay. Place this on a small plate for the children to take home. Modeling clay will not completely harden so the child can repeat this process at home with another object. They may find things of interest outside, near their homes. ▪ Show the children a book of common animal tracks. Seeing animal tracks in the mud or snow can help make clear to a child that dinosaurs also left tracks which may have later turned into fossils when they hardened.

Judy L. Zielinski, Maplewood, MN

3+

A Week of Protecting Our Planet

Science skills

This series of daily activities stimulates children to ask questions about the environment and encourages them to use fine motor skills.

Materials

Construction paper in these colors:
manila, light blue, dark blue, light gray, dark gray, yellow, orange, brown and white
Plastic dishpan large enough to hold a piece of 8½" x 11" (20.5 cm x 27.5 cm) construction paper
Small plastic cups
Flower seeds
Two plastic spoons
Tempera paint, blue and green
2 marbles
Masking tape
White school glue
Stickers of tropical fish, flowers, gold stars
Black crayons or markers
Potting soil
Two empty margarine tubs
Paper towels

What to do

Day One

1. The teacher cuts large manila circles, 7" to 8" (17.5 cm to 20 cm) in diameter, one for each child, and puts a piece of doubled-over masking tape in the bottom of the dishpan to hold the circle in place.
2. The teacher then puts blue paint in one empty margarine tub and green paint in the other and drops a marble into each container. With a spoon, she lifts each marble from the paint and drops it into the dishpan.
3. The child tips the dishpan gently side to side and back and forth to allow the marble to put paint over the manila circle. When it is finished, the circle picture should resemble the earth.
4. The teacher removes the marbles, wipes them on a paper towel and drops them back into the paint for the next child to use.
5. The children lay the circles aside to dry. When all the circles are dry, glue each onto a piece of dark blue construction paper entitled "Our Earth."
6. The children may cut a yellow moon to glue on the paper and add gold star stickers, too.

Day Two

1. Give each child a piece of manila paper to paint blue to represent the ocean. Entitle this paper "Watch What You Put in the Water."
2. On pieces of light blue and orange construction paper, the teacher traces each child's hand to make two fish. The children may cut out the fish.
3. When the painted paper is dry, the children can glue their fish in the water. They may also add fish stickers.

Environment

Day Three

1. The children cut different sizes and shapes of clouds from both colors of gray construction paper as well as a sun from the yellow paper. (Tearing shapes, for those who haven't mastered cutting, is fine, too.)
2. Give each child a piece of manila paper entitled "The Earth Needs Rain and Sun." The children glue the sun near one edge of the paper and two or three clouds of different sizes and shapes next to the other edge.
3. Children may wish to use crayons or markers to draw raindrops falling from their clouds.

Day Four

1. Help children design and cut out flower shapes from orange and yellow construction paper and stems with leaves from green paper.
2. Children paste their flowers onto a piece of manila paper entitled "Help Save Our Earth: Plant Flowers."
3. Then each child fills a small plastic cup with potting soil and plants three or four flower seeds in his cup. The teacher puts a piece of masking tape on each cup with the child's name on it.
4. The children take responsibility for watering their plants every few days.
5. When the plants are several inches tall, the children may take them home to plant.

Day Five

1. The teacher cuts brown strips for ax handles and white pieces into ax blades.
2. The children glue them together near one edge of a piece of manila construction paper entitled "Don't Hurt Our Forests."
3. The teacher traces each child's hand on green paper to make treetops and the children design and cut out tree trunks from brown paper.
4. The children glue the trunk and treetop near the ax.
5. You can save all of these papers and staple them together at the end of the unit with the earth picture on top to make a book about how to protect the environment.

More to do

More science: Talk about how to save electricity by turning off the lights when we leave the classroom. Remind the children to do this at home, too. ▪ Talk about what we can do at school to help conserve resources. ▪ Ask the children to contribute their ideas to a journal containing information on ways to help conserve energy and protect our forests and the animals that live in them. Each child can take home a photocopy of the journal.

Outdoors: Take nature walks to observe the plants and trees and watch them change as they grow.

Related books

Baby Beluga by Raffi
Blue Sea by Robert Kalan
Fish Eyes by Lois Ehlert
Flower Garden by Eve Bunting
The Freshwater Alphabet by Jerry Pallotta
The Listening Walk by Paul Showers
Rain Song by Lezlie Evans
Swimmy by Leo Lionni

Diane K. Weiss, Fairfax, VA

Small World, Big Words

Science skills
Children are encouraged to make observations and to develop their language skills.

Materials

Magnifying glasses
Markers
Chart paper

What to do

1. Choose an area to observe, anywhere from a field to the forest or playground.
2. Show the children how to hold a magnifying glass close to an object for observation. Looking closely at pebbles, sand and plants are good beginning activities.
3. Have children take turns using words to describe their small objects, for example, pebbles look sparkly, glittery, shiny.
4. Challenge the children to use new or different words each time. Some may even want to make up their own descriptive words.
5. Record the words on paper to keep track of variety and to use for comparing objects later.

More to do

Games: Ask each child to choose a small object secretly. The children then take turns describing their secret objects until someone guesses the item's identity. For example, my object is red, rough, glittery, hard and small. Is it a rock?

Language: Create a chart showing words the children use to describe each object:

Pebble	Leaf	Flower	Ant	Twig
shiny	smooth	colorful	wiggly	rough
hard	fuzzy	smooth	round	long
rough	jagged			bumpy
smooth				

Karen Johnson, Grand Rapids, MI

Case Dissolved

Science skills

Children are encouraged to ask questions about nature and to make predictions and observations.

Materials

A clear container in which 2-3 gallons (8-12 L) of water can be clearly viewed (an old fish aquarium or very large mayonnaise jar, for example)

Various items to put into the water container, such as salt, rocks, syrup, pepper

What to do

1. Place the clear container of water in the very center of a table where everyone will be able to see clearly. Place items to be tested close by.
2. Begin with an item that will most likely dissolve in water, such as salt. Pose the question, "Will it disappear or will you still be able to see it?" Pour in about a tablespoon (15 ml) of salt and closely observe the results. Make it clear that when the salt vanishes, it is because it has dissolved.
3. Move on to a solid object like a rock. Remember to ask the question first so the children may give their guesses. When the rock sinks to the bottom, explain that a rock is a "solid" and therefore can't dissolve. Continue with the rest of the items selected for this experiment.

More to do

Art: Try watercolor painting with the children. ▪ Make posters listing your findings of what dissolves in water and what sinks or floats, using magazine pictures to illustrate the experiments the children conducted.

More science: With the same tank of water (if it has not become too dirty or cloudy), conduct sinking and floating experiments, putting in items such as paper, corks, plastic spoons, metal spoons, lids, pencils and marbles. Ask the children to guess whether the items will sink or float.

*Penni L. Smith, Riverside, CA*

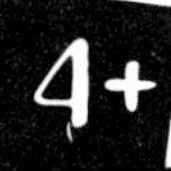

3+ Clean Water

Science skills

Children learn how filters clean debris from water.

Materials

Clear jars
Soil
Sand
Cheese cloth or cotton cloth
Rubber band

What to do

1. Pour water into a clear jar. Add some soil. Stir.
2. Spread the cheese cloth or cotton cloth over the opening of another jar and hold it in place with a rubber band. Pour sand onto the cloth.
3. Slowly pour the water with soil through the sand on the cloth and into the clean jar.
4. The water poured through the sand should be cleaner than the water in the original jar.

Related book

The Magic School Bus at the Waterworks by Joanna Cole

 *Monica Hay-Cook, Tucson, AZ*

4+ Weighing Waste

Science skills

Here's an experiment to raise the children's understanding of and enthusiasm for recycling.

Materials

Scale
Chart paper and marker
Classroom trash

What to do

This is a good project to help launch a study of recycling.

1. Throw all your classroom waste into a trash can lined with plastic bags, but before you take it out to be picked up by the trash collectors, weigh each bag on the scale. Do this for about one week.
2. Write the weight of the bags on a chart.

3. The second week, recycle as many things as you can, such as newspapers, aluminum and plastic bottles, and weigh only the trash you put out for the trash collectors.
4. Compare the weight of the bags this week with the week before. How much trash weight did you save? Congratulate the children on their recycling efforts.
5. Now that the children see how much is normally put into the trash that can actually be recycled, let them help to devise a system for recycling materials on a regular basis.

Related books

Recycle by Gail Gibbons

Where Does All the Garbage Go? by Melvin Berger

Monica Hay-Cook, Tucson, AZ

Litter Walk

4+

Science skills

In cleaning up a public space, children are encouraged to ask questions about their environment and to practice fine and large motor development.

Materials

Wartville Wizard by Don Madden

Plastic grocery bags with handles

Plastic gloves for each child

Polaroid camera

Safe area where there is human-made litter, for example, a playground, park or recreation area

What to do

1. Read the story *Wartville Wizard*. Discuss how the children's families get rid of their waste. Discuss the meaning of the word litter and the difference between human-made and natural litter. Children sometimes pick up sticks and leaves. Explain that this is natural litter.
2. Tell children that you will be going on a litter walk. Explain that they will be picking up human-made litter so they must wear gloves to protect their hands. Tell them not to touch any broken glass or items with sharp edges.
3. Take several pictures of the area before children pick up any litter, while they are picking up litter and after the area is clean. Later, post these on a bulletin board.
4. Take the litter back into the classroom. Dispose of the litter properly.

More to do

Language: Ask the children to dictate or write sentences about the litter walk. Staple them to the bulletin board.

More science: Before you dispose of the litter, select pieces of litter that are a sampling of what was found. Glue your selections to a large piece of cardboard. Write the sentence "Did you drop something?" on the cardboard. Display the litter collage in an area where other classes can see it.

 *Deborah A. Chaplin, Hot Springs, VA*

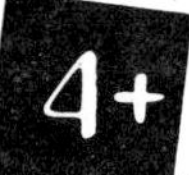

The Earth Is Our Only Home

Science skills

By looking close to home, children make observations about the environment and are encouraged to ask questions about recycling.

Materials

Box of biodegradable trash bags
Large poster board
Markers
Magazines
Glue

What to do

1. As a group, prepare a poster using pictures from magazines to help children understand what ecology and recycling are and how important they are for everyday living and for the future. Cut out pictures of plastic items such as dish soap, soda containers, and so on. Find something to illustrate aluminum cans, glass jars and bottles, etc. Cut out a picture of anything that is considered a recyclable product. The pictures on the poster can serve as reminders that those items can be used over again and need not be tossed out into our overcrowded landfills.
2. Check with various recycling centers to find out what they take and what they don't. List on the poster the many things that can be recycled, such as newspapers, telephone directories, magazines, glass jars and bottles, milk cartons or jugs, aluminum cans or clean foil, egg cartons, cardboard, etc. Now, with the children, start to think about how things can be improved in your classroom according to your poster.
3. Group clean-up can be fun and helpful. Teach your class the song, "We Need to Care for Earth," below. Hand out the recyclable trash bags. Go on a walk around your center, or a park area, gathering items that have been discarded. Assign one or two children to look only for aluminum cans, one or two to look for plastic bottles, others to look for newspaper, and so on. Encourage the children to bring in items to recycle from home and have their neighbors save their recyclables as well.
4. When you have collected enough, take a trip to a recycling center and cash in the money to buy seeds for a garden. Also, begin a compost bin to create mulch to use in your garden. Enlist the aid of a carpenter who can make a simple wooden box with a latched lid in which to make the mulch.
5. Explore other opportunities to gather together to make a better and cleaner world.

Original songs

Sing to the tune of "The Farmer in the Dell."

We need to care for Earth
We need to care for Earth

Environment

We're the only ones who can
We need to care for Earth.

We need to plant some trees
We need to plant some trees
We need trees so we can breathe
We need to plant some trees.

We need to make less trash
We need to make less trash
Recycling is a real good thing
We need to make less trash.

So, we need to help our Earth
We need to help our Earth
Every day along our way
We're going to help our Earth.

Penni L. Smith, Riverside, CA

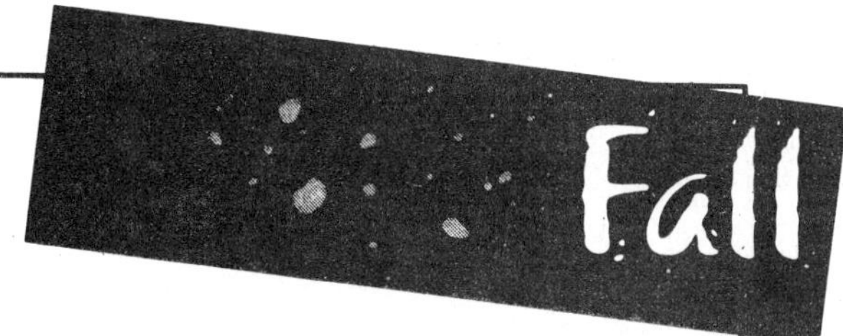

Signs of Fall Hunt

Science skills
Children first brainstorm, then hunt to find fall treasures.

Materials
Colored leaves
Other signs of fall
Pumpkins and squash
Large paper bag

What to do
1. Talk to the children about some signs of fall. Perhaps also read a story about fall.
2. Children help you make a list of some signs of fall. Think of as many as you can.
3. Take the children outside and hunt for the items on the list. Collect them in a large paper bag.
4. When you come back inside, look at each item and talk about it. Leave the items out on a special table for the children to explore.

More to do
More games: Hunt for signs of spring, summer and winter, too. Hunt for signs of various holidays, such as pumpkins for Halloween or evergreens for Christmas.

Related books
Fresh Fall Leaves by Betsy Franco
When Autumn Comes by Robert Maass

Susan Rinas, Parma, OH

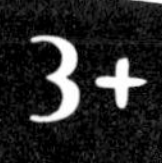

Woody Woodchuck and Sally Squirrel

Science skills
Through a charming story, children hear about hibernation and other wintertime habits of animals.

Materials
Stuffed animals or puppets

What to do
1. Tell the following story using stuffed animals or puppets to act out the story:

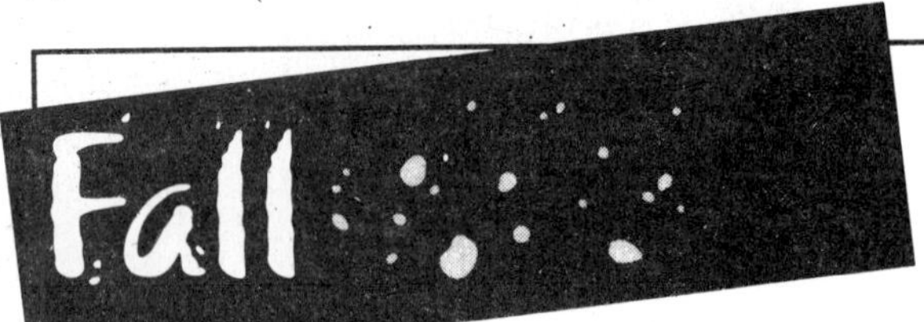

One fall morning Woody Woodchuck headed straight for Mrs. North's garden. Autumn winds were blowing leaves, red, orange, yellow and gold, right across his path. Woody scampered along even more quickly when he noticed the falling leaves and the wind. "I must eat as much as I can to fatten myself up. Soon winter will be here and I will sleep in my cozy underground burrow."

All of a sudden someone came racing along the path, knocking Woody over and falling over herself. It was Sally Squirrel. Her apron had been full of nuts that were now scattered all over the path. "Oh my, I have so little time left," Sally said. "Prince Autumn has come. I must gather many nuts and acorns, for once King Winter comes it will be difficult to find food." She looked up high in the treetop at her nest of leaves. Already she had buried nuts in the ground all around the tree, stuffed some in a hollow spot, and even carried a few to her nest.

She turned to Woody. "Excuse me, I'm sorry, I didn't hurt you did I? It's just that I'm in such a hurry! Do you understand?" Woody picked himself up and shyly shook his head. "No, frankly, I don't understand why you're hiding those nuts. Shouldn't you be eating as many as you can find?" "Oh no," said Sally. "I need to store those away to eat during the cold winter days when the trees are bare and little food will be found." "But don't you sleep underground all winter like I do?" asked Woody. "No, no!" Sally shook her head. "I spend a lot of time in my nest, but I'm up and about, too. I visit Mrs. North's bird feeder every morning for a sunflower seed breakfast. I lunch on nuts dug up from hidden stores...."

The wind seemed to sing a song:

"Squirrel Nutkin has a coat of gray
Quite the loveliest in the wood today.
Two bright eyes look round to see
Where the sweetest nuts may be."

Woody waved a shy good-bye and was soon eating the cabbages in Mrs. North's garden. Soon he would be plump and full and would spend the winter sleeping and dreaming in his burrow.

Sally began to bury an acorn. She would have plenty to eat during the winter. The autumn wind blew more leaves of red, orange, yellow and gold!

More to do

Art: Make a picture bulletin board with the children illustrating Sally climbing to her treetop nest and Woody sleeping in his underground nest. Show other animals who are asleep, such as chipmunks, or awake, such as deer.

Outdoors: Feed the birds during the winter.

Related books and recordings

Chipmunk Song by Joanne Ryder

Squirrels by Brian Wildsmith

"Come, Little Leaves" and "Hurry, Hurry, Hurry" in *Sing Through the Seasons: Ninety-Nine Songs for Children* edited by Society Brothers Staff

"Squirrel Nutkin" in *Sing Through the Day: Ninety Songs for Younger Children* edited by Marlys Swinger

Linda Atamian, Charlestown, RI

3+

An Observation Walk in Autumn

Science skills

Children ask questions about nature and practice classification and fine motor skills.

Materials

Four shoe boxes
Four index cards
Four crayons or markers: orange, red, brown and yellow

What to do

1. Using four index cards, print the name of one of the four colors listed above on each card. For example, print BROWN with a brown marker. Tape each card onto one of the shoe boxes.
2. Put the boxes on the science or discovery table.
3. The teacher brings four differently colored leaves into the classroom and shows them to the children. Discuss the four colors and find various objects with those colors in the proper room.
4. Take the children on an observation walk to gather various colored leaves.
5. Bring the leaves back to the classroom and children take turns placing them in the color-coded boxes.

More to do

More science: Keep the boxes on the science table for about a week so children may continue to add leaves and other collected natural items to them.

 *Elaine Commins, Atlanta, GA*

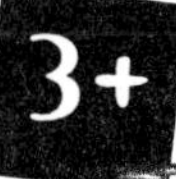
3+

Fall Wreath

Science skills

Children think about and search for signs of fall, then create their own display of natural seasonal items.

Materials

Heavy white paper (watercolor paper or tagboard works well)
Glue
Red or orange watercolor paints or crayons
Hole puncher
Red yarn
Fall objects such as dried leaves, milkweed seeds, acorns, pressed flowers, berries, wheat stalks

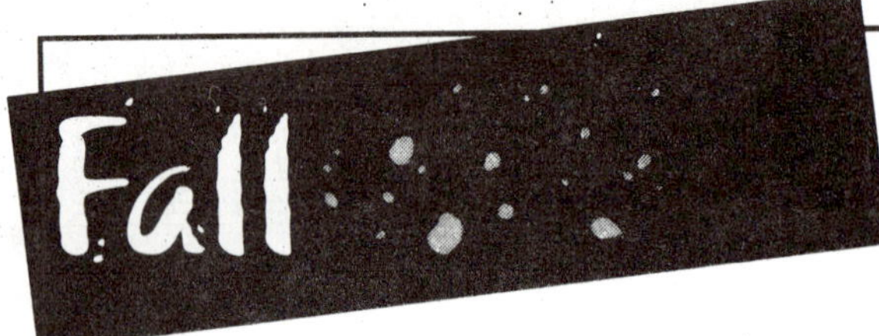

What to do

1. Cut wreath shapes out of paper and punch a hole at the top of each.
2. The children can paint or color the wreath shape. Let dry.
3. While the wreaths are drying, go outside on a fall hunt for items such as acorns, dried leaves, twigs, etc.
4. Back inside, spread the items out on a table. Let the children select the fall items they want for their wreath and glue them on.
5. When the wreaths are dry, tie yarn in a loop through the hole at the top of the wreath for hanging.

More to do

Art: Make other seasonal wreaths. For spring, make heart-shaped wreaths and use paper doilies and dried flowers tied with pink ribbons. For summer, make a beach wreath using dribbled sand, seaweed, shells, bay leaves, pebbles, etc. For winter, use cones from different evergreens (especially little hemlock cones); nuts like almonds, whole cinnamon and star-shaped anise, nutmeg gold stars and red ribbon.
Math: Collect extra fall items and place in a basket for sorting or counting practice.

Related books

Red Leaf, Yellow Leaf by Lois Ehlert
Chicken Soup with Rice by Maurice Sendak

Linda Atamian, Charlestown, RI

Leaves Change Color

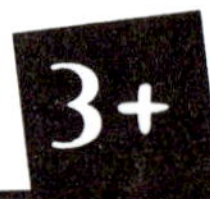

Science skills
Children learn new words for leaf pigments.

Materials

Why Do Leaves Change Color? by Betsy Maestro
Fall leaves of various colors

What to do

1. Read the book and discuss with the children the color change process.
2. Tell the children the names of the pigments responsible for the change: xanthophyll, carotene and anthocyanin.
3. Take the children on a fall walk to collect colored leaves.
4. Gather them together in a group and teach the pigment names using the leaves as visual aids and the rhyme below.

Original poem

Xanthophyll, xanthophyll
Pretty yellow fellow
When it turns old, he makes leaves gold
Xanthophyll is yellow.

Carotene, carotene
It's orange as can be
When fall is near, orange leaves are here
Carotene is orange.

Anthocyanin, anthocyanin
It makes red so bright
Inside the leaves it hides till fall
And turns leaves red out of sight!

 *Lisa M. Lang, Parkersburg, WV*

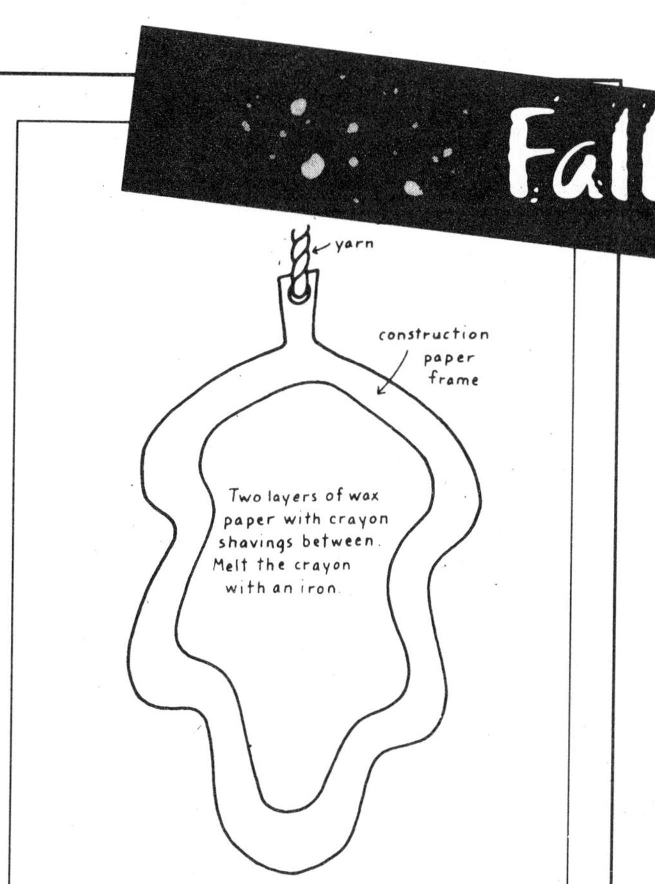

Fall Leaf Mobiles

Science skills
Children practice fine motor skills.

Materials

Leaf patterns
8½" x 11" (22.5 cm x 27.5 cm) paper
Scissors
Small sponges made by cutting a large sponge into 2" x 3" (5 cm x 7.5 cm) pieces
Small cups of tempera paint: red, yellow, orange, brown
String or yarn, 24" (60 cm) long
Stapler

What to do

1. Trace three or four leaves onto one 8½" x 11" piece of paper (see next page).
2. Make a copy of the leaf page for each child.
3. Show the children how to sponge paint the leaves.
4. Give each child a leaf page and let her sponge paint them.
5. After the pages are dry, the children may turn the paper over and sponge paint the whole backside of the paper. They may like to draw their own leaf designs to sponge paint.
6. When both sides are dry, ask the children to cut out the leaves.
7. Help the children attach the leaves to the length of yarn with a stapler.
8. Hang the leaf mobile by one end of the yarn and watch the falling leaves.

More to do

Art: Give each child a blank sheet of drawing paper and ask them to use brown crayons to draw a tree trunk. The children will enjoy using the sponge painting technique to make fall foliage on their tree.

Related books

Have You Seen Trees? by Joanne Oppenheim
Red Leaf, Yellow Leaf by Lois Ehlert
Squirrels by Brian Wildsmith

Barbara Saul, Eureka, CA

Fall Leaf Windows

Science skills

Children make observations and practice fine and large motor skills.

Materials

Assortment of fall leaves
Clear contact paper or wax paper
(if you use wax paper, you will also need liquid starch and an iron)
Newspaper or easel paper
Scissors
Construction paper
Stapler
Tape
Crayon shavings, optional

What to do

1. Take the children on a walk in the neighborhood to collect fall leaves, or ask them to bring fall leaves from home.
2. Working in small groups, ask each child to select 3 to 5 leaves.
3. If you use contact paper, cut a sheet about 11" x 17" (27.5 cm x 42.5 cm). Help each child arrange the leaves on half of the contact paper, sticky side up.
4. Fold the contact paper in half, matching edges and enclosing the leaves.
5. If you use wax paper, give each child two pieces, about 8" x 10" (20 cm x 25 cm).
6. Let the children arrange their leaves on one piece of wax paper. Crayon shavings may be sprinkled on top for additional color.
7. Paint the other piece of wax paper with a coat of liquid starch. Place the wax paper starch-side down on top of the leaves.
8. Cover the ironing surface with newspaper or easel paper.
9. Iron the two pieces of wax paper together, sandwiching the leaves between the two.
10. Help the children cut strips of the construction paper to make a frame for their leaf window.
11. Display the windows in a real window in the classroom.

More to do

Art: Use leftover leaves to make leaf rubbings. Cover some leaves with newsprint. Use the sides of crayons to gently rub the paper until an imprint is made.
Language: Brainstorm how the leaves are different from each other.
Math: Encourage the children to sort the leaves in their collections by shape, color, etc.

Barbara Saul, Eureka, CA

3+

Our Wreath

Science skills

Children practice social development as they work together on a fall class project.

Materials

Leaves, twigs, small pine cones, seeds
Glue
Ribbon (plastic or fabric)
Large piece of heavy cardboard
Scissors

What to do

1. Cut one large circle out of cardboard. Cut another smaller circle out of the center; the result should be a big doughnut shape.
2. Take a field trip outside with the children to collect leaves, twigs and small natural items reflective of the fall season.
3. Spread out all the leaves, twigs, etc. on an art table. Put the pre-cut wreath form in the center of the table.
4. Ask the children to select several of the items and take turns gluing some of the fall treasures onto the wreath. Note how with each child's addition the wreath is enhanced.

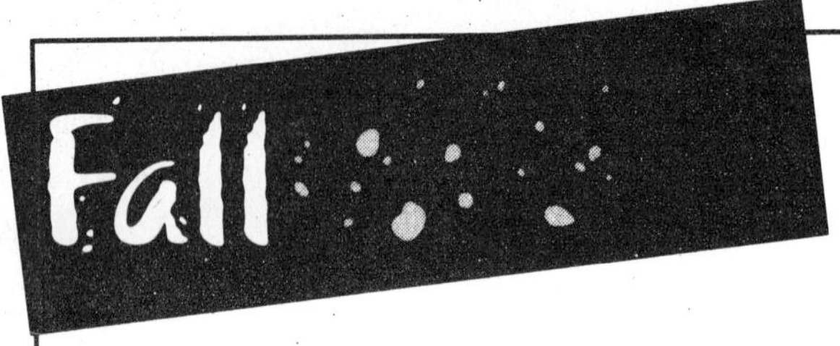

5. At the top of the wreath, the teacher can add a plastic or fabric bow.
6. Hang the fall wreath to remind the children of the fun you had working together on the project and as a focal point for continuing discussions of the fall season.

More to do

Language: Use this activity as an introduction to a discussion of the various changes in the outdoor world as fall arrives. Children could also describe the different colors and shapes of the natural items they collect, and compare their findings with those of other children.

 *Catherine McEntyre, Camarillo, CA*

October Science Table: Signs of Fall

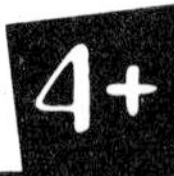

Science skills

Children practice observation and identification.

Materials

Large table
Construction paper in fall colors
7 or 8 same-sized shoe boxes, covered with contact paper
Yellow tagboard
Crayons
Leaves
Reference books about trees and leaves

What to do

1. Beforehand, make a sign reading "Signs of Fall" out of construction paper. Put the sign and the shoe boxes together in an area.
2. Make signs for the boxes, for example, oak, maple, poplar, sassafras, hickory, dogwood, etc. and one for "mystery" leaves. The signs can include the shape of the leaves, too.
3. Ask the children to bring in examples of leaves and then match them to the appropriate picture and box.
4. If there is no match, put the leaf in the mystery box.
5. Teacher and children look up mystery leaves in reference books.

More to do

Art: Make leaf place mats by placing 6 to 8 leaves on a piece of wax paper 12" x 18" (30 cm x 45 cm) and covering this with a second sheet of wax paper. Cover with padding. Slowly iron the surface to melt the wax. Trim the edges. ▪ Make leaf prints by first placing a leaf on newspaper and then rolling a paint-filled brayer over the leaf. Flip the leaf over onto a piece of paper and press gently.

Related books

Silly Sidney by Morgan Matthews
Trees of North America by C. Frank Brockman

Eileen E. Crocker, White Hall, MD

4+

Autumn Hunt

Science skills

On a walk on a crisp fall day, children ask questions about nature and practice fine and large motor skills.

Materials

Paper lunch bags
Paper
Pictures of fall finds
Markers, crayons

What to do

1. Talk with the children about how autumn is different from the other seasons. Discuss things they may find on a walk.
2. Give each child a paper bag and a list with pictures of things to look for on their autumn hunt.
3. When you return from your walk, the children can take their list and bag to the Art Center and make pictures of the things they found.

More to do

Art: Bring extra finds back for the Art Center. Children can glue and color their own autumn scenes.

More science: Bring your own finds back to display in the Science Center.

Related books

Fall Is Here, I Love It by Elaine W. Good
Look What I Did With a Leaf by Morteza E. Sohi
Why Do Leaves Change Color? by Betsy Maestro

Sandra Hutchins Lucas, Cox's Creek, KY

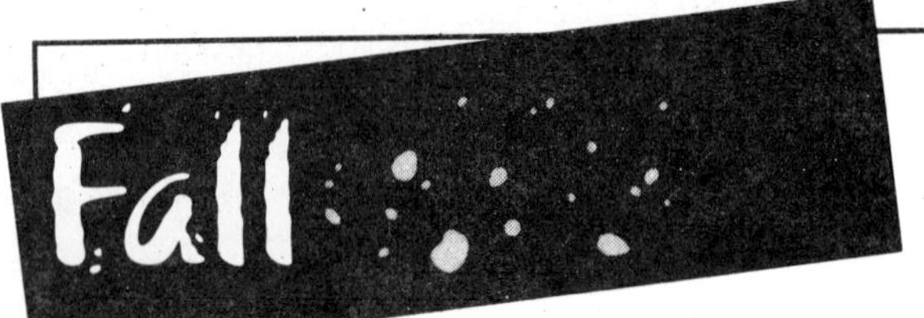

Musical Leaves

5+

Science skills

In this game, children learn identification and observation.

Materials

Leaves made of construction paper, fabric or real leaves from any tree native to the area in which you live
Small brown lunch bag
Portable cassette or CD player
Cassette or CD with children's music

What to do

1. If you use paper leaves, prepare them in advance. Also ahead of time, you should show pictures of various trees and identify their leaves. Let the children practice identifying various leaves.
2. Seat the children in a circle. Randomly choose a leaf, place it in the brown bag and close it up. Children should not see which leaf you choose.
3. Play music while the children pass the bag around the circle. When the music stops, the child with the bag takes out the leaf and identifies it.
4. Pick a new leaf to go in the bag. Play proceeds until each child has had at least one turn.

More to do

Art: Make a collage together from the leaves the children have collected.
More science: Take a fall walk and encourage the children to pick up leaves, or bring leaves from home. Identify them. ▪ Use silk or construction paper flowers to help the children learn to identify flowers.

Related books

Crinkleroot's Guide to Knowing the Trees by Jim Arnosky
Red Leaf, Yellow Leaf by Lois Ehlert
Why Do Leaves Change Color? by Betsy Maestro

Mary Rozum Anderson, Vermillion, SD

3+

Crushing Corn

Science skills
Using all their senses, children make observations and predictions and use fine and large motor skills.

Materials
Indian corn
Popcorn kernels
Flat rock, concave in the middle
Mortar and pestle
Field corn
Tray
Round rock
Big bowl

What to do
1. Show the children the different kinds of corn and let them use all their senses (except taste) to explore it.
2. Ask questions, closed and open ended, such as, could we eat the corn? What does it smell, feel, look like? What could we do with the corn?
3. Let children know what they will be doing with the corn by demonstrating step five. Explain that this is how Native Americans used to make food and how people in other cultures make their food now, for instance in Central and South America.
4. Children can take the corn off of the cobs and put the kernels into a plastic jar.
5. Put the Indian corn on the flat rock on a tray and crush with the round rock. You can also put the Indian corn in the mortar and crush it with a pestle.
6. Repeat step five using the field corn, then the popcorn.
7. Now put the crushed corn on the tray, and let the children play with it using their fingers.

More to do
Field trip: Visit a local farm that grows corn.

Original song and poem
Sing to the tune of "Ten Little Indians."

1 piece, 2 pieces, 3 pieces of corn
4 pieces, 5 pieces, 6 pieces of corn
7 pieces, 8 pieces, 9 pieces of corn
10 pieces that look so good!

Five Stalks of Corn

5 stalks of corn all standing in a field.
The first one said it's almost time to be picked.
Second one said look, there is a crow!
Third one said oh no! oh no!

Fourth one said let's sway in the wind.
Fifth one said I hear a noise.
Chug, chug went the tractor, crash went the corn!
Yum, yum said all
the little girls and boys.

Related book
Corn Is Maize: The Gift of the Indians by Aliki

Darleen Schaible, Stroudsburg, PA

Baking Corn Muffins

Science skills
The children practice a range of skills, such as observation, measurement, social development and fine motor.

Materials
Baking aprons or smocks
¾ cup (175 ml) flour
1½ teaspoon (7.5 ml) baking powder
_ cup (60 ml) oil
Large bowl
Measuring cups and spoons
Muffin papers or oil
¾ cup (175 ml) cornmeal
½ cup (125 ml) sugar
¾ cup (175 ml) milk
1 egg
Mixing spoon
Muffin tins
Oven

What to do
1. Ask the children to wash their hands and put on baking aprons.
2. Show them how to measure first the dry ingredients and then the wet ingredients into the bowl. Let them take turns so everybody has a chance to measure and/or add an ingredient. Mix well to combine.
3. Put muffin papers in muffin tins, or lightly oil the tins. Then fill muffin tins ⅔ full.
4. Bake in an oven at 350°F (180°C) for 25 to 30 minutes. Eat and enjoy!

Darleen Schaible, Stroudsburg, PA

Dandelion Dip

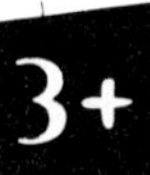

Science skills
Children learn about something unfamiliar by observing and using all their senses.

Materials

Freshly cut dandelion leaves (best in early spring)
Paper towels
Large tray for leaves
Two small clear glass bowls for dipping
Olive oil
Balsamic vinegar
Small paper plates

What to do

1. Take the children outdoors to gather fresh dandelion leaves. New early shoots are best!
2. Wash the leaves and dry them on paper towels. Place them on a tray.
3. Allow the children to serve themselves and to dip the leaves into the oil and then the vinegar.
4. Enjoy!

More to do

Math: Make a graph of the children's responses, their likes and dislikes. Bring a clump of dandelions into the classroom for observation. Conduct a survey on how many dandelions are in the children's yards.

Related books

Barney Bipple's Magic Dandelions by Carol Chapman
The Silver Dandelion Pop-up Surprise Book by Gill and John Speirs

Cathy Costantino, Carol Patnaude, Lynn R. Camara, Warwick, RI, and Darlene Maloney, East Greenwich, RI

3+

Food Colors

Science skills
Children make observations and predictions and use visual skills.

Materials

Paper plates in different colors
Pictures of food
Laminating machine or contact paper

What to do

1. Laminate uncolored pictures of food.
2. Have available the plates of different colors. You can spray paint plates if you can't find particular colors you want.
3. Have the children choose a picture of a food. Talk about food and the different colors that food is.

4. Encourage the children to place the pictures on the plate that is the color that their food should be.

Related book

Today Is Monday by Eric Carle

 *Sandra Hutchins Lucas, Cox's Creek, KY*

Jack Wax

Science skills

Children observe the effect of icy cold.

Materials

Pan of ice
Maple syrup
Toothpicks

What to do

1. Make a pan of solid ice.
2. Pour maple syrup over the top.
3. Lift the frozen syrup, jack wax, with toothpicks and eat! Yummy!

More to do

More science: We make syrup by tapping a maple tree, hanging a bucket on a spile, or spike, and then boiling down the sap.

Related book

Pancakes for Breakfast by Tomie dePaola

Andrea Clapper, Cobleskill, NY

Friendship Fruit Salad

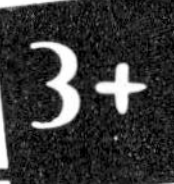

Science skills

The children practice fine motor skills and social development.

Materials

Assortment of fruits: apples, oranges, grapes, raisins, pineapple, bananas, pears, coconut, Maraschino cherries
Miniature marshmallows
Plastic knives
Large wooden spoon
Plastic spoons, one per child
Chart paper
Whipped topping, one container
Individual cutting boards, several
Small serving bowls, one per child
Markers

What to do

1. Introduce the concept of friendship by reading a poem, brainstorming related words/ideas or sharing a short story from *Frog and Toad Are Friends* by Arnold Lobel.
2. Emphasize the qualities of helping and sharing in relation to being a good friend.
3. Explain that the class will be making Friendship Fruit Salad for snack. Give each child a parent letter describing your class project and requesting the donation of one ingredient. (The ingredients list can be adjusted to match the number of children in your class.)
4. When all ingredients have arrived at school, let children wash their hands, wash and peel (if necessary) the fruit, and work in small groups to chop fruit and open cans.
5. After the children have prepared all ingredients, sit together as a class. Have individual children place each ingredient in the bowl as you write a rebus recipe on chart paper. When all ingredients have been added, stir and serve.

More to do

Art: Dip half of each of several different pieces of fruit in shallow containers of tempera paint to make fruit prints. Let the children use the fruit to make prints on brightly colored construction paper. When dry, the different fruit prints can be identified and labeled.
Language: Save seeds from several types of fruit for planting or sprouting. Keep a daily log to record class observations of the seeds' growth. ▪ Have children work in groups to write and illustrate stories about each seed. This is a great way to reinforce story sequence by emphasizing the idea of beginning, middle and end.

Related books

A Book of Fruit, photographs by Barbara H. Lember
Eating the Alphabet: Fruits and Vegetables from A to Z by Lois Ehlert
Growing Colors by Bruce McMillan

 *Rebecca M. McMahon, Scranton, PA*

Making Peanut Butter

3+

Science skills

Children observe and help with the making of a favorite food.

Materials

Roasted unsalted peanuts
Plastic spatula
Crackers
Blender
Peanut oil

What to do

1. Pour one cup (250 ml) of peanuts into the blender.
2. Add about 1 tablespoon (15 ml) of peanut oil.
3. Set the blender on "grind" and run it several minutes until the peanuts are ground smooth, stopping periodically to scrape the sides of the blender with the spatula.
   The following rhyme is fun to use with this activity:

   A peanut sat on the railroad track,
   His heart was all a flutter–
   A train came roarin' 'round the bend–
   "Toot! Toot! Peanut butter!"

4. Spread the peanut butter on crackers and enjoy!

More to do

Math: Let the children practice filling the measuring cup with peanuts and point out one-half, three-fourths and one cup.

Mary Jo Shannon, Roanoke, VA

Mystery Seeds

3+

Science skills

Children learn observation and matching skills.

Materials

Seeds from these fruits and vegetables: apple, orange, watermelon, squash, beans, peach,

plum, apricot, corn, mango, papaya, pumpkin, nuts, cherries, sunflower, tomato and cucumber
Whole fruits and vegetables
Index cards

What to do

1. Cut the whole fruits and vegetables in half to expose their seeds.
2. Make a simple matching game by extracting some seeds from the fruits and vegetables and gluing them on cards.
3. Children match the seed cards with the plant half.

More to do

More science: Children can take turns trying to identify the fruits and vegetables by smell and taste.

Related book

The Carrot Seed by Ruth Krauss

Susan R. Forbes, Holly Hill, FL

3+

Orange Juice

Science skills

Children make observations and predictions and use fine motor skills.

Materials

Oranges or grapefruits
Hand juicer
Cups
Vegetable brushes
Electric juicer
Marker

What to do

1. Wash the oranges with vegetable brushes.
2. Juice some with the hand juicer and some with the electric juicer.
3. Ask the children how many seeds they think are in an orange? How much juice do they predict they will get? Draw a line on a clear plastic cup and see how close the estimates are.
4. Plant the seeds.
5. Use the empty rinds to make bird feeders by filling them with birdseed and poking holes in the sides to hang them from a tree.

Kristina Davis and Anne M. Sullivan, Seminole, FL

The Fruity Tooty Riddle Game

3+

Science skills

Children practice social development and observation.

Materials

A tray with an apple, banana, lemon, orange, tomato, plum, kiwi, peach, grape, watermelon

What to do

1. First introduce the children to the fruits on the tray. Discuss why fruits are good for our bodies.
2. Now tell them that they are going to play the Fruity-Tooty Riddle Game.
3. Tell each child a riddle from the list that follows.
4. If a child tries to guess the answer and has trouble, other friends can help.
5. After a child has given the correct answer, he may select and eat the fruit that corresponds to the riddle.
6. Follow up the riddle game with a tasting party.

Riddles

1. *I am green on the outside, pinkish red on the inside and usually have black seeds. (Watermelon)*
2. *You can eat me as a fruit or squeeze me for juice. I have lots of vitamin C, and I am an orange color. (Orange)*
3. *I am round and red and I grow on a vine. Some people think I am a vegetable but I'm really a fruit. (Tomato)*
4. *I can be red or yellow or green. I grow on a tree, and I have a star inside. (Apple)*
5. *I am very sour inside and I can make your mouth pucker. (Lemon)*
6. *I am hidden inside a yellow skin. Monkeys as well as children like to eat me. (Banana)*
7. *I am brown on the outside and green within. I have the same name as a bird. (Kiwi)*
8. *I am purple on the outside. I am purple on the inside, and my name starts with a P. (Plum)*
9. *I grow on a tree, and my skin is very soft and fuzzy. I am a pinkish color, and I'm very sweet. I usually grow in the summer. (Peach)*
10. *Sometimes I'm green and sometimes I'm purple. If I am dried in the sun, I become a raisin. (Grape)*

Related recording

"Corner Grocery Store" by Raffi

Diann Spalding, Santa Rosa, CA

3+

The Veggie Game

Science skills

Children practice observation and work on their social development.

Materials

A tray with these vegetables on it: carrot, onion, celery, broccoli, potato, Brussels sprout, green pepper, head of lettuce, zucchini

What to do

1. Introduce the children to the vegetables on the tray.
2. Discuss why vegetables are good for our bodies.
3. Announce that you are going to play the Veggie Riddle Game.
4. Tell each child a riddle from the list that follows. Each tries to guess to which vegetable the riddle is referring. (If a child has trouble, then other friends in the circle may join in and help.)
5. After a child has given the correct answer, he may select and eat the vegetable from the tray that corresponds to the riddle.
6. Cut up the remaining vegetables, make a dip and have a tasting party to review.

Riddles

1. *I am long and orange and you can eat me raw or cooked. (Carrot)*
2. *I can be yellow, red, white or green. Sometimes I can be very hot. People often eat me on their hamburgers. (Onion)*
3. *I am crunchy and green. I often have little strings on me. Sometimes children enjoy eating me with peanut putter. (Celery)*
4. *I look like a group of little trees with stems and green leaves. I am very good for you. (Broccoli)*
5. *You can cook me many different ways; I can be mashed or fried or baked. I can be red, white, brown or even purple, and I have little eyes on my skin. (Potato)*
6. *I look like a green cabbage and I'm full of Vitamin C, but I am very cute and small. (Brussels sprout)*
7. *I am sometimes green, sometimes red and sometimes yellow. But I almost always have a bell shape. (Pepper)*
8. *I am long and green. Inside I am a whitish color. Some cooks use me in breads or cakes and as a vegetable for dinner. (Zucchini)*
9. *I am green and round. People use my leaves for salads or for sandwiches. (Lettuce)*

More to do

More science: Place vegetables in a bag. Have each child pick one vegetable out and tell what it is.

Related recording
"Corner Grocery Store" by Raffi

 *Diann Spalding, Santa Rosa, CA*

Dancing Raisins

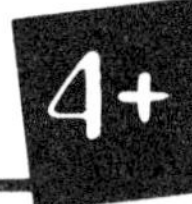

Science skills
Children have fun observing and making predictions in this experiment.

Materials
Chart paper
Clear plastic cups
Box of raisins
Marker
Club soda or flavored seltzer

What to do
1. Discuss the experiment with the children and talk about what you are going to do.
2. Describe how scientists make predictions called hypotheses and ask the children what their hypotheses about the experiment are. Write each hypothesis on chart paper.
3. Demonstrate the experiment by first filling a glass halfway with club soda or seltzer, then quickly putting five raisins in the glass, one at a time. Soon you will be able to see the raisins move up and down and do flips. The bubbles make them move.
4. Explain that the bubbles are filled with gas and when the bubbles cover the raisins, the raisins rise and appear to dance. Discuss the class hypothesis. Then you can give each child a glass and some raisins to repeat the experiment. The children can also taste the seltzer and raisins if they like.

More to do
Math: Provide the class with different types of seedless raisins, such as golden and brown. Ask them to taste each and graph their taste preference results.
Storytelling: Try using "If I Were a Raisin" as a class story title. Each child could contribute one silly sentence.

Related books
Eating the Alphabet: Fruits and Vegetables From A to Z by Lois Ehlert
The Very Hungry Caterpillar by Eric Carle

Karen Megay-Nespoli, Massapequa Park, NY

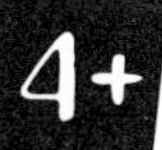

Fun With Fruit

Science skills
Children use language and visual skills, make comparisons and practice fine motor skills.

Materials
Book about fruits or vegetables
Magazines
Glue or paste
Crayons or markers and paper
Scissors
Poster board

What to do
1. Read your class a book about fruits or vegetables.
2. Ask the children to draw or cut out magazine pictures of favorite fruits or vegetables.
3. Paste these pictures on poster board to make a picture graph of the children's favorite fruits or vegetables. Label each food with its name.
4. Discuss the results of the graph, such as which fruit or vegetable was chosen by the most children. Tally the amounts next to the pictures.
5. Ask the children to bring in their favorite fruits or vegetables to make a salad to share with class.

More to do
More science: Learn about which fruits and vegetables grow on trees and which grow in the ground. Learn about the stages of growing these foods.

Related recording
"I Like to Eat Apples and Bananas" by Raffi

 *Deborah Hannes Litfin, Forest Hills, NY*

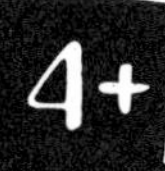

Is It Still Corn?

Science skills
Children observe as corn changes in form and appearance.

Materials
Popcorn
Indian corn
Wooden bowls
Corn on the cob
Dried feed corn
Clean, dry rocks

What to do

1. Display the different forms of corn. Let the children observe, touch and speculate on which type of corn kernel will become which type of familiar food.
2. Allow the children to crush the dried Indian corn kernels in wooden bowls using familiar rocks. Point out that the finished product is cornmeal. Put the cornmeal into an airtight container and save it for baking cornbread at a later time.
3. Try popping popcorn with the children and explain why the popcorn pops. Each kernel contains a drop of water and when that gets hot enough, it explodes.

Teresa J. Nos, Baltimore, MD

Solar Snacks

Science skills
Children make observations and use fine motor skills.

Materials

Fruit or vegetables suitable for drying: grapes, cranberries, bell peppers, mushrooms, apricots, apples, pears, plums, carrots
String
Clothes hangers
Safe plastic yarn needles
Clean nylon stockings, optional

What to do

1. Ask the children to bring one fruit or vegetable from home. Wash them.
2. Help the children string the fruit and vegetables onto string with the yarn needles (you may place larger fruit such as apples, pears, plums, etc., in a clean nylon stocking).
3. Attach strings and nylons to wire coat hangers and hang them in a clean dry area that receives a lot of sun. Allow them to dry undisturbed.
4. Small fruits and vegetables dry faster. Apples and other large fruits may take longer.
5. Taste your dried fruits and compare the difference between fresh and dried flavors and textures.

More to do

Math: You can display charts in your drying area. Children can mark off the days it takes for their food choice to dry and then visually compare bar graphs of how many days it takes for different foods to dry.
More science: Large groups can discuss wholesome foods and how air and sun can preserve foods through the dehydration process.

Dani Rosensteel, Payson, AZ

4+

Which Seed Is Which?

Science skills
Children are encouraged to ask questions about nature based on their observations.

Materials

Two trays, one tray with various fruits, nuts and vegetables and the other with corresponding seeds, cleaned and dried

Note: some of the selections could be: orange, apple, watermelon, walnuts, papaya, avocado, peach, apricot, mango, pumpkin, squash

What to do

1. Discuss the names of the various fruits and vegetables and nuts with the children.
2. Place the trays of food and seeds on a table and allow the children to observe and touch.
3. Encourage them to guess which seeds belong to which foods.
4. Cut up fruits and vegetables to show children the corresponding seeds.
5. Taste the foods.

More to do

More science: Plant and root the seeds to grow new plants.

Diann Spalding, Santa Rosa, CA

Which Seeds Belong to Which Food?

Science skills
Children make observations and predictions and check their hypotheses.

Materials

Fruits in season and their seeds
Glue
Chart paper
Poster board
Tray
Marker

What to do

1. Glue seeds onto a poster board.

2. Display a tray of the fruits on a table and let the children handle the fruits and see if they can guess which fruits belong to which seeds.
3. After everyone has guessed and you have written down all guesses on chart paper, cut open the fruits and find the seeds to match.

More to do

Math: Count how many seeds are in each fruit.

Snack: Have a fruit-tasting party.

Related book

Eating the Alphabet: Fruits and Vegetables From A to Z by Lois Ehlert

Holly Dzierzanowski, Austin, TX

Wiggle Worm Pie

Science skills

Children use fine motor and observation skills.

Materials

One foil cupcake cup per child
One small box of chocolate pudding for every eight children
A large resealable plastic bag
Mixer
Plastic spoons
Three chocolate cookies per child
2 cups (500 ml) milk per box of pudding
One gummy worm per child
Mixing bowl
Serving spoon

What to do

1. Place the cookies in the plastic bag and let the children crush them into crumbs.
2. Prepare the chocolate pudding according to package directions.
3. Each child puts a gummy worm in his foil cupcake cup, fills it with pudding and sprinkles cookie crumbs on top.
4. Use the recipe for measuring practice, too.

Related books

And So They Build by Bert Kitchen
Who Lives Here? by Rozanne Williams

Robin Works Davis, Keller, TX

Syrian Bread

Science skills

Children make observations, predict outcomes and engage in social development as well as fine and large motor skills.

Materials

¾ teaspoon (3.5 ml) yeast
⅛ cup (30 ml) vegetable oil
2 cups (500 ml) flour, plus extra flour for kneading and rolling dough
2 cooling racks
Mixing bowl
¾ cup (175 ml) warm water
⅔ teaspoon (3 ml) salt
Electric frying pan
Spatula
Measuring cups and spoons
Wooden spoon
Recipe printed on large easel paper and placed on a wall for reference

What to do

1. Plan this activity for a small group.
2. Gather all bread ingredients and utensils and place on the table before you invite the children to the activity. Ask the children to wash their hands.
3. Introduce the activity by talking about the recipe, ingredients, utensils and new vocabulary words.
4. Allow the children to measure the ingredients into the bowl, using the directions on the recipe card:

    Measure the yeast into the bowl.

    Add warm water and mix until yeast is dissolved. (Before they add the water, ask children to predict what will happen to the yeast.)

    Add the oil. Allow the children to observe the separation of the oil and water mixture and describe what they see. Stir.

    Add salt and stir, then add flour and stir.
5. Turn the dough onto a floured surface, and allow the children to knead the dough until it is smooth.
6. Separate the dough into five balls (the size of large eggs). Cover the balls and let them rise in a warm place for 20 minutes. Ask the children to predict what will happen to the dough.
7. While the dough is rising, the children can help wash the cooking utensils and clean the table area, getting it ready for the next steps. The teacher can also read the story, *Sitti's Secret* by Naomi S. Nye.
8. Back at the table, flour the table space in front of each child and give each a ball of dough. Remind the children that this is not playdough, and it should not be played with at this point.
9. Preheat a dry electric frying pan to 450°F (230°C) in a safe, well-supervised area.
10. Let the children roll out the dough to about ⅛″ (3 mm) thickness to form a circle about 7″ (17.5 cm).

11. The teacher places one dough round at a time into the preheated skillet, cooks it on one side for approximately 30 seconds, then flips it and cooks for another 30 seconds on the other side. If dough is thick, increase the cooking time.
12. Remove the bread from the skillet and place it on cooling rack. Repeat the process for the other dough balls.
13. Allow the children to eat the bread and ask them to compare the Syrian bread to the bread they eat at home. Talk about the smell, taste and texture of the bread.

More to do

Language: Let the children "write" their own recipes. Provide pencils, paper and a sample recipe book. Include magazines with food pictures that can be cut out and added to their recipes.

More science: Place a drop of dissolved yeast on a dish. Use a magnifying glass to look at it. ▪ Provide a variety of breads from different cultures. Let the children compare size, shape, color and texture of the breads. Break off a small piece of each, cover them and allow them to become moldy. Ask the children to predict which bread will mold first. Make a graph to chart their votes. Develop another chart to graph actual results. Compare charts. Talk about the fact that certain ingredients may hinder molding.

Related books

Bread, Bread, Bread by Ann Morris
Sitti's Secrets by Naomi S. Nye

Cheryl Collins, Hughson, CA

Let's Go Shopping Game

Science skills

This is a matching game in which children learn categorization and practice fine motor skills.

Materials

4" x 6" (10 cm x 15 cm) file cards
Pictures of foods, four of each
Laminating machine or contact paper, optional
3" x 5" (7.5 cm x 12.5 cm) file cards
Glue and scissors
Markers

What to do

To prepare the game:

1. Use the 4" x 6" cards to make four to six shopping lists and print shopping lists on each card.
2. On the 3" x 5" cards glue a picture of each food on the shopping list. This will be your draw pile of cards.

3. Laminate the cards if you wish.

To play the game:

1. Give each child a shopping list card.
2. Place the pictures of the food face down in a pile.
3. Have one child draw a card and look at his shopping list.
4. If the food is on the list he gets to keep it. If not, he places it back in the pile.
5. When a child finds all the foods on his list, he is finished shopping.

Janice Bodenstedt, Jackson, MI

A Tisket, a Tasket, What Is in My Basket? 3+

Science skills

Children learn to differentiate leaf shapes and numbers.

Materials

Empty laundry detergent box, cleaned and aired out
Clear tape
Classroom objects
Colored construction paper
Black marker

What to do

1. Beforehand, tape the construction paper over the box with clear tape.
2. With the marker, draw large and small question marks on the box.
3. Fill the box with things that pertain to that week's topic. For example, in fall cut various shapes of differently colored leaves from construction paper. Write numbers on the backs of the construction paper leaves from 1 to 10 in black marker, and laminate the leaves.
4. In class, ask the children to sit in a circle. The teacher can skip around the children, singing "A Tisket, a Tasket" and instead of singing "a brown and yellow basket," substitute the color of your basket.
5. Encourage each child to come up, reach into the box and pull out a colored and numbered leaf. They can tell you the color and the number on the leaf.
6. Change the contents of the box to go along with your current theme or the season.

Gloria C. Jones, California, MD

Whose Parent? 3+

Science skills

In this game, children use careful observation to match each child to his parent. Children in a class usually know each other's parents by sight, so they can all participate in finding the correct photo matches.

Materials

Photos of parents and children
Construction paper cut to give photos a ¼" (6 mm) border all the way around

Scissors and glue
Laminating machine or clear contact paper, optional

What to do

1. Take a photo of each child in your class, as well as one photo of each child's mother or father.
2. Glue photos onto construction paper and laminate, if possible.
3. The children match photos of children to their parents.

Jodi Sykes, Lake Worth, FL

3+

Color Musical Chairs

Science skills
Children practice auditory skills and vocabulary development.

Materials
Colored paper squares
Chairs
Tape
Music

What to do

1. Tape the different colored squares on the seats of the chairs, using a different color for each chair.
2. Play music as the children walk around the chairs. When the music stops, the children have to say what color paper is on their chair.

Related books
The Crayon Counting Book by Pam M. Ryan and Jerry Pallotta
Red, Blue, Yellow Shoe by Tana Hoban

Sandra Hutchins Lucas, Cox's Creek, KY

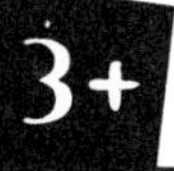

Ice Cube Mystery Game

Science skills
Children observe the qualities of water as it changes into ice.

Materials
Ice cube trays and water
Variety of items such as paper clips, vegetables, cotton balls, noodles

What to do

1. Let the children fill the trays with water.
2. Place a different item in each cubicle.
3. Place the trays in the freezer until they are frozen.
4. Talk about the changes the children think will take place. What will happen to the water? Will the items look different after the cubes melt?
5. Place the cubes onto a tray and see if the children can guess what item is in each cube.
6. Observe the changes as the cubes melt.

More to do

Art: Make colored ice cubes with food coloring and let the children paint with them on sturuy paper.

Cindy Winther, Oxford, MI

Follow My Directions

Science skills

Children practice large motor skills as well as social development

Materials

Large unbreakable objects, such as plastic cups, Styrofoam cups, empty cans, cartons, boxes
Blindfold

What to do

1. Set up an obstacle course with the objects. Ask one child to put on the blindfold. Note: some children may be uncomfortable wearing a blindfold.
2. The other children give directions for the blindfolded child to follow to avoid colliding with the obstacles.
3. Keep count of the number of obstacles the child knocks over. Change the course after each player.
4. Chart the results. Encourage the children to try the obstacle course again. Count how many obstacles they knock over this time. Compare the results of their first and second turns.

Monica Hay-Cook, Tucson, AZ

Life Cycle Bingo

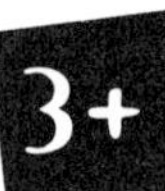

Science skills

Children make observations and are encouraged to ask questions about nature.

Materials

2 empty 1-quart (1 L) milk cartons
Glue
Paper and marker or drawing of the life cycle of a frog
Chips or markers of some sort
Contact paper

What to do

1. Cut the tops off of both milk cartons. The cut should be made as high up as the bottom is long so that all sides are the same length.
2. Fit the two bottoms together to form a cube. One open end should slide into the other.
3. Draw six stages of a frog's life. Each picture should be the same size as one side of your cube and should be in a row on one sheet of paper. Repeat this until you have five sets of pictures, illustrating egg, tadpole, tadpole with two legs, tadpole with four legs, tadpole with no tail, frog.
4. Cut one set apart and glue one picture to each side of your cube. You now have a die for your game. Cover your die and the four remaining strips of pictures with contact paper for durability.
5. Each child places a life cycle strip in front of her. Going around the table taking turns, the children roll the die and place a marker on the corresponding picture on their life cycle strip. The first child to cover all the pictures on her strip wins.

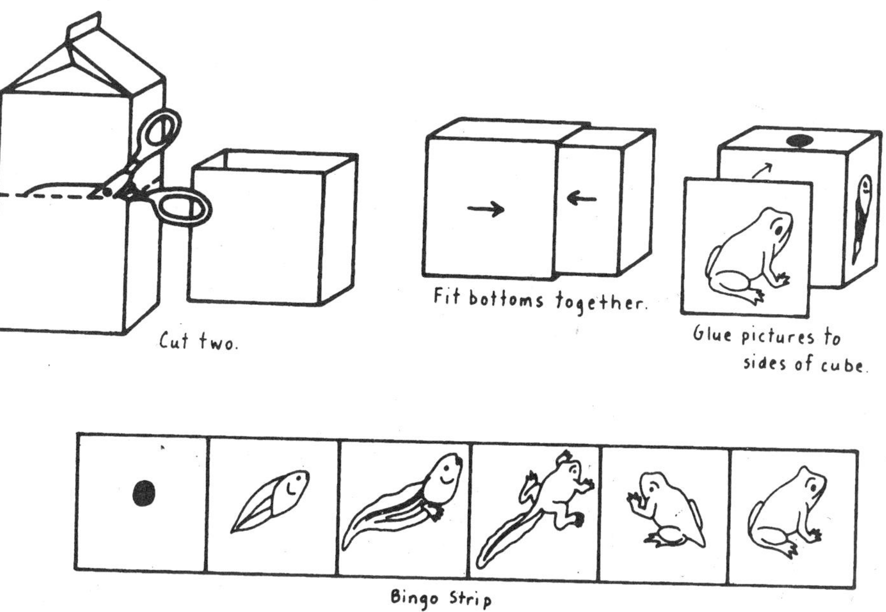

More to do

Math: You can write numbers by the pictures on the life cycle strip and use a real die. The children must then count the dots on the die and match them to the correct number. This game would be only for those children who have a good grasp of counting.

Ann Gudowski, Johnstown, PA

Moon Rock Hopscotch

3+

Science skills
Children practice large motor skills.

Materials
Chalk
Large sponge, painted gray for the moon rock

What to do
1. Draw a hopscotch game board on the pavement.
2. When it is time for each child to take a turn, give her the moon rock to throw. Use circles, crescents and semi-circles in the game board to represent the different phases of the moon.
3. When the moon rock lands on a particular shape, ask the child to identify the shape, as well as the numeral on it.

Related books
Goodnight, Moon by Margaret Wise Brown
The Moon Jumpers by Janice Udry
Papa, Please Get the Moon for Me by Eric Carle

Joyce Montag, Slippery Rock, PA

Name the Animal

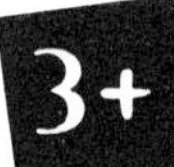

Science skills
A child must observe and draw conclusions in this game.

Materials
Scissors
Stickers and paints
Paper
Shoe box
Animal figures
Markers, crayons

What to do
1. Cut a hole in the top of the shoe box.
2. Ask the children to decorate the box with the stickers and paint.
3. Place all the figures in the box and ask each child to close her eyes and pick something out of the box.

4. Then describe to the child what the animal looks like, what sound it makes and where it lives. The child may guess which animal it is.
5. After each child has had a turn, ask her to draw a picture of the animal and where she thinks it lives.

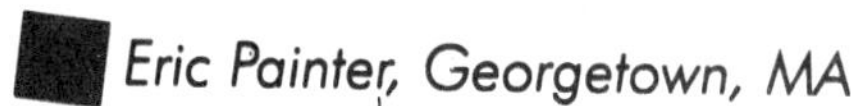
Eric Painter, Georgetown, MA

3+

Ten in a Plane

Science skills
Children practice large motor skills.

Materials
Chair or crate to stand on
Three hula hoops
Scarves

What to do
1. Place the chair or crate in the center of the room.
2. Position each of the three hoops approximately 1′ (30 cm) from the chair, place one hoop in front of the chair and one on each side of the chair.
3. Choose one child to be the pilot and ten children to jump from the chair or crate with parachutes. The rest will sing the song.
4. Have the children with "parachutes" form a line and jump in turn from the chair into one of the hoops. The child can use a scarf to simulate a parachute. Give each child a chance to jump.
5. Sing the following song to the tune of "There Were Ten in the Bed."
   There were ten in a plane and the pilot said,
   "Bail out, bail out!"
   They checked their chutes and one jumped out.

   Now there were nine in the plane and the pilot said . . . (Repeat until the last child jumps)

   Now there were none in the plane and the pilot said,
   "Good job, well done!"
   They gathered their chutes and all walked home.
   "Good bye, Good bye!"

Joyce Montag, Slippery Rock, PA

Walk-and-Balance

4+

Science skills

The children observe space and time relationships and cause and effect, as well as practice large motor skills.

Materials

Beanbag
2 paper cups
Cookie sheet
Tennis ball

What to do

1. Ask each child to perform the following balancing acts: walking with the beanbag balanced on her head; walking across the room holding a cup of water in each hand; and balancing the tennis ball on the cookie sheet.
2. After some practice, divide into teams and have relay races using the same balancing skills.

Monica Hay-Cook, Tucson, AZ

Occupation Musical Chairs

Science skills

Children practice vocabulary and language development, as well as large motor skills.

Materials

Chairs or rug square for each child
Occupation description cards, or simple pictures for younger children
Some form of music- or rhythm-making instrument

What to do

1. Make 10 to12 cards that briefly describe jobs people do in the community.
2. Gather children and chairs.
3. Explain that in this game of musical chairs, everyone will have a chair at the end, but on some chairs there will be a card that describes a job! If there's a card on a child's chair, you'll read about that job and the child can see if she can name the worker that does that job. For younger children you may only want to distribute a few cards, or you may wish to draw a simple picture instead of providing a written description.

4. Ask the children to march around the chairs in the same direction when you start the music, and then find a chair when the music stops.
5. Begin the music and circle the chairs with the children, placing cards on several chairs, then stop the music.
6. Help the children find chairs, then randomly read cards from those chairs that have them.
7. Encourage all the children to listen to other children's answers because that same card may be on their chair the next round!
8. Begin music and place cards out again as the children circle the chairs.

More to do

More games: Play an occupation guessing game like "Charades" in which the children act out the description on these cards and the other children try to name the worker. ▪ Play this musical chair game with any theme. You can place shapes, letters, numbers or animal pictures on the chairs.

Related book

What's It Like to Be a Police Officer by Michael Pellowski

Shirley R. Salach, Northwood, NH

4+

Feed Me

Science skills

In this game, the children practice memory and large motor skills.

Materials

Number strip (separate sheets taped together or a strip of paper, measuring about 1′ x 10′ or 30 cm x 3 m), marked off with numbers 1-10
9 blank index cards
One index card with a picture of a complete meal on it

What to do

1. Ask the children to name some things we can do to help keep our bodies healthy (e.g., eat healthy foods, sleep, exercise, wash hands before eating, clean our bodies, brush teeth, etc.).
2. Review the food groups briefly with the children. Can they give any examples of foods in these groups? Nutritionists help us to know how much of which foods we need to eat to stay as healthy as possible.
3. Show the children the blank cards and the one card with the meal picture on it and describe the game you will play. You may want to be the "hungry" person first to demonstrate.
4. Spread the sheet out with the index cards face down under each number. Mix up the cards so that nobody knows under which number the meal is hiding. The "hungry child" stands on "start" while the other children take turns telling her how to move (e.g., three steps forward,

one step backward). At each stop the "hungry child" looks at the index card to see if it is the one with the meal under it.

5. Other children continue to give commands to the "hungry child" until she has found the meal.
6. Each child takes a turn being the "hungry child."
7. Depending on the children's age level and how difficult it is for them to remember which numbers have already been checked, you can return the index cards to their face down position to encourage them to remember which ones were blank or collect them in your hand to eliminate repetition of blank cards.
8. Review by asking the children to name a few of the foods on the meal card, and which food group the foods belong to.

More to do

More science: Instead of including an entire healthy meal on the card, include foods from only one food group on several cards and challenge children to find the food for a specific group. ▪ Allow the "hungry child" to move according to the directions of friends, but then name the food group represented at every stop she makes. Encourage the children to make their own meal cards to play the game or take home.
Snack: Provide foods that were represented on the card.

Related book and recording

Bread and Jam for Frances by Russell Hoban
"Apples and Bananas" by Raffi

Shirley R. Salach, Northwood, NH

Flipping Flapjacks Game

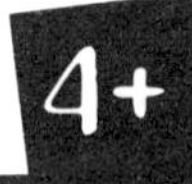

Science skills
Children practice fine motor skills and their eye-hand coordination.

Materials

Heavy cardboard
Markers, crayons
Markers
Scissors
Clear contact paper
Flapjack turners

What to do

To make the flapjacks

1. Cut 4" (10 cm) diameter circles from heavy cardboard to be the flapjacks. Draw and color a butter pat on one side of the flapjack and leave the other side blank. Cover each flapjack with clear contact paper. Cut 50 flapjacks—more for added fun!
2. Scatter the flapjacks all over the area to be used. Place some butter side up.

3. Divide your class into two teams. One team is the Butter Team, the other is the Plain Team.
4. Give each player a flapjack turner. (You can find these for pennies at thrift stores and yard sales.) The Butter Team wants all the flapjacks butter-side up, and the Plain Team wants all the flapjacks to be plain-side up.
5. Give the signal and everyone starts flipping the flapjacks with their turners. After a few minutes, give the signal to stop. You can then count how many of each are showing, and determine which team was working faster. Start the game again and see if the slower team can catch up.

More to do
Snack: Make flapjacks for snack time.

Related books
Cloudy With a Chance of Meatballs by Judi Barrett
Pancakes for Breakfast by Tomie dePaola

 *Valerie Chellew, Marshfield, WI*

4+

Who Is That Tapping on My Web?

Science skills
This game stimulates children's interest in and curiosity about nature.

Materials
Blindfold

What to do
1. During circle time, tell the children that a spider knows there is an insect in her web when she feels the movement of the insect.
2. Ask the children to form a circle and explain that you will select one child to be the spider and one child to be the insect. The spider will be blindfolded in the middle of the circle. After the spider is blindfolded, you will choose a child to be the insect by tapping on the child's head. You will then tell the child who is the insect to tap her feet so the spider will know where she is.
3. The child who is the spider must find the child who is tapping her feet.
4. When the spider catches the child playing the insect, the child playing the insect becomes the spider. This process continues until everyone has had a chance to be spider or insect.

More to do
Art: Provide the children with yarn, glue and paper and encourage them to make their own spider webs.

 *Linda Andrews, Sonora, CA*

Gardening

Carrot Tops

3+

Science skills
Children ask questions about nature and make observations.

Materials
Shallow dish or saucer
Water
Fresh carrots or even carrots that still have the greens attached

What to do
1. Talk about how the carrots grow from a little seed in such a way that the greens grow above the ground and the carrot grows underground.
2. Break off the greens from the top of the carrot, and slice about ½" (13 mm) from the top of the carrot.
3. Put the slice of carrot into the dish or saucer, flat side down, with enough water to reach half-way up the carrot slice.
4. Put the saucer in a sunny window, and continue replenishing the water.
5. After a few days you will see that the carrot greens are growing again.

More to do
Art: Use the discarded greens as paintbrushes, giving the children a new art medium.
More science: The carrot top activity can be a long-term project. Begin in the spring with carrot seeds, grow the seeds and transplant into a garden. In the summer and fall pull up the children's very own "home grown" veggies! ▪ Try using other vegetables or fruits to see if anything else will grow the same way (it is possible to get a pineapple top to "re-grow"). This past year we grew corn, carrots and pumpkins in our school garden, and the children were really thrilled to be able to eat something they'd grown from seed!
Snack: Eat the carrots raw for snack or at lunch time.

Diane Angus, Kittery Point, ME

Which One Will Grow First?

3+

Science skills
Children make observations and predictions

Materials

One clear plastic tumbler per child
Vegetable or flower seeds, two different packets
(for example, beans and carrots or sunflower and marigold)
Potting soil
Stickers
Chart paper
Water
Permanent marker

What to do

1. Discuss what seeds need in order to grow—sun, soil and water—and then show the children the two different types of seeds.
2. Write each child's name on a plastic tumbler.
3. Fill each tumbler three-quarters full with soil.
4. Ask the children to poke a hole in the soil and plant their two seeds.
5. Help each child water the seeds, and place the cups in a sunny location in the room.
6. Encourage the children to think about which of their seeds will sprout first. Glue the seed packets along the top of a large piece of chart paper. As each child states his prediction, let him put a sticker underneath the seed packet representing the prediction.
7. Discuss with the children the fact that our predictions don't always turn out to be correct. Check the seeds' progress daily and keep them moist.

More to do

More science: The children may prepare mini-science sketchbooks by stapling together four to five pieces of paper and leaving them in a basket, along with pencils and crayons. They can chart the progress of their seeds. Be prepared to take dictation and record the findings in their books.

 *Jodi Sykes, Lake Worth, FL*

How Seeds Grow

Science skills

Children make observations and are encouraged to ask questions about nature.

Materials

Many types of seeds: collect from fruit and outdoor plants and trees
Sponges
Grass seeds
Paper towels
Clear plastic cups
Plastic wrap
Tagboard
Plastic container
Soil
Bean seeds

Gardening

What to do

1. Examine and sort the various seeds you collected. Discuss their size, texture, color and where they were found.
2. Children can help make the seed chart. Use plastic wrap to enclose the seeds, label each on the chart and hang it in the classroom.
3. Wet a sponge and ask the children to drop grass seeds onto it. Now take the container and fill it with soil. Sprinkle on the grass seeds, add water and place the container in plastic wrap in the sun. Which grass grows first? Which is the stronger plant? Children, especially young ones, enjoy watching grass on the sponge. This can be done over and over again. Just pull off the grass, wash the sponge, and it is ready for the next batch.
4. Let the children feel the bean seeds. Plant a couple in soil, place in a sunny location and water as needed. Wet a paper towel and fold it to fit inside a plastic cup. Drop the seeds between the paper towel and the side of the cup and add some water to the bottom of the cup so that the paper towel can absorb it. Cover the top of the cup with plastic wrap to hold in moisture and put it inside a dark closet until the seeds start to sprout. Now put several seeds in a container and leave them alone. Children and teacher observe the seeds. Which seeds grew first? Which produced the strongest plant? Which didn't grow at all? Older children may chart the seeds' weekly growth.

More to do

Circle time: Children can pretend to be growing seeds. Ask them to curl up while the teacher tells a story about seeds planted in the ground. The sun shines and the rains come. Slowly the seeds start to grow and sprout. Soon they have roots. Then they begin to push through the ground. Soon they are plants. Children can also act out the story. Ask the children what type of seed they are pretending to be.

Snack: Children could make bean salad to eat with lunch or snack by mixing a 16 oz. (500 ml) can each of drained green beans, wax beans and kidney beans with an 8 oz. (250 ml) jar of Italian dressing.

Storytelling: You might tell the story *Jack and the Bean Stalk* during the bean experiment.

Garden in a Fish Bowl

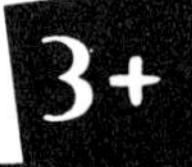

Science skills

This delightful long-term activity teaches observation skills and encourages questions about nature.

Materials

Fish bowl
Garden pea seeds
Water
Cotton balls
Clear plastic wrap
Chart paper and marker

What to do

1. Arrange a layer of cotton balls in the bowl.
2. Wet the cotton thoroughly; all water should be absorbed by the cotton.
3. Sprinkle the seeds over the cotton.
4. Cover the bowl with plastic wrap and place it near a window.
5. Watch each day. The seeds will sprout and eventually the vines will completely fill the bowl, creating a miniature jungle. When the peas sprout, you may wish to open the plastic covering and remove a seed to examine it.

More to do

Storytelling: Read or tell the story of *Jack and the Beanstalk.*

 *Mary Jo Shannon, Roanoke, VA*

3+

Growing a Garden

Science skills

As seeds grow, children learn observation skills and ask questions about nature.

Materials

Floor mat or plastic
Several 40 lb. (20 kg) bags of potting soil
Trowel, shovel, rake
Popsicle sticks
Tape
Camera
Wading pool
Corn and beans
Water cans
Index cards
Crayons
Ruler or tape measure

What to do

1. Place the floor mat underneath the wading pool.
2. Let the children place one to two inches (2.5 cm to 5 cm) of potting soil in the pool. Soil play can be fun before adding seeds!
3. Add the corn and beans to the soil, making sure they are covered, and water them. The seeds in the pool do not have to be outdoors to grow. The seeds should sprout within 2 to 8 days if the soil is kept moist but not saturated.
5. Make plant cards for the planted seeds by drawing on the index cards and placing them beside the seeds.
6. Watch the plants grow. As the seeds sprout, talk about the roots, stems, leaves, etc. that make up a plant, and how the seed opens to allow the plant to make a stalk.
7. Measure the plant's growth periodically.
8. Take photos of the planting process and the sprouting seeds to chart the growth.
9. If you have an outside garden, you can grow the plants from early spring through early fall.

Gardening

10. Add a scarecrow to the garden, if desired, using paper or small clothing stuffed with straw. Stand the scarecrow in the garden with a yardstick attached to its back.

More to do

Language: Make a storybook of the plant growth process. Allow the children to draw pictures of the step-by-step process each day. Notice how the drawings reflect what the children have experienced. This can be a cooperative storybook or each child may make one. Create titles and make sure to include any and all explanations of the pictures drawn.

More science: Plant seeds both inside and outside to compare the growth of the same items in different environments. Notice and discuss similarities and differences

Sand and water table: Have mud play or soil play at the water table. Add shovels, gardening tools, gardening gloves, seeds (grass or birdseed).

Related books

The Carrot Seed by Ruth Krauss
Growing Vegetable Soup by Lois Ehlert
The Tiny Seed by Eric Carle

Tina R. Woehler, Flower Mound, TX

Planting

3+

Science skills

Children have an opportunity for observation and fine motor play.

Materials

Rich, black soil
Tub
Water
Small trowels and hand rakes
Grass seed

What to do

1. For a new and different sensory experience, fill your water play tub with rich, black soil. Let the children explore the soil with their hands first; later you can add small trowels and rakes.
2. Later in the week, let the children add small amounts of water to half the tub. Talk about the differences between the feel and look of the wet and dry soil.
3. For a grand finale, let the children add grass seed to the tub and place it in front of a window. Encourage the children to water their grass daily and watch closely!

More to do

Math: Keep a growth chart of the grass growing in the water tub. Measure the growth each day and mark the chart.

More science: Let each child fill a plastic cup with soil and plant grass seed. Use round stickers to let each child create a face for his cup. As the seeds grow, the children can give their new "friend" a haircut.

Cindy Winther, Oxford, MI

3+ Seed Match-Up

Science skills
Children make observations and classify seeds

Materials

A variety of seed packages
Glue
Index cards

What to do

1. Remove the seeds from one of the packages and glue a few seeds onto an index card.
2. Glue the front cover of the seed package to another index card.
3. Repeat for each type of seed and seed package to make matching pairs. Allow the children to examine the seeds closely, and show the children the pictures on the packets. Talk about how each seed grows into the plant pictured on the packet.
4. After the cards dry, mix up the pairs and play matching games.

Laura Claire-Gremett, San Jose, CA

3+ Spring

Science skills
Children observe and make predictions and inferences.

Materials

Resealable plastic bags
Soil
Grass seed
Water

What to do

1. Fill two resealable plastic bags with a generous amount of soil.
2. Add a handful of grass seed and some water so the soil is moist but not soaked.

3. Close the bags and shake them so the soil and seeds mix.
4. Hang one bag in a window with southern exposure.
5. Hang the other bag in a window with northern exposure.
6. Both airtight bags will produce water droplets, and the continued "rain" will keep the soil wet.
7. Watch the bags to see which bag sprouts the seeds first. Encourage the children to try to explain why the seeds emerge first in the bag with southern exposure.

Ingelore Mix, Massapequa, NY

Sprout Garden

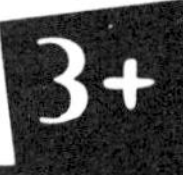

Science skills

Children observe seeds and sprouts and are encouraged to ask questions about nature.

Materials

Ice cube tray(s)
Water
Assortment of beans
Permanent marker

What to do

1. Encourage families to send in a bean.
2. Mark one child's name per cell on the ice tray on the inside of the cell so the name is visible.
3. Let each child place his bean in the cell.
4. When the tray is full, move it to a place in the classroom that receives light.
5. Ask the children to fill their bean cells with water.
6. Observe the growth and perhaps have a race to see which beans sprout fastest.
7. Keep the cells full of water 24 hours a day so they don't dry up. You may have to fill the cells every day as the beans grow.
8. Plant the sprouts in a garden.

Dani Rosensteel, Payson, AZ

Little Gardeners

Science skills

Children observe growing plants over many months and are encouraged to ask questions about nature.

Gardening

Materials

A small clear plastic cup for each child
Potting soil
Flower or vegetable seeds
Index cards
Poster board and markers
Magnifying glasses
Water, air and sunshine

What to do

1. Show the children how to fill their plastic cups about half full with potting soil.
2. Ask the children each to choose two or three seeds to plant in their cups. Give each child a magnifying glass so they may examine their seeds closely. Encourage them to notice details about the seeds and how they are the same or different. Let them draw pictures of their seeds on an index card. Keep the cards for later use. Post one child's representational drawing in the science area near your the cups. Print a large number 1 on another index card and post it next to the drawing.
3. Plant the seeds in the cups, and water them just enough to thoroughly wet the soil. Remind the children not to use too much water or their seeds will not sprout. Ask the children to draw a picture of the seeds in the cup. Keep these pictures for later use and post one under the seed picture in your science area, and put a large number 2 next to it.
4. Discuss how to care for the seeds. What do they need in order to sprout and grow properly? Make a poster about caring for your plants.
5. Care for the seeds until they sprout. Examine the new sprouts closely with a magnifying glass. Be sure to point out the developing root system, which may be visible through the clear plastic. Ask the children what they think has happened to the seed. Discuss the changes the seeds went through. If you have a Peabody Picture set, show the set that depicts the development of a seed. Explain how the water, sun and air combined to give the seed the right conditions to sprout into a plant. Encourage the children to draw a picture of their newly sprouted seedlings and put this with their other pictures. Post one drawing in the science area under the previous picture and a large number 3 next to it.
6. The children can now begin to use their index cards to order the stages of a plant's life cycle. Have them take out their cards and mix them up. Discuss how the plant looked when you first got it as a seed, and let them find their picture of the seed. Next discuss how you put the seed in the potting soil and gave it water, air and sunshine. The children can place their picture of the seed in the cup next to the first picture. Discuss what their plant looked like after it had sprouted, and let them place the drawing of the sprouted plant next to the second picture.
7. Care for the plants until they mature. When they have fully matured, the children can examine them closely again, using the magnifying glass if they wish. Encourage them to notice and describe how the plant has changed. Talk about ways in which the plant looks the same (it is still green, it still has leaves) and how it is different (it is taller, it has more leaves, it might have a flower or be producing some type of vegetable). The children can draw a picture of their mature plants. Add it to the previous drawings. Post one drawing in the science area under the previous ones with a large number 4 next to it.
8. Ask the children to use their cards again to correctly order the stages of a plant's development. Help them remember the various stages by asking open-ended questions such as, "What did your plant look like at first?" "What did you give the seed to help it sprout?" and "How did the seed change after you planted it?" Review the pictures posted in the science area and discuss each stage of the plant's development again.

Gardening

9. The children may take home their sprouted plants, or you may want to create a class garden (see More to do, below).

More to do

More science: You can create a garden in the playground area either by digging up a small portion of ground or by using containers. Help the children carefully transplant their plants from the cups to the garden. They can make markers with their names on them to help them identify their own plants (remember to laminate the markers since they will be out in the weather). You could add a Garden Helper position to your classroom Helper Chart and assign one child per week to water the garden. ▪ Discuss how the fruits and vegetables grown in gardens all over the world help us to live and be healthy and strong. Are there other creatures that benefit from a garden? Find out! Dig into your garden, once it is well established, and collect the dirt in a small container. Use your microscope or magnifiers to look for living things. What did you find there? Bugs and slugs and crawly things? Make a list of the bugs you discover and then return them to the garden. ▪ Keep a weekly journal about the development of the children's plants. Each week the children can draw a picture of their plants and dictate a sentence describing the changes noted that week. Create a cover, bind the pictures together into a book and you have a Little Gardener's Journal!

Original song

Sing to the tune of "Mary Had a Little Lamb."

Johnny had a little seed, little seed, little seed.
Johnny had a little seed, he put it in some soil.
He gave the seed sun, air and water; sun, air and water; sun, air and water.
He gave the seed sun, air and water,
And his seed did sprout.
Johnny had a little seed, little seed, little seed.
Johnny had a little seed but now he has a flower (or insert the name of the child's plant here).

Related books

City Green by DyAnne DiSalvo-Ryan
Dancers in the Garden by Joanne Ryder
From Seed to Plant by Gail Gibbons
A Handful of Seeds by Monica Hughes
How Plants Grow by Ron Wilson
Nana's Garden by Sophy Williams
Over Under in the Garden: A Botanical Alphabet by Pat Schories
The Plant Cycle by Nina Morgan
Seeds by George Shannon
The Tiny Seed by Eric Carle

Virginia Jean Herrod, Columbia, SC

3+

Plant a Bulb

Science skills
The children observe as bulbs grow and flower.

Materials

Flower pots, clay or plastic, one for each child
Small jars of acrylic paint
Small paintbrushes (watercolor brushes are fine)
Tulip bulbs, one for each child, plus two extras
Potting soil
Acrylic sealant, if pots are clay, available at art or paint stores
Permanent marker
Trowels or large spoons
Gardening gloves, optional

What to do

1. If you are using clay flowerpots, spray them with the sealant the day before doing this project.
2. In small groups, let the children paint their flowerpots with the acrylic paint. Use the permanent markers to write their names on the pots. Acrylic paint is water soluble so the brushes can be cleaned with water. Allow the pots to dry overnight.
3. Show the children pictures of flowering bulbs or read them a related book.
4. Give each child a bulb. Show the children where the roots come out of the bulb and out of which end the flower will grow.
5. In small groups, let each child plant his bulb in his flowerpot, using the potting soil and trowels or spoons.
6. Plant the two extra bulbs in separate pots.
7. Let the children water their bulbs and put them in a sunny place in your classroom.
8. Ask the children what the bulbs need to grow. Tell them you are going to do an experiment with one of the bulbs by putting it in a closet to see what will happen. Encourage the children to hypothesize what will happen to the bulb in the closet.
9. Mark on your class calendar the day that you planted the bulbs and each day count how many days it has been since.
10. Ask the children to water their bulbs regularly, once a week is probably fine.
11. When the bulbs begin to sprout, note which bulbs are sprouting. Are they all? Why or why not?
12. Compare the children's bulbs with the bulb in the closet.
13. Once they begin to sprout, graph each day how far the bulbs grow.
14. Just before the bulbs flower, send them home with the children.

Barbara Saul, Eureka, CA

Gardening

My Garden Pocket

4+

Science skills

Children practice observation and fine motor skills.

Materials

Books about gardening
Paper plates
Assorted colors of textured papers
Hole punch
Magazine clippings of flowers, insects, gardening tools and people gardening
Variety of gardening tools
Scissors
Glue
Paper curling ribbon, one yard per child
Unwrapped crayons
Craft sticks, ½" (13 mm) wide, 3 per child

What to do

1. Invite children to look at gardening books and to handle a variety of gardening tools. The tools could include a shovel, rake and digging fork.
2. Discuss the process of planting seeds and welcome children's comments about what they may already know about gardening.
3. To make the paper garden pockets, give each child one whole paper plate and one paper plate that has been cut in half.
4. Children may select several unwrapped crayons. Encourage them to illustrate the sky on the whole paper plate and to rub shades of soil and grass on their half paper plates.
5. Children place the two plates together and, using a hole punch, punch eight holes around the paper plates (or teachers may want to have holes already pre-punched).
6. Use the curling ribbon and lace through the two paper plates. Tie the two ribbons together.
7. Children may design their own paper flowers from a variety of textured papers or use the illustrated clippings from the magazines. The flowers and/or clippings can be affixed to craft

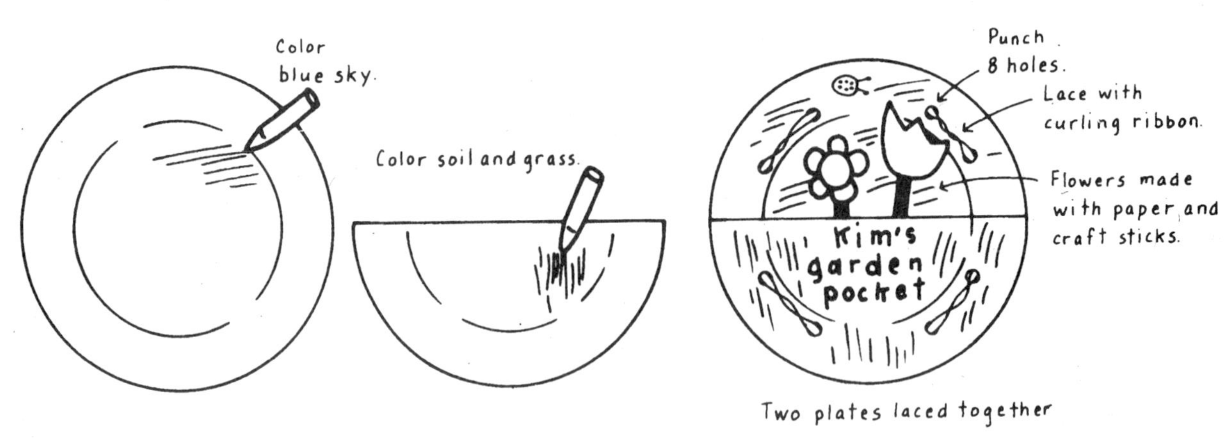

Two plates laced together

sticks using tape or glue. The children may color the craft sticks to represent the stems of plants. Children may want to embellish their stems with textured leaves (rubbings from leaves) and maybe add a friendly ladybug.

8. Organize and plant paper flowers between the two paper plates. Create garden stories, and please touch the flowers!

More to do

Math: Make a graphing chart with the following column headings: flowers, bugs, leaves. Count the flowers, bugs and leaves in each garden pocket and mark the appropriate column with the correct number of each item. How many flowers, bugs, leaves can you count?

Storytelling: Invite children to create a story garland. Document children's stories onto cut-out flower shapes and let the children use tape, glue, string or yarn to connect the flowers together. Display the garland across the classroom window.

Related books and recording

Creepy Crawlies by Cathy Kilpatrick
Planting a Rainbow by Lois Ehlert.
Linnea's Windowsill Garden by Christina Bjork
"Rain" words and music by Miss Jackie

Jill Loveless, Lee's Summit, MO

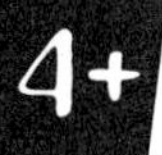

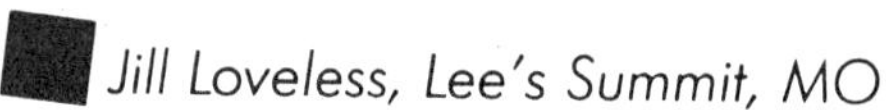

Butterfly Garden

Science skills

In this delightful outdoor activity, children use their creativity and practice social development.

Materials

Soil
Plastic cups
Sunny windowsill
Several of the following seeds: bee balm, foxglove, heliotrope, lilac, lupine, morning glory, nasturtium, pansy, Queen Anne's Lace, snapdragon, sunflower, sweet William, viburnum, yarrow

What to do

1. Discuss butterflies and describe the types of flowers that attract them. Tell the children that butterflies need a natural, chemical-free environment with a little shelter. A commercial butterfly house or a trellis with vines, such as morning glory, may be a shelter for a butterfly.
2. Decide on a place for your butterfly garden. It can be an established garden site, a window box or hanging planters. Let the children help select the place and design the garden, choosing plants in different colors, scents and heights. Include a bench or other seating if possible

and bricks or other absorbent rocks. The rock or brick can be doused with sugar water occasionally to give the butterflies an extra treat.

3. Plant the seeds in plastic cups. Keep them on a sunny windowsill and keep the soil moist. When the seedlings are about 2" (5 cm) tall, transplant them to your garden or pots and remember to water them. Now relax, and wait for the butterflies to come!

More to do

Art: Cut up clean plastic milk cartons into butterfly shapes and tape them to dowels. Let the children decorate the butterflies and use them as plant markers.
Math: Measure seedlings or count seeds.

Related books

Butterfly Story by Anca Hariton
Charlie the Caterpillar by Dom DeLuise
My Father's Hands by Joanne Ryder
Planting a Rainbow by Lois Ehlert
The Very Hungry Caterpillar by Eric Carle

Robin Works Davis, Keller TX

Seed Race

Science skills

This activity helps children with observation skills, stimulates interest in nature and allows them to practice number skills.

Materials

Assorted seeds in packets
Paper towels
Chart paper
Peanut butter jars, empty and washed
Water
Colored crayons or pencils

What to do

1. Ask the children to bring in seed packets.
2. Open and compare the many shapes and sizes of the seeds, keeping track of which seed belongs with which packet.
3. Line the jars with paper towels, and wet the towels thoroughly.
4. Push two seeds of each type between the towel and the jar so they can be seen through the glass and stay in contact with the wet paper.
5. Make a chart with a row of 14 blocks for each seed type. Label each row with the name of the seed and a picture of the plant and seed.
6. Color in a block each day until a seed sprouts. When it sprouts, stop coloring blocks in that row. Which seed sprouted first? Last? Read the chart.

More to do

Games: Create seed puzzles by gluing the picture from a seed packet on one end of a 4″ x 6″ (10 cm x 15 cm) piece of poster board. On the other end glue the seeds. Cut each card in half with a distinct shape pattern to create a set of puzzles. Match up the seeds with their plants.

Snack: Eat a seed snack. Try sunflower seeds, sesame seed and poppy seed crackers. ▪ Bake poppy seed muffins.

Related poem

Say the following poem and perform the actions:

Here is the seed, down in the ground, waiting here to grow (curl up in a ball on the floor)
First comes the rain (reach arms up and wiggle fingers down to floor)
Then comes the sun (reach arms up with hands in a circle)
Then it can grow and grow. (slowly rise from the floor and spread out arms)

 *Sandra Gratias, Perkasie, PA*

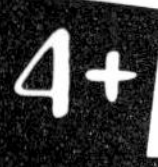

Sprouts and Roots

Science skills

Through observation, children are encouraged to ask questions about nature.

Materials

A variety of seeds
Empty glass jar
Sponge
Cups
Potting soil
Shovels
A sunny window

What to do

1. Dampen the sponge and place it in the bottom of the glass jar.
2. Place the seeds between the glass and the sponge.
3. Plant leftover seeds in cups filled with potting soil, one for each child. Water them and place them in a sunny spot.

4. Children can observe and compare the sprouts in the soil and the roots in the glass jar.
5. Keep both soil and sponge moist.

More to do

Games: What seed is this? Fold a piece of 18" x 24" (45 cm x 60 cm) poster board in half lengthwise. Cut the top half into sections, and glue seeds on top. Glue the corresponding seed packet to the bottom half.

Related books

The Carrot Seed by Ruth Kraus
Pumpkin Pumpkin by Jeanne Titherington

Teresa J. Nos, Baltimore, MD

Fun With Flowers

4+

Science skills

Children are encouraged to make observations and ask questions about nature.

Materials

Fresh flowers
Borax
Shallow box with lid
Glass or plastic vases
Instant oats

What to do

1. Discuss with the children the fact that many people make floral arrangements with fresh flowers. A florist would be a good guest, or make a trip to a flower shop.
2. Ask the children to help you arrange fresh flowers in one of the plastic containers. While you are arranging the flowers, talk about the different shapes and colors. Encourage the children to discuss different aspects of the arrangement they like and why they have chosen to arrange the flowers in a particular way.
3. Questions to spark discussion with the children while they are arranging:
   Are the flowers various shapes? What kinds of shapes do you see? Are the stems of some of the flowers too long or too short? Would you like help cutting some of the stems so they fit better into the vases? What color flowers are you placing together?
4. You can also dry fresh flowers at room temperature and use them for dried arrangements at other times of the year. If the children's age and abilities permit, have them mix together 1 cup (250 ml) borax and 2 cups (500 ml) oatmeal in a bowl. Pour half of the mixture into a shallow box, making a thin layer.
5. Place an assortment of flowers face down on the mixture in the box.
6. Help the children pour the remaining mixture over the flowers and cover with a lid.

7. Open the box in three to four weeks and gently shake the mixture off the flowers. They are ready to use for arrangements.

More to do

Art: Show the children pictures of floral paintings done by famous artists. Talk with them about the colors, flowers and brush stokes. Children may want to try to paint a picture of the flowers they arranged in the vases. Display the pictures and give each child a chance to tell about his or her artwork. ▪ Children can look through seed catalogs and observe many different varieties of flowers. They can cut out flower pictures from catalogs and glue them on white paper for individual or group collages. ▪ Children can design a garden of beautiful flowers! Encourage them to find flowers in the seed catalog and to color them into their paper garden. Talk about what flowers grow in your locations, but don't limit them to those flowers as they design their gardens.

More science: Talk with children about how flowers reseed themselves. Many children will have blown on a dandelion and scattered the seeds. Some may even have pulled seeds off flowers such as sunflowers. Explain that some flowers reseed themselves, and others we have to plant each year. Tell the children about some of the many ways flower seeds are transported. Some, like dandelion seeds, are very light and have parts that the wind will catch and carry away. Other seeds have little hooks that will stick on the fur of a passing animal, or a person's clothes, allowing the animal or person to carry them away.

Susan Thompson, Casper, WY

5+

Spring in Winter

Science skills

Children observe beautiful flowers growing in mid-winter and record and chart the flowers' growth.

Materials

Bulbs for paper whites, one for each child
Stones or marbles
Ruler, Unifix blocks or Cuisinaire rods
Clear plastic cups
Water
Chart with each child's name labeled

What to do

1. Place a scoop of stones or marbles in each cup, and place a bulb on top of the stones.
2. Add water to cover the stones and the bottom of the bulb, and place the cup in a sunny location where it will not be disturbed.
3. After the bulbs have sprouted, ask the children to measure their growth and record the results on the chart.

More to do

Art: Cut flower shapes out of sponges. Let the children paint a bouquet with flower prints.

More science: Plant bulbs outdoors in the fall, so in spring the children can find the sprouts.

Teresa J. Nos, Baltimore, MD

3+

Mud House

Science skills
The children observe the changes in mud "clay" as it hardens.

Materials

Mixing bowl
Soil
Water
Cookie sheet
Toothpicks
Large spoon
Grass
Loaf pan
Paint shirts
Oven

What to do

1. Mix together the soil, grass and water in the bowl. Add more water, grass or soil as needed until it is the consistency of clay.
2. Let the children touch, squeeze and mold the mixture for a few minutes and talk about how it feels.
3. Using the loaf pan as a mold, place enough of the mixture into the pan to mold it into the shape of a brick or rectangle.
4. Take it out of the loaf pan and place it on the cookie sheet. If desired, use toothpicks to draw windows, doors or even tiny brick shapes.
5. Bake in the oven on low for several hours, or bake in the sun for several days. Emphasize how mud is used to construct buildings.
6. Optionally, children could help construct a little diorama for their mud house.

More to do

More science: Add more grass and some twigs and use the mixture to build nests, beaver dams or caves.

Outdoors: Go for a walk and look for different types of homes.

Susan Rinas, Parma, OH

3+

Trio of Animal Habitats

Science skills
Children practice observation and sorting skills.

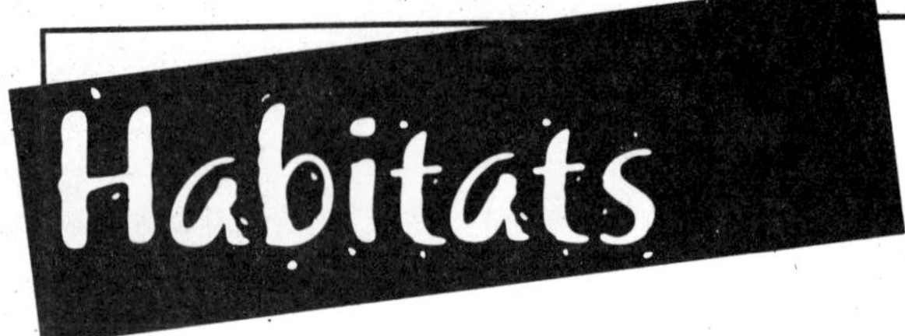

Habitats

Materials

Chart paper and marker
Small pictures of animals from various habitats: land, sea or air
A tray divided into three equal sections or a shoe box with taped-in cardboard dividers

What to do

1. Label each area in the bottom of the tray so that items can be sorted by land, air and sea (blue for water, brown/green for land, and light blue with cut-out of cloud or sun for air).
2. In a group, ask the children to think of animals that live in each area of the environment. Make a graph with a column for each habitat.
3. Take out the activity. Be sure to show the children how they are to sort, and what each picture stands for on the bottom of the tray.
4. You may also explain to the children the care to be taken with the items, how many children can use the activity at one time and how to put the activity away.

Melissa Browning, Milwaukee, WI

Indoor Pond

4+

Science skills

Over several weeks, children make and record observations and are encouraged to ask questions about nature.

Materials

Plastic wading pool
Water buckets
Goldfish
Aquarium filter
Crayons
Water
Tadpoles
Water plants
Drawing paper
Camera, optional

Note: You might want to send a note home with your children asking parents to donate these items.

What to do

1. Explain to the children that you are going to create an indoor habitat so you can watch living things grow right in the classroom. A habitat is a place where a plant or animal lives in nature. The habitat that you are going to create is a pond.
2. Ask the children to discuss what they already know about a pond and make a list of their thoughts on the chalkboard. Then ask them what they would like to learn about a pond and make a second list on the chalkboard.
3. Place the wading pool in a well-lit area of the room. Ask the children to help fill the pool about half full of water. Make sure to take the chlorine out of the water by letting the water "stand" overnight.

4. Next, allow the children to place the water plants throughout the pool. Also, place the aquarium filter in the center of the pond, making sure that you discuss water and electrical safety issues at this time.
5. The following day, let the children place several goldfish in the pond, as well as some tadpoles. You can purchase both of these at your local pet store if they have not already been donated. Discuss feeding rules and pond maintenance at this time. You might want to assign daily jobs.
6. Now ask the children to draw what they see in the pond. You might also want to take pictures of the pond, as this will help the children remember what the pond looked like when you first started this experiment. Point out the size of the fish, as well as the development of the tadpoles. This would be a good time to read several books on the life cycle of the frog.
7. Each week, ask the children to do another drawing and compare it to the ones they did earlier. If you started taking pictures, continue taking them throughout the duration of this experiment. Encourage the group to discuss the differences in the indoor pond over time, by asking such questions as, "Have the fish gotten larger? Did the plants grow? Is there algae in the pond? What is happening to the tadpoles?"
8. The children can keep track of the growth in the pond either with a large bulletin board where they can display their weekly drawings, or by placing the drawings in their individual portfolios.
9. After several weeks the children should understand what happens in a pond habitat, and you can dismantle the project. Many of the children may want to take home the inhabitants of the pond, for which you may want to consider a lottery system.

More to do

Art: Make watercolor paintings of the pond habitat.

Language: Let the children help write a song called "Old MacDonald Had a Pond" and also write about their favorite thing that lives in the pond.

Math: Help the children graph the growth of the inhabitants of the pond.

Related books

All About Ponds by Jane Rockwell
Amazing Frogs & Toads by Barry Clarke
Aquarium Take-Along Book by Sheldon Gerstenfeld
Chorus of Frogs by Joni Phelps Hunt
Fascinating World of Frogs and Toads by Maria Angels Julivert
Fish by Margaret Lane
Frogs, Toads, Lizards and Salamanders by Nancy Winslow Parker
In the Pond by Ermanno Cristini and Luigi Puricelli
In the Small, Small Pond by Denise Fleming
Life in the Pond by Eileen Curran
Lily Pad Pond by Bianca Lavies
From Tadpole To Frog by Wendy Pfeffer

Michael Krestar, White Oak, PA

This Is the House That We Built

4+

Science skills

Children are excited to watch a building under construction, and they document their observations.

Materials

Coloring items such as crayons, markers, paints
Hole punch
Ribbon, any kind
Plain white paper
Black marker

What to do

This is a great project if your school happens to be near the site of a new construction or a building undergoing a renovation or addition. In making your observations, supervise the children closely and keep them well away from the actual construction.

1. Discuss the different materials that homes are made of with the children.
2. Take children to visit a building site, if possible.
3. Discuss what they see and what they will see as days go by: machines, people at work, the building growing, etc.
4. Back at school, give the children paper and let them color a cover page for a book which they will make over the course of time it takes the workers to build the house.
5. If children can write, let them write the title; if not, let them dictate a title.
6. Take children back to the building site for visits. Have them add pages to illustrate the foundation, walls, ceiling, chimney, and so on. They can think of and dictate captions for each page. Take pictures of the house or building as it is going up to accompany the children's books.
7. As the building nears completion, discuss what the children think they might find inside. With this discussion, you could make pictures of the different rooms, furniture, perhaps even a staircase leading up or down, the fireplace, etc. They could even draw pictures of a family, perhaps pets, or other people who may use the new building.
8. If you know when moving day is, watch some of the things being moved inside. The children may want to add more pages to their books.
9. When the house is finished, the children's books should be near completion. Perhaps a landscaping picture could be the last page.
10. Collect the children's books and check for page sequence.
11. Punch holes to make the binder.
12. Lace the ribbon through the holes and tie with a bow.
13. Add the date and each child's name.

More to do

Blocks: Use wooden blocks, plastic interlocking blocks, gingerbread or milk cartons to build houses.

Dramatic play: Play house to help the children relate to what happens inside each of their homes. Find a large appliance box and let the children decorate it as a house.
Games: Play association games, for example, the children can name what goes with a house, such as a lawn, chimney, roof.
More science: To enhance listening skills, have a tape of construction sounds and let the children try to name the sounds.

Related books
A Home by Nola Langner Malone
Dinosaurs Travel: A Guide for Families on the Go by Laura Krasny Brown and Marc Brown
Mike Mulligan and His Steam Shovel by Virginia Lee Burton

Cindy Maloof, South Easton, MA

Animal Habitat Run

Science skills
Children are asked to make observations, inferences and predictions and use large motor skills.

Materials
Masking tape
Large pictures of land, water and sky
Room to run
Animal pictures

What to do
1. Using masking tape, divide the area to be used into three sections.
2. Place a picture of land, water or sky in each section by hanging them on a wall or mounting them on a box to make them more visible.
3. Tell the children that different animals live in different habitats: some in the water, some on land and some in the air. Some animals move about in more than one. For example, turtles usually live in the water, but also move on land. Show some animal pictures and ask the children to tell you in which habitat each can be found.
4. Explain that you are going to continue this game in the gym (or outside). Show the defined areas of habitats. You will then name an animal, or continue to show pictures, and the children will run to the habitat area in which they think each animal lives.
5. Try calling out two or more land animals in a row so the children will not automatically move to another area.
6. Children can imitate the movements of the animals, too.

More to do
Field trip: Take a walk to a forest or pond and look for animals living in those habitats.
More science: Provide small twigs and branch sections for the children to build animal homes.

Habitats

- Turn your room into a rain forest. Ask your children to make several lengths of paper chains out of green and brown construction paper. Hang these from the ceiling. Hide stuffed animals, like monkeys and birds, in silk trees that you have placed around the room. Have an environmental cassette playing in the background, such as thunderstorms and showers or a Brazilian rain forest. Try running a humidifier on high to simulate the humidity. ▪ Display forest animal foods such as acorns and other nuts, seeds and berries in the classroom.

Related books

The Deer in the Wood by Laura Ingalls Wilder
In the Snow: Who's Been Here? by Lindsay Barrett George
In the Woods: Who's Been Here? by Lindsay Barrett George
It's the Bear! by Jez Alborough
Night Tree by Eve Bunting

Valerie Chellew, Marshfield, WI

Slug and Salamander Safari

Science skills

This outdoor adventure encourages children to explore, observe and ask questions about nature.

Materials

Cotton swabs or ice cream sticks
Small jars or cages
Dark-colored construction paper

What to do

1. Obtain permission for children to go on a walk. Find a woodsy area where there are fallen branches and rocks.
2. Lift the rocks and branches to reveal slugs, bugs and salamanders.
3. Gently lift the creatures with fingers, sticks or cotton swabs, and place them into the jars. Encourage the children to observe them.
4. Place a slug on the dark paper to show how it leaves a trail.
5. Talk about the differences among the animals found in the same habitat and how they are alike.
6. Always return the animals to their habitats.

More to do

Art: Gather nature items while on a walk and make a habitat collage.
Games: Make a game in which the child matches the animal to its habitat: the bunny with its hold; the bird with its nest; the fish with water; the spider with its web; and people with their houses.

Related book
The Mixed-Up Chameleon by Eric Carle

Teresa J. Nos, Baltimore, MD

5+

Hermit Crab Home

Science skills
As architects of crab houses, children practice observation and fine motor skills and ask questions about nature.

Materials
A House for Hermit Crab by Eric Carle
Drawing paper
Crayons

What to do
1. Read the book *A House for Hermit Crab.*
2. Ask the children to draw and color a house for their hermit crab and then draw a hermit crab beside it.
3. Ask the children to dictate a story telling why their house would be a cozy or uncomfortable home for a hermit crab. The stories may be made into a class book.

More to do
Games: Play crab soccer or have hermit crab relays.
Math: Graph the hermit crab homes based on their coziness or suitability for a hermit crab.
More science: Let the children bring something from home that would make a good house for a hermit crab.

Stephanie Person, Kingsburg, CA

I Am Growing

3+

Science skills
This project stimulates the children's curiosity about nature and encourages fine motor development.

Materials
Construction paper

What to do

1. Send a piece of construction paper home with each child, along with a request that a parent or guardian trace his or her own hand on the paper and return it to school.
2. Help the child cut out the parent's hand.
3. Ask the child to place her hand inside the adult hand and trace around the child's hand.
4. Discuss how the adult hand and the child hand are alike and different. Discuss how much the child has grown since she was a baby and how much more growing she will do on the way to adulthood.

More to do
More science: For the children who have a baby brother or sister at home, send the hand drawing home again and ask the parent to trace the baby's hand inside the child's hand for further size comparison.
Snack: Serve each child a snack-size candy bar and a piece of fruit. Explain that some foods are "growing foods" because they provide nutrients the body needs to grow. Other foods, like candy bars, are "fun foods" but must be eaten in moderation because they do not help us grow and stay healthy.

Related book
Here Are My Hands by Bill Martin, Jr. and John Archambault

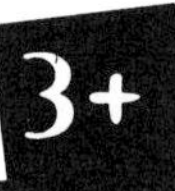

Ann Flagg, Clarion, PA

Happy Tooth, Sad Tooth

3+

Science skills
Tooth health provides a context for practicing classification skills.

Materials

Magazine pictures of nourishing food and junk food
Paper bag or box
2 posters, one with a happy tooth, one with sad tooth
Tape

What to do

1. Talk about the foods that are good for our teeth, and about the foods that have too much sugar and cause our teeth to decay. Put the magazine pictures in the bag or box.
2. Let each child draw a picture out of the bag and tape it to the correct tooth poster, the junk food on the sad tooth and the nourishing food on the happy tooth.

More to do

Snack: Extend your happy-sad tooth discussion to the lunch table. Prepare a happy-tooth nourishing snack to eat. Ask the children to help you prepare a list of happy-tooth snacks they like and distribute the lists to their parents. Ask the children to brush their teeth after lunch.

Related book

Going to the Dentist by Fred Rogers

Shirley Story, Lenoir, NC

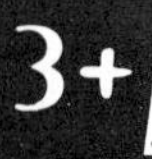

3+

Keeping Our Teeth Clean

Science skills

Children learn tooth hygiene and fine motor skills.

Materials

One sheet of 12″ x 18″ (30 cm x 45 cm) colored construction paper per child
One plain white paper towel for each child
Scissors
Glue

What to do

1. Talk about how we keep our teeth clean and healthy. Ask the children whether they brush at least two to three times a day.
2. Tell the children that they are going to make a giant toothbrush to help remind them to brush every day.
3. Fold each sheet of paper in half lengthwise. Mark off a 3″ x 8″ (7.5 cm x 20 cm) area on the lower corner of the paper, away from the fold, and ask the children to cut off the marked area.
4. Open the "toothbrush" and ask the children to lay the paper towel inside, extending one inch (2.5 cm) beyond the edge of the paper, then glue the paper closed.

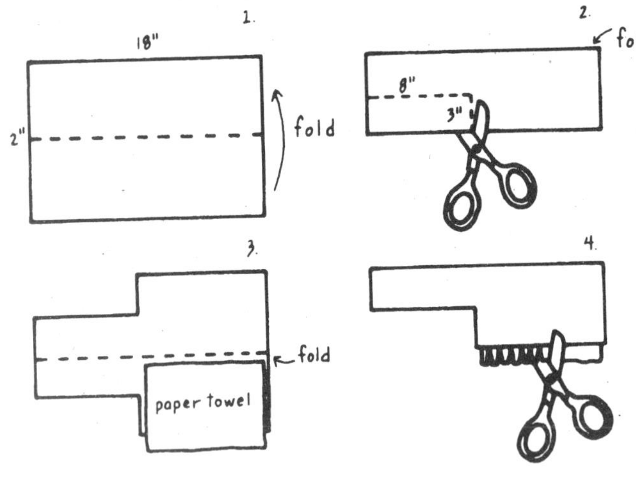

5. Let the children fringe the paper towel with scissors to form bristles.
6. Glue a tooth-brushing chart on the front of the toothbrush, so children can mark when they brush.
7. Let the children decorate their tooth brushes.

More to do

Art: Let the children paint with real toothbrushes.

More science: Invite a dentist to visit the class.

Related books

Arthur's Tooth by Marc Brown

Berenstein Bears Visit the Dentist by Stan and Janice Berenstein

Curious George Goes to the Dentist by Margaret Rey and Alan J. Shalleck

*Suzanne Maxymuk, Cherry Hill, NJ*

Safety Tips

Science skills

Children develop their language skills through working together.

Materials

Officer Buckle and Gloria by Peggy Rathman

What to do

1. Read *Officer Buckle and Gloria*.
2. Discuss safety tips.
3. Encourage children to come up with different safety tips.
4. Choose one child to name the safety tip and choose another volunteer to act it out.

More to do

Art: Ask the children each to draw a picture of a safety tip. Put these drawings together in a book.

Games: Without identifying the safety tips, encourage a child to act one out and let the others guess what it might be.

Related book
A Day in the Life of a Police Officer by Eric Arnold

 *Suzanne Maxymuk, Cherry Hill, NJ*

3+

Wash Off Those Germs

Science skills
Children learn about germs with this interesting experiment.

Materials
2 slices white bread
2 resealable plastic bags, one labeled "dirty hands" and the other labeled "clean hands"
Permanent marker

What to do
1. At circle time, talk about how we all have germs on our hands.
2. Ask children to look at their hands and see if they can see any germs.
3. Explain that when the children come in from the playground, everyone needs to touch the bread in the bag labeled "dirty hands." Then put the piece of bread in the bag and leave it in the science center.
4. Next, have everyone wash their hands and touch the other piece of bread, then put it in the resealable plastic bag and leave it in the science center.
5. Observe over the next few weeks and compare the mold on both pieces.
6. Show children how to wash their hands and, if they are interested, repeat the experiment.

Holly Dzierzanowski, Austin, TX

4+

Those Icky, Sticky Germs

Science skills
With this demonstration of the germ theory, children make observations and inferences.

Materials
2-3 cups (500 ml to 750 ml) moist, cooked rice
Newspaper or plastic to cover floor
Marker
Plastic bag or bowl
Large piece of paper

Health & Safety

What to do

1. Explain to the children that germs are very, very tiny organisms that can enter our bodies and make us sick. Germs are so small that you need a microscope to see them. Most of the time, the special germ fighters in our bodies stop the germs before we get sick, but sometimes we get colds and flu anyway.
2. Place the cooked rice in the plastic bag or bowl. Explain that the rice is the pretend germs.
3. Ask three to four children to stand side by side in a line. For easier clean-up, cover the floor where they will be standing with plastic or newspaper.
4. Let the first child in line dip her hand in the bag or bowl, squeeze the rice and release any loose rice in her hand.
5. This child shakes hands with the next child in line, that child shakes hands with the next, etc. All the children will have some rice on their hands.
6. Point out how easily the "germs" were spread from person to person.
7. Discuss with the children the fact that one way we can stop germs from spreading is to wash our hands. Ask the children when they think people should wash their hands to prevent the spread of germs. Record answers on large paper.

More to do

Art: With a white bar of soap, let the children make drawings on white construction paper. Brush over the soap drawing with watercolor paints. The paint will not stick to the soaped areas.
Cooking: Mix together 2 cups (500 ml) Ivory Snow Flakes and ½ cup (125 ml) water tinted with food coloring and form into balls. To make shaped soaps, press the mixture into candy molds. These soaps make great gifts, and the activity extends the germ/hand washing lesson to the home.
More science: Explain again that we can't see germs, but that they can be anywhere! Out of view of the children, spread a thin layer of petroleum jelly on doorknobs, faucet handles, tabletops or any item that is easily cleaned and that the petroleum jelly will not harm. Tell the children that as they play, they may find some "germ areas." If they touch something "greasy," they should immediately wash their hands so they don't spread the "germs." At the end of the day, ask the children where they found the "germs."

Original song

Those Icky Germs Are Always Around (sing to the tune of "Santa Claus Is Coming to Town")

You better use soap,
And wipe your hands dry.
It's important to do,
I'm telling you why—

Those icky germs are always around!

They're very sneaky,
And very quick.
Wash your hands well,
So you don't get sick—

Those icky germs are always around!

They're around when we are sleeping.
They're around when we're awake.
They're around on everything we touch,
So wash for goodness sake.

Oh...

You better use soap,
And wipe your hands dry.
It's important to do,
I'm telling you why—

Those icky germs are always around!

Related books

Body Battles by Rita Golden Gelman
Those Mean Nasty, Dirty Downright Disgusting But...Invisible Germs by Judith Rice

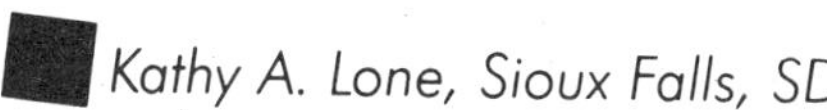
Kathy A. Lone, Sioux Falls, SD

4+

Safe or Not Safe

Science skills
Children practice classification and observation skills.

Materials

Pictures cut from magazines
Smiley faces and sad faces cut from cardboard
Laminating machine or clear contact paper

What to do

1. Cut out and laminate pictures showing things that are safe and things that are not safe (for example, child falling off a bike, mother cooking in the kitchen, baby riding in a car seat). Place the happy and sad faces on a table, along with a pile of the laminated pictures.
2. Talk to the children about safety and about things to do and to remember in order to keep ourselves safe.
3. Let the children choose pictures and take turns placing them under the right face, safe ones under the happy face, unsafe ones under the sad face.
4. This is a good time to review general safety rules, as well as to teach the children about dialing 911 in case of a true emergency.

More to do

Art: The children can illustrate their own ideas of safe and unsafe activities and situations.

Sandra Hutchins Lucas, Cox's Creek, KY

Holidays

Valentine Vine

3+

Science skills

Children make observations and measurements while creating a holiday gift.

Materials

Baby food jars
Red and pink construction paper
Glue
Beans
Potting soil

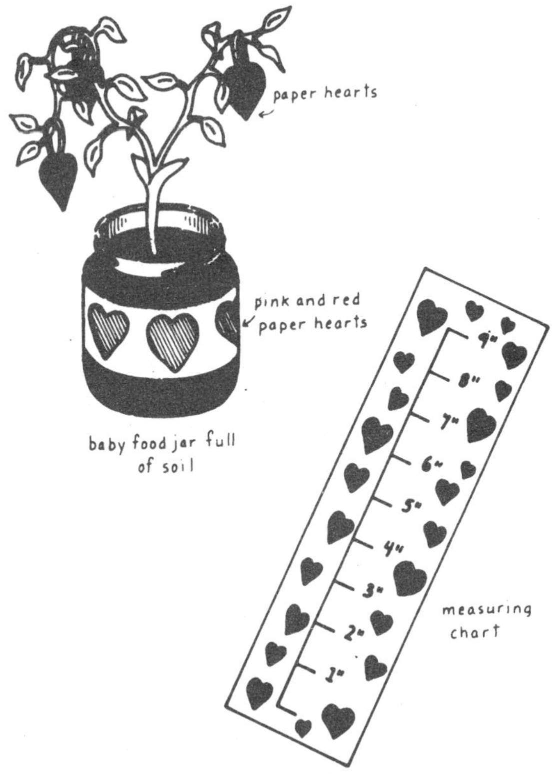

What to do

1. A few weeks before Valentine's Day help the children decorate the baby food jars by gluing on pink and red construction paper hearts.
2. Allow each child to place soil in the bottom of his jar and plant a bean sprout.
3. For the next two weeks help the children water and observe the sprouts, measuring the plants' growth with a Valentine's Day measuring chart.
4. Right before Valentine's Day decorate the vine with cut out paper hearts and allow the children to take them home for someone special.

Lisa M. Lang, Parkersburg, WV

Jingle Bells

3+

Science skills

Children make observations and inferences, draw conclusions and practice auditory skills.

Materials

2 very small jingle bells
2 medium-sized jingle bells
2 large jingle bells
2 extra large jingle bells (the type used as door decorations)
8 pieces of yarn, ribbon or string
Bag or basket

What to do

1. Before group time, tie the ribbons onto the bells.
2. Divide the bells into groups, one size bell for each group.
3. Place one group of bells on a table or the floor in front of you.
4. Hide the other bells in a bag or basket. They should not be visible to the children. Explain to the children that you are going to play a guessing game.
5. One by one, ring the visible bells for the children, asking the children to listen to the sound.
6. Ring one of the concealed bells and have the children guess which of the visible bells it sounds like. Continue to match all the bells.
7. Talk about tone, and the qualities of high, low, soft, loud.
8. Add these bells to your science center.

More to do

Music: Using pipe cleaners, attach jingle bells to the children's shoes. Walking becomes musical! Can they march out a tune with the bells on? ▪ Make "jingle sticks" by attaching bells and colored crepe paper streamers to popsicle sticks or jumbo craft sticks. ▪ Have a jingle parade with instruments from the music center. ▪ Play the matching game above using musical instruments. ▪ Ask the children to make a list of things with bells. Examine some of these other bells: doorbells, bells on timers, kitchen appliances, bicycles, etc.

Related song

Chant this little song:

Ring, ring, ring your bells
Ring them high and low.
Ring them left and ring them right,
Ring them fast and slow!

Related book

The Doorbell Rang by Pat Hutchins

Linda Ford, Sacramento, CA

Pumpkins

3+

Science skills

Children observe the growth of a pumpkin and make predictions and inferences.

Materials

From Seed to Jack-O'Lantern by Hannah Lyons Johnson, or another favorite pumpkin story
Flannel board story pieces:

Pumpkin seed
Pumpkin plant
Pumpkin
Jack-o-lantern

What to do

1. During circle time read *From Seed to Jack-O'Lantern,* or the story you chose.
2. As you read the story, place the flannel board pieces on the board in the order they come in the story.
3. After you finish the story, start a discussion by asking what was the first thing the brother and sister did in order to have a pumpkin. Plant a pumpkin seed. How did they take care of the pumpkin patch? They watered, weeded and made sure the plants got plenty of sunshine. What did they do with the pumpkin after it was grown? They made a jack-o-lantern for Halloween. Questions can be posed according to the story the teacher chooses to use.

More to do

Art: Make a reverse painting of a jack-o-lantern using these materials: tray, orange paint, cornstarch, water to mix the paint and pumpkin shapes. Place the materials on a table. The teacher will sprinkle the orange tempera and cornstarch onto the tray. Add enough water to mix the paint thoroughly. The paint should be thick, like finger paint. If you prefer, use premixed orange finger paint. Ask one child at a time to come over to the table, and give the child a pumpkin shape. Ask him to draw a face on the tray, and to gently lay the pumpkin down on the tray, covering the face. Let the child gently press on the pumpkin, and carefully lift the pumpkin from the tray. Set the pumpkin aside to dry, and later hang it up. ▪ Make crazy quilt pumpkins with these materials: scraps of fabric, pumpkin shapes, glue sticks. Let the children cut the fabric into small pieces. This is an excellent way to let them practice their scissors skills. When they are finished cutting up the fabric, push it into a pile in the middle of the table. Hand out the pumpkin shapes, and let the children use the glue stick to smear glue onto the pumpkin. Now they may choose fabric pieces, and put them down on the pumpkin in the glue. After the pumpkins are all done, hang them up. ▪ Make wallpaper pumpkins, using different kinds of wallpaper scraps. Ask the children to trace jack-o-lanterns out on the wallpaper. Let them cut out the pumpkins, and hang them up in the room. ▪ The teacher can make a classroom pumpkin patch on the bulletin board for hanging the above projects. Make a sign, Our Pumpkin Patch, and add a scarecrow. As the children finish their pumpkin projects, add them to the board.

Snack: Make pumpkin muffins for snack time.

Related books
How a Seed Grows by Helen J. Jordan
It's Pumpkin Time by Zoe Hall
The Pumpkin Patch by Elizabeth King
Pumpkin Pumpkin by Jeanne Titherington

Sherri Lawrence, Louisville, KY

3+

Scallop Shell Tree Ornaments

Science skills
Children are encouraged to ask questions about nature.

Materials
Scallop shells, one for each child
Glitter
Narrow ribbon or cord
White glue
Electric drill

What to do
1. Prepare the shells ahead of time by scrubbing them and drilling a hole at the base of each one.
2. Show a scallop shell with both halves attached. Read about shellfish and show pictures, explaining how an animal once lived inside the shell.
3. Demonstrate the easy way to draw a star with the white glue: first make a cross, then an X on top of the cross. Let the children draw their stars with the glue on the concave side of the shell.
4. Sprinkle the glue with glitter and shake off the excess. Allow to dry.
5. Attach a ribbon or cord hanger.

Mary Jo Shannon, Roanoke, VA

Holidays

Silver Polishing

3+

Science skills

This is an opportunity for observing and for developing fine motor and social skills.

Materials

Tartar-control toothpaste (not gel) or cream silver polish (toothpaste is non-toxic)
Small plastic containers, such as empty catsup or mustard cups from a fast-food restaurant
Small sponge
Soft cloth for polishing
A tarnished silver spoon or small bowl
Apron or smock

What to do

1. Squeeze some toothpaste into the container.
2. Use the sponge to apply the toothpaste to the silver, pointing out the dark tarnish.
3. Rub and observe changes.
4. Polish with the cloth and observe the shine.
5. Children may work on the silver once you have demonstrated. One child should not be expected to complete the project. It requires a lot of patience and effort. Let each child clean and shine a spot or two, then all can enjoy the beauty of their joint effort. Although it seems a chore to adults, children love to see the magic as the dull, dirty surface begins to gleam.

Thanksgiving Candles

4+

Science skills

Here is a delightful activity that provides an opportunity for observation and fine motor skill practice.

Materials

Electric skillet
Empty soup can with label removed
Crayon with paper wrappings removed
White votive candles, one for each child
Water
Paraffin wax
Spring-type clothespins
Waxed paper

What to do

1. Ahead of time, fill the electric skillet about half full with water. Place the empty soup can into the center of the pan. Put chunks of paraffin wax in the can, as well as the crayon. Turn the skillet on medium to melt the wax and crayon; stir frequently. Turn temperature down to low when wax and crayon have melted.
2. With the children, discuss the fact that the pilgrims made their own candles from wax. These people needed lots of candles since they did not have electric lights, and they made different sizes and colors of candles. To make candles, they dipped wicks into hot, melt-

ed wax many, many times until the candles were just the right size and shape. It was a lot of work for pilgrims, but very necessary!
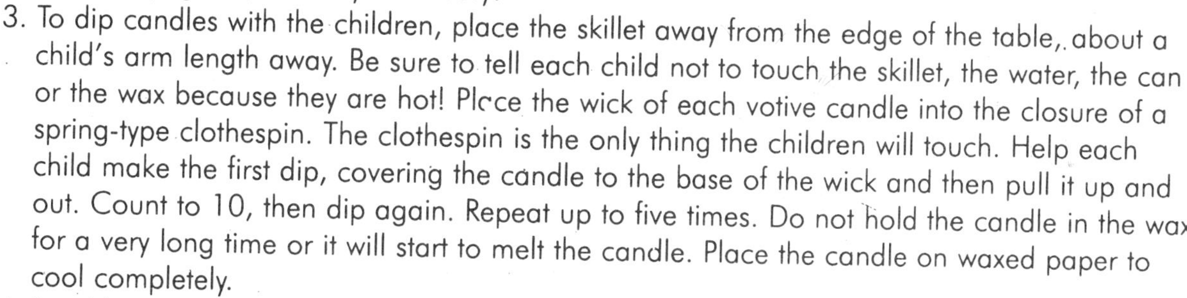
3. To dip candles with the children, place the skillet away from the edge of the table, about a child's arm length away. Be sure to tell each child not to touch the skillet, the water, the can or the wax because they are hot! Plcce the wick of each votive candle into the closure of a spring-type clothespin. The clothespin is the only thing the children will touch. Help each child make the first dip, covering the candle to the base of the wick and then pull it up and out. Count to 10, then dip again. Repeat up to five times. Do not hold the candle in the wax for a very long time or it will start to melt the candle. Place the candle on waxed paper to cool completely.
4. Send home directions for doing this activity at home. The children will want to make several!
5. We saved our candles for part of a holiday gift for parents. We thinned glue and used it to glue tissue paper squares to baby food jars. We placed the candles inside and wrapped them up.

More to do

More science: Encourage the children to plan a Thanksgiving celebration and to make the decorations. Use the candles in arrangements for the tables.

Related song

I'm a Little Candle (sing to the tune of "I'm a Little Teapot")

I'm a little candle
Short and thick.
Here is my wax
And here is my wick.
When I get all fired up
I just shout;
Watch me glow,
Then blow me out!

Valerie Chellew, Marshfield, WI

The Great Dreidl Race

5+

Science skills
Children make predictions and draw conclusions.

Materials
Assortment of four to six dreidls, made of metal, plastic, wood, clay
Large sheet of chart or graph paper
Marker
Timer

What to do

1. Although it is not necessary to introduce the dreidls as more than "tops used in a game played during the Jewish festival of Hannukah," it might be more meaningful to teach the game prior to engaging in this activity. You can find a complete explanation of the game, including detailed directions, in many nonfiction books about the celebration of Hanukkah.
2. Display the dreidls and ask the group, "How are these dreidls the same? How are they different?" Encourage a variety of responses and record on the chart paper descriptions of each dreidl, emphasizing the material(s) of which each is composed as its "identifier."
3. Allow the children to examine and spin the dreidls. Encourage predictions by asking, Which dreidl do you think can spin for a longer time than the others? Why? Guess which one will spin for the shortest amount of time.
4. Experiment by spinning each dreidl, timing the length of its spin and recording the results on the graph next to its description. Try involving the children as timekeepers and recorders. It would be fun to let the children take turns spinning. Or, for consistency of the spins and to remove the variables associated with differing levels of skill, you may want to do the spinning yourself. Repeat this step two to three times to get a more accurate sampling.
5. Discuss the results, comparing them to the class's original predictions. Then, help the class draw conclusions based on those results.

More to do
Math: Highlight the concepts of time measurement in the activity above.
Movement: Invite the children to move like dreidls to music in a clear, open area of the classroom. Make sure there is ample unobstructed space for your little spinners.
Snack: Bake and decorate delicious dreidl-shaped sugar cookies.

Marji E. Gold-Vukson, West Lafayette, IN

3+

And Now a Butterfly!

Science skills
This activity encourages questions about nature and the use of fine motor skills.

Materials
Cardboard egg cartons
Pipe cleaners
Glue
Tape
Paint and paintbrushes
Butcher paper
Scissors
Paper towels

What to do

1. On the first day, cut an egg carton in half lengthwise and poke two holes in one end. Help the child pull a pipe cleaner through the holes to make the antenna. Then the child paints her egg carton caterpillar. Children may want to name their caterpillars.
2. On the second day, the child can wrap the caterpillar up in a paper towel for a cocoon. The child can paint a large butterfly shape on the same day on butcher paper and cut it out.
3. On the following day, the children get to take their caterpillars out of the cocoon and glue them onto the butterfly shape, so that they are transformed into butterflies. You may need to tape the wings on as the glue dries or put a weight on the egg carton to hold it down. When the butterflies are dry, the children make them swirl through the air.

More to do
Movement: Watch a caterpillar change into a moth or butterfly. Act out being a tiny egg, then crawling around as a caterpillar, spinning a cocoon and finally flying with wings.

Related books
The Caterpillar and the Polliwog by Jack Kent
See How They Grow by Patricia Pearse
The Very Hungry Caterpillar by Eric Carle

Laura Durbrow, Lake Oswego, OR

Big Book of Butterflies

3+

Science skills

The children make observations and predictions and gain experience in sequencing.

Materials

Large handmade book with poster board on the front and back and white paper in the middle
Hole punch
Pipe cleaners
Crayons
The Very Hungry Caterpillar by Eric Carle

What to do

1. Each child will make her own big book. Read the story *The Very Hungry Caterpillar.*
2. Have a class discussion about all the different things a caterpillar might eat. Each day for several days the children draw pictures of these things in their books. After they finish each picture, punch a hole in the middle of it. Let them continue for about five to six days with the different things the caterpillar eats. On day seven, ask each child to draw the cocoon or chrysalis, and punch a hole in that as well.
3. The next day let the children draw a beautiful butterfly on the last page, with a hole where the head would be.
4. Now the children can tell the story, with their pipe cleaner "caterpillar" eating its way through all those foods, and then finally emerging as a butterfly.

Theresa M. Jarmuz, Lancaster, NY

Bringing Insects Indoors

Science skills

An insect in the classroom allows observation and stimulates discussion about nature.

Materials

Bug container and net

What to do

1. Take the children exploring outdoors. When you find an insect to observe, scoop up some of its habitat—the dirt and/or leaves surrounding it—and place the insect inside the container.

2. Bring the container indoors and let the children observe the insect for a few days. Explain to the children why it is very important to return the insect to its natural habitat.
3. Share insect facts with your class: all insects have six legs, two antennae and three body parts: the head, thorax and abdomen. Most progress from egg to adult insect.

Cindy Winther, Oxford, MI

3+

Bug Hunt

Science skills
Children closely observe insects.

Materials
Containers for collecting bugs
Magnifying glasses

What to do
1. At circle time read a book or show pictures of bugs and insects you may find in your area.
2. Ask the children if they know the story song "Bear Hunt." Tell them instead of a bear hunt you are going on a bug hunt. Pass out containers for bugs.
3. Sing as you go: We're going on a bug hunt, through the tall grass, through the mud, through the river, climb the mountain, etc., until you reach the area in which you will look for bugs. Allow the children to fan out and look for bugs to put in their containers. If you live in an area where there are dangerous bugs, be sure to tell the children to ask an adult before they touch a bug.
4. Encourage and assist the children to look under rocks, the bark of a tree, dead logs, and in or on plants. Help them put bugs in their containers.
5. When everyone has found at least one bug, return to the classroom. Be sure to go back down the mountain, through the river, etc.
6. Look at the bugs with a magnifying glass. After you are finished, you may return the bugs to their homes.

More to do
More science: Put some bugs in the science area or in an aquarium for a Bug Zoo. Provide the children with books so they can identify the bugs.

Helen DeWitt, Cochise, AZ

Fingerprint Bugs

3+

Science skills

Children make observations and use fine motor skills.

Materials

Washable ink pads
Pen
Paper

What to do

1. After a unit on insects, encourage the children to talk about their favorite insects.
2. Set out ink pads and ask the children to use one finger to make fingerprints. Five or six fingerprints together form a caterpillar. Two fingerprints with wings form a butterfly. One fingerprint with legs makes a spider. Use a pen to make legs and eyes.

Related books

I Wish I Were a Butterfly by James Howe
The Very Busy Spider by Eric Carle
The Very Hungry Caterpillar by Eric Carle

Sandra Hutchins Lucas, Cox's Creek, KY

I Can Fly!

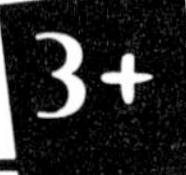

Science skills

As they act out a butterfly's life cycle, children become interested in nature.

Materials

Books about caterpillars and butterflies
Paper flowers
Scarves
Green paper leaves
Flexible exercise or nap mat

What to do

1. Examine books, pictures and models of caterpillars and butterflies.
2. Scatter paper leaves and flowers around the room.

3. Let the children crawl around the room on their bellies in search of leaves to munch (pretend munching only!).
4. One at a time, children crawl to the narrow end of the mat and are given two scarves. Take turns rolling up each child snugly in the mat.
5. The child wiggles and breaks free and flies around the room with scarf wings to visit flowers, sip nectar and lay eggs.

More to do

Art: Fold a 9" x 12" (22.5 cm x 30 cm) piece of construction paper in half, short end to short end. Trace half a butterfly on the fold and cut it out, but don't cut the fold. Open and dribble paint on the wing. Close and rub. Open to reveal "inkblot" decorated wings.

Games: Create a matching game by making pairs of matching paper butterflies with decorated wings. Hide one butterfly in the room. Give each child the matching butterfly, and let her find the mate.

Snack: Make a butterfly salad with half a banana for body and a half pineapple ring for each wing. Fill in the wings with cottage cheese and decorate with grape halves, peanuts and raisins.

Original poem

Say this poem and perform the actions with the children.

Roly Poly Caterpillar into a corner crept. (creep one hand up opposite arm)
Wound around himself a blanket, (winding motion with hands)
For a long time slept. (lay head on hands)
Roly Poly Caterpillar waking by and by, (pop head up)
Found himself with beautiful wings, changed to a butterfly! (hook thumbs together and flap hands)

Related books

Butterfly and Caterpillar by Barrie Watts
Look—a Butterfly by David Cutts
The Very Hungry Caterpillar by Eric Carle

Sandra Gratias, Perkasie, PA

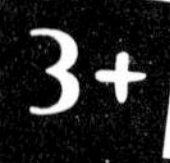

Ladybug Tickle Puppet

Science skills
Children make observations, then use creativity and fine motor skills to make a puppet.

Materials

Pictures and books about ladybugs
Two 6" (15 cm) paper plates for each child
Black construction paper
Stapler
Red and black crayons
Glue

Insects

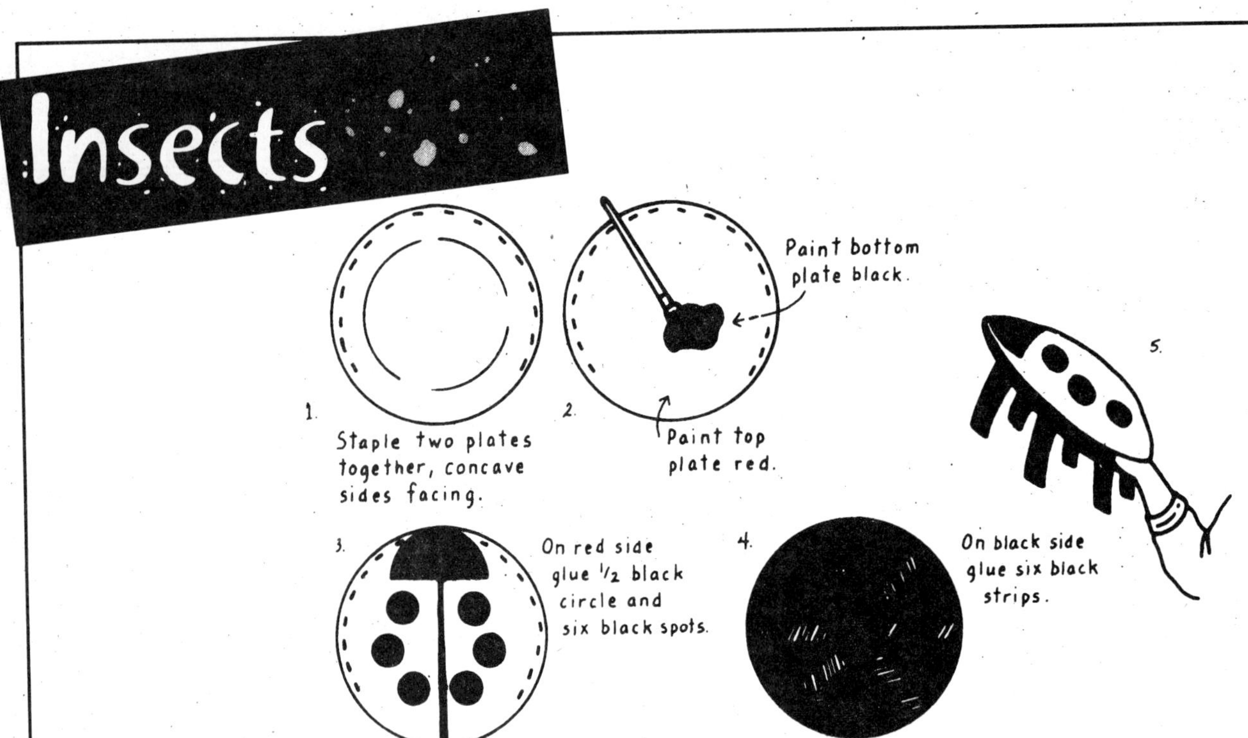

What to do

1. Read a book about ladybugs and allow the children to examine pictures.
2. Staple the plates together along the edges, three quarters of the way around. The concave sides of the plates should be facing each other.
3. Color the top plate red and the bottom plate black.
4. Cut out and glue black spots on the red side and 6 black strips for legs on the black side. Glue a black half-circle for the head on one end of the plate, opposite the open section.
5. The child inserts her hand in the open section of the edge and uses the ladybug as a puppet.
6. Older children may want to color both plates black and color a third plate red. Glue black dots on the red plate and cut it in half. Attach it to the puppet with a brass fastener so the red halves will open when the ladybug flies.

More to do

More science: Order a ladybug hatchery from a science catalog. Watch the life cycle of the ladybug. ▪ Compare ladybugs to other beetles.

Original song

Chant and do the hand motions:

Ladybug, Ladybug, red and black.
Ladybug, Ladybug with spots on its back.
Ladybug, Ladybug tickled me today.
Ladybug, Ladybug, (blow) fly away!

Related books

The Icky Bug Alphabet Book by Jerry Pallotte
The Ladybug and Other Insects by Pascale De Bourgoing

■ *Sandra Gratias, Perkasie, PA*

3+

Make a Caterpillar

Science skills

In making this caterpillar, children learn about what caterpillars look like and use their fine motor skills.

Materials

The Very Hungry Caterpillar by Eric Carle
Hole punch
Markers
Wiggle eyes
Egg cartons cut in half lengthwise, one per child
Pipe cleaners
Glue

What to do

1. Read *The Very Hungry Caterpillar* with the children to learn about the caterpillar's lite cycle. Then help them make their own caterpillars.
2. Cut the egg cartons in half lengthwise and glue on the wiggle eyes.
3. Punch holes for pipe cleaner legs and use the markers to color the caterpillar.

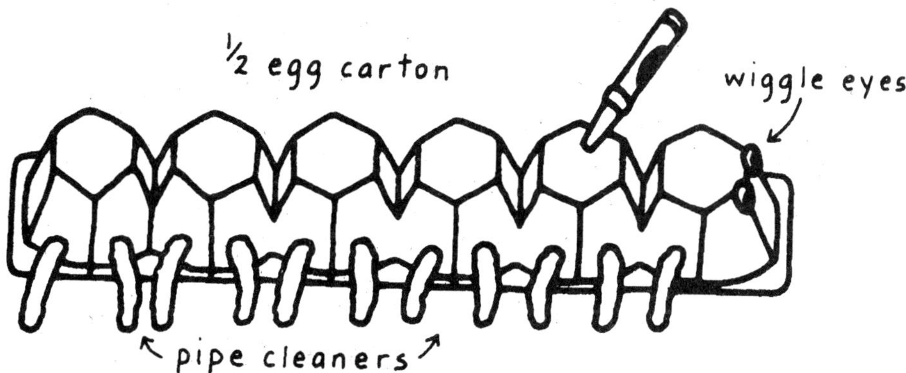

More to do

Art: Make butterfly finger puppets using paper coin roll covers. Punch a hole for pipe cleaner antennae and glue on two paper wings.

Dramatic play: Use a sock to be the very hungry caterpillar and have paper foods for him to "eat" through. With the sock over her arm, a child can slip her arm through the holes in the paper foods. Hide a butterfly inside the sock for the caterpillar to turn into.

Original poem

Caterpillar, caterpillar
Don't ask me why
You hang upside down
And change into a butterfly!

Related book

Creepy, Crawly Caterpillars by Mary Facklam

 *Andrea Clapper, Cobleskill, NY*

Observing Pill Bugs

Science skills

Children observe a living experiment.

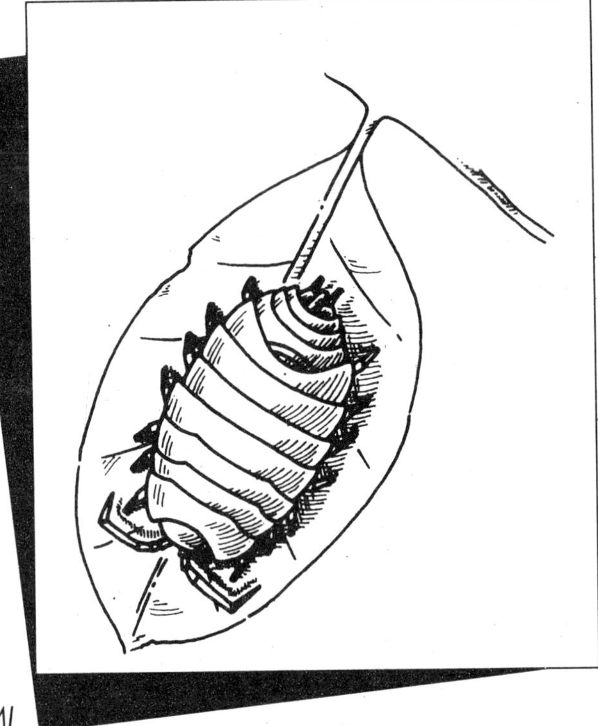

Materials

Clear container with lid
Soil
Leaves
Sticks
Rock
Pill bugs

What to do

1. Prepare the container for the pill bugs by layering the soil and creating hills. Add sticks and leaves and a rock. Dampen the soil and keep it moist throughout the experiment.
2. Enlist the children's help in collecting pill bugs. Place the bugs in their new home.
3. Observe the bugs for the next few weeks. The children will have fun watching the bugs feed on the leaves and decaying materials.

 *Cindy Winther, Oxford, MI*

Pizza Box Butterfly

Science skills

Children use creativity and fine motor skills.

Materials

One clean pizza box, any size, for each child
Yarn or string
Paint and paintbrush

Construction paper or tissue paper and glue
Markers, cotton balls or yarn bits or pieces of material
Pipe cleaners, optional
Hole punch or pointed scissors

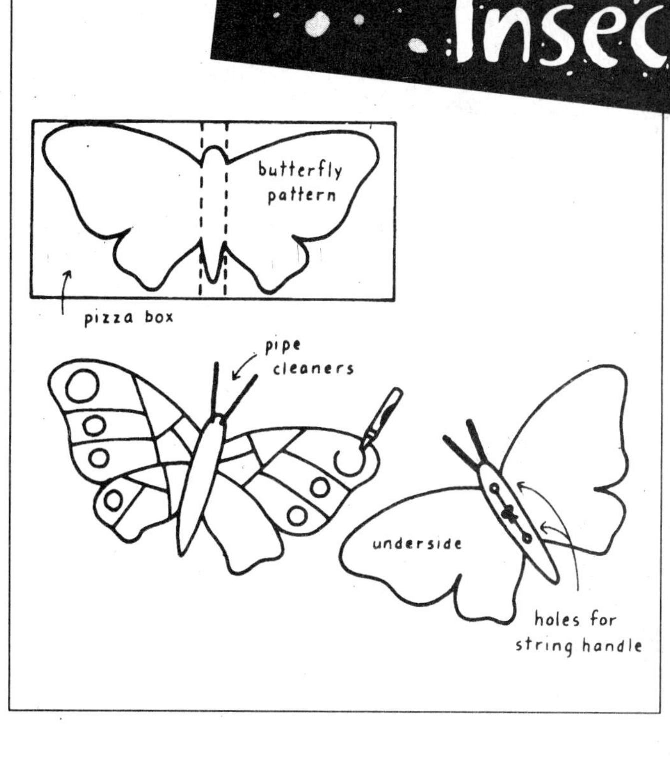

What to do

1. Pre-cut each side of the pizza box using the butterfly patterns shown below, or allow the children to create their own designs.
2. Let the children decorate the top or both sides of the butterfly using paint, glue, paper and other materials. You might suggest that the children decorate the butterflies symmetrically, so that one wing mirrors the other.
3. Punch two holes along the butterfly's "back" and lace string or yarn through the holes, tying the ends tightly together to make a handle on the butterfly's underside. Use pipe cleaners to create antennae.
4. Show the children how to slip their hands into the handles and move their arms to make the butterfly "fly."

Leslie Kvehn Meyer, Austin, MN

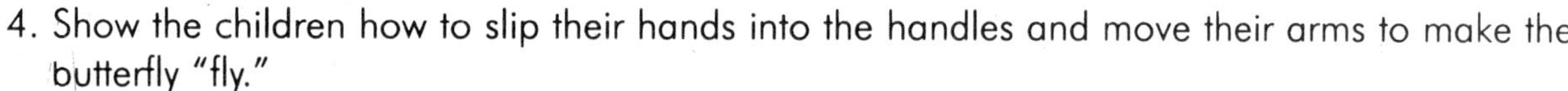

3+ Slither and Crawl

Science skills
The children observe closely and work on social skills.

Materials

22" x 28" (55 cm x 70 cm) sheet of white poster board
Reptile/insect wrapping paper with repeating pattern
Tape
Clear paper
Scissors

What to do

1. To create the game, cut the poster board in half and cut each half in half again to make four equal size rectangular pieces. These will be the game boards.
2. Cut out a portion of the wrapping paper to fit on each piece of poster board and tape it to the poster board. Now cover the prepared game board with contact paper.
3. Cut out individual reptiles and insects from the wrapping paper and cover them with contact paper. These are the game pieces.

4. To play the game, each player selects a game board. Place all game pieces face down in the middle of the table.
5. The first player selects a game piece from the pile and determines whether the game piece matches a reptile or insect on her game board.
6. If she makes a match, she places the game piece on her game board. If not, she returns the game piece face down to the pile of game pieces.
7. Play continues until the players have covered all their reptiles and insects.
8. Younger children can leave the game pieces face up. Also, they can work on covering the game boards with game pieces individually instead of in a game activity.
9. To vary the game, players might only match insects; then all reptiles drawn from the pile must be returned to the pile. Or they might match only reptiles and all insects drawn from the pile must be returned to the pile. Another variation might be to ask each player to draw a game piece from the pile and place it on another player's game board.

More to do

Art: Glue a popsicle stick to the back of one of each reptile or insect. The children can use these as puppets.

Games: This game can be made with any wrapping paper that has a repeating pattern so with the right wrapping paper it can be worked into any theme or unit. ▪ Using just the game pieces, each player draws a game piece from the pile and tries to act out the reptile or insect without saying a word, as in Charades. ▪ Use the game pieces to turn the matching game into a bingo type of game. Place all of the pieces into a container and then draw one piece out of the container at a time. The children cover each reptile or insect called on their game board.

Original song

Sing to the tune of "Mary Had a Little Lamb."

_________ *had a little snake, little snake, little snake.*
_________ *had a little snake that slithered all around.*
Every time he picked it up, picked it up, picked it up
Every time he picked it up, it wiggled all around.
It even tried to bite him once, bite him once, bite him once
It even tried to bite him once, which he did not allow.

Related books

Alpha Bugs by David Carter
The Best Bug to Be by Dolores Johnson
The Icky Bug Alphabet Book by Jerry Pallotta
Jimmy's Boa Bounces Back by Trinka Hakes Noble
The Mixed-Up Chameleon by Eric Carle
The Yucky Reptile Alphabet Book by Jerry Pallotta

Andria C. Donnelly, Sterling, VA

3+

Spiders

Science skills
After discussion and observation of spiders, children use fine motor skills to create a spider.

Materials

Small to medium size Styrofoam balls, one per child
1 large pipe cleaner each, any color
Black pipe cleaners for 8 legs each
Small wiggle eyes

What to do

1. Read some spider books with the children. Talk about how spiders are like insects and how they are different.
2. Sing "Eentsy-Weentsy Spider."
3. Discuss spiders and their role in nature and in the food chain and their size, color and shape.
4. Create your very own spider by gluing pre-cut pipe cleaners to a Styrofoam ball. Bend the ends of the legs up slightly to resemble a spider's foot. Glue on the eyes.
5. Glue on or poke one long pipe cleaner into the top of the spider for movement control.

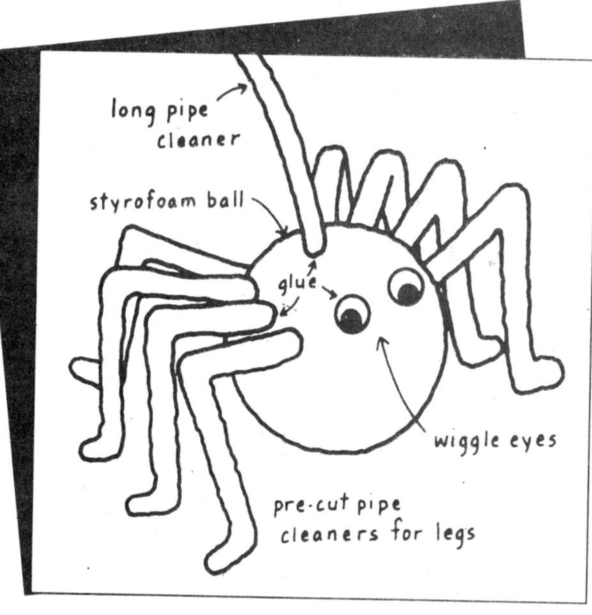

More to do

Language: Make a chart entitled "When I think of spiders ________" or "Spiders Are" or "How to Spin a Web." Ask the children to finish the sentence and record their responses on the chart.

More science: Draw a large web on a refrigerator-size piece of cardboard and cover with yarn. Let the children place their Styrofoam spiders in the web.

Related books

Anansi by Brian Gleeson
Be Nice to Spiders by Margaret Bloy Graham
The Fascinating World of Spiders by Maria A. Julivert
Miss Spider's Tea Party by David Kirk
Miss Spider's Wedding by David Kirk
Roly Poly Spider by Jill Sardegna
The Very Busy Spider by Eric Carle

Doris-Jane Smith, Lincolndale, NY

Insects

Squirmy Wormies

3+

Science skills

Worms and children get to know each other.

Materials

Worms
Chart paper
Large glass pie plate
Markers

What to do

1. Bring in several live worms from outdoors and place them on the glass pie plate. Let the children observe the worms and record their observations.
2. Let any child who wishes hold a worm. Talk about how the worms feel, look, etc. Ask the children, "Are worms insects?" Discuss why they answered yes or no.
3. Be sure to return the worms to their habitat.

More to do

Art: Using pieces of rug yarn, let the children dip the yarn into brown tempera paint and drag it across a piece of paper to make "worm tracks."

 *Cindy Winther, Oxford, MI*

Watching Monarchs

3+

Science skills

The children observe firsthand the life cycle of a butterfly.

Materials

Monarch caterpillar
Twenty small paper butterflies numbered 1-20
Two 12" (30 cm) cross stitch hoops
Stapler
Drawing paper
Chart paper
Milkweed
1 yard (1 m) of netting
Tape
Yarn
Crayons

What to do

1. First, make a butterfly cage. The butterfly cage will look like a bag, supported by the two hoops and suspended from the ceiling. Using the stapler, attach the netting to the hoops,

remembering to cover the bottom hoop with netting, too. When you are ready to hang the cage, use the yarn to suspend it from the ceiling.

2. Ask children and parents to look for a monarch caterpillar on milkweed plants near their homes in late August and early September. Bring in the caterpillar as well as some milkweed leaves for the caterpillar to eat and place them in the butterfly cage.
3. Daily, draw pictures to chart how the caterpillar changes in size and enters a chrysalis.
4. When the chrysalis forms, ask the children to predict on a chart "How many days before the caterpillar becomes a butterfly?" Write the predictions on the chart.
5. On the wall near the butterfly cage, each day tape the sequentially numbered butterflies to count the number of days that the caterpillar stays inside the chrysalis.
6. Continue drawing pictures weekly to illustrate how the chrysalis changes.
7. When the monarch emerges, note whether it is male or female.
8. Carry the cage outside to release your butterfly.

Related books

Amazing World of Butterflies and Moths by Louis Sabin
The Very Hungry Caterpillar by Eric Carle

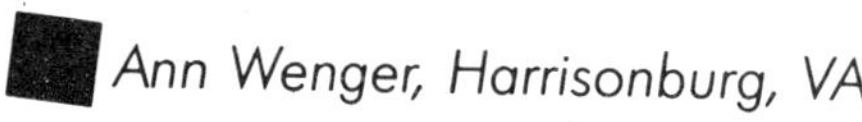

Ann Wenger, Harrisonburg, VA

Look at All Those Bugs

Science skills
The children make observations and use language skills.

Materials

Collection of bugs
Straight pins
Insect identification book
Flat piece of Styrofoam board
Magnifying glasses

What to do

1. Months before you study insects, start collecting real bugs. The insects must be dead for this activity.
2. Pin the bugs down to the Styrofoam board and label them using an insect book to identify them.

3. Put the board on the science table along with magnifying glasses.
4. Encourage the children to look at the bugs and to notice all the similarities and differences among them.

More to do

Art: Have a variety of art materials available (for example, egg cartons, pipe cleaners, wiggle eyes for older children) and let the children make their own bugs.

Holly Dzierzanowski, Austin, TX

Insects Forever

Science skills

Children are encouraged to make observations, use language skills and become interested in nature.

Materials

Small jars (baby food or other small plastic jars)
A variety of dead insects in the jars, one per jar
Paper
Magnifying glass
Word cards

What to do

1. Place the insect jars on display in a well-defined area. Label each jar with the insect's name printed clearly and place the word cards with the insects' names on them close by.
2. Ask the children to look at the jars with the magnifying glass. Encourage them to look for specific things related to each specimen, such as size, body color, number of legs, eye location, etc. They can also match the jars to the appropriate word cards.
3. The children can then use small pieces of paper to draw the insects, write their insect names at the bottom and put all of their pages together to make an individual science book.

Insect Body Part Puzzles

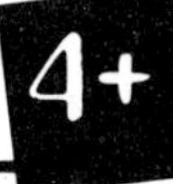

Science skills

Children practice new vocabulary words and use fine motor skills.

Materials

Pictures of two or three insects divided up into three sections
Scissors
Construction paper
Glue

What to do

1. Make a sketch of two or three insects, approximately 3″ x 6″ (7.5 cm x 15 cm). A fly, an ant and a butterfly work well.
2. Cut the insects into three equal rectangles, approximately 3″ x 2″ (7.5 cm x 5 cm).
3. Mix the rectangles up and arrange on a separate piece of paper, leaving a little space between each section. You may wish to make a border around each rectangle with a black marker.
4. Make copies of your sheet for each child.
5. Challenge children to cut up the rectangle sections and put the insects back together on a separate piece of construction paper.
6. Provide glue for them to reconstruct the heads, thoraxes and abdomens on their piece of construction paper.
7. While children are working, encourage use of new vocabulary, "thorax" and "abdomen."

More to do

More science: Do this same activity, only with arachnids consisting of two body part sections, the cephalothorax and abdomen (try a spider, scorpion, tick). ▪ Examine insects under magnifying glasses and try to find three body parts. ▪ Make a giant paper ant colony on your wall or a real ant colony in a jar.

Related book

The Icky Bug Alphabet Book by Jerry Pallotta

Shirley R. Salach, Northwood, NH

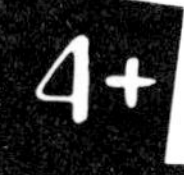

4+

The Life Cycle of the Butterfly

Science skills
Children use observation and fine motor skills.

Materials

The Very Hungry Caterpillar by Eric Carle
For each child:
Poster board piece, 9½″ x 12″ (23.5 cm x 30 cm)
3″ (7.5 cm) colored tissue paper squares
5 small pompom balls
Glue
Green construction paper and scissors
Egg carton cup sections
5 medium pompom balls

What to do

1. Read *The Very Hungry Caterpillar.*
2. Give each child one piece of poster board. Talk about the life cycle of the butterfly as you proceed.
3. Glue items in a large circle formation on the poster board, starting with one green leaf near

upper left corner, with a white punch dot on it for the egg (the children may design and cut out their own leaves).

4. Add five small pompom balls in a line to form the caterpillar, to the right of the leaf. Then, another green leaf with a bite cut out, to the right of the caterpillar. Five medium pompom balls show how the caterpillar has grown.
5. Trim the egg carton cup and press it down to the right of the caterpillar. Glue or tape the flared edges of the cup. This is the chrysalis.
6. Show the children how to pinch three squares of tissue paper in the center. Glue these to the right of the chrysalis. This is the emerging butterfly.
7. Print Life Cycle of the Butterfly at the top of the poster board. Draw arrows between each stage to show the cycle, ending at the butterfly.

More to do

Gardening: Plant a butterfly garden. Butterflies are attracted to purple, yellow and orange blossoms. Try planting fuchsias, violets, zinnias or butterfly bush in your garden. Will the butterflies find them?

Barbara Fischer, San Carlos, CA

Critter Cage

4+

Science skills

First children use fine motor skills to enclose a critter and then they observe the critter.

Materials

2 plastic coffee can lids of the same size
Wire cutters
Gloves
Hardware cloth
Wire
Tape

What to do

1. Measure the circumference of the lid.
2. Cut a length of hardware cloth to that measurement and cut the width as tall or as small as desired.
3. Roll the cloth into a cylinder shape and bend the edges inward.
4. Using wire, close up the seam.
5. Place one lid on the bottom and one on the top.
6. Capture a critter (insect) gently, and let it go after you've observed it.

More to do

Art: Using playdough or clay, let the children make bugs. Decorate with sticks, pipe cleaners, stones.
More science: Display an ant or ladybug farm.

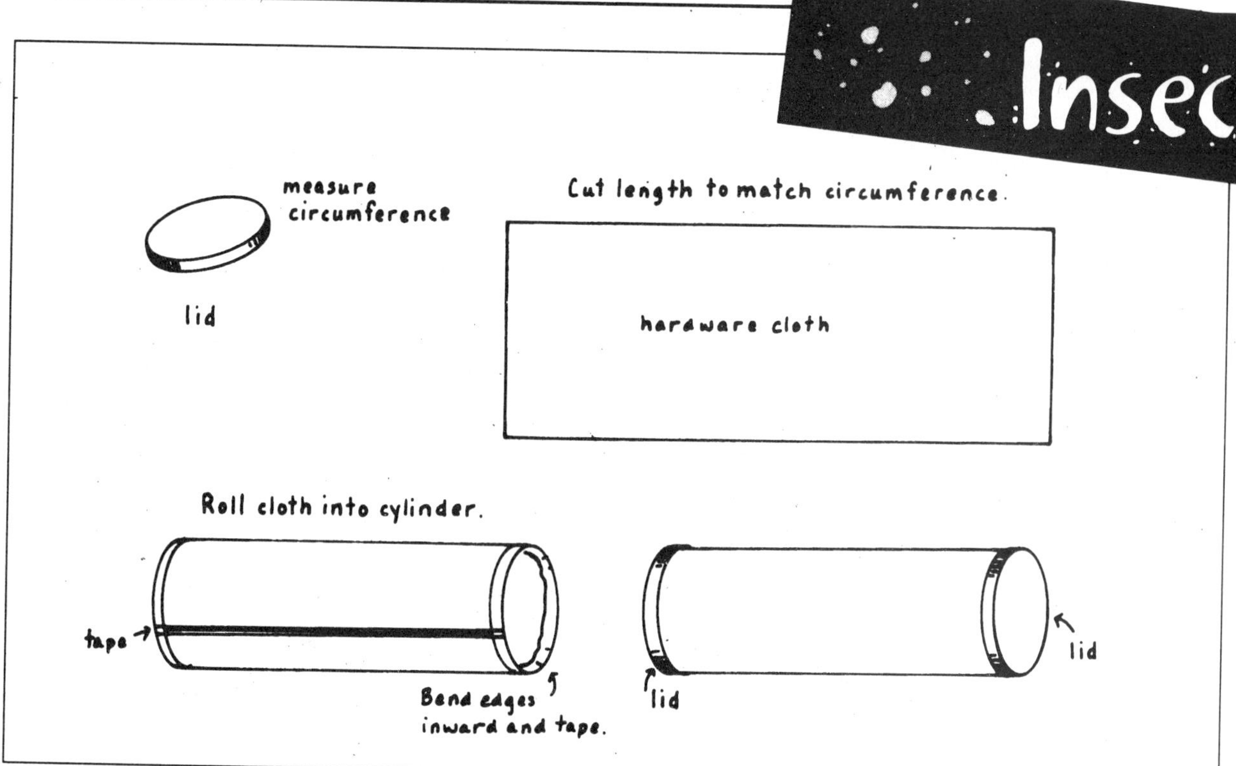

Snack: Make bug snacks, for example, crackers spread with peanut butter, with cheese curls for legs and raisin eyes.

Related books
The Very Busy Spider by Eric Carle
The Very Hungry Caterpillar by Eric Carle
The Very Quiet Cricket: A Multi-Sensory Book by Eric Carle

Teresa J. Nos, Baltimore, MD

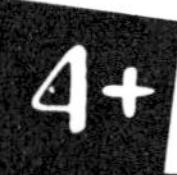

Flat-see the Fly Swatter

Science skills
This project encourages observation and the use of fine motor skills.

Materials
Paper towel rolls, tops slit 1″ (2.5 cm) on each side
Paintbrushes
6″ x 6″ (15 cm x 15 cm) pieces of cardboard, one for each child
Red felt or paper "smile strip" mouths
Chart paper with the poem written on it
Black paint
Crayons
Plastic wiggle eyes
Triangle-shaped felt or paper noses
Copies of Flat-see poem, one for each child

Insects

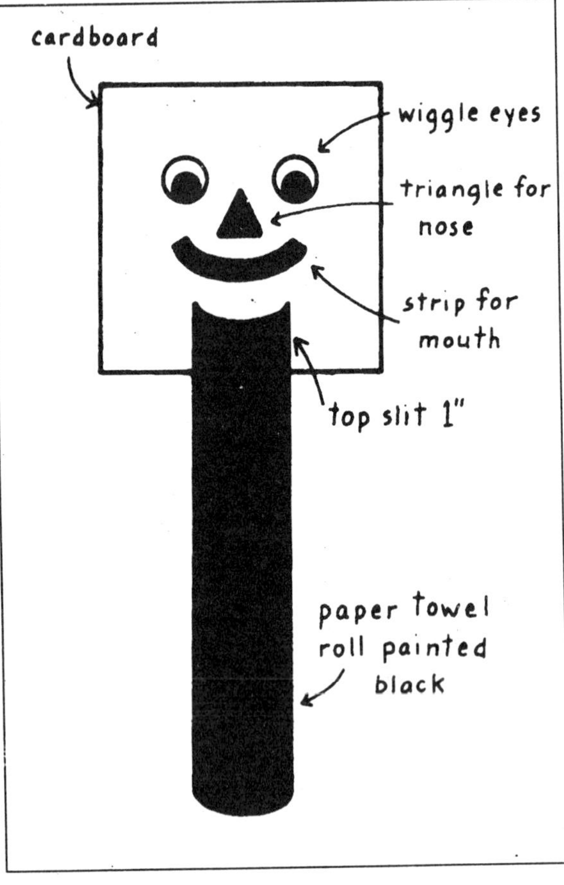

What to do

1. Discuss with the children why flies are pests. They feed on carrion, then spread germs, etc. Have Flat-see the fly swatter from the poem *Flat-see* (see below) on display for children to use as a guideline when making their fly swatters. Set up a paint center with black paint and paintbrushes. When children arrive in class, give them each a paper towel roll and send them to the paint center to paint it so it will be dry by the time they are ready to put the fly swatter together. Explain that this will be their fly swatter's handle.
2. During a science session, give each child one piece of cardboard, two wiggle eyes, one nose piece, one mouth piece and one copy of the poem.
3. Let the children color both sides of the cardboard and then glue the copy of Flat-see's poem on one side and the face pieces on the other side.
4. Once their handles are dry, the children can insert their cardboard faces into the slits at the top of the handle (you may want to use a little glue to reinforce).

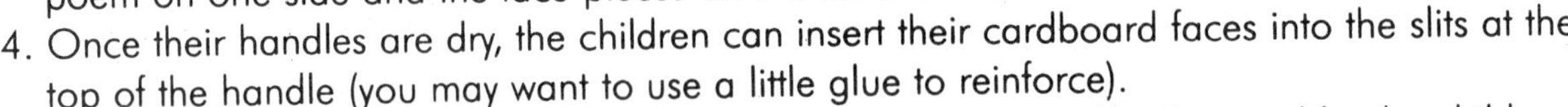

5. Have the chart paper posted for all to see. Read the poem to the class and let the children read it with you. Repeat the poem with the class, allowing the children to act out the swatting part. Show them how to swat with the face side up so they won't swat the eyes off of their fly swatter.

Original poem

Flat-see

When you see a fly go buzzing by
Make sure you give him a swat
Until he's lying flat.
He's full of germs, the uninvited guest
Otherwise known as the picnic pest.

Kathy Brand, Greenwood Lake, NY

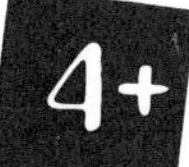

Hive Homes

Science skills
Children observe nature and practice fine motor skills.

Materials

Pictures of bees and hives
For each child:
Glue
Brown or deep gold tissue paper strips, 1½" x 6" (3.5 cm x 15 cm)
One small plastic bathroom cup
Paintbrush
One chenille bee on a wire
Small black construction paper half circle, ½" wide (13 mm)

What to do

1. Visit a bee keeper, if possible, or invite one to come visit your class. After discussing bees, help the children to make a bee.
2. Ask each child to place her cup upside down on the table and hold it down by putting her fingers on top.
3. Let her use a brush to paint glue all over the sides of the cup. After she twists strips of tissue into ropes, she may wrap them around the cup to completely cover the sides.
4. Now ask her to paint glue on top of the cup and cover it with more twisted tissue paper.
5. Insert the bee's wire between the tissue strips.
6. Glue the black half circle at the bottom edge of the cup to represent a door.

More to do

Art: Make a bee with a pantyhose container or large Easter egg. Color stripes on the pointed half of the egg. Glue paper wings on the rounded half. Add a face. You can insert a length of yarn before attaching the halves to hang or fly the bee. Use the bee with the poem on the next page.
Cooking: Taste honey from a comb. ▪ Eat popcorn dipped in honey. ▪ Make peanut butter balls by combining 1⅓ cups (325 ml)

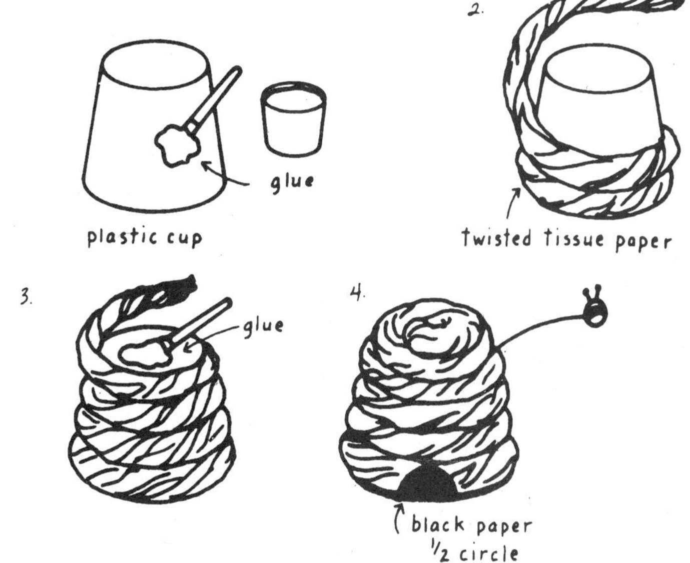

peanut butter, ⅔ cup (150 ml) honey and 1 cup (250 ml) milk powder. Roll into 1" (2.5 cm) balls, then eat!

Original poem

I like bumblebee, bumblebee buzzing.
I like bumblebee, bumblebee bu-uz-zing.
BUZZZZ

Sandra Gratias, Perkasie, PA

Bug Collecting

Science skills

Here children make observations and practice classification.

Materials

Books on insect identification, for example *Time-Life Book of Insects*
Baby food jars with lids
Magnifying glasses
Crayons
Outdoor area where bugs are likely to be found
Clear plastic cups, one or several for each child
Popsicle sticks
Drawing paper

What to do

1. Read several books about insects. Have the books available for the children to look at and read. Discuss the characteristics of a "true" insect versus a "bug." (True insects have three body parts and six legs, etc.)
2. Invite the children to go with you on an insect hunt. The rule is that you do not touch an insect. Children may move rocks and locate crawling insects, then carefully place their plastic cup over the insect. Demonstrate this procedure for the children so they see how not to squish the insect. The teacher will then scoot the insect into a baby food jar using the jar lid or popsicle stick.
3. Take the insects inside. Encourage the children to use magnifying glasses to examine the insects inside the jars. Have books available to help the children identify their insects. Sort the finds according to whether they are true insects or not. Encourage children to discuss what they are seeing, both in the jars and in the books. For example, "This one has six legs and three body parts."
4. Ask the children to draw a picture of their insects and dictate a sentence or two about them. Encourage them to include information about the looks of their insect, as well as where it was found.
5. Set the insects free where they were found.

More to do

Language: Say the well-known poem about ladybugs (Ladybug, ladybug, fly away home). Teach the children to recite the poem, then write it on chart story paper. Encourage the children to read the poem. Make word cards and let the children match the words to the chart story.

Math: Purchase plastic ants, spiders and flies. Use them as counters or put them together and have children sort them.

Snack: Make "ants on a log" by spreading peanut butter on celery and then putting raisin "ants" on the log.

Related books

Bugs by Nancy Winslow Parker and Joan Richards Wright
Creepy Crawlies by Cathy Kilpatrick
Icky Bug Alphabet Book by Jerry Pallotta
Icky Bug Counting Book by Jerry Pallotta
It's a Good Thing There Are Insects Big Book by Allan Fowler
Look at Insects by Rena Kirkpatrick

Deborah A. Chaplin, Hot Springs, VA

Butterflies Are Symmetrical

Science skills
Children use visual, classification and language skills.

Materials

Outline drawing of a butterfly
Color tiles
Pictures of butterflies, showing both wings
Attribute blocks
Cut-out shapes

What to do

1. Look at a picture of a butterfly. Build observation skills by asking the children if they notice anything about the left and right wings on the butterfly.
2. Guide the children to see that the colors, spots, stripes, etc. on one wing of the butterfly are identical to those on the other wing. One wing is a mirror image of the other. This is an example of symmetry but it is not necessarily important to introduce the word to the children.
3. Show the children the outline drawing of a butterfly. Place a large red triangle on the upper right wing.
4. Build the concept of symmetry by asking children a series of questions to clarify their thinking. Would there be a large green triangle on the upper left wing? Should a small red triangle be placed on the upper left wing? Does a large red triangle have to go on the bottom left wing? What shape should be placed on the upper left wing?
5. The children will agree that the large red triangle belongs on the upper left wing so that both

wings will look alike. Try the procedure again, using a different shape or combination of small shapes in one section of the wing. Let individual children place shapes on the opposite side to match. You can vary the complexity of the patterns you use in one wing for the children to reproduce in the other wing to suite the needs of particular children. For some, it may be appropriate to place two or three small identical shapes in one part of the wing and ask them to reproduce the number of shapes in the other wing. Others may be able to handle more complicated patterns.

More to do

Art: Provide each child with an outline drawing of a butterfly. At the art table, children can color, paint, or glue objects onto the wings so that the wings are mirror images of each other. ▪ Children may also enjoy painting one side of the butterfly's wings in an intricate pattern, and then folding the butterfly in half and pressing to transfer the pattern to the other wing. When they are dry, hang the butterflies with string, or affix them to a bulletin board decorated with flowers.
Field trip: If possible, visit a zoo with a butterfly garden to see butterflies up close.
More science: Notice the patterns on their wings, but remind the children not to catch them. Let the children explore the symmetry in their own faces. They can identify features that are on each side of their faces: eyes, ears, etc.

 *Kim Arnold, Big Flats, NY*

Firefly Fun

Science skills

Children get creative as they practice fine motor skills.

Materials

Black and green construction paper
Scissors
Pencil
Glue
Crayons
Tape

What to do

1. Color and cut out firefly patterns.
2. Let the children tear strips of green paper to serve as blades of grass and glue the grass onto the black construction paper.
3. Glue the fireflies to the black construction paper above the grass.
4. Poke a hole with the pencil on the dot at the back end of each firefly.
5. Tape the finished firefly picture to a bright window.

Original song

"Blink, Blink Firefly" (sing to the tune of "Baa, Baa, Black Sheep")

Blink, blink firefly,
Will you shine for me?

Yes sir, yes sir,
Can you see?

I'll shine for you,
We play hide and seek,
But promise not to catch me
If I blink.

Blink, blink firefly,
We'll have fun tonight,
I won't catch you,
And you will shine so bright.

Related books

Fireflies by Julie Brincloe
Sam and the Firefly by P. D. Eastman

 *Robin Works Davis, Keller, TX*

The Magic of Mirrors

3+

Science skills

Children learn about light and reflection.

Materials

Glass mirrors
Pans
Glue or paste
Scissors
Other mirrors (made from plastic, etc.)
Cardboard
Aluminum foil
Water

What to do

1. Explain to the children that today they will be doing an activity that centers on reflections. A reflection is the return of light from a surface.
2. Tell the children that the best reflections come from very shiny surfaces such as mirrors.
3. After you have discussed glass safety issues, display and distribute glass mirrors so that the children can see the shiny surfaces.
4. Ask the children what they notice about the mirrors. Try to get the children to notice the flat surface, the glare that is produced, that all of the mirrors are made of glass, etc.
5. Distribute the mirrors made from materials other than glass and ask the children to compare them to the glass ones. What things are the same about the mirrors? What things are different about the mirrors?
6. Tell the children that there are many things around our homes and in nature that reflect other objects. Have a brainstorming session with the children. Try to come up with a list of reflecting objects from both home and nature. You may want to do this on two sheets of large paper or on the chalkboard. Remind the children that the objects must be somewhat flat and shiny.
7. Tell the children that they are going to create two mirrors. One will represent nature while the other will represent the home.
8. Distribute the pans and let the children fill the pans with water to represent a pond or stream in nature.
9. Encourage the children to go around the room or even outside with their "water mirrors" to observe the reflections on the water. Discuss why the water creates reflections (it is a flat shiny surface).
10. Distribute the cardboard, aluminum foil, scissors and glue or paste.
11. Help the children cut a piece of foil to the size of the cardboard and then glue it to the cardboard to represent a household mirror.
12. Let the children repeat step nine with their foil mirrors.
13. Compare and contrast the results of the two mirrors. Did one reflect better than the other? Why? (Usually the water reflects better than the foil because it has a flatter surface.)

More to do

Art: Let the children look into a mirror and sketch what they see.
Storytelling: Ask the children to make up and tell stories about magic mirrors.

Related books

Moondance by Frank Asch
Reflections by Ann Jonas
Round Trip by Ann Jonas

Michael Krestar, White Oak, PA

Cat's Eye

Science skills
In this delightful activity, children learn about the connection between light and the ability to see objects.

Materials

Medium-sized cardboard box, about 3′ x 3′ (1 m x 1 m) with lid
Assortment of reflective materials: foil, mirror, cans, glass, tape, fluorescent objects, jewels, etc.
Glue
Black spray paint
Flashlight
Scissors
Tape
String

What to do

1. The teacher spray paints the inside of the box on all sides, bottom and top and then lets the box dry completely.
2. Next day, cut a viewing slot about 6″ x 3″ (15 cm x 7.5 cm) in the side of the box and a second hole next to it, so the flashlight can fit in and move around without difficulty.

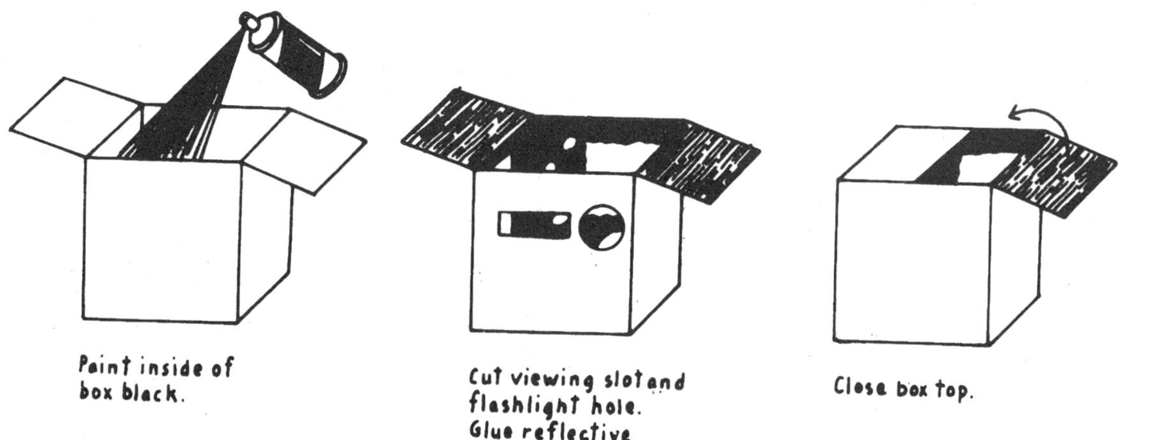

Paint inside of box black.

Cut viewing slot and flashlight hole. Glue reflective objects inside.

Close box top.

3. Ask the children to attach objects of their choice in the box. The teacher can help the children choose adhesive options that are best suited for the objects.
4. Once all the objects are inside the box, close the top and place it in the science area.
5. Now the children can take turns with the flashlight to look inside at the reflective objects.

More to do

More science: Discuss the safety issues of night activities, such as walking, biking, rollerblading, etc., and the importance of wearing white or reflective material on clothing so that cars can see you better.

Dani Rosensteel, Payson, AZ

Making Shadows

Science skills

In this exciting activity, children observe how shadows are created.

Materials

Large white sheet or a slide screen
Portable light

What to do

1. Hang a white sheet across the room. If you have a slide screen that can be positioned down low, this will also work.
2. Position a light so that it shines on the sheet. Darken the rest of the room as much as possible.
3. Discuss what shadows are. You can tell children that shadows are places of darkness created when something blocks light. Ask the children if they have ever seen their shadow.
4. Gather the children in front of the screen. Explain that you are going to play a game. Tell the children they will cover their eyes and turn their backs away from the screen. It is important for everyone to remain quiet. Tell the children that if they feel a tap on the shoulder to open their eyes and quietly come with you.
5. When a child is positioned behind the screen, ask the children to turn around and guess whose shadow they are seeing. Continue until everyone has had a turn. Experiment with having the children behind the screen face different directions or strike poses.

More to do

Movement: Assign each child a partner. Inform them that one is the leader and one is the shadow. Put on some music and let the leader move about the room while his shadow sticks with him and follows his every move. Be sure to allow time for children to switch positions.

Related book

Peter Pan by James M. Barrie

Connie Heagerty, Trumbull, CT

3+ Light and Shadow

Science skills

Children participate in making shadows and observing the effect of light.

Materials

Strong flashlight

Different objects around the classroom

What to do

1. Ask the children to pick up any object from around them, such as a block, a plate, a doll, a marker, etc.
2. Turn off the lights and pull the curtains to make the classroom as dark as possible.
3. Seat the children in front of a plain wall and let them take turns holding their objects in front of an illuminated flashlight which you hold so it shines steadily at the wall.
4. Encourage the children to look at the shadows they make. Ask questions such as, what shape is the shadow? Is it big or small? What happens when you move the object? Does the shadow move, too? What happens when you turn off the flashlight? Is the shadow still there?
5. Explain how things placed in front of a light make shadows, how shadows move and how we can make them bigger or smaller.

Manisha Segal, Burtonsville, MD

3+ Light Shapes

Science skills

A fun and easy project to help children uncover the mystery of shadows and learn about shapes.

Materials

4″ x 6″ (10 cm x 15 cm) rectangles

Scissors

Heavy paper

Flashlight

What to do

1. Cut different shapes (circle, triangle, heart, etc.) out of the center of each rectangle.
2. Ask the children if they know what a shadow is. Is it easier to see shadows when the lights are on or off? Why?
3. Show the shape cards to the children. Review the shapes.
4. Turn off the lights to darken the room.

5. Ask the children to predict what will happen when a flashlight is directed through the cut-out shapes.
6. Turn on the flashlight and aim the light through a shape so that the light shines on a nearby wall.
7. Ask the children what is projected on the wall. What makes a shadow?
8. Repeat with the remaining shapes.
9. Follow up this project by reading some books that explain shadows with the children.

Related books

Bear Shadow by Frank Asch
My Shadow by Susan Winter
Shadowville by Michael Bartalos

Elizabeth Thomas, Hobart, IN

Creating Heat

3+

Science skills

This simple experiment shows children the scientific principle of cause and effect.

Materials

2 small cardboard boxes
2 metal measuring cups
Piece of black paper and piece of white paper

What to do

1. Place a metal cup in each box.
2. Cover one box with white paper and one with black paper.
3. Place boxes in direct sunlight for several hours.
4. Uncover the boxes and let the children touch the metal cups.
5. Ask which is warmer.
6. Explain that darker colors absorb the light and heat while light colors reflect heat and light.

Cindy Winther, Oxford, MI

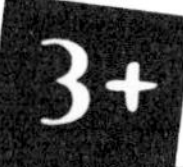

Effects of the Sun

Science skills
Children observe the effects of the sun.

Materials
Newspaper

What to do
1. Place a piece of newspaper outside in direct sunlight. Place another piece of newspaper indoors out of sunlight.
2. Observe the changes on both pieces of newspaper over the next week or so.
3. Bring the outside paper in and compare it to the indoor paper. Explain how sunlight can discolor the paper just as it discolors or tans a person's skin.

Cindy Winther, Oxford, MI

Faded Sun Prints

Science skills
Children observe the effects of the sun.

Materials
Colored construction paper, not fade-resistant type
Small objects such as buttons, charms, paper clips, pencils, lace, ribbons, etc.

What to do
1. Place the sheets of construction paper outside in direct sunlight.
2. Ask each child to arrange some objects on the paper to create a design.
3. Leave the paper with the objects in the sun for several hours.
4. When the children remove the objects, they will see the prints the objects left behind on the paper.

More to do
Art: The children can make frames for their sun prints.
More science: Allow other objects to fade in the sun, for example, other types of paper, cloth, ribbon, plastic, etc.

Melanie Lemen, Clear Spring, MD

Fading Colors

3+

Science skills

Children learn comparison skills.

Materials

Construction paper
Windows
Sunlight

What to do

1. Talk about how sunlight makes colors fade.
2. Tape squares of different color construction paper to the windows, making sure to have a sheet of each color left over to compare later.
3. Over the next two to three weeks pull the squares down periodically and compare them to the original color. Which colors faded the most? Which colors faded the fastest?
4. If you have access to windows in different areas of the building, watch to see if the colors fade differently depending on how much sunlight each area gets.

More to do

Art: When the experiment is over, glue the colored squares on bulletin board paper to make a giant rainbow. ▪ Paint with the colors that turn out to fade the most and the least.

Related book

Mouse Paint by Ellen Stoll Walsh

Suzanne Pearson, Winchester, VA

Learning About Light

3+

Science skills

Children practice their observation and language skills.

Materials

Variety of items to show how light travels, such as glass, cellophane, sheer fabric, cardboard, etc.

What to do

1. Experiment with different objects to see which ones allow light to travel through them by holding them up to a window.
2. Talk about "transparent"—it lets light shine through clearly; "translucent"—it lets light shine through but less clearly; and "opaque"—it does not let any light shine through at all.

Cindy Winther, Oxford, MI

3+ Mirror, Mirror

Science skills

When a child looks in a mirror, there is ample opportunity for learning about reflection.

Materials

2 mirror tiles, about 9" x 12" (22.5 cm x 30 cm), purchased from a home improvement store
Battery-operated candles
Piece of cardboard that can be folded like a book
Optional: various toys chosen from toy sets in classroom

What to do

Note: Keep in mind that the mirrors are breakable and use extra care in this activity.

1. Fold the cardboard into a "book" and glue the two mirrors on inside of it. Stand the book on edge in front of the child.
2. Sit down with each child in turn in front of the mirrors and encourage him to talk about himself, how he looks, hair color, etc.
3. Now the child may light the battery-operated candle and count the number of candles he sees by reflection.
4. Let the child put his hand against the mirror with only two or three fingers showing in the mirror. The reflection will make a monster claw.
5. The child may look at toys in the mirror so he can see halves of toys or the backs and fronts at the same time.

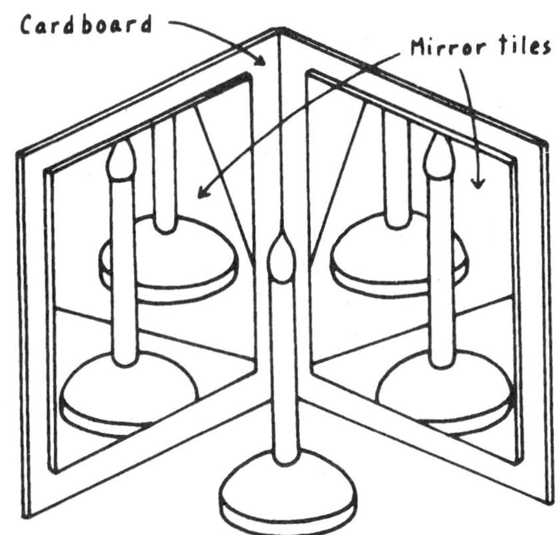

More to do

Art: Children might paint themselves on a mirrored surface or paint their portraits or that of a friend by mirror image.
Games: Mirror, Mirror on the Wall, Who Is the Tallest of Us All? Place a full-length mirror on its

side at the children's eye level. Let the children answer the questions, substituting other words or phrases for tallest: has the reddest dress, has the biggest smile of all, etc. Make the questions fit the situation, being careful not to be judgmental.

More science: In the play area, provide a full-length mirror on its side so children can see structures, front and back. The mirror will also make the structure look larger.

Related books

Mirror Magic by Seymour Simon

Snow White and the Seven Dwarfs, many versions

Helen Buemi, Binghamton, NY

My Own Constellation

4+

Science skills

Each child makes observations about light while making a personalized constellation.

Materials

Flashlight

Paper punch or sharp pencil

Chalk or star stickers

Black construction paper, one piece per child

Tape

What to do

1. Cut many small circles to the diameter of the lighted end of the flashlight out of the construction paper, enough for each child to have two or three.
2. Allow the children to use a paper punch or sharp pencil to make a few holes in each of their circles.
3. Tape a sheet of black construction paper onto a wall. From a distance of 12" to 18" (30 cm x 45 cm), hold a punched circle against the flashlight head and shine the light through the circle at the paper taped to the wall to reveal each child's constellation in turn. Use a new sheet of black paper for each child.
4. Let the children use chalk to draw their pictures or patterns over the stars on their paper.

More to do

Art: Use the constellation pictures to make a large mural or, if possible, a whole night sky that you can attach to the ceiling.

Language: During circle time ask each child to describe his constellation to the other children.

More science: Following steps one and two above, punch out real constellation patterns and shine them onto a wall for the children to identify.

Leslie Kvehn Meyer, Austin, MN

4+

Sunlight Tag

Science skills
In this game, children play with light and reflections.

Materials
Several metal canning lids, or any shiny, unbreakable object that a child can easily hold in his hand, such as a piece of cardboard covered with aluminum foil

What to do
1. The teacher can show the children how sunlight reflects off of canning lids and how the reflected light can move across the ceiling and the wall.
2. Ask all the children to try to focus their reflected light on the same spot simultaneously.
3. Now, ask them to try to chase and "tag" the teacher's reflected light with their own.
4. Caution the children never to shine the reflected light onto another person's face.

More to do
More science: Compare various materials, for example, aluminum foil, black cloth, white feathers, a clear plastic cassette case to determine which items have a shiny reflection. Which do not?

Original song
Chant or sing to the tune of "Ballin' the Jack."

First you let the sunlight into the room,
Let it touch your lid and watch it zoom,
Put it up the wall and down the door,
Around the desk and on the floor.
Never shine the light in someone's face.
Shining on the ceiling is a better place.
Put it up the wall and down the door,
Around the desk and on the floor.

Related books
The North Wind and the Sun by Jean de La Fontaine
Sunshine by Jan Ormerod
Who Gets the Sun Out of Bed? by Nancy Carlstrom

Christina Chilcote, New Freedom, PA

Adventures With Shadows

5+

Science skills

Children use light and shadows to make unique pictures.

Materials

Flashlight
Crayons
Various shadow pictures, created beforehand, for example, of scissors, toy truck, coffee mug, fork, butterfly
Paper
Assorted objects, such as comb, ball, box

What to do

1. Tell the children that you need their help to make some really special pictures. Tell them that they are going to have to help you catch the pictures before they disappear.
2. Pull the flashlight out of the box and tell them that it is a special tool that makes the pictures appear.
3. Ask the children what kind of picture they think will appear when you shine the flashlight on the ball. Shine the flashlight on the ball in such a way that the ball casts a shadow. For some objects, just setting them on the table works best. First, tape some paper to the table. Call on one of the children to come and trace around the outside of the shadow on the paper. When the child completes the tracing, turn off the flashlight and look at the shape he drew.
4. Create other pictures using the other objects.
5. Ask the children why they think the pictures appear. Help them draw the conclusion that the pictures are really shadows and shadows are created when light is blocked.
6. Show the children the shadow pictures you created beforehand using the other objects listed above. See if they can identify them.
7. Show the children how to make shadow figures on the wall with their hands.

More to do

Games: Play Shadow Tag on a sunny day in the early morning or late afternoon. The person who is "it" tags another person by stepping on their shadow. ▪ Make a matching game of objects and their shadows.

More science: Go outside and discover all the things that have a shadow at various times of day. ▪ Help the children draw their body silhouettes from their shadows on the sidewalk and then add the details.

Original poems

Poems adapted from *Think of Shadows* by Lillian Moore and Deborah Robinson.

Ground Hog Day

Ground Hog sleeps all winter snug in his soft warm fur.

He dreams of grassy shoots,
Of nicely newly nibbly roots—
Ah, at last he starts to stir.

With drowsy stare he looks out from his burrow
On fields of wintry snow.
What's that he sees? Oh no!
His shadow. We've six more wintry weeks to go.

Is There a Place?

Is there a place where shadows go when it is dark?
Do they play in the park?
Slip down the slides?
Run down streets?
Stretch high and shrink thin?
Do they spin in the wind and fly with the leaves?
Splash in the rain and hang from the wires to dry?
Do they miss us?
Are they glad to see the sun or sad?

Related books

Shadows Here, There, and Everywhere by Ron and Nancy Goor
What Makes a Shadow? by Clyde Robert Bulla

Michele Wistisen, Casper, WY

Sand Attraction

3+

Science skills

Children find magnetic material in beach sand using fine motor skills.

Materials

Magnets
Beach sand
Plastic trays with sides

What to do

1. Pour the beach sand into the trays and encourage the children to dip the magnets into the sand. Observe what happens.
2. If the magnets have black grains clinging to them, then the sand contains magnetite. Beach sand varies in magnetite content. Magnetite is a mineral called iron oxide (Fe_2O_4). It is an important iron ore that in another form we call rust.

More to do

Art: Create sand paintings using glue and sand on cardboard. Let the sand dry, then blow the loose sand away.
More science: Collect sand from different beaches as well as sand piles. Compare similarities and differences. Use see-through containers to compare the sand.

Related books

Science Book of Magnets by Niel Ardley
What Magnets Can Do by Allan Fowler

Jill Putnam, Wellfleet, MA

Painting With Magnets

Science skills

By making paintings, children observe magnetism.

Materials

Paint
Box
Magnets
Paper
Metal object

What to do

1. Place the paper in the box and put a few drops of thinned paint around the paper.
2. Now place a heavy metal object on the paper and move a magnet across the underside of the box.
3. As the metal object moves with the magnet, the paint will be dragged around, making designs.

Audrey F. Kanoff, Allentown, PA

3+

Pulling Power

Science skills
Children observe the strength of magnetism and test their prediction skills.

Materials

Strong magnet
Piece of paper
Cloth
Paper clip
Foil

What to do

1. Let the children try picking up just the paper clip with the magnet.
2. Now put a piece of paper over the clip and let them try to pick it up.
3. Next, put a piece of foil over the clip and try to pick it up.
4. Finally, put a piece of cloth over the clip and see what happens.
5. Each time the clip will stick to the magnet. The pulling power of a magnet is strong!

Cindy Winther, Oxford, MI

3+

Push and Pull With Magnets

Science skills
In play, children experiment with the attraction and repelling power of magnets.

Materials

Four small cars
Magnets
Glue
Box or tray to store the items

What to do

1. In advance, glue one magnet to the front and back of each car. Be sure to reverse the magnets on the front and back of each car, i.e., south on back and north on front.
2. Talk to the children about magnets and tell them that they need to be careful with the cars so the magnets do not fall off. Demonstrate how to experiment with the magnets.
3. Place the cars on a table and let the children see how the magnets will push away from each other, or pull to each other.
4. Ask the children why they think this is happening. Tell them that there is a north and a south pole to magnets, somewhat like their left and right hands and that neither of their hands ever change. Just as you can never shake your own hand, the same poles cannot stick together or shake hands.

Melissa Browning, Milwaukee, WI

Magnet Magic

3+

Science skills

Children will be thrilled to observe marbles magically leaping and moving.

Materials

Magnetic wand, found in most magnet kits
2-3 colored magnetic marbles
2-3 colored magnetic paper clips
One 16 oz. (500 ml) plastic bottle without label

What to do

1. Fill plastic bottle to the top with water.
2. Drop paper clips and marbles into the bottle.
3. The child or teacher holds the bottle (which is placed on the floor or on a table).
4. The child places the magnetic wand against the outside of the bottle. Hold the wand steady until the clips and marbles attach to the wand.
5. Have the child slowly slide the wand up the side of the bottle. Keep the wand on the bottle all the way up to the neck of the bottle.
6. When the wand gets to the top of the bottle, the clips and marbles will jump out of the bottle and onto the wand, forming a line. The children will be amazed!

Related books

1-2-3 Science by Gayle Bittinger
Mudpies to Magnets by R. Williams, R. Rockwell, E. Sherwood

Magnet Pole

Science skills
Children observe the properties of magnetism.

Materials

2 doughnut magnets
Small piece of wood
Wooden dowel
Drill

What to do

1. Drill a hole the size of the dowel in the piece of wood and glue the dowel into the hole.
2. Show the children how the doughnut magnet slides up and down the pole.
3. Talk to the children about the north and south ends of a magnet.
4. Let the children try to put the opposite sides of the magnets on the pole. The magnets cannot be pushed together. The children will think there's an invisible spring between them.

Related book

Marta's Magnets by Wendy Pfeffer

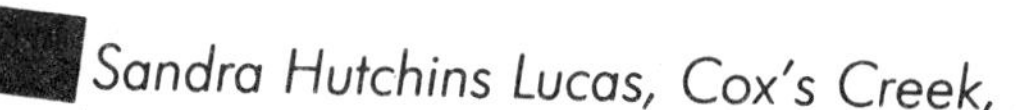
Sandra Hutchins Lucas, Cox's Creek, KY

3+

Let's Go Fishing

Science skills
As the children go fishing, they learn what is attracted to magnets and what is not.

Materials

Fish shapes cut out of plastic report covers
Large paper clips
Fishing poles made out of sticks with yarn tied on
Small tub or pool
A doughnut-shaped magnet attached to yarn

What to do

1. Attach large paper clips to the fish and place the fish in the pool.
2. Let the children "go fishing" with their fishing poles.
3. After the children have gotten the hang of it, throw in a few fish without clips. Be sure to talk about why they can't catch those fish.

More to do

More science: Put numbers on the fish. Encourage the children to "fish" for number 3 or number 5. ▪ Put shapes on the fish and ask the children to name each shape as it is caught.

Cindy Winther, Oxford, MI

Magic Racing Paper Clips

4+

Science skills

In this exciting game, children guess (predict) which magnet will finish first.

Materials

Two metal paper clips
Marker
Poster board, one piece
Two block magnets

What to do

1. The teacher makes a line with the marker 1" (2.5 cm) from the top and bottom edges on both sides of the poster board. The class sits on one side of the board and two children sit behind it as the teacher holds it up.
2. The two children hold their magnets at the bottom start line and the teacher places the two paper clips on the other side of the poster so that they are held in place by the magnets.
3. On the count of three the two racers move their magnets up to the finish line on the top as fast as they can without dropping the paper clips. The first one up wins the race. The children on the other side cheer on as they watch the paper clips move up as if by magic. Choose two new contestants each time and let each child have a turn.
4. Ask how the paper clips move and then explain how the magnets held on the back move the clips around.

More to do

More science: Ask the children to choose a few things from around the classroom and see if these things will be attracted to the magnet. You can give the children various metal things and allow them to experiment on their own.

Manisha Segal, Burtonsville, MD

Magnets

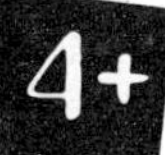

Magnet Animals

Science skills

The mouse magically and magnetically gets the cheese as the children practice observation skills.

Materials

One piece of white poster board, any size
Piece of cardboard or stiff paper
Paper clips
Glue
Crayons or markers in yellow, black, gray
Scissors
Magnet
Four wooden blocks

What to do

1. Draw a piece of cheese in the upper left-hand corner of the poster board. Draw a black circle in the lower right-hand corner.
2. Draw a mouse, about 1½" (3.5 cm) long, on cardboard or stiff paper and cut it out. On the back side of the mouse glue one or two paper clips and let dry.
3. Place the poster board on the blocks so that each corner is supported by a block.
4. Place the mouse on the black circle.
5. Hold the magnet underneath the poster board so that the magnet attracts the paper clips.
6. Now guide the mouse from the black circle to the cheese and back again to the black circle.

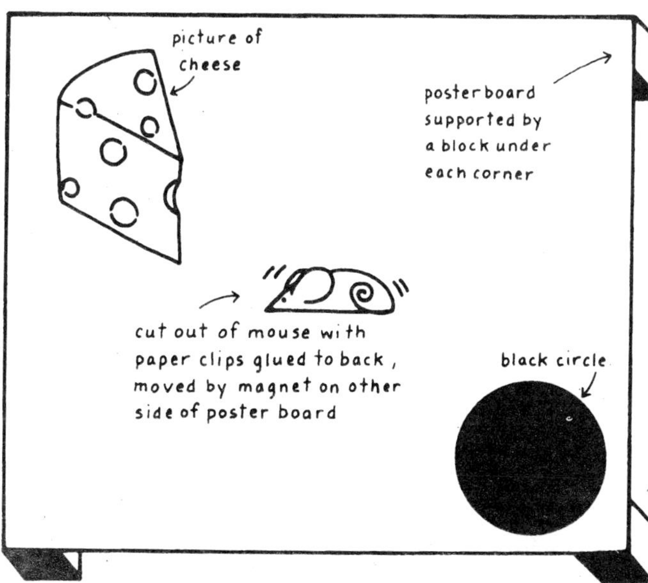

More to do

More science: Attach several paper clips together. Glue the half shell of a pistachio nut at one end of the paper clip chain to make the head of a snake. Draw a jungle on the white piece of poster board. Guide the snake through the jungle by the same method as above.

*Ingelore Mix, Massapequa, NY*

Magnet Power

4+

Science skills

Children observe magnetism firsthand and use fine motor skills.

Materials

1-liter clear plastic bottle with lid
Ball bearings
Water
2 large blocks
Colorful plastic covered paper clips
Nails
Paper shirt box
Magnet wands

What to do

1. Link paper clips into chains and place them in the empty bottle.
2. Fill the bottle with water and close it with the lid.
3. Use a wand to show that magnets even work through water
4. Now place the nails, clips and ball bearings in the box and balance the box between the two blocks so children can reach beneath.
5. Use magnet wand to show how magnets work through the box as well.

More to do

More science: Display and let the children play with many different games and toys that use magnets.
Movement: Let the children form teams of magnets so that when they get close to each other they "stick."

Teresa J. Nos, Baltimore, MD

Magnet Races

4+

Science skills

Children teach themselves about the workings of magnetism.

Materials

Paper
Ruler
Marker
Magnets of all shapes and sizes

What to do

1. Draw a starting line and finish line on a piece of paper.

2. Put one magnet on the starting line and put another magnet a little behind it.
3. Try to push the first magnet with the second one without having the magnets touch.
4. The children will learn through trial and error that poles must face each other and they'll learn about the strengths of various magnets.

More to do

Numbers: Measure with a ruler how far one magnet moves the other.

Related book

What Makes a Magnet? by Franklyn Branley

Karen Megay-Nespoli, Massapequa Park, NY

4+

Magnet Skaters

Science skills

The children observe magnetism and use fine motor skills.

Materials

Per child:
One construction paper strip, 1″ x 2″ (2.5 cm x 5 cm)
One 6″ (15 cm) plate
Fine point markers or colored pencils
One paper clip
One refrigerator magnet

What to do

1. Let each child draw a figure on the paper strip.
2. At the bottom of the strip fold a tab that is as wide as the paper clip.
3. Attach a paper clip to the tab.
4. Place the figure on top of the plate and hold a magnet underneath the plate so it catches the clip and makes the figure stand upright.
5. Slide the magnet against the bottom of the plate to make the figure on top skate and dance.

More to do

More science: Present a box filled with paper clips, marbles, crayons, buttons, etc. Ask the children to pick out the clips. Is there a fast way? ▪ Drop a metal object into a fish tank or behind some furniture. How can we retrieve it? ▪ Use a magnet to sort objects into a pile of metal and a pile of nonmetal.

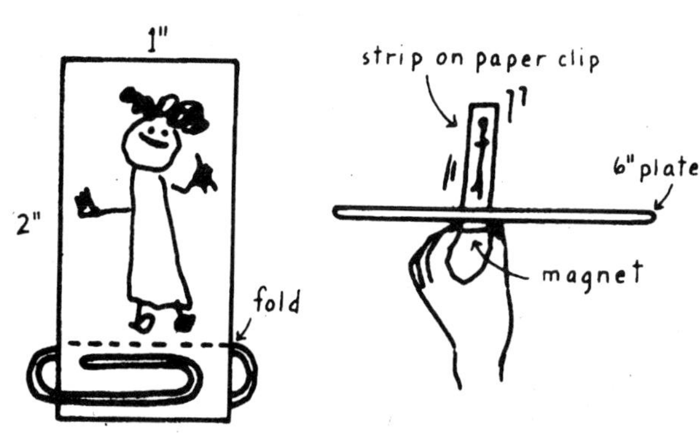

Sandra Gratias, Perkasie, PA

Magnets

4+

Science skills

Through observation, experimentation and using fine motor skills, children experience magnetism.

Materials

Magnets

Assorted metal and non-metal objects

What to do

Note: In advance, place various objects that are attracted to magnets around the room, such as scissors, coins, gem clips, utensils, etc.

Caution: Supervise closely.

1. Display one or two strong magnets and demonstrate how they work, using both objects that have attraction to magnets and others that do not.
2. Ask the children to walk around the class and pick up an object they think the magnet will attract.
3. Take turns showing their items and testing whether or not they are attracted. Let the class guess the answer before testing the items.
4. Have a follow-up discussion concerning the properties of objects that are attracted to magnets.

More to do

More science: Put all collected objects and the magnets on the science table with two boxes labeled Yes and No. Let the children take turns testing the items and putting them in the proper boxes.

 *Elaine Commins, Atlanta, GA*

Magnet Firefighters: Rushing to the Fire

Science skills

Here is a fun way for children to observe magnetism and develop fine motor skills.

Materials

2 pieces of white poster board
Markers
Pattern for the firefighters
Popsicle sticks
Laminate or clear contact paper
Multicultural crayons
Pattern for a fire truck
Disc magnets, 4 per firefighter (40 total)
Hot glue

What to do

1. Make 10 fire fighters about 3" (7.5 cm) tall, using multicultural crayons to show the many ethnic groups. Number the firefighters' hats from 1 to 10.
2. Mount each firefighter onto poster board and laminate or cover.
3. Draw a fire truck, a pole and other decorations on the large piece of poster board and laminate the entire board. This helps the firefighters to slide across the poster board.
4. On the back of each firefighter glue two disc magnets, one near the head and one near the feet.
5. Then put magnets onto the magnets that are already attached to the firefighters. Using hot glue, glue a popsicle stick to each of the top magnets. Make sure to write the number of the firefighter on one of the popsicle sticks. Do this with all 10 firefighters.
6. When the glue has dried, take the firefighter and popsicle stick apart, separating the magnets. Place the firefighter on the front of the poster board. Then line up the popsicle magnets behind the firefighter on the back of the board. Now, when you move the popsicle sticks, the firefighters will move. Recite this poem with the children and let them move the firefighters accordingly:

Ten brave fire fighters,
Standing in a row.
Ding dong rings the bell,
Down the pole they go.
Jump on the truck,
Ready to aim the hose.
Climb up the ladder,
Whoosh! Out the fire goes.

7. The children think it's magic. Show them that the magnets are doing the moving.
8. Show the children what happens when magnets don't attract. The firefighters fall off the board.

 *Debbie Barbuch, Sheboygan, WI*

4+

The Salt and Pepper Dance

Science skills

In this astonishing activity, children develop observation skills and curiosity about nature.

Magnets

Materials
Comb
Salt
Pepper

What to do
1. Pour the salt and pepper into a mound in the middle of a table.
2. Run the comb through your hair and then ask the children what they think will happen when you run the comb across the mound of salt and pepper.
3. Run the comb through your hair twice more and then run it across the salt and pepper.
4. The salt and pepper will separate because the comb becomes a static conductor and the pepper has magnetic elements in it.

Eric Painter, Georgetown, MA

You Can Make a Bird Fly

4+

Science skills
As they create a picture of nature, children learn about the power of magnetic attraction.

Materials
Construction paper
Markers
Glue or tape
Sticks or dowels, about 10" to 15" (15 cm to 37.5 cm) long
Crayons
Scissors
Magnets
Steel paper clips or bobby pins

What to do
1. Encourage the children to design, then cut out the top of a deciduous or evergreen tree from construction paper and glue it to the stick. Tape or glue one or two magnets about three-quarters of the way up the tree.
2. Ask the children to make pictures of birds and/or butterflies using construction paper and crayons. These should be no bigger than about 4" (10 cm) long. Cut out the pictures and slide the paper clip over the middle of the bird or butterfly's body, or attach it to the head area.
3. Gradually move the tree closer and closer to the bird or butterfly until the magnet attracts the paper clip on the bird. You may need to tilt the tree slightly. Watch the bird or butterfly fly to the top of the tree.

More to do
Art: Let the children create butterflies out of many types of materials: fabric, noodles, felt, clay, paints, etc.

Language: Read *The Giving Tree* by Shel Silverstein. Go around the room asking the children what they have been given and what they like to give to others.
Math: Ask the children to estimate how many paper clips one magnet could pick up out of a full box of paper clips and then try it.
More science: Find reference books with pictures of butterflies and/or birds for the children to study and appreciate. Put in the science area.

Jeannie Gunderson, Casper, WY

5+

Magnet Tray

Science skills
Children experiment and observe what is attracted to a magnet.

Materials

Plastic dinner tray or plate with one large and two small compartments
Horseshoe magnet
Small objects, such as safety pin, nail, paper clip, washer, cotton ball, piece of cloth, wooden popsicle stick, sponge, etc. (you might keep objects that magnets attract in a separate container and change the objects frequently to add interest)

What to do

1. Use a permanent marker to label the two small sections of the tray "Yes" and "No."
2. Place several objects in the large section.
3. Select one object at a time and test it with the magnet. If the magnet picks it up, put it in the "Yes" section. If the object isn't attracted, place it in the "No" section. Testing one object at a time prevents pulling all the metal objects out at the same time!

More to do

Language: Increase vocabulary by naming each object used and by categorizing the objects labeled "Yes" as all metal.
Math: Count the number of objects in the large section before you begin, then count the number in the "Yes" section and in the "No" section when you finish.
More science: Increase the difficulty and interest of the activity by adding some metals the magnet will not attract, such as copper, brass, silver and gold.

Mary Jo Shannon, Roanoke, VA

Measurement

Measure Lengths

3+

Science skills

Children learn about measurement tools and practice making comparisons.

Materials

Ruler
Wooden yard stick
Plastic and fabric tape measures
Roll-out tape measure
Folding yard stick
Items to measure: dolls, play cars, books, cups, toy animals and children

What to do

1. Talk about the names of the tools we use to take measurements.
2. Let the children measure to see which doll is tallest, which car is longest, which cup is widest, which animal is shortest, which book is narrowest, etc.

More to do

More science: Measure all the children's heights at the beginning and at the end of the year to see how much they have grown and show them on a ruler. ▪ Make the children's footprints at the beginning of the year by painting their feet with a foam brush and printing on paper, or drawing around the feet with a wide tip pen. ▪ Show the footprint of a baby sister or brother and measure the difference between it and the footprint of a child in the class.

Marilyn Harding, Grimes, IA

Sorting by Size

Science skills

Children learn to sort and classify, according to the criteria of small, medium and large.

Materials

Small, medium and large round items, such as apples, baseball, golf balls, ping pong balls, marbles
Box

What to do

1. Make three holes in the side of a box—one small, one medium, one large. Or use a long box and make the three different size holes on the same side.
2. Put in the various-sized objects. Shake or slide the box around until the objects roll out of the hole that is closest to their size.
3. Sort the round objects into piles by size.

More to do

Field trip: Visit an apple orchard, if possible. The children will be fascinated to see the machines used in orchards that work like the box in the activity above, sorting the apples by size.

Marilyn Harding, Grimes, IA

3+

How Heavy Is It?

Science skills

In this game, children make predictions, then test their predictions.

Materials

Items of varying weights, such as books, boxes, bricks, feathers, pencils, Styrofoam, wood blocks

What to do

1. Put out two items at a time. Without letting the children pick up the items, ask them which of the two they think is the heaviest.
2. After the children have made a guess, let them pick up the items to see if they were right.
3. Repeat the game with the other items.
4. If you want to make this more difficult, add a third item.

More to do

Math: Chart the children's answers to see how many times they guessed correctly and incorrectly.

Monica Hay-Cook, Tucson, AZ

Measurement

How Many Beanbags?

4+

Science skills
Children practice estimating.

Materials
A bucketful of same-size beanbags
A balance scale
Paper with pictures of objects in the room

What to do

1. You can purchase a balance scale or make one following the picture diagram.
2. Draw and write the following, using objects in the room, so that the children can weigh the objects on their own.

The [book] weighs ____ beanbags. The [block] weighs ____ beanbags.

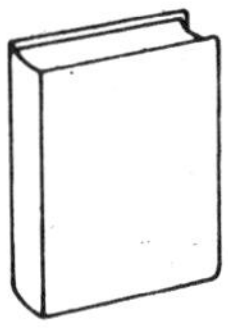

The [car] weighs ____ beanbags. The [purse] weighs ____ beanbcgs.

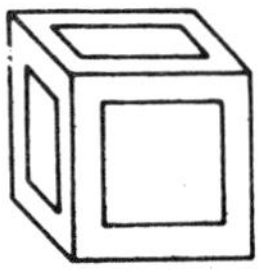

nut and bolt
eyelet
chain
metal tray

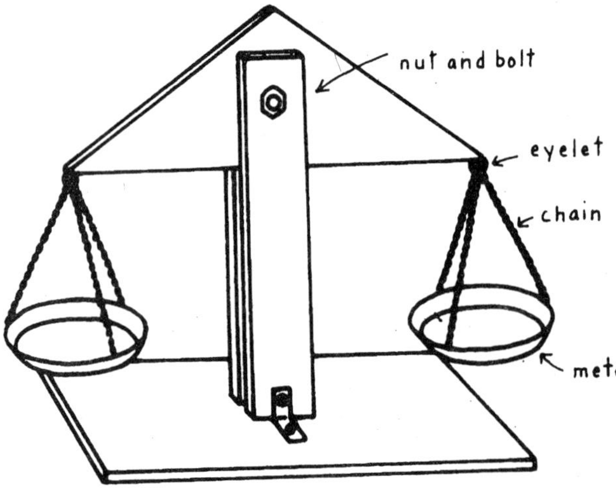

3. Ask the children to put an object on one side of the balance scale and then add enough beanbags to balance the scale. Now count the beanbags and record the numbers.
4. For variation, you could bring in other types of scales for the children to see and use, such as postal scales, food scales, bathroom scales, hanging scales.

Shirley Story, Lenoir, NC

4+

How Many Feet?

Science skills

Observation and counting are the skills children practice in this activity.

Materials

8-10 1′ (30 cm) rulers
Scissors
Paper with pictures of objects in the room
Heavy cardboard
Glue

What to do

1. Cut cardboard into eight to ten footprints, each 1′ long.
2. Glue one ruler on each footprint.
3. Draw pictures of objects in the room that children can measure. Add the following words so the children can measure objects on their own.

The ____ is ____ feet long. The ____ is ____ feet long.

The ____ is ____ feet long. The ____ is ____ feet long.

4. Ask the children to line the rulers up end to end along the item they are measuring and then count the rulers and record the number. Children can work in pairs.
5. As a variation, select one volunteer to lie down on the rug and help another volunteer to line up the rulers from the reclining child's head to his toes. Then the group can count to see how tall the child is.

Shirley Story, Lenoir, NC

Measurement

How Far?

4+

Science skills

This activity offers practice in observation as well as fine and large motor skills.

Materials

Jump, Frog, Jump! by Robert Kalan
Adding machine tape
Paper
Scissors
Masking tape or chalk
Tempera paint mixed for making handprints
Styrofoam trays

What to do

1. Read the book.
2. Talk about the way frogs move. Let the children brainstorm to think of other animals that move in a similar way.
3. Ask each child to pretend to be an animal that moves by jumping. Mark a starting line with masking tape or chalk. One at a time, let each child stand on the starting line and jump once as far as he can.
4. Using the adding machine tape, measure and cut a strip of paper the length of the child's jump.
5. Allow each child to measure his own tape using painted handprints as a nonstandard unit of measure. Stress the proper way to measure. Start at one end of the tape and proceed to the other. Handprints should touch but not overlap.
6. After you have measured all the jumps, you may choose to put the strips in order from shortest to longest.

More to do

More science: Encourage the children to use other non-standard units of measure such as blocks, straws, pipe cleaners, popsicle sticks, etc. to measure their jumps. Stress the difference in the number of units for each as well as the fact that the actual length of the tape did not change. Measure the jumps of a real frog.

Lyndall Warren, Milledgeville, GA

I Can't Believe My Eyes

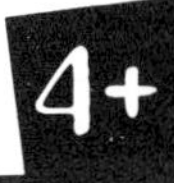

Science skills

Using water play, children make predictions and draw conclusions.

Materials

Non-breakable containers of different sizes: gallon (4 L), half-gallon (2 L), quart (1 L), pint (500 ml) and cup (250 ml), several of each

Water

Water play tub

What to do

1. Discuss the shapes and sizes of the different containers.
2. Encourage the children to predict which containers hold the same amount of water even though their shapes are different.
3. Place those containers into a water play tub and pour water into one selected container.
4. Do measuring by pouring water from one container to another.
5. Discuss the conclusions the children reach about containers of different shapes and their capacities.

Related book

Capacity by Henry Pluckrose

 *Sandra Fisher, Kutztown, PA*

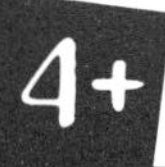

Measure Up

Science skills

Basketball's Dream Team inspires an activity in which children measure and compare.

Materials

String or yarn

Photos from sports magazines

Yardsticks or tape measures

Dream Team programs, or articles on them from sports magazines

What to do

1. Using a tape measure, measure a length of yarn as long as Shaqille O'Neal is tall and tape it to the wall.
2. Place a photo of Shaqille, cut from a magazine, at the top of the yarn, where his head would be.
3. Compare the children's heights to his height.
4. You may do this activity for each member of the Dream Team, and then compare the players' heights.

 *Tracie O'Hara, Charlotte, NC*

Measuring Inch by Inch

4+

Science skills

In this activity the children explore measurement.

Materials

Inch by Inch by Leo Lionni
Rulers
Gummi worms

What to do

1. Read *Inch by Inch*.
2. Discuss things that can be measured with a ruler and things that cannot. Examples: leaves can be measured, voices cannot; radios can be measured, radio music cannot.
3. Have rulers on hand to demonstrate how to find an inch, two inches, etc. Let the children practice.
4. Hand out one or two gummi worms to each child. Measure the worms and discuss how long they are. Children can eat the gummi worms.
5. Talk about some of the items measured by the inchworm in *Inch by Inch*. Discuss the difference between items in nature and human-made objects. Ask the children to name items in nature they might find around the school or at home (rocks, twigs, leaves, grass, etc.).
6. Weather permitting, take the children outside. Invite them to find and collect a few items in nature that are at least one inch long. If weather is inclement, explore items in the room.
7. Once back inside, measure the items the children collected. List the names and lengths of the items the children measured. Discuss the longest, shortest, fattest, hardest to measure, etc.

More to do

Art: Children can either make their own playdough or work with pre-made dough or clay. Remind the children about some of the items in nature they measured or named earlier. Let the children create an object from nature that is one inch long or wide, then one that is three inches, then whatever they choose. It can be a plant, an animal, a fish, a rock, etc. They can even invent their own animal or plant. Let each child talk about his creation and give its measurements.
Math: Make a graph of the length of the items the children found outside. ▪ Measure body parts such as heads, arms, fingers and feet with a tape measure or ruler.
More science: You could bring inchworms into the classroom so that the children can observe their movements.

Jeannie Gunderson, Casper WY

4+

Measuring for Self-Awareness

Science skills

Children measure and classify items using fine motor skills.

Materials

Paper and writing materials
Bathroom scales
Tape measures
Art materials
Smaller scales
Rulers and yardsticks
Possessions: shoes, coats, sweaters, favorite toys, classroom materials, any other items teachers and children wish to include

What to do

1. Introduce the activity with a short discussion about differences and similarities. Help the children design and create individual Measurement Books, using paper and art materials.
2. Let the children pick partners. Working with partners broadens self-esteem and enhances the children's social development.
3. Children measure and weigh each other and each other's possessions and record each other's measurements in their books.
4. Groups of children can make charts to include biggest, smallest, heaviest and lightest people and possessions.

More to do

More science: Add anything that the children can measure by weight, length or volume. As the curriculum continues to expand, so can the measurement activities.

 *Tom Gordon, Slippery Rock, PA*

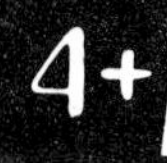

How Well Does Your Sport Move?

Science skills

Children make predictions, record the results of this exciting experiment, then compare their prediction to the result.

Materials

Variety of balls: football, tennis ball, soccer ball, hockey puck, golf ball, Ping-Pong ball, etc.
Paper (one per child) showing sketch of each ball to be used
Board to use as a ramp
Blocks
Pencils

Measurement

What to do

Note: With younger children, use only three balls at a time. Be sure to discuss appropriate use of the balls in this activity.

1. Show children the ramp and the balls. Ask them if they think that balls of different sizes, shapes and weights will roll the same distance when released at the top of the ramp. Write down their predictions.
2. Give each child a piece of paper showing the different balls to be used.
3. Have the children roll one ball at a time and place a block or other marker at the point where the ball stopped.
4. On their paper, children should write a number next to the picture of the ball. The ball that went the farthest should be given the number one, etc.
5. When the children are finished, compare their findings with their predictions.

More to do

Math: Measure the distance each ball went and make a class graph showing this information.

Melissa Browning, Milwaukee, WI

How Big Is a Whale?

Science skills

Children may experience the size of whales and how one might measure a whale.

Materials

White construction paper with pre-drawn people figures (draw 10 per child)
4 pieces of pre-measured string, 25′ (7.5 m), 60′ (18 m), 80′ (24 m), 100′ (30 m)
Scissors
Crayons
Large piece of paper

What to do

1. In advance, make a graph on the large piece of paper by dividing it into four sections top to bottom. Put a picture of a killer whale (25′) on the left side of the first section, a sperm whale (60′) below it in the next section and follow with the fin whale (80′) and the blue whale (100′) in the remaining sections.
2. Let the children each decorate 10 people on construction paper, to look like themselves, if they wish, and then cut them out.
3. Go outside and place each string on the ground, one at a time.
4. Ask the children to stand in a line holding hands and stretching their arms out.
5. Count how many children it takes to cover the length of each whale string.
6. Go back into class and place a paper child on the graph for each child it took to cover the length of each whale.

 killer whale 30'	7"
 sperm whale 60'	4yds
 right whale 70'	
 blue whale 100'	

More to do

Language: Discuss with children characteristics of whales, such as breaching, blowing, jumping. Write in journals a few of these characteristics. Draw pictures to go along with the descriptive words.

Original song

Ten Little Whales (sing to the tune of "Ten Little Pumpkins")

Ten little whales swimming out to sea,
One changed his mind and then there were nine.
Nine little whales swimming out to sea,
One left to migrate and then there were eight.
Eight little whales swimming out to sea,
One went to heaven and then there were seven.
Seven little whales swimming out to sea,
One did some tricks and then there were six.
Six little whales swimming out to sea,
One went to dive and then there were five.
Five little whales swimming out to sea,
One went to shore and then there were four.
Four little whales swimming out to sea,
One got free and then there were three.
Three little whales swimming out to sea,
One caught the flu and then there were two.
Two little whales swimming out to sea,
One stopped to rest and then there was one.
One little whale swimming out to sea,
He left to look for more fun and then there were none.

Related book

A Garden of Whales by Maggie Davis

Stephanie Person, Kingsburg, CA

A Heavy Rock

Science skills

This activity encourages observation, measuring and number skills.

Materials

A variety of rocks with numbers printed on them
Counting blocks or bears
A bucket balance scale
A piece of paper with two columns

What to do

1. In advance, prepare a chart on the piece of paper. In the left-hand column, draw a picture of each rock with its number on it. Leave the right-hand column blank so that the child can fill in the number of counters they need to make the scale even.
2. The teacher introduces the use of the balance scale and the care that must be taken with it. If necessary, demonstrate the experiment.

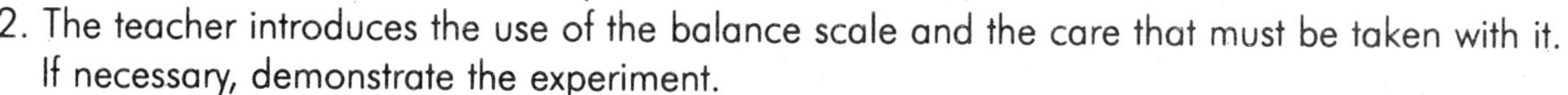

3. A child chooses a rock and places it on one side of the scale. On the other side of the scale, the child places the counting blocks or bears until the scale balances.
4. The child then counts the number of blocks he used and writes the number down in the right-hand column next to the appropriate rock picture. In turn, the children complete the activity with all of the rocks.
5. Later the teacher can gather the children's data on a graph and then do the activity again to check all of the data.

More to do

More science: Organize or rate the rocks according to weight or size. ▪ Include a pumice rock with other rocks of different sizes and materials to study the speed of sinking in water or to see whether any rocks float.

 *Melissa Browning, Milwaukee, WI*

5+

Measuring in Feet

Science skills

Children practice estimating, measuring and counting skills.

Materials

1′ (30 cm) rulers

Container for the rulers

What to do

1. Introduce the set of rulers to the children, explaining that each one is one foot long and that the children will be measuring things with them in the classroom.
2. Use the rulers to measure a familiar object in the room, such as a shelf, by laying out as many rulers as needed along the shelf's length, then counting the rulers.
3. Explain that if the object being measured is a little longer or a little shorter than the last ruler, it will only be measured "to the nearest foot." If it is a little more than the last one, don't count the extra; if it is almost as long as the last ruler, go ahead and count it.
4. Measure several familiar objects in the room. Be sure also to measure one of the children; ask the child to lie down and then place rulers in a straight line beside him from the top of his head to the bottom of his feet. Children love to measure each other this way, and they especially love to measure the teacher!
5. Return all rulers to the container and place the container where it is available to the children; invite them to choose this activity during free choice time.

More to do

More science: Use a larger set of rulers and measure objects or distances between objects on the playground. Point out that each one-foot ruler is divided into 12 inches, and measure objects to the nearest inch by first counting the rulers, then the inches on the last ruler to the end of the object being measured. ▪ Have a "measuring wall" with a wide piece of paper fastened securely to the wall from the floor to about five feet. Mark each child's height on the paper and let him write his name beside the mark. Then let each child measure his height from the floor to the mark in feet and inches. Measure once in the fall and again in spring to show the amount each person has grown during the school year. ▪ In a large open space, possibly outdoors, mark a line as a starting point and let the children make standing jumps from this point. Let each child mark where he lands by placing a plastic chip by the heel of his shoe. Then measure the distance from the starting point. To minimize any tendency to "stretch" the distance of the jump, the children could work in pairs with one jumping and the other measuring and then reversing their roles.

Related book

Inch by Inch by Leo Lionni

Susan Jones Jensen, Norman, OK

Shoe Skating

Science skills

Children explore friction, develop vocabulary and practice classification skills.

Materials

Uncarpeted floor space large enough to accommodate the group

What to do

1. Talk about skating, both on ice and in-line. Let the children pretend to skate on the floor. Why do some have an easier time than others? Friction! Depending on the soles of their shoes, some will slide more easily than others.
   Note: A child who is motor-impaired can work with a partner, who takes the shoe and rubs it on the floor to see if it slides or sticks.
2. Compare shoe soles of those who slid easily with the soles of those who stuck to the floor.
3. Classify the children's shoes, grouping sneakers, shoes, boots, etc.

More to do

Art: Children can dip the soles of old shoes in paint and make footprints on a mural or craft paper. Compare footprints.

More science: If appropriate, children can remove shoes and "skate" in their sock feet. Play a tape for background music.

Related books

Two Little Shoes by Razvan

Whose Shoes? by Brian Wildsmith

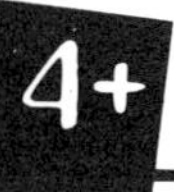

Racing Cars

Science skills

Children experiment with size and speed and use fine motor skills.

Materials

Plastic interlocking building blocks

Block bases with wheels and a ramp (or try a wooden board or sturdy cardboard over a set of 4 stairs)

What to do

1. This activity is best suited to a small group of children. Give each child a wheel base and blocks and help her think about building a race car that will go a long distance or will go fast. Then, she builds her car.
2. Test the cars by letting them roll down the ramp. Children initially figure that bigger is better, but once they have done a few trial runs and discovered that the tall cars have a tendency to tip over, they start modifying the cars. The slope of the ramp can be modified to see if that has an effect on time or distance. The children can make predictions, usually "mine's the fastest," and all can see the results immediately.

More to do

More science: You can extend this activity by measuring distance, measuring time and exploring concepts like bigger-smaller, longer-shorter, faster-slower. This encourages logical thinking and an understanding of cause and effect relationships.

Carol Nelson, Rockford, IL

De Colores

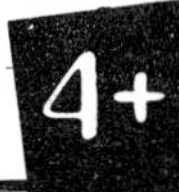

4+

Science skills

In this activity, children make observations and practice large motor skills.

Materials

Construction paper in multicultural colors
Musical tape or record and cassette or record player
Finger paints in primary colors
Tape

What to do

1. Arrange a table in an area with room to let children walk or propel a wheelchair around it.
2. Tape the multicultural construction paper all around the tops of the table and ask the children to stand around the table.
3. Practice marching and walking around the table, with everyone moving in the same direction.
4. Each child rolls up the sleeve of the arm next to the table. The teacher paints that hand, using different colors on different children.
5. Children march and walk around the table with their painted hands held high while the teacher plays music. When the music stops, the children put their handprints on the paper in front of them.
6. Continue until the paper is full of bright, colorful handprints.
7. The teacher may need to repaint hands occasionally.
8. The finished papers make a nice display with the words "De Colores" in the center.

More to do

Language: This activity lends itself to a discussion of differences and similarities among people.

Anne Lippincott, New Hartford, CT

Make a Machine

Science skills

Children experience space and time relationships and practice communication, social development and gross and fine motor skills.

Materials

None

What to do

1. Explain that machines are designed and made to help us in various ways. Ask the children to name a few machines and how they help us (for example, washing machines help us by automatically washing our clothes so that we don't have to scrub them).
2. Say, "We are going to build a machine with our bodies. But first we need to decide what our

Movement

machine is going to make or do." Some ideas: build a machine that will sweep dirt into a small pile or one that will mix bread into dough.

3. Start with one child and put her into place, giving her both an action and a sound to make. Some children will come up with their own ideas. Place the next child close to the first to "connect" the machine pieces, and so on, until every child is in place. Here are some movement ideas: lift one arm up, then down; a ballerina plié; head nod; head shake once; turn halfway around then back; knee up then down; bend over then stand up. Here are some ideas for sounds: boïng, ping, whoosh, beep, honk, shhh, whirr, snapping fingers, clap hands, stomp feet, pat tummy. These are limited only to your imagination! Be creative!
4. Be sure to assign one child to make the movement the machine was designed to do, for example, sweeping motion or mixing motion. You may also assign one person to be the power switch. Let the child hold out a pointer finger for the switch.
5. Now you are ready to turn the power switch on and see how every piece of the machine is moving and making its noise.
6. Turn the power off and let the children pretend that one piece of the machine has broken. Choose one child who no longer moves or makes a sound. Explain that in order for a machine to run all pieces and parts must work. Demonstrate this by trying to turn the power on. Each piece, no matter how small the movement or quiet the sound, is very important.
7. Now you can take out your gigantic "screwdriver and wrench" to fix the broken piece. Then turn the power back on.
8. Try a new machine or several smaller machines with fewer parts.

More to do

Field trip: Visit an automotive repair shop. Ask a mechanic to show the class the tools he uses to repair the cars and motors.

More science: In the workbench area, set out broken appliances and tools so the children can disassemble them to see the different parts of each machine.

Valerie Chellew, Marshfield, WI

Night Sights

Science skills

Children build vocabulary, practice social development and use fine and large motor skills.

Materials

Large yellow poster board full moon, 3′ (1 m) across
Dark blue and black scarves
Large white poster board stars, 14″ (35 cm) across, with silver glitter glued on
Small white or silver paper stars, 5″ (12.5 cm) across, glued to end of a 12″ (30 cm) dowel
Red and/or orange circles, 6″ (15 cm) in diameter, with red, orange and gold crepe paper streamers, taped to ends of 12″ (30 cm) dowels

Large open area for creative movement
Note: Have enough of each of the scarves, stars, shooting stars and comets for one-quarter of the children in the class.

What to do

1. While the children sit in a circle in a large open space, teach the poem "Star Light, Star Bright": Star light, star bright, the first star I see tonight. I wish I may, I wish I might, have the wish I wish tonight.
2. Pretend the sun has set and night has come. During the day, we usually see the sun. What do we see at night that is sometimes in the shape of a circle? Let's put our full moon up high on the wall or hang it from a wire. What color is the sky at night? Why is it dark? What other things might you see in the night sky (stars, clouds, airplanes, etc.)? If the children do not mention shooting stars and comets, ask them if they have ever seen a shooting star. What does it look like? What about a comet? What does it look like?
3. Divide the children into four groups. Explain to them that they are going to make their own dark night sky by swirling scarves in the air. Demonstrate for them by moving about in the open area, swirling a scarf all around. Move Group 1 to an open space and let each child in this group practice swirling a scarf in the air to make the night sky. After a short practice time, ask them to sit down and put their scarves on the floor behind them. Note: Be sure the children understand that your way of moving is not the only way. Their sky does not need to look exactly like yours. Encourage them to be creative.
4. Let's put some stars in our night sky. Demonstrate by holding a large star at chest height and slowly moving it up, down and around as you walk through the open area. Give Group 2 time to practice being stars. Then ask them to sit down, placing the stars on the floor behind them.
5. Add the shooting stars and comets. Demonstrate a shooting star by quickly moving the star through the sky and down a couple of times. Demonstrate a comet by moving through the space quickly holding the comet above your head so that the streamers trail behind. Give the shooting stars and then the comets time to practice. Sit down and place the star or comet on the floor behind them.
6. If your space is large enough, invite all the children to stand up with their props and to become the night sky altogether!
7. After each group has practiced its part, let the children rotate to another group. Every child should have a chance to be the sky, a star, a shooting star and a comet. At the end, collect the props and return to the circle. Say the "Star Light" poem once more.

More to do

Art: If you like, you could engage the children's imaginations by letting them help construct the props for this activity.
More science: You can expand on this activity in many ways, depending on the interests of the children, for example, discuss where the stars are during the day, why the moon is not always full and constellations such as the Big Dipper. ▪ Send a note home to parents with suggestions of things to look for on a clear night with their child, for example, the North Star, Big Dipper, shooting stars, satellites, etc.

Movement

Related poems
"Windy Nights" by Robert Louis Stevenson
"Winter Moon" by Langston Hughes

Jeanne Clark, Torrington, WY

3+ Water Glass Music

Science skills

As music floats out of the water glasses, children learn about vibrations.

Materials

4 glasses, at least 5½" (13.5 cm) tall
Metal spoon
Pint (500 ml) measuring cup

What to do

1. Let the children know that today they will discover how sounds are made. Ask them to press their lips together in a straight line and push air out to make a sound much like a horse snorting. Discuss the "tickle" they felt and tell them that all sounds are made from vibrations.
2. Fill the four glasses with the water amounts shown. You will want to try this ahead of time to verify the water amounts for your containers. Tap the filled glasses gently with the spoon. Ask the children to tell you which glasses make higher and lower sounds.

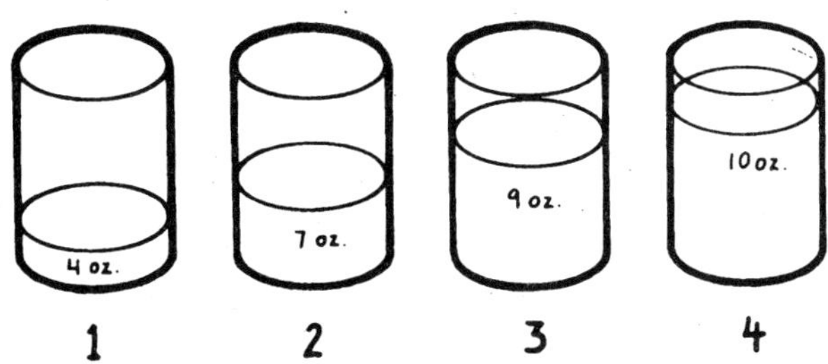

3. Play the sequence for the "Sounds Song" and help the children sing the song to the tune of "Mary Had a Little Lamb."

Lots of things can make a sound,
2 3 4 3 2 2 2

Make a sound,
3 3 3

Make a sound!
2 1 1

Ring! Crunch! Bang! Just look around.
2 3 4 3 2 2 2

Many things make sounds.
3 3 2 2 4

More to do

Math: Put large numbers on the glasses and let the children try to play them.

Movement: Tape an outline of a hand to the table edge under glasses 1 and 2, and an outline of a foot under glasses 3 and 4. When the indicated glasses are tapped, children clap hand or stamp feet to keep the rhythm.

Theresa A. Usilton, Easton, MD

Margarine Maracas

Science skills

Children sharpen their sense of hearing with this sound-identification activity.

Materials

Margarine container and lid for each child
Assorted small objects such as buttons, stones, Styrofoam pieces, seeds, bottle caps, etc.
Crepe paper streamers
Masking tape

What to do

1. Give each child a container and lid.
2. Let him experiment with the sounds of each object by placing the objects one at a time into the container, closing it and shaking it.
3. Describe the sounds with words such as soft, loud, quiet, musical, rough, etc.
4. Let the child select what he would like for his maraca. Place the object(s) inside and lay streamers over the edge to be held in place by the lid. Than seal the lid with tape.
5. Use the shakers for rhythm and movement activities.

More to do

Games: For a sound identification game, gather several bells with different pitches. Play each one several times while the children watch. Then ask the children to close their eyes while you play one bell. Now children open their eyes and a child points to the one the teacher rang. The child may then ring the bell himself. Repeat with the other bells. ▪ Matching Game: Place small objects into empty film or cat treat containers. Make two containers of each sound. Let children shake the containers and pair up the ones with matching sounds. Color the bottoms of the containers or use stickers to make the game self-correcting.

Sandra Gratias, Perkasie, PA

3+

Sounds Like the Slide

Science skills
Children use their sense of hearing to differentiate sounds.

Materials
Wood blocks
Bell
Slide whistle

What to do

1. Introduce each sound at a different location in the room, such as wood blocks at the door, bell on the rug and whistle at the slide.
2. Gather children in the center of the room.
3. Make a sound with one of the instruments. Children should go to the area of the room associated with that sound.
4. Make another sound. Children should move to the new location.
5. When children can do this easily, increase the difficulty by hiding the objects you use to make the sounds so there are no visual cues. Use three closely related objects, for example, three bells with different tones, three different rhythms played on a drum and three different melodies on a piano.

More to do
Movement: Match sounds to colors and then ask everyone wearing yellow to line up, sit down, etc. when you ring the bell. ▪ Instead of using three different room locations, associate three different movements, such as jumping, spinning and sitting, with the sounds.
Music: Use rhythms, sounds or songs to signal transitions such as clean-up, line-up and snack time.

Sandra Gratias, Perkasie, PA

3+

Twinkle, Twinkle

Science skills
Music, rhythm and light form the basis for children's observations.

Materials
5 or 6 flashlights

What to do

1. Children sit on the floor as a group.
2. Sing "Twinkle, Twinkle Little Star" several times until most of the children can follow along.
3. Give flashlights to five or six of the children.
4. Turn out the lights and encourage the children who have the flashlights to shine the lights on the ceiling and move the beams to the rhythm as the rest of the group sings the song.
5. Repeat until each child has had a chance to use a flashlight.
   Note: Be aware that some children may be afraid of the dark. Allow those children to sit by you or to stand in the doorway as they play the game.

More to do

Movement: Randomly tape enough cut-out stars to the floor so that each child will have one. Children perform some of the following gross-motor skills: walk around the stars, jump over the stars, sit beside a star, stand on a star, etc. ▪ Form a circle and sing Sally Go Round the Moon:

Sally go round the moon (slide to the left)
Sally go round the stars (slide to the right)
Sally go round the chimney top (slide to the left)
Every afternoon Boom! (jump and clap)

Music: Children with flashlights turn them on when the group sings the words "twinkle, twinkle" and turn them off for the rest of the song.

Related books

Goodnight, Moon by Margaret Wise Brown
Half a Moon, and One Whole Star by Crescent Dragonwagon

Joyce Montag, Slippery Rock, PA

Big Is Low, Small Is High

4+

Science skills

Children make observations, predictions and inferences and see cause and effect.

Materials

Xylophone
Jingle or sleigh bells in different sizes
Rubber bands
Piano, autoharp or guitar

What to do

1. Alternately play the largest key and smallest key of the xylophone and match your voice to the pitch. Identify notes as low and high, respectively.
2. Play bells the same way and place the low bell beside the low key and the high bell beside the high-sounding key.
3. Play the lowest and highest strings on the stringed instrument. Ask what the children notice

about the sizes of the keys or strings that made the high and low-sounding notes.

4. Show the rubber bands. Let children make predictions about which will sound low and high. Test the guesses.
5. If you have a piano available, open up the top to see the strings inside. Play low and high notes on the keys and see which strings the hammers strike.

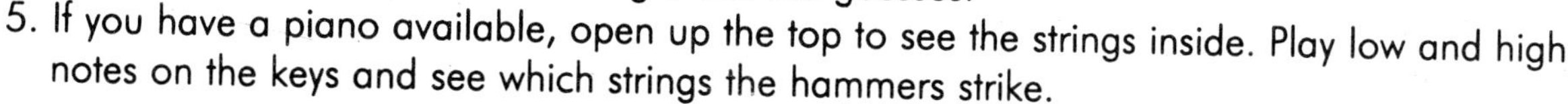

More to do

Art: Give each child a Styrofoam tray. Let him decorate it with crayons or permanent markers. Stretch rubber bands across it to make an instrument.

Field trip: Visit a school band or orchestra. Ask to hear different size drums or compare violin, viola, cello and bass, or flute and piccolo.

Music: Invite a church hand bell choir to bring a few bells for the class to hear.

Related books

The Banza by Diane Wolkstein

Berlioz the Bear by Jan Brett

Sandra Gratias, Perkasie, PA

5+

Sounds Everywhere

Science skills

Children learn to pay extra attention to the sounds in their surroundings by practicing observation.

Materials

Chart paper

Markers

A "nice weather" day

What to do

1. Sit in a circle and learn the song "Sounds Everywhere" (see illustration). Sing it a couple of times so that it is familiar. The children will learn a middle section to the song at the end of the lesson.
2. Ask children to sit quietly and listen very carefully. What sounds do we hear right now in the room? Make a list of "inside sounds" on chart paper.
3. Go outdoors to the playground, a yard or a park. Sit down in a circle and listen very carefully. What sounds do we hear now? Make a list of "outside sounds" on chart paper.
4. Talk about the sound lists. Which sounds are loud? Which sounds are soft? Which sounds happen in nature? Which sounds are from machines?
5. Learn the middle leader-echo section of "Sounds Everywhere" adding leader-echo words from your sound lists. Sing it several times to use most of the words on your lists.
   Take four sounds from the sound lists, for example trucks honking, children talking, dry leaves, water dripping, and form a spoken middle section for the song. The leader says

Music

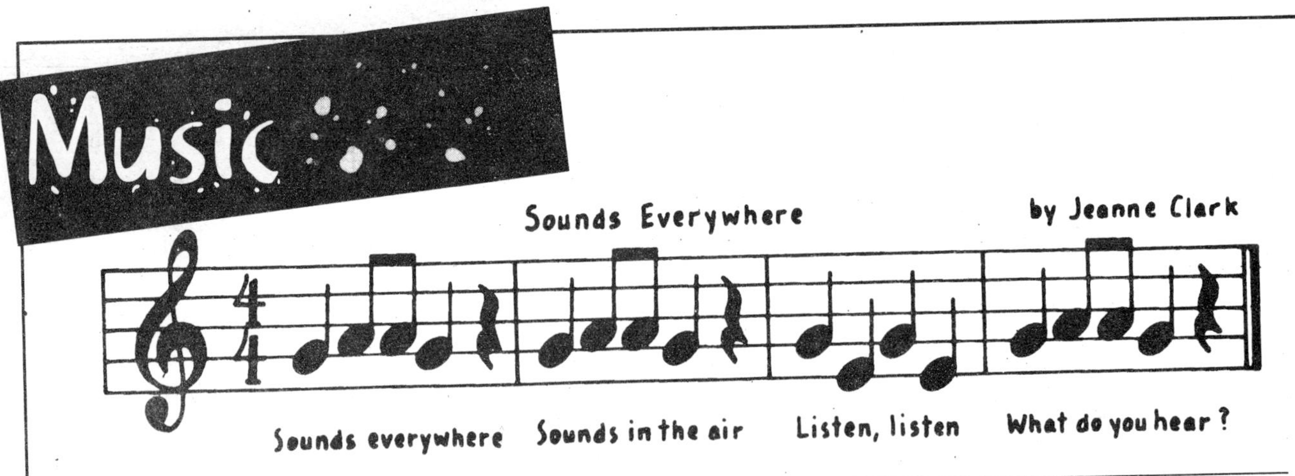

"trucks honking" and the children echo; the leader says "children talking" and the children echo, and so on. The last time through the singing section you could substitute "That's what we hear!" in place of "What do you hear?" The form of the song is to alternate singing and the leader-echo section.

More to do

Art: Working in groups, let the children create two murals with crayons and/or markers, one depicting the inside sounds and the other depicting outside sounds that they heard. Display the murals in your room or the hallway. Another option is to cut out magazine pictures depicting sounds and create collages. Take cards and print on them the names of the sounds depicted on the murals (e.g., car, leaves, bell, children) and attach the cards to the mural.

Games: Let the children play Charades, acting out sounds in silence. For example, a child might pantomime a ticking clock, or blowing wind or a laughing child. ▪ Invite another class to a "mini-performance of sounds." Show your murals and let the children tell what they learned. Conclude with "Sounds Everywhere" and/or the other fun sound songs with the audience participating.

More science: To expand on how sound is produced, do the "Good Vibrations" activity in *The Giant Encyclopedia of Circle Time and Group Activities for Children 3 to 6* by Gryphon House.

Music: Sing other songs that have sound effects added, for example "Old MacDonald Had a Farm" and/or "She'll Be Coming 'Round the Mountain."

Related book

The Listening Walk by Paul Showers

Jeanne Clark, Torrington, WY

3+ Worm House

Science skills

As they observe worms making tunnels, children ask questions about nature.

Materials

2 jars that fit inside one another
Newspaper
Sheet of black paper
Soil
Worms
Tape

What to do

1. Put the smaller jar inside the larger one.
2. Put the soil between the two jars. The smaller jar will prevent the worms from going into the center of the jar where you can't see them.
3. Gather worms from outside or buy them from a bait shop. Put the worms and the soil on a piece of newspaper on the floor. Observe the worms and discuss.
4. Put the worms in the worm house and put the black paper around the jar. After a while, remove the paper and observe how the worms are building tunnels. Keep the jar covered when no one is observing.
5. Be sure to return the worms to where you found them.

Carol Nelson, Rockford, IL

3+ Worms Worms Worms

Science skills

Children have fun playing with worms and making observations.

Materials

Real worms purchased at a bait shop or dug up by the children if you have a class garden
Tray or cookie sheet to put the worms on
Magnifier

What to do

1. Place the worms on the tray for the children to observe with the magnifier.
2. Don't be surprised if the children pick up the worms and play with them. Just remind them to be gentle.
3. Return the worms to the garden at the end of the day.

More to do

Art: Plastic worms, easily found in sporting goods departments, might make interesting painting tools. Painting with worms!

 *Marilyn E. Ewing, Richmond, TX*

Flower Dissection

3+

Science skills

Children practice observation, identification and fine motor skills.

Materials

Flowers collected from your personal flower garden, or ask a local florist for a donation of bouquet of slightly damaged flowers
Magnifying glasses
Diagram of the parts of a flower
Newspapers

What to do

1. Introduce the subject of flowers and display a diagram illustrating flower parts.
2. Cover a work area with newspaper for easy cleanup and give each child or group of children a flower.
3. Step by step, pull the flowers apart looking for each scientific part. Children love to do this. (Whoever gave them permission before to destroy a beautiful flower?)
4. Identify each part.

More to do

Art: Make a scrapbook using an old seed catalog with flowers for every letter of the alphabet. ▪ Have each child bring in one silk flower—or create an original flower with markers and construction paper—and use them to create an interesting bulletin board.
Field trip: Go for a walk in the neighborhood and look at flower gardens. ▪ Go for a nature walk and look for wildflowers. ▪ Visit a local florist.

Related books

Flowers by Ivan Anatta
Over Under in the Garden: A Botanical Alphabet by Pat Schories
The Reason for a Flower by Ruth Heller

Wanda K. Pelton, Lafayette, IN

Rock Critters

3+

Science skills

Children practice classification and use fine motor skills.

Materials

4-6 small rocks
A small piece of wood for each child, about 2" x 4" x 1" (5 cm x 10 cm x 2.5 cm), wood chips work fine
White glue
Small wiggle eyes
Moss or twigs

What to do

1. Tell the children that each of them is going to start a rock collection. Arrange for a walking field trip to find rocks, or ask the children to bring their own rock collections to school in boxes. Make sure they label their boxes with their names.
2. Let each child share a few favorite rocks.
3. Allow the children time to look at each other's collections.
4. Let the children pick partners and sort their rocks.
5. Ask the teams to explain to the class how they classified the rocks.
6. Ask older children to count the rocks in each category and write the number on paper to make a rock report.
7. Now help the children make "rock critters." Give each child a piece of wood and let her select four to six rocks.
8. She may glue two to three of her larger rocks onto the wood.
9. Glue smaller rocks onto the larger rocks to make critters' bodies.
10. Give each child wiggle eyes to glue on their top rocks.
11. Let each child use the moss or twigs to decorate her creation.

Barbara Saul, Eureka, CA

Rock Estimating

3+

Science skills

Children make predictions, and then test their predictions.

Materials

Rock collection with rocks of varying sizes
Large piece of white paper
Balance scale

What to do

1. Set out the rocks, the scale and the paper.
2. Let the children sit around the table so that every one can see the rocks and the paper.
3. Have a child choose a large rock and place it on the scale.
4. Ask the children how many smaller rocks they think it will take to lift the large rock.
5. List the children's responses on the paper.
6. Now let the children place rocks on the scale until the large rock balances.

More to do

More science: At circle time discuss the activity and why the children think the smaller rocks moved the large rock.

Related book

Alexander and the Wind-up Mouse by Leo Lionni

Linda M. Chase, Sonora, CA

Rock Rubbing

Science skills

In a water play variation, children discover the properties of rocks.

Materials

Collection of rocks of different textures

Individual wash tubs with water

What to do

1. Set up individual tubs of water and the rock collection on a worktable.
2. Give the children time to touch and examine each of the rocks. Point out the different textures, shapes, colors and sizes.
3. Ask the children what they think will happen when they rub one rock on another? Some of the rocks are going to make marks on the others.
4. Wet the rocks and then rub them together.

More to do

Snack: Make peanut butter rocks by mixing together 1 cup (250 ml) peanut butter, 1 cup (250 ml) powdered milk and ½ cup (125 ml) honey, and rolling the mixture into small balls or "rocks."

Related book

Anansi and the Moss-Covered Rock retold by Eric A. Kimmel

Linda M. Chase, Sonora, CA

3+

Rock Washing

Science skills
With more water play, children test their observation skills.

Materials

Individual wash tubs with water
Small brushes
Rocks, several for each child

What to do

1. Set up the table with a selection of rocks, brushes and individual tubs of water.
2. Ask the children what happens to the rocks when they get wet (they look darker and may feel slippery, etc.).
3. Let the children scrub the rocks. The appearance of the rocks may change further as the children scrub off dirt.

More to do

Cooking: Make "Stone Soup." Invite each child to bring a soup ingredient from home, add a clean stone and cook.
Language: Discuss the job of a geologist, places where rocks are displayed and the different types of rocks.
More science: Use a magnifying glass to examine the rocks.

Related book

Stone Soup by Marcia Brown

Linda M. Chase, Sonora, CA

Rocks

3+

Science skills

In this series of rock activities, children practice observing and classifying, predicting and inferring and use fine motor skills.

Materials

Rocks, stones, pebbles
Water
Stone or hot plate
Sylvester and the Magic Pebble by William Steig
Clear container
Saucepan
Paint and brushes

What to do

Gather a large collection of rocks, stones and pebbles. Children love bringing rocks from home. Here are various ways to use the rocks:

1. Classify them by size or weight; sort by size, color and texture.
2. Put the rocks on a balance scale and let the children predict and estimate how many small rocks will equal a large, how many foam blocks or other lightweight items will equal one rock, etc.
3. What happens when you freeze rocks; heat rocks?
4. Use rocks like chalk outside.
5. Put a large rock in a clear container of water that you have marked at the water level. What happens to the water level when you add the rock? Use the word displacement.
6. Paint rocks for paperweight presents or just for an art experience.
   Read *Sylvester and the Magic Pebble.*

Kristina Davis and Anne M. Sullivan, Seminole, FL

Sediment

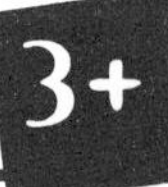

Science skills

Children are encouraged to ask questions about nature.

Materials

Clear plastic jar
Water
Any other items found on the playground that the children want to add: leaves, pebbles, sticks
Oil
Soil

What to do

1. Fill a large clear plastic jar with water, oil, different kinds of soil and other items.
2. Shake the jar and let it stand until the layers settle.
3. Talk about what the children observe.

Kristina Davis and Anne M. Sullivan, Seminole, FL

Bark Rubbings

Science skills
Children make observations and use fine motor skills.

Materials
White paper
Crayons or chalk

What to do

1. Take a nature walk with your class.
2. Point out the different varieties of trees.
3. Let the children examine and touch the bark of the various trees and describe the similarities and differences they observe.
4. In pairs, let the children make tree rubbings. One child can hold the paper while her partner rubs crayon or chalk lengthwise against the paper.

More to do
More science: Cut 1" (2.5 cm) slices from a trimmed tree branch. Let the children glue on pine cones, leaves, wildflowers, acorns, etc. Screw an eyebolt in the top of the plaque and spray with varnish.

Related book
A Tree Is Nice by Janice May Udry

Cindy Winther, Oxford, MI

Mountains and Valleys

3+

Science skills

In this fun activity, children make observations and use fine and large motor skills.

Materials

Large piece of corrugated cardboard
Masking tape
Flour and water
Tempera paint and paintbrushes
Old newspapers
Paper plates
Large bowl and spoon
Aprons or smocks

What to do

1. If possible, take the children on a field trip to the mountains. If not, talk about mountains and valleys using pictures and books.
2. On a cardboard base, show the children how to make piles of crumpled newspapers to build mountains. You may need to secure these somewhat with tape.
3. For mountain tops, make cuts from the edges to the centers of several paper plates and overlap the two cut edges to form cones. Tape these together and to the top of each mountain.
4. Ask the children to tear the newspaper into strips about 2" (5 cm) wide. Newspaper tears easily lengthwise.
5. Mix flour and water into a thick soup consistency in the bowl.
6. Wearing aprons or smocks, children dip the paper strips into the flour mixture. Remove the extra mixture by running the strips through index finger and thumb.
7. Put the strips on the mountains, building them up until you have a solid covering on the mountains. Let this dry for three to four days.
8. Paint the mountains and valleys with tempera paint and label them. If you took a field trip, you can label some of the landmarks you saw on your trip.

More to do

Games: Play "Go In and Out the Window" singing the words "go up and down the mountains."

Shirley Story, Lenoir, NC

Mr. and Mrs. Leaf

3+

Science skills

On a fall nature walk, children use observation skills to select leaves that can be used to make leaf "people."

Materials
Leaves, either green or changing colors, but not yet brown
Plastic bag
Scissors
White or light blue construction paper
White glue
Crayons

What to do

1. Go for a walk to gather various types and sizes of leaves and put them in the plastic bag.
2. Cut the stems off the leaves and decide if you want to make a leaf man, a leaf woman or both.
3. On the construction paper, draw the face and hair first, then glue on a small leaf as a hat.
4. Glue a large leaf as body and draw arms and legs.
5. Glue a skirt for a woman or two legs for a man.
6. Two small leaves of the same size will look like shoes when glued to the background paper.
7. You might press Mr. and Mrs. Leaf in or under a very heavy book.

More to do
Dramatic play: Let the children dramatize rain falling on trees in spring; leaves starting to grow; having a picnic under a shade tree in the summer; leaves falling from the tree in autumn and being raked, jumped in or bagged; and, finally, being a tree with no leaves in the winter.
Games: Show the outline of a maple leaf and let all the children hold up a maple leaf. Then show the outline of an oak leaf and again ask the children to match it.
Math: Combine all the unused leaves and then sort them by size or shape or color. ▪ Count leaves.

Original poem and song

Crunch and crackle all around
As brown leaves tumble to the ground.

They were really pretty—all colors on the tree
But they decided to come and play with me.

I rake them high into a giant pile
I do think those leaves must have a smile,

For they just know what I plan to do.
Then I run and jump in them, wouldn't you?

The Four Seasons (sing to the tune of "Frère Jacques")
It is summer. It is summer.
The leaves are green. The leaves are green.
Their shade is so cool now.
Their shade is so cool now.
Birds can be seen. Birds can be seen.

It is autumn. It is autumn.
Leaves are orange and brown. Leaves are orange and brown.

Some are red and gold, too.
Some are red and gold, too.
Then they float down. Then they float down.

It is winter. It is winter.
The trees are bare. The trees are bare.
The trees are resting now.
The trees are resting now.
No leaves anywhere. No leaves anywhere.

It is springtime. It is springtime.
New leaves appear. New leaves appear.
They will start to grow.
They will start to grow.
Summer is near. Summer is near.

Related book
Over and Over by Charlotte Zolotow

Mary Brehm, Aurora, OH

Nature Necklaces

Science skills
In this matching activity, children observe and compare items from nature.

Materials
Items from nature
Yarn
Cardboard
Clear contact paper

What to do
1. Beforehand, visit an area where the children can walk and where they can collect nature items. Collect items that the children will be able to find, such as leaves, seeds, flowers, one item for each child.
2. Back in the classroom, cut circles of cardboard small enough to be worn as a medallions but large enough to hold the gathered nature item.
3. Mount a nature item on each piece of cardboard.
4. Cover the cardboard and nature item with clear contact paper.

5. Punch a hole at the top of the cardboard circle, put a piece of yarn through the hole and tie it to make a necklace.
6. Give each child a necklace. Have her look closely at the item. Explain to the children that they will be going on a nature walk to look for items just like the ones on their necklaces. Walk to the area where you gathered the items and allow the children to look for items that match their Nature Necklaces.

More to do

Art: Gather extra items and use them to make a collage. Ask older children to draw a picture of their nature item.

Math: Make a graph representing the different types of nature items the children found. Record how many leaves, how many seeds, etc., they found.

Transitions: Use the different types of items on the necklaces as a transition tool: "Children with flower necklaces may line up. Children with leaf necklaces may line up…."

Sarah Dill, Madison, WI

3+

Nature Sort

Science skills

This activity will stimulate children's curiosity and interest in their environment and nature and children will learn to classify objects.

Materials

Several items from outdoors: seashell, bone, stick, pine cone, rock leaf, etc.
Several items from recycling: soda can, plastic water bottle, newspaper, etc.
Two large pieces of paper

What to do

1. Beforehand, label one large piece of paper NATURE and add an outdoor picture, label the other RECYCLE and add a picture of a recycling container.
2. With all the children sitting in a circle, introduce the concept of natural and wild places and how to take care of them.
3. Place all of the items in the middle of the circle of children and talk about each one.
4. Show the children the two sorting places and discuss what each means.
5. Let the children take turns choosing an object, labeling it and stating whether it is a natural thing that belongs in wild places or something that should be recycled (not left behind as litter) and placing it on the appropriate paper.
6. When you have sorted all the items, count the ones in each group and ask the children which category has the most.
7. Discuss the different recycling items, and how they might harm wildlife if they were left as litter.
8. Ask the children to think of other ways they can help take care of natural places.

More to do

Dramatic play: Set up the dramatic play area with camping items.

More science: Invite a Forestry Services employee to visit the classroom to talk about taking care of natural places and how to use these places with minimal impact.

Sand and water table: Fill the tactile table with natural items.

Carla Scholl, Fairplay, CO

Pressed Plants

Science skills

Children make observations, ask questions about nature and use fine motor skills.

Materials

Plants collected on a nature walk
Newsprint paper
Large clean paintbrushes
Construction paper
Corrugated cardboard
Phone books or other large books
Yarn or string
Glue

What to do

1. Go on a nature walk in search of beautiful plants. Allow each child to choose her own plant and bring it back to class.
2. In small groups, let the children gently clean their plants with the large brushes.
3. Give each child a piece of corrugated cardboard with a piece of newsprint on top. Let each child place her plant on the newsprint wherever she would like it.
4. Layer about five children's works on top of one another and place these between two phone books. Tie the phone books together with string or yarn to prevent movement.
5. Bring the phone book presses to circle time and use them as special chairs. Allow the helpers of the day to sit on them for added pressure.
6. After a day, untie the press and gently remove the paper. Take the top sheet off. This is the children's favorite part! Allow them to drizzle and drip glue all over the plants. It is okay to get some on the paper. Pick up the glue-covered plants and place them glue side down on a piece of construction paper.
7. Allow to dry.
8. Cover small pressed plants with clear contact paper and use them as book marks. These make fantastic Mother's or Father's Day presents. Alternatively, you could make a class book for the science corner of your classroom.

More to do

More science: Compare the different plant sizes, colors, types and shapes.

 *Ann Gudowski, Johnstown, PA*

Weighing and Sorting Nuts

Science skills
Children learn about comparing and classifying objects.

Materials
Balancing scale
Assorted nuts in their shells
Muffin tins or egg cartons

What to do
1. Set out a large container of nuts for children to explore. Have enough so that a few children can work together.
2. Now let them see the balancing scale and show them—or let them figure out themselves—how to balance the nuts, for example, two little ones weigh the same as one big one. Use vocabulary such as "more than," "less than," "heavier," "lighter," etc.
3. Add a muffin tin or an egg carton for sorting the nuts by shape, color or size.
4. Bring out a large wooden mallet for older children and assorted nut crackers so the children can crack the nuts and eat them.

More to do
Art: Use the cracked shells as a collage material. Allow the children to use the shells in other creative ways.
Cooking: Use the shelled nuts to cook with, for example, to make banana bread.

Related books
A Busy Year by Leo Lionni
Squirrels by Brian Wildsmith

Audrey F. Kanoff, Allentown, PA

Plant Prints

4+

Science skills

As they create art, children see the results of cause and effect.

Materials

Men's handkerchiefs or similar cloths, or porous paper, pale in color
A plant that was grown or picked by the children; a fern works especially well
A rubber-coated mallet

What to do

1. Lay the plant on a piece of cloth or paper and fold the cloth over top, covering the plant.
2. Let the children begin to gently hammer the cloth.
3. Unfold the cloth and discard the plant. You should have a beautiful print of the plant on the cloth or paper.
4. You can frame the prints as gifts for parents or use them to make special cards by cutting out the plant print and gluing it to construction paper.

Ann Gudowski, Johnstown, PA

Rock Collecting

4+

Science skills

In the process of making a collection, children make observations, have opportunities to ask questions about nature and use fine motor skills.

Materials

Rocks
2 or more shoe boxes
Large pieces of paper
Paper towel
Paper bags
Paint
Aluminum pie pans

What to do

1. Take the children on a nature walk and encourage them to collect rocks. Carry the rocks in the paper bags.
2. Bring the rocks back to the classroom and let the children sort the rocks by size into the shoe boxes.
3. Pour a small amount of paint into the pie pans. Give each child a large piece of paper.

4. Let the children press the rocks in the paint and then onto their papers to make rock prints. The children can print the rocks by size, for example, from largest to smallest, by color and texture or in any creative design.

Related book
Everybody Needs a Rock by Bryd Baylor

Elizabeth Thomas, Hobart, IN

4+

Seed Collection

Science skills
Children make collections, observations and practice fine motor skills.

Materials
Seeds from food
Masking tape
Poster board, cut into 24" x 4" (60 cm x 10 cm) pieces
Small resealable plastic bags
Glue
Marker

What to do
1. Each child collects seeds from foods they or others have eaten at home or at school. It may take a few days to build your collection. Keep each seed in a resealable plastic bag. Label by writing the child's name and type of seed on masking tape.
2. Each child receives a 24" x 4" piece of poster board, puts a drop of glue on the poster board and places a seed in the glue. The teacher writes the name of the seed next to it.
3. Each child may have as many seeds as desired. Eight seeds work well displayed in a single line.

More to do
Food: Many snacks, such as apples, kiwi, oranges, tomatoes, pears, string beans, etc. provide opportunities for discussions on the different families of seeds (vegetables and fruits), growing, gardening and plants and trees. Different seeds grow in different parts of the world—for example, Guam grows bananas. New Jersey does not grow bananas, but it grows blueberries.

Related recording
"Inch by Inch: The Garden Song" by David Mallet, recorded by Pete Seeger

Lauren Brickner-McDonald, Mountain Lakes, NJ

Seashore Shells and River Rocks

4+

Science skills

As they build collections, children make observations, comparisons and practice classification.

Materials

Large table
Plastic baskets for rocks
Blue paper strip made wavy to look like water
Signs for seashore shells, river rocks
Two clear plastic shoe boxes

What to do

1. Children and teachers bring in samples of shells and/or rocks and display them on two sides of a table with the appropriate signs.
2. Compare each side of the table. Some observations about shells might be that many are rough from turbulent water, that their forms are more varied than rocks, that their colors are lighter than rocks and that they can break easily. The children may observe about the rocks that many are smooth from water gently running over them, that their forms are more uniform, their colors are darker and their forms are sturdier than shells.
3. Display some examples in water so their colors will darken, especially the river rocks.
4. Put smaller shells and rocks in the baskets and classify each one by size, shape and color.

More to do

Art: To make shell and rock paintings or prints, dip the shells and rocks into shallow containers of tempera paint and press them onto construction paper.
Math: You can use the sorting activities suggested above as math exercises.

Related book

Seashells of North America by R. Tucker Abbot

Eileen E. Crocker, White Hall, MD

Volcano

4+

Science skills

In this exciting activity, children observe cause and effect.

Materials

Yogurt containers or plastic cups
Clay, playdough or papier-mâché
Vinegar
Baking soda
Red food coloring
Paint
Paintbrushes

What to do

1. Give each child a cup to place right side up on a work surface. Let her form a mountain shape around the cup with the clay, playdough or papier-mâché. Be sure she leaves a small opening at the top of the mountain shape.
2. When the mountain is dry, the children can decorate it with paint.
3. Now pour ¼ cup (60 ml) of vinegar into each cup.
4. Add just a few drops of red food coloring.
5. Add 1 teaspoon (5 ml) of baking soda and watch the volcano erupt. The children will want to make the volcano again and again.

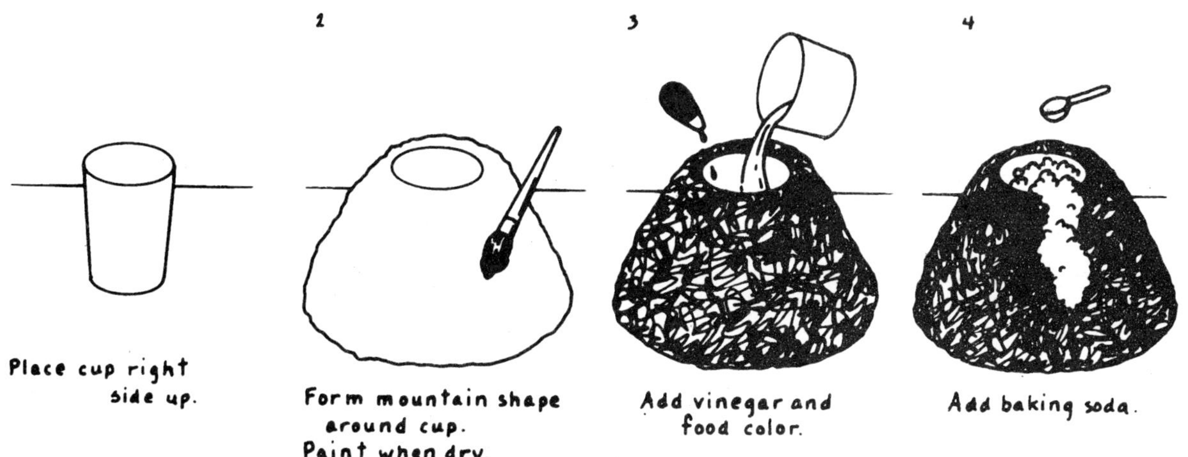

More to do

Food: Make a volcano snack by spreading cream cheese or peanut butter on a cracker and squeezing grape or strawberry jelly into a depression in the center.

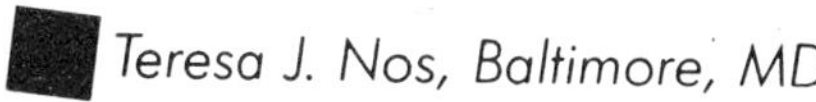
Teresa J. Nos, Baltimore, MD

Money Match Memory Game

3+

Science skills

In this matching game, children exercise their memories and practice classification skills.

Materials

2" (5 cm) cardboard or construction paper squares
At least two of as many different coins as possible
Clear contact paper

What to do

1. Prepare the pieces for a matching game. First, place a coin on each 2" square and then cover each square with contact paper. If you don't have enough preparation time, you can simply cover the coins with small paper cups.
2. Lay out the squares and allow the children to play a memory game by turning over two at a time to find a match.
3. For older children, you can vary the activity to make matches not only from identical coins but also from equal amounts, e.g., one quarter is a match for two dimes and a nickel. This version is easier using the paper cup method.

More to do

Art: Let the children make coin rubbings.
More science: Children can invent their own coins with faces, and worth any amount they choose, using juice lids, milk bottle tops, etc.

Related book

Alexander Who Used to Be Rich Last Sunday by Judith Viorst

Shirley R. Salach, Northwood, NH

Shiny Pennies

3+

Science skills

Children make observations, count and use fine motor skills.

Materials

Pennies
Clear plastic cups
Vinegar
Carpet pieces
Salt

What to do

1. Collect and set up all the materials on a table.
2. Talk about pennies, money and the proper handling of money.
3. Discuss two ways to make the pennies shine and assign the children to two groups. Demonstrate each method: rub the pennies on carpet until they shine, or drop the pennies into a vinegar and salt solution.
4. Make a comparison chart of the two methods showing which was better, quicker, messier, more fun, etc. Keep in mind that small cuts or scrapes on the children's hands will sting if vinegar or salt gets into them.

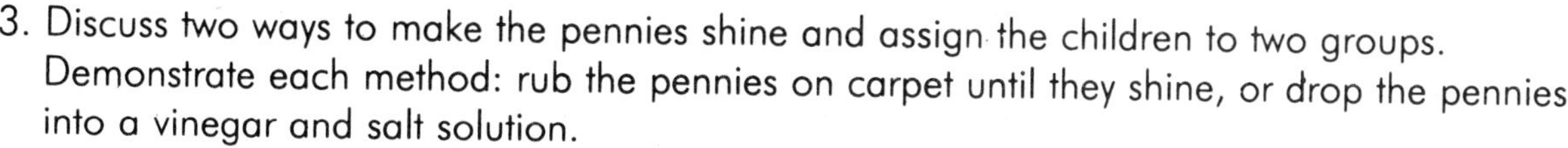

More to do

Language: What would I do with a shiny penny? Children's answers could be recorded in a class writing journal.
Math: Let the children count the pennies.

Related books

Peter and the Penny Tree
The Purse by Kathy Caple

Karen Megay-Nespoli, Massapequa Park, NY

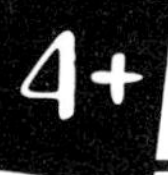

4+

Counting to Eleven

Science skills
In this exercise, children practice math skills.

Materials

12 Ways to Get to Eleven by Eve Merriam
Small groups of common objects for counting, such as buttons, tiles, chips
Resealable plastic bags

What to do

1. Read *12 Ways to Get to Eleven*.
2. Children follow the pattern from the book by counting items in the classroom to equal 11, for example, 4 erasers, 3 markers, 2 pointers, a meter stick and a chalk holder.
3. Prepare groups of simple objects in resealable plastic bags. Children select bags that will equal 11, for example, 3 spools of thread, 4 buttons, 3 wooden blocks, 1 toy truck.

More to do

Art: Children count out 11 crayons and draw a picture with 11 things in it.
Language: Write sentences containing the number 11. Borrow patterns from familiar stories or poems. ▪ Read stories with numbers in the titles: *The Wolf and the Seven Kids* by Jacob Grimm ad Wilhelm Grimm, *The Three Billy Goats Gruff* (many versions available), *101 Dalmations*

(Disney collection) and *Millions of Cats* by Wanda Gag. Don't forget the Dr. Seuss favorite, *The 500 Hats of Bartholomew Cubbins*.

Related books

How Many Bugs in a Box? by David A. Carter
How Many Snails? by Paul Giganti, Jr.

Barbara Hershberger, Watertown, WI

How Much Is It Worth?

5+

Science skills

In this game, the children learn classifying and math skills.

Materials

12 paper plates
Paper pennies, nickels and dimes or real pennies, nickels and dimes
Marker

What to do

1. Using paper or real coins, teach the children the names and values of the penny, the nickel and the dime. Observe and discuss the front side and the back of each coin.
2. Have the children count out equivalent groups, such as one nickel and five pennies; one dime and two nickels; and one dime and two nickels or one nickel and five pennies or ten pennies.

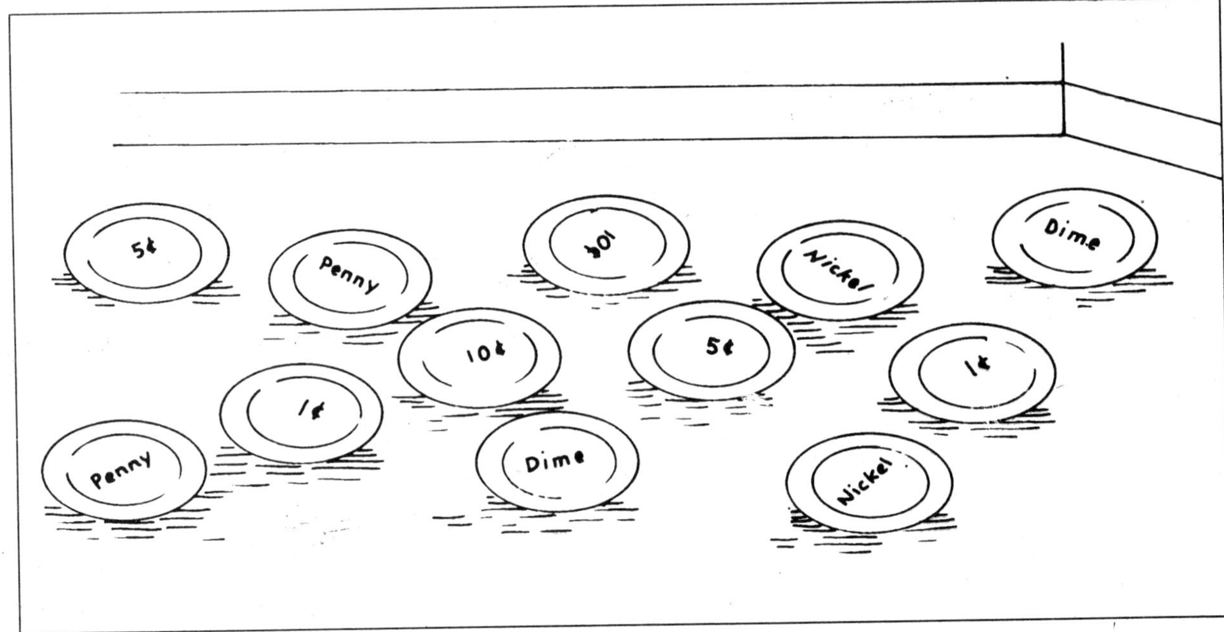

3. Write the name of each coin on two paper plates and the cents value of each coin on two paper plates, for a total of twelve plates.
4. Set out all twelve plates on the floor in a large area. Then ask the children to put one foot on the plate worth five cents. Keep in mind that there are four possible correct plates to choose from for their answer, the two plates labeled "five cents" and the two plates labeled "nickel." Continue posing questions while the children move around finding the correct plate to stand on. This gives them a chance to move around the room and also a chance to follow the crowd if they are unsure of the answer.
5. If your children are ready to moving on to quarters, discuss the value and appearance of the quarter and add more plates to the game to include the quarter in the game.

More to do

Math: Prepare little price tags and place them on books and toys around your room. The children can use the paper coins to purchase items at the "Classroom Store."

Related book

How Much Is a Million by David M. Schwartz

Judy Contino, Ozone Park, NY

Nursery Rhymes

The Eensie, Weensie Spider

3+

Science skills

Children experiment with and observe the power of water.

Materials

One 6' (2 m) length of 3" (7.5 cm) PVC pipe
One realistic rubber spider with 2"-3" (5 cm-7.5 cm) long body
For inside activity:
- Shower curtain or other floor protection
- Large flat container that will hold water

One bucket of water
Cups

What to do

1. If you are doing this activity inside, place the shower curtain on the floor.
2. On the shower curtain, place one end of the PVC pipe in the large container. At the other end of the pipe place the bucket of water, the cups and the spider.
3. To do this activity outside, place the PVC pipe on the ground. At one end place the bucket of water, the cups and the spider.
4. Let a child put the spider inside the PVC pipe. Using cups of water and lifting the end of the pipe, the child experiments to get the spider to go down the pipe as if it were a waterspout.

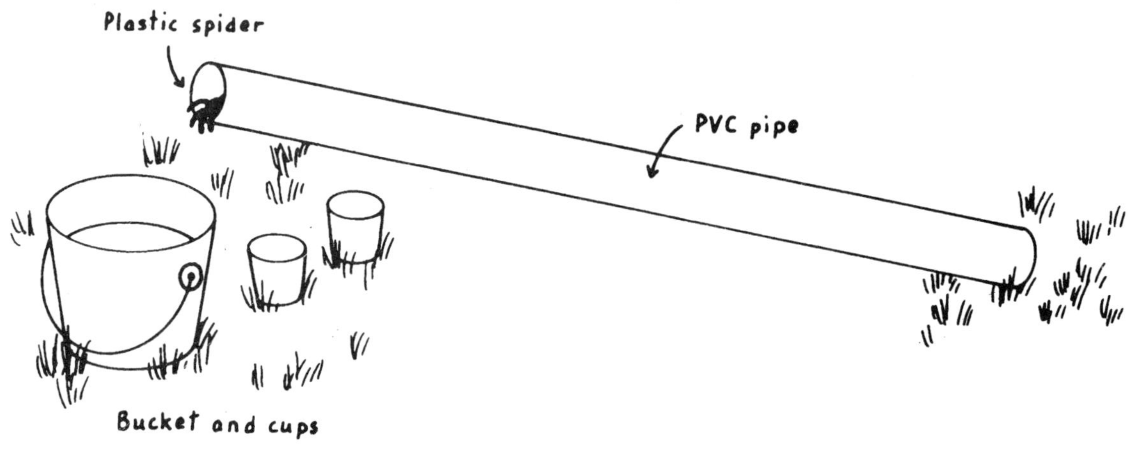

More to do

Art: Marble paint rain. Place a piece of white construction paper in a box with high sides. Put several dime-sized dollops of gray paint on the paper. Roll five to six marbles back and forth on the paper, spreading out the paint to resemble rain. Since marbles are a choking hazard, this activity requires adult supervision, or you may use golf balls instead of the marbles. ▪ Make handprint spiders. Let the child paint his hand a desired color, not too thickly. Make print of the palm and four fingers only on construction paper. Fold the paper across the center of the palm and rub gently to print a mirror image of other four legs of a spider. When the paint is dry, add ¼" (6 mm) round adhesive labels (sticky spots) for eyes.

More science: Let a real Daddy Long Legs crawl on the children. Let the children know that they should not pick up all spiders. ▪ Go outside on a spider hunt and observe spiders in their own habitat.

Outdoors: On a rainy day, watch rain go down a waterspout and see where it goes. ▪ Let the children use squirt bottles to make it rain on the sidewalk. Watch the sun "dry up all the rain."

Movement: Let the children be spiders and "wash the spider out" by sliding down the slide.

Carol Mead, Los Alamos, NM

3+

Humpty Dumpty

Science skills

By letting Humpty Dumpty fall, children practice observing and predicting skills.

Materials

Hard-boiled eggs
Mayonnaise
Bowls
Crackers or bread
Plastic forks and knives

What to do

1. Say the Humpty Dumpty nursery rhyme.

   Humpty Dumpty sat on a wall.
   Humpty Dumpty had a great fall.
   All the King's horses and all the King's men
   Couldn't put Humpty together again.

2. Talk about what happens when you break a raw egg. Can it be put back together again?
3. Ask the children to wash their hands and sit at a table. Give each child a hard-boiled egg.
4. Ask the children to put the egg on one hand they hold above the table. Gently bump the egg off their hands/walls, making the egg crack. Can the egg be put back together again? Now let the children eat their eggs.

More to do

Snack: Extend the activity by making egg salad. Peel an egg and place it in plastic bowl. Cut it up, mash it with the fork, add mayonnaise and mix. Spread the egg salad on crackers or bread. Eat and enjoy!

Phyllis Esch, Export, PA

Rhymes for a Reason

3+

Science skills

Here the teacher and children enliven the nursery rhymes by exploring the principles of balance, movement and measurement.

Materials

Book of Mother Goose Rhymes
Basket
Hard-boiled eggs
Spider puppet
Shawl
One candle in a candleholder
Brick or cardboard block

What to do

1. Jump-start those old nursery rhymes and explore the science of it all. Make it interesting and fun by starting the role-playing yourself.
2. Dress as old Mother Goose. Make use of a shawl, perhaps a hat, granny glasses, a stuffed goose. In your basket, have the props to bring your rhymes to life.
3. For Jack Be Nimble, jump over the candlestick—really! Then measure how tall the candle is. Then jump next to, behind or in front of the candlestick.
   Jack be nimble
   Jack be quick
   Jack jump over the candlestick
4. You can have Humpty Dumpty acted out by a leader or by all the children. Balance your hard-boiled egg on a real or cardboard brick wall. When Humpty falls, what happens? Can he be put back together?
5. For Little Miss Muffet, choose a Miss Muffet and use a puppet spider. Use the poem as a start for a study of spiders.
   Little Miss Muffet sat on a tuffet
   Eating her curds and whey
   Along came a spider
   And sat down beside her,
   And frightened Miss Muffet away.

More to do

Dramatic play: Put the props in the dramatic play center so the children can role play Mother Goose rhymes.

Related books

Be Nice to Spiders by Margaret Bloy Graham
Bently and Egg by William Joyce
Miss Spider's Tea Party by David Kirk
The Very Busy Spider by Eric Carle

Tracie O'Hara, Charlotte, NC

4+

Strength Test

Science skills
By building the little pigs' houses, children use gross and fine motor skills and make observations and predictions.

Materials

The Three Little Pigs (many versions available)
Sticks
Electric fan
Straw
Bricks

What to do

1. Read the children the story.
2. Separate the children into three groups. Give one group the straw, one the sticks and the last group the bricks.
3. Tell the children they are going to build a wall out of the things they have. Ask them which wall will be the strongest?
4. After the children finish the walls, put a fan next to each wall (supervise this step closely). See which one is the strongest and why.

Eric Painter, Georgetown, MA

The Food Pyramid

3+

Science skills

Children explore and classify objects.

Materials

Picture of the food pyramid, found on many cereal boxes
Masking tape
Empty food containers with labels showing contents

What to do

1. Collect empty food containers. Don't forget frozen foods and berry containers. Try to have something for each of the six food categories. Ask parents ahead of time to send a few containers with each child. If someone forgets, be sure to bring in extras.
2. Form the shape of a giant food pyramid with masking tape on your floor. Mark off the six sections with tape.
3. During circle time discuss the need for a variety of foods in a healthy diet. Show children a food pyramid. Explain the six categories and the daily serving suggestions for each: fats, oils and sweets (use sparingly); milk, yogurt, cheese and dairy (two to three servings); meat, poultry, fish, dry beans, eggs and nuts (two to three servings); vegetables (three to five servings); fruits (three to five servings); breads, cereals, pastas, rice and grains (six to eleven servings). Discuss with children which foods would go into each of the categories.
4. Then ask each child to place a container in the category they think it belongs. Let children help each other.
5. Afterwards, you can put the containers on shelves to have a grocery store. If you have a cart and register, children can shop for healthy foods. If you do not have these items, let children use their imaginations.
6. As a follow-up activity children can sort food into healthy and unhealthy categories.
7. At snack time ask children to which categories the food they are eating belong.

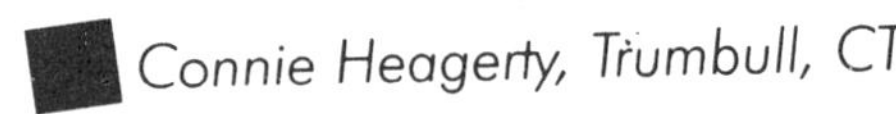

Connie Heagerty, Trumbull, CT

3+

Hungry Henry

Science skills

In this interactive game, children learn sorting skills.

Materials

Empty cereal box
Plastic food
Construction paper

What to do

Using a cereal box, make a puppet called "Hungry Henry" according to the directions given below. At group time, the children feed him using plastic food. The foods available to the children should include both nutritious and "junk" foods. As each child has a turn to select a food, she predicts whether Henry will like it or not. The puppet keeps nutritious foods in his mouth but "spits out" the junk food.

1. Cut the box in half on three sides but don't cut along the back of the box. On the back of the box, cut two small circle holes for fingers so you can open and close the box like a mouth.
2. Cover the box with construction paper and add decorations to make it into a head with a face—the open slit is where the mouth should be. Make sure the mouth is not too close to the bottom since the food pieces must fit in the box.

decorated cereal box

Christine Maiorano, Duxbury, MA

Nutrition

The Happy-Sad Food

3+

Science skills
In this sorting game, children practice observation and classification skills.

Materials

Two trays of food: one tray of healthy food such as an apple, orange, banana, potato, squash, nuts, onion, carrot; and one tray of unhealthy food such as candy, bubble gum, cupcake, sugar cube, lollipop, marshmallows
Two empty trays
Two signs, one with a Happy Face and one with a Sad Face

What to do

1. Allow children to observe trays of food.
2. Discuss which foods are healthy and unhealthy and why.
3. Let the children sort the foods into healthy and unhealthy categories and place them on the empty trays under the appropriate signs.

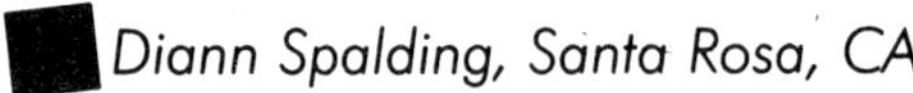

Diann Spalding, Santa Rosa, CA

Pretend Pizza

4+

Science skills
Children develop creative thinking and fine motor skills in preparing a favorite food.

Materials

Tan construction paper
Red, green and other colors of construction paper
Red fine-point markers
White glue
Two shades of yellow yarn, pre-cut into 1½" (3.5 cm) pieces
Scissors
Red crayons
Pencils
Thyme or oregano
Manila construction paper

What to do

1. Talk with the children about all the healthy foods you eat when you eat a pizza.
2. Make a pizza wedge pattern that the children can trace on tan paper and cut out.

3. Help the children trace around dimes or pennies on green paper for olives. Cut them out and color the centers with red crayon.
4. Trace around a fifty-cent piece on red paper. Cut these out and make red dots with markers. Glue thyme or oregano in the center of the red circles to give these pretend pepperonis a pizza smell.
5. Color the pizza red with a crayon, except for the crust area.
6. Make paper mushrooms out of construction paper and cut them out.
7. Glue all the ingredients randomly on the pizza: yarn cheese, olives, pepperoni, mushrooms and any other vegetable the children want to make.

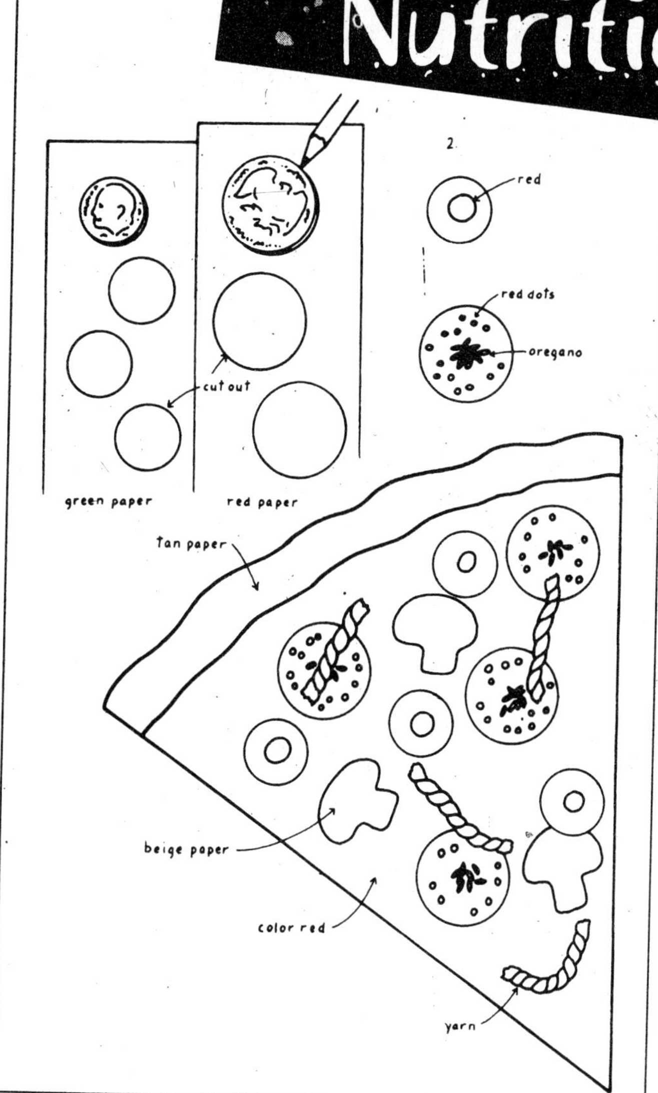

More to do

Cooking: Show the real ingredients of pizza. Feel and smell and perhaps even taste the ingredients, such as tomato sauce, pepperoni, sausage, yeast, flour, cheese, thyme, onion, green pepper, oregano, basil and olives. ▪ Compare the ingredients in terms of their place on the food pyramid chart. Why is pizza nutritious? ▪ Discuss the various types of pizza that you can make: veggie pizza, meat pizza, white cheese pizza. ▪ Have a pizza party. Either make it or order it and have it delivered. You might order or make several types of pizza so the children can have a taste of veggie pizza, for example, as well as the standard pepperoni. ▪ Visit a local pizza parlor and perhaps even tour the kitchen.

Dramatic play: Put the pretend pizzas in the cooking corner along with a chef's hat and apron, bowl, spoon and empty containers for pizza ingredients (tomato sauce, cheese, empty flour bags, etc.) Children can pretend to make pizza and serve it. ▪ Stock the shopping corner with containers for tomato sauce, etc. Let the children go shopping for pizza ingredients.

More science: Start a general nutrition discussion using pizza as an example. Talk about where food goes when you eat it and what happens to the food the body uses (vitamins and minerals are used by the body for energy and growth, etc.).

Original songs

Sing to the tune of "Did You Ever See a Lassie?"

Did you ever taste pizza, taste pizza, taste pizza?
Did you ever taste pizza? It tastes really good!
It has tomatoes and mushrooms.

Nutrition

It has bread dough and cheese.
Did you ever taste pizza? It tastes really good!

Did you ever taste veggie pizza, veggie pizza, veggie pizza?
Did you ever taste veggie pizza? It tastes really good!
It has broccoli and carrots.
It has green peppers and cheese.
Did you ever taste veggie pizza? It tastes really good!

Did you ever taste spaghetti, spaghetti, spaghetti?
Did you ever taste spaghetti? It tastes really good!
It has tomatoes and hamburger.
It has spaghetti and cheese.
Did you ever taste spaghetti? It tastes really good!

Sing to the tune of "Skip to My Lou."

Vitamins in the pizza are good for me,
Vitamins in the pizza are good for me,
Vitamins in the pizza are good for me,
Pizza tastes good and it begins with P.

Continue with verses about vegetables, eggs, tomatoes or any tasty pizza ingredient.

Related books

Eating the Alphabet: Fruits and Vegetables From A to Z by Lois Ehlert
The Human Body by Jonathan Miller

Mary Brehm, Aurora, OH

Foods We Liked As Babies

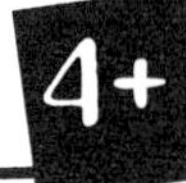

Science skills

Children learn how to compare information and chart the results.

Materials

Food survey form for parents to complete
Markers
Poster board or chart paper
Highlight pens

What to do

1. Create a survey for parents to complete and for the child to bring back to school.
2. Create a chart graph to record the results. Ask a group of children to record the survey results for each child.
3. Now record current food likes and dislikes of the children.
4. Compare and discuss how our tastes may change as we get older and how foods we do not care for today, we may enjoy later on.
5. Place the chart in the language or science area to record any further changes that may take place through the school year.

More to do

Snack: Discuss nutrition. Have "taste tests," and encourage children to try foods they once thought they disliked.

Related books

Bread, Bread, Bread by Ann Morris
Gregory, the Terrible Eater by Mitchell Sharmat

Dani Rosensteel, Payson, AZ

A School of Fish

3+

Science skills

This activity encourages children to then ask questions about nature.

Materials

Paper
String
Tape
Markers
Paint
Blue cellophane
Crayons

What to do

1. Cut out shapes of undersea life for children to paint. Older children can cut out their own.
2. Let the children paint the fish.
3. Hang the fish from the ceiling. Put blue cellophane on the classroom windows so it looks like you are all under the sea with fish swimming above.
4. The children can use crayons or markers to draw small fish shapes to tape to the blue cellophane.
5. When people look in the windows it is fun for the children to pretend to swim like fish. If possible, give each child a chance to look through the window at the class.

More to do

Language: Cut a piece of paper with wave shapes at the top. Ask the children to make up "fish stories" to dictate or write on the paper.
Math: Count fish crackers as you eat them at snack time.
More science: Look at photos of real undersea creatures.

Related books

Big Al by Andrew Clements
A House for Hermit Crab by Eric Carle
Swimmy by Leo Lionni

Laura Durbrow, Lake Oswego, OR

3+

Beach Under Glass

Science skills

By creating miniature oceans, children practice observation and fine motor skills.

Materials

Clear glass or plastic container, such as soda bottle, jam jar or mayonnaise jar, one for each child
Builder's sand, coarse grade, washed
Blue food coloring
Glue, waterproof or glue gun preferred
Small plastic fish and seaweed
Small shells and coral, washed
Water

What to do

1. Glue the plastic seaweed to the bottom of the jars and let the glue dry.
2. Now the children place washed shells, coral, fish and sand into the jars. Fill only one third of the containers with solid items and the remainder of the jars with water. Put one drop of blue food coloring in the water.
3. Seal the jars or bottles by putting glue on the tops and screwing the lids on tight to make them leak-proof. Let the glue set overnight.
4. The children may make waves by moving the jars back and forth, or ocean currents by using a circular motion.

More to do

Art: Make a smaller version of this activity by using a baby food jar. Spray paint the lid, glue rocks and seaweed to the lid and seal the jar. Using the lid as the base, you will have a very nice scene and paperweight.

Related book

Beneath Blue Waters: Meetings With Remarkable Deep-Sea Creatures by Deborah Kovacs and Kate Madin

Oceans

Exploring Seaweed

3+

Science skills

In exploring seaweed firsthand, children learn classifying skills.

Materials

Several dish tubs, wading pool or other large waterproof container

Seaweed

Chart paper

What to do

1. Gather some seaweed. If possible, find different types.
2. Make an identification chart with drawings and labels of the different types of seaweed and the different parts of the plant.
3. Put different types of seaweed in the dish tubs so the children can see and feel the differences among them..
4. Place the rest of the seaweed in the wading pool for further exploration. It is fun to add seashells and rubber sea animals to the pool.

Related book

Seashores by Joyce Pope

Ann Chandler, Felton, CA

Ocean in a Bottle

Science skills

Children learn about the properties of oil and water.

Materials

Clear plastic 1-liter bottle, empty

Water

Tape

Mineral oil, 1 pint (500 ml)

Blue food coloring

What to do

1. Pour mineral oil into the empty bottle and add water to fill.
2. Place five to six drops of blue food coloring in the bottle and shake.
3. Point out how the oil and water don't mix, which will be obvious because the oil will be clear and the water will turn blue.

4. Seal the bottle with a lid and tape it shut so it will not leak. You may even wish to seal with a hot glue gun.
5. Gently rock the bottle from side to side to simulate waves.

More to do

Art: Make a sandy collage using colored sand and glue.

Dramatic play: Fill a beach bag with things like a sweater, bathing suit, wool hat, suntan lotion, boots, sunglasses, etc. Ask the children to sort the clothes, finding the things needed on a trip to the beach.

Related books

A Day at the Beach by Mircea Vasiliu
At the Beach by Anne Rockwell

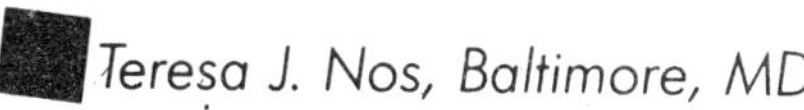
Teresa J. Nos, Baltimore, MD

3+

The Floating Sea Otter

Science skills
Children learn how otters live in the ocean.

Materials

Sea otter pattern to trace
Navy blue or turquoise construction paper
Medium-point black marker
White glue
One small seashell per child
Small seashells
Brown construction paper
Blue crayon or marker
12 mm wiggle eyes
White drawing or construction paper
Scissors

What to do

1. After talking about sea otters, help the children make one of their own.
2. Find areas on the globe where sea otters might live. Discuss ocean water pollution. How is it harmful to the sea otter? If the otter's fur is not clean, it will not be able to hold air bubbles and the otter could freeze to death from the cold water. The otter would not be able to float as well.
3. Make sea otter pattern and trace the otter and two arms and one hind leg on brown construction paper. Cut out the patterns.
4. Cut strip of blue paper 3" (7.5 cm) high and 12" (30 cm) long. Draw waves on the top edge with a blue crayon and cut out.
5. Draw one ear, nose, whiskers and a leg line with black marker and lines for toes on one paw and both feet.
6. Glue on the wiggle eye and the rear leg as shown.
7. Make a fold flap on one arm and glue it to the top of the otter and the other arm to back.
8. Glue the otter to white paper, then glue ocean waves, and then finally the shell between the paws.

Oceans

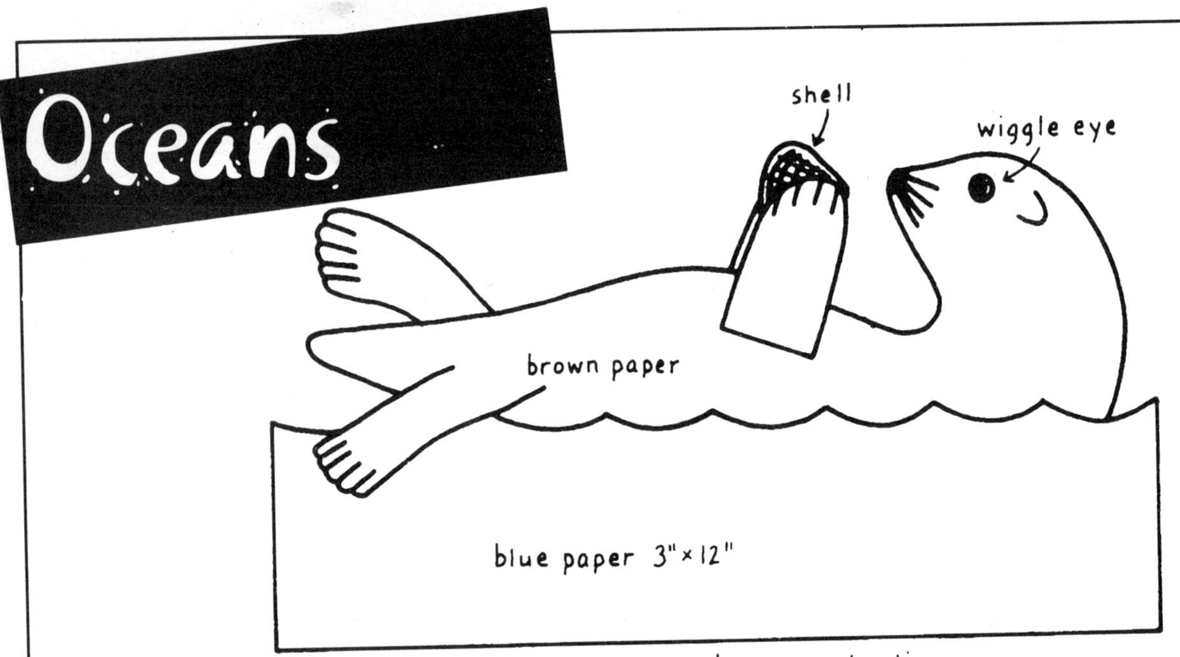

Draw nose, whiskers, ears, toes and leg lines.

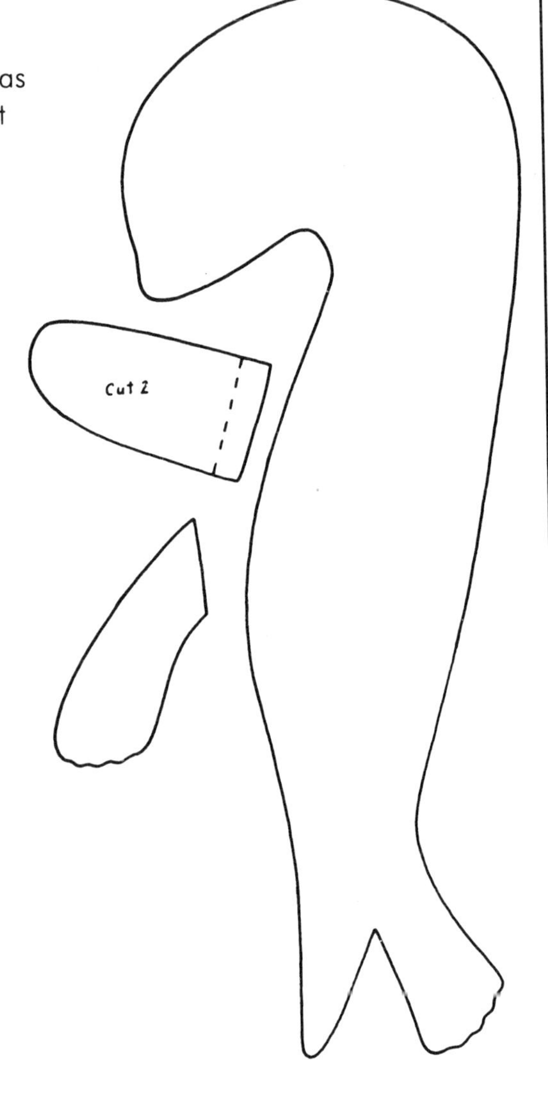

More to do

Sand and water table: Float objects in the water, such as a cork, sponge or air-filled balloon. What objects will not float? Put a penny, a nail and a heavy button in the water.

Special days: Have a designated sea otter day. Ask the children to bring plush otters, photos or pictures of otters to school.

Original poem

The Sea Otter

The cute little otter is very very shy.
His is quite furry with a whimper-like cry.
He grabs a sea urchin, starfish or clam shell
Tucks it in his skin pocket and gets a rock as well.

Then cracks the shell with the rock as he floats
On his back relaxing like a worthy row boat
Then rolls over and twists and squirms in quick time
To get rid of shell bits, food scraps or fish slime.

He eats and swims and nose dives at night
Using his whiskers and ears but not his sight.
When he wants to sleep, he gets a leaf of kelp
And wraps his blanket around himself.

His thick fur must be kept very, very clean
So it can trap air bubbles, but he is rarely seen.
He lives in the ocean and is playful and free
With his sweet face he is called "the clown of the sea."

Related books

Otter on His Own: The Story of a Sea Otter by Doe Boyle
Scamp's New Home by Joey Elliot
Zoobooks: Sea Otters, Wildlife Education, Ltd. staff

Mary Brehm, Aurora, OH

4+

Tide Pooling Field Trip

Science skills

On this delightful field trip, children learn observation, build vocabulary and use fine and large motor skills.

Materials

Each child will need a pair of rubber boots
Crayons
Blank book for each child
Many adults will be needed on this field trip
Watercolors

What to do

1. Read a tide table to find out when a low tide is expected and arrange to go on your field trip at that time.
2. Before the field trip, go to the tide pools and look at what kind of sea life lives there.
3. Tell the children before the trip that they are only going to LOOK at the animals in the tide pool. They are not to pick any up or take any home.
4. Divide the children up into groups of three to four per adult. Let each group explore the tide pools and discuss which animals they see in each one.
5. When the class returns to school, give each child a blank book with this poem written on the front page:

    We went to the tide pools, you and me
    And this is what we saw in the sea...
6. Still in small groups, ask each child to dictate one sea animal per page. The adult writes the animal names and the children illustrate to complete their book. Older children can copy the names of their sea animals.

More to do

Art: Let the children make "tide pools" out of Styrofoam bowls. Give them modeling clay to make the animals in their tide pools. When they are done, cut a piece of blue cellophane to fit over the opening of the bowl and glue it to the top. ▪ Let the children draw pictures of their tide pools and use crayons to color their pictures. Show the children how to do a watercolor wash on top of their drawings, to make the pictures look as if they are underwater.

Barbara Saul, Eureka, CA

Water, Water Everywhere!

4+

Science skills

Children observe how much water there is on Earth and practice eye-hand coordination.

Materials

Inflatable globe, beach ball size
Green and blue construction paper squares
Chart paper

What to do

1. Inflate the globe. Call a child's name and roll or toss the ball to him. When he catches the ball, ask him to call out where his fingers landed, either land or water.
2. Keep a tally on the chart paper of the number of "lands" and the number of "waters." For younger children, you can use green squares of paper to keep up with the amount of land and blue squares to tally the amount of water.
3. Give each child a chance to catch the ball. Be sure to record each time you roll or toss the ball.
4. After each child has had a turn, check to see if there is more land or water by counting the tally marks or the squares of paper.

More to do

Math: Use only squares of paper to record land and water amounts and graph the squares to provide visual comparison.

More science: Use a large floor map to allow the children to see all of the land and water on earth at once. Allow the children to pick out the large water sources that can be found on the map.

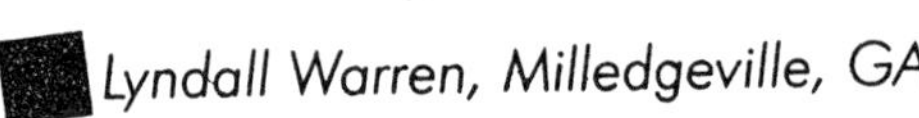

Hatching of a Sea Turtle

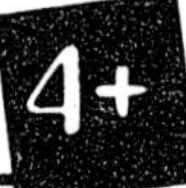

Science skills

Children observe a paper sea turtle hatching and develop fine motor skills.

Materials

Cardboard pattern to trace sea turtle and egg
Pencil
Black, white, brown, tan crayons
White glue
White drawing paper
Scissors
Pre-cut strip of white paper, 1" x 8" (2.5 cm x 20 cm)

What to do

1. Compare sea turtles, tortoises or land turtles and all kinds of freshwater turtles, such as Box Turtle, Snapping Turtle, Painted Turtle, Mud Turtle and the Spiny Soft-shell Turtle. Use the word "terrapin." This word refers to any kind of freshwater turtle. Use the word "carnivore," which is a meat-eating animal, such as the Snapping Turtle. All turtles have shells attached to their bodies. Turtles are reptiles and range in color from bright green to dark brown; some have colored spots, streaks or borders. Sea turtles' front legs are really flippers to help them swim. All female sea turtles lay their eggs in the beach sand and never see them hatch. The eggs are about the size of a ping pong ball and the female lays about 100 of them at a time.
2. Help the children make their own hatching sea turtle. Trace the shape of the sea turtle on cardboard and on white paper and cut them both out.
3. Now trace a large egg shape on the folded white paper and cut out the double egg, but do not cut on the fold.
4. Draw crack lines on the top side of the egg with a pencil. Open the egg up and cut the crack lines on the top side only.

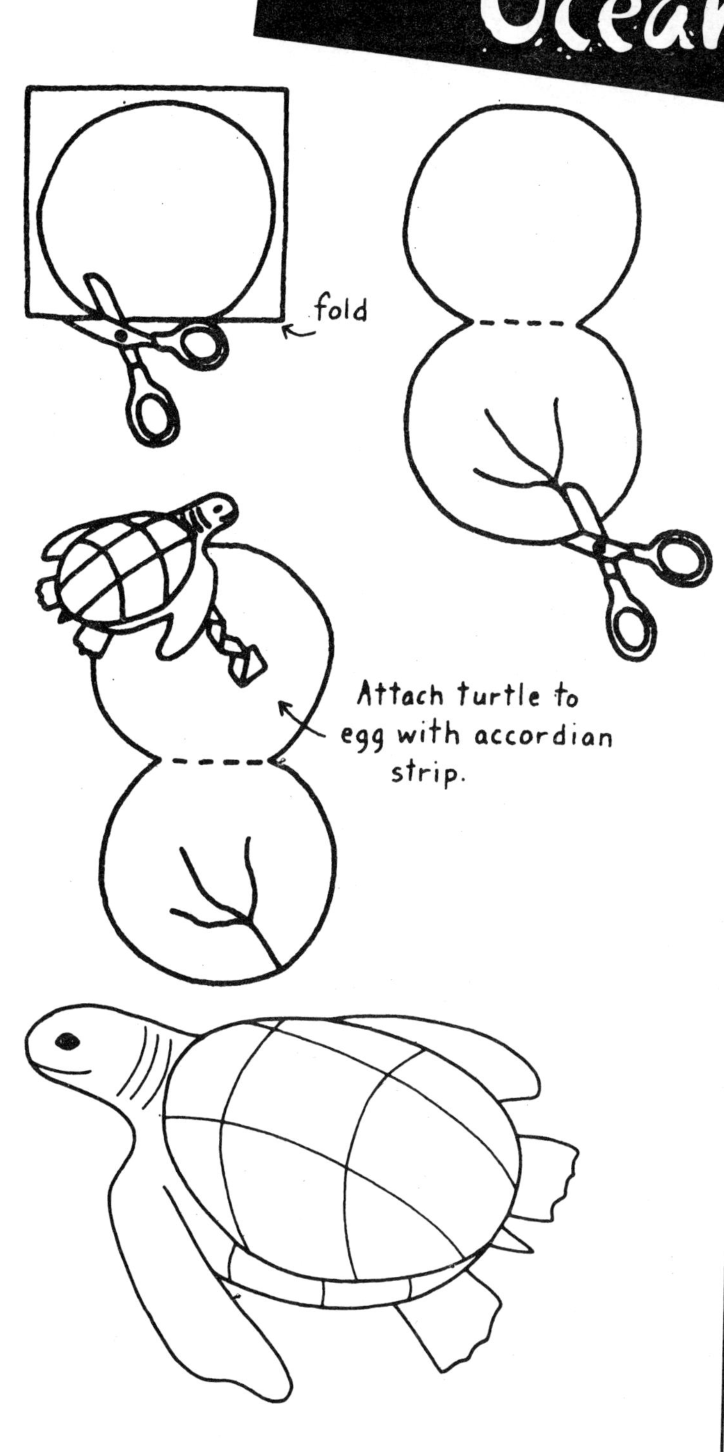

5. Draw an oval on the turtle's back with a pencil and color it to look like the turtle's shell. Also draw and crayon the turtle's eye, mouth and folded skin lines.
6. Accordion fold the 1" white paper strip and glue it to the inside center of the egg. Now glue the sea turtle to the last fold of the strip so that the head faces downward and the larger fin faces the bottom of the egg.
7. The sea turtle hatches by putting its head through the cracks in the top egg and then emerging altogether through the cracks. Children enjoy making the turtle hatch over and over again.

Oceans

More to do

Art: Make sea turtles out of clay or playdough.

Field trip: Visit a sea aquarium.

Math: Compare sizes of various turtles. Use pictures or paper cutout shapes of varying sizes.

More science: Find the ocean areas on a world globe where sea turtles probably live. Discuss why sea turtles are now an endangered species. How can we help protect them? Which turtles hibernate and where? Which kind of turtle lives in your area?

Storytelling: Tell turtle or tortoise fables or stories such as "The Tortoise and the Hare."

- Dramatize a favorite turtle story.

Original songs and poem

Sing to the tune of "Ten Little Indians."

One little, two little, three little turtles
Four little, little five, six little turtles
Seven little, eight little, nine little turtles.
Ten little turtles hatching.
Ten little, nine little, eight little, seven little . . .
One little turtle swimming.

Sing to the tune of "Did you Ever See a Lassie?"

Did you ever see a sea turtle, a sea turtle, a sea turtle?
Did you ever see a sea turtle swimming in the ocean?
He swims this way, he swims that way.
She swims this way, she swims that way.
Did you ever see a sea turtle swimming in the ocean?

The Life of a Sea Turtle (poem)

Teeny tiny sea turtle is hatching from its shell.
She'll have to climb out now from that deep sand well.

Then with her brothers and sisters, she walks toward the sea.
Here comes a hungry raccoon, so they had better flee.

Very tired now, she cradles in seaweed to sleep.
Then the hatchling looks for crabs and shrimp to eat.

After a year of the meat meal she eats seagrass instead,
Watching very carefully for fish that want her dead.

She swims to deeper waters until full grown and then
She'll swim all the way back to the same beach once again.

She will lay her eggs at night just as her mother had done.
And return to safe waters before the rising of the sun.

Related books

MacMillan Animal Encyclopedia for Children by Roger Few

Sea Turtle Journey: The Story of a Loggerhead Turtle by Lorraine A. Jay

Mary Brehm, Aurora, OH

4+

Let's Make Sand

Science skills

By making sand, children learn observation skills, develop their vocabulary and use fine and large motor skills.

Materials

Small amount of sand
Magnifying glass
Soft rocks
Towel
Small hammer or rubber mallet
Small bowl
Small shells
Resealabe plastic bag
Chart paper

What to do

1. Use this activity in the course of doing a unit on the ocean. Bring a bowl of sand to circle time. Slowly pass it around allowing the children to examine the sand with all their senses. Include a magnifying glass in the bowl.
2. Begin a discussion about the sand. Ask questions like, What color is it? How does it feel? What does it smell like? Lead the discussion to the question, "Where does it come from?" Write the children's answers on chart paper for all to see.
3. Lead the answers to shells, rocks and the force of water.
4. Put the rocks and shells into the resealable plastic bag and fold the towel around the bag.
5. One by one, let the children pound the towel with the hammer.
6. After all the children have had a turn, examine the contents. Ta da: sand!
7. Use the sand with glue for an art project, or put it in a tub with spoons, cups, magnifying lens, etc., for exploration.

Ann Gudowski, Johnstown, PA

Outer Space

Creative Constellations

3+

Science skills

The purpose of this activity is to stimulate children's curiosity and interest in nature.

Materials

Black construction paper
Rulers or anything with a straight edge
Self-adhesive foil stars
White crayons

What to do

1. Introduce the word "constellation," and show some examples in a book or on the drawing board.
2. Tell the children that they will make their own constellation.
3. Give each child a piece of construction paper, several star stickers, a ruler and a white crayon. The children arrange their stars on the paper.
4. Demonstrate how to use the ruler to connect the stars with white lines, and let the children connect the stars of their constellation.
5. Write the name of the child's constellation on the top of the paper, and hang all the children's constellations against a dark blue bulletin board to display.
6. Sing "Twinkle, Twinkle, Little Star."

More to do

Field trip: Visit a planetarium. • Visit the library and check out more books about the solar system.

Carla Scholl, Fairplay, CO

Seven Days of Outer Space Activities

Science skills

Here is a comprehensive series of fun activities to stimulate children's curiosity about the solar system.

Materials

Construction paper: yellow, dark blue, manila, red, green, white, black, orange, purple
Glue
Single-hole paper punch
Moon and star-shaped sponges or cookie cutters
Yellow poster board
Silver glitter
Yellow yarn
Yellow and black tempera paint
Plates or small pans

Stickers of spaceships, stars, American flags
Empty toilet paper and paper towel tubes
Scotch tape
Markers and crayons in all colors
Empty small plastic cups
White crayon or candle
Felt, as many colors as you like, cut into circles, rectangles and squares of varying size
Yellow tissue paper
Pictures of the Space Shuttle, rockets and astronauts

What to do

1. On Day One, help the children cut triangles from yellow construction paper. Each child needs four. Using a piece of dark blue paper, each child will paste his triangles together to make two stars on the blue sky. The teacher cuts a large star from yellow poster board for each child, and writes each name in glue. The children sprinkle glitter over the glue. The teacher punches a hole in the top of the star and puts yellow yarn through the hole to make necklaces for each child.
2. On Day Two, put yellow tempera paint on plates or in small pans. Using star and moon sponges or cookie cutters, each child paints on dark blue paper. The paper may be titled We're Off to Outer Space. Each child can add rocket or spaceship stickers.
3. For Day Three, make rocket ships. Give each child two pieces of manila paper cut to fit around a toilet paper tube and a paper towel tube. The children can use markers or crayons to decorate each of their rockets, and to draw windows and doors. The teacher tapes the paper around the tubes, and the children add flag stickers to each rocket. The teacher tapes an empty plastic cup to the top of each rocket for the capsule. The teacher also cuts small triangles of yellow poster board and tapes them to the bottoms of the tubes in three places to allow the rockets to stand upright.
4. On Day Four, the children draw a cluster of stars on light-colored construction paper using a white crayon or candle. The children use black tempera paint, watered down, to do a wash over the paper. As it dries, the stars become visible.
5. On Day Five, give each child a large piece of manila paper. Then help them cut different colors and sizes of circles, squares and rectangles. The children paste the shapes together to make robots. Now working in small groups of two or three, the children use the felt pieces to decorate their robots, at a table or on the floor.
6. For Day Six, the teacher tapes pieces of manila paper on the underside of a table, one at a time, for each child. Taking turns, the children lie on their backs under the table and color on the paper with crayons. When complete, each child's paper is labeled "Upside Down Drawing." We talk about the astronauts having to work over their heads and how tools and other objects float where there is no gravity. By discussing how it felt to lie on their backs to color, we get a sense of how the astronauts feel during weightlessness.
7. Finally, on Day Seven, the teacher gives each child a large circle cut from yellow poster board. The children brush glue all over the circles, and tear yellow tissue paper to cover the circle. When the circles are dry, the children may cut in from the other edges, fringing around the edge to make the sun's rays.

More to do

Dramatic play: Pretend to be astronauts going to the moon. Each child finds a spot on the floor to be his spaceship. Climb into them, buckle up and blast off. When you arrive in outer

space, go outside for a space walk, dodge a meteor shower and float around in space. When you are done with your walk, pull yourselves back to your spaceships and prepare to return to Earth.

Math: Cut different-sized stars from yellow paper and let the children take turns ordering them by size.

More science: Look at pictures of the Space Shuttle, spaceships and rockets. Talk about what is the same and what is different about each space vehicle. Look at pictures of what the people who go into space have to wear and discuss how it is different from what we wear. The U.S. Space Center in Huntsville, Alabama is an excellent source for material for all ages of children, and supplies free resources to teachers.

Related books and recordings

Draw Me a Star by Eric Carle
Papa, Please Get the Moon for Me by Eric Carle
What Is the Sun? by Reeve Lindbergh
"An Adventure in Space" from *On the Move with Greg and Steve*
"Twinkle, Twinkle, Little Star"

Diane K. Weiss, Fairfax, VA

Space Tours

3+

Science skills

In creating their own planets, children make observations and use creativity and fine motor skills.

Materials

Poster or model of the solar system
Balloons
Paper plates
Collage materials
Sand
For papier-mâché: flour, water, salt
Newspaper, torn into strips
Paint
Glitter
Glue
String

What to do

1. Discuss the solar system and show the poster or models of planets and the sun. Talk about the various aspects of the different planets, for example, how hot or cold they are, their position relative to the sun, whether they have water, air and other conditions needed to support life.
2. Help the children create their own planets using papier-mâché. Blow up one balloon for each child and layer newspaper dipped in the papier-mâché on it until it is completely covered. After the balloon is covered, attach a string to it, so it can be hung to dry. Simply lay a string on the balloon and put some papier-mâché newspaper over it.
3. Hang the balloons up to dry. This may take a while—as much as a couple of days—so plan ahead to have some interim activities to do during this stage. For example, ask the children

to dictate stories and draw pictures about their planets and the creatures that might live there. Let the children make their stories as funny, weird or outrageous as they like. Encourage them to include facts such as whether the inhabitants of this planet live on land, in the air or on water, what they eat, what they do for fun, whether they breathe oxygen, and if not, then how they live? Also, do these creatures have any special skills or talents?

4. Let the children use a variety of materials to decorate their planets. They can use paper plates that you tie or tape to the planet for Saturn-like rings. They can also use paint, collage materials, construction paper, glitter and colored sand or just about anything else to represent land masses and bodies of water on their planets.
5. Display the newly-formed solar system by hanging the planets around your room. Fishing line, attached to the light fixtures or corners of the windows, works very well. Be sure to put a label on each planet to identify the planet name and who created it.

More to do

Art: Be creative! You do not have to use a balloon. Who says planets always have to be round? You can create planets out of tissue boxes, small milk cartons, juice or soup cans or any material you happen to have laying around. Just cover them with papier-mâché and let the creative process take control! ▪ Make Space Scopes, using discarded paper towel tubes. Let the children decorate the outsides of their tubes in any manner they wish, using markers, crayons or poster paints. Avoid using glitter or any other type of glued-on materials, since these scopes will be used near the eyes and such decorations tend to fall off. Encourage the children to take their Space Scopes home and use them to observe the nighttime sky.

Games: Let the children run relay races or obstacle courses, as if they were floating in space. The object of the game is to move as fluidly as possible, as if floating weightlessly.

Movement: Play your best "spacey" music and encourage the children to dance as if they were floating in space. Enhance this activity by tethering your astronauts with lengths of soft yarn. Remind the children to move slowly and fluidly, as if they are weightless.

Related books

Other Worlds: A Beginner's Guide to Planets and Moons by Terence Dickinson

Our Solar System by Seymour Simon

The Planets by Gail Gibbon

The Sun's Family of Planets by Allan Fowler

Space Out: Jokes About Outer Space by Peter Roop

Virginia Jean Herrod, Columbia, SC

Outer Space

Moon Rocks

3+

Science skills

The children observe a substance changing from liquid to soild.

Materials

Plaster of Paris
Resealable plastic bags
Water

What to do

1. Allow the children to place the plaster of Paris in resealable plastic bags. Add some water, seal and mix. The bags will begin to get warm when the "chemical reaction" takes place.
2. As the plaster gets hard, break it into chunks and you have moon rocks! The fun in this is feeling the warmth of the plaster of Paris; the rocks are secondary, but the children love it!

Kristina Davis, Seminole, FL

Space Alien Slime

3+

Science skills

Children use their hands to explore an unusual mixture called "slime." Is it a solid or is it a liquid?

Materials

Large bowl
One wooden spoon or sturdy plastic spoon per child
Empty plastic ½ lb. (225 gm) margarine tubs with lids, one per child

Recipe per child
¼ cup (60 ml) cornstarch
5 teaspoons (25 ml) water
5 teaspoons (25 ml) water

What to do

1. Place cornstarch, water and food coloring into the bowl or the individual margarine tubs, and mix with a spoon until you have a thick paste. The mixture will be stiff. The children can mix with their hands if soap and water are easily available. Divide the mixture into the margarine tubs it you mixed il in one large bowl
2. Let the children handle the mixture: poke it, roll it, let it relax into a puddle, etc.
3. The "alien slime" will stay fresh for two or three days if you keep it in an airtight container.

4. The reason for the mixture's texture is that the cornstarch does not dissolve in the water, but remains suspended in the water. This gives the mixture its special "alien slime" properties.

More to do

More science: Compare sugar and water to the cornstarch and water combination. How is the sugar solution different? How is it the same?

Original poem

Space alien slime, it's red, blue or green,
And the quiver-iest, shiver-iest stuff that you've seen.
Poke it with your finger, and before you can say
"Boo!" the hole has gone away.
Rolled in your hand, it becomes a ball.
Left in a dish, it's a puddle. That's all.
Space alien slime, it's red, blue or green,
And the quiver-iest, shiver-iest stuff that you've seen.

Related books

Guys from Space by Daniel Pinkwater
Space Case by Edward Marshall

Christina Chilcote, New Freedom, PA

3+

Pop-Up Rockets

Science skills
Children learn about real rockets by making this model rocket.

Materials

Scissors
16-ounce (500 ml) plastic cup, one for each child
Plastic straws
Two pieces of construction paper, sizes 2" x 4" and 2" x 2" (5 cm x 10 cm and 5 cm x 5 cm)

What to do

1. Use pointed scissors to poke a hole in the middle of the bottom of the plastic cup. Make sure that a straw can slide easily through the hole.
2. Children cut the 2" x 2" square from corner to corner to create two triangles. Glue one triangle to one of the 2" sides of the rectangle to create the top of the rocket. Let the children cut the remaining triangle in half to create two smaller triangles. Glue the two triangles to the opposite end for the tail of the rocket. Tape the rocket to the straw, leaving about four inches of straw at the bottom.

Outer Space

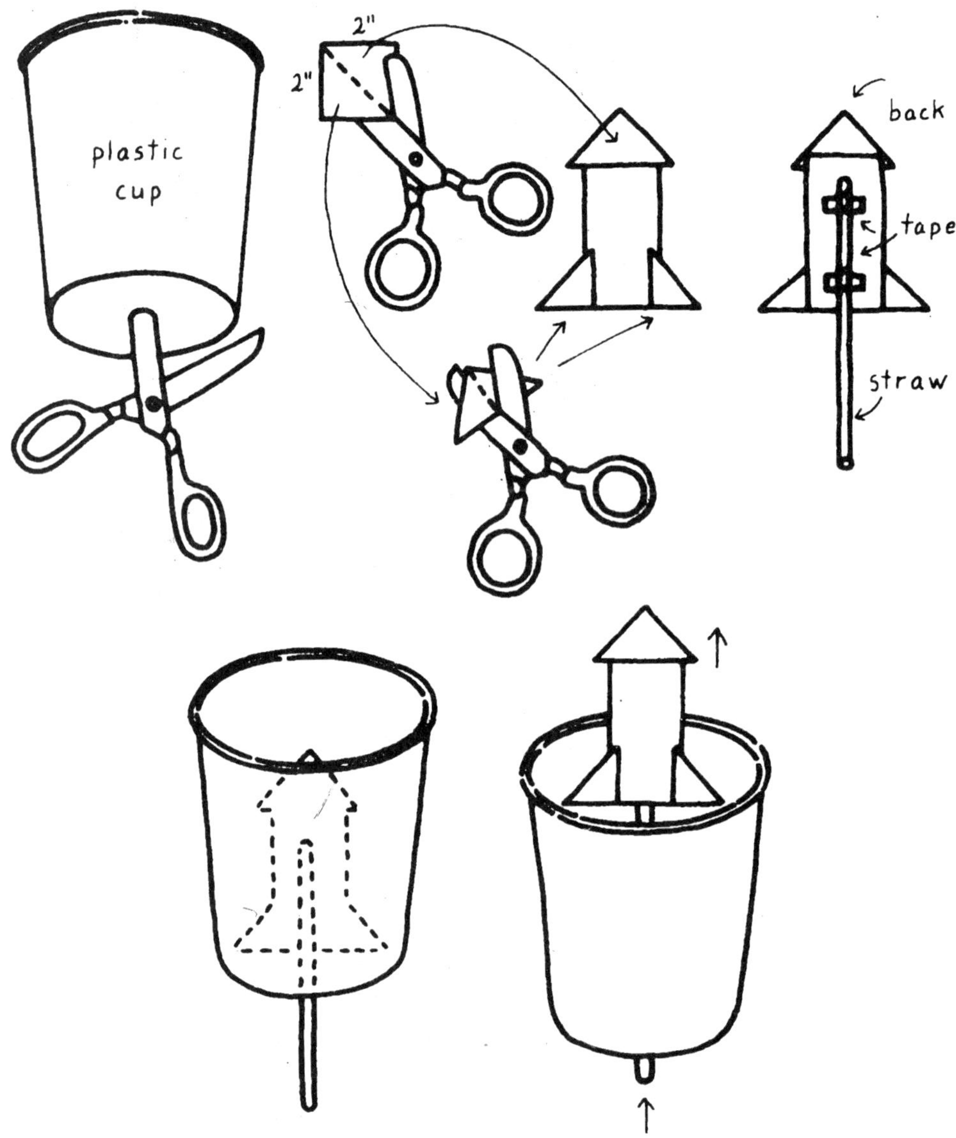

3. Place the bottom of the straw inside the cup and poke it down through the hole.
4. Children pull the straw down until the rocket disappears into the cup. Have a countdown and pop up the rockets when blast-off occurs.

Joyce Montag, Slippery Rock, PA

4+ Star Gazers

Science skills

This is a quick way for children to observe the constellations.

Materials

Book showing star constellations
Nails and hammer
Elastic bands
Black construction paper
Large juice cans with both ends removed and any rough edges covered with duct tape

What to do

1. Hold the juice can down on the black paper and trace around its end.
2. Using a book or guide, draw one of the constellation star patterns in the circle on the black paper.
3. Using a nail and hammer, poke holes in the paper where the stars should be. Supervise closely.
4. Put the black paper over the end of a can and hold it in place with an elastic band.
5. Look up to the light and see the constellations!

Related books

Starwatch by Ben Mayer
Nightwatch by Terence Dickinson

Andrea Clapper, Cobleskill, NY

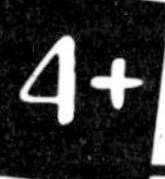

4+ Star Box

Science skills

Children experience a starry sky with this unique box.

Materials

Scissors
Large cardboard box
Glow-in-the-dark planet and star stickers
Paintbrush
Black or dark blue tempera paint
Glow-in-the-dark glue or paint

What to do

1. Cut a semi-circular hole in one side of the box.
2. Paint the inside and outside of the box and allow it to dry.
3. Stick planets and stars in a random pattern onto the inside of the box.

4. Fill in the dark background with dots of glow paint or glue to add depth.
5. Let the inside of the box absorb light.
6. Give children turns putting their heads in the box while they lie on the floor to give them a feeling of weightlessness.
7. Cover the hole to seal out any light. Enjoy the trip.

More to do

Art: Using paper towel rolls, make rocket ships. Children can decorate them with markers, stickers, refractive paper, glitter. ▪ Punch holes in the bottom of a cardboard oatmeal box in the patterns of constellations. Hold up to the light to view the stars.

Teresa J. Nos, Baltimore, MD

Star Shine

4+

Science skills

In this art project, children explore the qualities of stars.

Materials

9" x 12" or 12" x 18" (22.5 cm x 30 cm or 30 cm x 45 cm) dark-colored construction paper
Star-shaped cookie cutters
Newspapers
Glue
Glitter
Styrofoam tray

What to do

1. Study the stars with pictures of constellations, books and even a visit to the planetarium.
2. Let the children choose their paper and write their names on one side.
3. Pour a thin pool of glue into the Styrofoam tray. Children dip the cookie cutters into the glue and press them on their paper. Repeat as needed to create the constellation the child has imagined.
4. Sprinkle glitter over the paper, tilt the paper gently to cover all glued areas. Shake off the excess and reserve. Lay the papers flat to dry.

Related books

A Book About Planets and Stars by Betty Polisar Reigot
My Picture Book of the Planets by Nancy E. Krulik
The Planets in Our Solar System by Franklyn M. Branley
Stargazers by Gail Gibbons

Susan Oldham Hill, Lakeland, FL

4+

Edible Solar System

Science skills

In this delicious activity, children apply what they know about outer space to make real and imagined edible planets.

Materials

Various-sized round fruits, vegetables and nuts, such as red and green cabbage, grapefruit, lemon, lime, radish, grapes, walnuts, etc.

What to do

1. Give each food item a planet name based on its size.
2. Create your solar system by placing the planets in order on a table.
3. Let the children enjoy eating pieces of outer space.

Original song

Sing to the tune of "Twinkle, Twinkle, Little Star."

Lots of planets you will see,
Like Mars in this galaxy.
Neptune, Earth, Jupiter, plus
Mercury and Uranus.
Pluto, Saturn, Venus shine,
Count the planets, there are nine.

Patricia Moeser, McFarland, WI

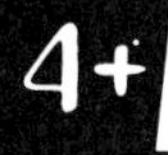

4+

Target Planet

Science skills

In this beanbag game, children learn about numbers and practice motor skills.

Materials

8″ (20 cm) diameter yellow circle labeled in the center with a number 10
9 5″ (12.5 cm) assorted-color circles each labeled in the center with a number from one to nine
Tape
Beanbag

What to do

1. Discuss the fact that there are nine planets that revolve around the sun.
2. Tape the sun and planets to the floor.
3. Encourage the children to take turns trying to throw a beanbag so that it lands on one of the circles.
4. The child should say the numeral on the circle his beanbag touched.
5. Children perform some activity to correspond to the number they hit with the beanbag, for example, clap nine times, jump four times, etc.

Joyce Montag, Slippery Rock, PA

Learning the Constellations

Science skills

Children use fine motor skills and observation, and begin to learn about numbers and letters.

Materials

Book on constellations
Hole punch
White chalk, optional
Black construction paper
White yarn

What to do

1. Trace a constellation on the black paper. Punch out holes where the major constellations are.
2. On the back of the paper, label the holes to match the pattern of the constellation using numbers or the alphabet. If desired, connect the stars of the constellations with white chalk.
3. Using a long piece of white yarn with a knotted end, let the child lace or sew, starting with the first letter or number until the design is complete.
4. Some easy constellations you can try are the Great Bear and the Lesser Bear, Big Dipper and Little Dipper, or even Pegasus and Draco the Dragon.
5. During story time, read Greek or Native American myths about these constellation creatures.

Related books

Draw Me a Star by Eric Carle
Papa, Please Get the Moon for Me by Eric Carle

Teresa Jarmuz, Lancaster NY

Science Centers in the Early Childhood Classroom

Here are a few things to keep in mind when you develop science centers for young children:

1. If it can't be touched, or survive repeated handling, the object should not be placed in a center, but rather should be used at group time, with an adult.
2. Children learn best through hands-on activities, so items in a science center should be touchable! This, of course, does not necessarily include any animals living in the center.
3. You should change the items in the center on a regular basis. If the children don't visit the science area, the science area needs changing, revitalizing, refreshing.
4. Include items that involve four of the senses, perhaps on a bookshelf with four shelves:
   Sight: viewers, magnifiers, color panels
   Hearing: sound canisters, bells, shakers, different noisemakers
   Touch: different fabrics to match by touch, sand paper, a feely box
   Smell: flowers, scent bottles, whole fruits, perfume samplers
   For obvious reasons there would not be a shelf for taste: it is dangerous to have children think they can put whatever they find into their mouths.
5. When putting plants in a science area remember to use non-toxic varieties. Your local poison control center or garden shop can help you find safe plants to use. Peppermint or other mint plants are a good choice. They are hearty plants and prolific growers, smell wonderful and are non-toxic if eaten. Children may assist in taking care of the plants.
6. No science area is complete without animals of some kind. Our center has had good luck with goldfish and crickets. Both are relatively inexpensive and easy to take care of. Crickets will reproduce within six to nine months and the children can take their own pet crickets home.
7. Another nice addition to the science area is a magnet board. The local auto supply store sells drip pans that make wonderful magnet boards when mounted on the back of a shelving or cubbie unit.

Linda Ford, Sacramento, CA

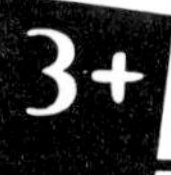
3+

The Great Wizdini

Science skills
A costumed character encourages children's interest in science.

Materials
Cape—blue and yellow satin, elastic, needle, thread, Velcro, gold fabric paint
Hat—poster board, blue and yellow satin, fabric glue, gold paint
Enthusiasm

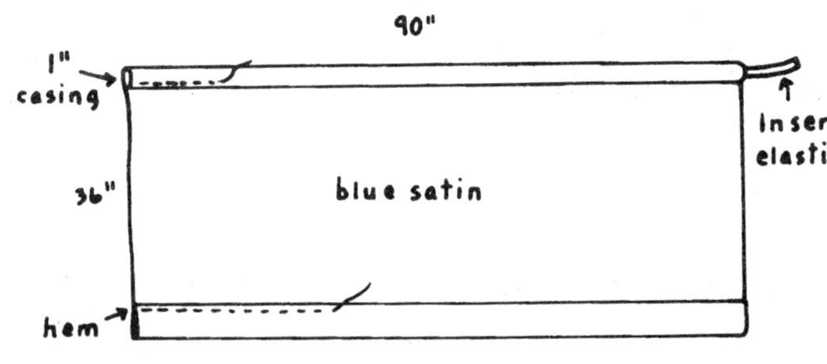

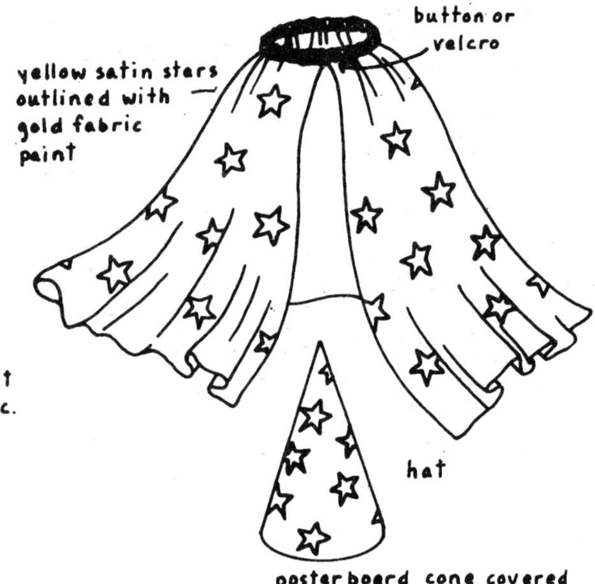

What to do

1. I have been teaching science to my preschool classes for 15 years but the response of the children when I created my "Wizdini" character has been so exciting. The interest and excitement levels have tripled.
2. To make the cape, use a piece of blue satin material 36" x 90" (1 m x 2¼ m). Make a 1" (2.5 cm) casing on one side of the 90" length and insert a piece of elastic long enough to fit comfortably around your neck. Hem the remaining sides. Add a piece of Velcro or a button at the neck. Glue yellow satin stars on the cape. I also outlined the stars with gold fabric paint.
3. Create a hat using poster board with more of the blue satin fabric. Add yellow stars and gold paint to the hat.
4. Whenever I do science with the children I enter the room dressed in my cape and hat, twirl around and announce, "I am the Great Wizdini! I've come to do science with you!" For my younger classes, I introduce the Wizdini beforehand using a picture of the Wizdini.

Cindy Winther, Oxford, MI

Pendulum Play

3+

Science skills

Children develop the scientific skill of observation.

Materials

Long board
Box or tray
Funnel
Salt
Large sheets of paper
2 classroom chairs
Yarn
Sand
Paint

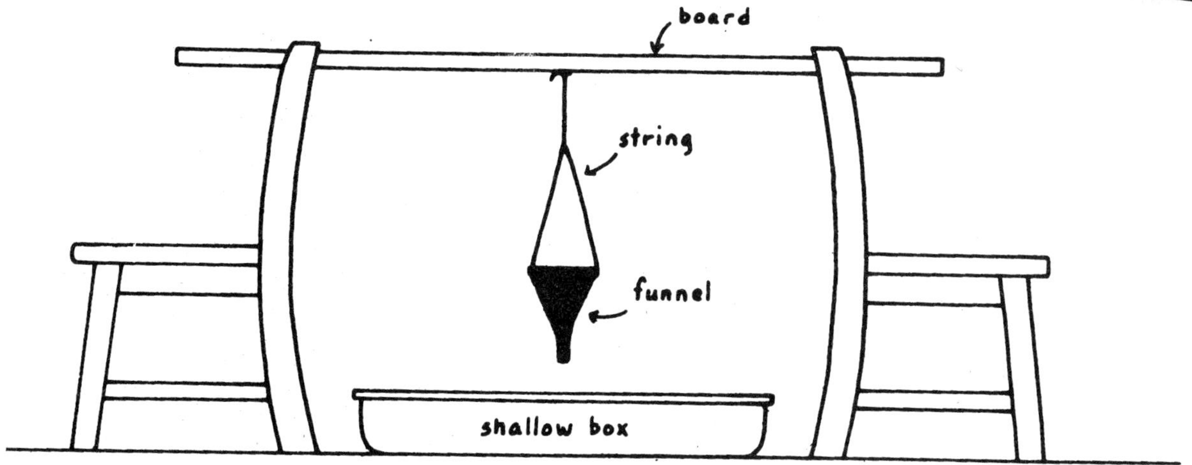

What to do

1. Outside, set the long board across two classroom chairs.
2. Place a large shallow box, such as one for under bed storage, under the board and hang the funnel from the middle of the board.
3. Fill the funnel with sand or colored salt.
4. Let the children swing the funnel and watch the designs, which are always elliptical and are named after the physicist Lissajoux. Next, you can move on to filling the funnel with paint and laying paper on the ground to make wonderful pictures!

Kristina Davis, Seminole, FL

3+

Pulling Pulleys

Science skills

With simple tools, children learn how scientific principles apply to everyday siuations.

Materials

Rope
Bucket
Sand

What to do

1. Tie the rope to the bucket.
2. Throw the rope over a short wall or fence.
3. Pour some sand into the bucket.

4. One child walks to the other side of the wall and pulls on the rope, lifting the bucket.
5. Show how builders and movers use a pulley to help in building and moving heavy items.

Related book

How Do You Lift a Lion? by Robert E. Wells

 *Monica Hay-Cook, Tucson, AZ*

Rip It, Tear It

Science skills

Children learn the scientific skill of careful observation.

Materials

Paper—construction, tissue paper, newspaper or magazines
Magnifying glass

What to do

1. Start with two pieces of construction paper.
2. Quickly rip one piece the long way, from top to bottom.
3. Quickly tear the second piece crosswise, from side to side.
4. Study the tears. Did one tear straighter than the other? That's because paper has grain. Use the magnifying glass to get a closer look.
5. Try the same process with other kinds of paper.

More to do

More science: Try the same procedure using cloth.

Original poem

Rip It and Tear It (chant)

Ripping and rolling it
Tearing and tucking it,
Squishing and squashing it,
Peeling and patting it,
Throwing and tossing it,

Catching and carrying it,
Taking it to the trash.

Monica Hay-Cook, Tucson, AZ

3+

Roll or Slide?

Science skills
Children learn to graph the results of their observations.

Materials
Board at least 2′ (60 cm) long
Variety of objects to test: plastic bowl, block, spool, pencil, a car, empty box, cardboard tube
Floor classification chart/graph for children to record findings

What to do
1. Prop one end of the board up at about a 45° angle.
2. Place one item at a time at the top of the board and let it go. Does it roll or slide? Repeat with the same item. Did you get the same result?
3. Put the item on the floor chart in the correct spot.
4. Move the top of the board up higher or down lower. Do you get the same results with the items you test?
5. Set up another board and place a "slider" or a "roller" at the top of each. Compare the speed of sliders against rollers. Put them in order of the fastest to the slowest. Change the angle of the boards and retest. Does this change affect the speed of any of the items?
6. Predict where on the floor the "rollers" will stop when you roll them down the board.

More to do
More science: This could lead to a discussion of inclined planes and wheels and other tools that help make work easier.

Diane Billman, Marietta, GA

3+

Sandbox Footprints

Science skills
Children learn how to look for similarities and differences.

Materials
Assortment of plastic animals
Sandbox, sand table or dishpan-type container with sand

What to do

1. Choose four or five plastic animal toys that will make different tracks in the sand. Slightly damp sand will hold a print better than dry sand.
2. Show the children that each animal makes a different footprint or pattern of prints in the sand. Compare the size, shape and pattern of the tracks.
3. Now let the children work in pairs or small groups. One child hides her eyes while another child chooses an animal to make prints in the sand.
4. The partner, who closed her eyes, tries to match the correct animal to the footprint. Children continue to take turns making tracks and hiding eyes.

More to do

Games: Again, children take turns hiding eyes, but this time one child chooses an animal to bury in the sand. When the other opens her eyes, she must decide which animal is missing from the group.

Outdoors: Take the children outside to look for real animal footprints. Areas with mud or near water are especially likely to have tracks. Try looking on snowy days, too.

Karen Johnson, Grand Rapids, MI

Science Tool Box

Science skills

Here are the basics for scientific exploration and experimentation.

Materials

Basket with a handle
Binoculars
Plastic color paddles
Linoleum color samples
Magnifying glasses
Tape measures
Prisms

What to do

I always keep plenty of child-safe scientific tools by the science table to enable the children to do their own experiments on classroom items. Keeping the tools stored in a handle basket allows us to take them outside to use in nature experiments. The tools can be used in teacher-directed activities, but also are great to encourage independent exploration and discovery. Add any other tools the children in your classroom might like.

Tracie O'Hara, Charlotte, NC

3+

Junk Drawer

Science skills

In this activity, children learn the important scientific skills of exploration and sorting.

Materials

Small items made of wood, plastic and metal
3 bowls
Large tray or flannel board

What to do

Sorting is an essential skill, but many children have only sorted objects according to color, shape and size, limiting their ability to see other attributes or properties. In this activity, the children sort items that are made of different materials.

1. Gather a large collection of odds and ends and put them out in a large basket with a tray.
2. Allow time for free exploration of the new items.
3. Introduce these words: wood, metal, plastic. For many children, these words are new. They can begin to label other items in the room according to what kind of material they are made from.
4. Place the items on a large tray or flannel board and put out three bowls or three circles of yarn. Allow the children to sort the items.
5. Encourage them to sort the items by other attributes.

 *Kristin Davis and Anne M. Sullivan, Seminole, FL*

3+

How Can They Float?

Science skills

In this fascinating experiment, children learn about making predictions and observation.

Materials

Brown "school" paper towel
Medium or large size plastic cups with wide tops, one for each child
Straight pins
Small keys
Other objects you may want to test
Water
Paper clips
Safety pins
Tacks
Toothpicks

What to do

1. Cut the paper towel into small pieces, about 2½" x 1½" (6.5 cm x 3.5 cm). Use brown "school" paper towels, which seems to work best, although regular paper towels work, too.
2. Fill the cups with water.
3. Carefully place a small piece of paper towel on the surface of the water. Holding the paper clip by the ends, carefully place it on the paper towel. It should stay on the surface and not sink. If it sinks, try this step again until it remains on the top of the paper.
4. When the paper clip is on the paper towel and floating, carefully poke around the edges of the paper towel with a toothpick until the towel sinks to the bottom.
5. The paper clip, or the other objects listed above, should float on the water. Surface tension is keeping it on the top. You can see small bubbles around the paper clip.
6. If you poke at the paper clip or other object with the toothpick, it will sink. You have broken the surface tension around the object, thus making it sink since it is heavier than water.
7. Although the paper clip, safety pin and straight pin will work the best, other small metal objects may work, as well. Perhaps trying a small nail, round paper fasteners, small washers, coins or rings may be fun. Ask the children what they think will happen with each object before you try it. Also try objects you know won't float at all to let the children know surface tension will not work with these objects because they are too heavy.

More to do

More science: Using this as a "magic" science trick will be fun for kids. First let them put the object in the water without the paper towel, and then you do the experiment with the paper towel. Asking the children why they think this is happening may produce some interesting answers.

Judy Zielinski, Maplewood, MN

Agua, Agua, Agua

Science skills

Children test the skill of observation in this activity.

Materials

Netting
Yarn
Masking tape
Pebbles
Clear container of water

What to do

1. Fill several 4" (10 cm) squares of netting with pebbles and tie them up with yarn.
2. Fill a container half full of water and mark the water level with masking tape.
3. Ask the children to brainstorm ways to raise the water level without adding more water.
4. Let the children add the netting packets of stones to the container of water.
5. Observe how the level rises. Explain that they are "displacing" the water.

6. Try taking out the packets of stones. What happens to the water level?

Related book

Agua, Agua, Agua by Pat Mora

Cindy Winther, Oxford, MI

3+

Magic Mixtures

Science skills

Children practice the scientific skills of exploration, observation and predicting.

Materials

Plastic smock for each child
¼ cup (60 ml) measuring cups or powdered drink scoops
Oil
Vinegar
Craft stick for each child
Large bowls
Flour
Baking soda
Colored water
Small container for each child

What to do

1. Put out on the table in large containers as much of the food items as you want the children to use. The larger the amounts the better! Gather the children at the science table, and ask them to put on their smocks.
2. Let the children explore the materials. Encourage them to use their measuring cups or scoops to mix the ingredients in any order, using their craft sticks, in their own containers.
3. You may want older children to tell what the ingredients are, and to predict what will happen.
4. Ask the questions, "What happened? What will happen if you add this?" Encourage them to put some vinegar with the soda to see a big surprise.

More to do

Language: Encourage the children to dictate to you a story about their magic mixture.
Math: Ask older children to count how many scoops of each ingredient they used in their own magic mixtures. Write these down to create their very own magic mixture recipe. You can keep these recipes for the next adventure with these ingredients.

Glenda Manchanda, Bemidji, MN

Science Process Skills

Beans

3+

Science skills

A series of bean activities develops observation skills.

Materials

Dried beans, different varieties
Cups
String
Funnels
Soil

What to do

1. Sort the dry beans by size, color, texture, etc.
   Note: Use caution with children who still put small objects in their mouths.
2. Set up a bean table with funnels and cups for the children to play with.
3. Plant the beans in clear plastic cups and graph how long they take to germinate.
4. Put some of the cups in a dark place. What is different compared to the bean plants placed in the sun?
5. Allow the beans to grow up a string, and measure and graph the growth over time.

 *Kristina Davis and Anne M. Sullivan, Seminole, FL*

Can You Hide It in Your Hand?

Science skills

This activity helps children develop their observation and prediction skills.

Materials

Variety of small objects: spool, short pencil, eraser, small box, tissue, block, crayon, large paper clip, key, golf ball, comb, shoe string
Basket

What to do

1. The child names an item she sees in the basket and predicts whether the item will fit in her hand.
2. The child picks up the item and wraps her fingers around it to try to hide the item. Ask, "Did you hide it in your hand? Did you predict correctly?"
3. For a variation provide three or four different-sized fabric pockets. The child chooses a pocket and predicts if an item will fit inside it or not.

More to do

Math: Compare your hand size with a friend's. Whose hand is bigger? Who has the biggest or smallest hand in the class? ▪ Trace your hand on a piece of paper and measure with Unifix cubes. Write the numeral somewhere on your paper. Have numeral models available for those who need help.

Related book

My Hands by Aliki

Diane Billman, Marietta, GA

How Does It Work?

Science skills

This activity encourages children to develop the scientific skills of observation, communication and creative thinking.

Materials

Five unusual gadgets or parts of gadgets, safe enough for the children to handle

Cards describing in words or symbols a variety of activities, such as washing dishes, building a doghouse, riding a pony, at least one per child

What to do

1. Ask the children to sit in a circle, and allow them to pass around and examine each of the gadgets.
2. Collect the gadgets and place them on the floor in the center of the circle.
3. Begin with a child who often produces creative responses. Let her draw an activity card from the deck and help her read the card aloud. Say, "Which one of the gadgets on the floor might you use to help someone (name the activity on the card)?" Encourage her to demonstrate how the item would be employed.
4. Now the child can return the gadget to the center of the floor, and you can ask another child to select an unused card from the deck, repeating the procedure in step 3. Continue until each child has had the opportunity to explore how a gadget might be used.

More to do

Language: Encourage children to describe their new inventions and to explain how they work and what they're used for.

More science: Supply your young inventors with safe gadget-building materials such as empty spools, drain stoppers, large metal bolts, rubber washers, pieces of broken gadgets, zippers, etc. Encourage them to create new, never-before-invented gadgets.

Marji E. Gold-Vukson, West Lafayette, IN

Science Process Skills

Let's See What Happens

Science skills
The children learn the basic process of doing science in this activity.

Materials
Determined by which experiments you do

What to do

1. Introduce the word "science" to the children and talk about how science is "seeing what happens."
2. Explain the following steps of science, and write them out or use picture symbols if possible:
   ASK—What will happen if . . .
   GUESS—I think this will happen . . .
   TRY—Test to see if your guess is what really happens.
   ANSWER—This is what happened.
3. Any simple exploration of the environment can demonstrate the "Let's See What Happens" process. For example:
   ASK—What will happen if I blow on a dandelion?
   GUESS—The flower will bend. The flower will turn. The "fuzzies" will fly off of the flower.
   TRY—The children each blow on a dandelion.
   ANSWER—The children observe the outcome, and use their own words to describe it and compare it to their guesses.
4. Apply the ASK, GUESS, TRY, ANSWER process to all science activities.
5. Remember to address safety. Remind children always to ask a grown-up whether it is okay to try something.

More to do
More science: Use the "Let's See What Happens" steps during art and play. For example, ask what happens if I mix red and yellow paint? What happens if I try the balance beam without holding my arms out? What happens if I stack the blocks with my eyes closed?

Suzanne Pearson, Winchester, VA

What's Inside?

Science skills
Children develop problem-solving skills, an essential science (and life!) skill.

Materials

Assortment of items, such as discarded small appliances
Containers
Various tools: screwdrivers, pliers, etc.
Safety glasses

What to do

1. Help children develop problem-solving skills by setting up a "What's Inside?" Center. This center will change over time but will always have in it a variety of items that have other items inside. Begin with discarded appliances or auto parts that have a lot of pieces inside. A carburetor from an auto junk yard or garage sale works well, or small kitchen appliances, telephones, cameras with lenses removed, a vacuum cleaner, clocks and hair dryers are good choices. Avoid things that might have glass or sharp parts, like a television. Caution: Cut off all electrical cords where they enter the appliance, and throw the cords away.
2. Put one or two items in the center along with various-size screw drivers, pliers and other appropriate tools. Provide safety goggles.
3. Encourage children to take apart the items to discover what's inside. Provide containers for them to put parts in as they dismantle the items. Discuss their findings and their hard work. Encourage prediction: "What do you think you will find inside? How many of those little round pieces do you think are in this toaster? How can we find out?"
4. As the children "gut" one item after another, encourage them to bring fresh items from home to this center. They'll think of many items. If they need help getting started, suggest broken video tapes or audio cassettes, switch boxes, a pillow, a tube of toothpaste or a back pack.

More to do

Art: As children explore art materials during the day, discuss what might be "inside" markers, paint cups, pencils, chalk, glue bottles and other items.
Language: Encourage children to bring in envelopes of junk mail. Open the envelopes and explore the contents. Children can "read" the junk mail, identifying letters and numbers, colors and familiar products.
More science: Let the children explore "what's inside" items in each area of the classroom. Discuss what they find inside and list their findings on a chart. Suggested places to explore include inside game boxes, inside pocketbooks or suitcases in the dramatic play area, inside paint cups at the easel, inside a drawer or cabinet, inside a pencil container, inside a box of animals at the block area, inside a canister in the cooking area, inside a pocket, inside the room, inside the building. Children will think of many more places to explore.
Snack: Cut miniature pita breads in half cross-wise, making pita pockets. Offer these with an assortment of fillings: shredded lettuce, chopped tomato, shredded or chunked cheese, sliced mushrooms, etc. Children stuff a pita pocket with their choice of fillings, then eat the pocket and "what's inside."

Related books

The Color Box by Dayle Ann Dodds
A House Is a House for Me by Mary Ann Hoberman
The Toolbox by Anne and Harlow Rockwell
Where's Spot? by Eric Hill

Barbara F. Backer, Charleston, SC

My Own Science Lab

4+

Science skills

This activity encourages the scientific skills of experimentation, observation and prediction.

Materials

Shoe box
Iron filings
Metal items
Magnifying glass
Contact paper
Magnets: bar, horseshoe and u
Non-metal items
Prisms

What to do

1. Cover a shoe box with contact paper.
2. Assemble the above items in the shoe box.
3. Encourage experimentation with the items to answer questions like: What happens when two magnets come into contact with one another? Do magnets pick up iron fillings? What objects were you not able to pick up with a magnet?
4. Look at the items through the magnifying glass. How does the magnifying glass make things look?
5. What does a prism do?

Monica Hay-Cook, Tucson, AZ

Shoe Box Science Sets

4+

Science skills

Here's a great way to organize your science area for self-discovery.

Materials

5 clear plastic shoe box-sized storage containers with contents as described below
Magnets, various types
Magnifying glasses, flashlight and other items with visual interest
Water bottle
Assorted small items, heavy and light
Assorted objects, metal and non-metal
Small kitchen scale
Items of varying, interesting textures

What to do

Start with these five basic experiments and add to your collection as new ideas arise.

1. Water Watch: Put in a water bottle for filling the storage container and assorted objects for a "sink or float" experiment.

2. Magnetic Magic: Use assorted magnets, such as horseshoe and wand types and various objects that are metal and non-metal for testing magnetic attraction.
3. Rate the Weight: For weighing experiments, put a small kitchen scale and an assortment of light and heavy objects to weigh in the third container.
4. Optical Tricks: Children will enjoy handling a variety of tools for exploring sight and light, such as magnifying glasses, prisms, kaleidoscopes, flashlight, unbreakable mirrors and translucent color paddles.
5. Touch Tester: Place a cloth to cover the top and sides of the open container, and items of various shapes and textures to identify by touch in the last container.

More to do

More science: You can apply the "shoe box set" idea to organize other materials, such as art supplies and manipulatives in your classroom. Each set is self-contained, compact, stackable, visible and easily accessible. This method of organization invites self-discovery and independence, and encourages children to classify materials for clean-up.

 *Susan A. Sharkey, La Mesa, CA*

4+

What's in a Machine?

Science skills

Children learn the scientific skills of observation and classification.

Materials

Old machines or gadgets that can be safely taken apart such as remote control, typewriter, telephone, radio
Child-size tools such as screwdrivers (flat head and Phillips), pliers, wrench, tweezers
Sorting baskets or bowls

What to do

Note: This activity requires constant adult supervision. Any items used for disassembly should not have batteries or sharp components.

1. Gather safe, small machines and gadgets from yard sales or ask parents to bring in appropriate items.
2. Prepare the science center for a small group of children.
3. Provide enough gadgets so that each child will have something to work on.
4. Invite the children to the science center table.
5. Allow the children to touch and explore the tools and give names to the tools. Explain the rules and demonstrate how to use each tool.
6. Give each child a gadget to take apart.
7. As gadgets are taken apart, children can sort and classify parts such as screws, bolts, wires, etc., into bowls or baskets.

More to do

Art: Children dip machine/gadget parts in paint and stamp their imprints on paper.

Math: Children develop a graph showing the number of screws, wires and other parts that were found in a particular machine.

More science: Invite a machine repair technician to visit the class and explain in more detail how a particular machine works.

Related book

Tools by Ann Morris

Cheryl Collins, Hughson, CA

How Many to Break It?

Science skills

Children learn the scientific skills of observation, estimation and prediction.

Materials

2 chairs
Long thin strip of paper, 10" x 2' to 4' (25 cm x 60-120 cm)
Marker
Masking tape
Rectangular unit blocks
Large poster board

What to do

1. As you set up the experiment, tell the children that often scientists "estimate" or guess about the results of an experiment; they're not sure what will happen, they think about what might happen, then try to make a good guess.
2. Set up the chairs, with the backs of the chairs facing each other, about 2 to 3 feet (60 cm to 1 m) apart.
3. Tape the paper to each seat, so that the paper spans the distance between the chairs.
4. Choose two children to sit in the chairs so the chairs do not tip over.
5. Have many blocks nearby. Let each child have one block to hold and examine.
6. On the chart, record the children's names and their guesses as to how many blocks it will take to break the paper.
7. One by one let the children add their blocks to the paper until it tears.
8. Review the chart.

More to do

Language: Encourage the children to draw or dictate a record of what happened.

More science: Supply the paper and tape, and allow experimentation by the children on their own.

Sharon Dempsey, Mays Landing, NJ

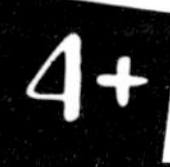

4+

What Made It Work?

Science skills
Children develop the scientific skills of observation and creative thinking.

Materials

Various tools, such as screwdrivers, pliers, hammers, tack removers, wire cutters, etc.
Large piece of corrugated cardboard or heavy box lid
Small appliances
Safety goggles
Glue, tape, wire

What to do

1. Ask parents and friends to save small appliances that no longer work.
2. Pick an appliance and discuss with the children what it was for and how the children think it worked.
3. Make sure that each child has a pair of safety goggles before beginning the next step.
4. Slowly and carefully help the children take apart as much of the appliance as they can.
5. Others can glue and tape the smaller pieces onto the piece of cardboard.
6. Label the pieces they recognize, like gears, magnets, wires, etc. The title of your board might be "See What Made Me Tick" for a clock or "See All the Pieces I Needed to Work." Children always seem to be amazed by all the pieces they find inside appliances.

 *Shirley Story, Lenoir, NC*

4+

How Fresh Is This Egg?

Science skills
In this egg-citing experiment, children practice the skills of observation and prediction.

Materials

Glass of water
Salt
Egg

What to do

1. Seat the children around the experiment table. Talk about where eggs come from and their uses.
2. Begin the experiment by choosing helpers. Ask one child to pour the water into the glass and another to pour the salt into the glass.

3. Before you drop the egg into the glass, encourage the children to predict what will happen. Tell them that if the egg sinks, it is stale; if it floats, it is fresh; and if it stands upright, it is old.
4. Compare the results with the predictions.
5. Older children could write the process in step format, for example:
   a. Pour water.
   b. Add salt.
   c. Drop in egg.

More to do

Art: Do this experiment during the Easter holiday, then decorate the eggs as an art project.
Math: Chart the predictions and the status of the eggs. Show the children that what we think might happen and what actually happens are often two different things.

Tammy M. Urquhart-Kibedy, Taylor, MI

Popcorn Up or Popcorn Down?

4+

Science skills

Children practice the skills of observation and prediction.

Materials

Tray
One 16-oz. (1 L) clear plastic bottle of water
One 16-oz. (1 L) clear plastic bottle of tonic water
¼ cup (60 ml) popcorn kernels, unpopped
Paper
Marker

What to do

1. Place both bottles of water on a tray and put the tray on a table.
2. Ask the children if the water in the bottles looks the same.
3. Open the plain bottle of water and drop an unpopped popcorn kernel into the water. Ask the children to watch what happens to the popcorn kernel.
4. Open the tonic water bottle and put another unpopped popcorn kernel in. Ask the children what happened to the popcorn kernels.
5. Ask the children why the popcorn kernel floated in the tonic water, but not in the regular water. What is the difference between the water in the bottles?
6. Record the children's answers on a large piece of paper.
7. Let the children continue to do the experiment themselves.
8. At circle time, discuss the answers the children gave and tell them about carbonation.

More to do

Art: Mix a few drops of liquid watercolor and water in a cup, and add a few drops of dish soap. Let the children blow bubbles in the cup with straws. Place a piece of paper on top of the cup to capture the bubbles. When the bubbles pop they make a design on the paper. ▪ Let the children

use gadgets and bubble solution for blowing bubbles. The gadgets might include strawberry baskets, fly swatters, pipe cleaners formed into a circle, etc.

Linda Andrews, Sonora, CA

4+

What Does Fire Need?

Science skills
By watching fire experiments, the children's curiosity and observation skills are challenged.

Materials
Chart paper
Matches
Pail of water
Marker
Candle
Small jar with top, such as a baby food jar

What to do
Caution: Point out that fire is dangerous, and that these experiments should be donely only by an adult. This would also be a good time to talk about fire safety.

1. Ask the children, "What do we know about fire and heat?" Chart their responses. Have a short talk about safety procedures during circle time.
2. As you light the candle, ask, "What does fire need to keep burning?" Now introduce these vocabulary words: air, heat and fuel. Fire must have all three in order to burn. Fuel is something that keeps the fire going, like gasoline keeps the car going and healthy food keeps your body going. What is the fuel here? The candlewick and wax are the fuels.
3. Light the candle; watch it burn for a few seconds.
4. Put the baby food jar over the lit candle and watch it burn. Watch the flame go out. Why did it go out? There is no air. Try this a few times.
5. Light the candle again. When you blow on the flame, why does it go out? Because there is less heat.

More to do
More science: After the experiments, chart the children's answers to: what do we know about fire and heat?

Ivy Sher, Sherman Oaks, CA

Wind Predictions

4+

Science skills

Children practice the skills of observation and prediction.

Materials

One feather
3″ (7.5 cm) Styrofoam ball
Block of wood
Hand-held cardboard or paper fan, one for each child
Paper and marker
Rubber ball
Rock

What to do

1. Place the feather on a hard surface, such as a table.
2. Ask the children to predict how many times they will have to wave the fan to move the feather across the table.
3. Record the predictions on paper.
4. Let the children wave the fans to produce air.
5. Repeat this process, using the balls, the block and the rock.
6. Ask open-ended questions about the process.
7. Discuss wind and air with the children.

More to do

Movement: Staple two tissue paper strips, each about 1′ (30 cm) long, to a tongue depressor. Put on some music and let the children dance with their streamers. Let them know that the streamers are moving because the children are moving the air as they dance.

Linda Andrews, Sonora, CA

Clowning Around

Science skills

Children learn about observations and predictions, and their curiosity about nature is stimulated.

Materials

Grease paints, different colors (paints that come in sticks or tubs are easy to work with)
A roll of paper towels
Old sock filled with approximately ¼ cup (60 ml) baby powder, tied off at the open end
Mirrors
Splatter aprons
Cold cream
1″ (2.5 cm) paintbrush, soft
Black eyeliner pencil
Camera

What to do

1. Start by setting everything out on a table and "painting" a red nose on yourself. Make a big show of it, and you will have no problem getting the interest of more than a few children.
2. Put aprons on the children, and one on yourself.
3. Demonstrate how to smear the cold cream all over your face. Use enough to just coat your face and rub it in. This will make it easier to apply the paints and remove them later.
   Note: Be sure to keep paint and cold cream away from eyes, nose and mouth.
4. Start dabbing paint on your face with your finger. Then smooth it out. (If you are teaching circles, make a circle around each eye, then around the mouth. If you are teaching triangles, use them or squares, stars, rainbows, etc.) Let the children be creative. As you help them apply the paints, watch the expressions change on their faces as they create new faces! If you make a mistake, just use a paper towel to wipe it off and try again.
5. Now for the science part: take the sock with the powder in it, and dab it on the painted areas of the children's faces. Note: Dab gently so the powder does not go into eyes, nose or mouth. Let the powder set just a few minutes and then use the paintbrush to brush the powder off. Now touch your face. The paint is dry. But it was sticky just minutes ago! It feels just like your face, doesn't it? Wow! You can even put water on and it won't come off.
6. Ask the children questions like, "What does it feel like now? Why did the paint change when we put powder on it? What made it change from sticky to dry?" The powder absorbs the grease in the paint.
7. Now you can draw lines around the dry colors with the eye liner pencil to help define the shapes. Don't forget to take a picture for review later.
8. Use the cold cream to remove the paint. Just smear some on and leave it a minute or two. Then use the paper towels to wipe it off. A second try will get any remaining color off.

More to do

Art: Provide brown paper shopping bags in the art center. Cut them flat and tape them together to form a life-size tent. Decorate the tent with crayons or paint. Hang it in the room and display the photos of the clown faces everyone made.

Dramatic play: Place clown clothes in the pretend or dress-up center. Clowns can wear over-sized shoes, ties, pants and shirts. Add scarves, hats and funny props.

More science: Place small amounts of grease paint in the science center. Demonstrate to the children how to use a paintbrush to apply the paint to paper instead of to their faces. Allow them to experiment with mixing colors and drying with baby powder. The children can predict which will dry the paint the fastest. Construct a graph and gather information to prove which guesses were correct.

Original poem

Here's a clown poem to say with the children once they're all painted up!

I am a clown as you can see.
Very soon I won't be me.
I put some paint upon my face.
Now I'm gone without a trace.

If you look hard
You will see
That this old clown
Is really ME!

Related books

Be a Clown by Mark Stolzenberg
The Circus by Mabel Harmer
Make-Up Art by Ron Freeman
Mudpies to Magnets by R. Williams, R. Rockwell and E. Sherwood
Transition Time: Let's Do Something Different by Jean Feldman

 *A. Gail Whitney, Dameron, MD*

Film Can Fun

Science skills

Children practice the scientific skills of observation, prediction and ordering.

Materials

Plastic 35-mm film canisters, black or gray but not transparent
Pennies and other objects, as described below
Sticky dots of two different colors
Markers
Balance scale

What to do

Try these challenging experiments!

1. To make sound shakers, separate 10 to 20 film cans into two sets. Mark each set with its own color dot on the top of each can.
2. Arrange the cans in pairs, one from each set. Fill each pair with small objects of matching quality and quantity. Examples might be two paper clips, five buttons, one penny, two marbles, etc.
3. Shuffle the pairs on a table. Challenge the children to shake the cans and place them in pairs by matching sounds.
4. Once they have arranged the cans, the children may remove the lids to see if the contents match.
5. To play a Penny Puzzler game, use 11 film cans and 55 pennies. Fill the cans with any number of pennies from 1 to 10. Label the bottom of each can with a sticky dot indicating the number of pennies inside.
6. Shuffle the cans on the table. Challenge the children to guess how many pennies are in each can by shaking and weighing them in their hands. Let the children arrange the cans in a row from 1 to 10, according to how many pennies they guess are in each can.
7. Once they have arranged the cans, the children can peek at the labels or remove the lids and count the pennies to check the results.
8. Use the balance scale to compare the weights of the penny cans.

More to do

Math: Use the pennies for counting activities. Place a jar of pennies next to a balance scale to invite self-discovery.

Music: Attach film cans filled with popcorn kernels, dried beans or rice to jumbo craft sticks with rubber bands. Use these rattles as rhythm instruments in your music area.

 *Susan Sharkey, LaMesa, CA*

Hot or Cold?

Science skills
Using thermometers, children practice observing and comparing.

Materials
Thermometers
Clear plastic cups
Warm and cold water

What to do
1. Show the children a thermometer and ask them what they think it might be. Ask them to tell things that they notice about the thermometer, for example, it has lines on it.
2. Explain the various uses of thermometers. Tell the children that there is something called mercury inside the thermometer, and the mercury expands and contracts when it becomes hotter or colder.
3. Tell the children to choose a partner, or you can pair them off.
4. Give each pair of children a thermometer.
5. Let the children move the thermometer from warm to cold water and observe which way the mercury moves. They will need help reading their thermometers.
6. After the children have had adequate exploration time, encourage them to discuss their observations as a class.

More to do
Language: Read seasonal books, such as *The Snowy Day* by Ezra Jack Keats, and encourage the children to tell you whether the mercury in a thermometer would be high or low in that type of weather.
Movement: Ask the children to crouch down and pretend that they are the mercury in a thermometer. Call out hot, warm, cool and cold. Let them move up and down as if they are the mercury.
Snack: Give the children freeze pops and let them squeeze the ice up and down like the mercury inside a thermometer.

Original poem
Up and down, the mercury goes.
Down means cold for fingers and toes.
Up, up, up as the weather gets hot.
Too hot? I hope not!

 *Lauren R. Zimmerman, Owings Mills, MD*

Class Tree

3+

Science skills
Children learn to be keen observers and become curious about nature.

Materials
Non-evergreen tree near the classroom
Camera

What to do

1. In the fall, take a walk outside and choose a "class tree." Take a color photograph of the tree with its brightly colored fall leaves. Hang the picture in the classroom for the children to see.
2. Take another photo when winter weather has taken all the leaves off the tree, another in spring of the budding tree and finally a summer photo of the tree in full foliage.
3. Make sure to display the tree pictures together as each season passes, so the children can see the changes in the tree.

More to do
More science: Make environmental discussions more concrete by discussing the effects of pollution, paper waste, etc., on the class tree.
Outdoors: Use the class tree in other ways, for example, as a place for a picnic, or for a leaf-raking expedition and jumping in the piles of leaves or to look for wildlife in it, etc.

Related book
The Giving Tree by Shel Silverstein

Suzanne Pearson, Winchester, VA

Tree Books

Science skills
This activity develops children's observations and fine motor skills.

Materials
8½" x 11" (21 cm x 27.5 cm) drawing paper
Tempera paints
Picture of a tree trunk
Paper cups

Fall

Winter

Spring

Summer

Small sponges, cut from a large sponge into 2" x 3" (5 cm x 7.5 cm) pieces
Crayons or felt-tipped markers
Pencils
Scissors
Stapler
Optional: pink or white tissue paper cut into 2" (5 cm) squares, white glue

What to do

1. To make the tree trunk pattern, fold a sheet of paper into fourths, and paste the outline of a tree trunk in each of the four sections. Leave enough space in each section so the children can add branches to the trunks. Draw lines between each of the four sections. Under each tree trunk write one of the four seasons: fall, winter, spring or summer. Duplicate the sheet of four trees for each child.
2. Read to the children a book about trees and their changes throughout the seasons. Discuss the changes with the class. Go outside and look at real trees.
3. Let the children cut on the lines so that they have four pages. Help those children who need it.
4. Complete the pages as follows: For fall, sponge paint fall colors onto the tree above the trunk. For winter, color the tree trunk and add bare branches. For the spring tree, use pastel colors to make blossoms on the tree or use tissue paper to make small flowers to glue onto the tree branches. For summer, paint or color green leaves on the tree.
5. After the pages dry, staple them together to make tree books.
6. Read aloud with the children the words under their trees.

More to do

More science: Plan a field trip to look at seasonal trees in a park, or take a walk in the neighborhood.

Related books

Have You Seen Trees? by Joanne Oppenheim
Red Leaf, Yellow Leaf by Lois Ehlert
Squirrels by Brian Wildsmith

Barbara Saul, Eureka, CA

The Four Seasons

3+

Science skills

Children learn about the seasons in this hands-on activity.

Materials

4 shallow trays
Water
Crushed leaves
Sand
Grass seed
Small animal and people figures
Small bowl
Masking tape

What to do

1. Beforehand, prepare the trays. For the spring tray, spread dirt on a tray, sprinkle it with grass seed and water the seeds. It will take a few days for the grass to grow. For the winter tray, freeze water in a tray. To make the fall tray, collect dried leaves, crush them and put them on a tray. For the summer tray, spread sand on the last tray and add a shallow bowl of water for a beach area. Add to the trays any other seasonal items, such as flowers, a plastic snowman or evergreen tree, a pumpkin and seashells.
2. Divide the science table into four parts using masking tape. Label each section with a season. For very young children, add pictures to depict the seasons. Place the trays on the appropriate section. Encourage the children to touch and handle the materials in the trays.
3. Use this hands-on approach to help children distinguish and interact with the seasons.

More to do

Games: Once the children can distinguish between the seasons, mix up the picture/word cards, and play a season identification game.

More science: Put the trays on the floor and let the children explore the sense of touch by feeling the contents of the trays with their bare feet.

 *Patricia Moeser, McFarland, WI*

3+

The Year-Round Pumpkin

Science skills

Children use all their senses to observe changes, and they are encouraged to ask questions about nature.

Materials

Ripe pumpkin
Carving tools
Garden area

What to do

1. Bring a pumpkin into the classroom.
2. Let children observe and explore it. How big around is it? Is it heavy? Are there any bumps or bruises?
3. Carve the pumpkin into a jack-o'-lantern and save the seeds.
4. Let the children explore the jack-o'-lantern by looking at the insides, at the pulp and by smelling and touching it.
5. Leave the jack-o'-lantern in the classroom for a few days. After Halloween is over, tell the children you will put the jack-o'-lantern out in the garden and they can watch what happens to it. Introduce the idea of decomposition, and observe the changes at regular intervals. Have any animals nibbled it? What color is it now? Is it still round?

6. By springtime most of the pumpkin will have decomposed. Discuss the fact that the pumpkin has become part of the soil and will now help the garden grow. Occasionally a seed that remained in the pumpkin will plant itself and grow!

More to do

Math: Estimate and then count how many seeds were in the pumpkin.

More science: Allow some seeds to air dry completely and save them to plant in the garden in the spring.

Snack: Wash and roast the pumpkin seeds for a snack.

Related books

Pumpkin, Pumpkin by Jeanne Titherington

The Seasons of Arnold's Apple Tree by Gail Gibbons

Sarah Dill, Madison, WI

Creating the Four Seasons

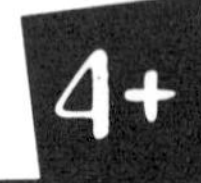

Science skills

As children illustrate the four seasons, they practice observation skills and use fine motor skills.

Materials

Poster board in blue, yellow, orange and green
Old greeting cards
Glue
Blue construction paper
Felt markers
Seasonal stickers
Paints
Old magazines
Scissors
Large coffee can
Rulers
Crayons
White paper

What to do

1. Make and display posters depicting the four seasons. The class can make these easily from poster board, blue for winter, yellow for summer, orange for autumn and green for spring (or let the children decide which color will make a good background for each season). Cut pictures from old magazines or greeting cards to paste on the poster boards or let the children color pictures depicting various "seasonal" activities and celebrations. You can make attractive edges for your posters from wallpaper sample books or construction paper. The posters make a wonderful group project for the class.
2. Using a large coffee can or something similar in diameter, pre-cut large circles from blue construction paper. With rulers and black felt markers, show the children how to mark off four sections on the circle. The children can use the crayons or markers to illustrate one season in each section any way they wish, or let them put stickers of the four seasons in each labeled section. Also, you can cut circle shapes from white paper and divide them, as above,

into four sections with a ruler and pen. This time the children can paint seasonal colors in each section, for example, white and gray or blue for winter; pink and green or pastels for spring; orange, yellow and brown for autumn; and yellow and gold for summer.

More to do

Field trip: Explore the seasons more by traveling to your local library to find music, books and stories that illustrate each season.

Penni L. Smith, Riverside, CA

4+

Spring Photo Shoot

Science skills

This activity encourages children to think about seasonal changes and organize their thoughts about the seasons.

Materials

Clipboard with paper and pencil
Camera, preferably Polaroid

What to do

1. Inside the classroom have a discussion on the changes we see in spring.
2. Now go on a walk to discover and observe the changes outdoors.
3. Let each child take his own photo of a spring change.
4. Be sure to note what each child is photographing.
5. Hang the developed photographs along with children's descriptions to make a mural in the classroom.

Sherri Scott, Hermitage, TN

Tasting Crystals

3+

Science skills
Children discover three different tastes.

Materials
3 soft drink caps per child
Salt
Lemonade drink mix
One small paper plate per child
Sugar

What to do

1. For each child, prepare a paper plate with a half teaspoon (2.5 ml) of salt in one cap, a half teaspoon of sugar in another cap and a half teaspoon of lemonade mix in the third cap.
2. During circle time, discuss the tongue and the sense of taste. Note that human tongues taste four basic tastes: sweet, sour, salty and bitter. If you have been growing crystals in class, also note that salt and sugar are crystals, while lemonade mix is a combination of various ingredients (check your label).
3. Explain that the children are going to try to identify which cap is salt, which is sugar and which is lemonade mix. Encourage them to use the terms salty, sweet and sour.
4. Present the paper plates to the children and demonstrate the fun tasting procedure of licking a finger and dipping it into the crystal, then licking it again to taste and identify.

More to do
More science: Make a graph on chart paper of each child's preferred taste—sweet, sour or salty.

Nancy M. Lotzer, Farmers Branch, TX

Bubble Wrap Fun

Science skills
Children use their bodies and their sense of hearing to make observations and draw conclusions, and they practice gross and fine motor skills.

Materials
Lengths of packing bubble wrap
Toy hammers
Tape
Plastic sewing needles

What to do

1. Save all the packing bubble wrap that you get in packaging and ask companies and stores to save you all of the wrap they get.
2. Tape the lengths of bubble wrap to the floor. Let the children hop and pop! Also encourage them to think of other body parts that can pop the bubbles, too, such as elbows, knees, shoulders and bottoms. Discourage the children from popping them with their heads or noses because the floor is hard!
3. Tape the bubble wrap to a table. Give the children toy hammers to pound and pop the bubbles or give them plastic sewing needles to pop them.
4. Place small pieces of bubble wrap in the sensory table. Let the children pop them only with their hands. Which way pops them the best?

Valerie Chellew, Marshfield, WI

3+

Distinguishing Sounds

Science skills

Using their sense of hearing, children make observations and draw conclusions.

Materials

5 to 6 different kinds of objects, such as pennies, paper clips, marbles, buttons, rocks, etc.
Empty black film containers
Tape recorder and tape

What to do

1. Fill matching pairs of film canisters with different objects.
2. Give each child a film container, and ask her to find the child with a matching sound by shaking the containers and listening to their different sounds. Ask the children to guess what might be in the container making that particular sound. Then mix them up and play the game again.
3. Make a tape of different familiar sounds in and around the classroom. Next, listen to it at group time and identify the sounds.

Related books

Hearing by Maria Rius
Polar Bear, Polar Bear, What Do You Hear? by Bill Martin Jr.
Sound All Around by Fay Robinson

Gina M. Duddy, Arlington MA

Seed-n-Feed

3+

Science skills

Children observe and compare types of animal feed.

Materials

Horsefeed
Dried beans
Hay or straw
Scoops
Buckets
Dried corn
Birdseed
Sifter
Shovels
Sensory table

What to do

1. Place all of the above items in the sensory table.
2. Talk about the smell and texture of each item and about who eats it. What sounds do the various feeds make as they're sifted, poured, etc.

   Note: Find a local farm or stable that can use the animal feed after the children are finished with it.

More to do

Movement: Practice animal walks: duck waddles, chicken squawk, cow stroll, horse gallop.

Related book

Animals Born Alive and Well by Ruth Heller
Baby Animals by Margaret Wise Brown
Big Red Barn by Margaret Wise Brown

 *Tina R. Woehler, Flower Mound, TX*

Name That Sound

3+

Science skills

Children learn about vibrations.

Materials

Bell
Scissors
Pennies
Spoons
Whistle
Paper
Cup of water
Bouncing ball
Hammer and wood block
Keys

What to do

1. Explain that the group is going to play a game using the sense of hearing. Explain that all sounds are caused by air movements called vibrations. When an object vibrates, the vibrations travel through the air.
2. Ask the children to close their eyes so they can concentrate on using only their sense of hearing. Ring the bell and ask the children to identify the sound.
3. Repeat the process, using different objects.

More to do

Music: Make a music shaker. Give each child a small paper plate. Encourage the children to decorate the backs of the plates with markers, wallpaper, paint, etc. Fold the plate in half and fill it with dried beans or bottle caps, and staple it shut. Be sure to form a marching band with your instruments!

Related book

My Five Senses by Aliki

Cindy Winther, Oxford, MI

3+

Listening Walk

Science skills
This is a fun activity for observing with the sense of hearing.

Materials

Tape recorder

What to do

1. Gather the children for circle time.
2. Show them the recorder and explain what it does.
3. Record your voice and each child's voice and play the tape back for the children. Explain that you are all going on a special walk and you'll take the tape recorder along. Say that if they are quiet, they will be able to record sounds.
4. Now take a walk through the building and outside, recording as you go, for example, a motor running on a vacuum, other children's voices, a pencil sharpener or pet animal noises. Outside you may hear birds, animals, traffic, etc. Encourage the children to make sounds such as crunching leaves, throwing rocks in a puddle, hitting a live tree and a dead tree with a stick. Listen to the different sounds.
5. Return to the classroom and play back the sounds. The children may be able to pick up recorded sounds they hadn't noticed on the walk, such as a plane flying over, a car horn or the distant bark of a dog.

More to do

Language: Leave the tape recorder on while the children are working or playing. Play it back at circle time and talk about how they spoke to each other. Congratulate children who spoke nicely to others. If you hear situations on the tape in which children could have spoken in a kinder manner to others, talk about it. Listen to yourself as you interact with the children. How or what could you have said or done differently?

More science: You might leave the tape recorder in the science corner with a blank tape, and let the children experiment making and recording sounds.

Helen DeWitt, Cochise, AZ

Hear! Hear!

Science skills

The children use a moment of silence to really listen.

Materials

Tape recorder
Paper
Marker

What to do

1. Ahead of time, make a tape recording of everyday noises at home. Some examples are: running water, door closing, television playing, radio playing, toilet flushing, telephone ringing, doorbell chiming, etc.
2. At circle time, talk to the children about hearing. Ask the children if they know how we hear. Tell them they are going to play a listening game. Request that they be totally silent for about a minute. Tell them ahead of time that you will signal them when that time is up. Inform them that during the minute of silence they will be listening for sounds both inside and outside the classroom. When the time is up, ask the children to tell what they heard. Make a list with two columns, one for inside and one for outside noises.
3. Play the tape recording, and ask the children to guess the noises.

More to do

Language: During free time call the children over one at a time and explain that you want them to say something into the tape recorder so you can record their voices. When you have recorded all the children, you can use this tape as another listening exercise. Play the tape and ask for the child who is talking on the tape to raise her hand. It's interesting to observe that some children will not be able to identify themselves at first. Save the tape to play later in the year.

Related books

The Five Senses edited by J. M. Parramon and J. J. Puig
Hearing by Maria Rius

Connie Heagerty, Trumbull, CT

Sound Shakers

Science skills
Children use their sense of hearing to guess what is inside containers.

Materials
Black film cannisters
Small items that will fit inside that cannisters (coins, salt, keys, beads, rocks, marbles, bells, buttons, etc.)

What to do
1. Introduce the sense of hearing by having the children close their eyes, listen carefully and describe any sounds they hear.
2. Pass a box of filled cannisters around the group, allowing each child to choose one, but to keep it closed.
3. One by one, ask each child to shake her cannister for all to hear, describe the sound, and then guess what object is making the sound.
4. Help the child open the cannister to see what the object is.
5. Let each child take a cannister home and put a tiny object in it. Instruct the children to bring the cannister back the next day to play the guessing game again.
Note: Use caution with children who still put small objects in their mouths.

More to do
Games: Play listening lotto.
Outdoors: Go for a walk in the building or outside and label many different sounds.

Related books
The Listening Walk by Paul Showers
The Five Senses Series (Hearing, Sight, Smell, Taste and Touch) by Maria Rius

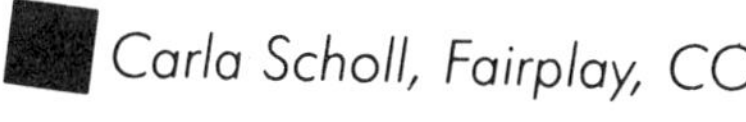
Carla Scholl, Fairplay, CO

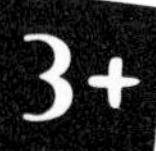

Shake Your Shaker and Listen

Science skills
In creating a shaker instrument, the children use fine motor skills and develop their sense of hearing.

Materials
Pictures of the outer ear and inner ear, optional
Crepe paper streamers in spring colors
10 small pebbles, marbles, etc. per child
Two 6½ (17 cm) heavy-weight paper plates per child
Markers
White glue
Optional: two 4" square pieces of paper per child

What to do
1. If possible, show a picture of the outer ear and the inner ear, and explain how we hear.
2. Cut streamers 8" (20 cm) long and ½" (13 mm) wide. You will need eight per shaker.
3. Place the 10 small objects on a plate, and glue the streamers around the edge of the plate.
4. Put glue on the outer rim of the plate, then put the other plate over the top so the edges meet.
5. Decorate the centers and edges of the plates with markers.
6. Use shakers as rhythm band instruments. March around the room.

More to do
Games: Lay out four or five animal beanbags. In turn, the children select which one they wish to catch by making the appropriate animal sound.
Language: Make the noise of an animal pictured on the shaker. ▪ Make various sounds behind a screen, unseen by the children, and ask the class to identify them.
More science: Teach spatial concepts using the shaker, such as high and low, under and over, between, right and left.
Music: Sing "Old MacDonald Had a Farm." ▪ Enhance auditory perception by playing the shakers loudly, softly, quickly, slowly, with an even and uneven beat.
Snack: Eat a crunchy snack, such as carrots, celery or rice cereal squares and listen for the sound.

Mary Brehm, Aurora, OH

What Do You Hear?

Science skills
On a nature walk, children hone their sense of hearing.

Materials
Tape recorder
Chart paper
Group of children
Marker

What to do
1. Gather the children and explain that you are going to take them on a fall or winter or spring walk. Explain that along the way, they are going to concentrate on their sense of hearing.
2. Generate a discussion about the different kinds of sounds they might hear on their walk.
3. Write down what the children think they might hear
4. Head out on your walk. Record the sounds of leaves crunching, birds chirping, twigs snapping, etc.

5. When you return to the classroom, play the tape for the children and see if they can identify the various sounds.
6. Look at the list of things the children thought they might hear. Compare this list to their actual experience.

Related book

My Five Senses by Aliki

Cindy Winther, Oxford, MI

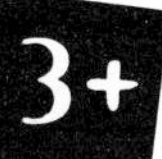
3+

Bring a Smell From Home

Science skills

Children make observations and predictions based on their sense of smell.

Materials

Empty film canister and lid with cotton ball inside
Note to parents explaining science activity
Extra film canister lids with slits cut with utility knife (only the teacher uses the knife)

What to do

1. Give each child a closed film canister to take home, along with a note to parents.
2. The parent is asked to help the child find something at home with a strong smell and put it in the film canister.
3. Explain to the child that the "smell" can be pleasant or unpleasant.
4. The following day, invite the children to share their "smells" one at a time by switching the closed lid on one film canister to the lid with the holes.
5. Pass each canister around. Ask each child to smell, but don't identify the smell until everyone has had a turn.
6. Bring extra "smells" from your house for the children who forget to bring theirs from home.

More to do

More science: Help the children use their noses all day long to smell aromas around the school.

Related book

My Five Senses by Aliki

Ann Wenger, Harrisonburg, VA

Hide and Smell

3+

Science skills

Children follow their noses to find the source of a fragrance.

Materials

Fragrant liquids, such as perfume, vanilla, cooking extracts, chocolate syrup, citrus oil, cinnamon oil, vinegar, maple syrup

Cotton balls

Jar lids

Index cards

What to do

1. Children should not be in the room as you prepare. This is a good activity to do first thing in the morning or after playground activity.
2. Choose one fragrance per day. Put that fragrance on cotton balls and put the cotton on the jar lids.
3. Hide the lids somewhere in the room no higher than children's noses. Be sure to put the lids behind other objects so they will not be easily seen.
4. Line up the children, and give each child a card. Have a sample of the scent on hand, so the children know what they are sniffing to find.
5. The object of the game is for children to use their noses to sniff around the room to find the source of the scent. When they do find one of the lids, they put their card on the place and go sit down. No other child may claim that lid. The children continue to search until they have all placed their cards.

Susan R. Forbes, Holly Hill, FL

Nose Detectives

Science skills

Children follow their noses to find a smelly substance.

Materials

Chunks of onion

Bowl

What to do

1. Hide a bowl filled with chunks of onion in the room and let the children hunt for it using their sense of smell.
2. Once they have found where you hid the onion, let the children take turns hiding it and seeking it.

Related book

Smelling by Kathy Billingslea Smith & Victoria Crenson

 *Cindy Winther, Oxford, MI*

Senses

3+ Smelling Bee

Science skills

Children use their sense of smell to guess the contents of mystery containers.

Materials

Variety of scented items, such as lemon, orange, peanut butter, chocolate, vinegar, spaghetti sauce, bubble gum, banana, etc.
Small film or yogurt containers
Cotton balls
Blindfolds

What to do

1. Place pieces of fruit in a container or put the liquid scents on cotton balls and put these into the containers and cover them.
2. Explain to the children how a "bee" works, and then blindfold a child and let her guess what the scent is, smelling-bee style. Smells can get very concentrated, so wait a moment after you take the lid off before you let the child take a sniff.
3. Older children can help each other at an independent workstation and can bring in their own scents to add variety. Of course scents should be approved by the teacher first, as some scents could be hazardous, such as alcohol, ammonia, bleach.

More to do

Language: Write the names of the scents on a paper plate or on construction paper.

 *Vicki Whitehead, Ft. Worth, TX*

3+ Smelling Jars

Science skills

Children use their sense of smell to sort containers.

Materials

Opaque film containers
One smell for each container (spices, cotton balls sprayed with perfume, shampoo, foods, coffee, lemon juice, etc.)
Hammer and nail

What to do

1. Use the nail and hammer to poke holes in the lids of the containers. (This step should be done only by adults.)
2. Fill the containers with many different smells.
3. The children can smell the smells and group them into two groups—"good" smells and "bad" smells.

More to do

Art: Draw pictures of the smells and have the children put the film containers on the matching picture.
Outdoors: Go on a walk and use your sense of smell to lead you where to go.

Related books

My Five Senses by Aliki
Sense Suspense by Bruce McMillan

Lisa Shattuck, Johnson City, NY

Goop

Science skills

Children learn about surprising chemical reactions.

Materials

Cornstarch
Water
Tub
Food coloring

What to do

1. This is fascinating for all ages. Pour a large amount of cornstarch into a dish tub. Add several cups of water along with food coloring as you stir. The mixture is easier to mix with your hands. You've added enough water when you pick up a handful of the mixture and it takes several seconds before it drips from your hands.
2. The Goop looks like it's wet, but when you pick up a handful, it feels dry. The heat from your body causes an endothermic reaction, which changes the "goop" to a liquid that drips through your fingers.

Cindy Winther, Oxford, MI

3+

Homemade Mud Puddles

Science skills

As they make messes, children use their sense of touch to observe and draw conclusions.

Materials

10 cups (2¼ kg) of used coffee grounds
(collect and store in a freezer until you have enough)
5 cups (1⅛ kg) dry oatmeal
2 small bowls
Spoons and scoops
1 large flat pan
2 cups (500 ml) salt
2 cups (500 ml) water
1 small pan for water

What to do

1. Place the coffee grounds in the large flat pan on a low table.
2. Place the salt, oatmeal and water in separate containers around the coffee grounds.
3. Explore the materials.
4. Ask how they feel. Rough? Gritty? Dry, wet, cold?
5. Add the spoons and scoops and encourage the children to mix the textures however they choose.

More to do

More science: Let the children take off their shoes and walk in their "Homemade Mud Puddles."
Outdoors: Go outside after a rain and splash in real mud puddles.

Peggy Eddy, Johnson City, TN

3+

Playing With Birdseed

Science skills

In this delightful activity, children exercise their sense of touch to their hearts' content.

Materials

Baby bathtub or other large tub
Measuring cups, spoons
Plastic pool
Variety of containers
Birdseed

What to do

1. Place the plastic tub inside the plastic pool.
2. Fill the tub with birdseed and add utènsils.

3. Allow the children to explore this new texture. Some children will just like running their hands through the seeds. Some children will enjoy pouring it into containers, measuring, comparing, etc.
4. The pool keeps this activity self-contained. The overflow falls into the pool and then you can easily clean it up. The pool also limits the number of children who can play at one time. Usually five children can fit in it comfortably. It's a good wintertime use for plastic pools. Note: When finished with the birdseed, scatter it outside for the birds to eat.

More to do

More science: Use the birdseed to make bird feeders by smearing peanut butter or rubbing suet onto pine cones and rolling the pine cones in birdseed. Hang the bird feeders with string on a tree branch.

Related books

Are You My Mother? by P. D. Eastman
The Best Nest by P. D. Eastman
Fly Away Home by Eve Bunting
Owl Babies by Martin Waddell

Audrey Kanoff, Allentown, PA

Please Touch

3+

Science skills

Children explore their sense of touch and use fine motor skills.

Materials

Large piece of paper
Miscellaneous collage materials
Textured fabric scraps
Glue

What to do

1. Cut out a large hand-shaped mural.
2. Give the children scraps of different textured materials to touch, such as fabrics, sandpaper, corrugated cardboard and cotton balls.
3. The children glue the different textures onto the hand. Discuss the sense of touch and ask what the children think the pieces feel like.
4. Display the finished collage mural on the wall with a sign that says, "Please DO Touch!"

More to do

Art: Make individual hand collages to take home.
Language: Write down the children's descriptive words as they touch textures.
Math: Set out fabric squares to sort and match by texture.

Related books

Don't Touch!, by Suzy Kline

Seven Blind Mice by Ed Young

Laura Durbrow, Lake Oswego, OR

3+ Manipulation Table

Science skills

A wonderful free exploration activity that encourages children to develop their senses.

Materials

A sand or water table (a bin or bucket will also work)
Small pieces of tissue paper
Straws

What to do

1. Put out a few of the following materials for the children to explore. This activity can be used every week with any topic of study.
   - Air—Straws and water
   - Animals—Snow and plastic bears and penguins; water and plastic fish
   - Beach—Sand, water and cups, spoons, forks, funnels
   - Birds—Birdseed and cups, spoons, etc.
   - Fall—Leaves, pine cones, acorns and magnifying glasses
   - Gardening—Tools, bulbs and dirt
   - Insects—Sand and plastic insects
   - Numbers—Only three at the center at one time
   - Sharing—Just being there
   - Storytime—Lead the children into pretending
   - Senses—Add a tape recording of waves, birds, etc.
   - Transportation—Sand and cars, boats and water, dirt and airplanes
2. The possibilities are endless. Ask the children for ideas.

Ann Gudowski, Johnstown, PA

3+ Sensory Experiences for the Sand and Water Table

Science skills

This activity focuses on the children's sense of touch.

Materials

Sensory table

Sand, water, birdseed, corks, cornstarch and water, dirt, Styrofoam pieces, whole walnuts in the shell, whole acorns in the shell, large buttons, large marbles, etc.

What to do

1. Each week or every other week fill your sensory table with one of the above materials.
2. Allow three to four children to work at a time.
3. Change the props every two weeks or so, as you wish.
4. When no one is using the table, it is time for you to add something new!

More to do

More science: Additional ideas for the sand table: add some water to make wet sand, cups and spoons, small containers, funnels, sifters, cars and trucks, plastic animals or dinosaurs, plastic eggs, etc. Or add food coloring, bubbles, ice cubes, boats, rubber fish, cups and funnels, baby dolls and sponges, dishes and sponges, plastic divers, etc.

Susan Myhre, Bremerton, WA

Sock Sense

Science skills

Children identify objects by the sense of touch in their feet.

Materials

6 socks, numbered 1 through 6

Various items, such as marbles, brush, glue bottle, ruler, an orange

Cards with the name of one object written on each

What to do

1. Discuss with the children the sense of touch. We can identify through touch the size, texture, temperature and shape of an object. There are many touch receptors scattered over our skin.
2. Put the items in the socks.
3. Children should take off one shoe and sock. They take turns pulling on socks and, using only their feet, feeling what is in each of the six socks.
4. Have the word cards on hand so the children can match what is in the socks with the correct words. For older children have extra words of objects that are not in the socks or use descriptive words.

Darlene D. Mueller, Columbia, MO

3+

Soft and Bright

Science skills

This is a quiet, tactile and fun way to focus on the sense of touch and to practice fine motor skills.

Materials

Plastic storage lids, shoe box size
3 sizes of brightly colored pompoms
Soft, brightly colored feathers
Plastic detergent scoops
Hinged tongs

What to do

1. Place one or two lids in the bottom of the sensory table. Fill each lid with lots of pompoms and the feathers.
2. Children use their hands and detergent scoops to take the pompoms off of the storage lid trays.
3. Children may also use the tongs to pick up individual pieces to develop fine motor skills.

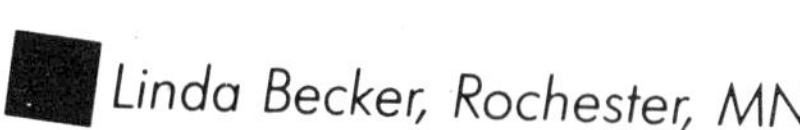
Linda Becker, Rochester, MN

3+

Five Senses Cube

Science skills

Children learn about the five senses through three-dimensional art.

Materials

Large cube-shaped box
Magazines
Scissors
Glue

What to do

1. Place the box in a learning center. Each day choose a sense that compliments your lesson plans and have the children find pictures from the magazines that relate to the sense.
2. Cut them out and glue on one side of the box in a collage. When finished, each side of the box will have pictures about one of the senses.

More to do

Games: Use your sense cube as a game at circle time. Give each child a chance to roll the cube. Encourage the child to name something (for instance) that smells, if noses land on top. Continue playing until everyone has had a turn.

Related books

The Five Senses Series (Hearing, Sight, Smell, Taste, and Touch) by Maria Rius
My Five Senses by Aliki

Janice Bodenstedt, Jackson, MI

Texture Boards

3+

Science skills

Children develop the ability to describe an experience.

Materials

Pieces of sturdy poster board or matte board
Other items with interesting textures, such as sandpaper, smooth contact paper, double-sided tape, seashells, rocks or pipe cleaners
Fabric clippings of various textures: corduroy, velour, fleece, etc.
Glue
Markers

What to do

1. Introduce the concept of touch by having the children feel and describe their clothing, the surface they are sitting on, their hair, etc.
2. Present the items and encourage the children to feel and describe them. They can try this with their eyes closed as well.
3. Give each child a piece of poster board and allow her to glue several different textures onto it.
4. Ask each child to describe her textures, such as spongy, sticky, sharp, rough, smooth, bumpy, fuzzy, etc., and write their words below the items.
5. When the texture boards are dry, you can display for peers, parents and visitors to feel and to read the children's descriptions.

More to do

Games: Play a "Tactile" Lotto Game.
More science: Make a feely box from the tall type of tissue box, and put in small objects for feeling and guessing.
Outdoors: Take a feeling walk inside or outside of the building. The children can walk with their eyes open, or they can choose a partner and wear a blindfold while they feel walls, trees or fences.

Carla Scholl, Fairplay, CO

3+

The Touching Game

Science skills

In this game, children learn to make educated guesses (estimations) and expand their vocabularies.

Materials

Objects for touching, such as sandpaper, fur, wood, a block, a sponge, a zipper, etc.

What to do

1. Ask the children to name each object.
2. Choose two children, one to put her hands behind her back and the other to select one of the objects and place it in the first child's hands. The challenge is to guess what the object is without looking and to think of a word to describe the object. You should encourage such words as fluffy, hard, scratchy, stretchy, etc.
3. Repeat the game with another pair of children.

More to do

Games: Extend the activity with an imagination game. Ask, "What do you imagine these would feel like? Clouds? Dinosaur skin? Stars? Lava? Porcupines? Angel wings?" Make a list of possible word choices, such as bumpy, soft, squishy, tickly, prickly, fluffy, etc.

Related books

Pat the Bunny by Dorothy Kunhardt
The Touch Me Book by Pat and Eve Witte

 *Iris Rothstein, New Hyde Park, NY*

3+

Treasure Box

Science skills

This fun activity allows children to make observations using several senses.

Materials

Shoe or boot box
Contact paper or wallpaper
Two 6" (15 cm) felt squares
Scissors
Glue

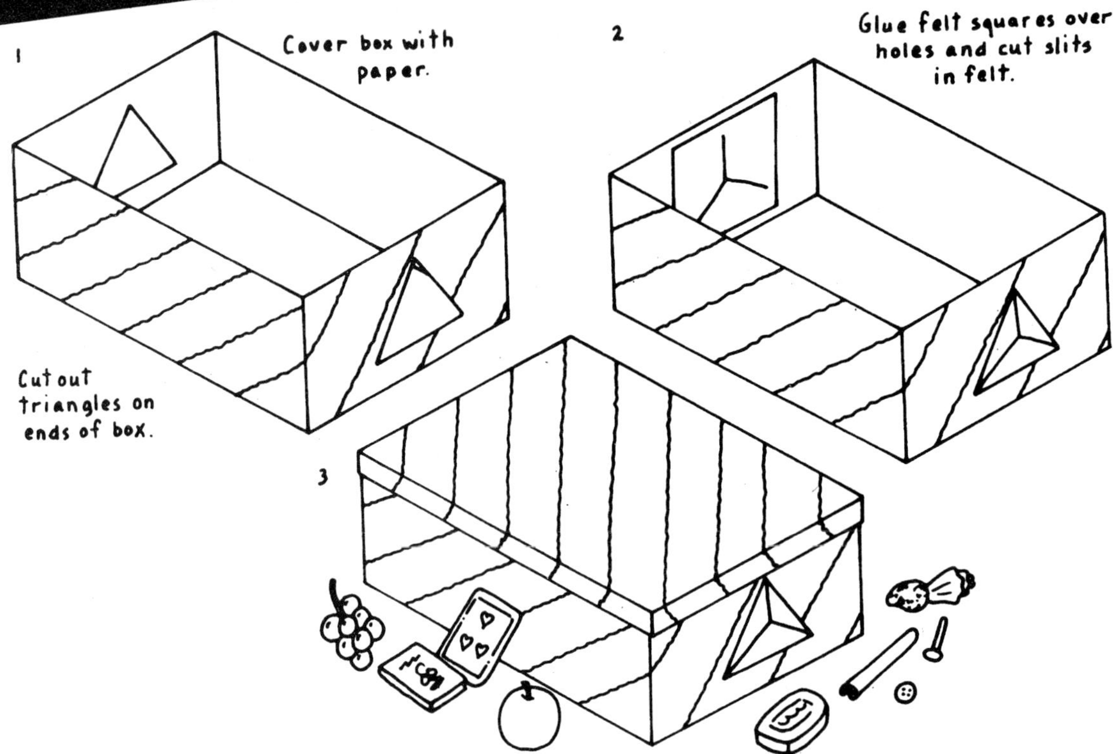

What to do

1. Cover the outside of the box with contact paper or wallpaper.
2. Cut two 4" (10 cm) triangles out on opposite sides of the box.
3. Glue the felt squares over the holes inside the box.
4. After the glue has dried, cut a slit in the felt, so that children's hands can slip through the holes.
5. Place a "mystery" object in the box.
6. Ask the children to sit on the floor and pass the box around. Using their senses of sight, smell, touch and hearing, allow the children to identify the mystery object. After they have identified the object, ask the children which sense helped them the most in the identification process.
   Here are some suggestions for objects for individual senses:
   Smell: perfume, vanilla, chocolate candy, peanut butter candy, cinnamon stick, vinegar, pickle juice, soap, mouthwash. Wrap solid items in gauze. Pour liquids on cotton balls, then place them in containers with holes.
   Hearing: Jingle bells, rocks, buttons, musical toys. Place items in plastic containers.
   Touch: fur, sandpaper, cotton, shell, small book, plastic cookie cutters.
   Sight: chicken or animal bones, plastic fruits or vegetables, playing cards.

Susan R. Forbes, Holly Hill, FL

3+

Texture Cards

Science skills

A simple, fun way for children to use their visual and tactile senses to notice details, similarities and differences in various materials.

Materials

Fabric scraps with different textures (corduroy, silk, tweed, burlap, cotton, netting)
Aluminum foil (crumpled, then opened up)
Glue
Sandpaper with various grits
Bubble wrap
Index cards

What to do

1. Cut scraps of fabric and other textured items listed.
2. Glue one swatch to each card.
3. Place in a basket in the science center for the children to explore and sort.

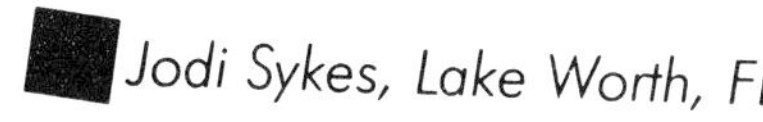
Jodi Sykes, Lake Worth, FL

3+

Pine Needle Sachet

Science skills

Children practice fine motor skills and use their senses to explore the properties of pine needles.

Materials

Assorted small evergreen boughs
Scissors
4" x 4" (10 cm x 10 cm) fabric squares, one per child
Gathering basket
Clear glass bowls
4" (10 cm) pieces of jute, one per child

What to do

1. Allow children to gather evergreen boughs or ask families to collect them.
2. Place the boughs in the gathering basket.
3. Give each child a clear bowl and pair of scissors.
4. Each child chooses a bough.
5. Show the children how to snip the needles into small pieces until their bowl is filled.

(Alternatively, the teacher could do the snipping.)

5. Place evergreen cuttings onto the fabric square.
6. Help the children gather the edges of the squares and tie with jute.
7. Gently squeeze the sachet to release the aroma.

More to do

More science: Identify various types of evergreen trees and chart their location.

Sand and water table: Add evergreen boughs or branches to sand table.

Related books

Have You Seen Trees? by Joanne Oppenheim

The Tree That Came to Stay by Anna Quinlen

Cathy Costantino, Carol Patnaude, Lynn R. Camara, Warwick, RI, and Darlene Maloney, East Greenwich, RI

Banana Kabobs

4+

Science skills

As they eat a treat, children use their sense of taste to classify flavors.

Materials

Bananas
Colored sugar
3 plates or pie pans
Chart paper and marker
Lemonade drink mix
Finely chopped salted peanuts
Skewers for kabobs, optional

What to do

1. Beforehand, peel the bananas and cut them into chunks. You will need three chunks per child. Put the drink mix, sugar and peanuts on separate plates. Have the skewers ready.
2. Let the children roll one piece of banana into each of the three "tastes." Slide the bananas onto a skewer if you are using them.
3. After everyone has rolled their bananas, they may eat the pieces. While the children are eating, ask questions to get them thinking about different tastes—salty, sweet and sour.
4. Write the three tastes on the board or chart paper. Ask the children to contribute the names of other foods that would fit into each taste category.

More to do

More science: Discuss taste buds. Let the children use mirrors to look at their taste buds. ▪ Have a model of the tongue available. As you discuss each taste, show the children where the taste buds for that taste are located.

Deborah A. Chaplin, Hot Springs, VA

4+

Do You Hear What I Hear?

Science skills
Record what children discover with their sense of hearing.

Materials
Chalkboard and chalk or chart paper and marker

What to do
1. On the chalkboard or a large piece of chart paper, write two headings, *Inside* and *Outside*.
2. Ask the children to take a seat and sit quietly. Tell them that you want them to listen carefully for a few minutes.
3. After a few minutes, ask for volunteers to tell you what kinds of sounds they heard. Write the words on the board or chart paper under the heading *Inside*.
   Note: Older children may write down the words for themselves.
4. Later in the day or another day, go for a walk outside around your building. Ask the children to listen for the many outside sounds. List the sounds they heard under the heading *Outside* when you return to the classroom.

Related book
My Five Senses by Aliki

Jennifer B. Strauzer, Jericho, NY

Our Eyes Are the Windows to Our World

Science skills
In this activity, children learn ways to appreciate their sense of sight.

Materials
Old pairs of sunglasses
Telescope
Kaleidoscope
Scissors
Glue
Paper plates
Binoculars
Mirrors
Old magazines
Balloons
Yarn
Paint

What to do

This activity stresses the importance of eyesight and reassures children who wear glasses or contact lenses.

1. Discuss features such as the color of one's eyes, explaining that the colored part of the eye is called the iris. The black circle of the eye is called the pupil, and is just a hole to let light through, so we can see. Set up a special area in the classroom to display sunglasses, binoculars, telescopes, mirrors and kaleidoscopes.
2. Try a simple game of Blindman's Bluff. Ask the children how they feel when they close their eyes. Point out that we should never take our eyesight for granted.
3. Allow children to browse through old magazines and find pictures of eyes in all colors. Blow up balloons for each child and tie a string on the knotted balloon end. Let the children carefully glue one pair of eyes they've cut from magazines onto their inflated balloon. They may add other facial features also, if they wish. Glue some yarn on the top of the balloon for hair. Encourage the children to give their balloon people the same eye colors and hair colors as they have or that a friend has. If they can't find the right eyes in magazines, cut them from construction paper or glue on wiggle eyes. Or children could look in magazines for the eyes of pets like dogs and cats and make their balloons into pet personalities. Make it a fun project.

More to do

Art: Make beautiful color wheels by asking the children to paint primary colors on paper plates.
More science: Discuss rainbows and ask the children to look for rainbow colors all around the classroom.

Penni L. Smith, Riverside, CA

Taste Testers

Science skills

In this interesting taste test, children use their senses of touch and taste and sight.

Materials

Saltine crackers
Baking cocoa
Sugar and salt
Chopped carrot and raw sweet potato
Chart paper
Lemon wedges
Clear corn syrup
Peeled apple and peeled raw potato slices
Seltzer and clear lemon soda
Marker

What to do

1. At circle time, talk about how your body tastes things. Explain that the tongue has special places to taste special tastes. Wait until everyone gets a sample of the item, then everyone tastes together.
2. Hand out the saltines, and let the children lick the tops. What do they taste?
3. Now hand out the small lemon pieces and let the children suck on them. These are sour.

4. Allow the children to smell the cocoa and then let each child take a small pinch to taste. It is bitter.
5. Put a drop of syrup on each child's finger. Lick it off. Sweet!

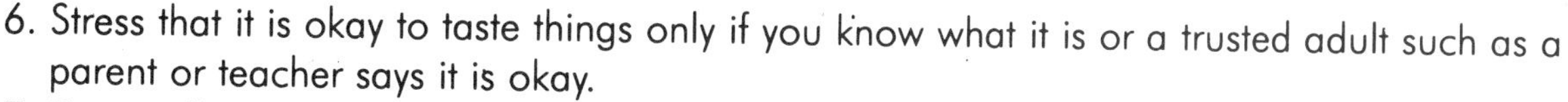

6. Stress that it is okay to taste things only if you know what it is or a trusted adult such as a parent or teacher says it is okay.
7. For small group time, introduce the dishes of similar-looking foods. Your eyes can't tell which is which. Sometimes your nose can't either. Only taste will tell for sure.
8. For each pair of foods, let the children make predictions as to which is sugar, apple, carrot, soda. Write down their predictions. Taste to check out the hypotheses.

More to do

Art: Make Mr. Yuk puppets with brown paper bags. Glue green circles onto the bottom flap. Draw features with black. Put green tongue under the flap. Use the puppets to discuss poisons.
Snack: Make gorp by mixing salty peanuts, sweet raisins and semisweet chocolate chips in a paper cup to eat for snack.

Sandra Gratias, Perkasie, PA

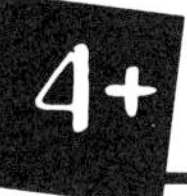

4+

Guess the Sound

Science skills
Children use their sense of hearing to draw conclusions.

Materials

Various familiar objects: scissors, pencil, block, sponge, book, etc.

What to do

1. Ask the children to name each object to be used in the activity. Use as few or as many as you think appropriate for the age and abilities of the children.
2. Drop each object on the floor and urge the children to listen carefully to the sound each one makes.
3. The child who is "It" sits on a chair with her back to the collection of objects.
4. A second child chooses one item and drops it on the floor behind the child who is "It."
5. The child who is "It" must try to guess which object the other child dropped just by using her sense of hearing. She may then look behind her to see if the guess was correct.

More to do

Games: Extend the activity by making a sound-sorting game. Children collect pictures of things such as a fire engine, kitten, lion, snowflakes, vacuum cleaner, etc. The challenge is to sort objects into bags labeled "LOUD" and "SOFT." Justify your choice by imitating the sound.

Original poem

Chant or sing:

Clap, clap, clap your hands,
Loud as can be.

Clap, clap, clap your hands,
Do it now with me.

Repeat, substituting the word "Softly" with an appropriate action. Let the children select other actions that can be done both loudly and softly.

Related books
My Five Senses by Aliki
Polar Bear, Polar Bear, What Do You Hear? by Bill Martin, Jr.

Iris Rothstein, New Hyde Park, NY

What's That Noise?

Science skills
Children use their sense of hearing for observation and learn guessing (estimating) skills.

Materials
Night in the Country by Cynthia Rylant
Tape of environmental sounds, optional
Tape player

What to do
1. Play a tape for the children of night noises in the country or other outdoor sounds.
2. Read the book.
3. After the story, ask the children to recall the sounds in the book, and what made the sounds. Determine whether the sounds are natural or human-made.
4. Take the class on a walking field trip to listen for sounds. Stop in several strategic locations and just listen. Record the sounds you hear at each location.
5. Return to the classroom and, using the tape as an aid, compile a complete list of the sounds you heard on the trip.
6. Emphasize the sound as well as the source, for example, chirps produced by birds, croaks produced by frogs, etc.
7. Classify the sounds as natural or human-made.
8. Brainstorm ideas of other sounds and their sources.

More to do
More science: Take an indoor field trip to listen for unique sounds within the school.

Lyndall Warren, Milledgeville, GA

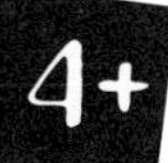

Sounds You Can See

Science skills

Children make predictions and observe the cause and effect of vibrations.

Materials

A hand drum with one open side
10" (22.5 cm) cookie tin with plastic wrap secured over the top
Shallow plate with water to cover the bottom
A few grains of uncooked rice
Wind up clock or a timer with a long ring
A plastic ruler

What to do

1. Ask the children if they can see sound. You may find there are some misconceptions about seeing the sound and seeing what produces the sound.
2. Put a spoonful of rice on top of the plastic wrap. Hold the drum above and near the cookie tin.
3. Ask the children what they think will happen to the rice when you hit the drum. Some may say that it will move. If so, query why.
4. Hit the drum and watch the rice dance.
5. Tell the children that when you hit the drum it made vibrations that they could see and hear.
6. Place the timer in a shallow plate of water. Wind and allow to ring. Point out to the children how they can see the water vibrate and hear the timer ring.
7. Place the ruler half way off the table. Place one hand over the end on the table. Give the other end a slap. Point out to the children that they can see the ruler vibrate and hear the sound it makes.

More to do

More science: Record various sounds that are familiar to the children. Have pictures of the sounds for the children to choose from. As you play the sound let the children touch the picture.

Related book

Mortimer by Robert Munsch

Michele Wistisen, Casper, WY

If You Couldn't See

4+

Science skills

Children experience what it might be like to be blind by using their sense of touch.

Materials

Small pitcher half-filled with water
Tray
Towels for clean-up
Plastic cup
Blindfold

What to do

1. Ask the children how they would learn to pour their juice if they couldn't use their eyes to see. Have a discussion about children who are not able to see.
2. Ask the question, "How would you know when your cup was filled with juice if you couldn't use your eyes?"
3. Demonstrate placing your finger on the inside top of the cup while you pour water, to help you tell if the cup is full.
4. Place a tray with the pitcher of water and the cup on the table.
5. Blindfold a child and let her try to pour water without spilling.
6. Allow the children to continue the experiment on their own.

More to do

More science: Contact a 4-H Club in your area to find out if it participates in the guide dog training program. If so, invite a guide dog trainer and guide dog to visit your school.
Movement: Invite the children to sit in a circle around you. Ask them to close their eyes and try to catch a pompom with a bell attached that you will throw to them. They must use their ears to hear when it is close to them. Ask them if it was easy or hard to catch the pompom without using their eyes.

Linda Andrews, Sonora, CA

Marshmallow Sense

4+

Science skills

Children use all five senses to make observations.

Materials

2 large fresh marshmallows for each child (mini-marshmallows could pose a choking hazard)
Chart paper and marker

What to do

1. Distribute one marshmallow to each child or one to each group of two children. Ask the children not to identify the object (the marshmallow) in front of them by name.
2. Ask the children to look at the object, but not touch it and brainstorm descriptive words. Accept all answers, for example, snowball, pillow, etc. Write responses on chart paper.
3. Ask the children to touch the object. How does it feel? Record all answers.
4. Let's smell it. What does this object smell like? Record the responses.
5. Can you hear it? Can it make any sound? Allow the children to drop their marshmallows onto a clean table if they wish. Continue to write down children's responses.
6. Give each child another marshmallow. Ask them to identify it by name. Those who wish may taste the marshmallow. Tell us how it tastes.
7. Discuss the children's responses and relate them to our five senses.

More to do

Art: Children may enjoy using their imaginations to dream up things they could do with marshmallows, then draw pictures of their ideas.

Language: Depending on the children's ages, you may want to encourage them to dictate or write a paragraph describing their marshmallow experience, highlighting their sensory discoveries.

Margery A. Kranyik, Hyde Park, MA

4+

Sounds Are Moving

Science skills

Children use their hearing to notice details, identify differences and recognize similarities.

Materials

Rope
Tape recorder
Emergency vehicle with siren
Cassette tape

What to do

1. Arrange for an emergency vehicle to come to your center at a specific time with the siren on. If you invite the same emergency vehicle and person to come prior to this activity to discuss community helpers, the excitement of the visit will not be such a distraction from the discussion of sound.
2. Listen for the emergency siren. As it comes closer, the sound will change. Record this sound on the tape recorder. Listen to the siren standing still nearby. You can listen to it and record it as it goes away again.
3. How was the sound different coming and going? How did movement affect it? Refer to the cassette to check the children's answers.
4. Talk to the children about sound. Explain that we hear high pitches and low pitches and that sound is vibrations or waves moving invisibly though the air from the object that made the sound to our ear.

Senses

5. Make sounds with your voice both high and low, then feel your throat and how it vibrates. Let the children try it.
6. Use a rope to demonstrate waves. Let a child hold one end of the rope while you or another child holds the other end. Ask the children to raise and lower their hands alternating and increasing in speed.
7. Observe how the rope makes waves. The faster the children go, the more waves, the slower they go, the fewer waves.
8. Explain that the fast waves are like the high pitches and the slow waves are like the lower pitches. This is the way sound waves travel in the air to your ear. You can also explain that when a noisy object moves, the sound (or pitch) changes.

More to do

More science: Talk about sound whenever you hear sounds during the day. Are they high pitches or low pitches? Are they moving or still?

Related books

The Magic of Sound by Larry Kettelkamp
The Science Book of Sound by Neil Ardley

Joyce Dowling, Clinton, MD

A Week of Exploration of the Five Senses

Science skills

Here is an opportunity for children to use all their senses for observation.

Materials

Old magazines
Construction paper
A tasty recipe
A box with a lid
Blindfold
Substances with different smells
Crayons
Scissors
Glue
Ingredients for the chosen recipe
Objects of different textures
Small paper cups
White paper
Records of lively music

What to do

1. Designate days of the week to work on each of the five senses, for example, Monday could be Sense of Smell Day, etc. Have the necessary items ready for that day.
2. For the Sense of Sight Day, instruct children to browse through magazines and cut out pictures that are pleasing to the eye and very colorful. Cut out pictures of eyes, trying to find all the hues of eye color. Glue the pictures in booklets of paper to keep, labeling the book, "My Sense of Sight Scrapbook."
3. For the Sense of Taste Day, select a recipe that will be flavorful and will allow the children to experience a variety of flavors (such as oatmeal cookies with cinnamon, nutmeg, allspice, etc.)

You can enhance the cookies' flavor by adding chocolate chips, raisins, nuts and spreading peanut butter or butter on them.

4. For the Sense of Touch Day, prepare a box with a lid, cutting a hole in the lid big enough for a hand to reach in to. Put variously textured objects inside the box, such as sandpaper, a carpet sample, marbles, rocks, a silk square sample, etc. Allow the children to reach a hand inside to feel the items. Ask them if they can name what they're touching, and if it is soft, or rough, or hard or smooth.
5. For the Sense of Smell Day, set up a smelling test. Place a variety of fragrant or interesting-smelling items in small paper cups. See if blindfolded children can name the items they smell and ask them to tell whether the smells are pleasant or unpleasant.
6. For the Sense of Hearing Day, give each child a large sheet of paper and bright crayons. Play the liveliest music you can find. Ask children to draw to the beat or rhythm of the song. Then try different types of music, such as something slow and thoughtful, like a classical piece. Share with the entire class the masterpiece artwork at the end of this session.

Penni L. Smith, Riverside, CA

4+

Pinch Strips

Science skills

Children use their sense of taste to describe foods.

Material

Heavy poster board
Markers
Scissors
Clear contact paper

What to do

1. Cut the poster board into 8" x 3" (20 cm x 8 cm) strips.
2. On each strip, draw four different circle faces expressing dislike, enjoyment, boredom, shock, or any other reaction one might have to a taste. Draw the same faces on the back of the strip in the same places, so the front and back are identical.
3. Cover the strips with clear contact paper for durability.
4. During a Taste unit, name some different foods. Each child willl "pinch" their strip next to the face that best shows how they like the taste. Pinching is done with the thumb and pointer finger.

More to do

More science: Pinch activities can be made for many different concepts such as faces showing sad, happy, scared and angry expressions. Use them by describing certain situations, then ask the children to "pinch" the face that shows how they would feel in that situation. For shapes name objects and ask the children to "pinch" the shape. For numbers ask the children to count how many times you clap, bounce a ball or turn around, and then "pinch" the correct number on the strip.

Valerie Chellew, Marshfield WI

The Nose Knows

4+

Science skills

Using only their sense of smell, children try to identify foods.

Material

Box

Variety of different smells (orange, peppermint candycane, chocolate, a flower, perfume, pepper, bubblegum, peanut butter, etc.)

Blindfold

What to do

1. This activity works best with a small group of children.
2. Discuss the sense of smell with the children. One of the suggested books could be read.
3. Show the children the items in the box. Let the children smell and identify each item.
4. Pick one child to stand up and be blindfolded. Choose one item and ask the child to identify it.
5. Can the child identify the scent? If not, give the child a hint or a choice between two different scents. (Does this smell like an orange or peanut butter, for example.)
6. Take the blindfold off the child and let him choose the next participant.
7. When the last child is finished, he gets to choose a scent in the box for the teacher to guess. The teacher can just close her eyes instead of being blindfolded.

More to do

Games: A similar game could be played for the sense of touch using a bag full of familiar items (a toothbrush, a ball, a pencil, etc.).

Related books

Don't Touch! by Suzy Kline

The Ear Book by Al Perkins

The Five Senses Series (Hearing, Sight, Smell, Taste, and Touch) by Maria Rius

The Magic of Sound by Larry Kettelkamp

My Five Senses by Aliki

Sense Suspense by Bruce McMillan

Seven Blind Mice by Ed Young

Christina Chilcote, New Freedom, PA

My Five Senses

Science skills
Children use all their senses to make observations and learn new vocabulary words.

Materials

Blackboard and chalk or chart paper and markers
Hearing: drum, alarm clock, bell
Smelling: flower, perfume, old shoe
Feeling: stuffed animal, balloon, textured material such as sandpaper
Container filled with a variety of objects
Tasting: apple, other foods or drinks
Seeing: pictures of a star, moon and sun

What to do

1. Ask the children to close their eyes and pretend that they are outdoors in a park. Encourage them to describe what they see, such as squirrels in trees and clouds in the sky. Similarly, discuss what they smell, feel, taste and hear.
2. After they open their eyes write "Five Senses" on the board or easel. Ask the children to describe what the words mean. Help explain that these are the abilities to see, hear, taste, smell and feel. List these "sense" words on the board, pointing to your eyes, ears, mouth, nose and hands as you write and discuss the words.
3. From a box or large bag invite one child at a time to remove an object; as a group discuss the "sense" used with that particular item.

Barbara J. Lindsay, Mason City, IA

Circle Book

3+

Science skills

This activity teaches children to recognize circles in their environment.

Materials

Round and Round and Round by Tana Hoban
Construction paper (black, gray, orange, yellow, white, red, various skin-tone colors, other assorted colors)
Glitter
Self-stick stars
Stapler
Scissors
Blue and orange paint
Sponge
Cotton swabs
Crayons
Strips of paper

What to do

1. In advance, draw nine circles (two brown and one each of black, gray, orange, yellow, white, red and skin-tone) for each child on construction paper. Gray circles should be a little smaller than the others. You may want to cut out circles for the younger children, but let the older children cut their own.
2. Set out the art supplies and circles on a table.
3. During circle time, read *Round and Round and Round.*
4. Ask the children to name some things that are round and tell them that today they will be making their own books of round objects.
5. Have the children choose a color for their covers, then cut out a cover circle for each book. Children love to have their books personalized, so write the child's name in the title (e.g., Andy's Circle Book).
6. Make the following suggestions for each page:
   "A circle is round like a pancake." A cotton swab dipped in blue paint can be used to make blueberries for the pancake. Point out that blueberries are round, too.
   "A circle is round like a tire." Using the black circle for the tire, paste the smaller gray circle in the center for the hubcap.
   "A circle is round like an orange." Children can sponge paint the orange circle with orange paint and then add a green stem to the orange.
   "A circle is round like a doughnut." Cut the center out of the brown circle and sprinkle with glitter.
   "A circle is round like the sun." Use the yellow circles for the sun.
   "A circle is round like a balloon." Children can color the white circles with crayons.
   "A circle is round like a ball." Children can decorate the red circle with paint, glitter, self-stick stars and strips of paper. Encourage them to be creative.
   "A circle is round like your face." Have the children draw eyes, a nose and a mouth on the skin-tone circle.
7. When the children have finished all the pages, add the cover and staple the book together.

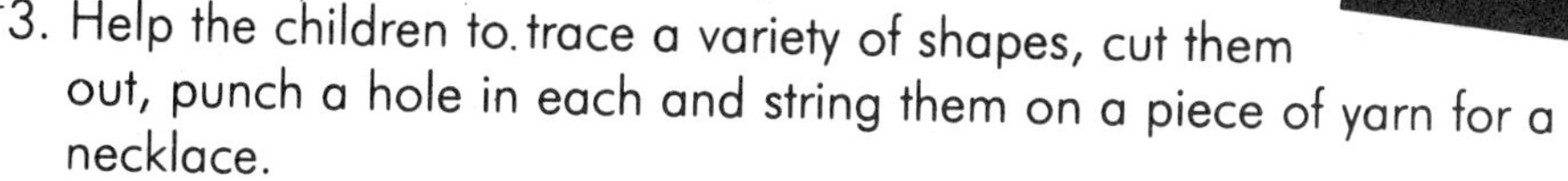

2. Demonstrate how to place the stencil over a piece of poster board and trace the shape.
3. Help the children to trace a variety of shapes, cut them out, punch a hole in each and string them on a piece of yarn for a necklace.
4. Talk about the different shapes and encourage children to name familiar objects they resemble.
5. When the children have completed their necklaces, help them label each shape. They may want to take the necklaces home to show their families.

More to do

Art: Use shape punches to make the holes in the shapes.

Games: Put several different shape pieces into a bag and have the children try to name the shape by feeling rather than seeing it. ▪ Hide shape blocks around the classroom and have the children go on a shape hunt. ▪ Take a walk through the building and ask children to identify the shapes of doors, windows, wall decorations, etc.

 *Carla Scholl, Fairplay, CO*

3+

Shape Pizzas

Science skills

Children cut out geometric shapes as toppings for a pretend pizza.

Materials

Unused personal-size pizza boxes and cardboard circles (available from pizza restaurants)
Construction paper (black, pink, white, red, green and yellow)
Paintbrushes
Red paint
Glue
Scissors
Air-dry clay

What to do

1. In advance, cut the cardboard circles to size (they must fit into the pizza boxes). Also mix the red paint and glue to make pizza "sauce" and cut out shape toppings from construction paper (or have the older children cut out the shapes themselves).
2. You can cut the construction paper shape toppings out in advance or assist as children cut out their own. Talk about which shapes resemble various pizza toppings.
3. Have the children roll lengths of clay and press it around the rim of the cardboard to form a crust.
4. Tell the children to paint inside the rim with the paint/glue mixture.
5. Have them add their choice of "toppings" (the following shapes cut from construction paper):

    yellow triangles—pineapple
    pink squares—ham
    black ovals—black olives
    red circles—pepperoni
    green ovals—green olives
    small white rectangles—onion

Toppings should stick when placed on top of paint/glue mixture. As the children put on the toppings, talk about their different shapes

6. They can store their pizzas in the pizza boxes when they have dried.

 *Valerie Chellew, Marshfield, WI*

Shapes All Around Us

Science skills

This simple game encourages children to use observation and matching skills to locate shapes in their environment.

Materials

Construction paper
Clear contact paper or laminate, optional
Scissors
Container

What to do

1. Cut basic shapes out of construction paper; laminate if possible.
2. Place shapes in a container.
3. Taking turns, have the children pull out a shape and look around the room for something that is the same shape. For example, they might say a block is a rectangle or the burners on the play stove are circles.

More to do

Game: Encourage the children to continue the game during free play or snack time. If they spot a particular shape, have them show a teacher. Keep a sticker chart with children's names showing how many of each shape they've found.

 *Suzanne Pearson, Winchester, VA*

The Shape of Our Environment

Science skills

Children use observation skills to hunt for shapes in the classroom.

Materials

Tagboard or poster board
Scissors
Chart paper and marker

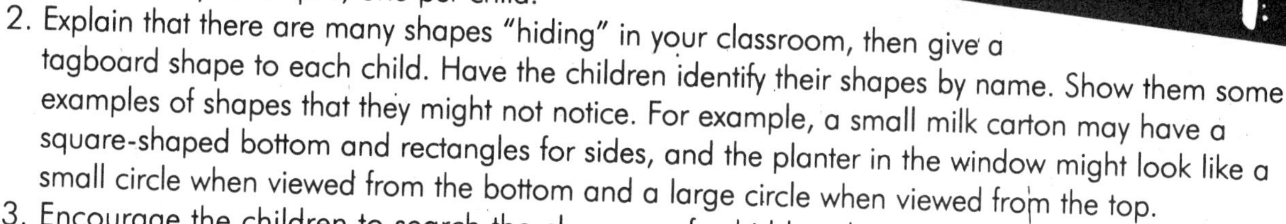

Shapes

What to do

1. Cut out simple 4" (10 cm) shapes from the tagboard. Use a variety of shapes, one per child.
2. Explain that there are many shapes "hiding" in your classroom, then give a tagboard shape to each child. Have the children identify their shapes by name. Show them some examples of shapes that they might not notice. For example, a small milk carton may have a square-shaped bottom and rectangles for sides, and the planter in the window might look like a small circle when viewed from the bottom and a large circle when viewed from the top.
3. Encourage the children to search the classroom for hidden shapes that match the tagboard shape they have been given.
4. Next, point out that there are many different shapes in the larger environment, too. Distribute additional shapes, if desired, identifying and discussing their physical properties.
5. Go outdoors for a scavenger hunt, finding as many varied and unusual items as possible to match the tagboard shapes your children are carrying. Findings may be called out, sketched, photographed or (if feasible) brought back as samples/specimens.
6. Ask, "Which shape did we find most often on our scavenger hunt?" Then make a chart of your class's findings.

Marji E. Gold-Vukson, West Lafayette, IN

4+

Mr. Square

Science skills

In this fun project, children practice fine motor and language skills.

Materials

Empty individual-size cereal boxes
Red felt
Yarn
Colored construction paper
Buttons or plastic eyes

What to do

1. Ahead of time, cut each box about three-quarters of the way in half width-wise. Fold each cut box so that its top and bottom meet, forming a square shape.
2. The children can match pieces of construction paper to the surfaces of the boxes and glue on.
3. Then, they can decorate their boxes with felt, yarn and buttons to make a face. Put red felt in the opening for a tongue.
4. Children place their hands in the box to work it as a puppet.
5. Find a square box to make a puppet. Say the Mr. Square rhyme (see below) as the children move the mouth for Mr. Square to talk.

More to do

Language: Use the puppets to put on a puppet show with the children's original scripts.

Original poem

I'd like to introduce myself.
My name is Mr. Square.

Shapes

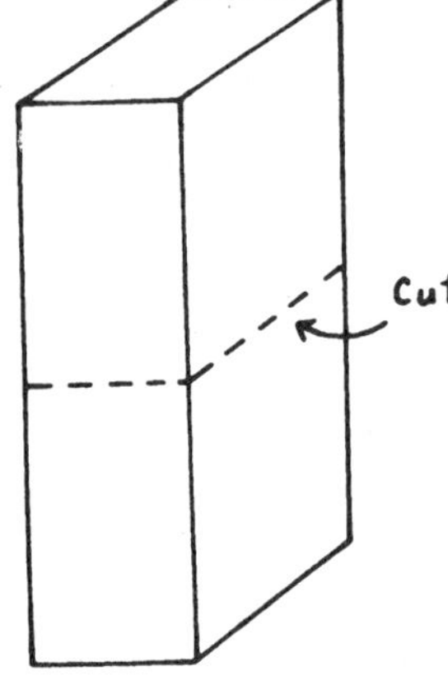

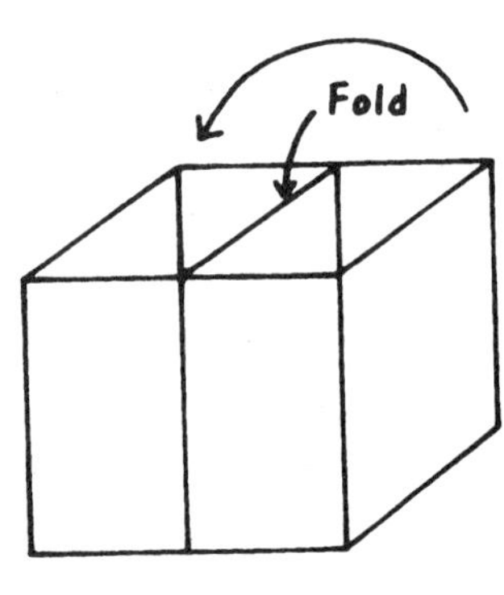

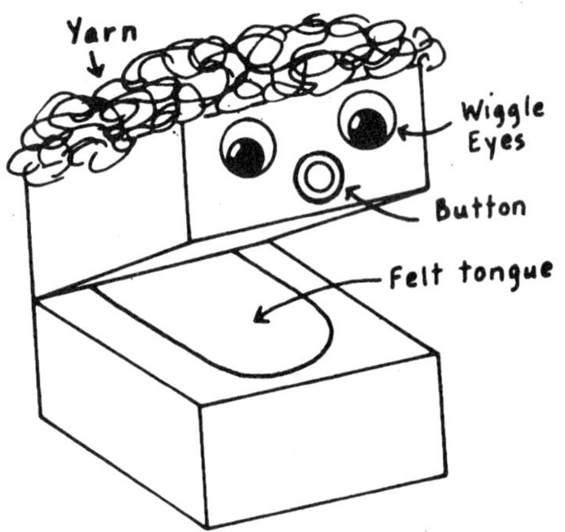

I look just like a box
And you can find me anywhere.

There's a funny thing about me.
If you measure every side,
You'll find that I am just as tall
As I am wide!

Beatrice Chawla, Vincentown, NJ

Create-A-Shape

Science skills

Children experiment with combining shapes to create new shapes.

Materials

Wooden unit blocks

What to do

1. Give children wooden unit blocks shaped like triangles, rectangles, squares, etc.
2. Talk about using shapes to create other shapes. For example, show the children how to use two triangles to form a square, two squares to form a rectangle, etc.
3. Have the children experiment with different combinations to form new shapes. Ask them what shapes they can make with two rectangles, four triangles, etc.
4. Encourage the children to create more complex designs such as an arrow, a house or an ice cream cone.

Suzanne Pearson, Winchester, VA

3+

Sign Language Reasoning

Science skills
Children practice nonverbal communication and learn about sign language.

Materials
Sign language book with clear illustrations or videotape of sign language demonstration
Note: If possible, consult with someone who is fluent in sign language.

What to do

1. In advance, select and practice simple signs that are easily related to the object or action they represent. Suggestions include signs for eat, stand, girl, boy, love, butterfly, soup, bowl, cup, drink, dance, fall, sit, swing, hat, coat, smile, tears, cry, hug, smell, hear, look, house, telephone, baseball, ball, time, toothbrush, horse, dog, cat and caterpillar.
2. Introduce the children to the concept of sign language. Explain that sign language is used by people who cannot hear and that it is entirely a visual language. Point out that hearing people learn sign language to communicate with non-hearing people, but they can also use sign language as a kind of secret code with friends who understand it or to communicate across a crowded room or while eating.

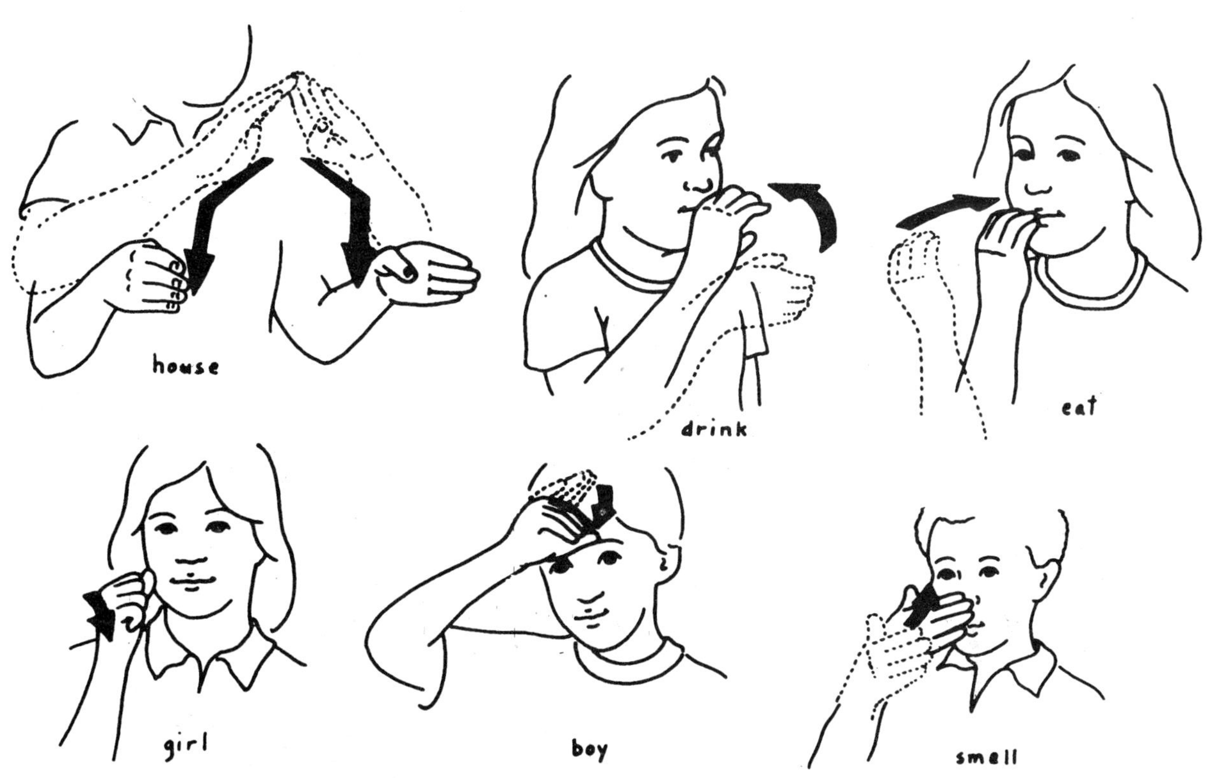

Sign Language

dog

cat

cry

stand

3. Demonstrate a few simple signs and ask children if they can guess why these signs were created to represent the spoken word. For example, ask them if they can see the movement of a butterfly in the fluttering of your hands as you sign it.
4. Now play a game to see if the children can guess the meaning of other signed words. This could be played like charades, but instead of pointing at the first child to correctly identify the sign, simply acknowledge that you heard the correct word and repeat it.

More to do

More science: Continue teaching signs as you do things throughout the day. Say, "You sign that this way. Can you guess why?" ▪ Teach children to sign their names using signs for letters of the alphabet.

Related books

American Sign Language Dictionary by Elaine Costello
Introduction to Sign Language and Signs You Already Know by Lawrence and Sharon Salows
Nursery Rhymes from Mother Goose: Told in Signed English by Harry Bornstein and Karen L. Salnier
Sesame Street Sign Language ABC with Linda Bove by Linda Bove
Simple Signs by Cindy Wheeler
Where's Spot? by Eric Hill

Joyce Dowling, Clinton, MD

3+

Signing the Colors

Science skills

Children practice sign language and prediction skills.

Materials

Baby oil
Small piece of wax colorant (red, blue, yellow)
Food coloring
4 to 5 plastic soda bottles
Water
Masking or electrical tape

What to do

1. Prepare the soda bottles in advance as follows. Fill half of a soda bottle with baby oil and add the red colorant. Let stand for about a week, then add water colored with yellow food coloring. The yellow will end up on the bottom and the red on the top. (Later, when the bottle is shaken, the two colors will mix to make the color orange; after a few moments, the colors will separate again). Do the same for the other bottles using any of these color mixtures: red and blue for purple; yellow and blue for green; blue and green for turquoise; red water and clear oil for pink.
   Note: Make sure the caps are on tight and taped to the bottle so that the children won't be tempted to open them up.

2. Before introducing the bottles, work on the signs for colors with the children.
3. When the children have learned the signs, show them the bottles. Ask them to sign the color in the top half of a bottle, then sign the color in the bottom half. Ask them to guess and show you the sign for the color they think they will see when you shake the bottles. Shake the bottles and see if they guessed right.

More to do

More science: Put the colored bottles out on the science table for the children to shake. Smaller children can lay the bottles on their sides to mix the colors if shaking them is too difficult.

Related books

Is It Red? Is It Yellow? Is It Blue? by Tana Hoban
Little Blue and Little Yellow by Leo Lionni
Mouse Paint by Ellen Stoll Walsh
Simple Signs by Cindy Wheeler

Debbie Barbuch, Sheboygan, WI

3+

Earth Paper Weights

Science skills
Children learn about the shape and colors of the Earth.

Materials

Self-hardening modeling dough, commercial or homemade
Food colors, blue and green

What to do

1. Using a globe, show children the location of their city. Talk about the shape of the Earth. Point out the difference between land and water.
2. Purchase or prepare a batch of self-hardening modeling dough.
3. Divide the dough into three equal portions. Leave one portion the natural color, add green food coloring to the second and blue food coloring to the third. Knead the dough until the colors are evenly distributed.
4. Give each child some dough of each color. As they play with it, talk about the Earth. Explain that some of the Earth is dry, like the desert; some of the Earth is moist and green with plant growth, like the forest; and some of the Earth is completely covered by water, like the ocean.
5. Have each child combine all the dough colors and form into a ball.
6. Let the dough air harden (or bake on low for several hours fo harden faster).

Self-Hardening Modeling Dough Recipe
1½ cups (375 ml) salt
4 cups (1L) flour
1½ cups (375 ml) water
1½ cups (375 ml) water
Mix together all ingredients and knead.

Susan Rinas, Parma, OH

Let's Go Spelunking

4+

Science skills

This activity stimulates an interest in caves and nature.

Materials

Black construction paper
Masking tape
Papier-mâché recipe
Paintbrushes
Flashlights
String
Newspaper
Brown paint
Plastic collection bags
Any items that might be found in a cave

What to do

1. Send a note home explaining that the class is going pretend spelunking the next day and ask that each child bring a small flashlight and a pair of boots (labeled with names).
2. Make several bats from black construction paper using the pattern provided. Hang them from the ceiling in the area that you designate as the "cave." Secure with tape.
3. Make stalactites and stalagmites from papier-mâché. Form cone shapes out of newspaper. Secure with masking tape. Dip narrow strips of newspaper into a thin mixture of flour and water and wrap around the cones. Let dry. Paint a pale brown. Hang the 'tites from the ceiling. Put the 'mites on the floor.
4. Other things you can add to your cave: small rocks, fossils, non-spring clothespins painted white for pretend bones, a fan blowing from a corner to make it cooler, a recording of water dripping and bats screeching, pans or trays of dirt, sand and gravel.
5. Explain that spelunking is cave exploring. Some questions to ask: What might you find in a cave? Would it be dark or light? Why? Do you think it would be warm or cold in a cave? What kind of equipment would you need to go spelunking (ropes, flashlights; warm clothes, boots, a plastic bag for collecting samples)? Would you move very fast or slow while you are exploring?
6. Tell the children to go and get their gear for their trip to the cave. Each child should be given a plastic bag for collecting two samples from the cave.
7. Turn on the flashlights before entering the cave. Have the children explore freely. Talk about the things they find.
8. After their explorations, bring the samples they found back to the classroom to show everyone. These samples will be treasured items!

More to do

Art: Mold playdough into cave shapes, stalagmites and bats.
Movement: Pretend to be bats flying around the cave (with the lights on for safety). Make your body into the shape of a stalagmite. Shadow dance in the light of a flashlight.

Valerie Chellew, Marshfield, WI

Spider Puppets

3+

Science skills

Children learn about spiders and use fine motor skills to make puppets.

Materials

Black construction paper
Wax paper sandwich bags
Wiggle eyes
Scissors
Glue

What to do

1. For each child in the class, cut out one circle about 4″ (10 cm) in diameter and eight strips about 1″ x 6″ (2.5 cm x 15 cm) from the black construction paper. The older children may want to cut out their own circles and strips.
2. Tell the children that they are going to make spider puppets. Give each child a wax paper sandwich bag, a circle and eight strips.
3. The children glue the black circle to one side of the bag, then glue the legs onto the circle. They may want to glue on wiggle eyes as well.
4. When the spider puppets are dry, have the children slip them onto their hands and put on a puppet show.

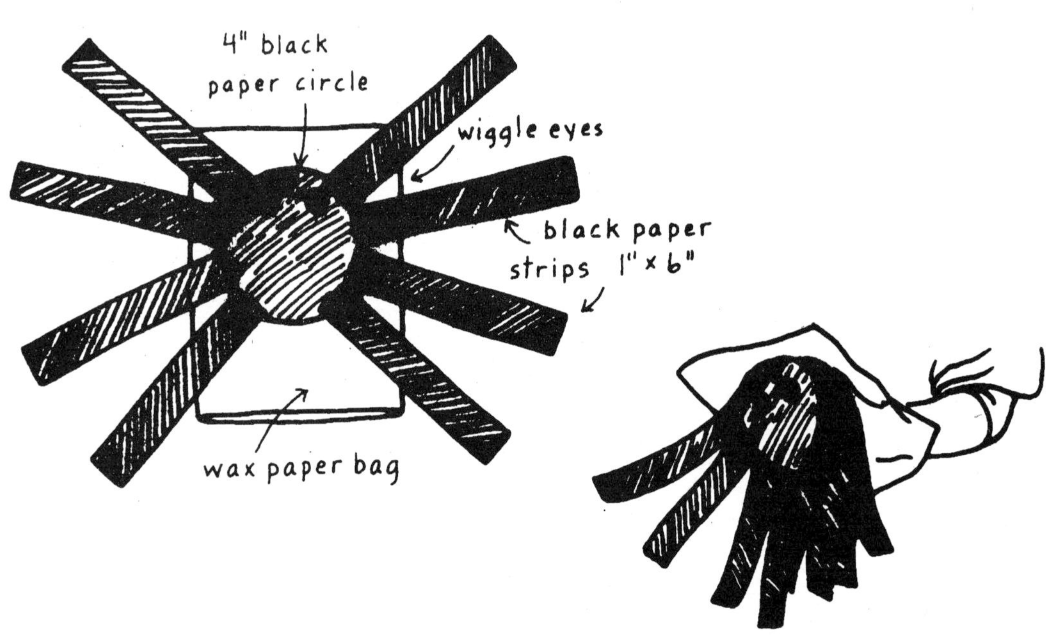

More to do

Art: Make ladybug puppets by gluing on red circles and black dots. ▪ Make butterfly puppets by cutting out butterfly parts and having children color them before gluing them onto the bag.

Language: Read *The Grouchy Ladybug* or *The Very Hungry Caterpillar* by Eric Carle.

Related book

The Very Busy Spider by Eric Carle

Audrey F. Kanoff, Allentown, PA

3+

Spider Web Prints

Science skills

Children create webs for their spiders.

Materials

Plastic paper plate holders
Paper
4 black pipe cleaners per child
Black paint
Egg carton section
Pencil

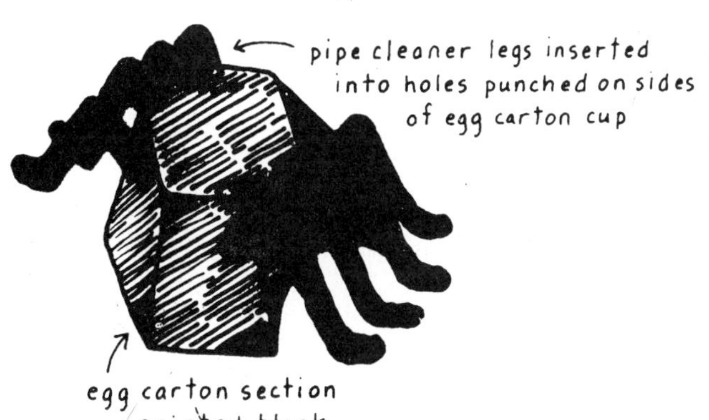

What to do

1. To make the web, children paint the bottom of a paper plate holder with black paint. While it is still wet, children lay a piece of paper on top, rub it and lift it off. This makes a realistic looking spider web.
2. To make the spider, give each child a single egg section of an egg carton. Children paint the sections black and let them dry, then turn their egg sections upside down and push four holes in the sides using the tip of a pen or pencil. You may need to do this for the younger children. Show the children how to push the four pipe cleaners through the holes so that they are sticking out through both sides (making eight legs).
3. Children can place their spiders on their webs.

More to do

Field trip: Take a walk and look for real spiders and their webs.

Audrey Kanoff, Allentown, PA

Spiders Have Eight Legs

Science skills

This activity reinforces an interesting fact about spiders.

Materials

Toilet paper tubes
Paintbrush
Tape
Yarn or string
Black paint
Black construction paper
Scissors

What to do

1. Children cover tubes with black construction paper or paint them black.
2. Have children cut eight strips of black paper and fold them fan style to form the legs.
3. Have the children tape four strips onto each side of tube.
4. To make the face, tell the children to cut out a small circle about the size of the tube opening and tape it over one end.
5. To hang the spiders, thread the string or yarn through the middle of the tube so some extends above and below the spider. When spider has been hung, the thread hanging down looks like it has been spun by the spider.

More to do

Language: Talk about how the spider is symmetrical, pointing out that both sides of the spider are exactly the same.

Ivy Sher, Sherman Oaks, CA

3+

Who's Caught in the Web?

Science skills

Children use tactile clues to determine if something has landed in their "web."

Materials

Two 10′ (3 m) pieces of sturdy string or lightweight rope
Picture or drawing of a fly
Four chairs
Picture or drawing of a spider
Tape

What to do

1. Place two chairs side by side, approximately 2′ (60 cm) apart. The chair backs should be facing the same direction, toward an open area.
2. Tie one end of each string to each chair back. Tape the picture of the spider to one chair back. Tape the picture of the fly to the other chair back.
3. Approximately 8′ (2.5 m) away, place the two remaining chairs side by side, about 3′ (1 m) apart. The chair backs should be facing the pictures of the spider and the fly. Tie the two remaining ends of string to these chair backs.
4. Have a child stand between the two strings, very close to the insect pictures. The child will lightly place fingers on both strings. The child should face the pictures.
5. The teacher or another child, standing at the other end of the strings, should lightly pluck one of the strings. The first child has to decide if there is a spider or a fly on the string "web."
6. Explain that this is how a spider knows if it has caught something on its web. The children can take turns playing this game.

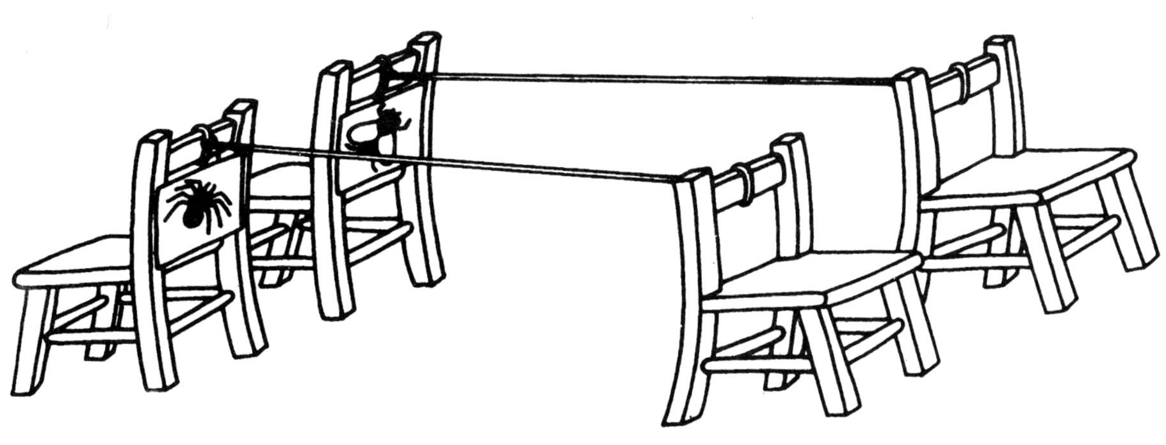

More to do

More science: Compare this kind of communication with the vibrations of a tin can (or paper cup) when part of a "string telephone."

Original song

Sing to the tune of "Itsy-Bitsy Spider."

Creepy, crawly spider,
Busy, buzzy fly.
Spider waits on the web,
As the fly zips by.
"Won't you come and join me?"
I heard the spider say.
But the fly was much too busy
And he just flew away.

Related books

The Itsy-Bitsy Spider by Iza Trapani
Old Black Fly by Jim Aylesworth
The Very Busy Spider by Eric Carle

■ *Christina Chilcote, New Freedom, PA*

Spiders

4+

Science skills

Children learn that spiders can be helpful, and they make 3-D models of spiders.

Materials

Be Nice to Spiders by Margaret Bloy Graham
Styrofoam balls: 1" (2.5 cm) and 1½" (3.75 cm), each child will get one-half of each size
Paintbrushes
String or wire for hanging
Toothpicks
Pipe cleaners, brown or black
Acrylic paint, brown or black
Paper clips
Clear spray paint or glitter spray, optional

What to do

Note: Decide whether you will be making brown or black spiders and purchase paint and pipe cleaners of the same color.

1. In advance, cut the Styrofoam balls in half and the pipe cleaners into 1" (2.5 cm) pieces (each child will get eight pieces).
2. Read *Be Nice to Spiders*. Discuss how the spiders in the story were able to help the other animals.
3. Give each child one half of each size Styrofoam ball. Have the children paint their balls and let them dry.

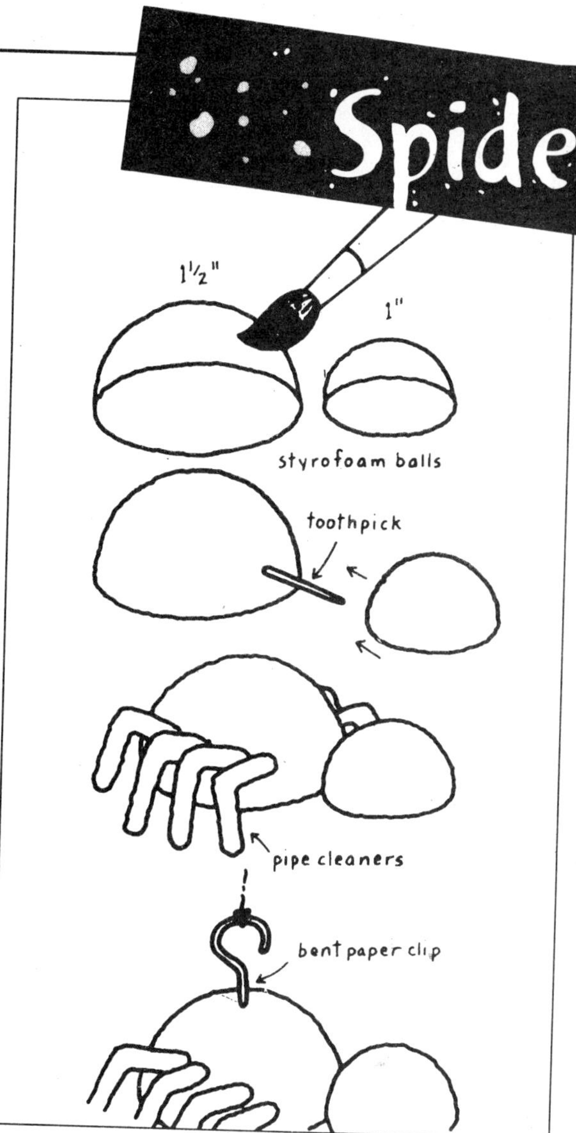

4. After the balls have dried (length of time depends on paint used), you may wish to spray them with clear paint or glitter spray before the children continue with the next step.
5. Have children assemble their spiders as follows: Use a toothpick to hold the head to the body. Stick four pipe cleaner "legs" in each side of the body. Bend each leg in half so that it forms the letter L (this will allow spiders to stand up).
6. To hang the finished spiders, bend a paper clip into an S shape and insert the small part of the S into the back of the spider. Suspend from the ceiling using wire or string.

More to do

Art: Make a large web on the bulletin board using prepackaged webs (usually sold around Halloween), string/yarn or fabric paint on paper. Attach the spiders to the web. You might use glow-in-the dark fabric paint and surprise the children by turning out the lights.

Related books

The Itsy-Bitsy Spider by Iza Trapini
Spiders by Gail Gibbons
A Very Busy Spider by Eric Carle

Deborah A. Chaplin, Hot Springs, VA

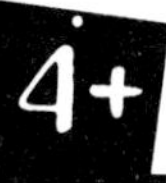

Sticky Spider Webs

Science skills
This activity stimulates interest in how spiders make their webs.

Materials

Chart paper and marker
Clear school glue or toothpicks and glue in tray
Construction paper
Crayons

What to do

1. In advance, draw a large spider web on chart paper.
2. Gather children around the large spider web. Ask them to tell you what they know about spider webs. Explain that spider webs are sticky. When a small insect comes into contact with the web, it may get stuck. A spider uses the web to gather food.

3. Give each child a piece of construction paper and crayons. Encourage him to create his own web and then draw a picture of an insect caught in the web. Write "Look! A ________ is caught in my web!" Help the child complete the sentence.
4. Using glue bottles or trays with glue and toothpicks, have the children trace over the web lines with glue to make them raised and sticky.
5. After the glue dries, encourage the children to feel the raised web lines.
6. Bind the pages together to make a class book titled "Look What the Spider Caught in Her Sticky Web!"

More to do

Snack: Serve something sticky for snack time such as caramel corn, rice crispy squares or bread with honey.

Related book

The Very Busy Spider by Eric Carle

Ann Flagg, Clarion, PA

Shiny Webs

Science skills

Children use fine motor skills to create shiny webs for hanging in the classroom.

Materials

White glue in squeeze bottles
Plastic wrap
Silver glitter
String

What to do

1. In advance, make glitter-glue by adding silver glitter to white glue.
2. Give each child a piece of plastic wrap and glitter-glue in a squeeze bottle.
3. Tell the children to draw spider webs on the plastic wrap using the glitter-glue. Demonstrate by making lines that look like spokes and connecting the spokes with arcs of glue.
4. Allow the webs to dry. As they do, they will pull away from the plastic wrap.
5. Using string, hang the shiny webs around the classroom. Have the children sing the song, "The Itsy Bitsy Spider."

More to do

Math: Discuss the geometric shapes formed by a spider web.

Related books
The Itsy-Bitsy Spider by Iza Trapini
Miss Spider's Tea Party by David Kirk
Spider's Web by Christine Back and Barrie Watts
The Very Busy Spider by Eric Carle

Robin Works Davis, Keller, TX

5+

Spiders Don't Get Stuck

Science skills
Children explore the mystery of spider webs and use fine motor skills.

Materials
Paper
Markers, two colors
Colored chalk, two colors

What to do
1. Ask the children if they know why spiders don't get stuck in their own webs. Explain that not all of the threads in a web are sticky. Spiders first spin vertical threads, which are not sticky, and then horizontal threads, which are. Insects get caught when they touch the sticky threads, but spiders "tiptoe" over them.
2. Give the children paper and have them draw the vertical lines of a spider web in one color and the horizontal lines in another.
3. Go outside and draw a large web with chalk on the playground. Draw the vertical lines in one color and the horizontal lines in another. Have children pretend they are bugs and try to walk across the web without stepping on the "sticky" lines.

More to do
Art: Use regular and double-sided tape to create the web on paper.
Movement: Do listening activities involving horizontal and vertical (e.g., lie down, stand up, hold out your arms, lift your arms).

Related books
I Love Spiders by Parker
The Itsy-Bitsy Spider by Iza Trapani

Ivy Sher, Sherman Oaks, CA

The Magnificent Story of Jack and the Beanstalk 3+

Science skills

Children listen to a favorite story and then observe how water and light magnify objects.

Materials

Cutouts of Jack, the giant, Jack's mother and the cow
Clear drinking straws
Clear one-gallon (4 L) jar
Celery stalk
Clear contact paper or laminate
Glue
Water
Wooden bead

What to do

1. Color and laminate story characters. Make sure to leave at least a ¼ inch (6 mm) of laminate around each cutout.
2. Glue clear straws to the backs of the characters for handles.
3. Fill the gallon jar three-fourths full with water.
4. Place story objects next to jar, then tell the following story:

Once upon a time, there was a boy named Jack. His family was very poor. (Hold up cutout of Jack.) One day, Jack was taking his cow to market (hold up Jack and the cow) when he met a man who traded Jack a magic bean for the cow. (Hold up wooden bead.)

Jack took the magic bean back to his mother. (Hold up the mother.) She was so angry, she threw the magic bean out the window. (Drop wooden bead into jar of water.) The magic bean grew larger! (Ask the children if they see how much bigger the magic bean looks now. The next morning, a large beanstalk had grown outside Jack's window. (Place celery stalk in the jar so that it leans to the side and children can see how it is magnified.)

Jack climbed up the beanstalk, high, high into the clouds. (Move the figure of Jack up the outside of the jar.) At the top was the castle of the evil giant! The giant had stolen a bag of gold from Jack's family many years before, leaving them penniless. When Jack entered the castle, he could see the giant counting the gold. (Lower the cutout of the giant into the water.) The giant said, "Fee, Fie, Foe, Fum, I smell the blood of an Englishman!"

(Lower the figure of Jack into the water.) Jack realized that being in the giant's castle made him big and strong, too. He quickly grabbed the gold and ran. But the giant ran after Jack. Jack climbed down the beanstalk as fast as he could, but he could see the giant was coming down after him. (Remove figure of Jack from the water.) Jack called to his mother to bring him an ax. He quickly chopped down the beanstalk. (Remove the celery from the water.) The giant came crashing to the ground. (Remove figure of giant from the water.)

And so, Jack and his mother got their gold back and lived happily ever after.

Illustrations by Erinn Valhkamp

More to do

More science: Encourage the children to put their hands into the jar of water and see how they are magnified. They do the same under running water. Help the children notice that there is no magnification. Explain that in order for something to magnify, it has to be curved, transparent and have light.

Dottie Enderle, Houston, TX

Find Cinderella Using Science

Science skills

Using a fairy tale, children become acquainted with the scientific process.

Materials

Cinderella (many versions available)

What to do

1. Read or tell the story *Cinderella*.
2. Think about the steps in the scientific process that follow and help the prince solve his problem.
   Steps in the scientific process:
   - observing
   - questioning
   - experimenting
   - recording results
   - drawing conclusions
   - reporting
3. Here's a possible solution to the prince's problem of finding Cinderella, using the scientific method:
   - The ball is over and Cinderella is gone. (observing)
   - The prince finds Cinderella's slipper. (questioning)
   - The prince tries the slipper on all the young girls. (experimenting)
   - The slipper fits Cinderella and no one else. (recording results)
   - The prince knows he's found Cinderella. (drawing conclusion)
   - The prince tells everyone this is Cinderella. (reporting)

More to do

More science: Try this process with other nursery rhymes or stories.

Monica Hay-Cook, Tucson, AZ

5 Minute Ice Cream

Science skills
Children use measuring skills to create a cool summer snack.

Materials

Milk
Vanilla
Ice cubes
Large (gallon or 4 L size) and small (sandwich size) resealable plastic bags
Sugar
Measuring cups and spoons
Salt
Spoons
Cups or bowls

What to do

1. Set out all the ingredients and measuring supplies on a large table.
2. Give each child a small and large bag.
3. Tell the children to put ½ cup (125 ml) milk, 1 tablespoon (15 ml) sugar, and ¼ teaspoon (1 ml) vanilla into the small bag. You may need to help the younger children with the measurements.
4. The children then seal their bags and shake or gently squeeze them to combine the ingredients.
5. Have the children place their sealed bags into the larger bags and add ice cubes (about one dozen) and six tablespoons (90 ml) of salt to the area around it in the large bag.
6. After carefully sealing the large bag, children should shake it for five minutes or until ice cream hardens.
7. When the ice cream is ready to eat, have the children pour it into the bowls or cups.

More to do

Dramatic play: Set up an ice cream shop with props from a local ice cream shop.
More science: Add primary food coloring and observe the mixing of two colors. Add various extract flavorings to change the flavor of the ice cream.

Kaethe Lewandowski, Centreville, VA

Camping Memory Game

3+

Science skills

Children practice memory skills and learn about outdoor camping.

Materials

Backpack filled with camping items such as flashlight, canteen, can of baked beans, pots and pans, binoculars, plastic tent stakes, rope, sunscreen, etc.

What to do

1. Talk about outdoor camping with the children. Ask if any of the children have been on a camping trip and encourage them to tell the group what it was like. Explain that when we go camping out in nature, we are away from such things as electricity, our own beds, etc. We want to take along the things that we will need, but not so many things that we become distracted from enjoying nature.
2. Pass the backpack around and have each child select one object from inside. The child tells the group what the object is, then some ways the object might be used on a camping trip.
3. When each child has had a turn, have the children place all of the objects in the center of the group.
4. Have all the children close their eyes. One child comes forward, removes an object from the pile and hides it. Ask the children to guess which object is missing.
5. The game continues in this way until each child has had a turn to guess and to hide an object.

More to do

Dramatic play: Pitch a free standing dome tent in the dramatic play center, and add firewood, cookware, sleeping bags, backpacks and other camping supplies.
Snack: Make trail mix with raisins, dry cereal, granola, chocolate chips, etc.
Special days: Invite a local forest ranger to visit the classroom and discuss outdoor safety issues.

Carla Scholl, Fairplay, CO

Water Painting

3+

Science skills

In this creative outdoor activity, children learn about evaporation.

Materials

Bucket of water
Paintbrushes

What to do

1. Take a bucket of water and some paintbrushes outside on a hot day.
2. Have children "paint" designs on sidewalks, brick walls and paved play areas using plain water.
3. Within a few minutes, the water paintings will begin to disappear. Talk about evaporation and how the warm sun evaporated the water into air.
4. Repeat the activity on a cool, cloudy day. Point out that the water paintings stay visible longer when the sun is not so hot.

More to do

Art: Mix a little bit of dry tempera paint in the water. Have children paint on white paper and leave the paintings outside. The water will evaporate and leave traces of the tempera paint behind.

Suzanne Pearson, Winchester, VA

Telephones

Our Telephone Book

4+

Science skills

The importance of knowing your phone number is reinforced in this group activity.

Materials

Real telephones
Hole punch
Index cards
Fasteners

What to do

1. Display a real telephone and talk to the children about why it is important for them to learn their phone number. Explain how to dial 911 in emergency situations.
2. Give each child an index card and tell him to take it home and bring it back with his name and phone number written neatly on one side. Encourage the children to ask for a parent's help when doing their card.
3. When all the cards have been returned, combine them to make a book. Punch holes along one edge and insert fasteners.
4. Place the book in the house center with one or more real phones (not hooked up). Encourage the children to dial their own phone numbers as part of their play.

More to do

Art: The children could make and decorate individual phone books using the telephone numbers of the other children.

Sandra Hutchins Lucas, Cox's Creek, KY

Telephones

4+

Telephone Technology

Science skills

Children experience different types of telephones.

Materials

Variety of telephones (cordless, rotary, speaker phone, push button)

What to do

1. Show children as many different types of phones as possible. Ask the children if any of the phones resemble a phone they have at home.
2. Discuss how the phones are similar and how they are different.
3. Place the phones in a play center for children to explore.

More to do

More science: Make "can" telephones and discuss how sound travels through the strings.

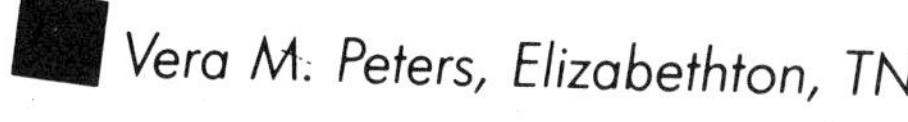

Vera M. Peters, Elizabethton, TN

Transportation

Track Painting

3+

Science skills

Children make and identify tread patterns of toy vehicles.

Materials

Paint (liquid tempera)
Small toy vehicles with moving wheels
Shallow trays
Paper

What to do

1. Pour paint into shallow trays.
2. Set out a variety of toy vehicles and paper.
3. Have the children roll the vehicles in the paint and then "drive" them on the paper.
4. Compare the tracks made by the different vehicles. Point out that some are wider or thinner than others, and note any differences in tread patterns that you see.
5. Encourage children to make straight or curvy lines by moving the cars in different ways.

More to do

Outdoors: Take a walk outside and look at tires on cars and trucks. ■ Ride bikes/tricycles through puddles and observe the tracks.

Suzanne Pearson, Winchester, VA

Wheels

Science skills

Through experimentation, children learn which shape rolls.

Materials

Cardboard
Scissors
Wooden dowels, pencils or metal rods

What to do

1. In advance, cut out two squares, two triangles and two circles from the cardboard. Connect each set of shapes by inserting a wooden dowel, pencil or metal rod through the center of each so the shapes can roll like a set of wheels.
2. Ask the children to roll each set of shapes across the table.

3. Which set of shapes rolls the best?

More to do

More science: Try rolling other shapes like octagons and rectangles.

Original poem

When you want a vehicle (or car)
To go along the ground.
Circle wheels work best
To go 'round and 'round and 'round.

Marilyn Harding, Grimes, IA

3+

Where Do They Travel?

Science skills

In this fun game, children match vehicles to appropriate scenes.

Materials

Magazines
Clear contact paper or laminate
Markers, crayons
Scissors
3 manila folders

What to do

1. In advance, cut pictures of various forms of transportation from magazines—or let the children cut them out. Laminate the pictures.
2. Decorate three manila folders, each with one of the following scenes: ground, air and water.
3. Have children sort the pictures into the proper folder. The children hypothesize what would happen if a particular vehicle tried to travel elsewhere. For example, ask "What would happen if a car tried to drive on the water?" or "Why can't a boat fly?"

More to do

Art: Children draw or paint pictures showing air, water and ground scenes and the appropriate forms of transportation.

Music: Have children sing and act out "Row, Row, Row Your Boat," pretending they are cars by moving about on hands and knees, and flying like an airplane by holding their arms out like wings. Substitute appropriate words to the tune, for example: drive, drive, drive your car, or fly, fly, fly your airplane.

Related book

This Is the Way We Go to School by Edith Baer

Suzanne Pearson, Winchester, VA

Similar or Different?

4+

Science skills

Children work on classification skills as they learn about boats.

Materials

Boating magazines and catalogs
Glue
Marker
Scissors
Index cards, any size

What to do

1. Find pictures of different kinds of boats in magazines and catalogs. Glue the pictures onto index cards. Write the names of the boats on other cards. Types of boats include:
   - tug
   - trawler
   - cutter
   - ferry
   - houseboat
   - ocean liner
   - sailboat
   - lobster boat
2. Ask the children to sort the boats by an attribute of their choice.
3. Encourage them to match the names of the boats to the correct pictures. Use books as references.
4. Classify boats by purpose (work or pleasure).
5. How are the boats similar and different?

More to do

Art: Invite the children to work together to paint a mural of boats, bridges and lighthouses.
Language: Ask the children to write or dictate a story about the boat of their choice.

Related books

Boats by Anne Rockwell
I Love Boats by Flora M. Donnell
The Little Red Lighthouse and the Great Gray Bridge by Hildegarde Swift
Sailing to the Sea by Mary Claire Helldorfer
Sarah's Boat by Douglas Alvord
Sven's Bridge by Anita Lobel
Workboats by Jan Adkins

 *Barbara Hershberger, Watertown, WI*

3+

Dandelion Seed Pictures

Science skills

Children observe the intricacies of a dandelion seed.

Materials

Black paper
Glue
Magnifying glass

What to do

1. On a windy day when dandelions have gone to seed, take the children outdoors to an area with many dandelions.
2. After children have each picked a dandelion, have them put some glue on black paper and blow the dandelion so the seeds get caught on the sticky surface.
3. Children then examine their seeds closely using a magnifying glass.

Related books

A Seed Is a Promise by Claire Merrill
The Tiny Seed by Eric Carle

 *Cindy Winther, Oxford, MI*

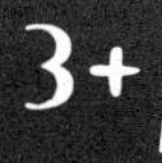

Seed Match

Science skills

Observation and memory skills are heightened with this fun game.

Materials

Resealable sandwich-size plastic bags
Seeds from fruits: oranges, apples, kiwi, bananas, etc.
Photograph or drawing of each fruit

What to do

1. Place the seeds from each fruit in a separate plastic bag. Add the pictures of the mature fruit and close.
2. Pass the bags around for children to examine.
3. Remove the pictures from the bags and invite the children to play a matching game by finding the seed bag that goes with each.

More to do

More science: Each child makes a set of seed bags to take home. These bags can be kept together by punching a hole in the corner and stringing them together with yarn. ▪ Children make bags using other objects from nature such as feathers and bird photos; seedlings, nuts or leaves with tree photos; and sand with desert or beach photos.

Related books

Pumpkin Pumpkin by Jeanne Titherington

The Seasons of Arnold's Apple Tree by Gail Gibbons

Susan Rinas, Parma, OH

Seeds Can Travel: Milkweed

Science skills

Storytelling helps children understand seed disbursal.

Materials

Milkweed pods

What to do

1. Tell the following story about Mel Milkweed, using a milkweed pod as a prop. Open the pod and take out a few seeds at the appropriate time.

   "It was very dark. Mel Milkweed had been lying very still for such a long time. He was waiting and waiting along with all the other seeds in the pod, waiting for the time when the pod would open and he and all the other milkweed seeds would fly out and travel to new places to live. He was getting very excited. He could feel the pod starting to loosen and open. The time was near! Suddenly a tiny bit of light shone into the pod. Then more light and finally Mel felt himself falling. His little parachute began to open. A gust of wind carried Mel up into the air toward a tree. He could see the other seeds in the air, too. Where would they all land? Where would he land? Would he hit the tree? Suddenly the wind took him away from the tree and into a field. He came down on a soft spot of ground. This would be a great place for Mel to live and grow into a milkweed plant. It would take a long time, but he knew he could do it!"

2. Invite children to examine milkweed pods and seeds. On a windy day take milkweed seeds outdoors and give each child a few to "fly." Watch how the wind carries them.

More to do

Language: Write a group story about what the milkweed seed might see and feel as it travels along. Older children may prefer to dictate their own story and draw a picture. Make into one book and read at story time.

More science: Try "flying " other types of seeds, such as dandelion seeds or maple seeds. ■ Sort of variety of seeds into two categories: those that the wind can carry and those it can't.

 *Irene A. Tegze, Mahwah, NJ*

3+

Apples

Science skills
Children explore the characteristics of apples.

Materials

Drawing paper
Apples, assorted types, sizes, colors
Chart paper (for graph)
Crock pot
Markers, crayons
Knife and cutting board (for adults only)
Water

What to do

1. Talk to children about how apples grow on trees. Encourage them to draw apple trees.
2. Bring in an assortment of apples. Invite the children to bring in apples as well.
3. Cut the apples into bite-sized pieces.
4. Have children taste the apples and use words such as sweet, sour, crunchy, mushy, etc., to describe how they taste.
5. Graph the different tastes and the numbers of children who preferred each one.
6. Cut up the remaining apples. Put the apple pieces and 1 cup (250 ml) of water into a crock pot and let cook until you have applesauce.

More to do

Art: Give the children a cup of red tempera paint and tell them to dip their fingers into the paint and make red "fingerprint" apples on the apple trees they drew earlier.

Barbara Saul, Eureka, CA

3+

Do Plants Need Water to Grow?

Science skills
Children learn the requirements of plants through experimentation.

Materials

2 green plants
Marker
Index cards
Water

What to do

1. Show the children two healthy green plants.
2. Explain that the class is going to do an experiment to see if plants need water to live and to grow.
3. Label one plant WATER and the other NO WATER.
4. Let the children water the plant labeled WATER as needed.
5. Ask the children to predict what will happen to each plant.
6. After two weeks, compare the two plants. Discuss the results. The dead plant could be put in a compost pile.

More to do

More science. Have each child plant a seed in a cup of soil to take home. (Marigold seeds grow quickly.)

Cindy Winther, Oxford, MI

Living Trees

Science skills

Children compare types of evergreens by touching and observing.

Materials

Branches, bark, needles, pine cones of evergreen trees

What to do

1. Place the evergreen materials on a large table and let the children explore them.
2. Talk about the various types of evergreen branches and needles. Explain that these are from living trees.
3. Take a walk in a park where there are evergreen trees and ask the children to point them out. Compare them in terms of size and shape.

Brenda Miller, Olean, NY

Nature Viewer

Science skills

Children learn about flowers through collecting and drying blossoms.

Materials

Collecting basket or box
Newsprint
White typing paper
Three-ring binder or notebook
Drying table or floor area
Heavy books
White glue in squeeze bottle
Plastic sleeves for three-ring binder

What to do

1. Take the children for a walk and collect a variety of blossoms in a basket or box. Try to identify the blossoms as you collect them.
2. Select a drying area that can be left undisturbed for several days, such as a table or a corner of the floor, and spread out several sheets of clean newsprint.
3. Have the children arrange the blossoms on the newsprint so they are not touching and cover them with another sheet of clean newsprint. Place some heavy books on top and leave undisturbed for three days.
4. Remove the books and the top layer of newsprint. Demonstrate how to carefully peel away any blossoms stuck to the newsprint. Ask the children to help.
5. Invite the children to create interesting arrangements with the dried blossoms on white paper. Tell them they can arrange the blossoms by color, size or type, or just put one blossom on a page. The children then glue on the blossoms one at a time. Allow to dry overnight.
6. When dry, carefully slip the glued blossom paper into the plastic sleeve and place it in the three-ring binder. Continue until all the blossom papers have been inserted in the book.
7. Place the book in an area of the classroom where everyone can enjoy it.

More to do

Art: Use the dried blossoms to decorate note cards or create framed pictures with blossoms. When plastic sleeves will not be used, cover the blossoms with clear adhesive plastic or wide shipping tape to protect them. ■ Create pictures with leaves instead of blossoms. ■ Use pictures of flowers and leaves from gardening magazines in place of real items.

Original poem

Blossom Fingerplay by MaryAnn Kohl © 1997

Little blossom, closed up tight, (hold one hand up like a fist, fingers and palm up)
Start to grow with all your might. (begin to unfold a few fingers slowly)
Big sun warm you, help you grow, (use other hand to send rays of sunlight)

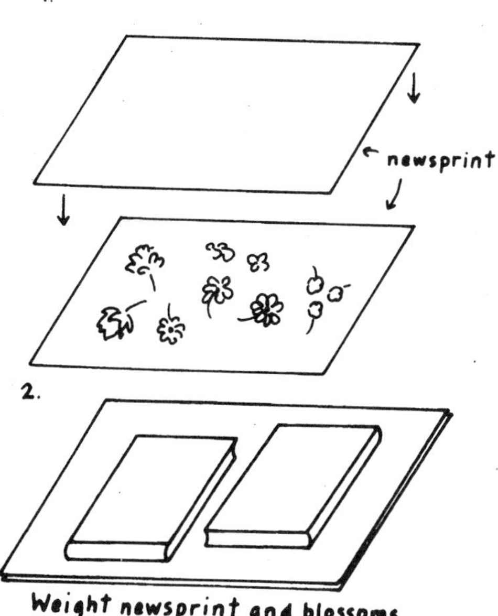

Weight newsprint and blossoms with heavy books.

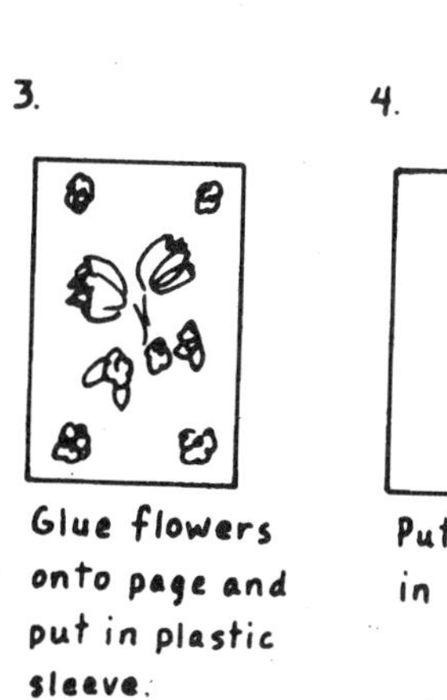

Glue flowers onto page and put in plastic sleeve.

Put pages together in binder.

Rain drops feed you, here you go. (use other hand to send raindrops, while opening blossom more and more)
When your time is almost right, (peek through visor of other hand at blossom)
BURST! and BLOOM! Oh, what a sight! (explode both hands into one fully formed flower, turning it and looking at it with proud admiration)

Related books

Chrysanthemum by Kevin Henkes
The Empty Pot by Demi
First Comes Spring by Anne Rockwell
Planting a Rainbow by Lois Ehlert
Plants That Never Ever Bloom by Ruth Heller
This Year's Garden by Cynthia Rylant

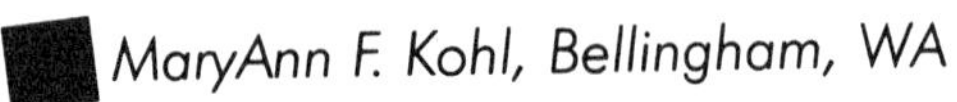
MaryAnn F. Kohl, Bellingham, WA

Mr. Day and Mr. Night

4+

Science skills

Children experiment with light and plants and draw conclusions.

Materials

Styrofoam cups
Potting soil
Geranium seeds
Paper labels
Glue
Digging sticks
Crayons
Watering can

What to do

1. Discuss what plants need to live: water, sunlight and soil.
2. Give each child two Styrofoam cups to fill with soil and a few geranium seeds.
3. Have the children color two labels each. One should say "Mr. Day" and the other "Mr. Night." Have children glue the labels on their plant cups.
4. Explain that the class will be conducting an experiment to see how important light is to the growth of a plant.
5. Invite the children to place Mr. Night plants in a dark spot, such as a classroom closet, and Mr. Day plants in a sunny place.
6. For three weeks, children water their plants and monitor the growth patterns.
7. After three weeks, tell the children to compare their Mr. Day and Mr. Night plants. Which plant is the largest? Greenest? Healthiest looking? Ask the children why they think one is larger than the other. What did Mr. Day have that Mr. Night did not? Why is sunlight necessary for the plants?

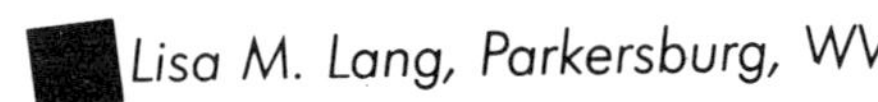
Lisa M. Lang, Parkersburg, WV

4+

What Makes Plants Grow?

Science skills
Experimentation shows the importance of water, sun and air to plants.

Materials
Seeds of fast growing plants
Flower pots or margarine tubs
Chart paper
2-liter drink bottle
Soil
Wanda's Roses by Pat Brisson
Markers
Popsicle sticks

What to do
1. In advance, plant seeds and wait for them to flower. Alternatively, you could purchase four already flowering plants such as marigolds.
2. Read _Wanda's Roses_. Discuss the three things that Wanda says her rosebush needs to grow.
3. Explain to the children that you will be conducting an experiment to find out how important it is for a plant to have air, water and sunlight. Have children predict the importance of each. Write down their predictions.
4. Describe the experiment. One plant will receive sunlight, water and air. A second plant will be given water and air, but it will be kept in a dark place such as in the closet, where it will receive no sunlight. The third plant will have air and sun but no water. The fourth plant will be given water and sun, but no fresh air (to do this, cut the top off the liter drink bottle and invert it over the plant; seal, but allow to open for watering).
5. On the popsicle sticks, draw the elements that each of the plants will be allowed to receive: a sun, water droplets and a cloud-like figure to indicate air.
6. Set the plants in their appropriate locations.
7. Ask the children to check on the plants each day. As a class, keep a log of the condition of each plant each day. Have the children dictate sentences about the conditions of the plants.
8. This experiment can end at any point. For example, you may decide to monitor the plants for several weeks but not let them die.

More to do
Dramatic play: Children become the plants and role play different scenarios such as "I have lots of sun, but no water. What do I look like?"
More science: Ask the children what might happen if the elements that were withheld were restored to the plant? Reverse the experiment and see how long it takes to restore the plants to a healthy condition.

 _Deborah A. Chaplin, Hot Springs, VA_

Pressing Leaves

4+

Science skills

Stimulate children's interest in the natural world through collecting leaves and then assembling them in a press to dry.

Materials

2 pieces of plywood, 16″ x 24″ (40 cm x 60 cm)
10 pieces of corrugated cardboard,
12″ x 20″ (30 cm x 50 cm)
Variety of leaves
Paper towels
2 belts or camping straps for tightening press

What to do

1. Take a nature walk and collect fresh leaves for pressing. Talk to children about what happens to the leaves on trees when the weather changes (they change color, fall to the ground, dry up).
2. Invite the children to help you assemble a leaf press in the following manner: Begin with a piece of plywood for the bottom, then one piece of corrugated cardboard followed by a paper towel. Arrange leaves on the paper towel, keeping them as flat as possible. Cover the leaves with another paper towel, then another piece of corrugated cardboard. Continue this pattern until all leaves are in the press (keeping a few leaves out to compare with pressed leaves at a later date), and top with the second piece of plywood.
3. Wrap belts or camping straps around the press and tighten.
4. Have children open the press and change the paper towels after about five days. Tighten up the press again. Depending on how wet your leaves were, you may need to change the paper towels again.

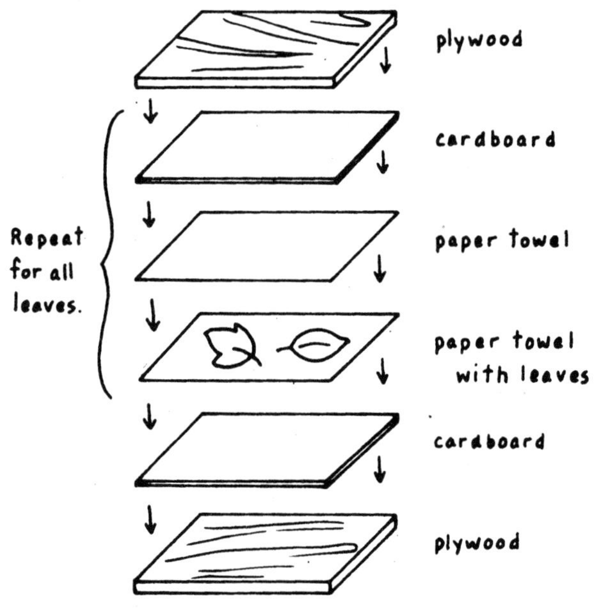

5. Leaves should be completely dry within four weeks. Compare them to leaves that were not pressed.

More to do

Art: Properly pressed leaves will last a long time. They can be used to make greeting cards or may be pressed between sheets of wax paper and hung in a window. Make a reusable place mat by mounting leaves with white glue on light cardboard and covering both sides with clear vinyl or laminate.

Math: Have children count the leaves and sort them by size, color, shape and variety.

Related books

Fresh Fall Leaves by Betsy Franco
Red Leaf, Yellow Leaf by Lois Ehlert
When Autumn Comes by Robert Maass
Why Do Leaves Change Color? by Betsy Maestro

Mark Crouse, Nova Scotia, Canada

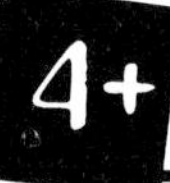
4+

Choose a Leaf

Science skills

Children learn about leaves through observation and the sense of touch.

Materials

Leaves
Chart showing leaves common to your area
Magnifying glasses

What to do

1. Divide children into pairs and give each pair three of the leaves.
2. With eyes closed, one child in each pair selects one of the leaves and feels it carefully.
3. The child's partner mixes the leaf with the other two.
4. The first child (with eyes still closed) then carefully feels all three leaves and tries to pick out the original leaf. The partner says whether the choice is right or wrong.
5. Have children in each pair switch places and repeat the activity.
6. Ask children to describe how they knew which was their original leaf.
7. Give children a magnifying glass and tell them to examine their leaves. Ask them if they can see the stem and veins, and if they notice any insect-made holes or variations in color.
8. Encourage the children to try to match the leaf to those on the chart.

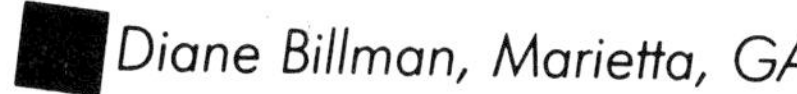
Diane Billman, Marietta, GA

How Much Will It Grow?

4+

Science skills

Stimulate children's curiosity and interest in the way plants grow.

Materials

Magic Growing Powder by Janet Quin-Harkin
Plant food or fertilizer
Marker
2 identical potted plants
Chart paper
Camera, optional

What to do

1. Read the book.
2. Review the purpose of the "magic growing powder" that was used in the story.
3. Relate the idea of "magic growing powder" to fertilizer or plant food.
4. Introduce the two identical potted plants and the plant food to the class.
5. Ask the children to make predictions about what might happen to each of the plants if all conditions are kept the same except that one is watered with tap water and one is watered with a plant food solution.
6. Measure and record the height of each plant. If possible, take a photo of the two plants side by side for comparison later on.
7. Place the plants in an area of the room where they will receive adequate light and be in easy reach of the children so they can assist in daily care and monitoring.
8. Water the plants appropriately, keeping a daily record of the care of each. Measure each plant and record the results after a few days. Continue to measure and record over a period of time so that the children can see the changes and evaluate the effectiveness of the plant food.
9. Photographs may also be made at the end of the experiment to demonstrate a "before and after" relationship to the children.

More to do

More science: Try this experiment with several types of plant food to determine the best product. Each child could keep a personal learning log to record the steps in the experiment and the results.

Lyndall Warren, Milledgeville, GA

4+

How Seeds Travel

Science skills
Children examine different kinds of seeds and learn how they travel.

Materials
Variety of different seeds

What to do
1. Collect a variety of seeds, either as a class or ahead of time.
2. Talk about what makes a weed different from other plants.
3. Ask children if they know how weeds can appear in places where no one has planted them. Explain how seeds travel (in the wind, on animals, in water, etc.).
4. Introduce seeds from the collection and discuss how each might travel. For example, if a seed has burrs, demonstrate how it can attach to clothing or other objects.

More to do
Art: Paint with weeds (weeds dipped in white paint and brushed onto dark paper make an interesting winter scene).
More science: Go for a nature walk and look for weeds growing in the ground. Pull the weeds out of the ground, noting the different types.

Related books
From Seed to Plant by Gail Gibbons
Seeds Pop-Stick-Glide by Patricia Lauber

Wanda K. Pelton, Lafayette, IN

5+

Plant Growth

Science skills
The children learn about plant growth firsthand.

Materials
Styrofoam cups, one per child
Soil
Corn seeds
Paper
Markers
Spoons
Watering bucket or cup and water
Markers, crayons, pencils

What to do

1. Set up a garden area near a windowsill.
2. The children write their names on Styrofoam cups.
3. Each child puts about five teaspoons (25 ml) of soil into his or her cup.
4. Show the children how to make a hole in the middle of the soil and drop in three corn seeds.
5. Help them water their seeds every few days.
6. Encourage each child to make a journal so that they can record the daily progress of their corn plants. They can decorate the cover and pages of the journals any way they wish.

More to do

Language: Write or tell a story about the plants titled: "How My Seed Became a Plant."

Related books

Billy the Bean by Maria Elena Buria
How a Seed Grows by Helene J. Jordan

Jennifer B. Strauzer, Jericho, NY

Water

3+

Floating Fruit

Science skills

Children experiment with estimating and prediction skills.

Materials

Half of a grapefruit and orange, hollowed out
Items to use as units of measure, such as bear counters
Large bowl of water

What to do

1. Place the fruit halves in the water. Ask the children to predict how many of the counters the fruit "boat" might hold before it sinks and whether the way the counters are placed inside will matter.
2. Give the counters to the children and let them experiment. Compare their predictions with what happens.

More to do

More science: Experiment with other types of fruit "boats" and small counting items, such as large buttons, play money, walnuts in the shell, etc.

 *Melissa Browning, Milwaukee, WI*

3+

Flood Fun

Science skills

In this activity, children experiment with the concepts of volume and capacity and practice counting skills.

Materials

Baby food jars
Water
Small objects such as marbles, coins
Large bowls
Pitcher

What to do

1. Place empty baby food jars in bowls.
2. Fill jars with water to the top.

3. Children drop in as many of each item as will fit and observe where the water goes.
4. Children count the number of items in each jar.

More to do

More science: Find a larger jar and mark lines on the outside with a marker or tape every ½ inch (13 mm), making a beaker. Place the baby food jar inside and repeat the experiment. Coloring the water helps. Find small toys and common heavy objects around the room. Drop them into the jar and see how much water is displaced. Drop in tablespoons of sand to observe water displacement.

Susan R. Forbes, Holly Hill, FL

How Did That Plant Grow? 3+

Science skills

This activity encourages children to ask questions about nature and to explore cause and effect relationships.

Materials

Paper the size of the back of the jar
Laminate or clear contact paper
Clear mailing tape
Crayons or markers
Glass or plastic jar
Water

What to do

1. On a piece of paper, draw a thin plant or flower. Color and laminate or cover with clear contact paper, leaving enough of an edge around the plant picture so that paper does not get wet.
2. Using clear mailing tape, adhere the picture to the outside of the jar so that when you look through the front of the jar, the plant picture is facing you.
3. During group time, show the class the jar with the plant picture. Ask them what they think might happen when you pour water into the jar.
4. Pour in the water. Water will greatly magnify the picture and make it look like the plant is growing before their eyes.
5. Ask the children how they think the plant grew so quickly. Explain that water can magnify things and make them look bigger than they are. Describe what it takes for a real plant to grow.

More to do

More science: Put the activity on the science table for children to experiment with. Place a cookie sheet with edges under this activity to keep the spills off the table.

Related books

Growing Vegetable Soup by Lois Ehlert
Jack and the Beanstalk (many versions available)

Debbie Barbuch, Sheboygan, WI

Discovering Different Environments

Science skills

In this activity, children observe and describe the properties of ice.

Materials

Ice cubes
Chart paper and marker
Snow (or shaved ice)
Cookie sheet
Paper cups
Sand
Water
3 large, shallow baking pans or bowls

What to do

1. Give each child a paper cup with an ice cube in it. Have the children describe the ice cubes to you. Adjectives they might use include cold, colorless, wet, slippery, tasteless, solid.
2. Ask: "What do you think makes ice stay frozen?" and "What do you think makes ice melt?" Chart the children's thoughts and predictions.
3. Show the children four different simulated environments and label them:
   ice skating rink (frozen water on a cookie sheet)
   snow (shallow pan full of snow)
   sandbox (shallow pan full of sand)
   swimming pool (shallow pan full of water)
4. Give each child a new ice cube in a cup. Ask the children to predict in which environment the ice cube will last the longest. Why?
5. Children give their pet ice cubes a name and take them on an adventure to the different environments.
6. When play is compete, go back to the prediction list to compare the results.

More to do

Language: Have the children dictate stories of their pet ice cube's adventures for a class book. Each child can illustrate a page.

More science: Wrap some ice cubes up in different materials (e.g., plastic wrap, foil, felt). Predict which will melt first, then observe. Compare results with predictions. Fill three bowls with ice cubes. Put one bowl in the freezer, one bowl in the refrigerator and one bowl on the table. Have the children predict what will happen with each bowl. Which will melt the fastest? Then watch and compare results.

Related book

The Snowy Day by Ezra Jack Keats

Gina M. Duddy, Arlington, MA

Water Flow Exploration

3+

Science skills

Children observe the flow of water through different size holes and draw conclusions.

Materials

Glue gun
Scoops of equal size from detergents or drink mixes
Container for water play (sink, tub, pan, water table, bucket, wading pool)
Water

What to do

Note: Step one should be done by an adult only.

1. Plug in glue gun. When it is hot, use it to melt holes into the sides and bottoms of the plastic scoops. Vary the size and the number of holes.
2. Place the scoops in the water play area.
3. While the children explore the scoops and the passing of water through them, ask them why the water is not staying in the scoop (cup, glass, etc.). Which scoop held water the shortest time? Which one let the water pass the fastest? Why does the water run out? Can you predict which of these will hold water the longest? Are all the scoops the same size? Do some hold more than others? Can you cover the holes so water does not run out? Measuring tools could be added to the activity.

Bev Schumacher, Ft. Mitchell, KY

Cubed Toy Freeze

Science skills

Children observe the relationship between water and ice.

Materials

Ice cube trays
Small toys
Water
Bowl of water or water table

What to do

1. Fill the ice trays with water and place one small toy in each section of the ice tray.
2. Freeze the ice trays for two to three hours and then release the ice cubes into a bowl of water or a water table.

3. Allow the children to play with the ice cubes until toys become visible. After the ice has melted, discover what's inside.
4. Allow the children to choose a small object or toy to place in the ice tray and refreeze the tray after filling it with water.
5. Place the ice cubes in the water table again and repeat the activity.

More to do

Movement: Make a tiled surface into a skating rink. Place colored tape in an oval or circle shape on the floor. Play classical music and allow the children to take off their shoes and skate around the rink in their socks. Make the shape large enough for a number of children to skate at the same time.

Snack: Enjoy frozen juice pops for snack. Mix a package of powdered drink mix in a pitcher and then pour it into empty ice trays. Put the trays in the freezer for 30 minutes, then add a popsicle stick to each section and freeze for another hour and a half. Pop out the cubes for a cool snack! You can also use paper cups instead of ice trays for this treat. Just cut away the cup and eat!

 *Tina R. Woehler, Flower Mound, TX*

3+

Icebergs

Science skills

Children examine and play with melting ice.

Materials

Bucket or water table
Freezer
Large bowl
Arctic play animals such as seals, beluga, walrus, humpback and orca whales, polar bears, etc.
Filled water balloons or milk cartons
Scissors
Water
Plastic sheet magnifiers

What to do

1. Discuss the type of environment in which such animals as seals, polar bears and walruses are found. Tell the children that you will be turning the water table into an Arctic zone for the day, complete with icebergs and animals.
2. Fill jugs or balloons with water and freeze six to eight hours.
3. Cut the balloons or jugs away from the ice.
4. Place the ice in a water table or bucket with about ½ to ¾ cup (125 ml to 175 ml) of warm water along with the animals.
5. Allow the children to play with the ice.
6. Discuss how the ice changes as it melts.
7. Add magnifiers for close-up observation of the changes in the ice.

More to do

Art: Use old markers on a tray of ice to create a unique coloring pad. As the ice melts it clears

Water

a new coloring area for the next designer.

Dramatic play: Put winter clothing such as mittens, coat, sled, hats, boots, etc., in the dramatic play area.

More science: Use shallow trays and freeze water in them for three to six hours. Remove the trays and place them onto a towel on a tabletop. Apply a few pieces of rock salt to create holes and begin the melting process. Be sure children do not eat the rock salt.

Outdoors: Watch the weather outside and take a walk, sled or build with ice and snow, if possible.

Sand and water table: Use snow in the water table with ice to enhance the winter effect.

Related books

Baby Beluga (soundtrack and book) by Raffi
Ice Is...Whee! by Carol Greene
The Jacket I Wear in the Snow by Shirley Neitzel
Little Polar Bear by Hans De Beer
Mama Do You Love Me? by Barbara M. Joosse
Playing Outdoors in the Winter by Dorothy Chlad

 *Tina R. Woehler, Flower Mound, TX*

Testing Water

Science skills

Children observe the effects of water on different materials.

Materials

Drawing paper
Water
Glass or syringe
Plastic bag
Fan
Crayons
Wax paper
Brown paper bag
Paper towels

What to do

1. To prepare for this activity, choose a volunteer to color on a few pieces of drawing paper. Have the child color hard in several separate areas on the paper.
2. Pour or drip small amounts of water onto the crayoned piece of drawing paper and the wax paper.
3. Wait a minute, then hold each paper up to see if the water has penetrated the paper or if the paper was waterproof.
4. Pour some water into the paper bag and into the plastic bag. After a few minutes, let the children feel the bottoms of both bags. Which is dry? Which is soggy?
5. Put two wet paper towels on a table. Aim a fan onto one of the paper towels for a few minutes and leave the other one to dry naturally. Which dries faster?

Original poem

Water, water, what will you do?
Can I hold you, or will you soak through?

3+

Will It Absorb?

Science skills

Children test various objects in water to see if they are absorbent.

Materials

Trays
Wooden block
Plastic toy
Rubber ball
Cotton balls
Water
Sponge
Tissue
Piece of cloth
Rubber eraser

What to do

1. Pour some water onto several trays.
2. Set the wooden block into the water on one tray and the sponge into the water in the other tray.
3. Observe for a few minutes, then pick up the block and the sponge to see what has happened.
4. Repeat the process with the other objects.

 *Marilyn Harding, Grimes, IA*

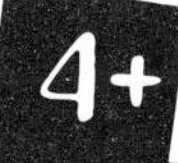

Will It Dissolve?

Science skills

Children experiment by adding substances to water and charting the results.

Materials

Chart paper and marker
Water
Various substances to test: salt, sugar, baking soda, flour, sawdust, Styrofoam pieces, etc.
Small clear plastic cups
Spoons, one per cup

What to do

1. In advance, make up a chart labeled "Dissolves" and "Doesn't Dissolve" with pictures for the children to record their findings.
2. The children choose one substance and spoon it into a cup of water.

3. After gently stirring, they decide if the substance dis solved or not, then place the cup of water on the classification chart.
4. When the children have completed testing all the available substances, ask them to look at the cups again and note any changes that may have occurred. Invite them to stir the water a second time and see if anything changes. Ask if they know why the substance did or did not dissolve.

More to do

More science: Watch powdered drink or dessert mix dissolve. Discuss the contents of these mixes. Is this consistent with the previous findings?

■ *Diane Billman, Marietta, GA*

Floaters and Sinkers

4+

Science skills

Children make predictions, observe objects in water and categorize them as sinkers or floaters.

Materials

Sink or tub
3 plastic trays or containers
Some small objects (blocks, nails, metal toys, wood, nuts, etc.)
Glue
Water
Chart paper
Markers
Magazine pictures

What to do

1. Fill tub with water. Arrange small objects on one tray. Label second tray "Sinkers" and the third tray "Floaters."
2. Invite children to work in pairs and test the items to see which ones sink and which ones float. After testing them, the children should set them on the appropriate tray.
3. Categorize sinkers and floaters by material (wood, metal, etc.) and make an experiment chart.
4. When the experiment is over, have children glue magazine pictures of different objects on chart paper under headings of "Sinkers" and "Floaters." Ask them why they made their choices.

More to do

More science: Observe what happens as the following dry items get wet or fill up with water in the tub: sponge, cloth, plastic bag (sealed with air inside), Styrofoam cup, empty metal can, noodles, cotton balls, yarn, string, cardboard and various papers (toilet tissue, towels, drawing paper). ■ Children fill four to eight baby food jars with different amounts of colored water. Older children can measure certain amounts of water into each jar. Screw the tops on the jars and float them in the tub. Observe the differences in the jars.

 *Susan R. Forbes, Holly Hill, FL*

4+

Magic Water

Science skills

Children experiment with mixing oil and water and draw conclusions.

Materials

4 clear plastic cups
Food coloring: red, blue, green, yellow
White construction paper cut into 2" x 4" (2.5 cm x 5 cm) strips
Water
Cooking oil
Tray

What to do

1. Place four clear plastic cups on a tray and pour water into the cups until they are half full.
2. Add a different food color to each cup and pour ¼" (6 mm) cooking oil on top of the colored water.
3. Have the children predict what color a strip of paper will be when it is dipped into a cup, then select a child to dip the paper into the selected cup. Repeat the process with the other cups.
4. Encourage the children to observe what happened to the strip and ask them why it did not turn the color of the water in the cup.
5. Point out the layers of oil and water in the plastic cup. Help the children reach the conclusion that because the strip was first covered with oil, the colored water would not adhere to it (oil and water do not mix).

More to do

More science: Ask a child to shake a bottle of oil-based salad dressing. Observe what happens. Point out how the water and oil will separate again after a few minutes.
Outdoors: Observe a puddle in a driveway or parking lot that forms over oil after it rains.

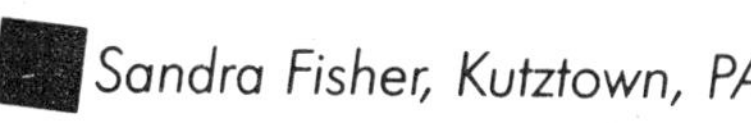
Sandra Fisher, Kutztown, PA

4+

Emulsion Fun

Science skills

In this activity, children compare the reactions of different objects when added to water.

Water

Materials

8-12 plastic jars with lids
Ingredients such as cooking oil, sand, soil, clay, salt, sugar, flour, dry tempera paint, oil-based paint
Labels
Water
Chart paper
Markers

What to do

1. Place ¼ cup (60 ml) of each ingredient listed above into a separate jar.
2. Add water to each jar and screw on the lid. Put a label on the outside.
3. Let each child take a jar and examine it. Has anything changed since you added the water?
4. Ask the children to shake the jars and see if anything changes.
5. Line the jars up on the counter and let them stand undisturbed for an hour. Compare the jars again. Has anything dissolved?
6. Make a chart showing the changes.

More to do

More science: Mix pebbles, sand, soils, oil and shells in a large clear jar. Place lid on securely and shake. Let the jar rest for one hour, then have children observe the layers. ■ Put a large jar filled with water on the table. Add 4 drops of food coloring, but do not stir or shake. Have children observe what happens.

Susan R. Forbes, Holy Hill, FL

Water Drops

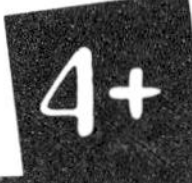

Science skills

Children use observation skills to categorize materials according to whether they repel or absorb water.

Materials

Chart paper
Small plastic container
Small pieces of various materials: newspaper, magazines, tissue paper, paper towels, plastic wrap, fabric cardboard, wax paper, piece of vinyl, wood, metal, aluminum foil, drawing paper, brick, etc.
Markers
Water in container
Medicine droppers

What to do

1. Ahead of time, make up a chart labeled "Repel" and "Absorb" with pictures for the children to record their findings.

2. The children drop water on the sample pieces of material and observe what happens. Does it absorb water or not?
3. The children then place the item on the chart in the right category.
4. When they have tried all the available materials, they can recheck. Did any of the materials that were originally placed in the repel category eventually absorb water?

More to do

Art: Do a crayon resist picture to show how wax repels water.

More science: Talk about how raincoats and boots help keep us dry. Ask why. What about umbrellas? Tents? Houses? How do ducks keep dry? This could lead to further investigation with oil and water.

Weather

Cloud Gazing

3+

Science skills

Children use observation skills and learn about different types of clouds.

Materials

Blankets or towels

What to do

1. Take the class outside and have children lie on the blankets. Encourage a discussion of the clouds. Ask how they look, how they might feel if touched.
2. Talk about the three main types of clouds. Explain that Cirrus clouds are white and feathery and are the highest clouds; Cumulus clouds are puffy and look like Cauliflower with a flat bottom; and Stratus clouds are low and look like wide gray blankets (drizzle or snow flurries may fall from them). .Point out the different types of clouds you see in the sky.

More to do

Art: Cut out white flannel shapes, similar to the ones in *It Looked Like Spilt Milk* by Charles G. Shaw. Let children use them to tell their own cloud stories.

Cindy Winther, Oxford, MI

Fluffy Clouds

3+

Science skills

Children begin to understand and recognize the different cloud types.

Materials

Little Cloud by Eric Carle
Cotton balls
Light blue construction paper
Glue

What to do

1. Show the children pictures or photos of the three main kinds of clouds, then discuss the appearance of the different types of clouds and the weather they bring: Cirrus—white, feathery, high clouds; Cumulus—puffy, low, shape-changing clouds; Stratus—wide, gray, low clouds.
2. Read *Little Cloud*. Let children discuss the story and any experiences they have had observing clouds.

3. Give each child a sheet of blue construction paper, glue and cotton balls. Let them make a cloud picture. They can make Cirrus, Cumulus or Stratus clouds by pulling the cotton balls into the desired shapes. If time permits, they can make more than one picture.

Related books

The Cloud Book by Tomie DePaola
Hi Clouds by Carol Greene
Weather Words and What They Mean by Gail Gibbons

 *Mary Rozum Anderson, Vermillion, SD*

3+

Rain Walk

Science skills

Children are encouraged to use their senses and language skills to experience the rain.

Materials

Rainboots
Chart paper
Raincoats or ponchos
Marker

What to do

1. On a rainy day (when there is no thunder or lightening), bundle the children into appropriate rain gear and take them on a rain walk. You may wish to take just a few children at a time.
2. Walk slowly and examine puddles, wet rocks and leaves, rain sliding down buildings, shiny objects, etc. Talk about how the rain feels on hands, faces, tongues and the sound rain makes when it hits hard or soft things. Look for animal hideaways.
3. Back inside, ask the children to talk about their walk using words that describe the feel and the sound of the rain. Write down their rain words.

More to do

More science: Collect wet rocks or other items and watch them as they dry.

Related books

Rain by Peter Spier
Rain Talk by Mary Serfozo
Spring Rain by Marchette Chute

Ann Chandler, Felton, CA

Rainwater Versus Faucet Water

3+

Science skills

Children compare rainwater and faucet water through experimentation.

Materials

Clear plastic glasses

Items that sink and float such as cotton balls, marbles, small piece of paper, paper clips, plastic block pieces, etc.

Sugar or other dissolvable powder, optional

Spoons

What to do

1. Collect rainwater in one glass and fill the other glass with water from the faucet.
2. Put both glasses on a table. Ask the children: Do they look alike? Do they smell alike? Why can we drink the water from our faucet but not from outside?
3. Have the children drop small items into the glasses. Ask the children: Does the same item float or sink in both faucet water and rainwater? Why or why not?
4. If desired, put a spoonful of sugar, or another powder that will dissolve in water, in both glasses. What happens? Does the sugar dissolve in both or in one and not the other? Why?

More to do

Language: Put on a recording of rain sounds. Ask the children to close their eyes and listen to the recording. When it is finished, talk about the sound of the rain. Tell the children to pretend that they are outside walking in the rain. What do they hear? Do cars sound different in the rain? Can they hear the splashing when they walk in the puddles? Can they hear birds chirping in the rain? Ask the children to tell about an experience they had in the rain.

Related books

Listen to the Rain by Bill Martin, Jr. and John Archambault

Rain by Peter Spiers

Rain Talk by Mary Serfozo

A Walk in the Rain by Ursel Scheffler

Cynthia A. Maloof, S. Easton, MA

3+

Do Raindrops Come in Different Sizes?

Science skills

This is a rainy day activity that allows children to observe raindrops in a cup of flour.

Materials

Paper cups
Flour sieve
Wax paper
Flour
Paper plates
Jar with lid, optional

What to do

1. You can make collection cups for each child or use one cup for a group of children. Fill the paper cups halfway with flour.
2. Set the paper cups outside in the rain for five minutes.
3. Bring them back inside and let them stand for about five more minutes.
4. Let each child sieve the flour in his cup onto a paper plate.
5. The flour that did not get wet with raindrops will pass right through the sieve. The flour that absorbed raindrops will stay on top of the sieve.
6. Pour the wet pellets of flour on a piece of wax paper. Let them dry and store them in the paper cup or a little jar with a lid.
7. Spend some time looking at the dried pellets. Are they all the same shape?
8. Take samples from different rainy days. Compare pellets from warm days, cold days, snow days and sleety days.

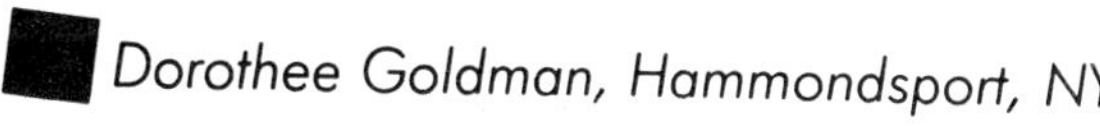

Dorothee Goldman, Hammondsport, NY

3+

Cloud Puffs

Science skills

Children work as a group to create a mural representing three types of clouds.

Materials

Blue bulletin board paper
Colored pencils, crayons, markers
Cotton balls
Construction paper
Glue
Tape

Weather

What to do

1. Explain to the children that they will be creating a mural. Put out a piece of blue bulletin board paper, large enough for all the children to work on at once.
2. Have the children draw a scene (of a town, neighborhood, woods, etc.) along the bottom third of the paper. Encourage the children to be creative.
3. When the children have finished the scene, discuss the three basic types of clouds: Stratus clouds are flat clouds that look like a blanket covering the sky. These clouds are closest to the earth. Cumulus clouds are puffy clouds that resemble a brain or head of broccoli. These clouds form higher in the sky, above the Stratus clouds. Cirrus clouds are wispy clouds that look like feathers or long blowing hair. These clouds form very high, above the Cumulus clouds, and are made up of ice crystals.
4. Have the children glue the cotton balls onto the paper in the shapes of the three different types of clouds. Make sure that the children remember to make a flat layer close to the Earth to signify the Stratus clouds, and wispy clouds at the very top of the paper to signify the Cirrus clouds.
5. Hang the mural where everyone can appreciate it.

More to do

Language: Encourage the children to make up a story about what is happening in the mural.

Related books

The Cloud Book by Julian May
Cloud Book by Tomie DePaola
How's the Weather? A Look at Weather and How It Changes by Melvin and Gilda Berger
Questions and Answers About Weather by M. Jean Craig
The Weather by Joy Richardson
Weather Forecasting by Gail Gibbons

Feel the Weather

Science skills

Through simulation, children can experience the weather right in the classroom.

Materials

Oscillating fan
Ice cubes
Spray bottle filled with water
Space heater, blower type

What to do

1. Wind: Ask the children, "How does it feel when the wind blows on your face and hair?" Turn on the fan and have the children feel the wind on the back of their heads and necks as well as on their faces.
2. Rain: Ask the children, "What happens when it rains?" Point the spray bottle (at mist setting)

over the children's heads and let them feel a gentle "rain."

3. Snow: Ask the children, "What happens when it snows and it is cold?"
   Give them ice cubes to rub on their faces and arms.
4. Heat: Ask the children, "How does it feel when it is hot?" Turn on the space heater and let them feel the warm air blowing from it.
   Note: Supervise closely the steps with the fan and the heater; be sure to warn children ahead of time not to touch these devices. Try placing a line with masking tape around the fan or heater. The children may not cross these lines with any part of their bodies.

More to do

More science: Dress flannel board dolls in appropriate clothes to match the weather.

 *Sandra Wallace Kayes, Philadelphia, PA*

3+

Fishing

Science skills

Children "fish" for clothes and classify them according to season.

Materials

12" (30 cm) wood doweling or plastic pipe
Drill (for adults only)
Magnet with hole in the middle
Juice lids from frozen concentrate
Sandpaper
8" (20 cm) cord or strong yarn
Glue
Pictures or stickers of clothing

What to do

Note: This activity uses a magnetic fishing pole. If you already have one, go to step 2. Step 1 is done by adults.

1. To make a fishing pole, cut dowel to 12" (30 cm) length and sand it smooth. Drill a hole through the rod near an end. String cord or rope through the hole and attach cord to the magnet. Be sure all knots are secure. For added safety, seal knots with glue.
2. Decorate lids with stickers or pictures of clothing for all different types of weather.
3. Put the lids into a fishing area (this could be the water table, the rug area, hula hoop, in a bike or car tire, plastic bin or box, etc.).
4. Talk about how our bodies feel when it is hot and when it is cold. Ask the children to name some clothes they wear in winter, in summer and in the seasons between.
5. Invite the children to go fishing for lids. When all the lids have been "caught," have the children sort the lids into different categories such as clothes we wear in summer, clothes we wear in winter, clothes we wear on our heads, clothes we wear on our feet, etc.

More to do

Math: To teach numbers, decorate one set of lids with numbers and the other with dots to represent the numbers. After children have fished for the lids, have them match the lids that go together. ■ To teach money value, glue on coins (one kind of coin per lid). After children have fished for lids, have them sort the lids by placing in boxes for pennies, nickels, dimes, etc. Older cnildren could make piles with the lids to represent amounts such as 30 cents, 40 cents, etc. ■ Reinforce telephone numbers by putting a single number on each lid and having childrer "fish" to get the numbers they need to build their own telephone number.

■ *Bev Schumacher, Ft. Mitchell, KY*

Flagpole Weather Watchers

3+

Science skills

Children observe the connection between weather and shadows.

Materials

Flagpole or suitable alternative

What to do

1. Use the school flagpole as a kind of weathervane. Take the children outside on sunny and cloudy days. Point out how shiny the flagpole is when the sun is shining and how the sun makes the pole cast a shadow on the ground. When it's cloudy, the pole doesn't shine and does not cast a shadow.
2. Remind children to "check the pole" to get a hint about the weather each day.
3. Ask the children what else might reflect sunlight and cast a shadow, for example cars, street signs and mailboxes. Encourage them to find something outside their homes to look at each morning to determine if it is sunny or cloudy.

More to do

Games: Play shadow tag.

Outdoors: Go on a "shadow and reflection" walk to find objects that reflect sunlight and/or cast a shadow.

■ *Suzanne Pearson, Winchester, VA*

Ice

3+

Science skills

Children experiment with ice and make predictions.

Materials

Ice cube tray
Food coloring
Freezer
Bowl of ice cubes
Water
Popsicle sticks
3 small clear containers

What to do

1. In advance, fill an ice cube tray with water (three-fourths full). Put three to four drops of food coloring in each cube and mix well. Break six popsicle sticks in half and place one in each cube (they will lay at an angle). Freeze.
2. Ask the children what ice is and how it forms. What conditions must be present for water to turn to ice? How does ice melt? What does it become when it melts? Ask if they've ever seen icicles or been ice skating.
3. Pass around a bowl filled with clear ice cubes for children to handle. Encourage them to describe what they feel.
4. Tell the children they are going to conduct an experiment. Put one ice cube in each of the three plastic containers. The children fill one container with warm water and one with cold water; the third container will have just a cube, no water.
5. Ask the children to speculate on which ice cube will melt first. Continue checking every five minutes until all are melted. Compare their predictions with what happened.

More to do

Art: Cover work area with newspaper and give each child a piece of white construction paper. Remove colored ice cubes from the tray and have the children paint with them, as though they were paintbrushes. When they finish, discuss what happened. Did the ice cubes get smaller? Did colors mix to form new colors? Was it like watercolor painting?

Connie Heagerty, Trumbull, CT

3+

Making Raindrops

Science skills

This activity encourages fine motor development and an interest in rain.

Materials

Pan
Water
Eyedroppers, various sizes

What to do

1. On a rainy day, take the class outside to observe raindrops. Point out how raindrops that fall on puddles cause ripples in them. Talk about how the ripples get bigger and bigger the farther out they go.
2. Go inside and invite the children to make ripples like the ones they saw outside. Give them eyedroppers and a pan of water. Show them how to make water go in and out of an eye-

dropper. Then they make ripples by letting drops fall into the pan.

More to do

Art: Use watered-down tempera paint and eyedroppers to make rain art.

Circle time: Everyone practices making rain sounds by snapping fingers, clapping hands or slapping legs. When the whole group gets going, it really sounds like a downpour!

Related book and song

It's Raining, It's Pouring by Kin Eagle

"It's Raining, It's Pouring"

Holly Dzierzanowski, Austin, TX

Single String Weather Mobile

Science skills

Children learn about weather in this fun art activity.

Materials

Cardboard
Construction paper: yellow, orange, white and blue
Glitter
Crayons
String
Scissors
Pencils
Glue
Hole punch

What to do

1. Create patterns out of cardboard for the sun, moon, raindrops and lightning.
2. The children trace the patterns on construction paper, cut them out and then color and decorate with glue and glitter. Talk about the shapes and the weather as they work.
3. When the shapes are dry, punch a small hole at the top of each and have the children attach a string for hanging. You may have to secure the string with tape.
4. Hang around the classroom.

Related books

Clifford and the Big Storm by Norman Bridwell
Goodnight Moon by Margaret Wise Brown
It Looked Like Spilt Milk by Charles G. Shaw
Little Cloud by Robert Tallon
Sky Fire by Frank Asch

Lisa Kingsley, North Franklin, CT

3+

Snowmen in May

Science skills
Children exercise their imagination and prediction skills.

Materials

Snowballs by Lois Ehlert
Small plastic plates
Tiny black beads
Snow
Toothpicks
Small buttons

What to do

1. Read the story *Snowballs* and discuss what must happen in order for it to snow. Talk about the temperature of the freezing point.
2. On a snowy day, take the children outside. Give each child a small plastic plate.
3. Invite the children to make tiny snowmen on their plates. They might use tiny black beads for eyes, toothpicks for arms and small buttons for decorating the front.
   Note: Use caution with young children who may still put small objects in their mouths.
4. Ask the children what might happen if the snowmen are taken indoors. Will they melt? Why?
5. Help the children place their snowmen in a freezer and tell them you will keep them there until spring. Explain how the freezer keeps the snowmen from melting.
6. Remove them from the freezer on a spring day and your class will have snowmen in May.

More to do

More science: Have a snowman melting party and allow the children to watch the snowmen melt. Discuss why this is happening.

Lisa M. Lang, Parkersburg, WV

3+

Temperature Tins

Science skills
This activity encourages temperature awareness and vocabulary development.

Materials

6 small tins with covers
Spray paint or contact paper
Clear caulk
Water (very warm, warm and cold)

What to do

1. Collect six tins of identical size.
2. Using spray paint or contact paper, decorate them so they look alike. (Adults do this step.)
3. Fill the tins with water. Two tins get very warm water, two get slightly warm water and two get cold water. Put on the covers. (If the tins leak, put some clear caulk on the inside seams and refill.)
4. Invite a small group of children to feel the water in the tins with their fingers and hands. Ask them to describe the temperature of the tins using words like warm, very warm and cold.
5. Ask the children to match the tins by their temperature (for example, to put the cold tins together, the warm tins together, etc.). When they are finished, ask the children how they knew which tins to pair together.

More to do

Storytelling: Read or tell the story of *The Three Bears*. Give the children the three covered tins (filled with very warm, warm and cold water) and pictures of the three bears. Ask them to pretend that the tins hold the bears' porridge and to guess which tin belongs to which bear. After making their guesses, they place a picture on the tin of the bear whose porridge is too hot, too cold and just right.

 *Debbie Barbuch, Sheboygan, WI*

Tissue Square Suncatchers

3+

Science skills

This activity will stimulate children's interest in the sun.

Materials

Tissue paper, red, yellow and orange
Newspaper
Liquid starch
Wax paper
White crayons
Scissors
Styrofoam tray
Paintbrushes
Black construction paper
Stapler

What to do

1. In advance, cut out lots of 1" (2.5 cm) squares of tissue paper in each color, or let the children help you cut out the squares. Spread newspaper on the work surface and pour starch into Styrofoam tray.
2. Talk about the sun and the heat and light it generates. Tell the children that they are going to make suncatchers.
3. Give each child a 9" x 12" (22 cm x 30 cm) piece of wax paper and two 9" x 12" (22 cm x 30 cm) pieces of black construction paper. Set out a pile of colored tissue paper squares.
4. Have each child paint starch over half of the wax paper and lay on overlapping tissue squares to fill the area, then repeat on other half. Wax paper should be filled to 1" to 2" (2.5 cm to 5 cm) from the edge.

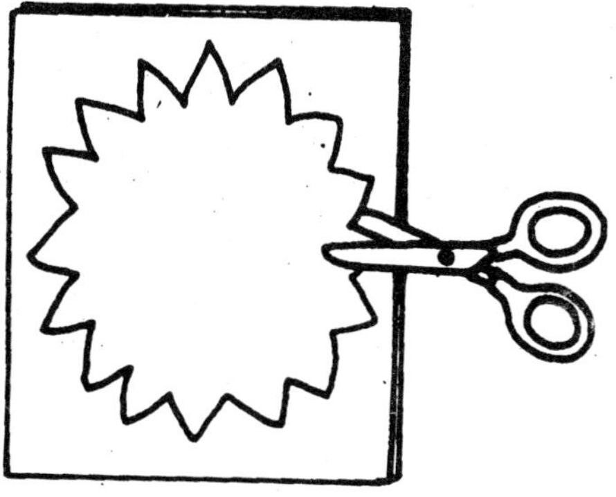

Holding two pieces of black paper together, cut out sun, leaving frame uncut.

Insert wax paper between sheets of black paper and staple edges.

5. The children then paint over the squares with more starch. Let dry overnight.
6. Using a white crayon, each child draws the outline of a sun on one of the sheets of black paper.
7. Holding both sheets of black paper together cut out the sun from the center only, leaving the frame around the edges uncut. Insert the decorated wax paper between the two black frames and staple all three together. (Some children may need help with this step.)
8. Let children tape their pictures to the window to catch the sun.

 *Susan Oldham Hill, Lakeland, FL*

3+

Tornado Art

Science skills

Children learn about tornadoes and do a related art project.

Materials

Thinned tempera paint, any color
Paper plates
Lettuce spinner with lid
Tornado tube or tornado pictures
Eyedroppers

What to do

1. Thin the tempera paint until watery. Set out the materials on a table.
2. Discuss tornadoes, including how they are formed and how we can find safety from them. Emphasize that winds swirl around very fast creating a tunnel. Demonstrate using the tornado tube or show pictures of tornadoes.
3. To make tornado art, have the children place a paper plate into the bottom of the lettuce spinner. (Some spinners have a point in the center that will hold the plate in place. If that is

the case, punch a hole through the center of each plate with pencil.)

4. Using the water droppers, children "dot" paint all over the plate. Place the lid on top, and have them spin it fast for several seconds. Open it up to see how it looks. Add more drops of paint if desired.
5. Invite the children to chant while spinning:

   Round and round and round it goes,
   Where it stops, no one knows.
   Twister, twister in a pot,
   Let's open it up and see what we've got!

More to do

Art: Place a paper plate with a hole in the center onto an old phonograph. Turn it so that the plate rotates around. Hold a marker, pressing lightly, onto the paper plate to make "swirlies" like a tornado. Demonstrate how you can move your hand just a little bit and the "swirlies" change size.

Field trip: Call the local news station and ask if a meteorologist would be able to show the class the machines and tools used to predict the weather.

Sand and water table: Put water and funnels in the water table. Show the children how water drains from the funnel in a circular motion by placing a small leaf on top. The leaf will rotate as the water drains out the bottom.

Valerie Chellew, Marshfield, WI

Umbrella Day

3+

Science skills

Observation skills are reinforced in this rainy day activity.

Materials

Umbrellas
Small paper drink umbrellas

What to do

1. Send home a note asking that each child bring in an umbrella on the next rainy day.
2. Take a walk on a rainy day. Listen to the sounds of the rain on the umbrellas. Point out all the different colors and styles of umbrellas that children bring in.
3. To celebrate the day, hand out small paper drink umbrellas (can be purchased at party stores). If the tips are sharp, break them off first.

More to do

Art: Children can wet paper shaped like an umbrella and paint it with watercolors. Add tissue paper raindrop shapes.

Math: Graph the colors of umbrellas that come to school.

Related books

Big Sarah's Little Boots by Paulette Bourgeoi
Mushroom in the Rain by Mirra Ginsburg
Umbrella by Taro Yashima
The Yellow Umbrella by Caitlin Dundon

Laura Durbrow, Lake Oswego, OR

3+

We Can Catch Raindrops!

Science skills
This art project encourages the children's curiosity about rain and develops both fine and large motor development.

Materials

White paper
Tissue paper, assorted colors
Paper clips

What to do

1. Tell the children they are going to make raindrop catchers.
2. Give each child one sheet of white paper and one sheet of colored tissue paper the same size. Have the children place the tissue paper on top of the white paper. Secure it with four paper clips, one on each side.
3. The next time there is a sprinkle of rain (not a downpour!), have the children take their rain catchers outside and catch some raindrops on their papers. Only a few raindrops are needed; papers should not get soaked.
4. Then, lay them out in your room to dry. Remove the clips and tissue paper. Pretty drops of color should appear on the white paper as the color leaches through.

Jodi Sykes, Lake Worth, FL

3+

I Am a Meteorologist

Science skills
The children learn about meteorology.

Materials

Large map of the world
Markers
Meteorologist's stick, optional
Small pieces of paper
Tape or putty for mounting

Weather

What to do

1. Discuss the weather and how and where people find out about the weather for the day. Explain to the children that the job of meteorologists is to track and predict weather.
2. Place the large map on the board.
3. Show the children some examples of how to draw types of weather: snow, sun, rain, wind and clouds.
4. Let children draw weather on small cards and mount them on the map.
5. During center time, they can tell the weather on the map.

More to do

Math: Use beads to lace how many sunny, cloudy, snowy or rainy days you have in a week or month.

Related book

The Dust Under Miss Merriweather's Bed by Susan Grohmann

Vera M. Peters, Elizabethton, TN

Weather Wise

Science skills

Children classify clothes according to their appropriateness for warm or cold weather.

Materials

Suitcase
Clothesline
Two signs: "Cold Weather" and "Warm Weather"
Clothing
Clothespins

What to do

1. In advance, pack a suitcase with clothing for different types of weather.
2. Hang two clotheslines at the children's level. Mark one with the "Cold Weather" sign and the other with the "Warm Weather" sign.
3. Talk about the weather and what people wear when it is hot, cold, etc. If possible, read a short poem or sing a song about the weather.
4. Show the suitcase to the children and explain that it contains different kinds of clothing.
5. Invite the children to come up (one at a time) and pick something from the suitcase. The child decides whether the article is something a person would wear in cold or warm weather and hangs it on the appropriate clothesline.
6. When all the items have been hung, ask the children to pick one item and suggest an activity where it might be used (e.g., bathing suit for swimming).

More to do

Dramatic play: Make the clothes available for dress-up.

Game: Play weather charades. Have children act out weather words like breezy, bright, cold, wet, rainy, hot, etc., as classmates try to guess them.

Snack: Make Crunchy Snowballs. Melt ¼ cup (60 ml) butter and 1 package of marshmallows in the microwave. Add 6 cups (1.5 L) rice cereal, 1 cup (250 ml) at a time, stirring constantly. Shape into snowballs. (Buttered hands help.) Shake balls in a bag with powered sugar.

Related book

The Wind Blew by Pat Hutchins

 *Vicki Whitehead, Ft. Worth, TX*

Weathering the Weather

Science skills

This activity reinforces weather-related concepts and encourages children to predict and draw conclusions.

Materials

Cardboard
Chart paper
Bowl of cold water with ice cubes in it
Pictures of clothing for different seasons
Markers
Bowl of very warm water
Two thermometers
Glue or tape

What to do

1. In advance, make a large cardboard thermometer but leave the area that represents the mercury white. Allow enough room on each side of the thermometer to affix the pictures of clothing.
2. Ask the children if they can define the word *weather* for you. You might say weather is a word we use to describe what it's like outside. Have the children describe different types of weather. Record their responses.
3. Ask if they know what the weather is like today without going outside. Tell them that a thermometer can be used to find out what the weather is like.
4. Show the cardboard thermometer and explain it can be used to find out the weather. Ask, "If the mercury (red liquid) in the thermometer is near the bottom, what do you think it's like outside? Is it hot or cold?" After allowing the children to make several guesses, tell them that you have a way of answering the question. Show the children the real thermometers and the two bowls of water.
5. Have a volunteer measure the temperature of the two bowls by placing one or more fingers in each. Ask the volunteer to describe the different temperatures.
6. Place one thermometer in each bowl and agree upon the amount of time they should be left in. When the time is up, remove the thermometers and examine them with the children. Record the temperature registered on each one. Point out that the mercury in the

thermometer from the bowl of hot water is near the top and the mercury from the thermometer in the cold water is near the bottom.

7. Ask the children the question from step four again. Now they should conclude that when the mercury is near the bottom of the thermometer, it is cold outside.
8. Ask the children what type of clothes they should wear when going outside in the cold. Explain that there are different types of clothes for all weather conditions. Distribute the clothing cutouts to the children.
9. Point to different levels on the cardboard thermometer. Ask the children to tell what type of clothing could be worn if it were that temperature outside. Allow the child holding the appropriate type of clothing to come up and glue or tape the cutout to the spot on the cardboard thermometer.
10. Continue until all the cutouts are affixed to the thermometer.

More to do

Language: Read *It's Raining Cats and Dogs* by Franklyn Mansfield Branley and make your own outlandish weather book. Have the children dictate what they would like to see raining down from the heavens and make illustrations for them. Create a cover and a title for the book and bind the pages together.

Related books

The Big Storm by Bruce Hisock
Sun Snow Stars Sky by Catherine Anholt

Virginia Jean Herrod, Columbia, SC

Weather Puppet

Science skills

This project encourages fine motor development and reinforces concepts related to weather.

Materials

6" (15 cm) paper plates
Markers or crayons
Construction paper
Crepe or tissue paper, blue and green
Craft sticks
Glue
Safety scissors
Cotton

What to do

1. Talk about various types of weather, such as sunny, snowy, windy, rainy, hot, etc.
2. Set out the craft supplies on a table and give each child a paper plate.
3. Explain that they are going to make weather puppets. Invite them to turn their plates into clouds, raindrops, snowflakes, the sun, etc. Wind puppets could have streamers cut from crepe or tissue paper. Clouds could be made of glued-on cotton. The sun could be made

from yellow construction paper. Encourage them to use their imaginations.

4. When the plates are decorated, have the children glue a craft stick to the back and extending below the plate as a handle.
5. Invite the children show their puppets to the class and talk about what kind of weather the puppet represents. Encourage them to talk about what they would do and wear in that type of weather.

More to do

Circle time: Save representative children's puppets to represent each type of weather. Use at circle time to identify and discuss the day's weather.

Margery A. Kranyik, Hyde Park, MA

Cloud Figures

Science skills

Children observe cloud formations and use fine motor skills to draw them.

Materials

Old bath towels or large piece of cloth
Construction paper
Colored pencils and/or crayons

What to do

1. Take the children outside and have them place their towels on the ground in a large, open area.
2. Explain that there are many different kinds of clouds and that scientists study their formations to predict weather such as rain and snow.
3. Have the children lie down on their towels and look at the clouds. Ask them to pretend that they are scientists and try to see things in the clouds. But instead of trying to see weather patterns, they should try to locate a cloud that resembles something else, i.e., a dog or a ship.
4. When the children have each located a special cloud, pass out the construction paper and colored pencils. Invite them to sketch the cloud formation. Children can repeat this activity and draw several cloud formations.
5. Back in the classroom, encourage children to share their pictures and talk about them. Talk about why two children looking at the same cloud might see two different things. Discuss how clouds change as air moves them across the sky.
6. Have the children predict how many of the cloud shapes they drew might still be visible in the sky, then test the predictions by going outside and looking at the sky.

More to do

Math: Make a graph showing the kinds of animals or objects seen by the children in the cloud formations. Discuss the type of cloud that most often looks like different fluffy shapes (Cumulus).

Related books

The Cloud Book by Julian May
Cloud Book by Tomie DePaola
Clouds by Thomas McGrath
Cloudy With a Chance of Meatballs by Judi Barrett
It Looked Like Spilt Milk by Charles G. Shaw
Sky Dragon by Ron Wegen

 *Michael Krestar, White Oak, PA*

Objects in Ice

Science skills
Children experiment with frozen water and make predictions.

Materials

Tiny toys
Water
Chart paper and marker
Large container
Freezer

What to do

1. Have children put the tiny toys into a container.
2. Pour in enough water to cover the objects, and freeze.
3. Ask the children to check the container throughout the day.
4. When the water is frozen solid, remove the block of ice and pass it around for everyone to handle.
5. Ask the children if they know how to get the toys out again and how long it might take for the ice block to melt if left out. Write down their suggestions and predictions. Try one or two of their suggestions.

More to do

Outdoors: On a cold winter day, take a walk and look on the ground for small ice patches. Give children sticks and let them poke at the ice to see if it is completely frozen.

 *Sharon Dempsey, Mays Landing, NJ*

Oobleck

Science skills
This activity encourages the development of language and fine motor skills.

Materials

Bartholomew and the Oobleck by Dr. Seuss
Mixing bowl
Water
Cornstarch
Durable plastic or wooden shapes or blocks, optional
Green food coloring
Rubber gloves
Water table or plastic tubs

What to do

1. Prepare oobleck as follows: Pour 2 cups (500 ml) of water and 8 drops of green food coloring into a large mixing bowl. Add 2 boxes of cornstarch and 1⅓ cups (330 ml) water. Use rubber gloves and a lifting motion with your fingers to blend mixture to an even consistency. The mixture should flow when you tip the bowl, yet feel stiff when you rub your finger across its surface. Add small amounts of water or cornstarch to alter as needed.
2. Pour the oobleck into a water table or into plastic tubs to place on tables. Cover to prevent the mixture from drying out. Set shapes/blocks aside for possible use.
3. Gather the children for a reading of Bartholomew and the Oobleck. In this charming story, a king becomes bored with the weather and orders a green, gummy, gooey substance called oobleck to fall from the sky.
4. After the story, invite the children to explore the amazing texture of the oobleck you have prepared. Props can be added to represent things in the kingdom that were covered with oobleck.

   Note: A more advanced version of this activity is described in *Oobleck: What Do Scientists Do? A Teacher's Guide* by Cary I. Sneider.

More to do

Art: Give the children green finger paints or playdough.
Snack: Add green food coloring to vanilla pudding for an ooblecky snack.

Related book

Cloudy With a Chance of Meatballs by Judi Barrett
(Great activities to do with this story can be found in *Story S-t-r-e-t-c-h-e-r-s: Activities to Expand Children's Favorite Books* by Shirley C. Raines and Robert J. Canady.)

Susan A. Sharkey, LaMesa, CA

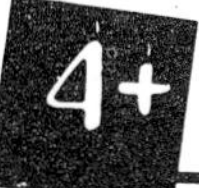

Piggies in a Blanket

Science skills
This experiment involves observing and recording data.

Materials

2 or more safe thermometers
Shoe boxes
Colored fabric pieces 6" x 6" (15 cm x 15 cm), one black and one white
Chart paper and marker

Weather

What to do

1. Read the temperature on the thermometers and record on a chart.
2. Place one thermometer in each shoe box, and have the children cover one thermometer with a white cloth and one with a black cloth.
3. Place the covered boxes in direct sunlight.
4. Wait several minutes, then lift the cloths and read the temperatures. Write the temperatures on the chart.
5. Compare the white-cloth temperature to the black-cloth temperature. Discuss how the color of the cloth might have affected the temperature and how the colors of our clothing may affect how much heat or cold we feel.

More to do

More science: Try the same experiment with cloth squares of other colors.

Dani Rosensteel, Payson, AZ

Instant Wind Storm

Science skills

The children observe the effects of wind.

Materials

Weather pictures, optional
Chalkboard and chalk or chart paper and marker
Collection of things, such as a rock, stick, feather, ball, leaf, hat, paper, toy car, tissue
Table fan
Pinwheels

What to do

1. Talk about the weather. Ask the children what they like most and what they like least.
2. You may wish to have some pictures of weather: a rainy day, a sunny day at the beach, lightning, snowy winter day, a tornado, a hurricane, etc. (Weather can be a scary thing for children, so remember to keep it fun.)
3. Ask the children: What does the wind sound like? Do you feel the wind inside?
4. Tell the children that you brought some wind with you today, and show them the table fan. It's not really wind, but it blows air like wind.
5. Turn the fan on low and let it blow the children's faces. Ask them how it makes them feel. Note: Supervise closely. Be sure to remind children not to touch or get too close to the fan.
6. Explain how wind can make things move and demonstrate with a pinwheel. Each child may wish to have a turn at this activity.
7. Demonstrate what else the wind can move by setting the fan on a table. One at a time set items from your collection on the table and let the children predict whether each will move when the fan is turned on.
8. Record your results by sorting items that move and don't move. List items on the chalkboard or chart paper.

More to do

Art: Paint by blowing paint on paper using a straw. ■ Make pinwheels, windsocks or kites.

Games: For fun, take some pillow feathers outside or in a large open area and see if the children can keep them in the air by blowing them or by fanning them with their hands. Balloons can also be used. ■ Let children blow Ping-Pong balls from one end of a table to the other.

Related books

Clifford and the Big Storm by Norman Bridwell
Fresh Fall Leaves by Betsy Franco
Millicent and the Wind by Robert Munsch
Sasha and the Wind by Rhea Tregebov
When Autumn Comes by Robert Maass
The Wind Blew by Pat Hutchins

■ *Mark Crouse, Nova Scotia, Canada*

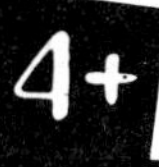

Roll of Thunder

Science skills

This activity reinforces auditory skills and develops an understanding of weather concepts.

Materials

How Thunder and Lightning Came to Be: A Choctaw Legend by Beatrice Orcutt Harrell
3 or 4 pairs of stones, various sizes
Chart paper
Markers

What to do

1. Briefly provide the scientific explanation for thunder and lightning.
2. Introduce the book listed above by explaining to the children that many stories and legends of the Native American people explain natural phenomena using great imagination and emphasize the close relationship between people and nature. Emphasize the fact that the story you are about to read is a legend. The book tells the story of two birds, Heloha and Melatha, who accidentally create thunder and lightning as a way to warn the Choctaw people of coming rainstorms.
3. Discuss the objects used in the story to create the sound of thunder and how this feat was accomplished. Then explain to the children that they, too, can make their own thunder in much the same way.
4. Place pairs of stones of various sizes on a table or tile floor. Use one pair of stones to demonstrate how they can be rolled together to create the sound of thunder when they collide, just like the eggs did in the story.

5. Let the children experiment with the different pairs of stones and combinations of pairs to determine the difference in the sounds made. Be sure to rein force such concepts as loud and quiet, hard and soft, slow and fast.
6. Help the children create a chart depicting the levels of sound made by each set of stones or a graph representing the set of stones each child feels best depicts the sound of actual thunder.

More to do

Art: Explain that the lightning bolt shape is found in many crafts made by Native American tribes, such as beadwork, traditional clothing and especially the shawl. Have the children tear a large piece of aluminum foil into strips and glue to construction paper to represent their interpretation of lightning. While children are completing this activity, ask such questions as, "What else happens when there is lightning?" and "Have you ever seen lightning?"
Language: Read the book Thunder Cake by Patricia Polacco, which tells the story of how Grandma finds a way to dispel her grandchildren's fear of thunderstorms. Discuss characteristics of thunderstorms that can make them seem scary. Then write a recipe for thunder cake. Use the class recipe to make and enjoy a special snack.
Music: Using their bodies and/or a variety of musical instruments, the children can create stormy sounds to match the words of familiar rhymes, for example, from, *Ring a Ring 'O Roses: Fingerplays for Preschool Children,* edited by Charles A. Hansen and Cynthia S. Stilley.

Related books

Flash, Crash, Rumble and Roll by Franklyn M. Branley
Her Seven Brothers by Paul Goble
The Story of Light by Susan L. Roth

Rebecca McMahon, Scranton, PA

Weather Forecaster

Science skills
Children use observation skills to describe the weather outside.

Materials

Drawing paper
Classroom calendar
Weather Forecasting by Gail Gibbons
What Will the Weather Be Like? by Lynda DeWitt
Crayons, markers
Weather symbols for calendar (clouds, rain drops, snowflakes, umbrella, etc.)

What to do

1. Discuss weather words, such as thunderstorm, rain showers, wind, sun, snow rainbow, tornado, hurricane, etc. Invite the children to pick one of the words and draw a picture of it.
2. Then, during circle time, read the books.

3. Tell the children that each day you will choose one child to be the weather forecaster for the class.
4. Have the first forecaster look out a classroom window for a few minutes. When the child rejoins the group, ask what the weather looks like today. Is it rainy, sunny, cloudy, etc.?
5. Have the child put the appropriate weather symbol on the calendar for that day.

More to do

Math: Set out a coffee can to catch the rain. Bring it in at the end of the day and let the children measure the amount of water collected. Write down the result. Continue this experiment for several more rainy days. Make a graph showing the amount of rain for each day.

Related books

1001 Questions Answered About the Weather by Frank Forrester
Cloudy With a Chance of Meatballs by Judi Barrett
Goodbye Thunderstorms by Dorothy Marino
How the First Rainbow Was Made by Ruth Robbins
I Like Weather by Aileen Fisher
Nature's Weather Forecasters by Helen Sattler
Raindrops and Rainbows by Rose Wyler
Windy Day by Janet Palazzo
What Makes the Weather by Janet Palazzo

Sherri Lawrence, Louisville, KY

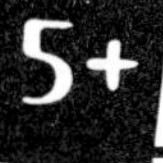

Jack Frost and Jane Thaw

Science skills

This lively game encourages large motor development and an awareness of weather and temperature.

Materials

Stocking cap
Sunglasses

What to do

1. Ask the children who wants to start the game by being Jack Frost and Jane Thaw. When two children have been chosen, give Jack a stocking cap to wear, and Jane a pair of sunglasses.
2. The other children run around the room trying to stay away from Jack Frost. If Jack Frost tags them, they must freeze until Jane Thaw tags them. When that happens, they melt and are free to run again.
3. Stop the game after a little while and select different Jacks and Janes until everyone has had a turn.

More to do

Games: Have a Winter Warm-up Relay. Lay out piles of the following items in a row: hats, scarves, jackets, mittens (not gloves). Divide the class into two teams. Start the relay by having the first two in line run to the pile of hats and put one on, then put on the scarves, etc., until they are dressed. Have them reverse the process by taking those items off again and placing them back in the piles. When they have finished, they run back to their teams and tag the next in line. Be sure to select large jackets and mittens for ease in dressing. Zipping or buttoning the jackets is not required.

Valerie Chellew, Marshfield, WI

3+

3-D Winter Wrap-Up

Science skills

Children learn about cold weather activities and clothing and exercise fine motor skills.

Materials

Jackets, mufflers, boots, etc.
Markers or crayons
Fabric strips, 24" x 1" (60 cm x 2.5 cm)
Construction paper
Scissors

What to do

1. Talk to the children about winter. Ask how people change their activities in the winter months (e.g., spend more time inside, do winter sports, eat hot soups and stews, wear winter clothing). Give children items to try on such as jackets, mufflers, boots.
2. Invite the children to draw pictures on 12" x 18" (30 cm x 50 cm) construction paper of themselves dressed for outdoor winter play, leaving off the scarf or muffler so they can add it later with fabric. The pictures should be large and fill the paper.
3. Each child then chooses a fabric muffler to add to his self-portrait. Using scissors, make a vertical slit in the paper on each side of the neck and insert the fabric strip through openings. Trim if necessary. The child can tie in front and fringe the ends.

Related books

Amy Loves the Snow by Julia Hoban
The First Snowfall by Anne and Harlow Rockwell
Five Little Foxes and the Snow by Tony Johnston
The Jacket I Wear in the Snow by Shirley Neitzel
The Mitten by Alvin Tresselt
Sadie and the Snowman by Allen Morgan

Susan Oldham Hill, Lakeland, FL

Colorful Snow

Science skills

Children make pretty snow while observing what happens when two colors are mixed.

Materials

Snow or ice
Large bowls, clear or white
Food coloring

What to do

1. Give children large bowls filled with snow or ice.
2. Children add a few drops of food coloring, com bining red and yellow, blue and yellow or blue and red in different bowls.
3. As the snow (ice) melts, children observe the mixing of the colors into a new color.

More to do

More science: Ask children what warmth does to snow. Have them set one bowl of fresh snow on a table inside and one bowl outside. Check both at 15-minute intervals and compare.

Related book

Little Blue and Little Yellow by Leo Lionni

Diane L. Shatto, Kansas City, MO

Frozen Bird Feeder

Science skills

Children explore the properties of ice while feeding birds in the winter.

Materials

Bowls
Birdseed
Small pine cones
Yarn
Freezer
Pieces of pine branch
Cranberries
Large paper cups
Water

What to do

1. Fill separate bowls with pieces of pine branch, birdseed, cranberries and small pine cones.
2. Have each child partially fill a paper cup with a mix of these items.
3. Make a loop with yarn and hang over edge of cup.
4. Let child pour water into cup. Be sure the end of the yarn is in the water.
5. Set the cups in the freezer.
6. When sculptures are frozen, peel away the cups and hang on a tree. Children will have fun watching for the first warm day to thaw their frozen bird feeders.

Related book

Birds by Susan Kuchalla

Cindy Winther, Oxford, MI

3+

Frozen Bubbles

Science skills

Children learn what cold temperatures do to a favorite summertime activity.

Materials

Bubble liquid
Bubble wands
Rubber gloves, optional

What to do

Note: Do this activity outside on a day when the temperature is lower than 32°F (0°C).

1. Give children the bubble liquid inside and let them blow a few bubbles to see how quickly they pop and disappear.
2. Bundle up and go outdoors to make bubbles. The children will observe how much slower the bubbles are to pop. When they do, they leave behind a frozen soap "skin."
3. Let the children catch the frozen bubbles with their mittens on. Ask, "Do these bubbles last longer than the indoor bubbles?"

More to do

More science: Use a pan and a very large bubble wand for longer, bigger bubbles to see if this makes any difference.

Original poem

Wind howls, snow blows,
Frozen fingers, frozen nose.
Frozen ears, frozen toes,
When snow howls, wind blows.

Related book

The Snowy Day by Ezra Jack Keats

Christina Chilcote, New Freedom, PA

3+

Glittering Snow Scene

Science skills

Children develop curiosity about snow with this creative winter art project.

Materials

Cards with snow scenes (cover only)
Cardboard
Pencils
Scissors
Glue
White meat trays, 8″ x 5¾″ (20 cm x 14.5 cm) and 1″ (2.5 cm) deep
Cotton batting or fluffy fiberfill pieces
Yarn for hanging
White or silver glitter
Tape

What to do

1. Invite the children each to choose a winter card scene.
2. Have children trace a 4″ x 6½″ (10 cm x 16 cm) cardboard rectangle on the back of the card (this is the size of the bottom of the tray) and then cut along the pencil line with scissors. (Some children may need help with this step.)
3. Children glue the card to the tray and decorate, gluing cotton or fiberfill to the tray edges and sprinkling on glitter.
4. Turn the tray over and write each child's name on back. Attach hanging yarn with tape.

More to do

Dramatic play: Invite children to take turns dramatizing their favorite winter activity.
Snack: Make snowflake-shaped sugar cookies.

Original poems

Chant the following poems together.

Tell Me About Snowflakes

Tell me about how snowflakes form out there in space.
Tell me how they fall down painting white every place.

Little tiny droplets of water come together like a crowd.
Then they become much bigger forming a little white cloud.

When the cloud is too heavy then they will drop as rain.
But if the rain gets much colder then snow will fall instead.

The snow will fall on the mountain, fall on the ground and on me.
But if the snow flakes fall on water, it will melt them, you see.

Making Sugar Cookies

Making sugar cookies
Is the most fun I know.
I measure, sift and stir
And roll out the dough.

I pat it with my hands
Which are clean, of course
And choose a cookie cutter;
A snowflake, star or horse.

I cut out lots of shapes
And a scrap of dough I eat.
I sprinkle my cookies with sugar
And lift to the cookie sheet.

After I make some more,
They go in the oven to bake.
I think that sugar cookies
Are a special treat to make.

Related books

Over and Over by Charlotte Zolotow
Snow by Roy McKee and P. D. Eastman

Mary Brehm, Aurora, OH

3+

Hibernating Bear

Science skills

This activity encourages children to ask questions about nature.

Materials

Bear puppet
Bag or box

What to do

1. Introduce your bear puppet after reading a story about bears (see suggestions below) at group time. Pull him out of a bag or box and surprise the children.
2. Have the bear tell the children that their song woke him up. Make him sound drowsy and maybe a bit grumpy.
3. He can explain how bears hibernate in the winter. He might mention other animals that hibernate in winter and ask the children questions about winter in general. What do they like to do in the snow? Do they hibernate, too?

More to do

Art: Look through magazines for pictures of bears and make a class collage.

Related books

Not This Bear by Bernice Myers
Sleepy Bear by Lydia Dabcovich

Laura Durbrow, Lake Oswego, OR

Ice Castle

3+

Science skills

In this activity, children observe how ice takes the shape of the container it was frozen in and how it reacts to salt.

Materials

Plastic containers, one per child
Freezer
Gloves and mittens
Chart paper and marker
Water
Water table
Salt shaker with salt

What to do

1. Have children fill small containers of different sizes with water and place in a freezer overnight.
2. Remove ice from containers and place in the water table.
3. Point out how the ice took the shape of the containers.
4. Encourage children to build a castle with the ice. They will need gloves or mittens, and they will need to cooperate with each other as each tries to stack his shape. Do the ice cubes stack the same way blocks do?
5. Sprinkle the ice with a salt shaker. The salt helps the ice pieces stick together. Ask the children if they know how this happens. Record their responses.
6. Ask the children if they can think of other ways to keep the pieces of ice together. Try a few.

More to do

Art: Freeze colored water in a cup with a stick. Children ice paint on porous paper.

Related books

The Penguin That Hated the Cold by Barbara Brenner
The Snowy Day by Ezra Jack Keats

Teresa J. Nos, Baltimore, MD

Ice Cube Race

Science skills

Children use observation and prediction skills in this activity.

Materials

Ice cubes
Plastic wrap
Chart paper and marker
Foil
Salt
Bowls

What to do

1. Place one ice cube in a bowl by itself.
2. Place one ice cube wrapped in a piece of foil in a second bowl.
3. Place one ice cube wrapped in a piece of plastic wrap in a third bowl.
4. Place one ice cube in a bowl filled with salt.
5. Ask the children to predict the order in which the ice cubes will melt.
6. Make a chart listing their predictions.
7. After an hour or so, check the cubes and talk about reasons why some melted faster than others.

More to do

Art: Try painting with ice cubes. Put a small amount of dry tempera on a piece of finger paint paper and put on a lively music tape. Give each child an ice cube and let him paint to the music.
Math: Graph the results of the experiment.

Cindy Winther, Oxford, MI

3+

Ice and Snow Play

Science skills
A simple song teaches children what squirrels, penguins and bears do in the winter.

Materials

Acorn nuts buried in a tub of snow (if it doesn't snow in your area, use leaves)
Penguin figures on a shallow tray of ice
Bear figures in a shoe box cave

What to do

1. Set out the above items in your science area during free playtime.
2. Use as props with the original song below (sing to the tune of "So Early in the Morning").

What can you do on a winter day?
What can you do on a winter day?
What can you do on a winter day,
So early in the season.

You can dig in the snow for nuts like a squirrel.
Dig in the snow for nuts like a squirrel.
Dig in the snow for nuts like a squirrel,
So early in the season.

You can skate like a penguin on frozen ice.
Skate like a penguin on frozen ice.
Skate like a penguin on frozen ice,
So early in the season.

You can sleep like a bear in a dark den.
Sleep like a bear in a dark den.
Sleep like a bear in a dark den,
So early in the season.

More to do

More science: Fill ice cube trays with water and drop an acorn in each cube. Freeze and let the children explore ways to free the acorn (set out salt shakers and safe tools to use).

Patricia Moeser, McFarland, WI

Indoor Snowman

Science skills

Children observe a melting snowman and chart its changing height over time.

Materials

Water table or tub
Mittens
Snow
Chart paper and markers

What to do

1. Fill the water table or tub with fresh snow.
2. Provide mittens so the children can experiment with the snow.
3. Invite them to make a snowman inside the tub.
4. Check the snowman every 15 minutes to observe what is happening.
5. Make a chart showing the height of the snowman and the new height as it melts.

Related books

The Snowy Day by Ezra Keats
A Winter Day by Douglas Florian

Cindy Winther, Oxford, MI

3+

Jack Frost Pictures

Science skills
An Epsom salt solution will amaze children as they watch it crystallize in an art project.

Materials

Epsom salt
Jar
Paintbrushes
Water
Paint cups
Dark construction paper

What to do

1. Mix a solution of equal amounts of water and Epsom salt in a jar and wait for the salt to dissolve. Pour into paint cups and add brushes.
2. Have the children paint a wet design on the dark paper with the Epsom salt solution. As the paper dries, the design whitens and begins to crystallize.

More to do

Art: Children can use wax crayons to draw a picture or design on the dark paper (emphasize pressing heavily). Paint with the Epsom salt solution over the crayon design. As it dries, the crystals will form on the paper wherever there is no crayon. This looks good with snowmen, snow forts and igloo drawings. ■ Children could glue a winter picture cut from a magazine on to construction paper, then paint over it with Epsom salt solution. When dry, staple a paper cut into the shape of a window pane over the painting to give it the Jack Frost effect you see on a frosty window in winter.

Sandra L. Nagel, White Lake, MI

3

Snowflake Catch

Science skills
Children use their observation and large motor skills as they catch and examine snowflakes.

Materials

Black construction paper
Snowflakes
Freezer
Magnifying glass

What to do

1. Put black construction paper in the freezer.
2. When it snows, the children take the frozen construction paper outside and catch snowflakes coming down.
3. Give them a magnifying glass to observe their flakes on the paper.

More to do

Art: Draw snowflake designs on paper. ■ Whip up Ivory Snowflakes with a little water into a spreadable texture. Use cotton swabs to paint snowflake designs on black paper.

Related books

The Snowman by Raymond Briggs
The Snowy Day by Ezra Keats
White Snow Bright Snow by Alvin Tresselt

■ *Jill Putnam, Wellfleet, MA*

Frost Walk

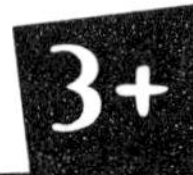

Science skills
Children use their observation skills to learn about frost.

Materials

Magnifying glass
Kitchen knife
Small containers

What to do

1. Invite the children to go on a frost walk. Look for frosty places.
2. Compare frost in sunny and in shady places. Compare frost on hard surfaces, on grass, on leaves, etc.
3. Examine frost through magnifying glasses.
4. Scrape some frost into small containers and watch what happens to it in the sun or shade.

More to do

More science: The day before, set out some small containers such as pie plates or ice cube trays filled with ice and let children handle to observe the properties of ice.

Related books

Fox's Dream by Tejima
Goodbye Geese by Nancy White Carlstrom

■ *Ann Chandler, Felton, CA*

3+

What Do the Salt Trucks Do?

Science skills
Children predict, then observe what happens to ice when salt is applied to it.

Materials
3 ice cubes
2 containers
Iodized salt

What to do
Note: This is a good activity for a snowy morning when children are likely to have noticed salt trucks on their street spreading salt.

1. Pass one ice cube around the group and ask children to tell something they know about it. Discuss its temperature, color, slipperiness, melting properties, etc. Mention some of the problems people have when there is ice on the ground (e.g., it's too slippery to walk or drive safely). Ask if the children have noticed salt trucks on the road. Explain that they spread salt to help melt the ice and make the roads safer for cars.
2. Place the two remaining ice cubes in separate containers. Pour a generous amount of salt on one, but none on the other. Ask children to predict what might happen.
3. Ask children to check the two containers periodically. After an hour or so (the rate of melting depends on many things, including the amount of salt used), reconvene the group. Ask them what has happened to the ice and if the salt made a difference.

More to do
Language: Talk about games or activities that depend on ice, such as ice skating or ice hockey.
More science: Will salt melt other materials in the room? Set up similar experiments with materials children would like to use. Observe what happens.

Related book
Ice Is...Whee! by Carol Greene

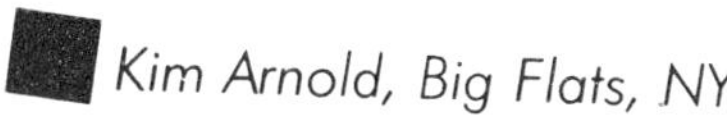

Kim Arnold, Big Flats, NY

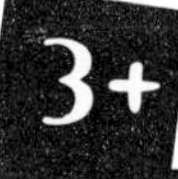

3+

When Snow Melts

Science skills
Children observe, measure and predict in this experiment.

Winter

Materials

Clear plastic containers, same size
Snow
Chart paper and marker

What to do

1. Mark three or four containers with a fill line, in exactly the same place on each container.
2. Invite the children to fill each container to the fill line with snow and place in different areas: in the freezer, the refrigerator, on a heater, in the room on a bookcase, etc.
3. Ask the children to check all the containers regularly throughout the day to see if the snow is melting.
4. Make a chart showing the results.

Related books

Sadie and the Snowman by Allen Morgan
The Snowy Day by Ezra Jack Keats
A Winter Day by Douglas Florian

■ *Andrea Clapper, Cobleskill, NY*

Winter Pine Tree

4+

Science skills

Children enjoy the beauty of pine trees in snow with this art activity.

Materials

Cardboard
Pencil
Stapler
Paintbrush
Green construction paper
Scissors
White tempera paint

What to do

1. Make a pine tree pattern out of cardboard.
2. The children use the pattern to trace two trees on construction paper, then cut them out and fold them in half vertically.
3. Staple the two folded trees together along the vertical line so the tree can stand up.
4. Have the children paint white tempera on tips of branches to resemble snow.

More to do

Field trip: Visit a tree farm or nursery, or take a walk and look for evergreens. Bring back pine cones for children to sort from largest to smallest, fattest to skinniest.
More science: Pass around branches from various types of evergreen trees. Label branches fir, blue spruce, white pine, hemlock, etc. ■ Get seedlings from your state conservation agency and plant in a public place as a beautification project.

Outdoors: Cover pine cones with peanut butter (mixed with lard) and birdseed for a bird feeder.

Original poems

The Pine Tree

I like the smell of the pine tree on a wintry day.
It looks so tall and green as near it I play.
I watch the birds fly to its branches so green.
Both summer and winter the birds can be seen.
It stands stately with its tip reaching high.
It looks like a green triangle touching the sky.

Feeding the Birds

I love to feed the little birds
In winter when it's cold,
For if they're never hungry
They'll live to be quite old.

I fill the feeder very full
Or drop seeds on the ground.
And then look out the window
But never make a sound.

For if I'm very quiet
The birds will come and go.
Blue, red, brown and black ones
Put on their special show.

If I were a hungry bird
Sitting in a snow-capped tree
I'd like the little boys and girls
Who bring the food to me.

Related books

American Trees by Russell Limbach
A Child's Book of Trees by Valerie Swenson
My Big Book of the Seasons illustrated by Eloise Wilken

Mary Brehm, Aurora, OH

What Melts?

Science skills

Children use their observation and predicting skills as they apply warmth to ice and other objects.

Materials

Warming tray
12 foil baking cups
2 ice cubes
2 peeled crayons
2 paper clips
2 tortilla chips
2 cubes of cheese
2 pieces of wood
Chart paper and marker

What to do

1. Turn on the warming tray and warn the children that it will get hot. Supervise closely.
2. Hold up each item and have the children predict whether or not the object will melt. Record their predictions on chart paper.
3. Have children place one of each item in the foil muffin cups.
4. Place one set of items on a nearby counter or table and the other on the warming tray. For example, one ice cube would be placed on the table and one on the tray.
5. Have the children observe the two sets to see which ones melt and which don't. Discuss their observations.

More to do

Art: Using aluminum foil, do crayon melting on the warming tray.
Cooking: Make nachos or melt chocolate.

Related books

Frosty the Snowman, many versions available
Snow by Kathleen Todd
Snow and Ice by Stephen Krensky
The Snowy Day by Ezra Jack Keats

Linda Ford, Sacramento, CA

Sparkling Suzie Snowflake

Science skills

Children learn about the properties of a snowflake and then use fine motor skills to cut one from paper.

Materials

White tissue paper
White glue
White crystal glitter
Safety scissors
Blue construction paper

What to do

1. In advance, cut out 6" (15 cm) squares of white tissue papers, one per child or let the children help cut them out.

1.

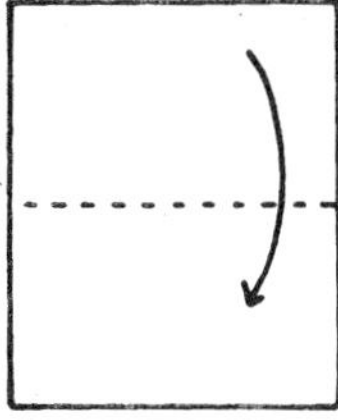

Fold paper in half.

2.

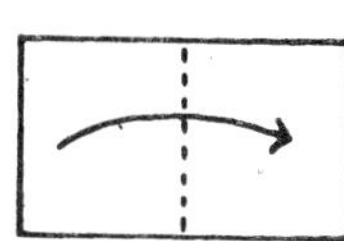

Fold in half again.

3.

Fold into thirds.

4.

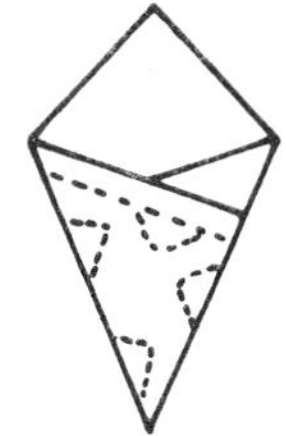

Cut top off at slant. Cut notches from all three sides.

2. Talk to the children about snowflakes and how they are formed. Explain that all snowflakes have six points but every design is different. Say that today they are going to make and decorate their own snowflakes.
3. Give the children the squares and show them how to make the following folds: fold it in half, then in half again, then in thirds. It will end up looking like an ice cream cone.
4. Help the children use safety scissors to cut off the top of their folded square with a slight slant, then cut out notches on all three sides.
5. Then the children can open the square and see the beautiful snowflake. Glue to the blue construction paper and decorate with glitter.

More to do

Art: Make a giant snowflake using the same folding and cutting procedure. Laminate with contact paper or cold laminating plastic. They should be large enough for children to hold and see the through center cuts, to pretend they are snowflakes.

Original songs

Sing to the tune of "Frère Jacques."

I'm a Snowflake

I'm a snowflake, I'm a snowflake.
(one child sings)
Yes, I am. Yes, I am.
(Child's name) is a snowflake. (class sings)
Yes he (she) is! Yes, he (she) is!

Suzie Snowflake

Suzie Snowflake, Suzie Snowflake
Floating down, floating down
You don't make any sound,
Twirling, twirling round and round.
Suzie Snowflake, Suzie Snowflake!

Suzie Snowflake, Suzie Snowflake
Wild and free, wild and free
Won't you come and dance with me?

Winter

Just don't get caught up in a tree!
Suzie Snowflake, Suzie Snowflake!

Suzie Snowflake, Suzie Snowflake
Soft and white, soft and white
You're so pretty in snow lace.
I think I can see your face.
Suzie Snowflake, Suzie Snowflake!

Related books
My Big Book of the Seasons by Eloise Wilkins
Sing a Song All Year Long by Connie Walters and Diane Trotten (songbook)
Snow by Roy McKie
White Snow, Bright Snow by Alvin Tresselt
Why Does It Snow? by Chris Arvetis

Mary Brehm, Aurora, OH

Glue to construction paper and decorate.

Index

Index

Index

Index

Index

Index

Index

Index

Index

Q, R

S

Index

Index

Index